The Chronicles of Japan

The Hsu-Tang Library of Classical Chinese Literature

Made possible by a generous gift from Hsin-Mei Agnes Hsu-Tang 徐心眉 and Oscar L. Tang 唐騮千, the Hsu-Tang Library presents authoritative, eminently readable translations of classical Chinese literature, ranging across three millennia and the entire Sinitic world.

Series Editors
Wiebke Denecke 魏樸和, *Founding Editor-in-Chief*
Lucas Klein 柯夏智, *Associate Editor*

Editorial Board
Cheng Yu-yu 鄭毓瑜
Wilt L. Idema 伊維德
Victor H. Mair 梅維恆
Michael Puett 普鳴
Xi Chuan 西川
Pauline Yu 余寶琳

The Chronicles of Japan

Matthieu Felt

Volume I

The Age of the Gods and
Legendary Sovereigns

OXFORD
UNIVERSITY PRESS

Oxford University Press is a department of the University of Oxford.
It furthers the University's objective of excellence in research, scholarship,
and education by publishing worldwide. Oxford is a registered trade mark of
Oxford University Press in the UK and in certain other countries.

Published in the United States of America by Oxford University Press
198 Madison Avenue, New York, NY 10016, United States of America.

© Oxford University Press 2026

All rights reserved. No part of this publication may be reproduced, stored in a retrieval system, or transmitted, in any form or by any means, without the prior permission in writing of Oxford University Press, or as expressly permitted by law, by license or under terms agreed with the appropriate reprographics rights organization. Inquiries concerning reproduction outside the scope of the above should be sent to the Rights Department, Oxford University Press, at the address above.

You must not circulate this work in any other form and you must impose this same condition on any acquirer.

Library of Congress Control Number is on file at the Library of Congress.

ISBN 978-0-19-760622-3

Printed by Sheridan Books, Inc., United States of America.

For David Lurie, who taught me how to read

Volume I

The Age of the Gods and Legendary Sovereigns

Contents

Acknowledgments xi
Introduction xiii

The Chronicles of Japan
    Book 1: Age of the Gods, 1 3
    Book 2: Age of the Gods, 2 71
    Book 3: Emperor Jinmu 127
    Book 4: Emperors Suizei, Annei, Itoku, Kōshō, Kōan, Kōrei,
        Kōgen, and Kaika 169
    Book 5: Emperor Sujin 187
    Book 6: Emperor Suinin 217
    Book 7: Emperors Keikō and Seimu 245
    Book 8: Emperor Chūai 293
    Book 9: Empress Jingū 305
    Book 10: Emperor Ōjin 349
    Book 11: Emperor Nintoku 375
    Book 12: Emperors Richū and Hanzei 427
    Book 13: Emperors Ingyō and Ankō 447
    Book 14: Emperor Yūryaku 477
    Book 15: Emperors Seinei, Kenzō, and Ninken 539
    Book 16: Emperor Buretsu 579

Appendix 1: Glossary of Kami in the Chronicles 593
Appendix 2: Songs in the Chronicles 623
Text-Critical Endnotes 627
Index of Key Names and Places 691

Acknowledgments

The invaluable support, advice, and guidance of numerous friends, colleagues, and instructors was essential to the completion of this translation. When I was a graduate student, David B. Lurie provided my first real instruction in reading the *Chronicles of Japan* in the original, and it is thanks to his animated and engaging teaching that I have both the skills to perform this translation and the interest to sustain the translation project. It is also thanks to David that I had the opportunity to learn from both Shinada Yoshikazu and Kōnoshi Takamitsu, two giants in the field of eighth-century Japanese literature. Instruction from many others during my graduate research in Japan was fundamental in building my reading and translation ability, including Tokumori Makoto, Yamada Jun, Kanazawa Hideyuki, Ishida Chihiro, Iwashita Takehiro, Matsuda Hiroshi, Nishizawa Kazumitsu, Ōura Seiji, Tetsuno Masahiro, and Tsukioka Masaharu. I must also thank Haruo Shirane, Liu Lening, and Li Feng for their thorough and engaging instruction in Classical Chinese and Japanese.

This translation itself would never have happened without the vision and drive of Wiebke Denecke, Founding Editor-in-Chief of the Hsu-Tang Library of Classical Chinese Literature. Wiebke's expansive vision of Chinese literature as World Literature, and her commitment to including in the corpus Korean, Vietnamese, and Japanese works written in Literary Sinitic, was directly responsible for bringing this volume into production. Wiebke also wrote on my behalf to support and fund my translation work. I would also like to thank Bryan Lowe for his encouragement and advocacy in bringing this project to completion. Finally, special thanks to Sarah G. Douglas for feedback and edits on the first round of drafts, and to Lucas Klein, Eleanor Goodman, and Alan Thwaits for their editorial suggestions and corrections.

This translation was completed with the support of an individual grant from the National Endowment for the Humanities. The NEH saw that I was provided with time, that most valuable of resources, to work on this project. The translation was also funded in part by a Humanities Scholarship Enhancement Grant from the University of Florida, and I thank Akintunde Akinyemi and Trysh Travis for their support of my work.

Friends and colleagues have been amazing resources on both things Japanese and matters generally during the past few years when this translation took shape. My sincere thanks to Nadia Kanagawa, Marjorie Burge,

Paula Curtis, Chris Smith, Ann Wehmeyer, Nan Ma Hartmann, Tom Gaubatz, Matthew Mewhinney, Malgorzata Citko-Duplantis, Scott Wilbur, Tyler Walker, Jae Won Chung, Glenda Chao, and James Gerien-Chen.

Finally, Norm and Kathy Younker and my wife, Tess, have been an enormous source of support over the years it has taken to bring this project together, and they have my heartfelt thanks.

Introduction

The Chronicles of Japan (*Nihon shoki* 日本書紀, 720 CE) is the first official history of the Japanese state and the single most valuable source of information about the life, language, culture, and customs of early Japan. Written in Literary Sinitic with vernacular Japanese notes and songs, the text combines frequent and poignant references to the Classical Chinese canon with regionally specific customs and anecdotes, blending its prestige language with local idiom. The juxtaposition of cosmopolitan and rustic creates a stimulating narrative that speaks on multiple levels. The *Chronicles* is also one of the most widely read works in the history of Japan, with over one millennium of notes, commentary, and treatises debating its meaning, significance, and nuances. No other text in Japan boasts such a long reading tradition. Even today, the *Chronicles* continues to be the preeminent source on Japanese origins, inspiring new adaptations in film, media, and video games into the twenty-first century.

The text, which begins with the Japanese creation story, is one of the oldest written sources documenting the unique and vibrant Japanese mythical narrative. This creation narrative segues into the foundation myth of the ancient Japanese state, established near present-day Nara by the legendary Emperor Jinmu in 660 BCE. The *Chronicles* then continues to record over 1,300 years of imperial governance, documenting both major domestic events and significant foreign interactions. These include the first arrival of Chinese classics in Japan, the introduction of the Chinese writing system, and the importation and adoption of Buddhism. Bit by bit, the mythical-legendary narrative of gods and sovereigns transitions into historical fact as the *Chronicles* narrates Japan's reimagination of itself as a sovereign empire and coequal power with China.

In contemporary Japan, the *Chronicles* is known by name to virtually everyone on the archipelago. Basic information about the *Chronicles*, along with that about *An Account of Ancient Matters* (*Kojiki* 古事記, 712 CE), is part of the standardized secondary school curriculum. These two texts are counted as the oldest written works on the archipelago and the primary sources for understanding where Japan came from and what it means to be Japanese. The language of both texts is inaccessible to most modern Japanese readers, but their creation narrative, along with numerous other myths and folk tales, are widely recognized, much like King Arthur and Guinevere are household names, even if the original text of *Historia regum*

Britanniae is seldom read in the English-speaking world. Because of its centrality to the definition and significance of Japanese origins, the *Chronicles* also has a long reception history, including commentary, treatises, picture scrolls, Noh plays, and other media, from the late eighth century until the present. Japanese publishers continue to release new critical editions of the text on a regular basis.

In the academy, the *Chronicles* is a cornerstone text for religion, history, linguistics, and literature. Stories of the kami, or Japanese deities, provide a basis for the Shinto religion, and while traditions of kami worship in the history of Japan are rarely linked to the *Chronicles*, the text is one of the oldest sources to describe these figures. The *Chronicles* also narrates the early history of Buddhism in Japan and the building of the first Buddhist temple. Much of the early historical material in the *Chronicles* is specious, but especially for the seventh century, the text constitutes an indispensable source of knowledge about the early court and the lineage groups that vied for power. The *Chronicles* is one of the earliest extant examples of a non-Sinitic people using Literary Sinitic in a non-Sinitic (Japanese) linguistic context to produce a long-form narrative, and while such borrowing certainly occurred in the eighth century on the Korean peninsula and elsewhere in East Asia, most of those examples do not survive. The *Chronicles* also contains a number of poems inscribed in the Japanese vernacular, making it one of only a handful of sources for Old Japanese. Finally, many narratives within the *Chronicles* are considered to have literary merit, and the text is one of the earliest examples of a Japanese written tradition.

The Japanese creation myth centers on the activities of the kami. Most of the kami in the mythical narrative are humanoid, and they engage in a variety of human activity, including farming, weaving, dancing, and sex. They also experience the gamut of human emotions, including jealousy, rage, pride, longing, and resentment. They woo, battle, and play mischievous tricks on each other, sometimes with fatal consequences. Their interactions are originally confined to heaven, but in time, extend also to the archipelago, known as the central reed plain land. After numerous missteps, betrayals, and intrigue, the kami at last establish a legitimate ruler of the central reed plain land, Jinmu's great-grandfather Ninigi. The myths from Ninigi to Jinmu, beginning in Book 2 of the *Chronicles*, take place on earth and see both Ninigi and Jinmu conquer the rampaging kami opposed to their dominion.

Once Jinmu founds the Yamato state late in Book 3 of the *Chronicles*, the text assumes the form of historical annals. Years are counted for the reign of each emperor and reset upon their death and succession. These annals include domestic politics, the genealogy of major clans, and diplomatic relations, but also folklore, religion, and vernacular Japanese poetry.

While the timeline, especially prior to the sixth century, is largely spurious, the *Chronicles* remains the most important source of material for ancient Japanese language, literature, religion, and history. The narrative ends in 697 CE, when Emperor Jitō 持統天皇 (645–703, r. 686–697) abdicated the throne in favor of her grandson. (As Japanese makes no distinction between the title used by male and female occupants of the throne, sovereigns, in this translation, will all be titled "emperor," "empress" being used to refer to the nonruling wife of a male emperor. The husbands of all four female emperors in the *Chronicles* were emperors themselves, so no male equivalent of "empress" is required.) While there are numerous succession disputes in the *Chronicles*, the text depicts the entire period, from Jinmu to Jitō, as a single lineage on its face, though a close reading will undoubtedly reveal interruptions and dynastic transitions that lie below the surface.

Author

The compilers of the *Chronicles* are named in its sequel, *The Continued Chronicles of Japan* (*Shoku Nihongi* 続日本紀, 797), as "Prince Toneri 舎人親王 (676–735), and others." Toneri was the son of Emperor Tenmu 天武天皇, (d. 686, r. 673–686) and Imperial Princess Niitabe 新田部皇女 (d. 699), Tenmu's niece. Imperial descent from both his maternal and paternal bloodlines made Toneri a plausible candidate for the throne, but the oath taken in 679 by Tenmu's adult sons, recorded in Tenmu 8.5 of the *Chronicles*, definitively established Toneri's half-brother Prince Kusakabe 草壁皇子 (662–689) as the legitimate heir. Toneri instead made a name for himself in the political arena. By the end of his life, Toneri reached the highest echelons of court aristocracy, proving himself an effective bureaucrat and administrator. Toneri played a major role in the Prince Nagaya Incident of 729, which consolidated Fujiwara control of the imperial court. Toneri was also involved in a 731 edict that expanded the roster of high-level aristocrats, a move that cemented the Fujiwara position. Outside of politics, Toneri also distinguished himself as a poet, and three of his compositions are preserved in the poetry anthology *Collection of Myriad Poems* (*Man'yōshū* 万葉集, final compilation c. 759). Toneri's son briefly ruled as Emperor Junnin 淳仁天皇 (733–765, r. 758–764), though historians widely agree that Junnin was only a figurehead for Kusakabe's great-granddaughter, Kōken 孝謙 (718–770; r. 749–758, r. 764–770 as Shōtoku 称徳). Nonetheless, Junnin's status elevated Toneri, who was posthumously honored with the title of Emperor Sudōjinkei 崇道尽敬皇帝. Toneri died of smallpox in 735.

There are many hypotheses regarding the identity of the "others," including refugees from the Korean state of Paekche, immigrants or captives from Tang dynasty China, and Ō no Yasumaro 太安万侶 (d. 723), author of *Ancient Matters*. Inconsistencies in orthography and narrative strongly suggest compilation by committee and the existence of multiple conflicting source documents. However, in the absence of compelling evidence otherwise, Toneri is best regarded as the main compiler and author of the *Chronicles*.

The compilation of the *Chronicles* marks the closing of an epochal seventh century for Japanese and Asian history. For most of the sixth century, the states of the Korean peninsula and Japanese archipelago enjoyed the fruits of diplomatic relations with both Northern and Southern Dynasties. When Sui and later Tang unified China, the possibility of dual patronage ended, and the states of Northeast Asia reorganized into three more centralized powers. Rule of the Korean peninsula—previously contested by Silla, Paekche, Koguryŏ, and the states of the Kaya Confederacy—was consolidated under Silla in 668. Parhae emerged from the ruins of Koguryŏ in 698. On the Japanese archipelago, the victors of a 672 coup reorganized the state on the basis of Korean and Chinese models of literate administration, and they renamed their state Japan (*Yamato, Nihon* 日本) and its ruler, emperor (*sumeroki, tennō* 天皇). The *Chronicles* is the official record of both this reorganization and the state that resulted from it. As such, every entry is a double statement: a historical fact, often of dubious provenance; and a matter of priority or import to the new Japanese state, which sought to write itself a backstory beginning with the creation of the world.

As a son of Emperor Tenmu, Toneri wrote *The Chronicles of Japan* with the intention of legitimating Tenmu's rule, an endeavor that pervades the whole *Chronicles* but is most evident in the later entries. The antepenultimate and penultimate book of the thirty-book text are devoted to Tenmu, giving him more coverage than any other emperor. The first of these two books recounts Tenmu's exploits in the 672 Jinshin war, in which he raised an army and took the throne by force. To a limited degree, alternative voices casting a more favorable light on Tenmu's rivals appear, but Toneri largely pushes these voices into the paratext, and in the main account he heralds Tenmu's victory over an illegitimate rival, the son of the previous ruler. The second book on Tenmu recounts the creation of the Yamato state, an effort continued by this successor and spouse, Emperor Jitō, in the last book of the *Chronicles*.

To a limited degree, the *Chronicles* seats Tenmu at the head of a new patrilinear dynasty that Kusakabe was intended to inherit. When Kusakabe died suddenly in his late twenties, Jitō took the throne before ultimately abdicating for Kusakabe's son, her own grandson. However, in the *Chronicles*, Toneri frames Tenmu and Jitō's new dynasty rather as the continuation of a long tradition. This emphasis on continuity characterizes the middle books of the *Chronicles*, which trace the occupants of the throne from the mythical Jinmu in 660 BCE to Jitō as if they formed a single dynasty called Japan.

INTRODUCTION   xvii

Numerous interruptions to the succession are patently obvious, namely following Buretsu, but also after Kaika, Chūai, Seinei, and Keitai. These interruptions perhaps reflect the fall and rise of distinct kingship lineages or polities on the archipelago prior to the seventh century. The orthodox order of previous reigns was probably established in Tenmu and Jitō's time; a recounting of past emperors is given at Tenmu's funeral as recorded in the *Chronicles*, and it appears in other early sources. However, Toneri weaves these lineages together in the *Chronicles* in a comprehensive and decisive fashion, using both historical narrative and historiographical form. As such, the reigns from Jinmu to Tenmu and Jitō are arrayed into a celebration of a long political heritage, with the latter two rulers as its capstones.

Structure and Influences

The *Chronicles* applies two textual forms. The first two books, which constitute the "Age of the Gods," are given as a main narrative with variants. The main narrative is divided into eleven sections, referred to in the paratext of this translation as S1, S2, etc. Each of these eleven sections is followed by a number of variants, which elaborate on parts of the main narrative or provide alternative accounts of events. These are referred to as S1.3, for example, for variant 3 of section 1. In some of the oldest manuscripts of the *Chronicles*, these variants are written in half-size characters, indicating that they were meant to be notes, but in manuscripts from the Urabe clan, they are given in full-size type with one level of indentation. The Kanbun 9 (1669) printed edition of the *Chronicles*, which is the basis for this and all other modern editions, derives from the Urabe manuscripts, and in this translation, variants are given in a smaller font face.

The length of the variants differs, but there is an internal logic to their placement in the text. The eleven variants of S5, for example, are ordered sequentially according to the part of S5 on which they comment. Confusingly, the variants often gainsay the account given in the main narrative. For example, the patron deity of the imperial house, the sun kami Amaterasu, is born three times and in three different ways, in S5, S5.1, and S5.6. The main narrative also relies on the variants for its own development. For example, the kami who conquer the archipelago in S9 are born as the result of an event, the death of Izanami, that does not happen in the main narrative of S5. The provision of alternative accounts likely derives from the *Annotated Records of the Three Kingdoms* (*Sanguozhi zhu* 三國志注), by Pei Songzhi 裴松之 (372–451). Because the variants also result in repeated information, the *Chronicles* frequently deploys "and so on" to simplify sections of narrative or lists of items.

The remaining twenty-eight books of the *Chronicles* use the annals style. The books have a prescribed format. Each begins with a pre-accession

(PA) narrative. If applicable, this narrative provides the father, mother, and maternal grandfather of the ruler, a comment on his demeanor, the age at which he became heir, the death of the previous ruler, and any narrative detail, such as a military campaign, that was required for his accession. Following the accession, each book generally gives the dates for the naming of the former empress as empress dowager, the burial of the previous emperor, the naming of a new empress, and a list of consorts with progeny. As seen, for example, in the very short accounts given for the eight emperors in Book 4 of the *Chronicles*, this information constituted the essential content for every reign, and its repetition provides a sense of regularity to the text and the imperial succession.

Volume 1 of this translation of the *Chronicles* contains the first sixteen books of the text. Books 1 and 2 contain the creation myths of Japan and are often called the "Divine Age" or "Age of the Gods." Book 3 records the mythical emperor Jinmu and the foundation of the Japanese state. The eight emperors in Book 4 were likely created to push the foundation of the realm back to the auspicious year 660 BCE. These reigns are often referred to as "absent histories" owing to the scant detail of each reign. Books 5, 6, and 7 present emperors Sujin, Suinin, Keikō, and Seimu. These three reigns are characterized by long narratives of conquest, visits from foreign emissaries, and religious rituals to placate the kami. Keikō's son and intended heir, Yamato Take, dies during a mission to conquer northeastern Japan, and after a brief rule by Keikō's younger son Seimu, the throne, in Book 8, goes to Chūai, Yamato Take's son. Chūai dies a young death as punishment for mocking the gods, and so his wife, Jingū, serves as regent until their son, Ōjin, is ready to succeed. Jingū is explicitly likened to Pimiko, Queen of Wa, from the Chinese historical record, and Book 9 describes Jingū's mythical conquest of Korea. The vernacular Japanese names of Keikō, Seimu, Chūai, and Jingū contain common elements, and these rulers are often imagined to constitute one cluster of related figures.

In Book 10, Ōjin is presented as the son of Chūai and Jingū, though his miraculous birth and unusual vernacular name have been taken to suggest a new dynastic lineage. Ōjin's son, Nintoku, succeeds him and, in Book 11, is described as the ideal sage ruler. Nintoku's lineage continues with the nine emperors appearing in Books 12 to 16. These reigns are shorter and filled with violence and intrigue. Of particular note is Book 14, on Yūryaku, who forms the martial alternative to the cultured reign of Nintoku. Books 12 to 16 also bear the most striking resemblance to the Five Kings of Wa who appear in several Chinese records covering the fifth and early sixth centuries. The last of these kings, named Bu 武 in the Chinese, is likely Yūryaku, but there are some inconsistencies in equating the four kings that precede him with the emperors named in the *Chronicles*. At the end of Book 16, Buretsu dies without an heir, and the succession continues with Keitai, a purported fifth-generation descendant of Ōjin, but almost certainly completely unrelated and thus indicative of a new dynastic lineage. So Volume 1 of this translation ends with the death of Buretsu, which conveniently occurs about halfway through the *Chronicles*.

Most books of the *Chronicles* also include more detailed entries on specific actions taken by the emperor. The emperor is the subject of most sentences, to the point that in the original text, sentences with the emperor as subject often abbreviate it; a subject of "the emperor" has been added in translation to conform with English grammatical demands. Years are counted from the accession of the emperor to the throne, with a few notable exceptions. Months follow the twelve-month Chinese lunisolar calendar, with intercalary months occasionally added to prevent the timing of the months from drifting too far from the astronomical solar year. The first day of a month is given using the sixty-count sexagenary cycle, with successive dates in the same month derived by counting forward from the first day of the month. In the paratext, dates are abbreviated to the relevant month. For example, the tenth year, tenth month, of Suiko's reign is referred to as Suiko 10.10, and Suiko PA refers to the pre-accession content preceding Suiko 1.1, the first year of Suiko's reign. Some books of the *Chronicles* also provide general information on the state or on foreign states, often with no specific date, just "that year" or "that month."

The *Chronicles* derives portions of its contents from works across the Classical Chinese canon, without citing these works directly. They include the *Writings of the Huainan Masters* (*Huainanzi* 淮南子), *Classified Extracts from Literature* (*Yiwen lei ju* 藝文類聚), *Records of the Historian* (*Shiji* 史記), *History of the Liu Song* (*Song shu* 宋書), *Classic of Poetry* (*Shijing* 詩經), *History of the Three Kingdoms* (*Sanguo zhi* 三國志), *History of the Former Han* (*Han shu* 漢書), *Classic of Changes* (*Yijing* 易経), *History of the Later Han* (*Hou Han shu* 後漢書), *Han Records of the Eastern Lodge* (*Dongguan Han ji* 東觀漢記), *Golden Light Sutra* (*Jin guang ming jing* 金光明経), and *History of Liang* (*Liang shu* 梁書), among others. These texts are deployed not only to create literal meaning, but also because they resonate with the content of the *Chronicles*. The Japanese Emperor Jinmu, for example, is likened to Emperor Gaozu of Han 漢高祖 (256–195 BCE) because both are dynastic founders. The Japanese Emperor Buretsu adopts passages that recall Di Xin of Shang 商帝辛 (1105–1046 BCE) because both marked the end of a dynastic cycle.

At several points, the annals of the *Chronicles* directly cites other texts. Some of these, such as the *History of Wei* (*Wei shu* 魏書) in the *History of the Three Kingdoms*, are extant, and some, such as the *Record of Paekche* (*Kudara ki* 百済記), are not. Modern Japanese editions of the *Chronicles* usually give these citations in half-size characters; in this translation, they are given as block citations using a smaller font size. The *Chronicles* includes a number of other notes in half-size characters that clarify details or dates; these are also given in half-size characters. However, to preserve reading ease, original notes providing alternative names for people and kami have been moved to the footnotes.

The possible existence of Japanese sources for the *Chronicles* is a never-ending topic of speculation among senior scholars and lay historians alike. Speculation begins with an entry for 620 CE given in Book 22 in which Prince Shōtoku 聖徳太子 (574–622) and Soga no Umako 蘇我馬子 (d. 626) compile the first history of Japan and a record of the emperors. This history of Japan was destroyed in a fire of 645, but the record of the emperors is saved. A 681 CE entry in Book 29 records Tenmu ordering the compilation of a record of the emperors. The preface of *Ancient Matters* claims that Tenmu also ordered a scholar to create a historical narrative. A generous reading of events finds congruence between these readings, or at least between the latter two. In truth, there is no way to know exactly what Japanese sources Toneri had at his disposal with a satisfactory level of certainty.

The language of the *Chronicles* is generally Literary Sinitic, and readers of Classical Chinese will have little difficulty reading most of the text in the original. Many of the emperors depicted in the text are legendary, and their exploits are not infrequently taken from Chinese histories, especially the *History of the Former Han* and the *History of the Later Han*, among others. However, personal and place-names use vernacular Japanese. A small number of quotations of direct speech in vernacular Japanese and languages of the Korean peninsula are also recorded using Chinese characters phonetically. There are ninety-five vernacular Japanese poems in Volume 1 of the *Chronicles*, which are inscribed in the vernacular and are not readable in Chinese. Japanese readers of the *Chronicles* have historically read the text by gloss. While modern Japanese editions of the text continue to contest the appropriate gloss for the text, a relatively stable set of readings has emerged based on the Kanbun 9 (1669) printed edition of the *Chronicles*, which is the basis for all modern editions of the text.

FIGURE 1 The 1669 (Kanbun 9) version of the *Chronicles*, held by Ibaraki University Library, page 1a. The large characters in the first line from the right indicate the book number, in the second line, the book title, and then the text begins from the third line. Small characters to the right of each line provide the primary Japanese vernacular glosses. Secondary glosses occasionally appear to the left of a character. *Kunten*, which indicate the Japanese word order, also appear to the left of some characters.

日本書紀卷第一

神代上

古天地未剖陰陽不分渾沌如雞子溟涬而含牙及其清陽者薄靡而爲天重濁者淹滯而爲地精妙之合摶易重濁之凝竭難故天先成而地後定然後神聖生其中焉故曰開闢之初洲壤浮漂譬猶游魚之浮水上也于時天地之中生一物狀如葦牙便化爲神號國常立尊

It is hard to imagine that the compilers of the *Chronicles* did not know of the existence of *Ancient Matters*. The differences in content, form, language, and objective between the texts suggest a deliberate effort to write a different kind of mythic-historical record. For the mythical books, *Ancient Matters* centers on the efforts of the heavenly gods and the influence of *musuhi*, a generative force, while the *Chronicles* applies the principles of yin and yang cosmology. The historical books of *Ancient Matters* foreground genealogical information on emperors and their retainers, while the emperors of the *Chronicles* are bureaucratic administrators issuing edicts to their courts. In form, *Ancient Matters* is not a chronicle, and years are only occasionally identified. In contrast, the *Chronicles* is organized by date. The language of *Ancient Matters* is a hybrid of Chinese and Japanese unique to the text, while the *Chronicles* uses Literary Sinitic in the style of a Chinese history. Finally, *Ancient Matters* restricts its scope to the ancient period; substantive entries about imperial reigns end in the early seventh century CE. Hence, the objective of *Ancient Matters* was likely to connect the people and events of antiquity to those of recent history. The *Chronicles* ends in 697 CE, and the two full books devoted to the reign of Emperor Tenmu show that the text emphasizes the legitimacy of Tenmu's rule and his place within a long succession of emperors. Despite these differences, the two texts have been read alongside each other since the early ninth century. In this translation, important differences between *Ancient Matters* and the *Chronicles* will be identified in the notes.

Contents

The *Chronicles* is organized into thirty books, which correspond to the historical dates in Table 1.

Book 1 begins with the creation of the world by the separation of yin and yang, then names the first three kami to appear. Variant texts alter the names and number of these kami. These first three kami, which all appear individually, are followed by four generations of kami that appear as pairs. Collectively, the first three kami and the four pairs are known as the "seven generations of gods." This phrase also appears in *Ancient Matters*, but in that narrative, the seven generations comprise two individual kami and then five paired kami, and the very first kami to appear are not part of the seven generations. The last of the paired kami are Izanagi and Izanami, the main agents of the Japanese creation myth. The pair stand atop the floating bridge of heaven, dip a spear into the sea below, then pull the spear out. The brine that drips off the spear forms an island, to which they descend and consummate their marriage. Izanami gives birth to the islands of the Japanese archipelago, the kami that inhabit it, and then three illustrious kami: Amaterasu, the sun goddess; Tsuku-yomi, the moon god; and Susano-o, a raging god of

INTRODUCTION   xxiii

TABLE 1 ORGANIZATION OF BOOKS IN THE CHRONICLES

BOOK	EMPEROR(S)	REIGN	BOOK	EMPEROR(S)	REIGN
1	Divine Age		16	Buretsu	499–506
2	Divine Age		17	Keitai	507–531
3	Jinmu	660–582 BCE	18	Ankan, Senka	534–539
4	Suizei, Annei, Itoku, Kōshō, Kōan, Kōrei, Kōgen, Kaika	581–98 BCE	19	Kinmei	540–571
5	Sujin	97–30 BCE	20	Bidatsu	572–585
6	Suinin	29 BCE–70 CE	21	Yōmei, Sushun	586–592
7	Keikō, Seimu	71–190	22	Suiko	593–628
8	Chūai	192–200	23	Jomei	629–641
9	Jingū	201–269	24	Kōgyoku	642–645
10	Ōjin	270–310	25	Kōtoku	645–654
11	Nintoku	311–399	26	Saimei	655–661
12	Richū, Hanzei	400–410	27	Tenji	662–671
13	Ingyō, Ankō	411–456	28	Tenmu (1)	672
14	Yūryaku	456–479	29	Tenmu (2)	673–686
15	Seinei, Kenzō, Ninken	480–498	30	Jitō	686–697

storms. Susano-o's bad behavior results in his parents banishing him to the distant Land of Ne. Before he departs, he ascends to heaven to see his sister Amaterasu. Amaterasu assumes he has come to steal her land and dons her armor and gathers her arms, but Susano-o protests his innocence, which he confirms via an oath that they share. One of the children that results from their oath is Oshi-ho-mimi. Susano-o then goes on to commit a number of atrocities in heaven, driving Amaterasu into seclusion in the heavenly rock cave. The heavenly kami hatch a plan to lure her out of the cave, and then banish Susano-o from heaven. Susano-o lands in the land of Izumo, in western Japan, saves the maiden Kushi-ina-da-hime from an eight-headed serpent, marries her, and then at last goes to the Land of Ne.

In Book 2, the action shifts from heaven to earth and follows Oshi-ho-mimi and his descendants. Oshi-ho-mimi marries a daughter of the heavenly kami Taka-mi-musuhi, and Taka-mi-musuhi wishes to see their son, his grandson, named Ninigi, rule the Japanese archipelago. Taka-mi-musuhi sends a succession of kami to the archipelago with orders to force the islands' rampaging gods into submission by securing an oath of fealty from their leader, Ō-kuni-nushi. Ō-kuni-nushi, a descendant of Susano-o, ruled the archipelago from his home in Izumo. Ō-kuni-nushi is at last vanquished, and Ninigi descends from heaven, landing in the southern part of Japan's southernmost major island, Kyushu. He marries a local kami, but when he expresses doubt that she became pregnant after only one night with him, his furious wife locks herself in an earthen chamber and sets it on fire, swearing that if the children are truly his, they will not be harmed. Two of their sons, known popularly as Umi-sachi-hiko ("Luck of the Sea") and Yama-sachi-hiko ("Luck of the Mountain") are talented at fishing and hunting, respectively. One day they agree to trade tools. Umi-sachi-hiko takes his younger brother's bow and arrow, and Yama-sachi-hiko takes his older brother's fishhook. However, they both fail to catch anything, and Yama-sachi-hiko loses the fishhook in the ocean. To retrieve it, he travels to the palace of the sea kami, where he retrieves the hook and marries the sea kami's daughter. After his return to Kyushu, she comes ashore to give birth to their son, Fuki-aezu, but in the process, is revealed to be a sea monster. Shamed, she returns to the sea and sends her younger sister to look after Fuki-aezu. When he grows up, he marries the sister, who has four sons.

Book 3 describes the foundation of the Japanese state by Fuki-aezu's youngest son, Jinmu, and the narrative moves from mythical time to historical time. In 667 BCE, Jinmu proposes to his son and older brothers that they leave Kyushu and found a state in a prosperous land to the east that he heard about from a local kami. They build a fleet and sail northeast along the Kyushu coast, then turn eastward through Japan's Inland Sea. They spend three years near Okayama preparing troops and rations, then continue east to Naniwa, present-day Osaka City. They attempt to enter the Nara Basin first from the west, but are repelled by its chieftain, Naga-sune-hiko. In addition, Jinmu's oldest brother is hit by an arrow and dies. Jinmu resolves to circle around and enter the Nara Basin from the east instead, with the sun at his back. His other brothers leave en route, but Jinmu arrives in the mountainous land of Kumano. Guided by a magical crow, his army enters the Nara Basin and defeats Naga-sune-hiko. Jinmu then founds his capital at Kashihara in 660 BCE, takes a new wife as empress, and builds a palace.

Book 4 is often called the "eight absent histories," referring to the scant historical detail given for each of the eight emperors it chronicles. First, a succession struggle results in Jinmu's youngest son becoming the next emperor, aided by his older brother, but having to kill their stepbrother, the son that Jinmu brought with him from Kyushu. The reigns of the next eight emperors follow a formulaic pattern in which they accede to the throne, name an empress and crown prince, build a palace, die, and are succeeded by their son. The book thus provides the bare minimum for how the *Chronicles* records a reign. The long historical period, in which many emperors live for one hundred years or more, also pushes the founding reign by Jinmu back to the auspicious year of 660 BCE.

Book 5 chronicles Emperor Sujin, also called the "first emperor to rule the state." Sujin receives this appellation because, while Jinmu founds the state, it is Sujin who institutes a system of taxation and who sends four generals in the four directions to put down rebellion and dissent. The loose relationship between Sujin and Jinmu owing to the clearly fabricated eight intervening emperors suggests that Sujin too was a foundational emperor. Much of Book 5 details his relationship with the kami of Mt. Miwa, a major site of ritual veneration on the eastern edge of the Nara Basin. The kami of this mountain causes a plague in the land, demanding that he be worshipped. He also marries Sujin's aunt, Yamato-to-to-hi-momo-so-bime. When the aunt dies, she is buried in the Hashihaka Tumulus, one of Japan's oldest keyhole tombs and the purported burial site for Queen Pimiko, a Japanese ruler mentioned in the Chinese histories. Sujin also moves the mirror associated with Amaterasu out of the palace and demands the treasures held in the Izumo Grand Shrine, suggesting a tightening relationship between the imperial court and ritual observances.

Book 6, the first substantive introduction of the Korean peninsula into the historical narrative, is centered on Sujin's son, Suinin. Suinin purportedly entertains a visitor from Mimana, a term used in the *Chronicles* to describe both the Korean state of Kŭmgwan Kaya and the broader coalition of polities on the southern Korean peninsula known as the Kaya Confederacy. Suinin is also visited by a mythical prince from Silla, who settles in Japan. This plot point is tied to Book 9, in which one of the prince's descendants, Empress Jingū, returns to Silla in a fantastical narrative of conquest. Among Suinin's other major accomplishments are the establishment of the Ise Grand Shrine, which is the final location of the mirror used to worship Amaterasu; the creation of the first imperial estate, a major tool for expanding imperial control; and the prohibition of following one's lord in death. Instead of burying alive the servants of deceased nobility alongside them, statuettes called *haniwa* would be used as burial goods.

In Book 7, Emperor Keikō has two sons, the older named Ō-usu, and the younger O-usu, known more popularly as Yamato Take. Yamato Take is frequently called Yamato Takeru, a reading for his name used from the late nineteenth century in Japanese sources and adopted in English as well, but the original reading, which I use in this translation, was Yamato Take. According to the *Chronicles*, during Keikō's reign, the inhabitants of southern Kyushu, the Kumaso, rebelled, though in truth, they were likely not part of the Japanese state at this time. Keikō himself goes to Kyushu and subdues numerous rebel leaders. After his return to his capital in the Nara Basin, the Kumaso rebel again, and Keikō sends Yamato Take to defeat them in his stead. After Yamato Take's successful return, the Emishi people of northeastern Japan rebel, and so Yamato Take goes out again to quell the uprising. This time, on his return, Yamato Take is poisoned by an evil kami, and he dies before he can make it back to his home. The language of the *Chronicles* speaks of Yamato Take as if he were a ruling emperor. Keikō is succeeded by his son, Seimu, and Seimu later dies with no heirs. Though Seimu rules for sixty years, his chronicle has only seven entries. Among them is the establishment of administrative divisions for the realm.

In Book 8, Yamato Take's son, Chūai, takes the throne, making good on the textual treatment of his father as an emperor. The Kumaso revolt again, but as Chūai prepares to attack, his wife, Empress Jingū, is possessed by several kami. These kami promise Chūai rule of the Korean peninsula and tell him to ignore the Kumaso, but since he cannot see the land to the west of the Japanese archipelago, Chūai rejects their commandment and attacks the Kumaso. The kami revoke their promise and instead insist that Chūai's son, still in the womb, will receive the lands of Korea. After failing to defeat the Kumaso, Chūai suddenly falls ill and dies at only fifty-two years of age. The empress, fearing a rebellion if the emperor's sudden death were known to his rivals, has four trusted servants perform a temporary burial in secret.

Book 9 is the only book not centered on a ruling emperor. After Chūai's death, Jingū summons the gods to possess her again and reveals their identities as Amaterasu, the oracle god Koto-shiro-nushi, and the three sea gods of the Sumiyoshi Grand Shrine. Jingū performs a number of other supernatural feats, and, heavily pregnant, sets out for Silla. The power of the kami carry her boat all the way to the Silla capital of Kyŏngju, twelve miles inland. The King of Silla immediately surrenders, followed by the kings of the other Korean states of Koguryŏ and Paekche, all swearing to regularly send tribute to Japan. Jingū returns and, after putting down a rebellion, rules as regent for her son for sixty-nine years. Book 9 also cites *Notes on the Emperor's Doings* (*Jin qi ju zhu* 晋起居注) to make Jingū appear to be the same figure as Pimiko.

After Jingū's death, her adult son Ōjin, the subject of Book 10, succeeds to the throne. Ōjin's reign is filled with exchanges with foreign states and with the Emishi people. Most notable, in 284–285 CE, lettered public servants arrive from Paekche. The first of these, Achiki, is noted to be a scholar of the Confucian Classics, and he becomes the founding ancestor of a clan of scribes. Achiki is followed by Wani, an even greater scholar, and Wani becomes the tutor of the crown prince. According to *Ancient Matters*, Wani also brought copies of *The Analects* (*Lun yu* 論語) and *The Thousand-Character Classic* (*Qianzi wen* 千字文) with him to Japan, though this more accurately describes the materials that an eighth-century Japanese person would begin with as reading and writing primers. A number of other immigrants, largely associated with textile production, later arrive from Wu. Ōjin's reign also sees the appearance and veneration of a powerful deity from Tsunuga on Japan's north-central coast, suggesting a non–Nara Basin point of origin for the imperial lineage from Ōjin.

Book 11 begins with an unusually long three-year period with an empty throne. Ōjin's two sons, one who was named crown prince, the other who was ultimately named the next emperor, Nintoku, continually defer the throne to one another until the crown prince at last kills himself to force Nintoku to become the next emperor. Nintoku's reign is a mixture of virtuous works and marital strife. Most famously, shortly after taking the throne, Nintoku looks upon his land from the top of a hill and sees few cooking fires burning, and so he invokes a tax holiday. His own palace falls into extreme disrepair, angering the empress, but Nintoku's virtuous rule is rewarded later when the people, now affluent, spontaneously come together to rebuild his palace. Later, Nintoku's pursuit of new consorts causes the empress to separate from him. Nintoku's rule is associated with the Osaka area, across the western mountains of the Nara Basin, and his tomb is usually considered to be the Daisenryō Tumulus, the largest tomb in Japan at over 2,000 feet wide and 2,700 feet long.

The reigns of two of Nintoku's sons, Richū and Hanzei, make up the annals of Book 12. Richū was named crown prince, but after Nintoku's death, narrowly escaped assassination thanks to the help of three trusted retainers, each associated with powerful clans: Heguri, Mononobe, and Aya. In 403, the fourth year of his reign, Richū allegedly sent scribes to the provinces of Japan for the first time, an entry influenced by Chinese records but also reflecting the development of literate administration in Japan at the time the *Chronicles* was being compiled. Hanzei's reign, only five years in length and with only four entries, is the shortest in the *Chronicles*.

Book 13 continues with Nintoku's fourth son, who ruled as Ingyō. Another mutual deferment opens the book, this time between Ingyō and his younger brother Ō-kusaka, and Ingyō is eventually convinced to accede to the throne by his consort. Ingyō's mysterious illness, which he had from a young age, is healed by a Silla doctor, and he rules for forty-two years. Of particular note is a 415 order that the proper genealogical lineages of aristocratic families be investigated and clarified owing to falsified claims and erroneous information. In the eighth-century court where the *Chronicles* was produced, heritage was important in determining privilege, and the suggestion that the true descendants of the kami were mixed up was frequently repeated elsewhere, including in the preface to *Ancient Matters*. Ingyō was succeeded by his son, Ankō, but after only three years on the throne, he was killed by his adopted stepson, whose father Ankō had killed on account of a slanderous accusation.

Book 14, on the violent and powerful Emperor Yūryaku, begins with a swift and brutal cull of the now numerous imperial princes. Upon the assassination of his brother Ankō, Yūryaku kills not only the assassin but also two of his brothers, who he suspects are involved in the plot. He also kills one of his uncles, a son of Richū, though it is through the bloodline of this uncle that the throne later stays within the descendants of Nintoku after the death of Yūryaku's son. Yūryaku's annals, one of the longest books in the *Chronicles*, is filled with numerous episodes demonstrating the emperor's savage personality and godlike strength. It also includes details on the successful Koguryŏ attack on the Paekche capital of Wiryesŏng, northeast of present-day Seoul. In his final edict, Yūryaku implores his ministers to ensure that his son Seinei be protected from his other son Hoshikawa, and that Seinei succeed him to the throne.

Book 15 covers three emperors, more than any other in the *Chronicles*. Yūryaku's son, Seinei, succeeds his father, but dies after only five years on the throne with no heir of his own. In the second year of Seinei's reign, a vassal discovers two grandsons of Richū who had gone into hiding when Yūryaku killed their father. When Seinei discovers the two brothers, he immediately has them brought to the palace and names the older brother, Ninken, crown prince. However, after Seinei's death, Ninken refuses to take the throne in deference to his younger brother Kenzō, who he insists was responsible for the two being discovered and rescued. In the interim, their older sister, Iidoyo, rules for eleven months before dying. Like Yamato Take, the *Chronicles* accords imperial status to Iidoyo, but she is not included in the traditional count of emperors. Kenzō at last succeeds, and after his death, Ninken rules for eleven years.

Book 16, one of the shortest in the *Chronicles*, is also one of the most complex. Its emperor, Buretsu, is the oldest son of Ninken, and the brief chronicle alternates between three narrative threads. One is Buretsu's courtship and his conflict with the son of his senior minister, which takes place in a series of nine poems. Another is the record of a succession crisis in Paekche, which ultimately sees the people rise up and depose their king. This story closely matches the chronology given in Korean sources, but differs widely in narrative details. Yet another is the numerous gruesome and cruel actions of Buretsu, such as tearing out a man's fingernails and making him dig up sweet potatoes by hand. Only the first of these three is shared with *Ancient Matters*. Since Buretsu had no heirs, it may be that the compilers of the *Chronicles* peppered his record with cruel deeds to explain why his line failed.

Reception

Reception of the *Chronicles* outside of Japan is extremely limited and unfortunately associated with Japanese wartime activity. During the early twentieth century, the *Chronicles* was interpreted to support military expansion of the Japanese empire. The *Chronicles* imagines the kingdoms on the Korean peninsula as tributary states of a Yamato empire, and this vision was construed by modern Japanese readers to suggest that Japan had a legitimate territorial claim to the Korean peninsula. Later, the phrase "eight directions under one roof" (*hakkō ichiu* 八紘一宇), which appears in the *Chronicles* as *hakkō iu* 八紘為宇, was interpreted as a divine mandate for Japanese conquest of the whole world. In the *Chronicles*, the first emperor, Jinmu, uses the phrase to indicate his subjugation of the entire Yamato area, the present-day Nara Basin. The phrase itself likely derives from *Rhapsody on the Shu Metropolis* (*Shudu fu* 蜀都賦), by Zuo Si 左思 (ca. 250–ca. 305). The *Chronicles*, along with *Ancient Matters*, also made up the canon for state-sponsored and organized Shinto religion. At the end of World War II, the *Chronicles* lost the status of scripture, the emperor renounced his divinity, Korea regained its independence, and Japanese military expansion was curtailed. However, the legacy of Japanese colonialism left the historical reception of the *Chronicles* in Asia, especially in Korea, as a topic of contention and resentment. I stress that this translation of the *Chronicles* does not endorse its facticity.

The reception of the *Chronicles* within Japan, especially in the premodern era, is long and rich. Because *The Chronicles of Japan* is one of the first records of the Japanese creation myths and served as the foundation of the first Japanese state, generations of Japanese commentators have used the text to explain their world and its fundamental forces. As worldviews changed over time, the interpretation of the *Chronicles* changed as well, and a history of this text's reading and reception doubles as a snapshot of Japanese intellectual history.

During the ninth and tenth centuries in Japan, the *Chronicles* was ensconced as a state classic and canonical text. This operation was accomplished primarily by court-sponsored readings of the *Chronicles*, in which a court scholar would read the text out loud from beginning to end as an official ceremony. Attended by high-ranking members of the court, these ceremonies ensured that the *Chronicles*, as opposed to *Ancient Matters* or other early histories of the Japanese state, would be the official, orthodox version of events. The court readings also broached the problem of vernacular reading. Because the *Chronicles* was read out loud in vernacular Japanese, the scholar performing the reading would also be required to assign vernacular readings to the Literary Sinitic text. Existing notes from these readings reveal that this was a complicated and contested process, often with debates over the correct vernacular reading and disagreements with the conclusions reached at earlier court readings. Importantly, scholars in the ninth and tenth centuries did not assume that there was an original vernacular version of the *Chronicles* used to produce the Literary Sinitic text that we have today, nor did they insist on a one-to-one translation from Chinese to Japanese.

In the late tenth, eleventh, and twelfth centuries, political power shifted away from the emperor, first to the Fujiwara regents, then to the Taira and Minamoto warrior clans. Public readings of the *Chronicles*, which reiterated the origins of imperial legitimacy, ended in 965. Active scholarship on the text reached a nadir. At the same time, the emerging occupations of professional poet and poetry instructor, which were at the height of high culture in the era, placed a special emphasis on origin anecdotes. In composing a poem, the poet was expected not only to demonstrate classical poetic tropes and vocabulary, but also to understand the context from which classical motifs derived and be able to provide an explanatory anecdote. It was not uncommon for these anecdotes to cite the *Chronicles*, sometimes accurately but usually speciously. As such, in this period, the *Chronicles* went from being a canonical text to being a nebulous repository of origin anecdotes. In this capacity, citations of the work grew outward from poetics into various other genres such as prose fiction, picture scrolls, and legal writings.

The thirteenth to fifteenth centuries saw a renewed interest in study of the *Chronicles*. The most significant early achievement was the commentary *Explanation of the "Chronicles"* (*Shaku Nihongi* 釈日本紀), written around the turn of the fourteenth century by the Urabe clan, which specialized in the study of this text. The *Explanation* collected many of the notes from ninth- and tenth-century court readings, and the authors of this text envisioned themselves as continuing this reading tradition. Their specialized knowledge of the *Chronicles* also gave them a claim to court privilege, as they could identify the proper historical procedure for such ceremonies as imperial accession. Other major works included new histories of Japan that relied on and actively cited the *Chronicles*. Crucially, all of these works also incorporated Buddhist ontological and cosmological tenets, as Buddhism was the dominant intellectual tradition of the era. Later materials also began to incorporate Zhu Xi Confucian metaphysics. The Buddhist epistemological paradigm that ruled the day asserted that knowledge was created by identifying parallels. Scholars identified commonalities between the *Chronicles*, Buddhist doctrine, Zhu Xi Confucian metaphysics, and Daoist ideals.

In the sixteenth century, the emphasis on parallels ultimately resulted in a new formulation that imagined the *Chronicles* to be the original and primary locus of truth, with Buddhist and Chinese works as supplements. Japan was the seed, China the stem, and India the flower, and this relation was confirmed by the return of the flower to its seeds, that is, by the spread of Buddhism through China to Japan. A new sect of Shinto, Yoshida Shinto, claimed that the *Chronicles* was holy scripture, and that its pages revealed the ultimate secrets and mysteries of the universe.

The seventeenth and eighteenth centuries were dominated by Confucian approaches to reading the *Chronicles*. One such approach was based on Zhu Xi

Confucian metaphysics and attempted to reinterpret the *Chronicles* on that theological grounding. An alternative, the Suika sect of Shinto, building on Yoshida traditions, made the *Chronicles* the holy scripture of a world governed by Zhu Xi Confucian metaphysical principles. The Suika approach found favor with the Tokugawa shogunate and samurai elite, who had reoriented state government on Confucian principles during the seventeenth century. The Suika approach attempted to overthrow the shogunate on behalf of the emperor—a movement that resulted in the dissolution of the Suika sect, but not before several major commentaries on the *Chronicles* were produced by Suika theologians.

From the mid-eighteenth through the nineteenth centuries, a new paradigm of reading that emphasized empirical methods slowly grew to dominate the intellectual scene. Several texts that claimed to predate the *Chronicles*, including the *Original Records of Previous Reigns and Past Matters* (*Sendai kuji hongi* 先代旧事本紀), were exposed as products of a later era. Suika scholarship on the *Chronicles*, which often referred to secret transmissions or forced the application of Zhu Xi Confucian metaphysics, met with harsh criticism. A new style of commentary that culled spurious readings and forced analogues took hold, culminating in the *Collected Explanations of the "Chronicles"* (*Shoki shikkai* 書紀集解, sometimes called *Shoki shūge*). The same approach led to the first-ever full commentary of *Ancient Matters*, namely, *Commentary on "An Account of Ancient Matters"* (*Kojiki-den* 古事記伝), by Motoori Norinaga (1730–1801). The publication of this work brought *Ancient Matters* out of the shadow of the *Chronicles* for the first time, even though its commentator relied heavily on the *Chronicles* to produce this commentary.

During the first half of the twentieth century, both *Ancient Matters* and the *Chronicles* were identified as holy texts for a state-sponsored Shinto cult focused on worship of the emperor as a living deity. Among scholars working on the first two books of the *Chronicles*, heated debates began between mythologists and theologians about how these books should be interpreted and what their significance was for modern Shinto. The historical books of the *Chronicles* were more problematic. Comparison with Chinese records and archeological excavations yielded little support for Jinmu's Japanese empire of 660 BCE. Historian Tsuda Sōkichi, writing in the early 1920s, suggested that the early emperors were fictitious, which was hardly contentious at the time. The first English translator of the *Chronicles*, W. G. Aston, had come to the same conclusion in 1896, a conclusion shared by many early modern Japanese readers. However, in 1940 Tsuda was put on trial and convicted of insulting the imperial dignity for his writings twenty years earlier. Also contentious were suggestions, largely in the later books of the *Chronicles*, that the Kaya Confederacy was under Japanese control. These suggestions were taken out of context to mean that Japan actually ruled the peninsula in the premodern era. Interpreted at its most extreme, the *Chronicles* was invoked to claim Japanese superiority over the entire world, on the basis of a statement cobbled together from Book 3, *hakkō ichiu* (eight directions under one roof 八紘一宇). A 1940 monument bearing this slogan was erected in Miyazaki Prefecture, which the *Chronicles* identifies as Jinmu's initial departure point.

At the end of World War II, Emperor Hirohito renounced his divinity, and the *Chronicles* went from sacred text back to state history. The secularization of the *Chronicles* opened it up to new avenues of academic study, but because of the perception that *Ancient Matters* was more authentically Japanese, study of the *Chronicles* lagged behind that of *Ancient Matters* throughout the twentieth century. However, both texts are counted among Japan's greatest classics, and as such are the subject of continuous adaptations and reimaginings. More recently, these adaptations have appeared in manga, anime, and video games, and while few Japanese people are directly familiar with the *Chronicles* through its original text, many of its most popular stories and kami are household knowledge. Most significantly, the *Chronicles* continues to serve as a key resource for the continually evolving discourse on Japanese identity.

The Text

Manuscript lineages of the *Chronicles* are divided into two general groups: non-Urabe and Urabe, referring to the Urabe clan that specialized in the study of the *Chronicles* in premodern and early modern Japan. The oldest non-Urabe manuscripts date from the tenth century, but these contain only portions of the text. Many non-Urabe manuscripts are of the first two books of the *Chronicles*, the "Age of the Gods." The most important distinction between the Urabe and non-Urabe editions is that some of the oldest non-Urabe editions write the variant texts that appear in the Divine Age in half-width characters, suggesting that these variants were originally intended to function as notes. Urabe editions write these variants in full-size characters with one additional level of indentation. This formatting benefitted Urabe clan interpretations of the *Chronicles* in medieval Japan, as the tradition of Shinto that came out of the Urabe editions, the Yoshida interpretation, relied on information contained only in the variant texts. For the modern reader, the most salient issue is that the early non-Urabe-lineage manuscripts of the *Chronicles* are all partial. Consequently, modern editions universally have their roots in Urabe-lineage manuscripts. The actual basis for nearly every modern edition of the *Chronicles* is the so-called Kanbun 9 edition, published in 1669. The Kanbun 9 edition is of further significance in that it contains vernacular glosses for the entire text of the *Chronicles*.

Though modern Japanese editions of the *Chronicles* generally hold the Classical Chinese text in common, the vernacular readings vary widely between editions. This variance results from editorial perspective, and there is no one right way to read the text. Some editions reproduce the vernacular readings from the Kanbun 9 edition as is, some editions incorporate historically attested readings that predate 1669, and some editions simply remove the vernacular glosses entirely. This translation is based primarily on the 1994–1995 five-volume Iwanami bunko edition, which is itself a corrected edition of the 1965–1967 Iwanami Nihon koten bungaku taikei edition. The original text provided with this translation mostly matches that given in the Iwanami bunko edition, though some elements have been amended after comparing with other modern editions and the 1669 Kanbun 9 edition. Similarly, the translation provided here is based primarily on the vernacular given in the Iwanami bunko edition, but again, it has been amended after consulting other editions.

In addition to the Iwanami bunko and Iwanami Nihon koten bungaku taikei editions, there are several significant modern editions. The 2021 Kōdansha Shinshaku zenyaku edition, while not yet complete, will undoubtedly be the gold standard for modern Japanese editions of the *Chronicles* for the rest of the twenty-first century. The 1994–1998 Shogakukan Shinpen koten bungaku zenshū edition uses an unorthodox set of vernacular readings, but contains many valuable notes and a modern Japanese translation. Also of note are the Yoshikawa kōbunkan Shintei zōho kokushi taikei, Shinto taikei, and Inoue Mitsusada–edited Chūō kōron editions, all of which are useful reference materials.

The translation provided here was based primarily on the vernacular glosses, because this is how Japanese readers have tended to engage with this text. There are several notable exceptions to this trend, but since the original text of the *Chronicles* itself includes vernacular reading notes, and since the earliest readings of this text appear to have centered on establishing vernacular readings, it is clear that the *Chronicles* has always been a hybrid text. I encourage readers to consult with modern Japanese editions that reproduce the vernacular glosses in cases where my translation seemingly departs from the Classical Chinese text. While I admit that no exact one-to-one meaning exists between Chinese, Japanese, and English words, the vernacular glosses by and large stay close to the Chinese. In cases where the vernacular gloss differs markedly from the Literary Sinitic, this translation gives priority to the gloss. For example, in S1.5, the character *ren* 人 is glossed "kami," and so it has been translated as "kami" and not as "human."

Previous Translations

The Chronicles of Japan was among the first Japanese works translated into English, by W. G. Aston in 1896. However, the complex structure of the text is not adequately reflected in his translation's paratextual elements. As such, it is difficult for the English reader to navigate the divisions and variant texts in the "Age of the Gods" and the parenthetical notes included in the annals of the original text. Aston also translated the more salacious sections of the work into Latin. Robert Borgen and Marian Ury addressed the inaccessibility of Aston's work with their "Readable Japanese Mythology" (1990), but their translation is only about forty pages in total, less than five percent of the original text, and there are few notes. Karl Florenz published two partial translations in German: Books 1 and 2 of the *Chronicles* as *Japanische Mythologie* in 1901, and Books 22 to 30 as *Japanische Annalen* in 1903. Florenz provides more notes than Aston, and the translation is of excellent quality though now quite dated. Florenz's earlier translations from the *Chronicles* (1892–1897) also influenced Aston, who thanks Florenz in the acknowledgments to his 1896 translation. In Russian, Liudmila Ermakova has published a translation of the *Chronicles* in two volumes (1997). Ekaterina Levchenko has published a Russian translation of the poetry from both the *Chronicles* and *Ancient Matters* as *Songs of "Kojiki" and "Nihon shoki"* (2019).

Ancient Matters has enjoyed broader translation. Basil Hall Chamberlain's 1882 translation was one of the first translations of any Japanese classic into English. Donald L. Philippi retranslated *Ancient Matters* in 1968, updating the translation and providing more accurate transliterations of the Old Japanese used for the names of kami. Poet Danno Yoko produced an eminently readable translation as *Songs and Stories of the Kojiki* in 2008. Two less widely read translations were done by Isobe Yaichiro in 1929 and Inoue Shunji in 1965. Finally, Gustav Heldt translated *Ancient Matters* in 2014. Heldt's translation is the definitive edition in English, and its extensive glossaries and paratextual elements are indispensable to the study of early Japan. Previous translations of *Ancient Matters* into English are of immense value for their scholarship, and each has its own distinguishing features.

Ancient Matters has enjoyed wide publication in other languages. In German, Klaus Antoni translated *Ancient Matters* as *Kojiki: Aufzeichnung alter Begebenheiten* in 2012. Previously, Iwao Kinoshita produced a partial German translation in 1940 as *Kozikï – älteste japanische Reichsgeschichte*. Unfortunately, the final sections of this translation were lost to a fire in 1944 before they could be printed. Iwao then repeated his translation work and published the remainder in German translation in 1976. In French, Masumi and Maryse Shibata translated *Ancient Matters* as *Kojiki: chronique des choses anciennes* in 1969, followed by Pierre Vinclair, who translated it in 2011 as *Kojiki: chronique des faits anciens*. Jooffrey Chassat translated Book 1 of *Ancient Matters* as *Kojiki, mythes choisis* in 2016. *Ancient Matters* has been translated into Italian twice, first by Mario Marega as *Ko-gi-ki: Vecchie, cose, scritte; libro base dello shintoismo giapponese* in 1938, and then by Paolo Villani as *Kojiki: Un racconto di antichi eventi* in 2006. In Polish, Wiesław Kotański translated the text as *Kojiki czyli Księga dawnych wydarzeń* in 1986. A Spanish translation by Carlos Rubio and Rumi Tani Moratalla was published as *Kojiki: Crónicas de antiguos hechos de Japón* in 2014. Finally, Liudmila Ermakova has published a Russian translation of Book 2 of *Ancient Matters* (1995).

My notes frequently refer to *Ancient Matters*, *Original Records*, *New Selected Records of Names and Titles* (*Shinsen shōjiroku* 新撰姓氏録), *Myriad Poems*, and provincial gazetteers known as *Gazetteers* or as *Records of Wind and Earth* (*Fudoki* 風土記). I encourage the reader to refer to the Heldt translation of *Ancient Matters*, the Bentley translation of *Sendai kuji hongi*, the Aoki translation of the *Provincial Gazetteers of Hitachi, Izumo, Harima, Bungo*, and *Hizen* (published as *Records of Wind and Earth*), and the Palmer translation of the *Provincial Gazetteer of Harima* (published as *Harima Fudoki*). Citations of nonextant provincial gazetteers in later texts, as well as *New Selected Records*, are invaluable for the study of the *Chronicles*. Unfortunately, these materials are not available in English. *Myriad Poems* is available in numerous partial translations, with those by Ian Hideo Levy, Edwin Cranston, and Alexander Vovin worthy of recommendation.

This Translation

Place-names are transliterated from Japanese into English. In many cases, these names have meanings associated with their geography and topography, much like Dublin ("dark pool"), but such translations are not given here. When possible, the modern equivalents of place-names in the text are given in the notes, though many locations remain unknown. Place-names identified in modern Japan are given with varying specificity, depending on available information. Japanese administration usually follows the pattern of city, prefecture, or of town, district, prefecture. When possible, a more specific "area" (Jp. *chō* 町) is given, which usually corresponds with a geographical area of several square blocks. A list of historical Japanese provinces and their approximate modern equivalents, along with a map, are provided in Map 1; prefectures are omitted when the equivalent province is given. North and South Korean locations are given as either city, province, or as town, province. For place-names well known in the English-speaking world, long vowels have been omitted in transliterations (Osaka, not Ōsaka). Note that a single name, for example, Ōsaka, may be used for multiple places, especially when transcribed in the Roman alphabet; when Ōsaka has a long vowel indicated, it refers to a location other than Japan's third-largest city.

The original text often uses the administrative divisions of district and province. In truth, this usage is anachronistic, as these geographic boundaries were not formally established until the late seventh century. From the standpoint of the *Chronicles*, they were created during the legendary reign of Emperor Seimu. Making matters more confusing, the word and character for "province" is the same as that used for "land" and "country." As such, when the word for province appears in the original text narrative prior to the Seimu book, it is translated as "land." For example, the Japanese designation *Ki no kuni* is translated as "the land of Ki" prior to Seimu and "Ki Province" after Seimu, reflecting the formalization of this geographical boundary. Lands outside the Japanese realm incorporate the word "land" into their place-name, for example, "the Land of Ne" or "the Land of Tokoyo."

Personal names in the *Chronicles* are often very long, potentially comprising a job or posting, a place-name, a title of nobility, a lineage group

MAP 1 Provinces of Old Japan

name, a personal or individual name, and finally, a suffix denoting affection or status. In Japanese, each of these elements is separated by the genitive marker "no" or "tsu." More on these individual elements and how they are treated in this translation follows. The guiding principle in this translation is to limit names so that they have only one genitive marker. This makes the names in the *Chronicles* more closely approximate Japanese names as they customarily appear in later periods, for example, Fujiwara no Michinaga 藤原道長 (966–1028) or Taira no Kiyomori 平清盛 (1118–1181). Of course, these monikers for Michinaga and Kiyomori would not have been used to address or write about these figures in their own lifetimes, and this is the case for the earlier era of the *Chronicles* as well. Earlier names in the *Chronicles* tend to be longer, and their semantic elements are of more value. Accordingly, the trend in this translation in addressing the long historical period narrated by the *Chronicles* is to reduce hyphenation as names become shorter and come to more closely resemble the customary format for Japanese names in later periods, that is, family name, genitive marker, and personal name, with no hyphenation. English transliterations of Japanese names in the Jinmu and Suizei books use hyphens, but by the Yūryaku book, set nearly one thousand years later in the narrative, many English transliterations of Japanese names omit the hyphens.

Place-names in Japanese often have a very close, sometimes indivisible, association with personal names, in the fashion of the "House of Windsor." In cases where the place-name is clearly separable, and because it is often of consequence to the narrative, it is given in this translation following the personal name and preceded by the preposition "of," such as "Oto-hime of Kazuraki." Some place-names later became lineage names, for example, Soga, Heguri, or Wani. These names refer to physical locations in the Nara Basin that were the base of operations for these lineage groups, but the place-names came to function as the name of the lineage itself. In these cases, names are given with the location as the lineage group name, for example, Soga no Umako.

In the ancient period, Japanese aristocratic families often had a *kabane*, or title of nobility. These titles were amended several times, and a wide variety appear in the *Chronicles*. In Japanese, they fall at the end of the name: "Wani-no-omi," but in this translation, they are relocated to the front, so "Omi of Wani." Titles indicating authority over a given geographic region use "of," and the definite article is added when the authority is, or appears to be, over a group of people instead: "Muraji of the Ōtomo." A full explanation of the changing standards for titles of nobility appears in the Introduction to Volume 2 of *The Chronicles of Japan*. During the period covered by Volume 1, these titles were not formally systematized. The following titles appear in this volume and are not translated: Omi, Muraji,

Provincial Miyatsuko, Allied Miyatsuko, Kimi, Atai, Inaki, Wake, Sukune, Obito, Kishi, Suguri, Tami no tsukai, and Agata-nushi.

Some titles of nobility are shared with elements of names. Sukune, for example, is used both as an affectionate suffix in a name and as a title of nobility. When it appears as a suffix with no lineage group listed, the Sukune usually becomes part of the name itself, and is here transliterated in the Japanese order: "Takeuchi no Sukune." When it is a title of nobility, it is relocated to the front, like other such titles: "Sukune of Murata." When it appears in the name of an emperor as a suffix of affection, it is transliterated with hyphenation: "O-asazuma-wakugo-no-sukune." When it appears with a lineage name and a personal name as a suffix of affection, it is given at the beginning of the name after the position and/or title of nobility, for example, "the Ō-omi, Sukune Soga no Iname," in order to avoid using multiple genitive makers. Note that the title of nobility for the Soga was Omi, and the treatment here admittedly introduces a potential ambiguity. In my opinion, such occasions are rare enough, and the figures they apply to are well enough known, that this ambiguity is acceptable in order to prevent names from becoming overly long throughout the entire text. Another important exception is Wake, which is often appended to male names as a term of endearment but blurs the line between title and name.

The *be*, or hereditary guild, refers a group of people usually charged with the production of a certain kind of product, such as ceramics, or with the fulfillment of a certain duty, such as guard. *Be* is always translated as "hereditary guild," but when an individual has a *be* in their title of nobility, the meaning of the *be* is not translated, as in "Muraji of the Tama hereditary guild," and a note is added indicating that the Tama were responsible for the production of jewels. When the group is referred to in the text, then the occupational role is translated: "the jewel-makers hereditary guild." The reason for this distinction is that when the titled individual is mentioned in the text, often the context has nothing to do with the etymological origins of his title. However, when the hereditary guild is mentioned, it is usually in the context of whatever specialization that group possesses.

Names of kami, Japanese deities, are transliterated in the text as in modern Japanese. Hyphens have been added to divide the names up based on semantic units. Names often contain genitive postpositions (*no, nu, na, tsu*), which have no meaning of their own. Because the meanings of these names is tightly connected to the narrative, translations of the names of kami are given in the Glossary of Kami. Not every name is precisely known, and there may be alternative meanings in some cases. Translations are also provided in the notes for the vernacular Japanese names of emperors. Translations for the names of other human figures are not provided unless relevant to the narrative. Many kami have multiple names within the *Chronicles*, and their names also may differ from those given in *Ancient Matters* and other sources. Kami names often differ slightly from how they appear in *Ancient Matters*. This translation gives names based on traditional readings from the *Chronicles*, but since the names in *Ancient Matters* tend to be used as the canonical names, usages from both texts, as well as from the *Gazetteer of Izumo Province*, *Gazetteer of Harima Province*, and *Original Records*, are provided in the glossary. The English translations used in the Heldt translation of *Ancient Matters* and the Old Japanese transliteration from the Philippi translation of *Ancient Matters* are also provided. Four kami who appear frequently in the text or notes—Izanagi, Izanami, Amaterasu, and Susano-o—have their hyphenation removed after the first instance. The first three generations of earthly rulers are referred to in the paratext by their abbreviated names: Ninigi, Oshi-ho-mimi, and Fuki-aezu.

Japanese emperors also have Chinese titles, which were assigned many decades after the *Chronicles* was first compiled. Consequently, within the text, emperors are referred to exclusively with their Japanese names. However, printed and manuscript copies of the *Chronicles* provide the Chinese titles, and in secondary sources emperors are referred to almost exclusively by their Chinese titles. In this translation, emperors are referred to using their Japanese names as given in the original text of the *Chronicles*, but in the notes and this Introduction, emperors are referred to using their Chinese names, in keeping with scholarly tradition. The names can be resolved using Table 2. The meaning and likely Chinese sources of these titles are provided in the notes at the opening of each emperor's book.

In principle, Korean names are transliterated from the modern Korean reading of the original Chinese characters. However, I frequently made exceptions owing to the difficulty of this enterprise. Some names originate in Korean Peninsula languages only loosely or not at all related to the language that ultimately became modern Korean, and their transliteration first from some peninsular language into Japanese using Chinese characters in the *Chronicles*, then back into modern Korean in this translation, is by nature imprecise. Some Korean names rely on the Japanese vernacular usage of a character; in these cases, the name cannot be directly transcribed into modern Korean. Also, I may give the names of mythical figures that likely have no relation to a historical Korean person using only Japanese. For example, the mythical Silla prince Ame-no-hi-hoko, whose name is clearly of Japanese origin, is given in Japanese. Moreover, because some Korean personal names from Paekche and the Kaya Confederacy are difficult to parse and could ultimately translate back into multiple Korean sounds, and because English and Japanese secondary scholarship mostly use the Japanese versions of these names, I provide the modern Japanese transliteration in Table 3.

TABLE 2 JAPANESE EMPERORS' NAMES, VOLUME 1

COUNT*	JAPANESE NAME(S)	SINITIC NAME	REIGN DATES†
1	Kamu-yamato-iware-hiko; Hiko-ho-ho-de-mi; Sa-no; Kamu-yamato-iware-hiko-ho-ho-de-mi	Jinmu	660–585 BCE
2	Kamu-nu-na-kawa-mimi	Suizei	581–549 BCE
3	Shiki-tsu-hiko-tamate-mi	Annei	549–511 BCE
4	Ō-yamato-hiko-suki-tomo	Itoku	510–477 BCE
5	Mima-tsu-hiko-kaeshi-ne	Kōshō	475–393 BCE
6	Yamato-tarashi-hiko-kuni-oshi-hito	Kōan	392–291 BCE
7	Ō-yamato-neko-hiko-futo-ni	Kōrei	290–215 BCE
8	Ō-yamato-neko-hiko-kuni-kuru	Kōgen	214–158 BCE
9	Waka-yamato-neko-hiko-ō-bibi	Kaika	157–98 BCE
10	Mi-maki-iri-biko-i-nie	Sujin	97–30 BCE
11	Ikume-iri-biko-isa-chi	Suinin	29 BCE–70 CE
12	Ō-tarashi-hiko-oshiro-wake	Keikō	71–130
13	Waka-tarashi-hiko	Seimu	131–190
14	Tarashi-naka-tsu-hiko	Chūai	192–200
	Okinaga-tarashi-hime	Jingū	201–269
15	Homuta	Ōjin	270–310
16	Ōsazaki	Nintoku	311–399
17	Ōe-no-izaho-wake, Izaho-wake	Richū	400–405
18	Mitsu-ha-wake	Hanzei	406–410
19	O-asazuma-wakugo-no-sukune	Ingyō	411–453
20	Anaho	Ankō	453–456
21	Ō-hatsuse-no-waka-take, Ō-hatsuse	Yūryaku	456–479
22	Shiraka-no-take-hiro-kuni-oshi-waka-yamato-neko, Shiraka	Seinei	480–484
23	Oke; Kume-no-wakugo	Kenzō	485–487
24	Oke; Ōshi; Ōsu; Shima-no-iratsuko; Shima-no-wakugo	Ninken	488–498
25	O-hatsuse-no-waka-sazaki, O-hatsuse	Buretsu	499–506

* The count of Japanese emperors has been frequently revised. The current count, determined by the Imperial Household Agency, does not include Jingū as an emperor.
† The reign dates given here, determined by the Imperial Household Agency based on the *Chronicles*, are not always consistent with *Ancient Matters* or even within the *Chronicles* itself.

INTRODUCTION   xli

TABLE 3 KOREAN TO JAPANESE NAMES

KOREAN NAME	JAPANESE NAME	ORIGINAL CHARACTERS
Ahwa	Aka	阿花
Ajikki	Achiki	阿直伎
Asuji	Ashuchi	阿首至
Ch'im	Hari	針
Ch'imnyu	Tomuru	枕流
Ch'ogo	Shōko	肖古
Chemaryŏ	Otomaro	弟麻呂
Chigo	Chiko	知古
Chikchi	Toki	直支
Chingma-nanagabigwe	Chikuma-nanahiku	職麻那々加比跪
Chinmojin	Maketsu	眞毛津
Chinsa	Shinshi	辰斯
Chŏng-mag-ihae	Chaku-maku-nige	適莫爾解
Chwaro	Saru	左魯
Hŏji-pŏrhan	Kochi-hotsukan	許智伐旱
Hyŏngmaryŏ	Emaro	兄麻呂
Imunji	Nimonchi	爾汶至
Iramaju	Iramasu	伊羅麻酒
Kaero	Kōro / Kasuri no Kishi	蓋鹵 / 加須利君
Kibon Han'gi	Koho-kanki	己本旱岐
Kijŏnji	Kedenchi	既殿至
King Muryŏng	Munei	武寧王
Koihae	Konige	古爾解
Konji	Konki	昆支王
Konji	Konki	琨支王
Kuisin	Kuishin	久爾辛
Kujŏ	Kutei	久氐
Kuksari	Kokusari	國沙利
Kun	Kishi	君
Kuryeji	Kureshi	久禮志
Kuryep'a	Kureha	久禮波
Kwago	Wako	過古
Kwishin	Kuishin	貴信
Kwisu	Kuisu	貴須
Lady Chŏkkye	Iketsuhime / Chiyakukei	池津媛 / 適稽女郎
Makko	Makuko	莫古

(continued)

TABLE 3 KOREAN TO JAPANESE NAMES (CONTINUED)

KOREAN NAME	JAPANESE NAME	ORIGINAL CHARACTERS
Makkohae	Makukoge	莫古解
Malgŭm-han'gi	Makimu-kanki	末錦旱岐
Malta	Mata	末多王
Malta	Matsuta	末多王
Mana	Mana	麻那
Mijilgiji-p'ajin-kan'gi	Mishikochi-hatori-kanki	微叱己知波珍干岐
Mijirhŏji-pŏrhan	Mishikochi-hotsukan	微叱許智伐旱
Mijuryu	Mitsuru	彌州流
Mok Manch'i	Moku manchi	木滿致
Momarijilji	Momarishichi	毛麻利叱智
Mongna Kŭnja	Mokura Konshi	木羅斤資
Mun'gŭn	Monkon	文斤王
Muniu	Monsu	汶洲王
Nagit'a-gappae	Nakata-kōhai	那奇他甲背
Noryuji	Nuruki	奴流枳
Noshil	Muro	奴室
Ŏch'ang	Mikura	御倉
Oryesabŏl	Ureshihotsu	汙禮斯伐
P'asa-maegŭm	Hasa-mukimu	波沙寐錦
Paekch'ung	Momotsuki	百衝
Paekkujŏ	Hakukuchi	百久至
Puramoji	Horamochi	富羅母智
Saa	Shiga	遺期
Sajibigwe (Pigwe)	Sachihiku (Hiku)	沙至比跪
Sasanogwe	Sasanako	沙々奴跪
Sema / Munyŏng / Sama	Shima / Munei / Shima	嶋王 / 武寧王 / 斯麻王
Shinjedo-wŏn	Shisetsu-hime	新齊都媛
Soch'ang	Okura	小倉
Sonagalchilchi	Sonakashichi	蘇那曷叱智
Suryuji	Suruki	須流枳
Tongsŏng	Tōsei	東城王
Tonoa Arasadŭng	Tsunuga Arashito	都怒我阿羅斯等
Ŭidarang	Otara	意多郎
Uryuyujoburi-chigan	Uru-sohorichika	宇流助富利智干
Usagi Arijilji Kan'gi	Ushiki arishichi kanki	于斯岐阿利叱智于岐
Wangin	Wani	王仁

INTRODUCTION   xliii

Sometimes it is unclear whether an individual is from Yamato (Japan) or one of the Korean states; in these cases, their names are simply reproduced in transcription from the Japanese. Chinese names are transliterated from the Mandarin reading of the original Chinese characters. I stress that modern Japanese, modern Korean, and modern Mandarin did not exist in their present forms at the time the *Chronicles* was compiled, and furthermore, that several languages were used on the Korean peninsula in antiquity.

The Korean states of Koguryŏ, Paekche, and Silla are given with their modern Korean names. While the *Chronicles* usually but not exclusively refers to these kingdoms as Koma, Kudara, and Shiragi, respectively, there rarely is confusion about which kingdom on the Korean peninsula is meant. However, in the case of states of the Kaya Confederacy, the *Chronicles* is inconsistent, especially in its usage of the terms "Kara" and "Mimana." Sometimes these terms refer to specific states of the confederacy, sometimes they refer to the entire confederacy, and sometimes the text is unclear. Furthermore, the states of the Kaya Confederacy were themselves in flux during the period narrated by the *Chronicles*. Because of this ambiguity, this translation reproduces the terminology used in the original text. The paratext uses the modern Korean names for these states when an identification between the state given in the *Chronicles* and a historically attested Kaya state can be surmised. Many place-names in Paekche either rely on the Japanese vernacular reading and cannot be directly transcribed into modern Korean, or transcribe a traditional reading from the era in which the *Chronicles* was compiled that is likely based on the language used in Paekche. That is, such place-names are transcribed as given in the original text. The treatment of place-names as they appear in the *Chronicles* in no way constitutes a political statement on the affiliation or constitution of the states of the Kaya Confederacy. The *Chronicles* imagines the states of the Korean peninsula as part of the Yamato realm, and while that sentiment is faithfully reproduced in this translation, as with the treatment of names, it should not be confused with historical fact or an expression of my opinion.

The translation uses a formal tone to convey the stiffness of the original text. The prose may occasionally sound repetitive to the reader, but this too is in keeping with the original written style. Direct speech that appears within the narrative occasionally uses a less formal style, which I render using more colloquial language or contractions, as appropriate.

There are ninety-five songs or poems in the first sixteen books of *The Chronicles of Japan*; the Japanese word *uta* can refer to either. These poems are written in the Japanese vernacular using Chinese characters to express their phonetic value. In Appendix 2, I have given the poems the numbers commonly given in modern Japanese editions of the *Chronicles*. Many of these poems also appear in *Ancient Matters*, though they sometimes have slightly different content, appear in different contexts, or have minor linguistic variations. The variance between the two texts suggests that while the poems imbue both works with a folklike quality, many of the poems have likely been edited and repurposed. For the same reason, their respective fit with the narrative context varies widely. Poems that appear in the 5-7-5-7-7 meter, such as Susano-o's famous first poem from the Age of the Gods, were likely refashioned to match what became the standard syllabic meter for Japanese vernacular poetry.

Japanese vernacular poetry from this period often makes use of so-called "pillow words," which precede certain nouns, usually place-names. For example, the place-names "Shiga" and "Ōtsu" may use the pillow word "sasanami no," meaning "of small waves." "Sasanami no Shiga" would then be a reference to Lake Biwa, which is the largest lake in Japan, and which dominates the Shiga region. Scholars disagree on whether pillow words should be translated into English or simply omitted. In this volume, I have adopted a case-by-case approach. When the meaning of a pillow word is known, and it contributes to the overall meaning of the poem in translation, I have provided a translation in English followed by a dagger (†). When the meaning is unknown, or when it is known but is not immediately related to the English translation of the poem, I have omitted the pillow word.

The variant texts and original notes in the *Chronicles*, combined with my footnotes and endnotes, result in several layers of annotation. Variant texts and original notes that contain narrative information are given within the main text of the translation, but in a smaller font. On the rare occasion when an original note occurs within a variant text, it is further enclosed in parentheses, since the entirety of the variant is already in a smaller font. Original notes appearing within longer quotations or poetry are also enclosed in parentheses, in addition to being given in a smaller font, to aid the reader in distinguishing them. I make an exception for original notes that provide alternative names of individuals or kami, which I have moved to the footnotes. Because these notes usually appear within lists of proper nouns, including them in the original text makes it difficult to keep track of how many kami or children are being discussed. These footnotes begin with the phrase "An original note . . ." to distinguish them from footnotes created for this translation.

My annotations are divided into footnotes and endnotes. The ultimate objective of this annotation style, in keeping with the guidelines of the Hsu-Tang Library, is to keep the main text as uncluttered as possible. Footnotes contain basic explanatory information required to understand the text. Endnotes contain further detail, including genealogical information, relevant content in other early Japanese texts, and references to works in the Classical Chinese canon.

The *Chronicles* contains 314 vernacular notes, brief entries that give the Japanese vernacular reading of a word or phrase. The style of these notes closely resembles the notation used for indicating South Asian vernacular words in translations of Buddhist texts into Classical Chinese, and this practice in Buddhist works almost certainly influenced its adoption in the *Chronicles*. As these notes appear in the oldest, handwritten manuscripts of the *Chronicles*, it is presumed that they are authentic. They suggest that even at the earliest stages of its creation, the *Chronicles* was meant to be read in the Japanese vernacular. In this translation, these notes have been omitted, as they have no English meaning, though they are retained in the original text. An exception is made when the vernacular notes are unorthodox, for example, when they address words from a separate variant text, because this suggests an alternative structure for the variant texts as a whole. In these cases, they have been moved to the footnotes and are distinguished by the opening "An original note . . . ."

The *Chronicles* is fairly consistent in its assignment of verbs for speaking, giving objects, and death. Accordingly, in this translation, emperors decree, proclaim, issue edicts, bestow objects on others, and expire, while lower-ranked individuals might perish or die. While this occasionally results in somewhat clumsy English, the distinctions are extremely important in understanding how the text imagines sovereignty and kingship. Similarly, emperors sometimes use the royal We. Because subjects are not always specified in Chinese and Japanese, standard first-person pronouns have been added for emperors, who are the subject of almost every sentence in the text. When a royal We is used in the Chinese text, it will appear in translation as well. The *Chronicles* also distinguishes between two different characters for the title of "mikoto" given to gods and important kami. Kami who were ancestors of the imperial clan and emperors use one character, while other kami and high-ranking figures use another. Since in this translation the title of "mikoto" is omitted for kami, and the *Chronicles* is very consistent in usage, application of this title can be safely assumed. The two cases in which a non-emperor receives the imperial title "mikoto," Yamato Take and Iidoyo, are identified in the notes.

As in *Ancient Matters*, the passage of time in the *Chronicles* is marked by the repeated use of several characters that at times function more like punctuation than as words: "then," "therefore," "thereby," "thereafter," "at that time," "before that," and so on. Many of these words have been faithfully reproduced in the translation, but their repetition makes the English clunky, especially when the passage of time or the transition to a new topic can be marked using paragraphs and punctuation marks. For this reason, I have taken the liberty of omitting some of these characters to improve readability. Similarly, I have added named subjects to some sentences to improve clarity, especially when the subject changes from the previous sentence or could be easily confused with others. This addition is especially pronounced in the annals, which often have "the emperor" as an assumed subject.

Weights and measure are sometimes confusing. The same character, for example, can be used for "span" and "shaftment," and there are instances in which the *Chronicles* appears to have confused the two. Measures appear in the original text using Chinese characters, but may not reflect the same unit as in China. Even in China, the value of measures changed over time. I have chosen measures that closely approximate Japanese ones, but they are not exact conversions. Measures are given in Table 4.

TABLE 4 UNITS OF MEASURE

JAPANESE UNIT	TRANSLATION	MEANING (JAPANESE)	MEANING (ENGLISH)
hiro	Fathom	Outstretched arms	Outstretched arms
tsuka	Hand	Width of fist	Across palm
tsuka (rice)	Bushel	Amount of rice from one *shiro*	Eight dry gallons
shaku	Span	Tip of thumb to tip of middle finger	Tip of thumb to tip of little finger
ata	Shaftment	Eight *sun*	Across palm, including outstretched thumb
sun	Inch	Width of thumb	Width of thumb
jō	Ten feet	Ten *shaku*, about three meters	Ten feet
chō (*chōbu*)	Hectare	Ten *hectares*, about 99 square meters	100 meters squared OR 10,000 square meters
shiro	Square rod	Area to produce one *tsuka* of rice, about 23 square meters, used before Taika reforms	One quarter of a chain in length, squared, about 25 square meters

神代上

古天地未剖、陰陽不分、渾沌如鶏子、溟涬而含牙。及其清陽者、薄靡而爲天、重濁者、淹滯而爲地、精妙之合搏易、重濁之凝竭難。故天先成而地後定。然後、神聖生其中焉。

故曰、開闢之初、洲壤浮漂、譬猶游魚之浮水上也。于時、天地之中生一物。狀如葦牙。便化爲神。號國常立尊。至貴曰尊、自餘曰命。並訓美擧等也。下皆效此。次國狹槌尊。次豐斟渟尊。凡三神矣。乾道獨化。所以、成此純男。

一書曰、天地初判、一物在於虛中。狀貌難言。其中自有化生之神。號國常立尊。亦曰國底立尊。次國狹槌尊。亦曰國狹立尊。次豐國主尊。亦曰豐組野尊。亦曰豐香節野尊。亦曰浮經野豐買尊。亦曰豐國野尊。亦曰豐䶊野尊。亦曰葉木國野尊。亦曰見野尊。

---

1   Unlike *Ancient Matters* of 712, in which heaven and earth already exist at the beginning of the narrative, the *Chronicles* starts with the formation of the universe itself. In the Main Version, the emphasis on yin and yang and its associated binaries is maintained throughout the creation process.

Book 1
Age of the Gods, 1

Section 1: Separation of Heaven and Earth, Three Generations of Gods

Main Version

Of old, when heaven and earth were still unparted and yin and yang undivided, the swirling mass was like the inside of an egg.¹ Within those murky depths sprouted a bud. The clear and bright rose up and became heaven, while the heavy and turbid stagnated and became earth. The ethereal essences coalesced effortlessly, but the heavier sediment coagulated crudely. Thus, the heavens formed first, while the earth stabilized later. Afterward, kami appeared within.ⁱ

Thus it is said that when heaven and earth first emerged, the land floated like frolicking fish on the surface of the water. At some point in time, a single thing burgeoned within heaven and earth. Its shape was like a budding reed. Then it became a kami. It was called Kuni-no-toko-tachi.

<small>Kami are given the title *mikoto*, written with the character for 'honored,' out of esteem. This title is also written with the character for 'life.' This applies to all the kami that follow.</small>

Next was Kuni-no-sa-tsuchi. Next was Toyo-kumu-nu. In all, there were three kami. They came into being solely by way of heaven. For this reason, they took male form.²

Section 1, Variant 1

One text says, When heaven and earth first divided, a thing existed in the sky. Its form is difficult to express. From within it, a kami spontaneously came into being called Kuni-no-toko-tachi and also Kuni-no-soko-tachi. Next was Kuni-no-sa-tsuchi, also called Kuni-no-sa-tachi. Next was Toyo-kuni-nushi, also called Toyo-kumi-no, Toyo-kabu-shino, Uki-funo-no-toyo-kai, Toyo-kuni-no, Toyo-kuhi-no, Hako-kuni-no, and Mi-no.³

---

2 This second paragraph is usually interpreted as a pivot from a world-creation story to the Japanese mythological tradition, though it has also been argued that it is rather a repeated explanation of the creation of the entire world. The character used for kami in this paragraph differs from that used in the first paragraph and also those used in Variants 3 and 5, though they are all given the vernacular Japanese gloss of "kami." The distinction between the two characters used for "mikoto" indicates a status difference among kami, including deified humans, such as emperors. Heaven is associated with yang power and masculinity, which is why these three kami appear as male deities.
3 The names of these kami describe land rising out of the water.

一書曰、古國稚地稚之時、譬猶浮膏而漂蕩。于時、國中生物。狀如葦牙之抽出也。因此有化生之神。號可美葦牙彥舅尊。次國常立尊。次國狹槌尊。葉木國、此云播擧矩爾。可美、此云于麻時。
一書曰、天地混成之時、始有神人焉。號可美葦牙彥舅尊。次國底立尊。彥舅、此云比古尼。
一書曰、天地初判、始有俱生之神。號國常立尊。次國狹槌尊。又曰、高天原所生神名、曰天御中主尊。次高皇産靈尊。次神皇産靈尊。皇産靈、此云美武須毗。
一書曰、天地未生之時、譬猶海上浮雲無所根係。其中生一物。如葦牙之初生埿中也。便化爲人。號國常立尊。
一書曰、天地初判、有物。若葦牙、生於空中。因此化神、號天常立尊。次可美葦牙彥舅尊。又有物。若浮膏生於空中。因此化神、號國常立尊。

Section 1, Variant 2

One text says, Of old, when the land was young, when the earth was young, it hovered like floating oil.[4][ii] At some point in time, something came into being within the land shaped like a budding reed bursting forth. Thus, there appeared a kami called Umashi-ashikabi-hikoji. Next was Kuni-no-toko-tachi. Next was Kuni-no-sa-tsuchi.

Section 1, Variant 3

One text says, When heaven and earth were mixed together, at first there was a kami called Umashi-ashikabi-hikoji.[5] Next was Kuni-no-soko-tachi.

Section 1, Variant 4

One text says, When heaven and earth first divided, in the beginning, some kami came into being together. One was called Kuni-no-toko-tachi. Next was Kuni-no-sa-tsuchi. It also says that the name of the kami that appeared in the High Heavenly Plain was Ama-no-mi-naka-nushi. Next was Taka-mi-musuhi. Next was Kamu-mi-musuhi.[iii]

Section 1, Variant 5

One text says, When heaven and earth had still not come into being, they were like clouds floating on the sea[iv] without connecting roots. A single thing burgeoned within. It was like a reed first budding out of the mud. Then it became a kami called Kuni-no-toko-tachi.

Section 1, Variant 6

One text says, When heaven and earth first divided, there was something like a reed bud that burgeoned in the sky. Thereby it became a kami called Ama-no-toko-tachi. Next was Umashi-ashikabi-hikoji. Also, something else, like floating oil, sprouted something in the sky[6] that became a kami called Kuni-no-toko-tachi.

---

4 An original note adds the vernacular Japanese in both this variant and Variant 1.
5 An original note adds the vernacular Japanese for "hikoji," though the word already appeared in Variant 2.
6 Variant 6 clarifies the references to reeds and grease in other variants by connecting one with heaven and the other with earth.

次有神。埿土煑尊埿土、此云于毗尼。沙土煑尊。沙土、此云須毗尼。亦曰埿土根尊・沙土根尊。次有神。大戸之道尊一云、大戸之邊。大苫邊尊。亦曰大戸摩彦尊・大戸摩姫尊。亦曰大富道尊・大富邊尊。次有神。面足尊・惶根尊。亦曰吾屋惶根尊。亦曰忌橿城尊。亦曰青橿城根尊。亦曰吾屋橿城尊。次有神。伊弉諾尊・伊弉冉尊。

　一書曰、此二神、青橿城根尊之子也。

　一書曰、國常立尊生天鏡尊。天鏡尊生天萬尊。天萬尊生沫蕩尊。沫蕩尊生伊弉諾尊。沫蕩、此云阿和那伎。

凡八神矣。乾坤之道、相參而化。所以、成此男女。自國常立尊、迄伊弉諾尊・伊弉冉尊、是謂神世七代者矣。

　一書曰、男女偶生之神、先有埿土煑尊・沙土煑尊。次有角樴尊・活樴尊。次有面足尊・惶根尊。次有伊弉諾尊・伊弉冉尊。樴、橛也。

Section 2: Four Generations of Paired Gods

Main Version

Next there were the kami U-hiji-ni and Su-hiji-ni.[7] Next there were the kami Ō-to-no-ji and Ō-toma-be.[8] Next there were the kami Omo-taru and Kashiko-ne.[9] Next there were the kami Izana-gi and Izana-mi.

Section 2, Variant 1

One text says, These two kami were children of Ao-kashi-ki-ne.[10]

Section 2, Variant 2

One text says, Kuni-no-toko-tachi gave birth to Ama-no-kagami, who gave birth to Ama-no-yorozu, who gave birth to Awa-na-gi, who gave birth to Izanagi.[11]

Section 3: Seven Generations of Gods

Main Version

In all, there were eight kami.[12] The ways of heaven and earth mixed together, and they came into being. Because of this mixing, these kami formed as male and female pairs. The kami from Kuni-no-toko-tachi to Izanagi and Izanami are called the Seven Generations of Gods.[v]

Section 3, Variant 1

One text says, For the male and female kami that came into being as pairs, the first pair was U-hiji-ni and Su-hiji-ni. Next was Tsuno-kui and Iku-kui.[13] "Kui" means "peg." Next was Omo-taru and Kashiko-ne. Next was Izanagi and Izanami.

---

7   An original note adds the alternative names U-hiji-ne and Su-hiji-ne; "ne" means that the kami has a sex.
8   Original notes add the alternative names Ō-to-no-be for Ō-to-no-ji and Ō-toma-hiko / Ō-toma-hime and Ō-tomi-ji / Ō-tomi-be for the Ō-to-no-ji / Ō-toma-be pair.
9   They differ from the other pairs in that their names do not have any shared element. Kashiko-ne foreshadows the words of praise used by Izanagi and Izanami to each other in Section 4, perhaps uttered by Kashiko-ne at the "face-complete" character of Omo-taru. An original note adds the alternative names Aya-kashiko-ne, Imu-kashiki, Ao-kashiki-ne, and Aya-kashiki for Kashiko-ne.
10 Ao-kashiki-ne is an alternative name of Kashiko-ne from the Main Version of Section 2. This variant suggests a matrilineal model of genealogical accounting.
11 This variant proposes an entirely different lineage for Izanagi, the significance of which is unclear.
12 These eight kami appeared as four pairs in the Main Version of Section 2.
13 These names suggest the sharp, brisk emergence of something resembling a peg or stake.

伊奘諾尊・伊奘冉尊、立於天浮橋之上、共計曰、底下豈無國歟、廼以天之瓊瓊、玉也。此云努。矛、指下而探之。是獲滄溟。其矛鋒滴瀝之潮、凝成一嶋。名之曰磤馭慮嶋。二神、於是、降居彼嶋、因欲共爲夫婦、産生洲國。便以磤馭慮嶋、爲國中之柱、柱、此云美簸旨邏。而陽神左旋、陰神右旋。分巡國柱、同會一面。時陰神先唱曰、憙哉、遇可美少男焉。少男、此云烏等孤。

TABLE 5 SEVEN GENERATIONS OF GODS

GENERATION	ANCIENT MATTERS	CHRONICLES, MAIN VERSION
1	Kuni-toko-tachi	Kuni-toko-tachi
2	Toyo-kumu-nu	Kuni-no-sa-tsuchi
3	U-hiji-ni and Su-hiji-ni	Toyo-kumu-nu
4	Tsuno-kui and Iku-kui	U-hiji-ni and Su-hiji-ni
5	Ō-to-no-ji and Ō-toma-be	Ō-to-no-ji and Ō-toma-be
6	Omo-taru and Kashiko-ne	Omo-taru and Kashiko-ne
7	Izana-gi and Izana-mi	Izana-gi and Izana-mi

Section 4: Birth of the Land of Eight Great Islands

Main Version

Izanagi and Izanami stood atop the floating bridge of heaven and together made a plan, saying, "Is there not land in the depths below?"[14] They then took the jeweled spear of heaven and thrust it downward to search, and thereby found the blue sea.[15] The brine that dripped from the spear tip congealed and formed an island. The island's name was called Onogoroshima. The two kami then went down to dwell on the island, became husband and wife, and wished to give birth to the land. They then used Onogoroshima as a pillar in the center of the land. The male kami went around on the left, and the female kami went around on the right.[16] They went around the pillar of the land and met face to face. At that time the female kami first intoned,[17] "How wonderful: I have met a beautiful young man!"

---

14 Here Izanagi and Izanami, together and of their own accord, plan and execute the creation of the Japanese archipelago. "Floating bridge of heaven," the established translation of this phrase, evokes a horizontal structure in English, but in Old Japanese, "hashi" could also refer to a vertical connector, such as a ladder.
15 Commentators disagree as to whether this refers to an actual body of water or is rather a metaphor for the state of the world before any land had formed.
16 Because yang is associated with masculinity and the left, the male goes left, and the female goes right. In the Main Version, the pillar is the island itself.
17 The verb used here is for verse and other ritualistic speech patterns.

陽神不悅曰、吾是男子。理當先唱。如何婦人反先言乎。事既不祥。宜以改旋。於是、二神却更相遇。是行也、陽神先唱曰、憙哉、遇可美少女焉。少女、此云烏等咩。因問陰神曰、汝身有何成耶。

對曰、吾身有一雌元之處。

陽神曰、吾身亦有雄元之處。思欲以吾身元處、合汝身之元處。於是、陰陽始遘合爲夫婦。

及至產時、先以淡路洲爲胞。意所不快。故名之曰淡路洲。廼生大日本日本、此云耶麻騰。下皆效此。豐秋津洲。次生伊豫二名洲。次生筑紫洲。次雙生億岐洲與佐度洲。世人或有雙生者、象此也。次生越洲。次生大洲。次生吉備子洲。由是、始起大八洲國之號焉。即對馬嶋、壹岐嶋、及處處小嶋、皆是潮沫凝成者矣。亦曰水沫凝而成也。

The male kami said, unhappily, "I am the man here. According to principle I should be the one to intone first. How can a woman reverse that and speak before me? Things are already unpropitious. We must go around again." The two kami went back and met again. This time, the male kami intoned first. "How wonderful: I have met a beautiful young woman!" he said. Then he asked the female kami, "Has some part of your body come into form?"

She answered, "My body has a place that is the source of femininity."

The male kami said, "Likewise, my body has a place that is the source of masculinity. I want this source in my body to be one with the source in yours." Thus the male and female kami consummated their union and became the first husband and wife.

When the time of birth came, first came the island of Awaji as the placenta. The two were displeased, and so named it Awaji.[vi] Then the island Great Yamato of Rich Autumns was born. Next were the islands of Iyo-no-futana. Next was the island of Tsukushi. Next were the twin islands of Oki and Sado. This is the model for twin births in the human world. Next was the island of Koshi. Next Ō Island. Then Kibiko Island. Thus the moniker "Land of Eight Great Islands"[18] first came into use.[vii] Then Tsushima and Iki, and then the other small islands, all came to be, owing to the coagulation of the froth of the seawater. It is also said that they were formed from the coagulation of the froth of the fresh water.

---

18 A historic name for the Japanese archipelago; in this version and the variants that follow, along with *Ancient Matters*, there are eight islands listed to explain the name, though the specific islands differ between versions. It is likely that the "eight" of the title simply meant "many," but the compiler of the *Chronicles* took the moniker literally.

一書曰、天神謂伊弉諾尊・伊弉冉尊曰、有豐葦原千五百秋瑞穗之地。宜汝往脩之、廼賜天瓊戈。於是、二神立於天上浮橋、投戈求地。因畫滄海、而引舉之、即戈鋒垂落之潮、結而爲嶋。名曰磤馭慮嶋。二神降居彼嶋、化作八尋之殿。又化竪天柱。陽神問陰神曰、汝身有何成耶。

MAP 2 Islands of Japan birthed by Izanami

Section 4, Variant 1

One text says, The kami of heaven spoke to Izanagi and Izanami saying, "There is an abundant reed plain land of fifteen hundred autumn harvests. You should depart and rule it." Then they bestowed upon the two kami the jeweled spear of heaven. Thereupon Izanagi and Izanami stood on the floating bridge of heaven and thrust the spear down to search for land. In doing so, they stirred the blue sea, and when they pulled the spear back up, the brine that dripped down from the spear's point congealed and made an island. Its name was Onogoroshima. The two kami descended to dwell on that island and erected an eight-fathom shrine. They also erected the pillar of heaven. The male kami then asked the female kami, "Has something in your body taken form?"

對曰、吾身具成而、有稱陰元者一處。

陽神曰、吾身亦具成而、有稱陽元者一處。思欲以吾身陽元、合汝身之陰元。云爾。即將巡天柱、約束曰、妹自左巡。吾當右巡。既而分巡相遇。

陰神乃先唱曰、姸哉、可愛少男歟。

陽神後和之曰、姸哉、可愛少女歟。遂爲夫婦、先生蛭兒。便載葦船而流之。次生淡洲。此亦不以充兒數。

故還復上詣於天、具奏其狀。時天神、以太占而卜合之。乃教曰、婦人之辭、其已先揚乎。宜更還去。乃卜定時日而降之。故二神、改復巡柱。陽神自左、陰神自右。

既遇之時、陽神先唱曰、姸哉、可愛少女歟。

陰神後和之曰、姸哉、可愛少男歟。

然後、同宮共住而生兒。號大日本豐秋津洲。次淡路洲。次伊豫二名洲。次筑紫洲。次億岐三子洲。次佐度洲。次越洲。次吉備子洲。由此謂之大八洲國矣。瑞、此云彌圖。姸哉、此云阿那而惠夜。可愛、此云哀。太占、此云布刀磨爾。

一書曰、伊奘諾尊・伊奘冉尊、二神、立于天霧之中曰、吾欲得國、乃以天瓊矛、指垂而探之、得磤馭慮嶋。則拔矛而喜之曰、善乎、國之在矣。

She answered, "My body is completely formed and has a place called the source of femininity."

The male kami said, "My body too is completely formed, and has a place called the source of masculinity. I wish to unite the source of masculinity in my body with the source of femininity in your body. And so on." Then they prepared to go around the pillar of heaven, and the male kami proposed, "My lady, go around from the left side. I'll go around on the right." The two kami went around and met again.

The female kami first intoned, saying, "How wonderful, a charming young man!"

The male kami then replied saying "How wonderful, a charming young woman!" And so they became husband and wife, and first gave birth to Hiru-ko.[19] Then they put him in a reed boat and cast him adrift. Next born was Awa Island.[20] This child too is not included in the count of their children.

After this, they returned up to heaven and reported the results in full. At that time, the heavenly kami divined using the greater divination.[21] Then they instructed Izanagi and Izanami, saying, "The female's words were uttered first. Return back again." An auspicious day was divined, and they descended from heaven. Then the two kami went around the pillar again. The male kami went around from the left, and the female from the right.

When they met, the male kami intoned first, saying, "How wonderful, a charming young woman!"

The female kami replied afterward, saying, "How wonderful, a charming young man!"

After this they did the same as before with the shrine, where they dwelt together and gave birth to children. The first was called the island Great Yamato of Rich Autumns. Then the island of Awaji. Then the island of Iyo-no-futana. Then the island of Tsukushi. Then the triplets of the Oki Islands. Then the island of Sado. Then the island of Koshi. Then Kibiko Island. For this reason, the place is called the Land of Eight Great Islands.

Section 4, Variant 2

One text says, The two kami Izanagi and Izanami stood within the mist of heaven and said, "We wish to find land." Then, taking the jeweled spear of heaven, they thrust it down and searched and found the island of Onogoroshima. Pulling back the spear, they rejoiced, saying, "Fantastic! There is land!"

---

19 Hiru-ko (leech child), whose name suggests an incomplete form, is connected to Ebisu, a popular medieval Japanese fishing kami.
20 It is not clear to what island this statement refers, as there are multiple islands in Japan by this name. Awaji appears later as one of the eight islands of the archipelago.
21 Divination was usually performed by interpreting the cracks that appeared on turtle plastrons and/or deer scapulae when burnt. Writing was an essential technology for this manner of divination. In eras when these myths were taken literally, this passage prompted much speculation about the potential existence of writing in the Japanese archipelago before the importation of Chinese characters.

一書曰、伊奘諾・伊奘冉、二神、坐于高天原曰、當有國耶、乃以天瓊矛、畫成磤馭慮嶋。

一書曰、伊奘諾・伊奘冉、二神、相謂曰、有物若浮膏。其中蓋有國乎、乃以天瓊矛、探成一嶋。名曰磤馭慮嶋。

一書曰、陰神先唱曰、美哉、善少男。時以陰神先言故、爲不祥。

更復改巡。則陽神先唱曰、美哉、善少女。遂將合交。而不知其術。時有鶺鴒、飛來搖其首尾。二神見而學之、即得交道。

一書曰、二神合爲夫婦、先以淡路洲・淡洲爲胞、生大日本豐秋津洲。次伊豫洲。次筑紫洲。次雙生億岐洲與佐度洲。次越洲。次大洲。次子洲。

一書曰、先生淡路洲。次大日本豐秋津洲。次伊豫二名洲。次億岐洲。次佐度洲。次筑紫洲。次壹岐洲。次對馬洲。

一書曰、以磤馭慮嶋爲胞、生淡路洲。次大日本豐秋津洲。次伊豫二名洲。次筑紫洲。次吉備子洲。次雙生億岐洲與佐度洲。次越洲。

AGE OF THE GODS 1: S4.3–S4.8

Section 4, Variant 3

One text says, The two kami Izanagi and Izanami were in the High Heavenly Plain and said, "Could there be land?" Then, taking the jeweled spear of heaven, they stirred and formed Onogoroshima.

Section 4, Variant 4

One text says, The two kami Izanagi and Izanami said to each other, "Within what appears like floating oil there may be land." Then taking the jeweled spear of heaven, they stirred and formed an island. It was named Onogoroshima.

Section 4, Variant 5

One text says, The female kami intoned first, saying, "Wonderful, a charming young man!" But the female kami had spoken first, which made it unpropitious.

They went around again. Then the male kami intoned first, saying, "Wonderful, a charming young lady!" They were about to couple but did not know how. Then a wagtail flew to them, shaking its head and tail. The two kami saw this and, by imitating, were able to join in union.[22]

Section 4, Variant 6

One text says, The two kami joined in union and became husband and wife. First came the island of Awaji, or Awa, which was the placenta. Then they gave birth to the island Great Yamato of Rich Autumns. Then the island of Iyo. Then the island of Tsukushi. Then the twin islands of Oki and Sado. Then the island of Koshi. Then Ō Island. Then Ko Island.[viii]

Section 4, Variant 7

One text says, First born was the island of Awaji. Then the island Great Yamato of Rich Autumns. Then the island of Iyo-no-futana. Then the Oki Islands. Then the island of Sado. Then the island of Tsukushi. Then the Iki Islands. Then Tsushima.

Section 4, Variant 8

One text says, With the island of Onogoroshima as the placenta, they then gave birth to Awaji Island. Then the island Great Yamato of Rich Autumns. Then the island of Iyo-no-futana. Then the island of Tsukushi. Then Kibiko Island. Then the twin islands of Oki and Sado. Then the island of Koshi.

---

22 Perhaps because the tail feathers of the wagtail bob up and down, suggesting undulation of the hips.

一書曰、以淡路洲爲胞、生大日本豐秋津洲。次淡洲。
次伊豫二名洲。次億岐三子洲。次佐度洲。次筑紫洲。
次吉備子洲。次大洲。

一書曰、陰神先唱曰、姸哉、可愛少男乎。便握陽神
之手、遂爲夫婦、生淡路洲。次蛭兒。

次生海。次生川。次生山。次生木祖句句廼馳。次生草祖草
野姬。亦名野槌。既而伊弉諾尊・伊弉冉尊、共議曰、吾
已生大八洲國及山川草木。何不生天下之主者歟。

於是、共生日神。號大日孁貴。大日孁貴、此云於保比屢
咩能武智。孁音力丁反。一書云、天照大神。一書云、天照大日孁尊。
此子光華明彩、照徹於六合之內。故二神喜曰、吾息雖多、
未有若此靈異之兒。不宜久留此國。自當早送于天、而授以
天上之事。是時、天地相去未遠。故以天柱擧於天上也。

次生月神。一書云、月弓尊、月夜見尊、月讀尊。其光彩亞
日。可以配日而治。故亦送之于天。

Section 4, Variant 9

One text says, With the island of Awaji as the placenta, they then gave birth to the island Great Yamato of Rich Autumns. Then the island of Awa. Then the island of Iyo-no-futana. Then the triplets of the Oki Islands. Then the island of Sado. Then the island of Tsukushi. Then Kibiko Island. Then Ō Island.

Section 4, Variant 10

One text says, The female kami first intoned, saying "Wonderful, a charming young man!" Then she grasped the male kami's hand, and they became husband and wife and gave birth to the island of Awaji. Next was Hiru-ko.

Section 5: The Birth of Amaterasu and Susano-o

Main Version

Next they gave birth to the sea, then the rivers, then the mountains, and then the ancestor of trees Ku-ku-no-chi, and then the ancestor of the grasses Kaya-no-hime, or No-zu-chi.[23] Thereupon, Izanagi and Izanami conferred with each other, saying, "We have already given birth to the Land of Eight Great Islands, as well as the mountains and rivers, grasses and trees. Why should we not produce one fit to rule this realm?"[24]

Then, they together gave birth to the sun kami, called Ō-hiru-me-no-muchi.[25] This child shone radiantly, and her light extended throughout the six quarters.[26] Thereupon, Izanagi and Izanami rejoiced, saying, "Though our offspring are many, there has never been one like this sublime child. She ought not to reside in this land at length. We must promptly send her up to heaven and entrust her with the affairs of heaven above." At that time, heaven and earth were still not distantly separated from each other. So, using the pillar of heaven, Izanagi and Izanami sent her up to heaven.

Next they gave birth to the moon kami.[27] His radiance was second to the sun. For this reason, he was made to share her governance. Therefore he too was sent to heaven.

---

23 In the previous section, these kami thrust the jeweled spear of heaven into the blue sea. The sea born here refers to the waters governed by the Yamato state. In *Ancient Matters*, many of the kami of these natural features are named, but they are abbreviated here.
24 I use "realm" here with the dual meaning in Chinese of "the entire world" and "a circumscribed geographical area."
25 An original note adds, "Other writings give Ō-hiru-me the names Ama-terasu-ō-mi-kami and Ama-terasu-ō-hiru-me." She is commonly known as Amaterasu.
26 That is, east, west, north, south, up, and down, which is to say the whole world.
27 An original note adds, "Other writings name the moon kami Tsuku-yumi or use two written variations of Tsuku-yomi."

次生蛭兒。雖已三歲、脚猶不立。故載之於天磐橡樟船、而順風放棄。

次生素戔嗚尊。一書云、神素戔嗚尊、速素戔嗚尊。此神、有勇悍以安忍。且常以哭泣爲行。故令國內人民、多以夭折。復使靑山變枯。故其父母二神、勅素戔嗚尊、汝甚無道、不可以君臨宇宙。固當遠適之於根國矣、遂逐之。

一書曰、伊弉諾尊曰、吾欲生御宙之珍子、乃以左手持白銅鏡、則有化出之神。是謂大日孁尊。右手持白銅鏡、則有化出之神。是謂月弓尊。又廻首顧眄之間、則有化神。是謂素戔嗚尊。卽大日孁尊及月弓尊、並是質性明麗。故使照臨天地。素戔嗚尊、是性好殘害。故令下治根國。珍、此云于圖。顧眄之間、此云美屢摩沙可梨爾。

一書曰、日月旣生。次生蛭兒。此兒年滿三歲、脚尚不立。初伊弉諾、伊弉冉尊巡柱之時、陰神先發喜言。旣違陰陽之理。所以、今生蛭兒。次生素戔嗚尊。此神性惡、常好哭恚。國民多死。靑山爲枯。故其父母勅曰、假使汝治此國、必多所殘傷。故汝可以馭極遠之根國。次生鳥磐橡樟船。輙以此船載蛭兒、順流放棄。次生火神

28 In the Main Version, Hiru-ko is born in Section 5 along with his sister "Hiru-me" (sun-woman, that is, Amaterasu). He previously appeared in Variants 1 and 4 of Section 4.
29 An original note adds, "Other writings give Susano-o the names Kamu-susa-no-o and Haya-susa-no-o."
30 It is not clear where the humans killed by Susano-o in this section came from; the central concern of the *Chronicles* mythology is the origins and genealogy of the imperial clan, not of the people of the archipelago.

Next they gave birth to Hiru-ko.[28] Even when he reached three years of age, his legs still did not permit him to stand. So Izanagi and Izanami placed him in a heavenly hardened camphor boat and cast him into the winds.

Next they gave birth to Susa-no-o.[29] This kami was brazen and cruel in disposition. Moreover, he incessantly wept and wailed. He caused many people of the land to die before their time.[30] He even caused the verdant mountains to wither. Thus the two kami, his father and mother, decreed to Susano-o,[31] "You lack proper principles and are unfit to rule this realm. Begone, to the distant Land of Ne."[32] They then drove him out.

Section 5, Variant 1

One text says, Izanagi said, "I want to have extraordinary children who will rule this realm." Then he took in his left hand a mirror made of an alloy,[33] through which a kami called Ō-hiru-me came into being. He took in his right hand the mirror made of alloy, through which a kami called Tsuku-yumi came into being. Then Izanagi turned his head, and when he looked back, a kami called Susano-o came into being. Ō-hiru-me and Tsuku-yumi were both bright and beautiful, so they were made to shine upon the realm. Susano-o was cruel and loved hurtful acts, so he was made to descend to and rule the Land of Ne.

Section 5, Variant 2

One text says, The sun and the moon were already born. Next born was Hiru-ko. When this child reached three full years of age, he still could not stand. In the beginning, when Izanagi and Izanami went around the pillar, the female spoke her joyous words first. This went against the principle of yin and yang. For this reason, Hiru-ko was born. Next Susano-o was born. This kami had an evil character, and he often took pleasure in weeping and raging. Many people in the land died, and verdant mountains withered. So his father and mother decreed, "If we had you rule this land, much destruction would certainly ensue. Therefore, you shall rule the distant Land of Ne." Next born was the smooth hardened camphor boat.[34] They immediately placed Hiru-ko in this boat and cast it adrift. Next born was the fire kami

---

31 The verb used here for "decreed" is usually reserved for imperial proclamations. This suggests that the Main Version of the *Chronicles* takes Izanagi and Izanami to be the legitimate rulers of the realm referred to at the beginning of this section.
32 The Land of Ne is sometimes assumed to refer to Yomi, the land of the dead, because in another variant, Izanami dies and goes to Yomi, and later Susano-o insists on going to the land of his mother though he has no mother in the Main Version of the *Chronicles*. "Ne" means root and suggests that this land is underground.
33 Made of copper and tin, that is, bronze. Such mirrors were significant prestige goods imported from China or the Korean peninsula and have been found in significant numbers in early tombs on the archipelago.
34 Literally, "bird-hardened," recalling how water birds move through the water. This "bird-hardened" boat is here cast adrift in the sea, while the "heavenly hardened" boat of the Main Version is cast into the winds.

軻遇突智。時伊弉冉尊、爲軻遇突智、所焦而終矣。其且終之間、臥生土神埴山姬及水神罔象女。即軻遇突智娶埴山姬、生稚產靈。此神頭上、生蠶與桑。臍中生五穀。罔象、此云美都波。

一書曰、伊弉冉尊、生火產靈時、爲子所焦而神退矣、亦云神避。其且神退之時、則生水神罔象女及土神埴山姬、又生天吉葛。天吉葛、此云阿摩能與佐圖羅、一云與曾豆羅。

TABLE 6 Section 5, variant structures

	MAIN VER.	VARIANT 1	2	3	4	5	6	7	8	9	10	11
Birth of plants and trees	✓						✓					
Birth of 3 or 4 special children	✓	✓	✓	✓			*					
Death of Izanami			✓	✓	✓	✓	✓					
Death of fire kami							✓	✓	✓			
Visit to Yomi							✓			✓	✓	
Purification after Yomi							✓			✓	✓	
Governance charges							✓				✓	
Food kami episode												✓

* = Follows purification

Kagu-tsu-chi. At that time, because of Kagu-tsu-chi, Izanami was burned and died.[35] When she was dying, she lay down and gave birth to the earth kami Hani-yama-hime and the water kami Mitsu-ha-no-me.[36] Kagu-tsu-chi took Hani-yama-hime as his wife, and they had a child, Waka-musuhi. Silkworms and mulberry trees grew atop this kami's head, and within his navel, the five grains.[37]

Section 5, Variant 3[38]

One text says, When Izanami gave birth to Ho-musuhi, she was burned by the child and died, or passed away. When she died, she gave birth to the water kami Mitsu-ha-no-me and the earth kami Hani-yama-hime, and also to Ama-no-yosa-tsura.

---

35 This is the first variant in which Izanami dies when giving birth to the fire kami, the same myth that appears in *Ancient Matters*.
36 The earth kami is born at this moment because of the association between fire and clay used for ceramics. The case of the water kami is less clear. The traditional Fire Suppression Festival prayer (Hoshizume no matsuri norito 鎮火祭祝詞) from the tenth century suggests that Izanami recognized the destructive potential of Kagu-tsu-chi and wanted to provide a counter to the fire kami.
37 The exact composition of the "five grains" varies according to source, but could involve rice, varieties of millet, barley and wheat, and pulses.
38 Variants 3, 4, and 5 are alternative accounts of the last half of Variant 2 and do not correspond with the Main Version.

一書曰、伊弉冉尊、且生火神軻遇突智之時、悶熱懊
惱。因爲吐。此化爲神。名曰金山彥。次小便。化爲
神。名曰罔象女。次大便。化爲神。名曰埴山媛。
一書曰、伊弉冉尊、生火神時、被灼而神退去矣。故
葬於紀伊國熊野之有馬村焉。土俗祭此神之魂者、花
時亦以花祭。又用鼓吹幡旗、歌舞而祭矣。
一書曰、伊弉諾尊與伊弉冉尊、共生大八洲國。然後、
伊弉諾尊曰、我所生之國、唯有朝霧、而薰滿之哉、
乃吹撥之氣、化爲神。號曰級長戸邊命。亦曰級長津
彥命。是風神也。又飢時生兒、號倉稻魂命。又生海
神等、號少童命。山神等號山祇。水門神等 號速秋津
日命。木神等號句句廼馳。土神號埴安神。然後、悉
生萬物焉。

　　　至於火神軻遇突智之生也、其母伊弉冉尊、見焦而
化去。于時、伊弉諾尊恨之曰、唯以一兒、替我愛之妹
者乎、則匍匐頭邊、匍匐脚邊、而哭泣流涕焉。其涙墮
而爲神。是即畝丘樹下所居之神。號啼澤女命矣。遂拔
所帶十握劒、斬軻遇突智爲三段。此各化成神也。復劒
刃垂血、是爲天安河邊所在五百箇磐石也。即此經津主
神之祖矣。復劒鐔垂血、激越爲神。號曰甕速日神。次
熯速日神。其甕速日神、是武甕槌神之祖也。亦曰甕速
日命。次熯速日命。次武甕槌神。復劒鋒垂血、激越爲
神。號曰磐裂神。次根裂神。次磐筒男命。一云、磐筒
男命及磐筒女命。復劒頭垂血、激越爲神。號曰闇龗。
次闇山祇。次闇罔象。

Section 5, Variant 4

One text says, When Izanami was giving birth to the fire kami Kagu-tsu-chi, she was troubled by the heat. Then she vomited, and her vomit became a kami called Kana-yama-biko. Then she urinated, and her urine became a kami called Mitsu-ha-no-me. Next she defecated, and her feces became a kami called Hani-yama-hime.

Section 5, Variant 5

One text says, When Izanami gave birth to the fire kami, she was burned and died. Therefore, she was buried in Arima Village in Kumano, Kii Province.[ix] The residents there venerate the spirit of this kami. When the flowers bloom, they venerate her with flowers. They also use drums, wind instruments, and flags to venerate her with song and dance.

Section 5, Variant 6

One text says, Izanagi and Izanami gave birth to the Land of Eight Great Islands together. After this, Izanagi said, "There is a morning fog in the land we have produced, clouding it over." Then he blew the cloud away, and the air he exhaled became a kami, called Shi-naga-to-ma and also Shi-naga-tsu-hiko, a kami of the wind. Then when Izanagi weakened from hunger, a child was born, called Uka-no-mi-tama.[x] Then the kami of the sea was born, called Wata-tsu-mi. The kami of the mountains was called Yama-tsu-mi. The kami of the harbors was called Haya-aki-tsu-hi. The kami of the trees was called Ku-ku-no-chi. The kami of the earth was called Hani-yasu. After this, all things of the world were born.

When the fire kami Kagu-tsu-chi was born, his mother, Izanami, was burned and died. At that time, Izanagi was resentful and said, "I exchanged my beloved for just this one child." Then he crawled at her head and crawled at her feet, wailing and weeping in sadness. His tears fell and became a kami. This kami came to dwell at Uneo in Konomoto and is called Naki-sawa-me. Then Izanagi drew the ten-hand sword he wore and cut Kagu-tsu-chi into three pieces, each of which became a kami. Also, the blood that dripped from the sword blade became the innumerable rocks along the bank of the river of heaven. These were the ancestors of the kami Futsu-nushi. The blood that dripped from the sword guard ran off and became kami called Mika-no-haya-hi and Hi-no-haya-hi. The kami Mika-no-haya-hi was the ancestor of Take-mikazu-chi. It is also said that Mika-no-haya-hi was first, then Hi-no-haya-hi, then Take-mikazu-chi. The blood that dripped from the sword tip ran off and became kami called Iwa-saku, then Ne-saku, then Iwa-tsutsu-no-o, also called Iwa-tsutsu-no-o and Iwa-tsutsu-no-me. The blood that dripped from the sword pommel ran off and became kami called, in order, Kura-okami, then Kura-yama-tsu-mi, then Kura-mitsu-ha.

然後、伊奘諾尊、追伊奘冉尊、入於黃泉、而及之共語。時伊奘冉尊曰、吾夫君尊、何來之晚也。吾已飡泉之竈矣。雖然、吾當寢息。請勿視之。伊奘諾尊不聽、陰取湯津爪櫛、牽折其雄柱、以爲秉炬、而見之者、則膿沸蟲流。今世人夜忌一片之火、又夜忌擲櫛、此其緣也。

　時伊奘諾尊、大驚之曰、吾不意到於不須也凶目汙穢之國矣、乃急走廻歸。

　于時、伊奘冉尊恨曰、何不用要言、令吾恥辱、乃遣泉津醜女八人、一云泉津日狹女、追留之。故伊奘諾尊、拔劒背揮以逃矣。因投黑鬘。此即化成蒲陶。醜女見而採噉之。噉了則更追。伊奘諾尊、又投湯津爪櫛。此即化成筍。醜女亦以拔噉之。噉了則更追。後則伊奘冉尊、亦自來追。是時、伊奘諾尊、已到泉津平坂。一云、伊奘諾尊、乃向大樹放尿。此即化成巨川。泉津日狹女、將渡其水之間、伊奘諾尊、已至泉津平坂。故便以千人所引磐石、塞其坂路、與伊奘冉尊相向而立、遂建絶妻之誓。

　時伊奘冉尊曰、愛也吾夫君、言如此者、吾當縊殺汝所治國民日將千頭。

　伊奘諾尊、乃報之曰、愛也吾妹、言如此者、吾則當産日將千五百頭。因曰、自此莫過。即投其杖。是謂岐神也。又投其帶。是謂長道磐神。又投其衣。是謂煩神。又投其褌。是謂開囓神。又投其履。是謂道敷神。其於泉津平坂、或所謂泉津平坂者、不復別有處所、但臨死氣絶之際、是之謂歟。所塞磐石、是謂泉門塞之大神也。亦名道返大神矣。

　伊奘諾尊既還、乃追悔之曰、吾前到於不須也凶目汙穢之處。故當滌去吾身之濁穢、則往至筑紫日向小戶橘之檍原、而祓除焉。遂將盪滌身之所汙、乃興言曰、上瀨是太疾、下瀨是太弱、便濯之於中瀨也。因以生神、號曰八十枉津日神。次將矯其枉而生神、號曰神直日神。次大直日神。又沈濯於海底。因以生神、號曰底津少童命、次底筒男命。又潛濯於潮中。因以生神、號曰中津少童命。次中筒男命。又浮濯於

After this, Izanagi pursued Izanami and entered the Land of Yomi, and then they spoke with one another.[xi] At that time Izanami said, "My esteemed husband, why have you come so late? I have already eaten the food of Yomi. I am about to rest, however, so do not look at me."[xii] Izanagi did not listen, and secretly took his hallowed comb,[39] broke off the tooth from the end, and made it into a torch. But when he looked at Izanami, pus spurted and insects crawled out. At present, people avoid carrying a single torch at night or throwing down a comb at night, and this is the reason.

At that, Izanagi said with great alarm, "I have needlessly come, without thinking, to a wretched, polluted land," and he quickly sought to escape back.

Then Izanami said with resentment, "Why didn't you listen to my warning? You have shamed me." She dispatched the Eight Crones of Yomi to pursue and stop him. Izanagi drew his sword and, swinging it behind him, fled. In his flight, he cast away his black headpiece, and it transformed into grapes. The crones gathered and ate them. When they finished eating, they continued their pursuit. Izanagi then threw down his hallowed comb, which changed into bamboo shoots. The crones picked and ate them. When the crones finished eating, they continued their chase. After this, Izanami herself came in pursuit. By this time, Izanagi was already at the border of Yomi. (It is also said that Izanagi faced a large tree and relieved himself, and his urine changed into a great river. While the Eight Crones of Yomi were trying to cross the river, Izanagi had reached the border of Yomi.[40]) When he got there, he blocked the border path with a boulder that would take one thousand men to move, turned toward Izanami, and said an oath of divorce.

In response, Izanami said, "My beloved husband, if you say such a thing, I will strangle one thousand people of the land you govern each day."

Izanagi replied, "My beloved wife, if you say such a thing, I will cause fifteen hundred children to be born every day."[41] Then he said, "Do not come beyond this point," and threw down his staff, which became the kami Fu-na-to. Then he threw down his belt, which became the kami Naga-chi-iwa. Then he threw down his robe, which became the kami Wazurai. Then he threw down his pants, which became the kami Aki-kui. Then he threw down his shoes, which became the kami Chi-shiki.[xiii] The border to Yomi may not refer to a physical place, but rather simply to the moment between the cessation of breath and actual death. The boulder that blocks the way is the great kami Yomi-to-ni-fusakari-masu. Another name for it is the great kami Chi-gaeshi.

Izanagi returned and said remorsefully, "I have gone to a terrible, filthy place. So I will go to clean the filth from my body." He then went to Awakihara in Tachibana, Odo, Himuka, Tsukushi, to cleanse himself. When he had finally prepared to wash the filth from his body, he declared, "The current in the upper shallows is very fast, and in the lower shallows very weak. Therefore, I will wash in the middle shallows." This caused a kami to be born, called Yaso-maga-tsu-hi. Then, to correct this deviation, another kami was born, called Kamu-nao-hi. Next was Ō-nao-hi. Then he sank and bathed in the depths of the sea. This caused a kami to be born, called Soko-tsu-wata-tsu-mi. Next was Soko-tsu-tsu-no-o. Next, he bathed in the middle of the sea. This caused another kami to be born, called Naka-tsu-wata-tsu-mi. Next was Naka-tsu-tsu-no-o. Then he bathed floating upon

---

39 Named Yutsu-no-tsuma-gushi, meaning "hallowed handheld comb."
40 An original note adds that the crones were also called the long-dwelling women of Yomi.
41 This exchange explains the phenomenon of population growth. However, the *Chronicles* never explains where the people who are to be killed came from.

潮上。因以生神、號曰表津少童命。次表筒男命。凡有九神矣。其底筒男命・中筒男命・表筒男命、是即住吉大神矣。底津少童命・中津少童命・表津少童命、是阿曇連等所祭神矣。

然後、洗左眼。因以生神、號曰天照大神。復洗右眼。因以生神、號曰月讀尊。復洗鼻。因以生神、號曰素戔嗚尊。凡三神矣。已而伊弉諾尊、勅任三子曰、天照大神者、可以治高天原也。月讀尊者、可以治滄海原潮之八百重也。素戔嗚尊者、可以治天下也。是時素戔嗚尊、年已長矣。復生八握鬚髯。雖然不治天下、常以啼泣恚恨。故伊弉諾尊問之曰、汝何故恆啼如此耶。

對曰、吾欲從母於根國、只爲泣耳。

伊弉諾尊惡之曰、可以任情行矣、乃逐之。

一書曰、伊弉諾尊、拔劒斬軻遇突智、爲三段。其一段是爲雷神。一段是爲大山祇神。一段是爲高龗。又曰、斬軻遇突智時、其血激越、染於天八十河中所在五百箇磐石。而因化成神、號曰磐裂神。次根裂神、兒磐筒男神。次磐筒女神、兒經津主神。倉稻魂、此云宇介能美拕磨。少童、此云和多都美。頭邊、此云摩苦羅陛。脚邊、此云阿度陛。熯火也。音而善反。龗、此云於箇美。音力丁反。吾夫君、此云阿我儺勢。滄泉之竈、此云譽母都俳遇比。秉炬、此云多妃。不須也凶目污穢、此云伊儺之居梅枳枳多儺枳。醜女、此云志許賣。背揮、此云志理幣提爾布俱。泉津平坂、此云餘母都比羅佐可。尿、此云愈磨理。音乃弔反。絕妻之誓、此云許等度。岐神、此云布那斗能加微。檍、此云阿波岐。

一書曰、伊弉諾尊、斬軻遇突智命、爲五段。此各化成五山祇。一則首、化爲大山祇。二則身中、化爲中山祇。三則手、化爲麓山祇。四則腰、化爲正勝山祇。五則足、化爲䨄山祇。是時、斬血激灑、染於石礫樹草。此草木沙石自含火之緣也。麓、山足曰麓、此云簸耶磨。正勝、此云麻沙柯。一云麻左柯豆。䨄、此云之伎。音鳥含反。

the surface of the water. This caused a kami to be born, called Uwa-tsu-wata-tsu-mi.[42] Next was Uwa-tsu-tsu-no-o. There were nine kami in all. Among these kami, Soko-tsu-tsu-no-o, Naka-tsu-tsu-no-o, and Uwa-tsu-tsu-no-o are the three great kami of Suminoe. Soko-tsu-wata-tsu-mi, Naka-tsu-wata-tsu-mi, and Uwa-tsu-wata-tsu-mi are the kami venerated by the Muraji of Azumi.[43]

After this, he washed his left eye. This caused a kami to be born called Amatera-su-ō-mi-kami. He also washed his right eye. This caused a kami to be born called Tsu-ku-yomi. Also, he washed his nose. This caused a kami to be born called Susano-o. Altogether, three kami were born. Izanagi then decreed a charge for each of the three children, saying, "Amaterasu shall rule the high plain of heaven. Tsuku-yomi shall rule the manifold saltwater waves of the blue sea. Susano-o shall rule the earthly realm." At that time Susano-o was already grown, and his beard was eight hands long. However, Susano-o did not rule his realm, but rather was constantly crying and wailing. So Izanagi asked him, "Why do you cry so incessantly?"

Susano-o replied, "I want to follow my mother to the Land of Ne; that is why I cry."

Izanagi then said with displeasure, "Go where you wish," and banished him.

Section 5, Variant 7

One text says, Izanagi drew his sword and killed Kagu-tsu-chi, cutting him into three pieces.[44] One piece became the kami Ikazuchi. One piece became the kami Ō-yama-tsu-mi. One piece became the kami Taka-okami.[45] It is also said, When he struck Kagu-tsu-chi, the blood gushed out and stained countless rocks in the eighty rivers of heaven. This produced a kami called Iwa-saku. Next was Ne-saku. Their children were Iwa-tsutsu-no-o and Iwa-tsutsu-no-me. Their child was the kami Futsu-nushi.

Section 5, Variant 8

One text says, Izanagi killed Kagu-tsu-chi, cutting him into five pieces. These became five mountain kami. The first was from the head, which became Ō-yama-tsu-mi. The second came from the body, which became Naka-yama-tsu-mi. The third was from the hands and became Ha-yama-tsu-mi. The fourth came from the hips and became Ma-saka-yama-tsu-mi. The fifth came from the feet, which became Shigi-yama-tsu-mi. At the time, blood gushed out and stained the rocks, pebbles, trees, and grass. This is why trees, grass, pebbles, and rocks are included in the element of fire.

---

42 Soko-tsu-wata-tsu-mi, Naka-tsu-wata-tsu-mi, and Uwa-tsu-wata-tsu-mi, all with "sea" in their name, are venerated at the Shikaumi Shrine in the port city of Fukuoka.
43 Muraji was a title of nobility granted to lineage groups outside the imperial clan and used in the late sixth and early seventh centuries. "Azumi" refers to the Fukuoka region in Northern Kyushu. These three kami, all with "harbor" in their name, are venerated at Sumiyoshi Grand Shrine in the port city of Osaka.
44 Original notes add the vernacular Japanese for words from Variants 6 and 7 together at the end of this variant; Variant 7 may have been considered a variant of Variant 6, rather than a freestanding variant of the main narrative.
45 These three kami parallel those that appear when Izanagi kills Kagu-tsu-chi in Variant 6.

一書曰、伊弉諾尊、欲見其妹、乃到殯斂之處。是時、伊弉冉尊、猶如生平、出迎共語。已而謂伊弉諾尊曰、吾夫君尊、請勿視吾矣。言訖忽然不見。于時闇也。伊弉諾尊、乃舉一片之火而視之。時伊弉冉尊、脹滿太高。上有八色雷公。伊弉諾尊、驚而走還。是時、雷等皆起追來。時道邊有大桃樹。故伊弉諾尊、隱其樹下、因採其實、以擲雷者、雷等皆退走矣。此用桃避鬼之緣也。時伊弉諾尊、乃投其杖曰、自此以還、雷不敢來。是謂岐神。此本號曰來名戶之祖神焉。所謂八雷者、在首曰大雷。在胸曰火雷。在腹曰土雷。在背曰稚雷。在尻曰黑雷。在手曰山雷。在足上曰野雷。在陰上曰裂雷。

一書曰、伊弉諾尊、追至伊弉冉尊所在處、便語之曰、悲汝故來。

　　答曰、族也、勿看吾矣。伊裝諾尊、不從猶看之。故伊弉冉尊恥恨之曰、汝已見我情。我復見汝情。

　　時伊弉諾尊亦慙焉。因將出返。于時、不直默歸、而盟之曰、族離。又曰、不負於族。乃所唾之神、號曰速玉之男。次掃之神、號泉津事解之男。凡二神矣。及其與妹相鬪於泉平坂也、伊弉諾尊曰、始爲族悲、及思哀者、是吾之怯矣。

　　時、泉守道者白云、有言矣。曰、吾與汝已生國矣。奈何更求生乎。吾則當留此國、不可共去。是時、菊理媛神亦有白事。伊弉諾尊聞而善之。乃散去矣。但親見泉國。此既不祥。故欲濯除其穢惡、乃往見粟門

Section 5, Variant 9

One text says, Izanagi wanted to see his wife, so he went to the building where the corpse is held before burial. At that time, Izanami seemed as if she were alive, and she came out and they spoke together. Then Izanami said, "My beloved and esteemed husband, do not look upon me." As soon as she finished speaking, she vanished. It was dark. Izanagi lit a torch to see, and at that time Izanami was bloated and swollen, and eight kinds of thunder were resting upon her.[46] Izanagi, being very alarmed, fled back from whence he had come. Then the thunders all got up to chase him. At that time there was a large peach tree at the edge of the road. Izanagi hid at the base of this tree, collected the fruit there, and threw it at the thunders, who all fled. This is why peaches have the power to block evil spirits. Then Izanagi threw down his staff, saying, "Past this point, thunders may not come." The staff is the kami Fu-na-to, whose original name was Ku-na-to-no-sae. Concerning the eight thunders, the one on her head was Ō-ikazuchi, the one on her breast was Ho-no-ikazuchi, the one on her stomach was Tsuchi-ikazuchi, the one on her back was Waka-ikazuchi, the one on her bottom was Kuro-ikazuchi, the one on her hands was Yama-no-ikazuchi, the one on her legs was No-no-ikazuchi, and the one on her genitals was Saku-ikazuchi.

Section 5, Variant 10

One text says, Izanagi pursued Izanami to the place where she was and said, "I was sad at your passing, so I came."

Izanami then replied, "My kin, do not look upon me." Izanagi disobeyed her directions and looked, so Izanami was shamed and resentful. She said, "You have looked upon my true figure, and I have seen your true character."

In turn Izanagi was shamed, and so he prepared to depart. However, he did not return in silence, but rather broke their alliance, saying, "We are divorced." Then he said, "I will not be defeated by my kindred." The kami from his saliva was called Haya-tama-no-o. Next, the kami from their severed connection was Yomo-tsu-koto-saka-no-o. In all, there were two kami. Izanagi quarreled with his wife at the entrance to Yomi and then said, "At first, I grieved for you and missed you. I was weak and foolish."

At that time, the gatekeeper of Yomi said that he had a message from Izanami: "You and I have already given birth to the land. Why do you want to continue living? I must stay in this land and cannot depart with you." Then the kami Kukuri-hime also said something. When he heard this, Izanagi praised her and departed. However, he had seen the Land of Yomi, and this was not good. Accordingly, he wanted to bathe and cleanse himself of the contamination, so he went and looked upon the water at Awanomito and

---

46 The Eight Thunder Gods also appear in *Ancient Matters*, but have different names and associated body parts, and they come from the corpse of the fire kami.

及速吸名門、然此二門、潮既太急。故還向於橘之小門、而拂濯也。于時、入水吹生磐土命。出水吹生大直日神。又入吹生底土命。出吹生大綾津日神。又入吹生赤土命。出吹生大地海原之諸神矣。不負於族、此云宇我邇磨穊茸。

一書曰、伊弉諾尊、勅任三子曰、天照大神者、可以御高天之原也。月夜見尊者、可以配日而知天事也。素戔嗚尊者、可以御滄海之原也。

　　既而天照大神、在於天上曰、聞葦原中國有保食神。宜爾月夜見尊、就候之。

　　月夜見尊、受勅而降。已到于保食神許。保食神、乃廻首嚮國、則自口出飯。又嚮海、則鰭廣鰭狭亦自口出。又嚮山、則毛麁毛柔亦自口出。夫品物悉備、貯之百机而饗之。是時、月夜見尊、忿然作色曰、穢哉、鄙矣、寧可以口吐之物、敢養我乎、廼拔劒擊殺。

　　然後、復命、具言其事。時天照大神、怒甚之曰、汝是惡神。不須相見、乃與月夜見尊、一日一夜、隔離而住。是後、天照大神、復遣天熊人往看之。是時、保食神實已死矣。唯有其神之頂、化爲牛馬。顱上生粟。眉上生蠒。眼中生稗。腹中生稻。陰生麥及大小豆。天熊人悉取持去而奉進之。

　　于時、天照大神喜之曰、是物者、則顯見蒼生、可食而活之也。乃以粟稗麥豆、爲陸田種子。以稻爲水田種子。又因定天邑君。即以其稻種、始殖于天狭田及長田。其秋垂穎、八握莫莫然、甚快也。又口裏含蠒、便得抽絲。自此始有養蠶之道焉。保食神、此云宇氣母知能加微。顯見蒼生、此云宇都志枳阿鳥比等久佐。

於是、素戔嗚尊請曰、吾今奉教、將就根國。故欲暫向高天原、與姉相見而、後永退矣。

　　勅許之。乃昇詣之於天也。

at Hayasuhinato, but at these two places the current was very fast. That being the case, he went back to Odo in Tachibana and cleansed himself there. When he entered the water, his breath produced the kami Iwa-tsutsu. When he left the water, his breath produced the kami Ō-nao-hi. He entered again, and his breath produced the kami Soko-tsutsu, and when he got out, his breath produced the kami Ō-aya-tsu-hi. He entered yet again, and this time his breath produced Aka-tsutsu, and when he got out, it produced various kami of the earth and sea.

Section 5, Variant 11[xiv]

One text says, Izanagi decreed a charge for each of his three children, saying, "Amaterasu shall rule the high plain of heaven. Tsuku-yomi shall share rule of heavenly affairs with the sun. Susano-o shall rule the blue sea."

Amaterasu was already up in heaven and said, "I have heard that in the central reed plain land below lives the kami Uke-mochi. Tsuku-yomi, go and see."

Tsuku-yomi received this decree, descended, and went immediately to Uke-mochi. Thereupon, Uke-mochi turned her head and faced the land and grain came out of her mouth. Then she faced the sea, and both wide-finned and narrow-finned fish came out of her mouth. Then she faced the mountains, and both coarse-haired and smooth-haired animals came out of her mouth. Then she prepared all these various delicacies and placed them on one hundred tables for a feast. At that, Tsuku-yomi angrily said, "How filthy, how vile, that you should dare feast me with things you vomit from your mouth!" He then drew his sword and slew her.

Afterward, he returned and reported in detail. In response, Amaterasu said angrily, "You are an evil kami. I do not wish to see you." Thus the sun and moon are estranged. Later Amaterasu dispatched Ama-no-kuma-hito to go and investigate. At that time Uke-mochi was already dead, but from the crown of her head came forth cows and horses. From her forehead grew foxtail millet, and from her brow, silkworms. From inside her eyes came barnyard millet, and from inside her stomach, rice. From her genitals came barley and large and small beans.[xv] Ama-no-kuma-hito collected all these things and went back and presented them to Amaterasu.

When she saw them, Amaterasu said with pleasure, "These things shall be eaten as sustenance by the people of the world." Hence, foxtail and barnyard millet, barley and beans, became the seed crops of dry fields, and rice became the seed crop of paddy fields. Also, Amaterasu appointed a village chief of heaven. Then for the first time, rice seeds were planted in both the long and narrow paddy fields of heaven. The drooping rice ears grew eight hands long by autumn and were very good. Also, taking silkworms in her mouth, she reeled off thread. This was the beginning of sericulture.

Section 6: The Oath of Amaterasu and Susano-o

Main Version

Then Susano-o made a request, saying "I will now humbly receive this order and withdraw to the Land of Ne. Before I leave, I want to go to the high plain of heaven for a time and see my sister, for afterward I shall be gone forever."[xvi]

"Granted," decreed Izanagi. Then Susano-o went up to heaven.

是後、伊弉諾尊、神功既畢、靈運當遷。是以、構幽宮於淡路之洲、寂然長隱者矣。亦曰、伊弉諾尊、功既至矣。德亦大矣。於是、登天報命。仍留宅於日之少宮矣。少宮、此云倭柯美野。

　始、素戔嗚尊昇天之時、溟渤以之鼓盪、山岳爲之鳴响。此則神性雄健使之然也。天照大神、素知其神暴惡、至聞來詣之狀、乃勃然而驚曰、吾弟之來、豈以善意乎。謂當有奪國之志歟。夫父母既任諸子、各有其境。如何棄置當就之國、而敢窺覦此處乎。

　乃結髮爲髻、縛裳爲袴、便以八坂瓊之五百箇御統、御統、此云美須磨屢。纒其髻鬘及腕、又背負千箭之靫千箭、此云知能梨。與五百箭之靫、臂著稜威之高鞆、稜威、此云伊都振起弓彇、急握劒柄、蹈堅庭而陷股、若沫雪以蹴散、蹴散、此云倶穢簸邏邏箇須。奮稜威之雄誥、雄誥、此云烏多稽眉。發稜威之噴讓、噴讓、此云擧廬毗。而徑詰問焉。

　素戔嗚尊對曰、吾元無黑心。但父母已有嚴勅、將永就乎根國。如不與姉相見、吾何能敢去。是以、跋涉雲霧、遠自來參。不意、阿姉翻起嚴顏。

　于時、天照大神復問曰、若然者、將何以明爾之赤心也。

After this, Izanagi, having completed his divine task, prepared to depart from the world. To that end, he built a hermitage on the island of Awaji and hid himself away in quiet isolation forever. It is also said that Izanagi having completed his task, his divine virtue was great. Then he ascended to heaven and made a report. Afterward, he stayed in the Lesser Palace of the Sun.[xvii]

When Susano-o first ascended to heaven, the great sea churned and groaned, and the mountains and hills cried out. This was due to the kami's fierce nature. Amaterasu[47] already knew of this kami's violence and evil, and upon hearing the manner of his coming, her face changed color and she said with surprise, "My younger brother has come, but how could he mean well? Surely, he intends to steal my land. Our parents already gave charges to us children, making us keep within our own boundaries.[xviii] Why has he abandoned the land he is supposed to go to and dared to come calling here?"

Then she tied her hair up over her ears and bound her skirt into trousers. She took a long eight-span string of innumerable beads and wrapped it around her hair buns and arms.[xix] She also put on her back a quiver of one thousand arrows and a quiver of five hundred arrows, strapped to her elbow a fiercely loud-sounding arm protector,[48] waved the tip of her bow, and firmly gripped her sword hilt. She stamped on the hard ground so that her legs sank in up to the thigh, and then kicked and spread the dirt around like powdered snow. She shook with a fierce roar and issued a fierce shout, then interrogated him straightaway.

Susano-o replied, "I never had any impure intentions. But our parents have already made a strict decree that I am to go to the Land of Ne forever. But how could I go there without seeing my older sister? For this reason, I have tread on the clouds and mists and come from afar. I did not expect my sister to be so angry."

At that, Amaterasu asked him in return, "Supposing that to be true, how can you make the purity of your intentions clear?"

---

47 "Amaterasu" is given as an alternative name in a note in the Main Version of Section 5, but here it is used in the text along with "sun kami."
48 A sound would be produced when the bowstring struck the arm protector.

對曰、請與姉共誓。夫誓約之中、誓約之中、此云宇氣譬能美儺箇。必當生子。如吾所生、是女者、則可以爲有濁心。若是男者、則可以爲有淸心。

於是、天照大神、乃索取素戔嗚尊十握劒、打折爲三段、

濯於天眞名井、嚙然咀嚼、嚙然咀嚼、此云佐我彌爾加武。而吹棄氣噴之狹霧吹棄氣噴之狹霧、此云浮枳于都屢伊浮岐能佐擬理所生神、號曰田心姫。次湍津姫。次市杵嶋姫。凡三女矣。

既而素戔嗚尊、乞取天照大神髻鬘及腕所纏、八坂瓊之五百箇御統、濯於天眞名井、嚙然咀嚼、而吹棄氣噴之狹霧所生神、號曰正哉吾勝勝速日天忍穗耳尊。次天穗日命。是出雲臣・土師連等祖也。次天津彦根命。

是凡川內直・山代直等祖也。次活津彦根命。次熊野櫲樟日命。凡五男矣。

是時、天照大神勅曰、原其物根、則八坂瓊之五百箇御統者、是吾物也。故彼五男神、悉是吾兒、乃取而子養焉。又勅曰、其十握劒者、是素戔嗚尊物也。故此三女神、悉是爾兒、便授之素戔嗚尊。此則筑紫胸肩君等所祭神是也。

49 The agreement is called an "ukei," which required a stated hypothesis that would be tested during the course of the oath.

He replied, "I ask that we make an oath together.[49] During the course of this oath, children will surely be born. If the children I bear are female, then you can consider my intentions to be impure. If they are male, then please believe my intentions to be pure."

At this, Amaterasu demanded and took Susano-o's ten-hand sword, struck it, and broke it into three pieces. These she rinsed in the truly named well of heaven and crunched up in her mouth. A kami was born in the thin mist of breath she exhaled, called Ta-kori-hime. Next was Tagitsu-hime. Next was Ichi-ki-shima-hime.[xx] In all, there were three female kami.

Thereupon Susano-o appealed for and took the long eight-span string of innumerable beads wrapped around Amaterasu's hair buns and arms. This he rinsed in the true well of heaven and crunched up in his mouth. A kami was born in the thin mist of breath he exhaled, called Masa-ka-a-katsu-haya-hi-ama-no-oshi-ho-mimi. Next was Ama-no-ho-hi, the ancestor of the Omi of Izumo and the Muraji of Haji. Next was Ama-tsu-hiko-ne, ancestor of the Atai of Ōshikōchi and Yamashiro.[50] Next was Iku-tsu-hiko-ne. Next was Ku-mano-kusu-hi. In all, there were five male kami.[51]

Upon this, Amaterasu decreed, "If we inquire into origins, the long eight-span string of innumerable beads was mine. Therefore, these five kami are all my children." Then she took them to raise them. Then she again decreed, "The ten-hand sword was yours, Susano-o. Therefore, these three female kami shall all be your children." Then she bestowed them upon Susano-o. These are the kami venerated by the Kimi of Munakata in Tsukushi.[52]

---

50 Omi and Atai are nobility titles that were awarded to lineage groups in ancient Japan, along with Muraji, which appeared earlier.
51 This is the first of many notes in the *Chronicles* that identifies the earthly progeny of the kami. Each of the five male kami is given the title "mikoto" in the original, but the Chinese character used demarcates Oshi-ho-mimi's superior status. The Omi of Izumo originated from Ōgun District, Izumo Province (present-day Matsue City, Shimane Prefecture), and were the lineage of the Provincial Miyatsuko of Izumo. The Muraji of the Haji were a lineage group associated with ceramics, including funerary goods, and were, by extension, responsible for tomb management. The Atai of Ōshikōchi and Yamashiro were the lineage groups for the Provincial Miyatsuko of Kōchi Province (present-day Osaka Prefecture) and Yamashiro Province (present-day Kyoto Prefecture).
52 Kimi is a title of nobility. Tsukushi is the old name for Kyushu. The Kimi of Munakata originated from Munakata District, Chikuzen Province (present-day Munakata City, Fukuoka Prefecture).

一書曰、日神本知素戔鳴尊、有武健凌物之意。及其上至、便謂、弟所以來者、非是善意。必當奪我天原、乃設大夫武備。躬帶十握劒・九握劒・八握劒、又背上負靫、又臂著稜威高鞆、手捉弓箭、親迎防禦。

　是時、素戔鳴尊告曰、吾元無悪心。唯欲與姉相見、只爲暫來耳。

　於是、日神共素戔鳴尊、相對而立誓曰、若汝心明淨、不有凌奪之意者、汝所生兒、必當男矣。言訖、先食所帶十握劒生兒、號瀛津嶋姬。又食九握劒生兒、號湍津姬。又食八握劒生兒、號田心姬。凡三女神矣。

　已而素戔鳴尊、以其頸所嬰五百箇御統之瓊、濯于天渟名井、亦名去來之眞名井而食之。乃生兒、號正哉吾勝勝速日天忍骨尊。次天津彦根命。次活津彦根命。次天穗日命。次熊野忍蹈命。凡五男神矣。

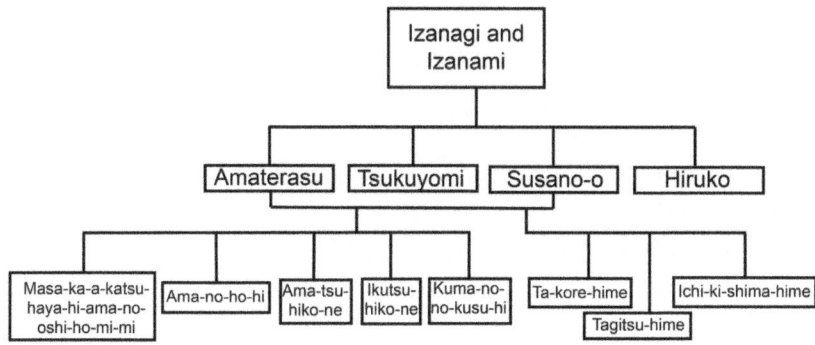

FIGURE 2   Genealogy of kami in Sections 5 and 6

Section 6, Variant 1

One text says, The sun kami already knew that Susano-o was of a violent nature and wrongful heart. Thus, when he ascended and arrived, she thought, "The reason my younger brother has come is not because he means well. Surely, he will steal my heavenly plain." She then prepared for him like a brave male warrior. She armed herself with a ten-hand sword, a nine-hand sword, an eight-hand sword, bore a quiver on her back, wore a fiercely loud-sounding arm protector on her forearm, and took her bow and arrows in hand. Then she went out to meet and repel him.

In response, Susano-o addressed her, saying, "I never had any impure intentions. I wanted only to meet my older sister. I have come for only a short time."

Then the sun kami and Susano-o stood face-to-face while she made an oath, saying, "If your heart is pure and you do not have any thieving, wrongful intentions, the children you give birth to will be male."[53] When she finished speaking, she first ate the ten-hand sword she wore and produced a child called Oki-tsu-shima-hime. Again, she ate the nine-hand sword and produced a child called Tagitsu-hime. Again, she ate the eight-hand sword and produced a child called Ta-kori-hime. All together there were three female kami.

This being done, Susano-o took the long string of innumerable beads from around his neck, rinsed it in the frothing well of heaven, also called the true inviting well, and ate it. This produced a child called Masa-ka-a-katsu-haya-hi-ama-no-oshi-ho-ne. Then Ama-tsu-hiko-ne. Then Iku-tsu-hiko-ne. Then Ama-no-ho-hi. Then Kumano-oshi-ho-mi. Altogether there were five male kami.[54]

53 Variant 1 suggests that it was instead the sun kami who provided the trial for the oath. This variant also confirms that Amaterasu in the Main Version is the same figure as the sun kami. In the variants for Section 6, despite differing details, Amaterasu always produces three female kami, and Susano-o's intentions are always proved pure.
54 The name of this first kami, Oshi-ho-mimi, differs slightly, with "ne" replacing "mimi." The meaning is unchanged. The name of the final kami has swapped "kusu-hi" for "oshi-ho-mi."

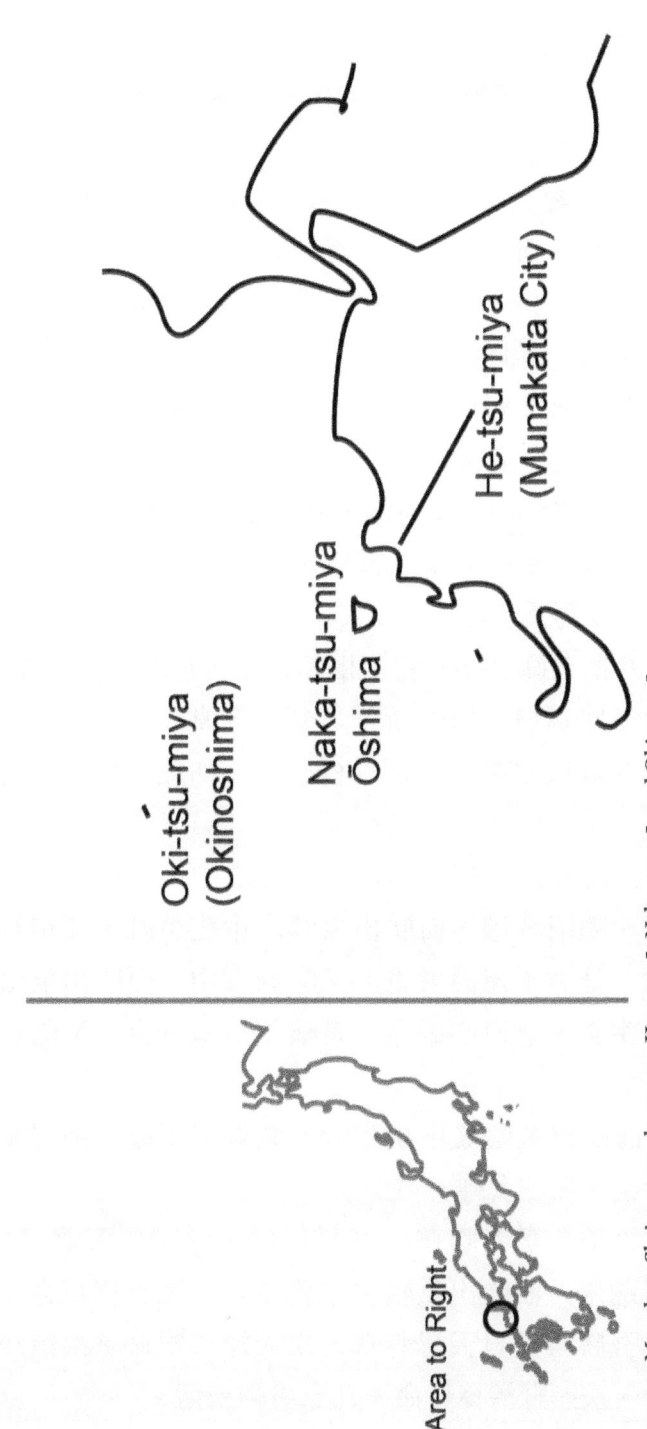

MAP 3 Munakata Shrines, now known as He-tsu-gū, Naka-tsu-gū, and Oki-tsu-gū

故素戔嗚尊、既得勝驗。於是、日神、方知素戔嗚尊、固無惡意、乃以日神所生三女神、令降於筑紫洲。因教之曰、汝三神、宜降居道中、奉助天孫、而爲天孫所祭也。

一書曰、素戔嗚尊、將昇天時、有一神。號羽明玉。此神奉迎、而進以瑞八坂瓊之曲玉。故素戔嗚尊、持其瓊玉、而到之於天上也。是時、天照大神、疑弟有惡心、起兵詰問。

素戔嗚尊對曰、吾所以來者、實欲與姉相見。亦欲獻珍寶瑞八坂瓊之曲玉耳。不敢別有意也。

時天照大神、復問曰、汝言虛實、將何以爲驗。

對曰、請吾與姉、共立誓約。誓約之間、生女爲黑心。生男爲赤心。

乃掘天眞名井三處、相與對立。是時、天照大神、謂素戔嗚尊曰、以吾所帶之劒、今當奉汝。汝、以汝所持八坂瓊之曲玉、可以授予矣。如此約束、共相換取。

已而天照大神、則以八坂瓊之曲玉、浮寄於天眞名井、囓斷瓊端、而吹出氣噴之中化生神、號市杵嶋姬命。是居于遠瀛者也。又囓斷瓊中、而吹出氣噴之中化生神、號田心姬命。是居于中瀛者也。又囓斷瓊尾、

而吹出氣噴之中化生神、號湍津姬命。是居于海濱者也。凡三女神。

於是、素戔嗚尊、以所持劒、浮寄於天眞名井、囓斷劒末、而吹出氣噴之中化生神、號天穗日命。次正哉吾勝勝速日天忍骨尊。次天津彥根命。次活津彥根命。次熊野橡樟日命。凡五男神云爾。

Thus Susano-o proved victorious in the trial. Because of this, the sun kami knew that Susano-o truly had no evil intentions. Thus, the three female kami that the sun kami produced were made to descend to Tsukushi. She ordered them, saying, "You three kami, go down and dwell in the middle circuit, attend on the heavenly descendant, and perform veneration on behalf of the heavenly descendant.[55]

Section 6, Variant 2

One text says, When Susano-o prepared to ascend to heaven, one kami, called Ha-aka-ru-tama, went out to greet him and presented him with a brilliant eight-span jade curved jewel.[56] Then Susano-o, carrying this jade jewel, went up to heaven. At that time, Amaterasu thought that her younger brother had evil intentions and doubted him, and so mobilized troops and interrogated him.

Susano-o replied, "The reason I have come is truly to see you, older sister. Also, I wanted to offer you this treasured jade curved jewel. I dare not have any other intention."

Amaterasu asked him again, "How can we test whether what you say is truth or lies?"

He replied, "I ask that my older sister and I make an oath together. During the test, if my children are female, believe that my intentions are impure. If they are male, believe that my intentions are pure."

Then they dug three true wells of heaven and stood face to face. Then Amaterasu told Susano-o, "I will present you the sword I am armed with. You will give me the jade curved jewel you hold." As the oath specified, they exchanged objects.

Amaterasu floated the jade curved jewel in the true wells of heaven and bit off the head of the jewel. The kami that came into being from the breath she exhaled was called Ichi-ki-shima-hime.[57] This kami dwells in Oki-tsu-miya. Then she bit off the middle of the jewel, and the kami that came into being from the breath she exhaled was called Ta-kori-hime. This kami dwells in Naka-tsu-miya. Then she bit off the tail of the jewel, and the kami that came into being from the breath she exhaled was called Tagitsu-hime. This kami dwells in He-tsu-miya. In all, there were three female kami.

Thereupon Susano-o floated the sword he held in the true wells of heaven and bit off the sword tip. The kami that came into being from the breath he exhaled was called Ama-no-ho-hi. Next was Masa-ka-a-katsu-kachi-haya-hi-ama-no-oshi-hone. Next was Ama-tsu-hiko-ne. Next was Iku-tsu-hiko-ne. Next was Kumano-kusu-hi. In all, there were five male kami.

---

55 The "middle of the way" is unclear here, but based on Variant 3, presumably refers to northern Kyushu. The "heavenly descendant" usually refers to Oshi-ho-mimi's son Ninigi, but this kami has not yet been born.
56 The curved jewel is known as a *magatama*, a comma-shaped bead common in ancient Japan.
57 In the Main Version and Variant 1, the resultant kami are born or produced, suggesting a mixture of yin and yang, but in Variants 2 and 3, they come into being, that is, they spring forth from nothing.

一書曰、日神與素戔嗚尊、隔天安河、而相對乃立誓約曰、汝若不有姧賊之心者、汝所生子、必男矣。如生男者、予以爲子、而令治天原也。

　於是、日神先食其十握劒化生兒、瀛津嶋姬命。亦名市杵嶋姬命。又食九握劒化生兒、湍津姬命。又食八握劒化生兒、田霧姬命。

　已而素戔嗚尊、含其左髻所纒五百箇統之瓊、而著於左手掌中、便化生男矣。則稱之曰、正哉吾勝。故因名之、曰勝速日天忍穗耳尊。復含右髻之瓊、著於右手掌中、化生天穗日命。復含嬰頸之瓊、著於左臂中、化生天津彦根命。又自右臂中、化生活津彦根命。

　又自左足中、化生熯之速日命。又自右足中、化生熊野忍蹈命。亦名熊野忍隅命。其素戔嗚尊所生之兒、皆已男矣。故日神方知素戔嗚尊、元有赤心、便取其六男、以爲日神之子、使治天原。即以日神所生三女神者、使降居于葦原中國之宇佐嶋矣。今在海北道中。號曰道主貴。此筑紫水沼君等祭神是也。熯、干也。此云備。

Section 6, Variant 3

One text says, The sun kami faced Susano-o across the Tranquil River of Heaven and made an oath, saying, "If in your heart there is no intention to disturb, the children you bear will certainly be male. If they are males, they will become my children, and I will order them to govern the heavenly plain."

Thereupon, the sun kami first ate her ten-hand sword, and the child that came into being was called Oki-tsu-shima-hime, also called Ichi-ki-shima-hime. Then she ate her nine-hand sword, and the child that came into being was called Tagitsu-hime. Then she ate her eight-hand sword, and the child that came into being was called Ta-kiri-hime.

Then Susano-o took in his mouth his long string of innumerable beads that tied up his left hair bun, then put it in the palm of his left hand, and a male kami came into being. Then he said, "Truly, I have won." For this reason, the child was named Kachi-haya-hi-ama-no-oshi-ho-mimi. Then he took in his mouth his long string of innumerable beads that tied up his right hair bun, then put it in the palm of his right hand, and Ama-no-ho-hi came into being. Then he took in his mouth the jewel adorning his neck, placed it on his left forearm, and Ama-tsu-hiko-ne came into being. Then from his right forearm, Iku-tsu-hiko-ne came into being. Then from his left leg, Hi-no-haya-hi came into being. Then from his right leg, the child that came into being was Kumano-oshi-ho-mi, also called Kumano-oshi-kuma.

The children born of Susano-o were all male. So the sun kami knew that Susano-o had pure intentions. Then she took these six male kami as her children and made them rule the heavenly plain. The three female kami born of the sun kami were made to descend and dwell on Usa Island in the central reed plain land. Now they are in the northern sea circuit,[58] and are called Michi-nushi-no-muchi. These kami are venerated by the Kimi of Minuma[59] of Tsukushi.[xxi]

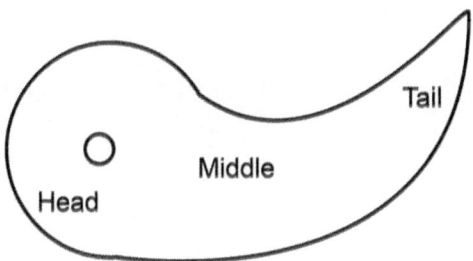

FIGURE 3 Magatama

---

58 It is unclear what the "northern sea route" refers to. The Korean peninsula is one possibility.

59 The Kimi of Minuma are presumably a lineage group from northern Kyushu; the location appears in Keikō 4.2 and 18.7.

是後、素戔嗚尊之爲行也、甚無狀。何則天照大神、以天狹田・長田爲御田。時素戔嗚尊、春則重播種子、重播種子、此云璽枳磨枳。且毀其畔。毀、此云波那豆。秋則放天斑駒、使伏田中。復見天照大神當新嘗時、則陰放屎於新宮。又見天照大神、方織神衣、居齋服殿、則剝天斑駒、穿殿甍而投納。是時、天照大神驚動、以梭傷身。

由此、發慍、乃入于天石窟、閉磐戶而幽居焉。故六合之內常闇、而不知晝夜之相代。

于時、八十萬神、會於天安河邊、計其可禱之方。故思兼神、深謀遠慮、遂聚常世之長鳴鳥、使互長鳴。亦以手力雄神、立磐戶之側、而中臣連遠祖天兒屋命、忌部遠祖太玉命、掘天香山之五百箇眞坂樹、而上枝懸八坂瓊之五百箇御統、中枝懸八咫鏡、一云眞經津鏡。下枝懸青和幣和幣、此云尼枳底。白和幣、相與致其祈禱焉。

60 These fields were created in Variant 11 of Section 5. Susano-o's destruction of the ridges would case the rice paddies to dry out, while the release of the horses would damage the crop and make it impossible to harvest. In *Ancient Matters*, Susano-o's destruction of Amaterasu's fields is explicitly linked to his victory in the oath, but in the Main Version here, no strict causation is established.
61 The feast of first rice is a religious ritual, traditionally in the eleventh month, in which the first rice to be harvested is presented to the kami.
62 The backward flaying of the colt is specified by the vernacular gloss reading, but would otherwise be indistinguishable from a normal flaying.

Section 7: Evil Acts of Susano-o

Main Version

Henceforth, Susano-o's actions truly lacked proper principles. That is to say, Amaterasu set up the narrow paddies and long paddies of heaven as her own. Susano-o, in the spring, double-planted the seedlings. He also broke down the ridges around the paddies. In the autumn, he released heavenly mottled colts and made them lie down in the paddies.[60] Later, when he saw Amaterasu planning to celebrate the feast of first rice,[61] he secretly defecated in the feast shrine. Also, upon seeing Amaterasu weaving the clothing of the kami while in the sacred weaving hall, he flayed a heavenly mottled colt backward,[62] made a hole in the hall's tiled roof, and threw the colt inside. At this, Amaterasu was so surprised that she injured herself with the weaving shuttle.

For these reasons, Amaterasu was angered, went immediately into the rock cave of heaven, closed the stone door, and dwelt within. Hence, it was dark in all six quarters, and the alternation of day and night was unknown.

At this time, all the kami[63] met together on the banks of the Tranquil River of Heaven and planned how they should supplicate her. Thereupon, the kami Omoi-kane, with deep consideration and far-reaching thought, at last gathered the long-crying birds of Tokoyo and made them long-cry to one another.[64] Also, the kami Ta-jikara-o hid beside the stone door. The distant ancestor of the Muraji of the Nakatomi, Ama-no-koyane, and the distant ancestor of the Inbe, Futo-dama, dug from the Heavenly Mt. Kagu an innumerably branched true sakaki tree.[65] On its upper branches they hung a long eight-span string of innumerable beads, and in its middle branches an eight-shaftment mirror, and on the lower branches blue-paper and white-paper streamers.[66] They prayed together for supplication.

---

63 In the original, the precise number of 800,000 is given. The wording contrasts with the variants, which use "various kami" or "many kami."

64 Tokoyo appears for the first time in reference to these birds; in Variant 6 of Section 8 and in Suinin 90.2, there is a Land of Tokoyo across the sea, but there is no "land" designator here. Omoi-kane is called Omoi-kane of Tokoyo in *Ancient Matters*.

65 The Nakatomi and the Inbe lineage groups were allied miyatsuko associated with state ritual. The sakaki tree is used in Shinto ritual, as are the paper streamers that appear below. What dimension is being given for the mirror is unclear. Confusingly, a Heavenly Mt. Kagu (Ama-no-kagu-yama) exists in both heaven and on earth, in present-day Nara Prefecture.

66 An original note adds that the mirror was also called a "mafutsu mirror," but the meaning of this word is unclear.

又猨女君遠祖天鈿女命、則手持茅纏之稍、立於天石窟戶之前、巧作俳優。亦以天香山之眞坂樹爲鬘、以蘿、蘿、此云此舸礙。爲手繦、手繦、此云多須枳。而火處燒、覆槽置、覆槽、此云于該。顯神明之憑談、顯神明之憑談、此云歌牟鵝可梨。

是時、天照大神、聞之而曰、吾比閉居石窟。謂當豐葦原中國、必爲長夜。云何天鈿女命噱樂如此者乎、乃以御手、細開磐戶窺之。

時手力雄神、則奉承天照大神之手、引而奉出。於是、中臣神・忌部神、則界以端出之繩。繩、亦云、左繩端出。此云斯梨俱梅儺波。乃請曰、勿復還幸。然後、諸神歸罪過於素戔鳴尊、而科之以千座置戶、遂促徵矣。至使拔髮、以贖其罪。亦曰、拔其手足之爪贖之。已而竟逐降焉。

一書曰、是後、稚日女尊、坐于齋服殿、而織神之御服也。素戔鳴尊見之、則逆剥斑駒、投入之於殿内。稚日女尊、乃驚而墮機、以所持梭傷體、而神退矣。故天照大神謂素戔鳴尊曰、汝猶有黑心。不欲與汝相見、乃入于天石窟、而閉著磐戶焉。於是、天下恆闇、無復晝夜之殊。

故會八十萬神於天高市而問之。時有高皇產靈之息思兼神云者。有思慮之智。乃思而白曰、宜圖造彼神之象、而奉招禱也。故即以石凝姥爲冶工、採天香山之金、以作日矛。又全剥

Also, the distant ancestor of the Kimi of Sarume, Ama-no-uzu-me, took in her hand a spear wrapped with grass, stood in front of the rock cave of heaven, and adroitly performed a mimic dance.[67] She turned a true sakaki tree from the Heavenly Mt. Kagu into her headdress, took hanging moss as her shoulder fringe, made a ceremonial fire, overturned a stock tank to use as her stage, and performed a dance imitating divine possession.

When Amaterasu heard her, she said, "I am shut away in this rock cave. Presumably, the abundant central reed plain land is in a state of permanent darkness. How can Ama-no-uzu-me jokingly make light in this fashion?" Then she used her hand to open the stone door a crack and peeked out.

When she did, Ta-jikara-o took Amaterasu's hand and pulled her out, and the kami of the Nakatomi and Inbe strung up a rope barrier behind her.[68] Then they implored her, "Please do not go back inside." Afterward, the various kami charged Susano-o for his crimes, fining him one thousand tables of offerings and pressing him for their collection. They had his hair pulled out to atone for his crimes. It is also said that they removed the nails of his hands and feet to make him atone. Having done this, they at last banished him downward.

Section 7, Variant 1

One text says, After this, Waka-hiru-me was in the sacred weaving hall weaving the august garments of the kami.[69] Susano-o saw her and then flayed a mottled colt backward[70] and threw it inside the hall. Waka-hiru-me was startled and fell from the loom, injured herself with the shuttle that she held, and died. Accordingly, Amaterasu told Susano-o, "You still have impure intentions. I do not want to see you." Then she went into the heavenly rock cave and shut the stone door. Upon doing so, the realm was perpetually dark, and there was no distinction between day and night.

Consequently, all the kami assembled at the High Heavenly Market and made an inquiry. At that time the kami Omoi-kane, the son of Taka-mi-musuhi, had an idea as a result of thoughtful consideration. He revealed his thoughts, saying, "We should make a likeness of the kami and invite her out." Thereupon, Ishi-kori-do-me was designated the artist, and she took metal from Heavenly Mt. Kagu and made a sun-halberd. Also, she completely skinned

---

69 The name Waka-hiru-me suggests some connection to Amaterasu (Ō-hiru-me). A younger sister or daughter have been proposed by commentators, but there is no definitive identification. She may accord with the kami Ame-no-hata-ori-me in *Ancient Matters*. The prefix -*mi*, meaning "august," appears frequently in the *Chronicles* and *Ancient Matters*. Its translation as "august," now somewhat archaic, follows the translations of Chamberlain and Aston.

70 The backward flaying is specified here by both the characters and the vernacular gloss reading.

眞名鹿之皮、以作天羽鞴。用此奉造之神、是卽紀伊國所坐日前神也。石凝姥、此云伊之居梨度咩。全剝、此云宇都播伎。

一書曰、日神尊、以天垣田爲御田。時素戔嗚尊、春則塡渠毀畔。又秋穀已成、則冒以絡繩。且日神居織殿時、則生剝斑駒、納其殿內。凡此諸事、盡是無狀。雖然、日神、恩親之意、不慍不恨、皆以平心容焉。

及至日神當新嘗之時、素戔嗚尊、則於新宮御席之下、陰自送糞。日神不知、俓坐席上。由是、日神、擧體不平。故以恚恨、廼居于天石窟、閉其磐戶。

于時、諸神憂之、乃使鏡作部遠祖天糠戶者造鏡。忌部遠祖太玉者造幣。玉作部遠祖豐玉者造玉。又使山雷者、採五百箇眞坂樹八十玉籤。野槌者、採五百箇野薦八十玉籤。凡此諸物、皆來聚集。

時中臣遠祖天兒屋命、則以神祝祝之。於是、日神方開磐戶而出焉。是時、以鏡入其石窟者、觸戶小瑕。其瑕於今猶存。此卽伊勢崇祕之大神也。

已而科罪於素戔嗚尊、而責其秡具。是以、有手端吉棄物、足端凶棄物。亦以唾爲白和幣、以洟爲靑和幣、用此解除竟、遂以神逐之理逐之。送糞、此云俱蘇摩屢。玉籤、此云多摩俱之。秡具、此云波羅閉都母能。手端吉棄、此云多那須衞能餘之岐羅毗。神祝祝之、此云加武保佐枳保佐枳枳。逐之、此云波羅賦。

一書曰、是後、日神之田、有三處焉。號曰天安田・天平田・天邑幷田。此皆良田。雖經霖旱、無所損傷。其素戔嗚尊之田、亦有

a true deer and made a heavenly bellows. Using these, she made and presented a likeness, which is now the kami Hi-no-mae in Kii Province.^xxii

Section 7, Variant 2

One text says, The sun kami had used heavenly field hedges to set up her paddies. In the springtime, Susano-o filled in the ditches and broke the ridges. In the fall, when the grain had ripened, he used braided rope to claim the paddies for his own. Furthermore, when the sun kami was in the weaving hall, he flayed a live mottled colt and threw it into the hall. All these many things are examples of his lack of proper principles. Despite this, the sun kami, being of gracious and kind disposition, did not blame him or resent him. All these things she bore with an even temperament.

When the time came for the feast of first rice for the sun kami, Susano-o secretly defecated underneath her seat in the feast hall. The sun kami, not knowing, simply sat upon her seat. As a result, the sun kami's constitution became uneven, and she therefore became angry and immediately went to dwell in the heavenly rock cave and closed its stone door.

At that time, the various kami worried and had made the distant ancestor of the mirror makers, Ama-no-nuka-do, make a mirror.[71] The distant ancestor of the Inbe, Futo-dama, made paper streamers. The distant ancestor of the jewel makers, Toyo-tama, made jewels.[72] Also, Yamazu-chi was made to collect many stakes from an innumerably branched true sakaki tree, and No-zu-chi was made to collect many bamboo shoots from an innumerably bladed field. With all of these things, the various kami came and assembled.

At that time the distant ancestor of the Nakatomi, Ama-no-koyane, prayed a divine prayer. Thereupon, the sun kami opened the stone door and came out. At that time, the mirror was put into the stone cave, and where it struck the door, it acquired a small defect, a defect that still exists. This mirror is the great kami venerated at Ise.

Shortly thereafter the kami fined Susano-o for his crimes and demanded the objects needed for his expiation. Thereupon, his fingernails were made into auspicious things to be cast away, and his toenails into inauspicious things to be cast away. Also, his saliva was made into white paper streamers, and his nasal mucus[73] into blue paper streamers. Using these things, the kami finished the expiation, and then at last they banished him according to the principle of a divine banishing.

Section 7, Variant 3^xxiii

One text says, After this, the sun kami had rice paddies in three places, called Heaven's Tranquil Paddies, Heaven's Even Paddies, and Heaven's Village Assembly Paddies. All were good fields. Even after prolonged rain or drought, they sustained no damage. Susano-o also had

71 The mirror makers were a lineage group of allied miyatsuko from the Shikishimo District of Yamato Province (present-day Tawaramoto, Shiki District). They were promoted to muraji in Tenmu 12.9. Ama-no-nuka-do appears here and in Variant 3 written with different characters.
72 The jewel makers were a lineage group of allied miyatsuko. Groups with similar names were widely dispersed, making a precise identification difficult.
73 Glossed with the vernacular Japanese for "drool," but the translation here follows the character.

三處。號曰天樴田・天川依田・天口銳田。此皆磽地。雨則流之、旱則焦之。故素戔嗚尊、妬害姉田。春則廢渠槽、及埋溝、毀畔、又重播種子。秋則挿籤、伏馬。凡此惡事、曾無息時。雖然、日神不慍、恆以平恕相容焉、云々。

至於日神、閉居于天石窟也、諸神遣中臣連遠祖興台產靈兒天兒屋命、而使祈焉。於是、天兒屋命、掘天香山之眞坂木、而上枝懸以鏡作遠祖天拔戶兒石凝戶邊所作八咫鏡、中枝懸以玉作遠祖伊弉諾尊兒天明玉所作八坂瓊之曲玉、下枝懸以粟國忌部遠祖天日鷲所作木綿、乃使忌部首遠祖太玉命執取、而廣厚稱辭祈啓矣。

于時、日神聞之曰、頃者人雖多請、未有若此言之麗美者也。乃細開磐戶而窺之。是時、天手力雄神、侍磐戶側、則引開之者、日神之光、滿於六合。故諸神大喜、即科素戔嗚尊千座置戶之解除、以手爪爲吉爪棄物、以足爪爲凶爪棄物。

乃使天兒屋命、掌其解除之太諄辭而宣之焉。世人愼收己爪者、此其緣也。

既而諸神、噴素戔嗚尊曰、汝所行甚無賴。故不可住於天上。亦不可居於葦原中國。宜急適於底根之國、乃共逐降去。于時、霖也。素戔嗚尊、結束青草、以爲笠蓑、而乞宿於衆神。

衆神曰、汝是躬行濁惡、而見逐謫者。如何乞宿於我、遂同距之。是以、風雨雖甚、不得留休、而辛苦降矣。自爾以來、世諱著笠蓑、以入他人屋內。又諱負束草、以入他人家內。有犯此者、必債解除、此太古之遺法也。

是後、素戔嗚尊曰、諸神逐我。我今當永去。如何不與我姉相見、而擅自徑去歟、廼復扇天扇國、上詣于天。

rice paddies in three places, called Heaven's Stumpy Paddy, Heaven's Riverside Paddy, and Heaven's Sharp-Mouth Paddy.[74] They were rocky fields. When it rained, they got washed away, and in times of drought, they dried up. So Susano-o was jealous of his sister's fields and damaged them. In the spring, he broke the irrigation pipes and filled in the ditches, broke down the ridges separating the paddies, and double-planted the seedlings. In the autumn, he re-staked the paddies to claim them as his own and made horses lay down in the paddies. He continued all of these improper deeds without ceasing. Despite this, the sun kami did not blame him, and always bore him with an even temper, and so on.

Then the sun kami went and closed herself in the heavenly rock cave, and the various kami dispatched the distant ancestor of the Muraji of the Nakatomi and the child of Ko-goto-musu-hi, Ama-no-koyane, and made him pray. Ama-no-koyane then dug up a true sakaki tree from Heavenly Mt. Kagu. On the upper branches, he hung an eight-shaftment mirror made by the distant ancestor of the mirror makers and the child of Ama-no-nuka-do, Ishi-kori-tobe. On the middle branches he hung an eight-shaftment curved jewel made by the ancestor of the jewel makers and child of Izanagi, Ama-no-akaru-tama. On the lower branches, he hung barkcloth made by the distant ancestor of the Inbe of Awa Province, Ama-no-hi-washi. Then he made the distant ancestor of the Obito[75] of the Inbe, Futo-dama, hold these objects and pray an expansive, sincere, and fervent encomium.

When the sun kami heard this, she said, "These days people say many things, but there have never been any words as beautiful as these." Then she opened the stone door a crack and peeked out. Ama-no-ta-jikara-o was waiting alongside the stone door, and when he pulled it open, the light of the sun kami filled the six quarters. The various kami were greatly pleased. They fined Susano-o one thousand tables for his expiation. His fingernails were made into auspicious things to be cast away, and his toenails into inauspicious things to be cast away. Ama-no-koyane was put in charge of the ritual prayer for the expiation and made to recite it. People of this world are careful with their nails for this reason.

After this, the various kami denounced Susano-o, saying, "Your actions have been extremely unrighteous. On account of them, you cannot live in heaven, nor can you dwell in the central reed plain land either. Quickly be gone to the far-off Land of Ne." Then together they chased him out. At that time, there was prolonged rain. Susano-o bound green grass into a hat and raincoat, and begged lodging of the many kami.

The many kami said, "Your actions have been impure, and so you have been banished as punishment. How can you ask us for lodging?" In the end, they all rejected him. Then, though the wind and rain were very strong, he could not find a place to stay, and he became bitter. Ever since that time, in our world, one avoids going into someone else's house while wearing a hat and raincoat. If someone violates this point of etiquette, expiation will certainly be demanded. This is a rule passed down to us from very long ago.

Afterward, Susano-o said, "The various kami have banished me. I will depart forever. But how can I just depart in this fashion and not see my sister?" He then again shook the heavens and rattled the earth, and ascended to heaven.

---

74 Heaven's Village Assembly Paddy and Heaven's Mouth-Sharp Paddy are translated according to the literal meaning of the characters; the meaning is unclear.
75 A title of nobility.

時、天鈿女見之、而告言於日神也。日神曰、吾弟所以上來、非復好意。必欲奪之我國者歟。吾雖婦女、何當避乎、乃躬裝武備、云々。

於是、素戔嗚尊誓之曰、吾若懷不善、而復上來者、吾今囓玉生兒、必當爲女矣。如此則可以降女於葦原中國。如有清心者、必當生男矣。如此則可以使男御天上。且姉之所生、亦同此誓。

於是、日神先囓十握劒、云々。素戔嗚尊、乃輻轤然、解其左髻所纒五百箇統之瓊綸、而瓊響瑲瑲、濯浮於天渟名井。囓其瓊端、置之左掌、而生兒、正哉吾勝勝速日天忍穗根尊。復囓右瓊、置之右掌、而生兒、天穗日命。此出雲臣・武藏國造・土師連等遠祖也。次天津彥根命。此茨城國造・額田部連等遠祖也。次活目津彥根命。次熯速日命。次熊野大角命。凡六男矣。

於是、素戔嗚尊、白日神曰、吾所以更昇來者、衆神處我以根國。今當就去。若不與姉相見、終不能忍離。故實以清心、復上來耳。今則奉覲已訖。當隨衆神之意、自此永歸根國矣。請姉照臨天國、自可平安。且吾以清心所生兒等、亦奉於姉。已而復還降焉。廢渠槽、此云祕波鵝都。捶籤、此云久斯社志。興台產靈、此云許語等武須毗。太諄辭、此云布斗能理斗。輻轤然、此云乎謀苦留留爾。瑲瑲乎、此云奴儺等母母由羅爾。

是時、素戔嗚尊、自天而降到於出雲國簸之川上。時聞川上有啼哭之聲、故尋聲覓往者、有一老公與老婆、中間置一少女、撫而哭之。素戔嗚尊問曰、汝等誰也。何爲哭之如此耶。

對曰、吾是國神。號脚摩乳。我妻號手摩乳。此童女是吾兒也。號奇稻田

When Ama-no-uzu-me saw him, she reported it to the sun kami. The sun kami said, "My brother has come up without good intentions. He certainly wants to steal my land. Woman though I am, why should I flee?" She straightaway put on military gear, and so on.

Then Susano-o made an oath, saying, "If I have come again with evil in my breast, the children born when I now chew up this jewel will certainly be female. In that case, the girls will descend to the central reed plain land. If I have pure intentions, they will certainly be male. In this case, the boys will be made to rule heaven. For those children that my sister produces, this oath will be the same."

Thereupon, the sun kami first chewed her ten-hand sword, and so on. Susano-o then untied the long string of innumerable beads wrapped round and round his left hair bun, and they made a clear sound when he rinsed them in the true well of heaven. When he bit the end of the jewel and placed it in his left palm, the child born was Masa-ka-a-katsu-kachi-haya-hi-ama-no-oshi-hone. Again, when he bit the right jewel and placed it in his right palm, the child born was Ama-no-ho-hi,is the distant ancestor of the Omi of Izumo, the Provincial Miyatsuko of Musashi, and the Muraji of the Haji. Next was Ama-tsu-hiko-ne,is the distant ancestor of the Provincial Miyatsuko of Ubaraki and the Muraji of the Nukatabe.[76] Next was Iku-tsu-hiko-ne. Next was Hi-no-haya-hi. Next was Kumano-no-ō-sumi. There were six male kami in all.

At this point, Susano-o said to the sun kami, "The reason I have come up again is that the many kami have exiled me to the Land of Ne. If I were not to see my older sister, I would not be able to bear the separation. So I truly came up again with only pure intentions. Now my audience with my older sister is complete. In accordance with the will of the many kami, I will presently depart forever for the Land of Ne. May my older sister shine upon heaven and earth and be in complete peace. Also, I present the children that I produced with a pure heart to my older sister." Then Susano-o again returned downward.

Section 8: Susano-o Defeats the Eight-Headed Serpent

Main Version

At this time, Susano-o descended from heaven to the headwaters of the Hi River in the land of Izumo.[xxiv] There he heard, from the headwaters, the sound of weeping and wailing. He went looking for the sound, and there was an old man and an old woman. Between them was a young girl, whom they were consoling and for whom they were weeping. Susano-o asked them, "Who are you? Why are you crying like this?"

The old man replied, "I am a kami of the land, called Ashi-nazu-chi. My wife is called Te-nazu-chi.[77] This child is my daughter, called Kushi-ina-da-

---

76 The Nukatabe were a widely dispersed lineage group of allied miyatsuko.
77 The names of the parents refer to comforting actions toward a child.

姫。所以哭者、往時吾兒有八箇少女。每年爲八岐大蛇所吞。今此少童且臨被吞。無由脱免。故以哀傷。

素戔嗚尊勅曰、若然者、汝、當以女奉吾耶。

對曰、隨勅奉矣。

故素戔嗚尊、立化奇稻田姫、爲湯津爪櫛、而插於御髻。乃使脚摩乳・手摩乳釀八醞酒。幷作假庪假庪、此云佐受枳八間、各置一口槽、而盛酒以待之也。

至期果有大蛇。頭尾各有八岐。眼如赤酸醬。赤酸醬、此云阿箇箇鵝知。松柏生於背上、而蔓延於八丘八谷之間。及至得酒、頭各一槽飮。醉而睡。

時素戔嗚尊、乃拔所帶十握劒、寸斬其蛇。至尾劒刃少缺。故割裂其尾視之、中有一劒。此所謂草薙劒也。

草薙劒、此云倶娑那伎能都留伎。一書云本名天叢雲劒。蓋大蛇所居之上、常有雲氣、故以名歟。至日本武皇子、改名曰草薙劒。素戔嗚尊曰、是神劒也、吾何敢私以安乎、乃上獻於天神也。

然後、行覓將婚之處。遂到出雲之淸地焉。淸地、此云素鵝。乃言曰、吾心淸淸之。此今呼此地曰淸。於彼處建宮。

hime.⁷⁸ We weep because in the past we had eight daughters. Every year one is swallowed by a giant eight-headed serpent.⁷⁹ Now this maiden will be swallowed as well. There is no way to avoid it. So we grieve."

Susano-o then decreed, "If that is the case, why not give this girl to me?"

They replied, "We shall present her to you, as you decree."

So Susano-o changed Kushi-ina-da-hime into a hallowed comb and inserted her into his hair bun. Then he made Ashi-nazu-chi and Te-nazu-chi make repeatedly fermented wine and, at the same time, make temporary platforms for eight settings. On each of these, he placed a barrel, filled it with wine, and waited.

Time passed and at last the giant serpent appeared. It had eight heads and eight tails. Its eyes were as red as cherries, pine and oak grew on its back, and it stretched across eight mountains and eight valleys as it crawled. When it got to the wine, each head went into a barrel and drank. Intoxicated, it slept.

Susano-o drew the ten-hand sword he wore and cut the serpent to shreds. When he got to the tails, the blade of his sword developed a small notch. So he cut open the tails and examined them, and within one was a sword. This is the sword now known as Kusa-nagi.

One text says, That the real name of the sword was Ama-no-mura-kumo,⁸⁰ but perhaps because above the serpent there were always clouds, it was thus named. In the time of Imperial Prince Yamato Take, the name was changed to Kusa-nagi.⁸¹

Susano-o said, "This is a divine sword. How could I dare to make it my own?" And so he presented it to the heavenly kami.

Afterward, he searched for a place to get married, and at last, he reached Suga in Izumo. There he declared, "My mind is refreshed." And so now this place is called Suga. He built a shrine there.

---

78 "Kushi" is a pun for "stakes" used to demarcate paddy fields and "comb," which she is transformed into.
79 The eight-headed serpent could be interpreted as simply having "many" heads; the number eight is repeated many times in this section.
80 Meaning "heavenly gathering clouds."
81 Meaning "grass mower." The details concerning this note are given in the Keikō book.

或云時、武素戔嗚尊歌之曰、

夜句茂多兔	やくもたつ
伊弩毛夜覇餓岐	いづもやへがき
兔磨語昧爾	つまごめに
夜覇餓枳都倶盧	やへがきつくる
贈廼夜覇餓岐廻	そのやへがきゑ

乃相與遘合、而生兒大己貴神。因勅之曰、吾兒宮首者、即脚摩乳・手摩乳也。故賜號於二神、曰稲田宮主神。已而素戔嗚尊、遂就於根國矣。

一書曰、素戔嗚尊、自天而降到於出雲簸之川上。則見稲田宮主簀狹之八箇耳女子號稲田媛、乃於奇御戸爲起而生兒、號淸之湯山主三名狹漏彥八嶋篠。一云、淸之繋名坂輕彥八嶋手命。又云、淸之湯山主三名狹漏彥八嶋野。此神五世孫、即大國主神。篠、小竹也。此云斯奴。

一書曰、是時、素戔嗚尊、下到於安藝國可愛之川上也。彼處有神。名曰脚摩手摩。其妻名曰稲田宮主簀狹之八箇耳。此神正在姙身。夫妻共愁、乃告素戔嗚尊曰、我生兒雖多、毎生輒有八岐大蛇來呑。不得一存。今吾且產。恐亦見呑。是以哀傷。素戔嗚尊乃教之曰、汝可以衆菓釀酒八甕。吾當爲汝殺蛇。二神隨教設酒。

By one account, At this time, Susano-o sang,

Eightfold clouds rise;†
The eightfold hedge of Izumo!
To enclose my wife,
I build an eightfold hedge.
Oh, that eightfold hedge!⁸²

Then they consummated the marriage and gave birth to their child, the kami Ō-ana-muchi. Susano-o then decreed, "The caretakers of my child's shrine shall be Ashi-nazu-chi and Te-nazu-chi. Therefore, I bestow upon these two kami the title Ina-da-no-miya-nushi. Then Susano-o at last went to the Land of Ne.

Section 8, Variant 1

One text says, Susano-o descended from heaven to the headwaters of the Hi River in Izumo. Then he saw Ina-da-no-miya-nushi-suga-no-ya-tsu-mimi's daughter, called Ina-da-hime, and then built a wedding-house.⁸³ The child that was born was called Suga-no-yu-yama-nushi-mi-na-saro-hiko-ya-shima-shino. Another account says Suga-no-kake-na-saka-karu-hiko-ya-shima-de. Also said is Suga-no-yu-yama-nushi-mi-na-saro-hiko-ya-shima-no. This kami's fifth-generation descendent is the kami Ō-kuni-nushi.

Section 8, Variant 2

One text says, At this time, Susano-o went down to the headwaters of the E River in the land of Aki.ˣˣᵛ There was a kami there named Ashi-nazu-te-nazu.⁸⁴ His wife's name was Ina-da-no-miya-nushi-suga-no-ya-tsu-mimi. This kami was pregnant. Both husband and wife were worried and addressed Susano-o, saying, "Though we have had many children, every time they are born, the eight-headed giant serpent soon comes and swallows them. Not one has been able to live. We will have a child now and fear that it too will be swallowed. That is why we are grieving."

Then Susano-o instructed them, saying, "Use a lot of fruit to brew eight vats of wine. I will then kill the serpent for you." The two kami prepared the wine in accordance with his instructions.

---

82 This song is written in the 5-7-5-7-7 syllabic meter of traditional Japanese poetry and taken to be the first ever Japanese vernacular poem.
83 In the Main Version, Ina-da-no-miya-nushi is the same name that Susano-o gives to the old man and old woman. Here it is appended with "susa-no" (of Susa), the name of a place in Izumo and a reference to Susano-o, and "ya-tsu-mimi" (many mysterious powers).
84 Ashi-nazu-te-nazu is the combination of the names of the old man and the old woman in the Main Version.

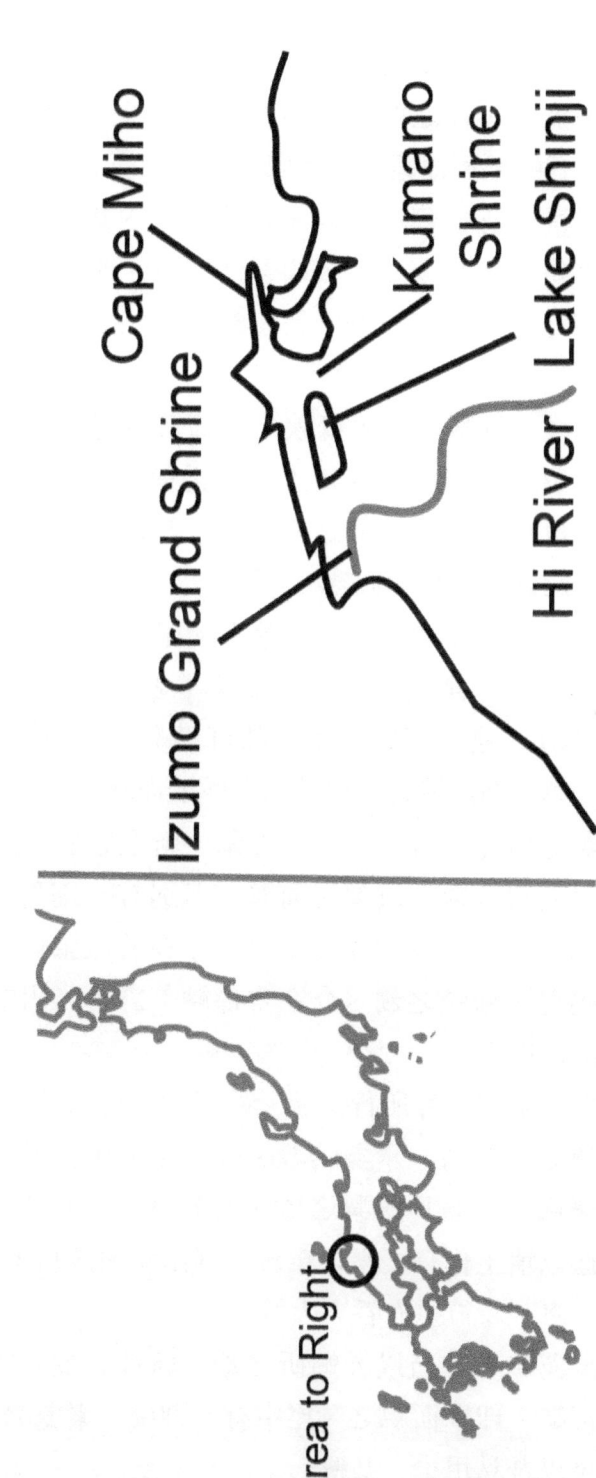

MAP 4 Izumo region. The Hi River has since been redirected to empty into Lake Shinji

至產時、必彼大蛇、當戸將吞兒焉。素戔嗚尊勅蛇曰、汝是可畏之神。敢不饗乎、乃以八甕酒、毎口沃入。其蛇飮酒而睡。素戔嗚尊、拔劒斬之。

　至斬尾時、劒刃少缺。割而視之、則劒在尾中。是號草薙劒。此今在尾張國吾湯市村。卽熱田祝部所掌之神是也。其斷蛇劒、號曰蛇之麁正。此今在石上也。

　是後、以稻田宮主簀狹之八箇耳生兒眞髮觸奇稻田媛、遷置於出雲國簸川上、而長養焉。然後、素戔嗚尊、以爲妃而所生兒之六世孫、是曰大己貴命。大己貴、此云於褒婀娜武智。

一書曰、素戔嗚尊、欲幸奇稻田媛而乞之。脚摩乳・手摩乳對曰、請先殺彼蛇、然後幸者宜也。彼大蛇、毎頭各有石松。兩脇有山。甚可畏矣。將何以殺之。素戔嗚尊、乃計釀毒酒以飮之。蛇醉而睡。

　素戔嗚尊、乃以蛇韓鋤之劒、斬頭斬腹。其斬尾之時、劒刃少缺。故裂尾而看、卽別有一劒焉。名爲草薙劒。此劒昔在素戔嗚尊許。今在於尾張國也。其素戔嗚尊、斷蛇之劒、今在吉備神部許也。出雲簸之川上山是也。

一書曰、素戔嗚尊所行無狀。故諸神、科以千座置戸、而遂逐之。是時、素戔嗚尊、帥其子五十猛神、降到於新羅國、居曾尸茂梨之處。乃興言曰、此地吾不欲居、遂以埴土作舟、乘之東渡、到出雲國簸川上所在、鳥上之峯。時彼處有吞人大蛇。

　素戔嗚尊、乃以天蠅斫之劒、斬彼大蛇。時斬蛇尾而刃缺。卽擘而視之、尾中有一神劒。素戔嗚尊曰、此不可以吾私用也、乃遣

When the time came to give birth, sure enough the serpent came to the door to swallow the child. Susano-o then decreed to the serpent, "You are a truly formidable kami. I dare not neglect treating you to a feast." Then he poured the eight vats of wine into each mouth. The serpent drank the wine and fell asleep. Then Susano-o drew his sword and killed it.

While he was cutting the tail, the blade of his sword got a small notch. He cut open the tail and looked, and there was a sword inside the tail. This sword is called Kusa-nagi. Presently this sword is in the village of Ayuchi in Owari Province. It is the kami that the priests of Atsuta venerate and attend.[xxvi] The sword that killed the serpent is called Orochi-no-aramasa. It is presently in the Isonokami Shrine.[xxvii]

Afterward, Ma-kami-furu-kushi-ina-da-hime, the child born of Ina-da-no-miya-nushi-suga-no-ya-tsu-mimi, moved to the headwaters of the Hi River in Izumo and grew up there. Sometime later, Susano-o made her his wife, and she thereby gave birth to a child whose sixth-generation descendent was Ō-ana-muchi.[85]

Section 8, Variant 3

One text says, Susano-o wanted to marry Kushi-ina-da-hime and sought her hand. Ashi-nazu-chi and Te-nazu-chi replied, "Please first kill that serpent, and afterward you may marry her. As for the giant serpent, each head has boulder-rooted pine trees on it, and from the side it looks like a mountain. It is truly terrible. How will you kill it?" Susano-o made a plan, brewed foul wine, and made the serpent drink it. The serpent became intoxicated and fell asleep.

Susano-o, with his sword Orochi-no-kara-sahi, then cut off its heads and cut open its stomach. When he cut its tail, the blade of his sword got slightly notched. So he cut open the tail and looked, and there was another sword inside. It is named Kusa-nagi. This sword was with Susano-o a long time ago. Now it is in Owari Province. The sword that Susano-o used to cut the serpent is now with the priests in Kibi.[xxviii] The place where the serpent was slain is in Izumo, at the mountain at the head of the Hi River.[86]

Section 8, Variant 4

One text says, Susano-o's conduct lacked proper principles. So the various kami fined him one thousand tables, and then in the end they banished him. At that time, Susano-o, leading his son the kami I-takeru, descended to the Land of Silla[87] and dwelt in the place Soshimori.[xxix] Then he said, "I do not wish to dwell in this land." He made a boat out of clay[88] and crossed over to the east, to the headwaters of the Hi River in the land of Izumo, and then to the peak of Torikami.[xxx] At that time and in that place, there was a giant snake that swallowed people.

Susano-o, with his sword Ama-no-hae-kiri, slew this great serpent. When he cut the serpent's tail, his blade got notched. So he cut the tail open and looked, and inside there was a divine sword. Susano-o said, "I should not keep this for my own use." Then he dispatched

---

85 An original note gives the vernacular for Ō-ana-muchi, though this name appeared already in the Main Version.
86 The final sentence does not make sense as written; a subject has been added.
87 The Kingdom of Silla on the Korean peninsula.
88 Perhaps for lack of trees for wood.

五世孫天之葺根神、上奉於天。此今所謂草薙劒矣。
　　　初五十猛神、天降之時、多將樹種而下。然不殖韓地、盡以持歸。遂始自筑紫、凡大八洲國之內、莫不播殖而成靑山焉。所以、稱五十猛命、爲有功之神。即紀伊國所坐大神是也。
一書曰、素戔嗚尊曰、韓鄕之嶋、是有金銀。若使吾兒所御之國、不有浮寶者、未是佳也。乃拔鬚髯散之。即成杉。又拔散胸毛。是成檜。尻毛是成柀。眉毛是成橡樟。已而定其當用。乃稱之曰、杉及橡樟、此兩樹者、可以爲浮寶。檜可以爲瑞宮之材。柀可以爲顯見蒼生奧津棄戸將臥之具。夫須噉八十木種、皆能播生。
　　　于時、素戔嗚尊之子、號曰五十猛命。妹大屋津姬命。次枛津姬命。凡此三神、亦能分布木種。即奉渡於紀伊國也。然後、素戔嗚尊、居熊成峯、而遂入於根國者矣。棄戸、此云須多杯。柀、此云磨紀。
一書曰、大國主神、亦名大物主神、亦號國作大己貴命。亦曰葦原醜男。亦曰八千戈神。亦曰大國玉神。亦曰顯國玉神。其子凡有一百八十一神。

his fifth-generation descendent, the kami Ama-no-fuki-ne, to present it to heaven. This sword is now called Kusa-nagi.

At first, I-takeru, when he descended from heaven, came down bringing many tree seeds. However, he did not plant them in the Land of Kara; rather, he brought all of them back to Yamato with him.[89] Then beginning in Tsukushi, he planted them throughout the Land of Eight Great Islands, and there was no mountain that was not verdant. For this reason, I-takeru was given the name Isao-shi. He is the great kami living in Kii Province.[90]

Section 8, Variant 5

One text says, Susano-o said, "On the islands of the Land of Kara[91] are gold and silver. If there are no boats in the land that my child rules, it will not be good."[92] Then he pulled out his beard and scattered it. This became cedar. He also pulled out the hair of his chest and scattered it. This became cypress. The hair from his buttocks became yew. The hair from his brow became camphor. After that, he established their uses, declaring "The two trees cedar and camphor should be used for making boats. Cypress should be used as timber for making auspicious shrines. Yew should be used as a tool for making coffins for the people of this world. The seeds of the many fruit trees that have all been planted should be used for food."

At that time, Susano-o's son was called I-takeru. That kami's younger sister was Ō-ya-tsu-hime. Next was Tsuma-tsu-hime. Together these three kami also widely planted tree seeds. Then they crossed over to the land of Kii. Afterward, Susano-o, who was dwelling at the peak of Kumanari, at last went to the Land of Ne.[93]

Section 8, Variant 6[xxxi]

One text says, The kami Ō-kuni-nushi—also called Ō-mono-nushi, Kuni-tsukuri-no-ō-ana-muchi, Ashi-hara-no-shi-ko-o, Ya-chi-hoko, Ō-kuni-tama, or Utsushi-kuni-tama—had children numbering 181 kami in all.[94]

---

89 Kara is the Korean peninsula. Here it is contrasted with the Land of Eight Great Islands, that is, the Japanese archipelago.
90 The old name of Kii Province was Ki-no-kuni, "tree land."
91 Referring to the Korean peninsula, despite its not being an island.
92 "My child" could refer to either Oshi-ho-mimi or to Ō-kuni-nushi. Gold and silver and the characters "floating treasure" used to write "boats" refer to the legendary oracle decree of Empress Jingū described in Chūai 8.9.
93 Kumanari also appears as Waninari and Kumanu; the last of these might refer to Kumano, a place-name in both Kii and Izumo. Modern commentators have suggested a Korean etymology as well.
94 Ō-kuni-nushi appeared in Variant 1. The number 181 is a stand-in for "many."

夫大己貴命、與少彦名命、戮力一心、經營天下。復爲顯見蒼生及畜産、則定其療病之方。又爲攘鳥獸昆蟲之災異、則定其禁厭之法。是以、百姓至今、咸蒙恩頼。

嘗大己貴命謂少彦名命曰、吾等所造之國、豈謂善成之乎。

少彦名命對曰、或有所成。或有不成。是談也、蓋有幽深之致焉。

其後少彦名命、行至熊野之御碕。遂適於常世鄉矣。亦曰、至淡嶋、而緣粟莖者、則彈渡而至常世鄉矣。

自後、國中所未成者、大己貴神、獨能巡造。遂到出雲國、乃興言曰、夫葦原中國、本自荒芒。至及磐石草木、咸能強暴。然吾已摧伏、莫不和順。遂因言、今理此國、唯吾一身而已。其可與吾共理天下者、蓋有之乎。

于時、神光照海、忽然有浮來者。曰、如吾不在者、汝何能平此國乎。由吾在故、汝得建其大造之績矣。

是時、大己貴神問曰、然則汝是誰耶。

對曰、吾是汝之幸魂奇魂也。

大己貴神曰、唯然。迺知汝是吾之幸魂奇魂。今欲何處住耶。

對曰、吾欲住於日本國之三諸山。故即營宮彼處、使就而居。此大三輪之神也。此神之子、即甘茂君等・大三輪君等、又姬蹈鞴五十鈴姬命。又曰、事代主神、化爲八尋熊鰐、通三嶋溝樴姬、或云、玉櫛姬。而生兒姬蹈鞴五十鈴姬命。是爲神日本磐余彦火火出見天皇之后也。

Ō-ana-muchi combined his power with Sukuna-biko-na, and their intentions became one, and they made the realm. Also, for the people of this world and domesticated animals, they established the methods for curing diseases. They also established rules for suppressive incantations to exorcise the calamities caused by birds, beasts, and insects. Subjects all continue to enjoy these blessings even now.[95]

At one point, Ō-ana-muchi said to Sukuna-biko-na, "The land we have made, is it not good and complete?"[96]

Sukuna-biko-na replied, "Some places are complete, and some are not." This conversation likely has a deep and profound meaning.

After this, Sukuna-biko-na went to the bluff of Kumano, and in the end went to the Land of Tokoyo. It is also said that he went to the Island of Awa, climbed a millet stalk, launched himself off to cross over, and arrived in the Land of Tokoyo.[xxxii]

After he departed, some places within the land were not complete, and Ō-ana-muchi by himself went throughout and made them so. Finally, he reached the land of Izumo and decreed, "The central reed plain land was originally vast and uncultivated. Even the rocks, grass, and trees were completely unruly. However, I have conquered, and nothing is out of order." Finally he said, "Now the ruler of this land is myself alone. Is there anyone that should rule this realm together with me?"

At that time, a divine light shone from the sea. Suddenly, something came floating in and said, "If we did not exist, how could you have pacified this land? Because we exist, you could undertake the task of creating this great land."

Then Ō-ana-muchi asked, "And so who are you?"

They replied, "Your spirit of fortune and your spirit of discernment."[97]

Then Ō-ana-muchi said suddenly, "Just so. I knew that you were my spirit of fortune and my spirit of discernment. Now, where do you wish to live?"

They replied, "We wish to dwell in Mt. Mimoro, in the land of Yamato." So he made a shrine there and had them go and dwell there. These are the kami of Ōmiwa. Their children are the Kimi of Kamo and Ōmiwa.[xxxiii] Also Hime-tatara-i-suzu-hime. In addition, it is said that the kami Koto-shiro-nushi transformed into an eight-fathom shark,[98] and had intercourse with Mizo-kui-hime of Mishima, by one account Tama-kushi-hime. They had a child, Hime-tatara-i-suzu-hime, who became the empress to Emperor Kamu-yamato-iware-hiko-ho-ho-de-mi [Jinmu].[xxxiv]

---

95 The gloss for "blessings" here is "mitama no fuyu," a word used to gloss different characters in later books to describe the spiritual power of the emperor, and meaning "august spirit exertion."
96 Commentators disagree on whether this is meant to be a serious question or a rhetorical one. Either interpretation is possible.
97 Literally, "fortune spirit" and "mysterious spirit," two of four kinds of spirits that comprise the divine, along with spirits of peace and spirits of violence.
98 The character for "shark" literally means "bear crocodile" and is sometimes translated as such. However, crocodiles are not native to Japan, and commentators generally agree that "shark" is the intended meaning.

初大己貴神之平國也、行到出雲國五十狹々小汀、而且當飮食。是時、海上忽有人聲。乃驚而求之、都無所見。頃時、有一箇小男、以白蘞皮爲舟、以鷦鷯羽爲衣、隨潮水以浮到。大己貴神、即取置掌中、而翫之、則跳囓其頰。乃怪其物色、遣使白於天神。

　于時、高皇産靈尊聞之而曰、吾所産兒、凡有一千五百座。其中一兒最惡、不順教養。自指間漏墮者、必彼矣。宜愛而養之。此即少彦名命是也。顯、此云于都斯。蹈鞴、此云多多羅。幸魂、此云佐枳彌多摩。奇魂、此云俱斯美挖磨。鷦鷯、此云娑娑岐。

At first, when Ō-ana-muchi was pacifying the land, he went to the small beach of Isasa in the land of Izumo and was going to eat.[xxxv] At that time, a human voice suddenly came across the sea. Surprised, he searched, but did not see anything. After some time, there was a small man using the skin of a rough potato pod as a boat and the feathers of a wren as clothing.[99] He floated along as the current took him. Ō-ana-muchi took the man and placed him in the palm of his hand and examined him, and the man jumped up and bit him on the cheek. Thinking the man's appearance strange, Ō-ana-muchi dispatched a messenger to report to the heavenly kami.

At that time, Taka-mi-musuhi heard of this and said, "In all, I have born fifteen hundred children. Among them, one was badly behaved and would not follow instructions. He slipped between my fingers and fell; this must be him. Love him and raise him." This was Sukuna-biko-na.

---

99 The rough potato plant (*Metaplexis japonica*) is in the milkweed family. Its elliptical seed pods split open when ripe, and the silky, threadlike seeds travel on the wind.

神代下

天照大神之子正哉吾勝勝速日天忍穗耳尊、娶高皇産靈尊之女栲幡千千姬、生天津彦彦火瓊瓊杵尊。故皇祖高皇産靈尊、特鍾憐愛、以崇養焉。遂欲立皇孫天津彦彦火瓊瓊杵尊、以爲葦原中國之主。然彼地多有螢火光神及蠅聲邪神。復有草木咸能言語。故高皇産靈尊、召集八十諸神、而問之曰、吾欲令撥平葦原中國之邪鬼。當遣誰者宜也。惟爾諸神、勿隱所知。

僉曰、天穗日命、是神之傑也。可不試歟。於是、俯順衆言、即以天穗日命往平之。然此神佞媚於大己貴神、比及三年、尚不報聞。故仍遣其子大背飯三熊之大人、大人、此云于志。亦名武三熊之大人。此亦還順其父、遂不報聞。

故高皇産靈尊、更會諸神、問當遣者。僉曰、天國玉之子天稚彦、是壯士也。宜試之。於是、高皇産靈尊、賜天稚彦天鹿兒弓

---

1 Historically speaking, the division between parts 1 and 2 of the "Age of the Gods" has been between the so-called seven generations of heavenly kami, from Kuni-no-toko-tachi to Izanagi and Izanami, and the five generations of earthly kami, from Amaterasu to Fukiaezu. However, the main version mentions the name of Amaterasu only once, at the opening of the book, and the primary driver of the plot of Section 9 is the heavenly kami Taka-mi-musuhi. Amaterasu's role in the main version of part 2 is limited to being the parent of Oshi-ho-mimi. Oshi-ho-mimi was the first male kami born during the oath testing of Amaterasu and Susano-o.

2 Taka-mi-musuhi is called the "imperial ancestor" upon the birth of his grandson Ninigi, the "imperial grandson" or "imperial descendant." The appellation "heavenly kami" or "heavenly grandson" is used for Ninigi when he is in dialogue with earthly kami as a

Book 2
Age of the Gods, 2

Section 9: Pacification of the Central Reed Plain Land, Descent of Ninigi

Main Version[1]

The son of the great kami Amaterasu, Masa-ka-a-katsu-kachi-haya-hi-ama-no-oshi-ho-mimi, wed the daughter of Taka-mi-musuhi, Taku-hata-chi-ji-hime, and she gave birth to Ama-tsu-hiko-hiko-ho-no-ninigi. His imperial ancestor Taka-mi-musuhi especially favored him and raised him with care.[2] Ultimately, he wanted to establish his imperial grandson Ama-tsu-hiko-hiko-ho-no-ninigi as the ruler of the central reed plain land.[3] However, in that land were many kami shining bright like lightning bugs and evil kami buzzing noisily like flies. Also, the grass and trees could all speak. So Taka-mi-musuhi summoned the many kami to assemble and asked them, "I want to rule and pacify the evil spirits of the central reed plain land. Who would be appropriate to dispatch? Should you various kami know, do not hide your thoughts."

All said, "Ama-no-ho-hi[4] is a superior kami. Should we not try him?" Taka-mi-musuhi consented to what they said, and Ama-no-ho-hi went to pacify that land. Yet this kami succumbed to flattering the kami Ō-ana-muchi for favor, and even after three years passed, there was no report back. So Taka-mi-musuhi also dispatched the kami's son, Ō-se-ii-no-mi-kuma-no-ushi, also known as Take-mi-kuma-no-ushi. This kami also went along with the will of his father, and in the end, there was no report back.

So Taka-mi-musuhi again met with the various kami and asked them who should be dispatched. All said, "The child of Ama-no-kuni-tama, Ame-waka-hiko, is a valiant warrior. We should try him. And so Taka-mi-musuhi bestowed upon Ame-waka-hiko a heavenly fawn bow

---

marker of hierarchical relations. Ninigi's legitimacy as a ruler thus derives from his status as the imperial grandson of the imperial ancestor Taka-mi-mushi, not his status as a heavenly kami or his descent from a heavenly kami, as in *Ancient Matters*. In Chinese historiography, the phrase "imperial grandson" can refer to any son of a crown prince, but in the main version of Book 2 of the *Chronicles*, it is exclusively used to refer to Ninigi.

3   This moniker is used throughout the variants of Sections 5 to 8, but only once, and in the alternative form "rich central reed plain land," in the main narrative, in Section 7. That is to say, while the variant texts present different and conflicting versions of events, their augmentative role is indispensable to the contents of the main narrative.

4   Oshi-ho-mimi's younger brother.

及天羽羽矢以遣之。此神亦不忠誠也。來到即娶顯國玉
之女子下照姬、亦名高姬亦名稚國玉。因留住之曰、吾亦欲馭
葦原中國、遂不復命。

是時、高皇產靈尊、怪其久不來報、乃遣無名雉伺之。
其雉飛降、止於天稚彥門前所植植、此云多底婁湯津杜木之
杪。杜木、此云可豆邏。時天探女天探女、此云阿麻能左愚謎。見、
而謂天稚彥曰、奇鳥來居杜杪。天稚彥、乃取高皇產靈尊所
賜天鹿兒弓・天羽羽矢、射雉斃之。其矢洞達雉胸、而至
高皇產靈尊之座前也。

時高皇產靈尊、見其矢曰、是矢、則昔我賜天稚彥之矢
也。血染其矢。蓋與國神相戰而然歟。於是、取矢還投下
之。其矢落下、則中天稚彥之胸上。于時、天稚彥、新嘗休
臥之時也。中矢立死。此世人所謂、反矢可畏之緣也。

天稚彥之妻下照姬、哭泣悲哀、聲達于天。是時、天國
玉、聞其哭聲、則知夫天稚彥已死、乃遣疾風、擧尸致天。
便造喪屋而殯之。即以川鴈、爲持傾頭者及持帚者、一云、
以鷄爲持傾頭者、以川鴈爲持帚者。又以雀爲舂女。一云、乃以川
鴈爲持傾頭者、亦爲持帚者。以鴻爲尸者。以雀爲舂者。以鷦鷯爲哭
者。以鵄爲造綿者。以烏爲宍人者。凡以衆鳥任事。

and heavenly viper arrows and sent him. This kami too was disloyal. Upon arriving, he married Utsushi-kuni-tama's daughter, Shita-teru-hime, also called Taka-hime or Waka-kuni-tama.[5] For this reason, he stayed there, saying, "I want to rule the central reed plain country," and in the end he never reported back.

In time, Taka-mi-musuhi thought it strange that no report had come back for so long, and so he dispatched an unnamed pheasant to investigate. This pheasant flew down and perched atop a hallowed cinnamon tree planted in front of Ame-waka-hiko's gate. Ama-no-sagu-me saw it and so told Ame-waka-hiko, "A strange bird has come and is in the cinnamon tree." Ame-waka-hiko then took the heavenly fawn bow and heavenly viper arrows that Taka-mi-musuhi had bestowed upon him and shot the pheasant dead. The arrow passed through the pheasant's breast and landed before Taka-mi-musuhi.

When Taka-mi-musuhi saw the arrow, he said, "This arrow is one that I bestowed upon Ame-waka-hiko long ago. The arrow is stained with blood, perhaps because he has been fighting with the kami of the land." He then took the arrow and returned it, throwing it downward. The arrow went down and struck Ame-waka-hiko in his upper chest. At that time, Ame-waka-hiko was laying down to rest after the feast of first rice. When hit by the arrow, he died instantly. This is the origin of the popular saying, "Fear a returning arrow."

Ame-waka-hiko's wife, Shita-teru-hime, wailed and cried in grief, and her voice reached all the way to heaven. When Ama-no-kuni-tama heard her wailing, he knew that Ame-waka-hiko had died, and so sent a swift wind to lift the corpse up to heaven. Then he made a tomb and performed the ritual of temporary interment. The river geese arranged the body and carried the brooms, and the sparrows polished the rice.[6]

Another account says that the chickens arranged the body and the river geese carried the brooms. Yet another account says that the river geese arranged the body and also carried the brooms, the kingfishers ate the food, the sparrows polished the rice, the wrens did the crying, the kites made the cerements, and the crows prepared the food. All of the birds were given a charge.

---

5 Utsushi-kuni-tama is an alternative name for Ō-ana-muchi.
6 The precise role of the geese here is unclear. "Arranged the body" is written with the characters "held hang head" and is glossed "kisari," based on *Ancient Matters*, but the meaning of this vernacular word is unclear.

而八日八夜、啼哭悲歌。

先是、天稚彦在於葦原中國也、與味耜高彦根神友善。味耜、此云婀膩須岐。故味耜高彦根神、昇天弔喪。時此神容貌、正類天稚彦平生之儀。故天稚彦親屬妻子皆謂、吾君猶在、則攀牽衣帶、且喜且慟。

時味耜高彦根神、忿然作色曰、朋友之道、理宜相弔。故不憚污穢、遠自赴哀。何爲誤我於亡者、則拔其帶劒大葉刈、刈、此云我里。亦名神戸劒。以斫仆喪屋。此即落而爲山。今在美濃國藍見川之上喪山是也。世人惡以生誤死、此其緣也。

是後、高皇産靈尊、更會諸神、選當遣於葦原中國者。僉曰、磐裂磐裂、此云以簸娑窶。根裂神之子磐筒男・磐筒女所生之子經津經津、此云賦都主神、是將佳也。

時有天石窟所住神、稜威雄走神之子甕速日神、甕速日神之子熯速日神、熯速日神之子武甕槌神。此神進曰、豈唯經津主神獨爲丈夫、而吾非丈夫者哉。其辭氣慷慨。故以即配經津主神、令平葦原中國。

二神、於是、降到出雲國五十田狹之小汀、則拔十握劒、倒植於地、踞其鋒端、而問大己貴神曰、高皇産靈尊、欲降皇孫、君臨此地。故先遣我二神、驅除平定。汝意何如。當須避不。

For eight days and eight nights, they wailed and cried in saddened verse.

Prior to this, when Ame-waka-hiko was in the central reed plain country, he was close to the kami Aji-suki-taka-hiko-ne. For this reason, Aji-suki-taka-hiko-ne ascended to heaven to mourn. At that time, this kami's appearance resembled that of Ame-waka-hiko when he was alive. Thus, Ame-waka-hiko's parents, siblings, wife, and child all said, "Our lord still lives!" Then they clutched at Aji-suki-taka-hiko-ne's belt and were half-overjoyed and half-bewildered.

Aji-suki-taka-hiko-ne's countenance changed to one of anger, and he said, "The principle of friendship is that we should mourn one another. Accordingly, not fearing the pollution of death,[7] I have come from afar to grieve. Why am I being mistaken for the deceased?" Then he drew the sword that he wore, Ō-ha-kari, and used it to cut down the tomb. Another name for the sword was Kan-to.[8] It fell and became a mountain. Now it is in Mino Province, at the headwaters of the Ayumi River, and is called Mt. Moyama.[i] People avoid mistaking the dead for the living for this reason.

After this, Taka-mi-musuhi again assembled the various kami to select who should be dispatched to the central reed plain land. All said, "The kami Futsu-nushi, son of Iwa-tsutsu-no-o and Iwa-tsutsu-no-me, who are themselves the children of the kami Iwa-saku-ne-saku, would be good."[9]

At that time, among the kami living in the heavenly rock cave was the kami Itsu-no-o-hashiri, and his son the kami Mika-no-haya-hi, and his son the kami Take-mikazu-chi. Take-mikazu-chi emerged, saying, "Why is Futsu-nushi alone called a hero? Am I not a hero?" His tone was fierce. So he accompanied Futsu-nushi and was ordered to pacify the central reed plain land.

The two kami then descended to Itasa Beach in the land of Izumo. They drew their ten-hand swords and planted their handles into the ground, then sat upon the tips of the blades. Then they questioned Ō-ana-muchi saying, "Taka-mi-musuhi wants to make his imperial grandson descend and rule this land. To that end, he dispatched us first to drive out and quell the unruly kami here. What do you intend to do? Will you withdraw, or no?"

---

7 Corpses were considered sources of pollution in ancient Japan.
8 Ō-ha-kari means great-blade sword. Kari is derived from Korean k'al for "knife." Kan-to means "divinely sharp."
9 Iwa-saku-ne-saku appears as the two kami Iwa-saku and Ne-saku in Variant 6 of Section 5. The figures Taka-mi-musuhi, Futsu-nushi, and Take-mikazu-chi only appear in the variant texts of Book 1, creating a major narrative inconsistency between the main versions of Books 1 and 2.

時大己貴神對曰、當問我子、然後將報。

是時、其子事代主神、遊行在於出雲國三穗三穗、此云美保之碕。以釣魚爲樂。或曰、遊鳥爲樂。故以熊野諸手船、亦名天鴿船。載使者稻背脛遣之。而致高皇產靈尊勅於事代主神、且問將報之辭。

時事代主神、謂使者曰、今天神有此借問之勅。我父宜當奉避。吾亦不可違。因於海中、造八重蒼柴柴、此云府璽籬、蹈船枻船枻、此云浮那能倍而避之。使者既還報命。

故大己貴神、則以其子之辭、白於二神曰、我怙之子、既避去矣。故吾亦當避。如吾防禦者、國內諸神、必當同禦。今我奉避、誰復敢有不順者。乃以平國時所杖之廣矛、授二神曰、吾以此矛卒有治功。天孫若用此矛治國者、必當平安。今我當於百不足之八十隈、將隱去矣。隈、此云矩磨泥。言訖遂隱。於是、二神、誅諸不順鬼神等、一云、二神、遂誅邪神及草木石類、皆已平了。其所不服者、唯星神香香背男耳。故加遣倭文神建葉槌命者則服。故二神登天也。倭文神、此云斯圖梨俄未。果以復命。

Ō-ana-muchi replied, "Ask my son, and after that I will give you my answer."

At that time, his son, the kami Koto-shiro-nushi, had gone out to Cape Miho to engage in some sport fishing.[ii] By one account, he was hunting birds for sport. So the two kami Futsu-nushi and Take-mikazu-chi dispatched their messenger Ina-se-hagi in a double-sided boat of Kumano.[10] When he arrived, he relayed Taka-mi-musuhi's decree to Koto-shiro-nushi and asked him for his response.

Koto-shiro-nushi told the messenger, "Now the kami of heaven have questioned us about this decree. My father had best withdraw, nor will I oppose you." Accordingly, he made an eightfold hedge of green brushwood in the ocean, stepped upon the bow of the boat, and withdrew. The messenger returned forthwith and made a report.

So Ō-ana-muchi, in accordance with his son's words, said to the two kami, "My son upon whom I rely has already withdrawn. Therefore, I too shall withdraw. If I resisted, the various kami in this land would certainly do the same and resist. Now I submit this land to you and withdraw. Who will dare to defy you?" Then he handed the two kami the broad-bladed halberd with which he had pacified the land to use as a staff, saying, "I, with this halberd, became ruler. If the heavenly descendant uses it to rule the land, surely it will be at peace.[11] Now I will hide myself and depart to a distant land."[12] Saying this, he at last concealed himself. Thereupon, the two kami Futsu-nushi and Take-mikazu-chi killed all the various evil kami who would not submit.

> Another account says that the two at last killed the evil kami and also the grass, tree, and stone kami, and all were pacified. At this time, the only insubordinate was the star kami Kaga-se-o-no-mi. So they additionally dispatched the weaver kami Take-hazu-chi, and the star kami yielded.

Then they ascended to heaven and at last reported their results.

---

10 An original note adds, "The boat was also named the Heavenly Pigeon Boat." This boat could move through the water like a pigeon on the wing. Kumano is present-day Wakayama Prefecture and is known as a supplier of wood for making boats. This boat was paddled on both sides, and so required two hands.

11 Perhaps Ō-ana-muchi is suggesting that the halberd be thrust into the ground as a staff. A similar usage as a marker of conquest appears in the Jingū book.

12 The "distant land" to which Ō-ana-muchi promises to retreat is given literally as "a road with less than one hundred but more than eighty turns."

于時、高皇産靈尊、以眞床追衾、覆於皇孫天津彦彦火瓊瓊杵尊使降之。皇孫乃離天磐座、天磐座、此云阿麻能以簸矩羅。且排分天八重雲、稜威之道別道別而、天降於日向襲之高千穗峯矣。既而皇孫遊行之狀也者、則自槵日二上天浮橋、立於浮渚在平處、立於浮渚在平處、此云羽企爾磨梨陀毗邇而陀陀志。而膂宍之空國、自頓丘覓國行去、頓丘、此云毗陀烏。覓國、此云矩貳磨儀。行去、此云騰褒屢。到於吾田長屋笠狹之碕矣。

其地有一人。自號事勝國勝長狹。皇孫問曰、國在耶以不。

對曰、此焉有國。請任意遊之。故皇孫就而留住。

時彼國有美人。名曰鹿葦津姫。亦名神吾田津姫。亦名木花之開耶姫。皇孫問此美人曰、汝誰之女子耶。

對曰、妾是天神娶大山祇神、所生兒也。皇孫因而幸之。即一夜而有娠。

皇孫未信之曰、雖復天神、何能一夜之間、令人有娠乎。汝所懷者、必非我子歟。

故鹿葦津姫忿恨、乃作無戶室、入居其內、而誓之曰、妾所娠、非天孫之胤、必當爨滅。如實天孫之胤、火不能害。即放火燒室。始起烟末生出之兒、號火闌降命。是隼人等始祖也。火闌降、此云褒能須素里。次避熱而居、生出之兒、號彥火火出見尊。次生出之兒、號火明命。是尾張連等始祖也。凡三子矣。

久之天津彦彦火瓊瓊杵尊崩。因葬筑紫日向可愛此云埃之山陵。

13 Ma-toko-ō-fusama, or "true bed coverlet."
14 Ninigi's question is not whether land physically exists, but whether the kind of superlative land, filled with superlative things, as referred to in this kami's name, exists.
15 An original note adds, "She is also named as Kamu-ata-tsu-hime and Ko-no-hana-no-saku-ya-hime."

Taka-mi-musuhi draped his imperial grandson Ama-tsu-hiko-hiko-ho-no-ninigi with a resplendent coverlet[13] and made him descend. The imperial grandson departed the heavenly rock seat, pushed apart the eightfold clouds of heaven, cleared the way with a fierce road-clearing, and descended from heaven to the peak of Takachiho in So, in Himuka.[iii] From there, the imperial grandson's passage was as follows: from the floating bridge of heaven above the twin peaks of Kushihi, he stood in a wide place on a floating island. Then he passed through a barren land, and from a succession of hills he searched for land. He arrived at Cape Kasasa in Nagaya in Ata.[iv]

There was a man in that land who called himself Koto-katsu-kuni-katsu-naga-sa. The imperial grandson asked him, "Is there land, or not?"[14]

He replied, "There is land. Please go forth at your pleasure." Thus, the imperial grandson went and dwelled there.

At that time there was a beautiful woman in that land named Ka-ashi-tsu-hime.[15] The imperial grandson asked this beautiful woman, "Whose daughter are you?"

She replied "I am the child of a heavenly kami who married[16] the kami Ō-yama-tsu-mi."

The imperial grandson summoned the woman to his bedchamber, and in one night she became pregnant. Thinking he had been deceived, the imperial grandson said, "Heavenly kami though I may be, how could I impregnate someone in just one night? The child you carry is surely not mine."

Thus Ka-ashi-tsu-hime became angry and spiteful, and so she made a chamber with no entrance or exit and dwelt inside. Then she swore an oath, saying, "If the child I carry is not the heir of the heavenly grandson, then it will surely burn. But if it is truly the heir of the heavenly grandson, the fire will not harm it." Then she lit a fire and incinerated the chamber. The child born before the smoke had risen was called Ho-no-susori.[v] He is the ancestor of the Hayato.[17]

Next, the child born when the heat of the fire retreated was named Hiko-ho-ho-de-mi.[vi] Next, the child born was called Ho-no-akari. He is the ancestor of the Muraji of Owari.[18] In all, there were three children.

After a long time, Ama-tsu-hiko-hiko-ho-no-ninigi expired.[19] He is buried in E Tomb in Himuka in Tsukushi.[vii]

---

16 The verb used here makes clear that in the main narrative, Ō-yama-tsu-mi is a female kami. This passage also reveals that Ninigi is not the only heavenly kami to have descended to earth.
17 The Hayato were a group of people living in southern Kyushu who resisted Japanese imperial rule into the eighth century CE.
18 Present-day Mie Prefecture.
19 This verb is reserved for emperors.

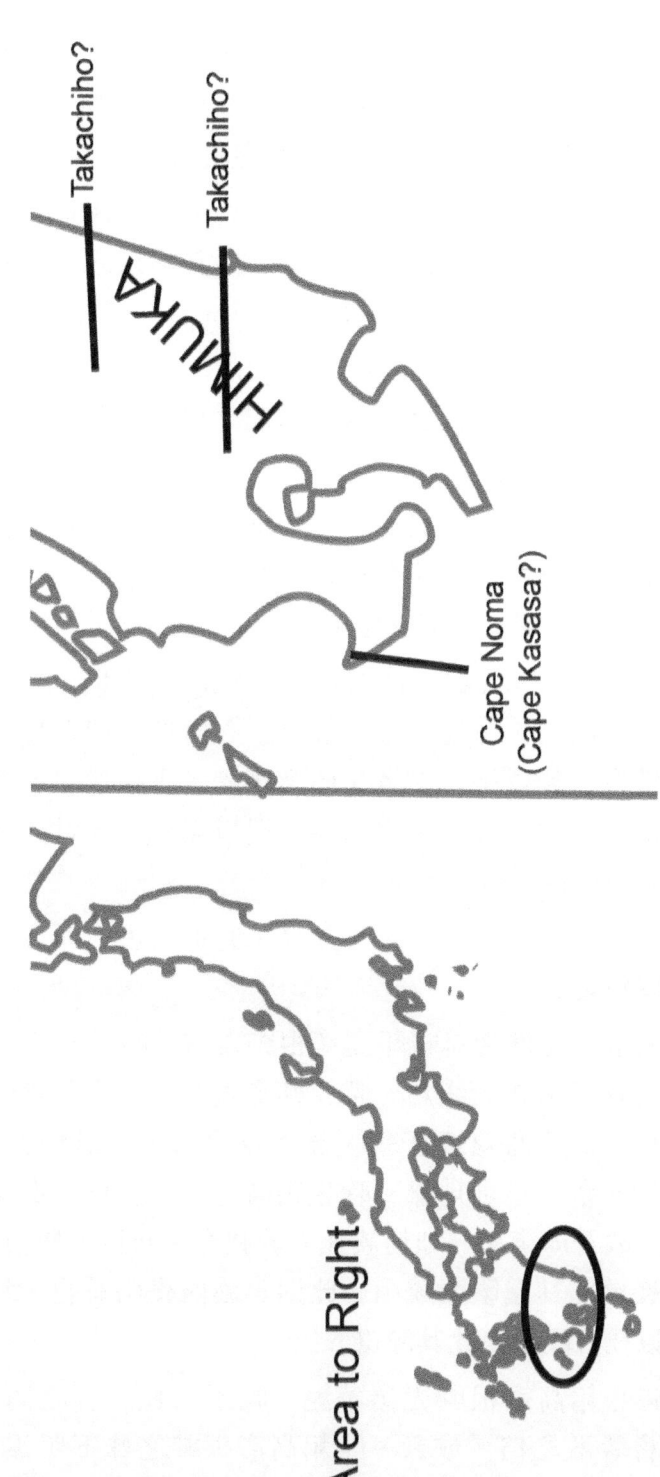

MAP 5 Descent of Ninigi

一書曰、天照大神、勅天稚彥曰、豐葦原中國、是吾兒可王之地也。然慮、有殘賊强暴橫惡之神者。故汝先往平之。乃賜天鹿兒弓及天眞鹿兒矢遣之。

天稚彥受勅來降、則多娶國神女子、經八年無以報命。故天照大神、乃召思兼神、問其不來之狀。時思兼神、思而告曰、宜且遣雉問之。

於是、從彼神謀、乃使雉往候之。其雉飛下、居于天稚彥門前湯津杜樹之杪、而鳴之曰、天稚彥、何故八年之間、未有復命。

時有國神。號天探女。見其雉曰、鳴聲惡鳥、在此樹上。可射之。天稚彥乃取天神所賜天鹿兒弓・天眞鹿兒矢、便射之。則矢達雉胸、遂至天神所處。

時天神見其矢曰、此昔我賜天稚彥之矢也。今何故來、乃取矢、而呪之曰、若以惡心射者、則天稚彥必當遭害。若以平心射者、則當無恙。因還投之。即其矢落下、中于天稚彥之高胸。因以立死。此世人所謂、返矢可畏之緣也。

時天稚彥之妻子、從天降來、將柩上去、而於天作喪屋殯哭之。

先是、天稚彥與味耜高彥根神友善。故味耜高彥根神、登天弔喪大臨焉。時此神形貌、自與天稚彥恰然相似。故天稚彥妻子等、見而喜之曰、吾君猶在。則攀持衣帶。不可排離。時味耜高彥根神忿曰、朋友喪亡。故吾即來弔。如何誤死人於我耶、乃拔十握劒、斫倒喪屋。其屋墮而成山。此則美濃國喪山是也。世人惡以死者誤己、此其緣也。

時味耜高彥根神光儀華艷、映于二丘二谷之間。故喪會者歌之曰、或云、味耜高彥根神之妹下照媛、欲令衆人知映丘谷者、是味耜高彥根神、故歌之曰、

Section 9, Variant 1

One text says, The great kami Amaterasu decreed to Ame-waka-hiko, "The rich central reed plain land is where my child is meant to rule. However, upon reflection, there are treacherous, violent, evil kami there. So first you will go there and pacify them." Then she bestowed upon him a heavenly fawn bow and true heavenly fawn arrows and sent him.

Ame-waka-hiko received this decree and went down. There he then took many wives who were daughters of earthly kami. Eight years passed, and there was no report back. So Amaterasu summoned the kami Omoi-kane and asked him about the reports not forthcoming. Omoi-kane thought about the matter and said, "Best send a pheasant to inquire into this matter."

Then, in accordance with this kami's plan, Amaterasu made a pheasant go and investigate. The pheasant flew down and, from the top of a hallowed cinnamon tree planted in front of Ame-waka-hiko's gate, cried out "Ame-waka-hiko! Why, after eight years' time, have you still made no report back?"

An earthly kami called Ama-no-sagume saw the pheasant and said, "A bird with an unpleasant cry is atop that tree. You should shoot it." Ame-waka-hiko took the heavenly fawn bow and true heavenly fawn arrows that he had received from the heavenly kami and shot the pheasant. The arrow passed through the pheasant's breast and, in the end, reached the place where the heavenly kami were.

The heavenly kami Amaterasu saw this arrow and said, "This is an arrow I bestowed upon Ame-waka-hiko long ago. Why has it come here now?" Taking the arrow, she took an oath, saying, "If this arrow was let loose with impure intentions, then Ame-waka-hiko will certainly meet with destruction. If it was shot with pure intentions, then he will be without accident." She then threw it back. The arrow went down and struck Ame-waka-hiko in the upper chest, and he died straightaway. This is the origin of the popular saying, "Fear a returning arrow."

Ame-waka-hiko's wife and child came down from heaven, went back up with a casket, and then in heaven built a tomb and mourned him at his temporary interment.

Sometime before this, Ame-waka-hiko had been good friends with the kami Aji-suki-taka-hiko-ne. As such, Aji-suki-taka-hiko-ne went up to heaven and mourned Ame-waka-hiko with great wailing. The kami's appearance was naturally very similar to that of Ame-waka-hiko. Hence, when Ame-waka-hiko's wife and children saw him, they exclaimed happily, "Our lord still lives!" Then they clung to his belt and could not be separated from him. In response, Aji-suki-taka-hiko-ne said angrily, "My friend is dead. So I came to mourn. Why am I being mistaken for a dead man?" Then he drew his ten-hand sword and cut down the tomb. The structure fell and became a mountain. This is Mt. Moyama in Mino Province. This is the reason that people dislike being mistaken for the dead.

At that time, Aji-suki-taka-hiko-ne shone brilliantly and beautifully, and his light filled the space of two hills and two valleys. Accordingly, the people who came to mourn sang. It is also said that the younger sister of Aji-suki-taka-hiko-ne, Shita-teru-hime, wanted the multitudes to know that the shining one who filled the hills and valleys with light was Aji-suki-taka-hiko-ne. The song went,

阿妹奈屢夜	あめなるや
乙登多奈婆多廼	おとたなはたの
汚奈餓勢屢	うながせる
多磨廼彌素磨屢廼	たまのみすまるの
阿奈陀磨波夜	あなたまはや
彌多爾	みたに
輔柁和柁邐須	ふたわたらす
阿泥素企多伽避顧禰	あぢすきたかひこね

又歌之曰、

阿磨佐箇屢	あまさかる
避奈菟謎廼	ひなつめの
以和多邏素西渡	いわたらすせと
以嗣箇播箇柁輔智	いしかはかたふち
箇多輔智爾	かたふちに
阿彌播利和柁嗣	あみはりわたし
妹慮豫嗣爾	めろよしに
豫嗣豫利據禰	よしよりこね
以嗣箇播箇柁輔智	いしかはかたふち

此兩首歌辭、今號夷曲。

　既而天照大神、以思兼神妹萬幡豐秋津媛命、配正哉吾勝勝速日天忍穗耳尊爲妃、令降之於葦原中國。是時、勝速日天忍穗耳尊、立于天浮橋、而臨睨之曰、彼地未平矣。不須也頗傾凶目杵之國歟、乃更還登、具陳不降之狀。

　故天照大神、復遣武甕槌神及經津主神、先行駈除。時二神、降到出雲、便問大己貴神曰、汝將此國、奉天神耶以不。

　對曰、吾兒事代主、射鳥遨遊、在三津之碕。今當問以報之。乃遣使人訪焉。

對曰、天神所求、何不奉歟。

> Like beads strung together
> on the neck,
> on the ankles,
> of the young weaver maiden
> in heaven,
> his light spans two valleys,
> Aji-suki-taka-hiko-ne.

Again she sang:

> At the shallows crossed
> by the countryside woman
> in far-off heaven,†
> at the depths of the rocky riverside,
> she strings her net.
> Like drawing the gaps of the net closed,
> draw near, draw close,
> at the depths of the rocky riverside.

These two songs are now called "Rustic Tunes."[20]

Shortly thereafter, the great kami Amaterasu arranged for Masa-ka-a-katsu-kachi-haya-hi-ama-no-oshi-ho-mimi to marry Yorozu-hata-toyo-aki-tsu-hime, the younger sister of the kami Omoi-kane, and she made them descend to the central reed plain land. At this time, Kachi-haya-hi-ama-no-oshi-ho-mimi stood on the floating bridge of heaven, looked down, and said, "This land has still not quieted down. It is a needlessly unruly and wretched land." He promptly returned upward and spoke in detail of why he would not descend.

So Amaterasu dispatched anew the kami Take-mikazu-chi and Futsu-nushi to go first and drive out the unruly kami. Thus, the two kami descended to Izumo, and then they asked the kami Ō-ana-muchi, "Will you submit this land to the heavenly kami or not?"

He replied, "My son, the kami Koto-shiro-nushi, is hunting birds for sport at Cape Mitsu. I shall presently ask him and report back." Then he dispatched a messenger to make inquiry.

The reply said, "This land is sought by the heavenly kami. How could we not submit it to them?"

---

20 This is the first of numerous instances in the *Chronicles* in which poems are named or suggested to go with a particular tune.

故大己貴神、以其子之辭、報乎二神。二神乃昇天、復命而告之曰、葦原中國、皆已平竟。

時天照大神勅曰、若然者、方當降吾兒矣。且將降間、皇孫已生。號曰天津彥彥火瓊瓊杵尊。時有奏曰、欲以此皇孫代降。

故天照大神、乃賜天津彥彥火瓊瓊杵尊、八坂瓊曲玉及八咫鏡・草薙劒、三種寶物。又以中臣上祖天兒屋命・忌部上祖太玉命・猨女上祖天鈿女命・鏡作上祖石凝姥命・玉作上祖玉屋命、凡五部神、使配侍焉。因勅皇孫曰、葦原千五百秋之瑞穗國、是吾子孫可王之地也。宜爾皇孫、就而治焉。行矣。寶祚之隆、當與天壤無窮者矣。

已而且降之間、先驅者還白、有一神、居天八達之衢。其鼻長七咫、背長七尺餘。當言七尋。且口尻明耀。眼如八咫鏡、而𤾨然似赤酸醬也。即遣從神往問。時有八十萬神、皆不得目勝相問。

故特勅天鈿女曰、汝是目勝於人者。宜往問之。天鈿女、乃露其胸乳、抑裳帶於臍下、而咲噱向立。

是時、衢神問曰、天鈿女、汝爲之何故耶。

對曰、天照大神之子所幸道路、有如此居之者誰也。敢問之。

衢神對曰、聞天照大神之子、今當降行、故奉迎相待。吾名是猨田彥大神。

時天鈿女復問曰、汝將先我行乎。抑我先汝行乎。

對曰、吾先啓行。

天鈿女復問曰、汝何處到耶。皇孫何處到耶。

Ō-ana-muchi reported his son's words to the two kami. The kami ascended to heaven and reported, saying "Subjugation of all in the central reed plain land is complete."

At that, Amaterasu decreed, "If that is the case, then I will make my son descend." But while she was preparing to send him down, her imperial grandchild, called Ama-tsu-hiko-hiko-ho-no-ninigi, was born. Oshi-ho-mimi beseeched Amaterasu, saying, "I entreat you to make this imperial grandchild descend instead."

Amaterasu then bestowed upon Ama-tsu-hiko-hiko-ho-no-ninigi three treasures: an eight-shaftment curved jewel, an eight-shaftment mirror, and the sword Kusa-nagi.[21] She also made the remote ancestor of the Nakatomi, Ama-no-koyane; the remote ancestor of the Inbe, Futo-dama; the remote ancestor of the Sarume, Ama-no-uzu-me; the remote ancestor of the mirror makers, Ishi-kori-do-me; and the remote ancestor of the jewel makers, Tama-no-ya, in all five kami of hereditary guilds, accompany and attend upon him. Then she decreed to her imperial grandchild, "The abundant reed plain land where rice grows for fifteen hundred years is a land my descendants are meant to rule. You, my imperial grandchild, shall go and rule. Go! And may the prosperity of your heavenly lineage never be exhausted so long as heaven and earth endure."

When he was about to descend, the kami in his vanguard returned and said, "There is a kami at the crossroads of heaven. His nose is seven shaftments long, and his back is over seven spans long; his height must be seven fathoms. Also, his mouth and his buttocks shine bright red, and his eyes are like an eight-shaftment mirror shining red as a bladder cherry." The kami attending upon him were dispatched to make inquiry, but among all the kami, none could withstand his gaze in order to question him.

So it was specially decreed to Ama-no-uzu-me, "Your gaze exceeds that of others. You should go and make inquiry." Ama-no-uzu-me exposed her breasts, pushed down the drawstring of her skirt below her navel, and then laughing, mockingly went to face the kami at the crossroads.

When he saw her, the kami at the crossroads asked, "Ama-no-uzu-me, for what reason do you do this?"

She ignored him and asked, "Who occupies the road upon which the child of the great kami Amaterasu will proceed?"

The kami at the crossroads replied, "I heard that the child of the great kami Amaterasu will presently descend. Thus, I wait to receive him. I am the great kami Saru-ta-hiko."

Ama-no-uzu-me asked him again, "Will you go before me, or shall I go before you?"

He replied, "I will begin and clear the way."

Ama-no-uzu-me asked him again, "Where will you go, and where shall the imperial grandson go?"

---

21 These bestowals, along with the five patron kami, connect this variant with the heavenly rock cave narrative in Section 7 of Book 1.

對曰、天神之子、則當到筑紫日向高千穗樴觸之峯。吾則應到伊勢之狹長田五十鈴川上。因曰、發顯我者汝也。故汝可以送我而致之矣。天鈿女、還詣報狀。

皇孫、於是、脫離天磐座、排分天八重雲、稜威道別道別、而天降之也。果如先期、皇孫則到筑紫日向高千穗樴觸之峯。

其猨田彥神者、則到伊勢之狹長田五十鈴川上。即天鈿女命、隨猨田彥神所乞、遂以侍送焉。時皇孫勅天鈿女命、汝宜以所顯神名、爲姓氏焉。因賜猨女君之號。故猨女君等男女、皆呼爲君、此其緣也。高胸、此云多歌武娜娑歌。頗傾也、此云歌矛志。

一書曰、天神、遣經津主神・武甕槌神、使平定葦原中國。時二神曰、天有惡神。名曰天津甕星。亦名天香香背男。請先誅此神、然後下撥葦原中國。

是時、齋主神、號齋之大人。此神今在于東國檝取之地也。

既而二神、降到出雲五十田狹之小汀、而問大己貴神曰、汝將以此國、奉天神耶以不。

對曰、疑、汝二神、非是吾處來者。故不須許也。

於是、經津主神、則還昇報告。時高皇產靈尊、乃還遣二神、勅大己貴神曰、今者聞汝所言、深有其理。故更條而勅之。夫汝所治顯露之事、宜是吾孫治之。汝則可以治神事。又汝應住天日隅宮者、今當供造、即以千尋栲繩結爲百八十紐。其造宮之制者、柱則高大。板則廣厚。又將田供佃。又爲汝往來遊海之具、高橋・浮橋及天鳥船、亦將供造。又於天安河、亦造打橋。又供造百八十縫之白楯。又當主汝祭祀者、天穗日命是也。

He replied, "The child of the heavenly kami shall go to the peak of Kushifuru in Takachiho, in Himuka, in Tsukushi. I will go to the headwaters of the Isuzu River in Sanagata, in Ise."[viii] Then he said, "You are the one who revealed me. Hence, you should see me to my destination." Ama-no-uzu-me returned and reported these events.

Thereupon, the imperial grandson departed from the heavenly rock seat, pushed apart the eightfold clouds of heaven, cleared the way with a fierce road-clearing, and descended from heaven. Finally, as stipulated earlier, the imperial grandson arrived at the peak of Kushifuru in Takachiho, in Himuka, in Tsukushi.

Saru-ta-hiko arrived at the headwaters of the Isuzu River in Sanagata in Ise. Ama-no-uzu-me, as Saru-ta-hiko had requested, ended up seeing him off. At that time, the imperial grandchild decreed to Ama-no-uzu-me, "You shall take the name of the kami that you revealed as your own family name." And so he bestowed upon her the name Kimi of Sarume. For this reason, both the men and women of the Sarume are called Kimi.[22]

Section 9, Variant 2

One text says, The heavenly kami dispatched the kami Futsu-nushi and Take-mikazu-chi to subjugate the central reed plain land. At that time the two kami said, "There is an evil kami in heaven named Ama-tsu-mika-hoshi, also called Ama-no-kagase-o. First we will kill this kami, and afterward we will descend and clear out the central reed plain land."

At that time, there was a kami in charge of seeking auspicious signs called Iwai-no-ushi.[23] This kami is presently in Katori in the land of Azuma.[ix]

Later the two kami descended to Isodasa Beach in Izumo, and they asked the kami Ō-ana-muchi, "Will you submit this land to the heavenly kami or not?"

He replied, "I have doubts about whether you two kami were sent to me. Hence, I cannot permit this."

Thereupon, the kami Futsu-nushi ascended back to heaven and made a report. Taka-mi-musuhi then dispatched the two kami back again, decreeing to Ō-ana-muchi, "Now, what you have said has profound reasoning to it. Therefore, I will pronounce my decrees one by one. The everyday matters now governed by you shall be ruled on by my grandson. You may rule on matters divine.[24] Also, we will build the shrine of Ama-no-hi-sumi, where you shall live.[x] One hundred eighty knots will be tied into a mulberry-bark rope of one thousand fathoms, and the plans for the shrine construction will employ tall, grand pillars and broad, thick boards. Also, I grant you cultivated fields. And to facilitate your comings and goings to the sea for sport, I also grant you a bridge, a pier, and a heavenly bird-boat. Also, a bridge shall be built over Heaven's Tranquil River. Also, I grant you a white shield with many strings. Also, I designate an official to venerate you: Ama-no-ho-hi.[25]

22 Kimi was a title of nobility, and as such was usually used only with male names, but as this note makes clear, in the case of the Sarume, Kimi is the family name, and hence was used by both the males and females of this lineage group.
23 This same charge is given to the kami Michi-no-omi in the Jinmu book, also prior to a martial conflict. Presumably, this kami was sought out before the pacification of the land, but those details are not recorded here.
24 The division of rulership is literally between "visible" matters and "divine" matters, or as Ō-ana-muchi will later call them, "matters unseen."
25 Ama-no-ho-hi was recorded as the ancestor of the Omi of Izumo in the main version of Section 6. In the main version of Section 9, Ama-no-ho-hi was one of the kami who failed to pacify the central reed plain land.

於是、大己貴神報曰、天神勅教、慇懃如此。敢不從命乎。吾所治顯露事者、皇孫當治。吾將退治幽事。乃薦岐神於二神曰、是當代我而奉從也。吾將自此避去。即躬披瑞之八坂瓊、而長隱者矣。

　故經津主神、以岐神爲鄕導、周流削平。有逆命者、即加斬戮。歸順者、仍加褒美。是時、歸順之首渠者、大物主神及事代主神。乃合八十萬神於天高市、帥以昇天、陳其誠款之至。

　時高皇產靈尊、勅大物主神、汝若以國神爲妻、吾猶謂汝有疏心。故今以吾女三穗津姬、配汝爲妻。宜領八十萬神、永爲皇孫奉護、乃使還降之。

　即以紀國忌部遠祖手置帆負神、定爲作笠者。彥狹知神爲作盾者。天目一箇神爲作金者。天日鷲神爲作木綿者。櫛明玉神爲作玉者。乃使太玉命、以弱肩被太手繦、而代御手、以祭此神者、始起於此矣。且天兒屋命、主神事之宗源者也。故俾以太占之卜事、而奉仕焉。高皇產靈尊因勅曰、吾則起樹天津神籬及天津磐境、當爲吾孫奉齋矣。汝天兒屋命・太玉命、宜持天津神籬、降於葦原中國、亦爲吾孫奉齋焉。乃使二神、陪從天忍穗耳尊以降之。

　是時、天照大神、手持寶鏡、授天忍穗耳尊、而祝之曰、吾兒視此寶鏡、當猶視吾。可與同床共殿、以爲齋鏡。復勅天兒屋命・太玉命、惟爾二神、亦同侍殿內、善爲防護。又勅曰、以吾高天原所御齋庭之穗、亦當御於吾兒。

　則以高皇產靈尊之女號萬幡姬、配天忍穗耳尊爲妃降之。故時居於虛天而生兒、

Thereupon, the kami Ō-ana-muchi replied, "The heavenly kami's decree is quite courteous. How could I dare to not comply with this order? The everyday matters over which I govern will be ruled on by the imperial grandchild. I will withdraw and rule on matters unseen. Then he presented the kami Ku-na-to to the two kami and said, "This one will attend on you in place of myself.[26] Forthwith I shall withdraw." Then he adorned himself with a sacred eight-shaftment jewel and hid himself away forever.

Accordingly, the kami Futsu-nushi, with the kami Ku-na-to as guide, traveled the land extensively and subjugated it. Those who resisted were put to death, and those who yielded were praised. During this time, the leaders who yielded were the kami Ō-mono-nushi and Koto-shiro-nushi. They assembled all of the kami at the High Heavenly Market[27] and led them up to heaven to express the extent of their loyalty.

Then Taka-mi-musuhi decreed to Ō-mono-nushi,[28] "If you take a kami of the land as wife, I will presume that you still have inhospitable intentions. So I will presently arrange for my daughter, Mi-ho-tsu-hime, to be your wife. Lead all of the kami in paying deference to the imperial grandson forever." He then made them return downward.

Accordingly, the distant ancestor of the Inbe of Ki Province, the kami Ta-oki-ho-oi, was installed as the maker of hats, the kami Hiko-sashiri as the maker of shields, the kami Ame-ma-hitotsu as the maker of metals, Ama-no-hi-washi as the maker of cottons, and Kushi-akaru-dama as the maker of jewels. Then having Futo-dama bear a thick sash upon his humble shoulders, he venerated this kami in place of the imperial grandson; this was the beginning of worship of Ō-mono-nushi. Also, Ama-no-koyane, as the original supervisor of divine ritual matters, was thus made to perform divination by drum in attendance on this observance. Taka-mi-musuhi decreed accordingly, "I shall hereby erect a heavenly shrine dwelling and heavenly rock barrier for ritual worship on behalf of my descendants. You two, Ama-no-koyane and Futo-dama, shall take this heavenly shrine and descend to the central reed plain land and perform ritual worship on behalf of my descendants." He then made the two kami descend as attendants to Ama-no-oshi-ho-mimi.

At that time, the great kami Amaterasu took in her hand a treasured mirror and bestowed it upon Ama-no-oshi-ho-mimi and blessed him, saying, "My child, gazing upon this treasured mirror shall be as if you gaze upon me. You should keep it in your same room, and share the same building, as a mirror for ritual worship. She then decreed again to Ama-no-koyane and Futo-dama, "I want you two kami also to attend on him within the same building and protect and defend him well." She also decreed, "The rice from my fields in the High Heavenly Plain used to venerate the kami will be entrusted to my child.

Then Taka-mi-mushi's daughter, Yorozu-hata-hime, was arranged as Ama-no-oshi-ho-mimi's wife and made to descend. However, while she was in the air, she gave birth to a child,

---

26 Ku-na-to is written using the same characters as those for the kami Fu-na-to, who emerges from Izanagi's discarded staff in Section 5, but here they are glossed differently. In either case, this is a crossroads kami.

27 This market also appears in Variant 1 of Section 7, but that market was in heaven and the one in this variant is on earth. The "heavenly" attribute derives from the latter's location as a starting point for ascending to heaven.

28 Ō-mono-nushi is given as an alternative name for Ō-ana-muchi in Variant 6 of Section 8, but as they are venerated differently, in this variant the two are different entities. Worship of Ō-mono-nushi in order to effectively govern the realm is recapitulated in Sujin 7.

號天津彥火瓊瓊杵尊。因欲以此皇孫代親而降。故以天兒屋命・太玉命、及諸部神等、悉皆相授。且服御之物、一依前授。然後、天忍穗耳尊、復還於天。

故天津彥火瓊瓊杵尊、降到於日向襲日高千穗之峯、而膂宍胸副國、自頓丘覓國行去、立於浮渚在平地、乃召國主事勝國勝長狹而訪之。

對曰、是有國也。取捨隨勅。

時皇孫因立宮殿、是焉遊息。

後遊幸海濱、見一美人。皇孫問曰、汝是誰之子耶。

對曰、妾是大山祇神之子、名神吾田鹿葦津姬、亦名木花開耶姬。因白、亦吾姉磐長姬在。

皇孫曰、吾欲以汝爲妻、如之何。

對曰、妾父大山祇神在。請以垂問。

皇孫因謂大山祇神曰、吾見汝之女子。欲以爲妻。

於是、大山祇神、乃使二女、持百机飲食奉進。時皇孫謂姉爲醜、不御而罷。妹有國色、引而幸之。則一夜有身。

故磐長姬。大慙而詛之曰、假使天孫、不斥妾而御者、生兒永壽、有如磐石之常存。今既不然、唯弟獨見御。故其生兒、必如木花之、移落。一云、磐長姬恥恨、而唾泣之曰、顯見蒼生者、如木花之、俄遷轉當衰去矣。此世人短折之緣也。

是後、神吾田鹿葦津姬、見皇孫曰、妾孕天孫之子。不可私以生也。

皇孫曰、雖復天神之子、如何一夜使人娠乎。抑非吾之兒歟。

called Ama-tsu-hiko-ho-no-ninigi. Taka-mi-musuhi thus wanted this imperial grandson to change places with his parents and descend.[29] Therefore, he bestowed upon him in turn Ama-no-koyane and Futo-dama and the patron kami of the various hereditary guilds.[30] Also, as before, clothing was bestowed upon him. Afterward, Ama-no-oshi-ho-mimi returned to heaven.

And so Ama-tsu-hiko-ho-no-ninigi descended to the peak of Takachiho in Kushihi in Himuka, then to the barren land of Munasō, and from a succession of hills he searched for the land and passed through. He stood in a wide place on a floating island, then summoned the ruler of the land, Koto-katsu-kuni-katsu-naga-sa, and questioned him.

He replied, "There is land here. Take it or leave it, however you decree."

The imperial grandchild therefore built a palace and rested.

After this, he went to the beach and saw a young woman. The imperial grandson asked, "Whose daughter are you?"

She replied, "I am the daughter of the kami Ō-yama-tsu-mi. My name is Kamu-ata-ka-ashi-tsu-hime. I am also called Ko-no-hana-saku-ya-hime." Then she added, "I also have an older sister, Iwa-naga-hime."

The imperial grandchild said, "I want you to be my wife. What say you?"

She replied, "My father is the kami Ō-yama-tsu-mi. Please ask him."

The imperial grandchild then said to the kami Ō-yama-tsu-mi, "I see you have a daughter. I want her to be my wife."

At this, the kami Ō-yama-tsu-mi had his two daughters bring one hundred tables of food and drink to present to their guest. The imperial grandchild thought that the older sister was ugly, so he did not summon her to his bedchamber and instead dismissed her. The younger sister was the most beautiful in the land, and he shared his bed with her. Then, in one night, she became pregnant.

The older sister Iwa-naga-hime was greatly shamed and cursed him, saying, "If the heavenly grandson had summoned me instead of dismissing me, the lifespan of the child I bore him would have been as long as a stone's. Now it is not to be, as you summoned only my younger sister. Therefore, the child she bears him will certainly fall like a tree or flower." Another account says, Iwa-naga-hime was shamed and angry, and so she spat and cried out, saying, "Like a tree or flower, people will quickly change with the passage of time, then wither and die." This is why people have short lives.[31]

Afterward, Kamu-ata-ka-ashi-tsu-hime looked at the imperial grandchild and said, "I am pregnant with the child of the heavenly grandson. I should not bear it in secret."

Then the imperial grandson said, "Child of the heavenly kami though I may be, how could I impregnate someone in one night? Perhaps the child is not mine."

---

29 It is not explicit that Taka-mi-musuhi ordered the switch between Oshi-ho-mimi and Ninigi, but the word "parent" suggests that Oshi-ho-mimi is not the subject of the sentence. Given the use of "imperial grandson," "Taka-mi-musuhi" makes the most sense as the subject.
30 Who this patron kami was is disputed. It could refer to the kami earlier mentioned in connection with worship of Ō-mono-nushi, the five occupational groups mentioned in Variant 1, or some other unspecified kami.
31 By convention, less than thirty or sixty years.

木花開耶姬、甚以憼恨、乃作無戶室、而誓之曰、吾所娠、是若他神之子者、必不幸矣。是實天孫之子者、必當全生、則入其室中、以火焚室。于時、燄初起時共生兒、號火酢芹命。次火盛時生兒、號火明命。次生兒、號彥火火出見尊。亦號火折尊。齋主、此云伊播毗。顯露、此云阿羅播貳。齋庭、此云踰貳波。一書曰、初火燄明時生兒、火明命。次火炎盛時生兒、火進命。又曰火酢芹命。次避火炎時生兒、火折彥火火出見尊。凡此三子、火不能害。及母亦無所少損。時以竹刀、截其兒臍。其所棄竹刀、終成竹林。故號彼地曰竹屋。

時神吾田鹿葦津姬、以卜定田、號曰狹名田。以其田稻、釀天甜酒嘗之。又用淳浪田稻、爲飯嘗之。一書曰、高皇產靈尊、以眞床覆衾、裹天津彥國光彥火瓊瓊杵尊、則引開天磐戶、排分天八重雲、以奉降之。

于時、大伴連遠祖天忍日命、帥來目部遠祖天槵津大來目、背負天磐靫、臂著稜威高鞆、手捉天梔弓・天羽羽矢、及副持八目鳴鏑、又帶頭槌劍、而立天孫之前。

遊行降來、到於日向襲之高千穗槵日二上峯天浮橋、而立於浮渚在之平地、膂宍空國、自頓丘覓國行去、到於吾田長屋笠狹之御碕。時彼處有一神、名曰事勝國勝長狹。故天孫問其神曰、國在耶。

Ko-no-hana-saku-ya-hime was extremely shamed and vengeful, and so made a chamber with no entrance or exit, then swore, "If the child I carry is of another kami, then it will surely meet with disaster. If it is truly the child of the heavenly grandson, then it will surely live." Then she went inside the chamber and set the chamber on fire. The child born when the flame began to burn was called Ho-no-su-seri. Next, the child born when the fire peaked was called Ho-no-akari. The next child born was called Hiko-ho-ho-de-mi, and also called Ho-no-ori.

Section 9, Variant 3

One text says, First, the child born when the fire was bright was Ho-no-akari. Next, the child born when the blaze peaked was Ho-no-susumi, also called Ho-no-suseri. Next, the child born when the blaze retreated was Ho-no-ori-hiko-ho-ho-de-mi. In all, there were three children, and the fire was not able to hurt them. Also, the mother was not harmed in the slightest. At the time, she used a bamboo knife to cut the children's umbilical cords. The knife was then discarded and eventually became a bamboo forest. As a result, the place is named Takaya, or Bamboo Building."[xi]

At that time, Kamu-ata-ka-ashi-tsu-hime used divination to select a rice field and named it Sanada. The rice from this field was used to brew heavenly sweet wine for the feast of first rice. She also cooked rice from paddy fields for the feast of first rice.

Section 9, Variant 4

One text says, Taka-mi-musuhi wrapped Ama-tsu-hiko-kuni-teru-hiko-ho-no-ninigi in a resplendent coverlet, pulled open the stone door of heaven, pushed apart the eightfold clouds of heaven, and had him descend.

At that time, the distant ancestor of the Muraji of the Ōtomo, Ama-no-oshi-hi, led the distant ancestor of the Kume hereditary guild,[32] Ame-kushi-tsu-ō-kume, put on his back a heavenly stone quiver, put on his elbow a fierce loud-sounding arm protector, and took in his hands a heavenly sumac bow and heavenly viper arrows. He also took many-holed signal arrows and wore a sword with a bulbous pommel and led the vanguard for the heavenly grandson.

Going down, Ninigi arrived at the floating bridge of heaven above the two peaks of Kushihi in Takachiho, in So, in Himuka. He stood in a wide place on a floating island, passed through a barren land, and from a succession of hills searched for the land and passed through. He arrived at Cape Kasasa in Nagaya in Ata. At that time, there was one kami there. His name was Koto-katsu-kuni-katsu-naga-sa. So the heavenly grandchild asked this kami, "Is there land?"

---

32 The Ōtomo and Kume were hereditary guilds associated with military matters.

對曰、在也。因曰、隨勅奉矣。故天孫留住於彼處。其事勝國勝神者、是伊弉諾尊之子也、亦名鹽土老翁。
一書曰、天孫幸大山祇神之女子吾田鹿葦津姬。則一夜有身。遂生四子。故吾田鹿葦津姬、抱子而來進曰、天神之子、寧可以私養乎。故告狀知聞。

是時、天孫見其子等嘲之曰、姸哉、吾皇子者、聞喜而生之歟。

故吾田鹿葦津姬、乃慍之曰、何爲嘲妾乎。

天孫曰、心疑之矣。故嘲之。何則雖復天神之子、豈能一夜之間、使人有身者哉。固非我子矣。

是以、吾田鹿葦津姬益恨、作無戶室、入居其内誓之曰、妾所娠、若非天神之胤者必亡。是若天神之胤者無所害。則放火焚室。

其火初明時、蹈誥出兒自言、吾是天神之子。名火明命。吾父何處坐耶。

次火盛時、蹈誥出兒亦言、吾是天神之子。名火進命。吾父及兄何處在耶。

次火炎衰時、蹈誥出兒亦言、吾是天神之子。名火折尊。吾父及兄等何處在耶。

次避火熱時、蹈誥出兒亦言、吾是天神之子。名彥火火出見尊。吾父及兄等何處在耶。

然後、母吾田鹿葦津姬、自火爐中出來、就而稱之曰、妾所生兒及妾身、自當火難、無所少損。天孫豈見之乎。

對曰、我知本是吾兒。但一夜而有身、慮有疑者、欲使衆人皆知是吾兒、幷亦天神能令一夜有娠。亦欲明汝有靈異之威、子等復有超倫之氣。故有前日之嘲辭也。柂、此云波茸、音之移反。頭槌、此云箇步豆智。老翁、此云烏膩。

He replied, "There is." Then he added, "As you decree, it shall be submitted to you." So the heavenly grandchild stayed in that place. This kami Koto-katsu-kuni-katsu was a child of Izanagi. He is also called Old Man Shio-tsu-chi.

Section 9, Variant 5

One version says, The heavenly grandson summoned the daughter of the kami Ō-yama-tsu-mi, Ata-ka-ashi-tsu-hime. Consequently, she was impregnated in one night, and ended up with four children. Ata-ka-ashi-tsu-hime came forth carrying the children, saying, "These are the children of a heavenly kami, so how could they be raised as I please? I am here to inform you of their birth."

At this, the heavenly grandson looked at the children and jeered, "How wonderful! These are my children, I'm very happy to hear of their birth."

Ata-ka-ashi-tsu-hime was angered and asked, "Why do you jeer?"

The heavenly grandson said, "I have doubts in my heart, and so I jeer. Child of the heavenly kami though I may be, how could I make someone with child in just one night? Truly, these are not my children."

Because of this, Ata-ka-ashi-tsu-hime was resentful and made a chamber with no entrance or exit, shut herself up inside, and swore an oath, saying, "I have given birth. If these are not the children of a heavenly kami, they will surely perish. If they are the children of a heavenly kami, they will not be harmed. Then she set fire to the chamber.

When the fire began to brighten, a child stamped its feet and said, "I am a heavenly kami's child, named Ho-no-akari. Where is my father?"

Next, when the fire peaked, a child stamped its feet and said, "I am a heavenly kami's child, named Ho-no-susumi. Where are my father and older brother?"

Next, when the blaze waned, a child stamped its feet and said, "I am a heavenly kami's child, named Ho-no-ori. Where are my father and older brothers?"

Next, when the heat from the fire retreated, a child stamped its feet and said, "I am a heavenly kami's child, named Hiko-ho-ho-de-mi. Where are my father and older brothers?"

Afterward, their mother Ata-ka-ashi-tsu-hime came out from the burnt remains and declared, "There is not the slightest bit of harm from fire to myself or the children I bore. The heavenly grandson saw this, did he not?"

He replied, "I knew from the first that these were my children. However, I thought that there might be doubters because you became pregnant in one night, and I wanted to make all the people know that these were my children, and that the heavenly kami can impregnate someone in one night. Also, I wanted to make clear your mystical powers and the superlative nature of these children. Hence, I jeered when I spoke the other day."[33]

---

33 Original notes here give the vernacular for words from Variants 4 and 5.

一書曰、天忍穗根尊、娶高皇產靈尊女子栲幡千千姬萬幡姬命、亦云高皇產靈尊兒火之戶幡姬兒千千姬命、而生兒天火明命。次生天津彥根火瓊瓊杵根尊。其天火明命兒、天香山、是尾張連等遠祖也。

及至奉降皇孫火瓊瓊杵尊、於葦原中國也、高皇產靈尊、勅八十諸神曰、葦原中國者、磐根木株草葉、猶能言語。夜者若熛火而喧響之、晝者如五月蠅而沸騰之、云々。

時高皇產靈尊勅曰、昔遣天稚彥於葦原中國、至今所以久不來者、蓋是國神、有強禦之者。乃遣無名雄雉往候之。此雉降來、因見粟田・豆田、則留而不返。此世所謂、雉頓使之緣也。故復遣無名雌雉。此鳥下來、爲天稚彥所射、中其矢而上報、云々。

是時、高皇產靈尊、乃用眞床覆衾、裹皇孫天津彥根火瓊瓊杵根尊、而排披天八重雲、以奉降之。故稱此神、曰天國饒石彥火瓊瓊杵尊。于時、降到之處者、呼曰日向襲之高千穗添山峯矣。及其遊行之時也、云々。

到于吾田笠狹之御碕。遂登長屋之竹嶋。乃巡覽其地者、彼有人焉。名曰事勝國勝長狹。天孫因問之曰、此誰國歟。

對曰、是長狹所住之國也。然今乃奉上天孫矣。

天孫又問曰、其於秀起浪穗之上、起八尋殿、而手玉玲瓏、織絍之少女者、是誰之子女耶。

答曰、大山祇神之女等、大號磐長姬。少號木花開耶姬。亦號豐吾田津姬。云々。皇孫因幸豐吾田津姬。則一夜而有身。皇孫疑之、云々。

遂生火酢芹命。次生火折尊。亦號彥火火出見尊。母誓已驗。方知、實是皇孫之胤。然豐吾田津姬、恨皇孫不與共言。皇孫憂之、乃爲歌之曰、

Section 9, Variant 6

One text says, Ama-no-oshi-ho-ne wed the daughter of Taka-mi-musuhi, Taku-hata-chi-ji-hime-yorozu-hata-hime. It is also said that he wed Chi-ji-hime, granddaughter of Taka-mi-musuhi and daughter of Ho-no-to-hata-hime. The child that was born was Ama-no-ho-akari. Next born was Ama-tsu-hiko-ne-ho-no-ninigi-ne. The child of Ama-no-ho-no-akari, Ama-no-kako-yama, is the distant ancestor of the Muraji of Owari.

The imperial grandson Ho-no-ninigi was to descend to the central reed plain land, and Taka-mi-musuhi decreed to the all the various kami, "In the central reed plain land, even the roots of boulders, stumps of trees, and blades of grass can speak. At night it is as noisy as a bonfire, and in the day as agitated as flies in midsummer." And so on.

At that time, Taka-mi-musuhi decreed, "In ancient times I dispatched Ame-waka-hiko to the central reed plain land, but now he has not returned for a long time. Perhaps among the kami of the land there is a powerful resistor." And so on. He then dispatched an unnamed pheasant to go and see. This pheasant came down and saw fields of millet and fields of beans, and stayed without returning. This is why we say that pheasants are "one-way messengers." So he dispatched another nameless pheasant. This bird came down and was shot by Ame-waka-hiko. Hit by the arrow, it ascended and reported. And so on.

At that time, Taka-mi-musuhi used a resplendent coverlet to wrap the imperial grandson Ama-tsu-hiko-ne-ho-no-ninigi-ne, pushed apart the eightfold clouds of heaven, and had him descend. Hence, this kami is styled Ame-kuni-nigi-shi-hiko-ho-no-ninigi. The place that he descended to was called the peak of Mt. Sohori in Takachiho, in So, in Himuka. He traveled around, and so on.

He arrived at Cape Kasasa in Ata, and at last climbed Takashima in Nagaya. When he inspected that land, there was a man named Koto-katsu-kuni-katsu-naga-sa. The heavenly grandson asked him, "Whose land is this?"

He replied, "This is where I, Naga-sa, dwell. Now, however, I submit it to the heavenly grandson."

The heavenly grandson further asked him, "Atop the high wave crests sits an eight-fathom building, and within it are young women weaving with beads jangling. Whose daughters are they?"

He replied, "They are the daughters of the kami Ō-yama-tsu-mi. The older is called Iwa-naga-hime and the younger is called Ko-no-hana-saku-ya-hime, also called Toyo-ata-tsu-hime. And so on."

The imperial grandson then summoned Toyo-ata-tsu-hime, and in one night made her pregnant. The imperial grandson had doubts, and so on.

At last, Ho-no-suseri was born. Next to be born was Ho-no-ori, also called Hiko-ho-ho-de-mi. They were proof of their mother's oath. They are truly known to be the progeny of the imperial grandson. However, Toyo-ata-tsu-hime resented the imperial grandson and would not speak with him. The imperial grandson was saddened at this and sang,

憶企都茂播	おきつもは
陛爾播響戻耐母	へにはよれども
佐禰耐據茂	さねどこも
阿黨播怒介茂響	あたはぬかもよ
播磨都智耐理響	はまつちどりよ

　　燻火、此云裒倍。喧響、此云淤等娜比。五月蠅、此云左魔倍。添山、此云曾褒里能耶麻。秀起、此云左岐陀豆屢。

一書曰、高皇産靈尊之女天萬栲幡千幡姫。一云、高皇産靈尊兒萬幡姫兒玉依姫命。此神爲天忍骨命妃、生兒天之杵火火置瀨尊。

　　一云、勝速日命兒天大耳尊。此神娶丹舄姫、生兒火瓊瓊杵尊。一云、神皇産靈尊之女栲幡千幡姫、生兒火瓊瓊杵尊。

　　一云、天杵瀨命、娶吾田津姫、生兒火明命。次火夜織命。次彦火火出見尊。

一書曰、正哉吾勝勝速日天忍穗耳尊、娶高皇産靈尊之女天萬栲幡千幡姫、爲妃而生兒。號天照國照彦火明命。是尾張連等遠祖也。次天饒石國饒石天津彦火瓊瓊杵尊。此神娶大山祇神女子木花開耶姫命、爲妃而生兒。號火酢芹命。次彦火火出見尊。

兄火闌降命、自有海幸。幸、此云左知。弟彦火火出見尊、自有山幸。始兄弟二人相謂曰、試欲

Though seaweed from the depths
draws near to the beach,
a shared bed
she has no intention of granting.
Oh, plovers of the beach![34]

Section 9, Variant 7

One text says, The daughter of Taka-mi-musuhi was Ama-yorozu-taku-hata-chi-hata-hime. Another account says, The daughter of Taka-mi-musuhi's child Yorozu-hata-hime was Ta-ma-yori-hime. This kami became the wife of Ama-no-oshi-hone and give birth to the child Ama-no-ki-ho-ho-oki-se.

Another account says, The child of Kachi-haya-hi, Ama-no-ō-mimi, wed Ni-kutsu-hime, and she gave birth to the child Ho-no-ninigi. Another account says that he wed the daughter of Kamu-musu-hi, Taku-hata-chi-hata-hime, and the child Ho-ninigi was born.

Another account says, Ama-no-kise wed Ata-tsu-hime, and the child Ho-no-akari was born. Next was Ho-no-yo-ori. Next was Hiko-ho-ho-de-mi.

Section 9, Variant 8

One text says, Masa-ka-a-katsu-haya-hi-ama-no-oshi-ho-mimi wed the daughter of Ta-ka-mi-musuhi, Ama-yorozu-taku-hata-chi-hata-hime. As his wife, she had children, one called Ama-teru-kuni-teru-hiko-ho-no-akari. He is the distant ancestor of the Muraji of Owari. Next was Ama-no-nigi-shi-kuni-no-nigi-shi-ama-tsu-hiko-ho-no-ninigi. This kami wed the daughter of Ō-yama-tsu-mi, Ko-no-hana-saka-ya-hime. As his wife, she had children, one called Ho-no-suseri. Next was Hiko-ho-ho-de-mi.

Section 10: The Brothers Luck-of-the-Mountain and Luck-of-the-Sea

Main Version

The older brother, Ho-no-susori, had a natural talent for ocean fishing, and the younger brother Hiko-ho-ho-de-mi had a natural talent for mountain hunting. Once, the two brothers spoke to one another, saying, "Let's try

---

34 In Japanese poetry, plovers suggest two lovers being together. Ninigi uses "plovers" to contrast his solitude.

易幸、遂相易之。各不得其利。

兄悔之、乃還弟弓箭、而乞己釣鉤、弟時既失兄鉤。無由訪覓。故別作新鉤與兄。兄不肯受、而責其故鉤。

弟患之、即以其横刀、鍛作新鉤、盛一箕而與之。兄忿之曰、非我故鉤、雖多不取、益復急責。故彥火火出見尊、憂苦甚深。行吟海畔。

時逢鹽土老翁。老翁問曰、何故在此愁乎。對以事之本末。老翁曰、勿復憂。吾當爲汝計之、乃作無目籠、內彥火火出見尊於籠中、沈之于海。即自然有可怜小汀。可怜、此云于麻師。汀、此云波麻。於是、棄籠遊行。忽至海神之宮。

其宮也、雉堞整頓、臺宇玲瓏。門前有一井。井上有一湯津杜樹。枝葉扶疏。時彥火火出見尊、就其樹下、徒倚彷徨。良久有一美人、排闥而出。遂以玉鋺、來當汲水。因舉目視之。乃驚而還入、白其父母曰、有一希客者。在門前樹下。

海神、於是、鋪設八重席薦、以延內之。坐定、因問其來意。時彥火火出見尊、對以情之委曲。海神乃集大小之魚逼問之、僉曰、不識。唯赤女赤女、鯛魚名也。比有口疾而不來。

exchanging our talents," and so traded them. But both failed to gain any benefit from this.

The older brother regretted it, so he returned the younger brother's bow and arrows, and asked for his fishhook back. But by that time, the younger brother had already lost the older brother's fishhook and could not find it anywhere. So he made a new fishhook and gave it to his older brother. The older brother refused to take it and demanded his original fishhook back.

The younger brother, troubled by this, used his sword to forge new fishhooks, filling a winnowing basket with them, and he gave them to his brother. The older brother said angrily, "If it is not my original fishhook, I won't take it, no matter how many fishhooks you make," and continued to vex him. As a result, Hiko-ho-ho-de-mi's grief was especially keen, and he howled as he went to the seaside.

There he met Old Man Shio-tsu-chi. The old man asked him, "Why are you crying here?" The younger brother told him what happened, and then the old man said, "Do not despair. I will come up with a plan for you." Then he made a basket with no gaps, put Hiko-ho-ho-de-mi inside the basket, and sank it into the sea. The basket naturally made its way to a charming little beach. There Hiko-ho-ho-de-mi discarded the basket and went on foot, eventually reaching the palace of the sea kami Wata-tsu-mi.

At this palace, the walls were neatly kept and the roof of the tower gleamed like jewels. Before the gate was a well, and above the well was a hallowed cinnamon tree whose leaves and branches stretched in every direction. Hiko-ho-ho-de-mi went to the base of the tree and loitered there. After some time, a beautiful young woman pushed open the gate and came out. She carried a precious pitcher to draw water. Looking up, she saw him, was startled, and returned inside. She told her father and mother, "We have a strange visitor. He is at the base of the tree by the gate."

Wata-tsu-mi prepared many layers of cushions for seating and led him inside. After seating him, the sea kami asked why he had come. Hiko-ho-ho-de-mi replied with the particulars of the situation. Wata-tsu-mi then assembled the fish great and small and interrogated them. They all said, "We know not, but the red seabream has a sore mouth and so did not come."

固召之探其口者、果得失鉤。

已而彥火火出見尊、因娶海神女豐玉姬。仍留住海宮、已經三年。彼處雖復安樂、猶有憶鄉之情。故時復太息。豐玉姬聞之、謂其父曰、天孫悽然數歎。蓋懷土之憂乎。

海神乃延彥火火出見尊、從容語曰、天孫若欲還鄉者、吾當奉送。便授所得釣鉤、因誨之曰、以此鉤與汝兄時、則陰呼此鉤曰貧鉤、然後與之。復授潮滿瓊及潮涸瓊、而誨之曰、漬潮滿瓊者、則潮忽滿。以此沒溺汝兄。若兄悔而祈者、還漬潮涸瓊、則潮自涸。以此救之。如此逼惱、則汝兄自伏。

及將歸去、豐玉姬謂天孫曰、妾已娠矣。當產不久。妾必以風濤急峻之日、出到海濱。請爲我作產室相待矣。

彥火火出見尊已還宮、一遵海神之教。時兄火闌降命、既被厄困、乃自伏罪曰、從今以後、吾將爲汝俳優之民。請施恩活。於是、隨其所乞遂赦之。其火闌降命、即吾田君小橋等之本祖也。

後豐玉姬、果如前期、將其女弟玉依姬、直冒風波、來到海邊。

Thus, he summoned the red seabream, and when he searched its mouth, he ended up finding the lost fishhook.

Eventually, Hiko-ho-ho-de-mi [Jinmu] married the daughter of Wa-ta-tsu-mi, Toyo-tama-hime. And so he stayed and dwelt in Wata-tsu-mi's palace, and three years passed. He enjoyed great comfort there, yet he felt homesick. From time to time he let out great sighs. Toyo-tama-hime heard them and told her father, "The heavenly grandson frequently sighs in sorrow. He is probably suffering from homesickness."

The sea kami took Hiko-ho-ho-de-mi aside and frankly told him, "Heavenly grandson, if you wish to return to your land, I will send you back." Then he gave him the fishhook they had gathered and advised him, "When you are about to give this fishhook to your brother, secretly call it a hook leading to poverty, then after that give it to him." He also gave him the jewel of high tide and the jewel of low tide, and advised him, "If you submerge the jewel of high tide, the tide will immediately come in. Use this to drown your older brother. If your brother regrets his actions and pleads for help, then submerge the jewel of low tide, and the tide will naturally go out. Thereby you can rescue him. If you torment him like this, then your older brother will surrender of his own accord."

When Hiko-ho-ho-de-mi was about to depart, Toyo-tama-hime told the heavenly grandson, "I am pregnant. It will not be long before I give birth. On a day when the wind and waves are fierce, I without fail will go out to the seaside. Please make a birthing hut for me and wait there."

Hiko-ho-ho-de-mi returned shortly thereafter to his palace and did as the sea kami had instructed him. Thereupon, his older brother Ho-no-susori was tormented and surrendered to punishment of his own accord, saying, "From now on, I will be your subject and jester. Please spare my life." In accordance with his request, he was forgiven. Ho-no-susori is the original ancestor of the Kimi Ohashi of Ata.[35]

Later, Toyo-tama-hime squarely braved the wind and waves and went as promised to the seaside along with her sister, Tama-yori-hime. As the

---

35 In the main version of Section 9, Ho-no-susori was identified as the ancestor of the Hayato. Records from the eighth century claim that this group performed dances when presenting tribute. Ata is a place-name turned family name. Ohashi is presented here as a personal name, but it is uncharacteristic in the *Chronicles* for a personal name to be given when identifying lineage. There is speculation that it might be a family name despite the syntax.

逮臨產時、請曰、妾產時、幸勿以看之。天孫猶不能忍、竊往覘之。豐玉姬方產化爲龍。而甚慙之曰、如有不辱我者、則使海陸相通、永無隔絶。今既辱之。將何以結親昵之情乎、乃以草裹兒、棄之海邊、閉海途而俓去矣。故因以名兒、曰彦波瀲武鸕鷀草葺不合尊。
　後久之、彦火火出見尊崩。葬日向高屋山上陵。
一書曰、兄火酢芹命能得海幸。弟彦火火出見尊、能得山幸。時兄弟欲互易其幸。故兄持弟之幸弓、入山覓獸。終不見獸之乾迹。弟持兄之幸鉤、入海釣魚。殊無所獲。遂失其鉤。
　是時、兄還弟弓矢、而責己鉤、弟患之、乃以所帶橫刀作鉤、盛一箕與兄。兄不受曰、猶欲得吾之幸鉤。於是、彦火火出見尊、不知所求。但有憂吟。乃行至海邊、彷徨嗟嘆。
　時有一長老、忽然而至。自稱鹽土老翁。乃問之曰、君是誰者。何故患於此處乎。彦火火出見尊、具言其事。老翁即取囊中玄櫛投地、則化成五百箇竹林。因取其竹、作大目麁籠、內火火出見尊於籠中、投之于海。一云、以無目堅間爲浮木、以細繩繫著火火出見尊而沈之。所謂堅間、是今之竹籠也。
　于時、海底自有可怜小汀。乃尋汀而進。忽到海神豐玉彦之宮。其宮也城闕崇華、樓臺壯麗。

time of birth approached, she requested, "When I give birth, please do not look at me." But the heavenly grandson could not resist, and he secretly went and spied on her. As Toyo-tama-hime was giving birth, she changed into a dragon. Then full of shame, she said, "If you had not embarrassed me, then we would have traversed land and sea and never have been parted for eternity. Now you have shamed me. How can we be bound by intimate feelings?" Then she wrapped the child in thatch, discarded it on the seaside, closed the path to the sea, and departed. For this reason, the child was named Hiko-nagisa-take-u-kaya-fuki-aezu.

A long time after this, Hiko-ho-ho-de-mi expired. He is buried atop Mt. Takaya in Himuka.[xii]

Section 10, Variant 1

One text says, The older brother, Ho-no-suseri, was skilled at getting the bounty of the sea, and the younger brother, Hiko-ho-ho-de-mi, the bounty of the mountains. One time, the brothers wanted to exchange their skills. So the older brother took in hand the skillful bow of the younger brother and went into the mountains to seek game, but in the end, he did not even see an animal's dried tracks. The younger brother took in hand the skillful fishhook of the older brother and went to the sea to fish, but did not catch anything. Furthermore, he lost the fishhook.

When the older brother returned the younger brother's bow and arrows, he demanded his fishhook back. The younger brother, being on the spot, used the sword he wore to make fishhooks, filled a winnowing basket with them, and gave the basket to his older brother. The older brother refused to take it, saying, "No, I want my skillful fishhook."

Thereupon, Hiko-ho-ho-de-mi did not even know where to look, and simply grieved. Then he went to the seaside to pace back and forth, crying.

At that time, an old man suddenly arrived. He called himself Old Man Shio-tsu-chi. He asked, "Who are you? Why are you crying here?" Hiko-ho-ho-de-mi told him the situation in detail. The old man then took from his bag a black comb and threw it on the ground, and it transformed into a dense bamboo forest. Then he took the bamboo and made a loose, roughly woven basket, put Hiko-ho-ho-de-mi inside the basket, and threw it into the sea. (Another account says that he used a basket with no gaps as a raft, tied Hiko-ho-ho-de-mi to it with a cord, and sank it. This was the bamboo basket.)

At that point, in the depths of the sea, there was a charming little beach. Following along the beach, he soon arrived at the palace of the sea kami, Toyo-tama-hiko. As for the palace, the barbican was ostentatious and imposing, and the towers were magnificent. Outside the

門外有井。井傍有杜樹。乃就樹下立之。

良久有一美人。容貌絕世。侍者群從、自內而出。將以玉壺汲水。仰見火火出見尊。便以驚還、而白其父神曰、門前井邊樹下、有一貴客。骨法非常。若從天降者、當有天垢。從地來者、當有地垢。實是妙美之。虛空彥者歟。一云、豐玉姬之侍者、以玉瓶汲水。終不能滿。俯視井中、則倒映人咲之顏。因以仰觀、有一麗神、倚於杜樹。故還入白其王。

於是、豐玉彥遣人問曰、客是誰者。何以至此。

火火出見尊對曰、吾是天神之孫也。乃遂言來意。

時海神迎拜延入、慇懃奉慰。因以女豐玉姬妻之。故留住海宮、已經三載。是後火火出見尊、數有歎息。豐玉姬問曰、天孫豈欲還故鄉歟。

對曰、然。

豐玉姬即白父神曰、在此貴客、意望欲還上國。

海神、於是、總集海魚、覓問其鉤。有一魚、對曰、赤女久有口疾。或云、赤鯛。疑是之吞乎。

故即召赤女、見其口者、鉤猶在口。便得之、乃以授彥火火出見尊。因教之曰、以鉤與汝兄時、則可詛言、貧窮之本、飢饉之始、困苦之根。而後與之。又汝兄涉海時、吾必起迅風洪濤、令其沒溺辛苦矣。於是、乘火火出見尊於大鰐、以送致本鄉。

先是且別時、豐玉姬從容語曰、妾已有身矣。當以風濤壯日、出到海邊。請爲我造產屋以待之。

是後、豐玉姬果如其言來至。謂火火出見尊曰、妾今夜當產。請勿臨之。

gate was a well, and beside the well was a cinnamon tree. He went to the base of the tree and stood there.

After some time, a beautiful young woman appeared. Her good looks were otherworldly. With a group of attendants, she came from within and was going to draw water into a precious jug when she looked up and saw Hiko-ho-ho-de-mi. She was startled and returned, and said to the kami her father, "There is a noble guest at the base of the tree beside the well in front of the gate. His features and build are uncommon. If he is descended from heaven, he will have a heavenly aura, and if he came from earth, he will have an earthly aura. He is very attractive; perhaps he is the kami Sora-tsu-hiko."[36] (Another account says that Toyo-tama-hime's attendants drew water with a precious bucket, but somehow could not fill it completely. When they looked down into the well, they saw the reversed reflection of a laughing face. Hence, they looked up and saw an attractive kami leaning against the cinnamon tree. Then they returned inside and told their king.)

Toyo-tama-hiko sent someone to ask, "Who are you, guest? Why have you come?"

Ho-ho-de-mi replied, "I am the descendant of a heavenly kami." Then he told them the reason he had come.

The sea kami reverently greeted him, led him inside, and treated him with the utmost courtesy. He arranged for his daughter, Toyo-tama-hime, to be his wife. So Ho-ho-de-mi stayed and dwelt in the palace of the sea kami for three years. After all this, Ho-ho-de-mi sighed from time to time. Toyo-tama-hime asked him, "Does the heavenly grandson wish to return to his homeland?"

"Of course," he replied.

Toyo-tama-hime spoke to the kami her father saying, "Our noble guest wishes to return to the land above."

The sea kami then assembled all of the fish of the sea and searched, asking about the fishhook. One fish replied, "The red seabream has had a sore mouth for a long time. (By one account, it was the red tai). Perhaps she swallowed the hook?"

Hence, he summoned the red seabream, looked in her mouth, and found the fishhook there. He took it and gave it to Hiko-ho-ho-de-mi. Then he instructed him, saying, "When you give this hook to your older brother, curse it, saying, 'This fishhook is the origin of poverty, the beginning of hunger, the root of suffering.' Then give it to him. When your older brother goes out to sea again, I without fail will cause a fast wind and high waves and make him suffer by drowning him." Then he mounted Ho-ho-de-mi on a great shark and sent him to his homeland.

Prior to all that, when they were to part, Toyo-tama-hime calmly told him, "I am with child. I will go out to the seaside on a day when the wind and waves are swift. Please build a birthing hut for me and wait there."

Afterward, Toyo-tama-hime came as promised. "I will give birth tonight," she said. Then she asked Ho-ho-de-mi, "Please do not look at me."

---

36 Sora-tsu-hiko means "sky lord." Toyo-tama-hime has trouble placing Hiko-ho-ho-de-mi because he is a heavenly kami born on earth. The sky is in between heaven and earth.

火火出見尊不聽、猶以櫛燃火視之。時豐玉姬、化爲八尋大熊鰐、匍匐逶虵。遂以見辱爲恨、則徑歸海鄕。留其女弟玉依姬、持養兒焉。所以兒名稱彥波瀲武鸕鷀草葺不合尊者、以彼海濱產屋、全用鸕鷀羽爲草葺之、而甍未合時、兒卽生焉故、因以名焉。上國、此云羽播豆矩儞。

一書曰、門前有一好井。井上有百枝杜樹。故彥火火出見尊、跳昇其樹而立之。于時、海神之女豐玉姬、手持玉鋺、來將汲水。正見人影、在於井中、乃仰視之。驚而墜鋺。鋺旣破碎、不顧而還入、謂父母曰、妾見一人、在於井邊樹上。顏色甚美、容貌且閑。殆非常之人者也。

時父神聞而奇之、乃設八重席迎入。坐定、因問來意。對以情之委曲。時海神便起憐心、盡召鰭廣鰭狹而問之。皆曰、不知。但赤女有口疾不來。亦云、口女有口疾。卽急召至、探其口者、所失之針鉤立得。於是、海神制曰、儞口女、從今以往、不得吞餌。又不得預天孫之饌。卽以口女魚所以不進御者、此其緣也。

及至彥火火出見尊將歸之時、海神白言、今者、天神之孫、辱臨吾處。中心欣慶、何日忘之。乃以思則潮溢之瓊、思則潮涸之瓊、副其鉤而奉進之曰、皇孫雖隔八重之隈、冀時復相憶、而勿棄置也。因教之曰、以此鉤與汝兄時、則稱貧鉤、滅鉤、落薄鉤。言訖、

Ho-ho-de-mi did not listen, and even lit a comb on fire to see her. Toyo-tama-hime had transformed into an eight-fathom shark and was wriggling on the ground like a snake. Resentful that she had been shamed, she promptly returned to her home in the sea. She left her younger sister Tama-yori-hime to raise the child. The reason the child was called Hiko-nagisa-take-u-kaya-fuki-aezu was that the seaside birthing hut was entirely roofed with cormorant feathers as thatch, and at its peak, the roof had not yet come together when the child was born. Thus, it was so named.

Section 10, Variant 2

One text says, In front of the gate there was a frothing well. Above the well was a hundred-branched cinnamon tree. So Hiko-ho-ho-de-mi climbed the tree and waited there. In time, the daughter of the sea kami, Toyo-tama-hime, came out holding a precious pitcher and was going to draw water. Upon seeing someone's reflection in the well, she looked up and saw him. Startled, she dropped the pitcher, which shattered into pieces, and without looking back, returned inside and told her father and mother, "I saw someone in the tree beside the well. His countenance was very beautiful, and his bearing refined. Surely, he is no ordinary individual."

The kami, her father, upon hearing this, thought it strange, but promptly spread many layers for seating and welcomed him inside. Once Hiko-ho-ho-de-mi was seated, the sea kami asked him why he had come, and Hiko-ho-ho-de-mi replied with the particulars of the situation. The sea kami was moved to sympathy, and so summoned all the wide-finned and narrow-finned fish without exception and asked them about it. They all said, "We do not know, but the red seabream has a sore mouth and did not come." (It is also said that the kuchime[37] was concerned about her mouth.) He summoned her with haste, and when she arrived, he searched her mouth and immediately found the fishhook that was lost. Then the sea kami warned her, saying, "You, kuchime, from now on shall not eat fishing bait. Also, you cannot be served to the heavenly grandson." For this reason, the kuchime is not presented at the emperor's table.

When Hiko-ho-ho-de-mi was about to return, the sea kami told him, "On this occasion, the descendant of the heavenly kami has deigned to visit my home. I am greatly pleased and will never forget this day." Then, along with the fishhook, he presented a jewel that made the tide come in as one wished and a jewel that made the tide go out as one wished, and said, "Imperial grandson, though we be separated by a road of innumerable bends, I hope that from time to time we will remember each other and not forsake our bonds." Then he instructed him, "When you give this fishhook to your older brother, pronounce it a hook leading to poverty, a ruinous hook, a hook causing destitution. Once you have said that,

---

37 It is unclear what fish "kuchime" refers to or if it is different from the red seabream.

以後手投棄與之、勿以向授。若兄起忿怒、有賊害之
心者、則出潮溢瓊以漂溺之。若已至危苦求憨者、則
出潮涸瓊以救之。如此逼惱、自當臣伏。

　　時彥火火出見尊、受彼瓊鉤、歸來本宮。
一依海神之教、先以其鉤與兄。兄怒不受。故弟出潮
溢瓊、則潮大溢、而兄自沒溺。因請之曰、吾當事汝
爲奴僕。願垂救活。

　　弟出潮涸瓊、則潮自涸、而兄還平復。已而兄改
前言曰、吾是汝兄。如何爲人兄而事弟耶。

　　弟時出潮溢瓊。兄見之走登高山。則潮亦沒山。
兄緣高樹。則潮亦沒樹。兄既窮途、無所逃去。乃伏
罪曰、吾已過矣。從今以往、吾子孫八十連屬、恆當
爲汝俳人。一云、狗人。請哀之。

　　弟還出涸瓊、則潮自息。於是、兄知弟有神德、
遂以伏事其弟。是以、火酢芹命苗裔、諸隼人等、至
今不離天皇宮墻之傍、代吠狗而奉事者矣。世人不償
失針、此其緣也。
一書曰、兄火酢芹命、能得海幸。故號海幸彥。弟彥
火火出見尊、能得山幸。故號山幸彥。

　　兄則毎有風雨、輒失其利。弟則雖逢風雨、其幸
不忒。時兄謂弟曰、吾試欲與汝換幸。弟許諾因易之。
時兄取弟弓失、入山獵獸。弟取兄釣鉤、入海釣魚。
俱不得利。空手來歸。

　　兄即還弟弓矢、而責己釣鉤、時弟已失鉤於海中、
無因訪獲。故別作新鉤數千與之。兄怒不受。急責故
鉤、云々。

turn your back and throw it to him. Do not face him when you give it to him. If your older brother gets angry and intends to cause you harm, take out the jewel of high tide and drown him. If, thus afflicted, he seeks forgiveness, take out the jewel of low tide and save him. If you torment him like this, he will surrender to you of his own accord." Hiko-ho-ho-de-mi received the jewels and hook and went back to his home palace.

Precisely following the instructions of the sea kami, Hiko-ho-ho-de-mi first gave the fishhook to his older brother. The older brother was angry and would not receive it. So the younger brother took out the jewel of high tide, and the tide surged in, and the older brother began to drown. He pleaded, saying, "I will become your servant. Please deign to save my life."

The younger brother took out the jewel of low tide, and the tide naturally went out, and the older brother recovered. But shortly thereafter, the older brother amended what he had said earlier, saying, "I am your older brother. How can the older serve the younger?"

Then the younger brother took out the jewel of high tide again. The older brother saw it and ran to climb a high mountain, and when the tide submerged the mountain, the older brother climbed a tall tree, and the tide submerged the tree. The older brother was trapped, with nowhere he could flee. And so he surrendered to punishment, saying, "I was wrong. From now on, my descendants and my descendants' descendants shall always serve as your jesters. (Another account says, Serve as your dogs.) Please have pity on me."

The younger brother again took out the jewel of low tide, and the tide naturally went out. At this, the older brother knew that the younger brother had godly powers and at last surrendered to his younger brother. So it is that Ho-no-suseri's progeny, the various Hayato, even now do not leave from inside the emperor's palace walls and serve him in place of barking dogs. This is also the reason that people do not blame others for lost fishhooks.

Section 10, Variant 3

One text says, The older brother, Ho-no-suseri, was skilled at getting the bounty of the sea. Thus he was called Umi-sachi-hiko. The younger brother, Hiko-ho-ho-de-mi, was skilled at getting the bounty of the mountains. Thus he was called Yama-sachi-hiko.

The older brother lost his prey whenever the wind was blowing or it was raining, but there was no change in the bounty of the younger brother even when he met with wind and rain. One time, the older brother told the younger, "I want to try exchanging our talents." The younger brother agreed, and they exchanged them. The older brother took the younger brother's bow and arrows and went into the mountains to hunt game, and the younger brother took the older brother's fishhook and went to the sea to catch fish. They both lost their quarries and returned home empty-handed.

The older brother then returned the younger brother's bow and arrows and demanded his fishhook back. By that time, the younger brother had already lost the fishhook in the ocean and had no means by which to get it back. So he made several thousand new fishhooks and gave those to him instead. The older brother was angered and would not accept them and further pressed for his original fishhook, and so on.

是時、弟往海濱、低徊愁吟。時有川鴈、嬰羂困厄。即起憐心、解而放去。須臾有鹽土老翁來、乃作無目堅間小船、載火火出見尊、推放於海中。則自然沈去。忽有可怜御路。故尋路而往。自至海神之宮。

是時、海神自迎延入、乃鋪設海驢皮八重、使坐其上。兼設饌百机、以盡主人之禮。因從容問曰、天神之孫、何以辱臨乎。一云頃吾兒來語曰、天孫憂居海濱、未審虛實。蓋有之乎。

彥火火出見尊、具申事之本末。因留息焉。海神則以其子豐玉姬妻之。遂綣綿篤愛、已經三年。

及至將歸、海神乃召鯛女、探其口者、即得鉤焉。於是、進此鉤于彥火火出見尊。因奉教之曰、以此與汝兄時、乃可稱曰、大鉤、踉䠙鉤、貧鉤、癡騃鉤。言訖、則可以後手投賜。已而召集鰐魚問之曰、天神之孫、今當還去。儞等幾日之內、將以奉致。

時諸鰐魚、各隨其長短、定其日數。中有一尋鰐、自言、一日之內、則當致焉。故即遣一尋鰐魚、以奉送焉。

復進潮滿瓊・潮涸瓊二種寶物、仍教用瓊之法。

又教曰、兄作高田者、汝可作洿田。兄作洿田者、汝可作高田。海神盡誠奉助、如此矣。

時彥火火出見尊、已歸來、一遵神教、依而行之。其後火酢芹命、日以襤褸、而憂之曰、吾已貧矣。乃歸伏於弟。弟時出潮滿瓊、即兄舉手溺困。還出潮涸瓊、則休而平復。

先是、豐玉姬謂天孫曰、妾已有娠也。天孫之胤、豈可產於海中乎。故當產時、

The younger brother then went to the seaside and paced with his head hung low and cried. Just then there was a river goose distressed because it was caught in a trap. Moved to sympathy, the younger brother untangled it and set it free. Before long, Old Man Shio-tsu-chi came. He turned a basket with no gaps into a small boat and loaded Hiko-ho-ho-de-mi into it, then pushed it into the sea to drift, and it sank all by itself. In no time at all, there was a charming road, and so he followed the road and in due course arrived at the palace of the sea kami.

At that time, the sea kami himself welcomed Hiko-ho-ho-de-mi and led him inside, spread many layers of sea lion pelts, and had Hiko-ho-ho-de-mi sit on them. The sea kami also prepared one hundred tables for feasting and thoroughly executed the duties of a host. Then he casually asked Hiko-ho-ho-de-mi, "Descendant of the heavenly kami, why have you deigned to come?" (Another account says, My child came and told me, "The heavenly grandson is crying by the seaside," but I do not know if that was true or not. Was that the case?)

Hiko-ho-ho-de-mi told him the details of the matter from beginning to end. Soon enough he came to stay there. The sea kami then arranged for his daughter, Toyo-tama-hime, to be his wife, and three years passed in deep harmonious love.

When it came time to return, the sea kami then summoned the Seabream Lady, searched her mouth, and obtained the fishhook. He presented this fishhook to Hiko-ho-ho-de-mi and offered him instruction, saying, "When you give this to your older brother, loudly pronounce it a useless hook, a recalcitrant hook, a hook leading to poverty, a hook of fools. Once you have said that, you should turn your back and throw it down to him." After this he summoned the sharks and asked them, "The descendant of the heavenly kami is about to return. How many days will it take for each of you to deliver him?"

The sharks then each determined the number of days on the basis of their lengths. Among them was a one-fathom shark who said, "I will deliver him in one day." So he sent the one-fathom shark to take Hiko-ho-ho-de-mi back.

The sea kami also presented him with two treasures: the jewel of high tide and the jewel of low tide. In addition, he instructed him, saying, "If your older brother makes rice paddies in high, dry places, make your paddies in low-lying, wet places. If your older brother makes rice paddies in low-lying, wet places, make your paddies in high, dry places." The sea kami truly and earnestly aided him in this fashion.

Once Hiko-ho-ho-de-mi had returned, he precisely followed the instructions of the sea kami and acted accordingly. Afterward, Ho-no-suseri grew shabbier by the day, and crying, he said, "I am totally destitute," and surrendered to his younger brother. Then the younger brother took out the jewel of high tide, and the older one threw up his hands as he was tortured by drowning. Conversely, when Hiko-ho-ho-de-mi took out the jewel of low tide, the tide went out, and the situation returned to normal.

Prior to this, Toyo-tama-hime told the heavenly grandson, "I am pregnant. It is the heir of the heavenly grandson; how can the child be born in the sea? So when it is time to give

必就君處。如爲我造屋於海邊、以相待者、是所望也。
　故彥火火出見尊、已還鄕、即以鸕鶿之羽、葺爲産屋。屋蓋未及合、豐玉姬自馭大龜、將女弟玉依姬、光海來到。時孕月已滿、產期方急。由此、不待葺合、俓入居焉。已而從容謂天孫曰、妾方產、請勿臨之。
　天孫心怪其言竊覘之。則化爲八尋大鰐。而知天孫視其私屛、深懷慙恨。
　既兒生之後、天孫就而問曰、兒名何稱者當可乎。
　對曰、宜號彥波瀲武鸕鶿草葺不合尊。言訖乃涉海俓去。
　于時、彥火火出見尊、乃歌之曰、

飫企都鄧利	おきつとり
軻茂豆勾志磨爾	かもづくしまに
和我謂禰志	わがゐねし
伊茂播和素邏珥	いもはわすらじ
譽能據鄧馭刳母	よのことごとも

亦云、彥火火出見尊、取婦人爲乳母・湯母、及飯嚼・湯坐。凡諸部備行、以奉養焉。于時、權用他婦、以乳養皇子焉。此世取乳母、養兒之緣也。
是後、豐玉姬聞其兒端正、心甚憐重。欲復歸養。於義不可、故遣女弟玉依姬、以來養者也。于時、豐玉姬命寄玉依姬而奉報歌曰、

birth, I will without fail come to where you are. If you could build a hut for me by the sea and wait there, it would fulfill my wishes."

So after Hiko-ho-ho-de-mi returned to his land, he used the feathers of a cormorant as thatch for a birthing hut, but the roof was still not completely joined when Toto-tama-hime, riding a great turtle and leading her younger sister Tama-yori-hime, made the sea glow and came forth. The pregnancy had already come to term, and the time for delivery soon arrived. Hence, she did not wait for the thatching to come together, but rather immediately went inside the hut. After doing so, she calmly told the heavenly grandson, "I am to give birth. Please do not enter."

The heavenly grandson was suspicious of her words and secretly spied on her and saw that she had transformed into an eight-fathom great shark. Knowing that the heavenly grandson had peeped at her, she was deeply shamed and resentful.

After the child was born, the heavenly grandson went and asked her, "What should we name the child?"

She replied, "He should be called Hiko-nagisa-take-u-kaya-fuki-aezu." Once she said that, she crossed the sea and departed.

At that time, Hiko-ho-ho-de-mi sang,

On the island†
where the geese land
in the deep sea,
I slept together
with my beloved, whom I shall not forget[38]
for all my life.

It is also said that Hiko-ho-ho-de-mi gathered women to be wet nurses, to prepare warm drinking water and chew food and to give warm baths. All of the various hereditary guilds were set up to raise the child. They nursed the imperial prince with the milk from another woman. This is the origin of having wet nurses for raising children in the present.

Afterward, Toyo-tama-hime heard how beautiful the child was, and her heart was heavy with longing. She wanted to return and raise the child, but when she considered what that would mean, she could not. So she sent her younger sister, Tama-yori-hime, to go and raise it. At that time, Toyo-tama-hime sent with Tama-yori-hime a reply to the poem, which, when sung, went,

---

38 The verb suggests a conscious effort to forget something, making this rendition of the poem stronger than that in *Ancient Matters*, where the verb suggests a natural kind of forgetting.

阿軻娜磨廼	あかだまの
比訶利播阿利登	ひかりはありと
比鄧播伊珮耐	ひとはいへど
企弭我譽贈比志	きみがよそひし
多輔妬勾阿利計利	たふとくありけり

凡此贈答二首、號曰擧歌。海驢、此云美知。跟踦鉤、此云須須能美膩。癡騃鉤、此云于樓該膩。

一書曰、兄火酢芹命、得山幸利。弟火折尊、得海幸利、云々。

弟愁吟在海濱。時遇鹽筒老翁。老翁問曰、何故愁若此乎。

火折尊對曰、云々。

老翁曰、勿復憂。吾將計之。計曰、海神所乘駿馬者、八尋鰐也。是竪其鰭背而在橘之小戸。吾當與彼者共策、乃將火折尊、共往而見之。

是時、鰐魚策之曰、吾者八日以後、方致天孫於海宮。唯我王駿馬、一尋鰐魚。是當一日之內、必奉致焉。故今我歸、而使彼出來。宜乘彼入海。入海之時、海中自有可怜小汀。隨其汀而進者、必至我王之宮。宮門井上、當有湯津杜樹。宜就其樹上而居之。言訖即入海去矣。

故天孫隨鰐所言留居、相待已八日矣。久之方有一尋鰐來。因乘而入海。毎遵前鰐之教。

時有豐玉姬侍者、持玉鋺當汲井水、見人影在水底、酌取之不得。因以仰見天孫。即入告其王曰、吾謂我王獨能絶麗。今有一客。彌復遠勝。

海神聞之曰、試以察之。乃設三床請入。於是、天孫於邊床則拭其兩足。於中床則據其兩手。於內床則寬坐於眞床覆衾之上。海神見之、乃知是天神之孫、益加崇敬、云々。

> Though people say
> that the light
> of a shining jewel is splendid,
> I find that your figure
> is even more so!

The two songs are now called "High Tunes."

Section 10, Variant 4

One text says, The older brother Ho-no-suseri caught the bounty of the mountains, and the younger brother Ho-no-ori caught the bounty of the sea, and so on.

The younger brother was at the seashore crying. Then he met Old Man Shio-tsutsu. The old man asked him, "Why are you crying like this?"

Ho-no-ori replied, and so on.

The old man said, "Do not despair. I will make a plan." Planning, he said, "One swift steed ridden by the sea kami is an eight-fathom shark. His dorsal fin stands straight up at Odo in Tachibana. I will devise a strategy together with him." Then leading Ho-no-suseri, the old man took the younger brother to see him together.

When they got there, the shark stated his plan, saying, "In eight days, I could deliver the heavenly grandson to the palace of the sea kami. However, the swift steed ridden by my king is a one-fathom shark, and he can surely deliver you in one day. Therefore, I will go back and have him come here. You should ride him out to sea. When you go out to sea, in due course there will be a charming beach. Proceed along this beach and without fail you will reach the palace of my king. There is a hallowed cinnamon tree near the well at the palace gate. You should climb up this tree and stay there." Once he had said this, he departed out to sea.

So the heavenly grandson did as the shark said and stayed in the tree, waiting as eight days passed. After some time, a one-fathom shark indeed came. Accordingly, he rode it and went to sea and did everything just as the earlier shark had instructed.

Thereupon, an attendant of Toyo-tama-hime, holding a precious pitcher, came to draw water and saw a human figure in the depths of the water and so could not draw the water. She in turn looked up and saw the heavenly grandson. Then she went inside and reported to her king, saying, "I thought my king's beauty to be unsurpassed, but now we have a guest who far outstrips you."

The sea kami heard this and said, "We will test him." Then he set up bedding in three places and asked him to come in. The heavenly grandson wiped both his feet with the outermost bedding, placed both hands on the middle bedding, and then sat cross-legged upon the coverlet enveloping the innermost bedding. The sea kami saw this and thus knew that he was a descendant of the heavenly kami, and he revered and honored him all the more. And so on.

海神召赤女・口女問之。時口女、自口出鉤以奉焉。赤女即赤鯛也。口女即鯔魚也。

時、海神授鉤彦火火出見尊、因教之曰、還兄鉤時、天孫則當言、汝生子八十連屬之裔、貧鉤・狹々貧鉤。言訖、三下唾與之。又兄入海釣時、天孫宜在海濱、以作風招。風招即嘯也。如此則吾起瀛風邊風、以奔波溺惱。

火折尊歸來、具遵神教。至及兄釣之日、弟居濱而嘯之。時迅風忽起。兄則溺苦、無由可生。便遙請弟曰、汝久居海原。必有善術。願以救之。若活我者、吾生兒八十連屬、不離汝之垣邊、當爲俳優之民也。於是、弟嘯已停、而風亦還息。故兄知弟德、欲自伏辜。而弟有慍色、不與共言。

於是、兄著犢鼻、以赭塗掌塗面、告其弟曰、吾汙身如此。永爲汝俳優者。乃擧足踏行、學其溺苦之狀。初潮漬足時、則爲足占。至膝時則擧足。至股時則走廻。至腰時則捫腰。至腋時則置手於胸。至頸時則擧手飄掌。自爾及今、曾無廢絶。

先是、豐玉姬、出來當産時、請皇孫曰、云々。皇孫不從。豐玉姬大恨之曰、不用吾言、令我屈辱。故自今以往、妾奴婢至君處者、勿復放還。君奴婢至妾處者、亦勿復還。遂以眞床覆衾及草、裹其兒置之波瀲。即入海去矣。此海陸不相通之緣也。一云、置兒於波瀲者非也、豐玉姬命、自抱而去。久之曰、天孫之胤、不宜置此海中、乃使玉依姬持之送出焉。

The sea kami summoned the Akame and the Kuchime and questioned them. Then the Kuchime took the fishhook out of her mouth and presented it. The Akame is the red sea-bream, and the Kuchime is the mullet.

When the sea kami gave the fishhook to Hiko-ho-ho-de-mi, he instructed him accordingly, saying, "When you return this fishhook to your older brother, the heavenly grandson shall say, 'For your descendants in perpetuity, this will be a hook leading to poverty or a hook leading to starvation.' Once you have said that, spit three times and give it to him. Also, when your brother goes to sea, the heavenly grandson should go to the beach and call upon the winds. Call upon the winds by humming. If you do this, I will incite the wind of the deep sea and the wind of the seaside, causing swift waves, and torture him with drowning."

Ho-no-ori returned and exactly followed the kami's instructions. On the day his older brother went fishing, the younger brother stood on the beach and hummed. Just then a fast wind arose, and the older brother was tortured with drowning. There was nothing he could do to stay alive. So he said to his brother from afar, "You were at sea for a long time, and must have some useful tactics. I beg you to save me. If you let me live, my descendants in perpetuity shall never be far from your walls and will be your subjects and jesters." Upon this, the younger brother stopped humming, and the wind and waves calmed. Thereby the older brother knew the power of the younger brother and surrendered to punishment of his own accord. However, the younger brother bore an angry expression and would not speak with him.

At this, the older brother stripped to his loincloth, smeared red clay on his palms and face, and said to his brother, "Thus have I soiled my body. Forever shall I serve as your jester." Then he walked by raising and stamping his feet to imitate how he had struggled while drowning. First, when the water reached his feet, he went on tiptoes as if performing divination. Then when it reached his knees, he raised his feet up. Then when it reached his thighs, he ran around. Then when it reached his waist, he twisted his waist. Then when it reached his sides, he placed his hands on his breast. Then when it reached his neck, he threw his hands up and flapped them about. From that time until now, this performance never ceases.

Prior to this, when Toyo-tama-hime was about to give birth, she asked the imperial descendant, and so on. The imperial descendant did not follow her request. Toyo-tama-hime resented him and said, "You did not heed my words and caused me shame. Hence, I will go now. If my servants arrive where you are, do not return them. If your servants arrive where I am, I will not return them." Then she wrapped the child in resplendent bedding and grass and placed it on the beach, then went out to sea. This is the reason that one cannot travel between land and sea. (Another account says, Placing the child on the beach would be wrong, so Toyo-tama-hime carried it off.) After a long time, she said, "The heir of the heavenly grandson should not dwell in the sea." Then she sent Tama-yori-hime to carry the child away.

初豐玉姬別去時、恨言既切。故火折尊知其不可復會、乃有贈歌、已見上。八十連屬、此云野素豆豆企。飄掌、此云陀毗盧簡須。

彥波瀲武鸕鷀草葺不合尊、以其姨玉依姬爲妃。生彥五瀨命。次稻飯命。次三毛入野命。次神日本磐余彥尊。凡生四男。久之彥波瀲武鸕鷀草葺不合尊、崩於西洲之宮。因葬日向吾平山上陵。

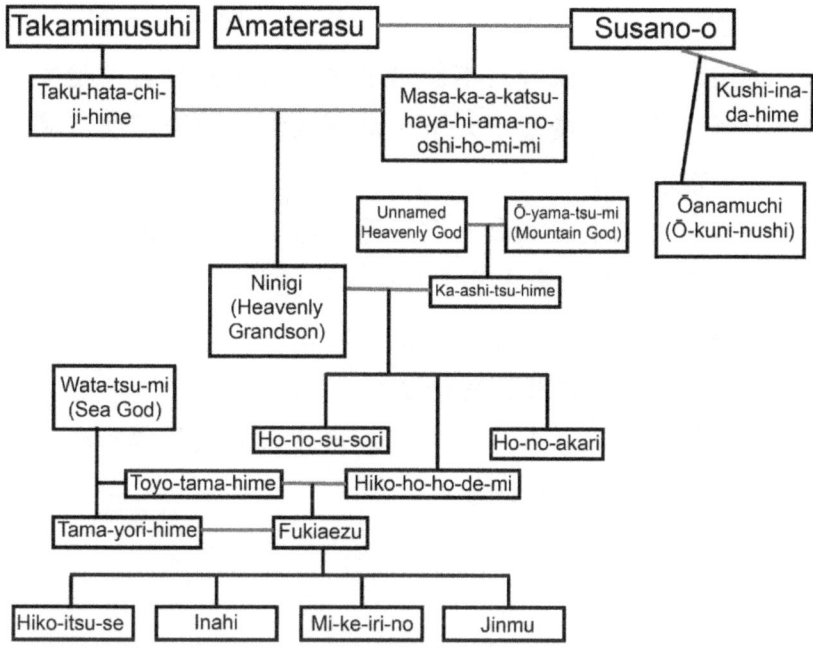

FIGURE 4 Genealogy of kami in Sections 9, 10, and 11

At first, when they parted, Toyo-tama-hime was seriously resentful. Hence, Ho-no-ori knew that he would never meet her again, and so he sent her a poem. It can be seen above.

Section 11: Children of Fuki-aezu

Main Version

Hiko-nagisa-take-u-kaya-fuki-aezu took his aunt Tama-yori-hime as his wife, and they had a child, Hiko-itsu-se. Next was Ina-hi. Next was Mi-ke-iri-no. Next was Kamu-yamato-iware-hiko [Jinmu].[39][xiii] In all, there were four sons. After a long time, Hiko-nagisa-take-u-gaya-fuki-aezu expired at his palace in the west of the land. Accordingly, he was buried atop Mt. Aira in Himuka.[xiv]

---

39 Now known as the first Japanese emperor, Jinmu.

一書曰、先生彥五瀨命。次稻飯命。次三毛入野命。次狹野尊。亦號神日本磐余彥尊。所稱狹野者、是年少時之號也。後撥平天下、奄有八洲。故復加號曰神日本磐余彥尊。

一書曰、先生五瀨命。次三毛野命。次稻飯命。次磐余彥尊。亦號神日本磐余彥火火出見尊。

一書曰、先生彥五瀨命。次稻飯命。次神日本磐余彥火火出見尊。次稚三毛野命。

一書曰、先生彥五瀨命。次磐余彥火火出見尊。次彥稻飯命。次三毛入野命。

Section 11, Variant 1

One text says, First born was Hiko-itsu-se. Next was Ina-hi. Next was Mike-iri-no. Next was Sa-no [Jinmu], also called Kamu-yamato-iware-hiko. Sa-no was his name when he was young.[xv] Later he pacified the realm and ruled the eight islands. For this reason, his name was changed to Kamu-yamato-iware-hiko.

Section 11, Variant 2

One text says, First born was Itsu-se. Next was Mi-ke-no. Next was Ina-hi. Next was Iware-hiko, also called Kamu-yamato-iware-hiko-ho-ho-de-mi.

Section 11, Variant 3

One text says, First born was Hiko-itsu-se. Next was Ina-hi. Next was Kamu-yamato-iware-hiko-ho-ho-de-mi. Next was Waka-mi-ke-no.

Section 11, Variant 4

One text says, First born was Hiko-itsu-se. Next was Iware-hiko-ho-ho-de-mi. Next was Hiko-ina-hi. Next was Mi-ke-iri-no.

神日本磐余彥天皇　神武天皇

神日本磐余彥天皇、諱彥火火出見。彥波瀲武鸕鷀草葺不合尊第四子也。母曰玉依姬。海童之少女也。天皇生而明達。意礭如也。年十五立爲太子。長而娶日向國吾田邑吾平津媛、爲妃。生手研耳命。

　　及年卅五歲、謂諸兄及子等曰、昔我天神、高皇產靈尊・大日孁尊、舉此豐葦原瑞穗國、而授我天祖彥火瓊々杵尊。於是、火瓊々杵尊、闢天關披雲路、驅仙蹕以戻止。是時、運屬鴻荒、時鍾草昧。故蒙以養正、治此西偏。皇祖皇考、乃神乃聖、積慶重暉、多歷年所。自天祖降跡以逮、于今一百七十九萬二千四百七十餘歲。而遼邈之地、猶未霑於王澤、遂使邑有君、村有長、各自分疆、用相凌躒。抑又聞於鹽土老翁。曰、東有美地。青山四周。其中亦有乘天磐船而飛降者。余謂、彼地、必當足以恢弘大業、

Book 3
Emperor Jinmu

The Emperor Goes Eastward

Emperor Kamu-yamato-iware-hiko [Jinmu] was originally named Hiko-ho-ho-de-mi.[i] He was the fourth child of Hiko-nagisa-u-gaya-fuki-aezu. His mother was called Tama-yori-hime. She was the younger daughter of Wata-tsu-mi. This emperor was astute from the time of his birth and was of resolute spirit.[ii] At fifteen years of age, he became crown prince. After he grew up, he took Ahira-tsu-hime, from the village of Ata, land of Himuka, as his princess, and she gave birth to Ta-gishi-mimi.

When he reached forty-five years of age, he told his older brothers and son,

> Of old, our heavenly kami Taka-mi-musuhi and Ō-hiru-me bestowed upon our heavenly ancestor Hiko-ho-no-ninigi this fertile reed country of rice ears.[1] Then Ho-no-ninigi pulled open the heavenly rock door, pushed the clouds from the way, and, preceded by his vanguard, arrived here. At that time, the world was still young, and all was dark. Thus he brought enlightenment to those in darkness and ruled this western region. Our imperial grandfather and imperial father,[2] as divine sages, accumulated fortune and increased prosperity, and now many years have passed. From the descent of our heavenly grandfather until now, it has been more than 1,792,470 years, but lands far away have still not been steeped in kingly favor. There, every town has its ruler, every village has its chief, every region marks its borders, and they fight among themselves. Also, I heard from Old Man Shio-tsu-chi that in the east there is a beautiful land surrounded on four sides by verdant mountains. In the center there is someone who flew down riding the stone boat of heaven. I believe that land most certainly to be satisfactory for the expansion of our imperial

---

1   Jinmu's use of this moniker from a variant, and his appeal to both Amaterasu and Taka-mi-musuhi as his divine patrons, serve to bring together the differing accounts in the "Age of the Gods" into a single narrative in Book 3, the beginning of the historical record.
2   Ho-ho-de-mi and Fuki-aezu.

光宅天下。蓋六合之中心乎。厥飛降者、謂是饒速日歟。何不就而都之乎。

諸皇子對曰、理實灼然。我亦恆以爲念。宜早行之。是年也、太歲甲寅。

其年冬十月丁巳朔辛酉、天皇親帥諸皇子舟師東征。至速吸之門。時有一漁人乘艇而至。天皇招之、因問曰、汝誰也。

對曰、臣是國神。名曰珍彥。釣魚於曲浦。聞天神子來、故即奉迎。

又問之曰、汝能爲我導耶。

對曰、導之矣。天皇勅授漁人椎橿末、令執而牽納於皇舟、以爲海導者。乃特賜名、爲椎根津彥。椎、此云辭毗。此即倭直部始祖也。

行至筑紫國菟狹。菟狹者地名也。此云宇佐。時有菟狹國造祖。號曰菟狹津彥・菟狹津媛。乃於菟狹川上、造一柱騰宮而奉饗焉。一柱騰宮、此云阿斯毗苔徒鞅餓離能宮。是時、勅以菟狹津媛、賜妻之於侍臣天種子命。天種子命、是中臣氏之遠祖也。

十有一月丙戌朔甲午、天皇至筑紫國岡水門。

十有二月丙辰朔壬午、至安藝國、居于埃宮。

乙卯年春三月甲寅朔己未、徙入吉備國。起行

---

3 Nigi-haya-hi here shows that, along with the father of Ka-ashi-tsu-hime in Section 9 of the "Age of the Gods," heavenly kami besides Ninigi had descended to the central reed plain land. The ancestry of Nigi-haya-hi is not given in the *Chronicles*, but his descendants, the Mononobe, are recognized as imperial subjects. A descent narrative for Nigi-haya-hi is given in the later *Original Records*, which identifies him the older brother of Ninigi.

lineage, which shall illuminate the realm. It must be the center of the world, and I think that the one who flew down is Nigi-haya-hi.³ Why should I not go there and build a capital?

The various imperial princes replied, "These words shine with the light of reason. We have been thinking the same thing. We should go soon." It was the year of the Wood Tiger [667 BCE].⁴

In the winter of that year, on the fifth day of the tenth month, the emperor himself led the various imperial princes and a fleet eastward to conquer. When they arrived first at the port of Hayasui, a fisherman in a small boat approached them. The emperor beckoned him and asked, "Who are you?"

"Your servant is a kami of the land, called Uzu-hiko," he replied. "I was fishing at the seaside and heard that a child of the heavenly kami had come. So I have come to welcome him."

The emperor questioned him again, asking, "Can you be my guide?"

He replied, "I shall guide you." The emperor decreed that a chinquapin rod be given to the fisherman so that he could grasp its tip and use it to pull the emperor's boat and guide it through the sea. Then the fisherman was specially granted the name Shihi-no-ne-tsu-hiko. He is the first ancestor of the Atai of Yamato.ⁱⁱⁱ

Going on, the emperor arrived in Usa, in the land of Tsukushi. At that time, the ancestors of the provincial Miyatsuko of Tsukushi were called Usa-tsu-hiko and Usa-tsu-hime, and they built a one-pillar victory shrine at the headwaters of the Usa River and presented a feast to the emperor. The emperor decreed that Usa-tsu-hime be bestowed upon his attendant Ama-no-tane as his wife.⁵ Ama-no-tane is the distant ancestor of the Nakatomi.⁶

Eleventh month, ninth day. The emperor arrived at the port of Oka in the land of Tsukushi.ⁱᵛ

Twelfth month, twenty-seventh day. The emperor arrived in the land of Aki and stayed in E Palace.ᵛ

Year of the Wood Rabbit [666 BCE], spring, third month, sixth day. The emperor moved into the land of Kibi, where he built a temporary

---

4   The sexagenary cycle used to measure years in Chinese history appears here for the first time. Later entries specify specific months or days. In the Chinese lunisolar calendar, the new year falls in late January or February of the Gregorian calendar and marks the beginning of spring.
5   An original note adds that Usa is a place-name.
6   Presumably, Ama-no-tane is a descendant of Ama-no-koyane, the first ancestor of the Nakatomi.

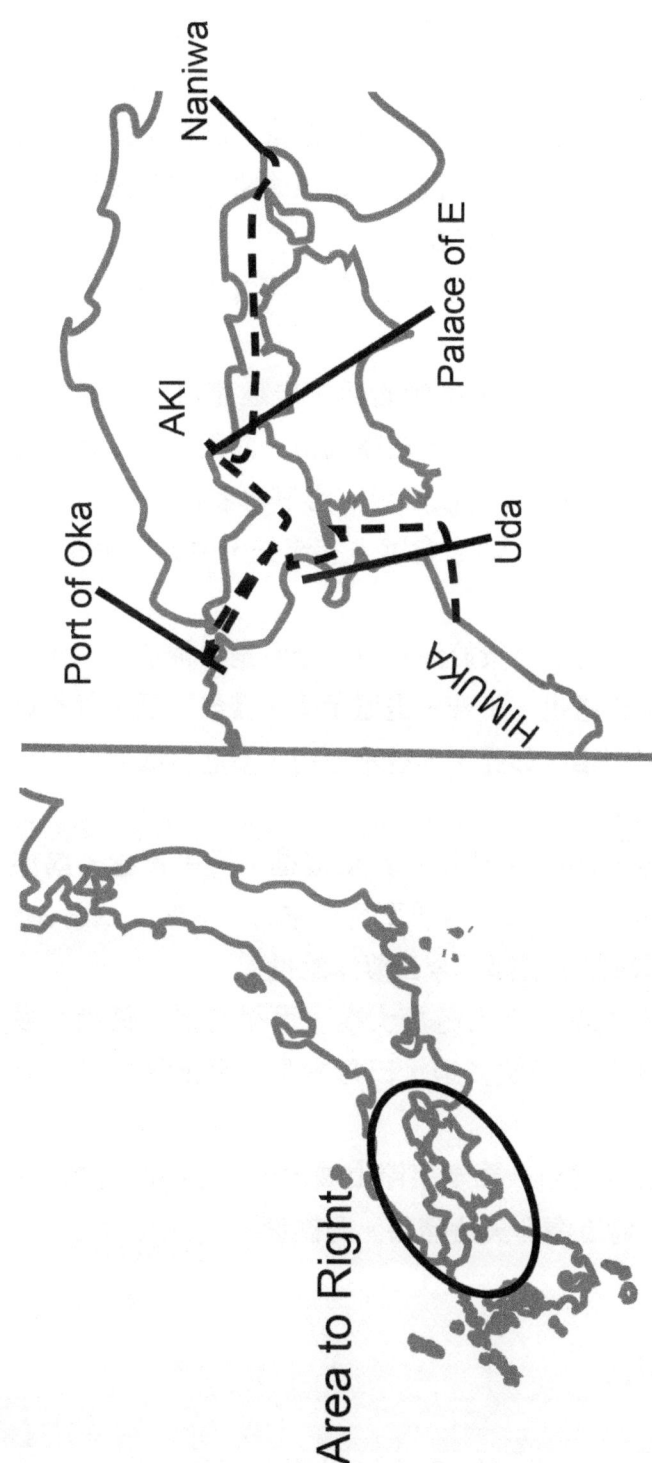

MAP 6 Jinmu's voyage to Naniwa. Jinmu's fleet left Himuka and traveled up the inland sea to Naniwa.

館以居之。是曰高嶋宮。積三年間、脩舟檝、蓄兵食、將欲以一擧而平天下也。

戊午年春二月丁酉朔丁未、皇師遂東。舳艫相接。方到難波之碕、會有奔潮太急。因以名爲浪速國。亦曰浪花。今謂難波訛也。訛、此云與許奈磨盧。

三月丁卯朔丙子、遡流而上、徑至河內國草香邑靑雲白肩之津。

夏四月丙申朔甲辰、皇師勒兵、步趣龍田。而其路狹嶮、人不得並行。乃還更欲東踰膽駒山、而入中洲。時長髓彥聞之曰、夫天神子等所以來者、必將奪我國、則盡起屬兵、徼之於孔舍衞坂、與之會戰。有流矢、中五瀬命肱脛。皇師不能進戰。

天皇憂之、乃運神策於沖衿曰、今我是日神子孫、而向日征虜、此逆天道也。不若、退還示弱、禮祭神祇、背負日神之威、隨影壓躡。如此、則曾不血刃、虜必自敗矣。

僉曰、然。

於是、令軍中曰、且停。勿須復進。乃引軍還。虜亦不敢逼。却至草香之津、植盾而爲雄誥焉。雄誥、此云烏多鶏縻。因改號其津曰、盾津。今云蓼津訛也。

初孔舍衞之戰、有人隱於大樹、而得免難、仍指其樹曰、恩如母。時人因號其地、曰母木邑。今云飫悶迺奇訛也。

五月丙寅朔癸酉、軍至茅渟山城水門。亦名山井水門。茅渟、此云智怒。時五瀬命矢瘡痛甚。乃撫劒

7　An original note adds that Yamaki Port was also called Yamai Port.

residence and stayed. It was called Takashima Palace.[vi] Over the course of three years, he prepared his ships and stored up rations, as he wanted to pacify the realm in one fell swoop.

Year of the Earth Horse [663 BCE], spring, second month, eleventh day. The emperor led the imperial army eastward, with the fore of each boat seeming to touch the aft of the boat in front of it. They arrived at the cape of Naniwa, where they encountered a swift current. Hence, the land was named Namihaya-no-kuni, or Land of Swift Waves. It was also called Namihana. Now it is called Naniwa, a corruption.[vii]

Third month, tenth day. Traveling upstream, they arrived at the harbor of Aokumo-no-shirakata in Kusaka Village in the land of Kōchi.[viii]

Spring, fourth month, ninth day. The imperial army outfitted its troops and marched toward Tatsuta. However, the road was steep and narrow, and they could not pass through in rank.[ix] They backtracked and went east by crossing Mt. Ikoma, entering the country's interior. When they did, Naga-sune-hiko heard of them and said, "The reason that these children of the heavenly kami have come must be to steal my land." He promptly mustered his own troops and blocked the imperial army at Kusae Hill, where the two sides engaged.[x] A stray arrow hit Itsu-se in the lower leg, and the imperial army was unable to advance.

The emperor, distressed by their defeat, went over many unfathomable stratagems in his mind. "Now, although I am a descendant of the sun kami," he said, "I attacked the enemy while facing the sun. This violates heavenly reason. Rather, we should retreat and feign weakness, venerate the kami of heaven and earth, put the energy of the sun kami at our backs, and tread them down before us like our own shadows. If we do this, the enemy will surely surrender of their own accord without blood staining our swords."

"So be it," everyone said.

At that, he ordered the army, "Hold for now. Do not advance." They pulled back. The enemy did not dare pursue them. They retreated to the harbor of Kusaka, planted their shields, and roared. Hence, this port was renamed Tate-tsu, or Shield Harbor. Now it is called Tadetsu, a corruption.

Previously, during the battle of Kusae, one man hid inside a large tree and thus avoided injury. So he pointed to the tree and said, "My debt of gratitude is akin to that for my own mother." Accordingly, people at the time named this place Omoki-mura, or Mother Tree Village. Now it is called Omonoki, a corruption.

The Emperor Circles around the Nara Basin

Fifth month, eighth day. The army arrived at Yamaki Port in Chinu.[7][xi] At that time, Itsu-se's arrow wound caused him great pain. Seizing the hilt of

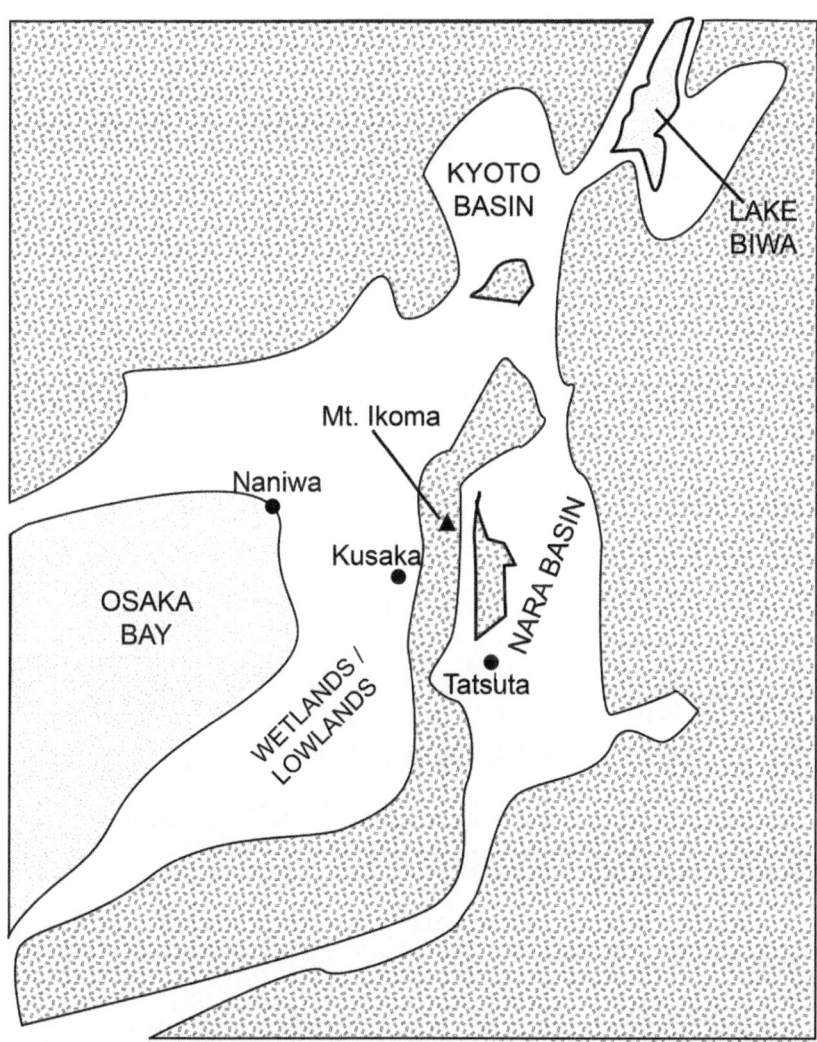

MAP 7 Initial approach to the Nara Basin. In antiquity, Osaka Bay and the delta formed by the Yodo River flowing south from Lake Biwa allowed crossing by boat far inland. Jinmu first attempted to enter the Nara Basin near Tatsuta, along the course of the Yamato River, retreated to Kusaka, attempted to enter by crossing Mt. Ikoma, then retreated again and took to the sea.

而雄誥之曰、撫劒、此云都盧瑟能多伽彌屠利辭魔屢。慨哉、大丈夫、慨哉、此云宇黎多棄伽夜。被傷於虜手、將不報而死耶。時人因號其處、曰雄水門。進到于紀國竈山、而五瀬命薨于軍。因葬竈山。

六月乙未朔丁巳、軍至名草邑。則誅名草戸畔者。戸畔、此云妬鼙。遂越狹野、而到熊野神邑、且登天磐盾。仍引軍漸進。海中卒遇暴風。皇舟漂蕩。時稻飯命乃歎曰、嗟乎、吾祖則天神、母則海神。如何厄我於陸、復厄我於海乎。言訖、乃拔劒入海、化爲鋤持神。三毛入野命、亦恨之曰、我母及姨並是海神。何爲起波瀾、以灌溺乎、則蹈浪秀而往乎常世郷矣。

天皇獨與皇子手硏耳命、帥軍而進、至熊野荒坂津。亦名丹敷浦。因誅丹敷戸畔者。時神吐毒氣、人物咸瘁。由是、皇軍不能復振。

時彼處有人。號曰、熊野高倉下。忽夜夢、天照大神、謂武甕雷神曰、夫葦原中國猶聞喧擾之響焉。聞喧擾之響焉、此云左揶霓利奈離。宜汝更往而征之。

武甕雷神對曰、雖予不行、而下予平國之劒、則國將自平矣。

天照大神曰、諾。諾、此云宇每那利。

時武甕雷神、登謂高倉曰、予劒號曰䫹靈。䫹靈、此云赴屠能瀰哆磨。今當置汝庫裏。宜取而獻之天孫。

his sword, he roared, "How infuriating! This hero has suffered injury at the enemy's hand and will die before he can exact his revenge." People at the time hence named this place O-no-minato, or Manly Port. The army advanced to the land of Ki, to Kamayama.[xii] Itsu-se perished[8] on the march. He was buried at Kamayama.

Sixth month, twenty-third day. The army arrived at the Nakusa Village and put to death a person called Nakusa-tobe.[9][xiii] Continuing on, they passed through Sano and arrived at Miwa Village in Kumano.[xiv] There the emperor climbed a shield-shaped boulder, then led the army gradually onward. When they took to the sea, there suddenly arose a violent wind that carried off the emperor's boat. At that time, Ina-hi sighed and said, "Alas! My ancestors are heavenly kami, but my mother's side is descended from the kami of the sea. Why did I meet trouble on land, only to again have troubles at sea?" Once he had said this, he drew his sword and thrust it into the ocean, and it transformed into the kami Sai-mochi. Then Mike-iri-no said with disgust, "My mother and aunt are also sea kami. Why do they cause great waves to rise and try to drown me?" Then, treading upon the waves, he went to the Land of Tokoyo.

Bereft of his brothers, the emperor, with only the imperial prince Tagishi-mimi, led the army and advanced, and they arrived at Arasaka Harbor in the land of Kumano.[10][xv] They put to death a person called Nishiki-tobe. But then the kami spewed a poisonous gas that sickened the people and enfeebled them. For this reason, the imperial army could not remobilize.

At that place, there was a man called Kumano Takakuraji. That night, he suddenly saw Amaterasu appear in a dream and tell Take-mikazu-chi, "I still hear the clamor of fighting from the central reed plain country. You should go back and conquer it."

Take-mikazu-chi replied, "Even if I do not go, if I lower the sword I used when I pacified the land, the country will be quelled as a matter of course."

Amaterasu said, "Indeed."

Then Take-mikazu-chi hastily said to Takakura, "My sword is called Futsu-no-mi-tama. I will put it in the back of your storehouse right now. You should take it and present it to the heavenly grandchild."

---

8 Use of this less prestigious verb reflects Jinmu's superior status.
9 Derived from the place-name Nakusa. The precise meaning of "tobe" is unclear, but it seems to refer to a local authority.
10 An original note adds that Arasaka was also called Nishiki Beach.

高倉曰唯唯而寤之。明旦、依夢中教、開庫視之、果有落劍、倒立於庫底板。即取以進之。

　于時、天皇適寐。忽然而寤之曰、予何長眠若此乎。尋而中毒士卒、悉復醒起。

　既而皇師、欲趣中洲。而山中嶮絶、無復可行之路。乃棲遑不知其所跋渉。時夜夢、天照大神訓于天皇曰、朕今遣頭八咫烏。宜以爲鄕導者。果有頭八咫烏、自空翔降。

　天皇曰、此烏之來、自叶祥夢。大哉、赫矣。我皇祖天照大神、欲以助成基業乎。

　是時、大伴氏之遠祖日臣命、帥大來目、督將元戎、蹈山啓行、乃尋烏所向、仰視而追之。遂達于菟田下縣。因號其所至之處、曰菟田穿邑。穿邑、此云于介知能務羅。于時、勅譽日臣命曰、汝忠而且勇。加能有導之功。是以、改汝名爲道臣。

　秋八月甲午朔乙未、天皇使徵兄猾及弟猾者。猾、此云字介志。是兩人、菟田縣之魁帥者也。魁帥、此云比鄧誤廼伽瀰。時兄猾不來。弟猾卽詣至。因拜軍門、而告之曰、臣兄々猾之爲逆狀也、聞天孫且到、卽起兵將襲。望見皇師之威、懼不敢敵、乃潛伏其兵、權作新宮、而殿內施機、欲因請饗以作難。願知此詐、善爲之備。

Takakura said "Yes, sir," and woke up. The next morning, in keeping with the instructions in the dream, he opened the storehouse and looked inside, and there a fallen sword was standing on its hilt on the storehouse floor. He took it and presented it to the emperor.

At that time, the emperor was sound asleep. Suddenly, he awoke and said, "Why did I sleep so long?" The poisoned soldiers completely came to their senses as well.

Thereupon, the imperial army wanted to make for the central land, but the mountains were steep, and there was no appropriate route. Caught in a conundrum, not knowing where to step or how to cross, Amaterasu instructed the emperor in a nighttime dream, saying, "We will now dispatch Ya-ta-garasu; you should use it as a guide in this land."[xvi] Sure enough, Ya-ta-garasu flew down from the sky.

"The coming of this crow no doubt accords with my auspicious dream," the emperor said. "Superb! My imperial ancestor Amaterasu wishes to aid me in establishing the foundations of this heavenly endeavor."

At that time, the distant ancestor of the Ōtomo, Hi-no-omi, led the Kume,[11] and as the general for their army, he treaded the mountain paths and cleared the route by looking for and heading toward the crow, and looking upward, he pursued it. At last they arrived at Uda, in the district of Shimotsu. So they named the place where they arrived Ukachi Village of Uda.[xvii] On that occasion, the emperor decreed praise for Hi-no-omi, saying, "You are loyal and valiant, on top of which you successfully guided us. I rename you Michi-no-omi, for you to henceforth use."

Autumn, eighth month, second day. The emperor summoned E-ukashi and Oto-ukashi. These two men were the chieftains of Uda District. E-ukashi did not come, but Oto-ukashi promptly attended. Making obeisance at the camp gate, he reported, "My older brother E-ukashi is planning a rebellion. When he heard that the heavenly grandchild arrived, he mustered troops to attack, but seeing the strength of the imperial army, he feared that he would be no match, so he made his troops go into hiding and built a new provisional palace. Inside he has rigged a booby trap. He wants to invite you to a banquet, then spring the trap and kill you. I want you to know of this deceit and be prepared for him."

---

11 In Variant 4 of Section 9 of the "Age of the Gods," Ama-no-oshi-hi is given as the ancestor of the Ōtomo and leader of the Kume hereditary guild, which suggests that Hi-no-omi is a descendant of this kami.

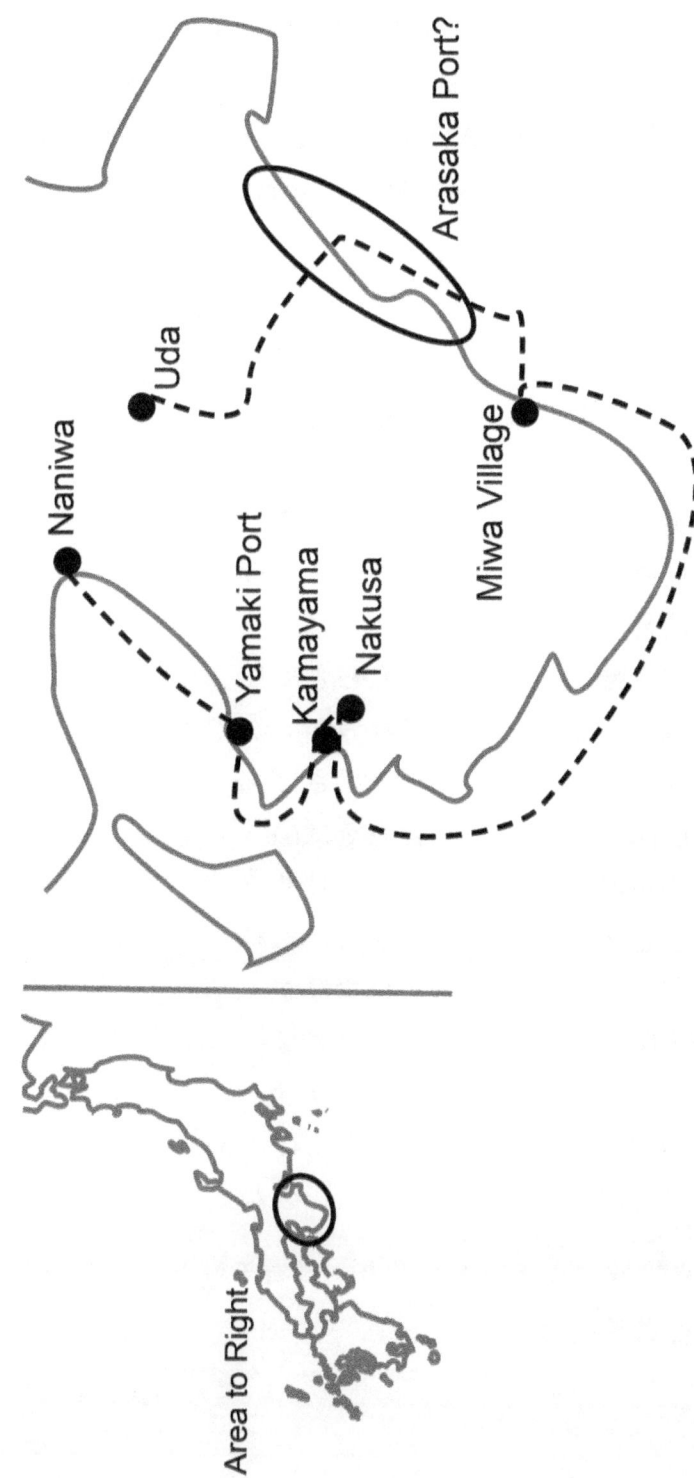

MAP 8 Entering the Nara Basin. Jinmu's fleet sailed around the Kii Peninsula and entered the Nara Basin overland from the southeast.

天皇即遣道臣命、察其逆狀。時道臣命、審知有賊害之心、而大怒誥嘖之曰、虜爾所造屋、爾自居之。爾、此云飫例。因案劒彎弓、逼令催入。兄猾、獲罪於天、事無所辭。乃自蹈機而壓死。時陳其屍而斬之。流血沒踝。故號其地、曰菟田血原。

　已而弟猾大設牛酒、以勞饗皇師焉。天皇以其酒宍、班賜軍卒。乃爲御謠之曰、謠、此云宇哆預瀰。

于儺能多伽機珥	うだのたかきに
辭藝和奈陂蘆	しぎわなはる
和餓末菟夜	わがまつや
辭藝破佐夜羅孺	しぎはさやらず
伊殊區波辭	いすくはし
區旎羅佐夜離	くぢらさやり
固奈瀰餓	こなみが
那居波佐麼	なこはさば
多智曽麼能	たちそばの
未廼那鶏句塢	みのなけくを
居氣辭被惠禰	こきしひゑね
宇破奈利餓	うはなりが
那居波佐麼	なこはさば
伊智佐介幾	いちさかき
未廼於朋鶏句塢	みのおほけくを
居氣儾被惠禰	こきだひゑね

　是謂來目歌。今樂府奏此歌者、猶有手量大小、及音聲巨細。此古之遺式也。

The emperor then dispatched Michi-no-omi to investigate this rebellion. When he did, Michi-no-omi knew all the details of the harm that E-ukashi intended to cause, and he erupted with rage, saying, "You wretch! As for the building you had made, go inside yourself!" Then he grasped his sword, drew his bow, and attacked to force him inside. E-ukashi could come up with no excuse for his crime against the emperor, and so stepped into his own trap and was crushed to death. Michi-no-omi dragged out the body and decapitated it, and the blood that flowed reached up to one's ankle. So this place is called Uda-no-chi-hara, or Bloody Field of Uda.

After this, Oto-ukashi prepared large amounts of beef and wine to thank the imperial army with a feast. The emperor distributed the wine and beef to the army, then composed a poem.

> At the high hunting ground in Uda,
> I wait upon
> the sandpiper, whose trap I strung.
> I caught no sandpiper,
> I caught a whale,
> a majestic whale.†
> If your first wife
> asks for trimmings,
> carve a side
> with no meat on it,
> like a beechnut.
> If your second wife
> asks for trimmings,
> carve a side
> abundant and meaty,
> like an acorn.[12]

This is called a "Kume Song." In the present, when this song is performed at the Bureau of Music, it includes clapping to the beat and changes in the volume of the voice.[13] This way of performing it remains with us from olden times.

---

12 In the first half of the poem, Jinmu refers to catching the older brother, the whale, rather than the younger, the sandpiper. In the second half, he likens this to his preference for the second, likely younger, wife.

13 The Bureau of Music was a bureaucratic organ of various Chinese imperial governments. A similar organ, the Gagakuryō, was created at the Japanese court in 701 CE.

是後、天皇欲省吉野之地、乃從菟田穿邑、親率輕兵巡幸焉。至吉野時、有人出自井中。光而有尾。天皇問之曰、汝何人。

　對曰、臣是國神、名爲井光。此則吉野首部始祖也。

　更少進、亦有尾而披磐石而出者。天皇問之曰、汝何人。

　對曰、臣是磐排別之子。排別、此云飫時和句。此則吉野國樔部始祖也。

　及緣水西行、亦有作梁取魚者。梁、此云揶奈。天皇問之。對曰、臣是苞苴擔之子。苞苴擔、此云珥倍毛菟。此則阿太養鸕部始祖也。

　九月甲子朔戊辰、天皇陟彼菟田高倉山之巓、瞻望域中。時、國見丘上則有八十梟帥。梟帥、此云多稽屢。又於女坂置女軍、男坂置男軍。墨坂置燠炭。其女坂、男坂、墨坂之號、由此而起也。復有兄磯城軍、布滿於磐余邑。磯、此云志。賊虜所據、皆是要害之地。故道路絶塞、無處可通。

　天皇惡之。是夜自祈而寢。夢有天神訓之曰、宜取天香山社中土香山、此云介遇夜摩以造天平瓮八十枚、平瓮、此云毗邏介。幷造嚴瓮、而敬祭天神地祇。嚴瓮、此云怡途背。亦爲嚴呪詛。如此、則虜自平伏。嚴呪詛、此云怡途能伽辭離。天皇祇承夢訓、依以將行。

　時弟猾又奏曰、倭國磯城邑、有磯城八十梟帥。又高尾張邑、或本云、葛城邑也。

　有赤銅八十梟帥。

14　Yoshino is a district in the southern part of present-day Nara Prefecture.
15　The Kunisu performed ritual duties at the imperial accession ceremony and other, seasonal events.
16　The Yoshino River.
17　These places are all in Uda, but only Sumisaka, the western pass from Haibara, is clearly attested. The name Kunimi ("land-see") suggests a survey point. The names Me-saka (woman hill), O-saka (man hill), and Sumi-saka (charcoal hill) are derived from the character of their respective garrisons.

Later the emperor wanted to investigate the land of Yoshino, so he left Ukachi Village of Uda and personally led a lightly armed detachment of troops to tour there.[14] When they arrived in Yoshino, a man came out of a well who shined and had a tail. The emperor asked him, "Who are you?"

He replied, "I am a kami of the land, called I-hika." He is the first ancestor of the Obito of Yoshino.

Proceeding a little further, there was another man with a tail who pushed aside a boulder and came out. The emperor asked him, "Who are you?"

He replied, "I am the child of Iwa-oshi-waku." He is the first ancestor of the Kunisu of Yoshino.[15][xviii]

They followed the river going west,[16] and there was a man catching fish at a fishing weir. The emperor asked him, and he replied, "I am the child of Nie-motsu." He was the first ancestor of the Ukai of Ada.[xix]

The Emperor Conquers the Nara Basin

Ninth month, fifth day. The emperor climbed to the peak of Mt. Takakura in Uda and surveyed the land. At that time, atop Kunimi Hill there were many enemy generals, a detachment at Mesaka, the main enemy force at Osaka, and live charcoal placed at Sumisaka.[17] The names Mesaka, Osaka, and Sumisaka are derived from these circumstances. Also, the army of E-shiki filled Iware Village.[xx] The places the bandits were using as bases were all strategic positions. So the roads were blocked, and there was no way to get through.

The emperor hated this situation, and that night he prayed for a revelation before he went to sleep. In his dream the heavenly kami instructed him, saying, "You should take clay from within the shrine of Heavenly Mt. Kagu and use it to make eighty heavenly platters. At the same time, make fierce jars and venerate the kami of heaven and earth.[18][xxi] Also, purify yourself, and recite a curse. If you do this, the enemy will be conquered as a matter of course." The emperor humbly received the instructions from this dream and prepared to carry them out.

Around the same time, Oto-ukashi addressed the emperor, saying, "The eighty[19] enemy generals of Shiki are in Shiki Village in the land of Yamato. Also, the many enemy generals of Akagane are in Takaohari Village.[20][xxii]

---

18 As in Sujin 10.9, the earth from Heavenly Mt. Kagu serves as stand-in for the land of the Yamato realm itself, and seizing it refers to taking control of the realm. Aside from their special use as ritual objects, it is unclear what "fierce jars" refers to.
19 A number simply meaning "many," but here used as a parallel for the number of earthen vessels that Jinmu will throw later in the episode.
20 An original note adds that Takaohari Village is also called Kazuraki Village.

此類皆欲與天皇距戰。臣竊爲天皇憂之。宜今當取天香山埴、以造天平瓮、而祭天社國社之神。然後擊虜則易除也。

天皇既以夢辭爲吉兆。及聞弟猾之言、益喜於懷。乃使椎根津彥、著弊衣服及蓑笠、爲老父貌。又使弟猾被箕、爲老嫗貌、而勅之曰、宜汝二人、到天香山、潛取其巓土、而可來旋矣。基業成否、當以汝爲占。努力愼歟。

是時、虜兵滿路、難以往還。時椎根津彥、乃祈之曰、我皇當能定此國者、行路自通。如不能者、賊必防禦。

言訖徑去。時群虜見二人、大咲之曰、大醜乎大醜、此云鞅奈瀰儞句。老父老嫗、則相與闢道使行。二人得至其山、取土來歸。

於是、天皇甚悅、乃以此埴、造作八十平瓮・天手抉八十枚手抉、此云多衢餌離。嚴瓮、而陟于丹生川上、用祭天神地祇。則於彼菟田川之朝原、譬如水沫而有所呪著也。天皇又因祈之曰、吾今當以八十平瓮、無水造飴。飴成、則吾必不假鋒刃之威、坐平天下。乃造飴。飴即自成。又祈之曰、吾今當以嚴瓮、沈于丹生之川。如魚無大小、悉醉而流、譬猶柀葉之浮流者、柀、此云磨紀。吾必能定此國。如其不爾、終無所成、乃沈瓮於川。

All of them intend to resist and fight you. In my heart, I am worried for you. You should take clay from Heavenly Mt. Kagu and make eighty heavenly platters, then venerate the kami of heaven and earth. Afterward, if we attack the enemy, they will easily be swept away."

The emperor had already believed his dream to be auspicious, but when he heard the words of Oto-ukashi, he was even more pleased. Then he had Shihi-no-ne-tsu-hiko wear ragged clothes and a straw raincoat and sedge hat to disguise him as an old man, and he made Oto-ukashi wear a grain sifter[21] to disguise him as an old woman. Then he decreed, "You two go to Heavenly Mt. Kagu and secretly take dirt from the peak, and then come back here. The success or failure of the foundation of the heavenly endeavor will be determined by your deeds. Give it your best!"

At that time, enemy troops filled the roads, and it would be difficult for them to go and come back. And so Shihi-no-ne-tsu-hiko made an oath, saying, "If our emperor is to establish the state, we will be able to pass on the road as a matter of course. If it is not to be, then the bandits will certainly stop us."

After he finished speaking, they went forth. A group of enemies saw the two of them and laughed loudly, saying, "Disgusting! Look at this old man and old woman!" Then they vacated the road so that they could pass. The two were able to go to the mountain, take the clay, and return.

The emperor was absolutely delighted, and using this clay, he made eighty heavenly platters and eighty hand-scooped fierce jars, climbed to the headwaters of the Niu River, and used them to venerate the kami of heaven and earth. Then at Asabara by the Uda River, the water foamed—a sign of a curse.[xxiii] Then the emperor continued with an oath, saying, "I now will use these eighty platters and make sweets without using any water. If the sweets come together, then I will pacify this realm without resorting to threat of arms." He then made sweets, and they formed all on their own. In another oath he said, "I will now take the heavenly jars and submerge them in the Niu River. If fish both large and small become intoxicated[22] and float along in the current like the fallen needles of a nutmeg-yew, then I will certainly establish this state. If this does not happen, then in the end it shall not come to pass." When he submerged the jars in the river, their

---

21 A woven basket of bamboo or other material used to remove husks from grain. Worn on the head, it would conceal the face.
22 Wine would be served to the kami in ritual vessels, which explains the drunken behavior of the fish.

其口向下。頃之魚皆浮出、隨水喰唒。

　時椎根津彦、見而奏之。天皇大喜、乃拔取丹生川上之五百箇眞坂樹、以祭諸神。自此始有嚴瓮之置也。

　時勅道臣命、今以高皇産靈尊、朕親作顯齋。顯齋、此云于圖詩怡破毗。用汝爲齋主、授以嚴媛之號。而名其所置埴瓮爲嚴瓮、又火名爲嚴香來雷。水名爲嚴罔象女。罔象女、此云瀰菟破廼迷。糧名爲嚴稻魂女。稻魂女此云于伽能迷。薪名爲嚴山雷。草名爲嚴野椎。

　冬十月癸巳朔、天皇嘗其嚴瓮之粮、勒兵而出。先擊八十梟帥於國見丘、破斬之。是役也、天皇志存必克。乃爲御謠之曰、

伽牟伽筮能	かむかぜの
伊齊能于瀰能	いせのうみの
於費異之珥夜	おほいしにや
異波臂茂等倍屢	いはひもとほる
之多儺瀰能	しただみの
之多儺瀰能	しただみの
阿誤豫	あごよ
阿誤豫	あごよ
之多太瀰能	しただみの
異波比茂等倍離	いはひもとほり
于智弖之夜莽務	うちてしやまむ
于智弖之夜莽務	うちてしやまむ

　謠意、以大石喩其國見丘也。

　既而餘黨猶繁、其情難測。乃顧勅道臣命、汝宜帥大來目部、作大室於忍坂邑、盛設宴饗、誘虜而取之。

　道臣命、於是、奉密旨、掘窨於忍坂、而選我猛卒、與虜雜居。陰期之日、酒酣之後、吾則起歌。汝等

mouths faced downward, before long the fish all floated up and went along with the current, opening and closing their mouths.

Shihi-no-ne-tsu-hiko saw this and reported it to the emperor. The emperor was greatly pleased, so he uprooted a true sakaki tree with innumerable branches from the headwaters of the Niu River and used it to venerate the various kami. From this began the practice of placing fierce jars for worship.

Then the emperor decreed to Michi-no-omi, "Now I will personally perform open ritual worship of Taka-mi-musuhi. I will use you as the ritual officiator and bestow upon you the name Itsu-hime. I name the ritually placed clay jars Itsu-he, the fire Itsu-no-kagu-tsu-chi, the water Itsu-no-mitsu-ha-no-me, the rations Itsu-no-uka-no-me, the firewood Itsu-no-yama-tsu-chi, and the grass Itsu-no-no-zu-chi.

Winter, tenth month, first day. The emperor ate the food from the fierce clay jars, put his troops in order, and moved out. They first attacked the many enemy generals at Kunimi Hill, where they broke through and executed them. At this battle, the emperor's attitude was one of certain victory. Accordingly, he composed a poem.

> Like snails
> that crawl about
> on the great boulders
> of Ise,
> where the divine winds blow,†
> like snails
> my troops,
> my troops
> like snails
> that crawl about—
> strike now and end them,
> strike now and end them![xxiv]

As for the meaning of the song, the great boulders are a metaphor for Kunimi Hill.

After some time, their remaining foes were still numerous, and their future intentions were difficult to fathom. So the emperor thought it over and decreed to Michi-no-omi, "Take charge of the greater Kume detachment and build a great hall in Osaka Village.[xxv] Prepare a massive feast, then invite the enemy and kill them."

Michi-no-omi secretly received these orders, dug a pit dwelling in Osaka, selected his bravest soldiers, and mixed them among the enemy. He had secretly told them, "After we are tipsy, I will stand up and sing. When you

聞吾歌聲、則一時刺虜。已而坐定酒行。虜不知我之有陰謀、任情徑醉。時道臣命、乃起而歌之曰、

於佐箇廼	おさかの
於朋務露夜珥	おほむろやに
比苔瑳破而	ひとさはに
異離烏利苔毛	いりをりとも
比苔瑳破而	ひとさはに
枳伊離烏利苔毛	きいりをりとも
瀰都瀰都志	みつみつし
倶梅能固邏餓	くめのこらが
勾鵄都都伊	くぶつつい
異志都々伊毛智	いしつついもち
于智弖之夜莽務	うちてしやまむ

時我卒聞歌、倶拔其頭椎劒、一時殺虜。虜無復噍類者。皇軍大悅、仰天而咲。因歌之曰、

伊莽波豫	いまはよ
伊莽波豫	いまはよ
阿阿時夜塢	ああしやを
伊莽儀而毛	いまだにも
阿誤豫	あごよ
伊莽儀而毛	いまだにも
阿誤豫	あごよ

今、來目部歌而後大哂、是其緣也。又歌之曰、

| 愛瀰詩烏 | えみしを |
| 毗儀利 | ひだり |

all hear me singing, immediately and jointly stab the enemy." After some time, they all sat down, and the wine was making its rounds. The enemies had no knowledge of the secret plan and drank to their heart's content. Then Michi-no-omi stood up and sang,

> In the great hall
> in Osaka,
> no matter how many people
> are inside,
> no matter how many people
> come inside,
> fiercely, fiercely
> the young Kume
> hold their bulbous-pommel swords,
> their stoneware bulbous-pommel swords—
> strike now and end them!

Just when the soldiers heard the song, they together drew their bulbous-pommel swords and immediately killed the enemies. Not one enemy soldier remained. The imperial army was greatly pleased and looked to heaven and laughed. Thereupon they sang,

> Just now,
> just now,
> ha, ha, serves you right!
> For now,
> we young ones;
> for now,
> we young ones![23]

In the present, the Kume laugh after singing, and this is why. Then they sang again:

> Though people say
> that one Emishi

---

23 "Just now" refers to the enemies that have just been struck down. "For now" suggests that enemies may attack again, but the Kume will fight them with the same spirit leading to victory.

毛々那比苔	ももなひと
比苔破易陪廼毛	ひとはいへども
多牟伽毗毛勢儒	たむかひもせず

此皆承密旨而歌之。非敢自專者也。

時天皇曰、戰勝而無驕者、良將之行也。今魁賊已滅、而同惡者、匈々十數群。其情不可知。如何久居一處、無以制變。乃徙營於別處。

十有一月癸亥朔己巳、皇師大舉、將攻磯城彥。先遣使者、徵兄磯城。兄磯城不承命。更遣頭八咫烏召之。時烏到其營而鳴之曰、天神子召汝。怡奘過、怡奘過。過、音倭。

兄磯城忿之曰、聞天壓神至、而吾爲慨憤時、奈何烏鳥若此惡鳴耶、壓、此云飫襲。乃彎弓射之。烏即避去。

次到弟磯城宅、而鳴之曰、天神子召汝。怡奘過、怡奘過。時弟磯城慄然改容曰、臣聞天壓神至、旦夕畏懼。善乎烏、汝鳴之若此者歟、即作葉盤八枚、盛食饗之。葉盤、此云毗羅耐。因以隨烏、詣到而告之曰、吾兄々磯城、聞天神子來、則聚八十梟帥、具兵甲、將與決戰。可早圖之。

天皇乃會諸將、問之曰、今兄磯城、果有逆賊之意。召亦不來。爲之奈何。

諸將曰、兄磯城黠賊也。宜先遣弟磯城曉喩之、幷說兄倉下・弟倉下。如遂不歸順、然後舉兵臨之、亦未晚也。倉下、此云衢羅餌。乃使弟磯城開示

is worth one hundred men,
they do not resist us!²⁴

These songs were all sung as part of the secret orders, and were not just sung impromptu.²⁵

At that time, the emperor said, "The way of a good general is to be victorious in battle without gloating. Now the enemy leaders have already been destroyed, but a dozen groups of the same evildoers are wreaking havoc. It is impossible to know what they have planned. How can we linger in one place, and not prepare for what will come?" Then he moved the camp to another place.

Eleventh month, seventh day. The imperial army mobilized their forces to attack the lords of Shiki. First, the emperor dispatched a messenger to summon E-no-shiki, but E-no-shiki would not obey the order. Subsequently, he dispatched Ya-ta-garasu to summon him. The crow went to his camp and cried, "The child of the heavenly kami summons you, c'mon, c'mon!"

E-no-shiki said angrily, "When I heard that the kami Ama-no-osu had come, I took exception. Why is this crow making such an obnoxious cry?" Then he drew his bow and shot at it, and the crow fled.

Next, the crow went to the house of Oto-shiki and cried, "The child of the heavenly kami summons you, c'mon, c'mon!" Oto-shiki, fearful, sat up straight and said, "When I heard that the kami Ama-no-osu had come, I was filled with fear from morning to night. It is well that you cry like this, crow." Then he prepared eight platters using leaves, filled them, and fed the crow. He then departed in accordance with the crow's summons and reported to the emperor, "My older brother, E-shiki, heard that a child of the heavenly kami had come, so he assembled many enemy generals, prepared arms and armor, and resolved to fight. Quickly, think of a plan!"

The emperor assembled his various generals and asked them, "Right now, E-shiki is planning a rebellion. I summoned him, but he did not come. What shall we do?"

The various generals said, "E-shiki is a crafty enemy. You should first send Oto-shiki to convince him, and to persuade E-kuraji and Oto-kuraji at the same time. If they do not surrender, it will not be too late afterward to raise troops and go to battle." And so he made Oto-shiki go to explain

---

24 The Emishi first appear in the historical record in Keikō 27 as non-imperial people from northeastern Japan.
25 That is, the songs were included in the secret orders that Jinmu issued to Michi-no-omi.

利害。而兄磯城等猶守愚謀、不肯承伏。
　時椎根津彦、計之曰、今者宜先遣我女軍、出自忍坂道。虜見之必盡銳而赴。吾則馳馳勁卒、直指墨坂、取菟田川水、以灌其炭火、儵忽之間出其不意、則破之必也。
　天皇善其策、乃出女軍以臨之。虜謂大兵已至、畢力相待。先是、皇軍攻必取、戰必勝。而介冑之士、不無疲弊。故聊爲御謠、以慰將卒之心焉。謠曰、

哆々奈梅弓	たたなめて
伊那瑳能椰摩能	いなさのやまの
虛能莽由毛	このまゆも
易喩者摩毛羅毗	いゆきまもらひ
多多介陪麼	たたかへば
和例破椰隈怒	われはやゑぬ
之摩途等利	しまつとり
宇介譽餓等茂	うかひがとも
伊莽輸開珥虛禰	いますけにこね

　果以男軍越墨坂、從後夾擊破之。斬其梟帥兄磯城等。
　十有二月癸巳朔丙申、皇師遂擊長髄彦。連戰不能取勝。時忽然天陰而雨氷。乃有金色靈鵄、飛來止于皇弓之弭。其鵄光曄煜、狀如流電。由是、長髄彦軍卒皆迷眩、不復力戰。長髄是

the stakes, but E-shiki and the others still maintained their foolish plans and would not agree to yield.

At that time, Shihi-no-ne-tsu-hiko made a plan, saying, "We should first send a detachment on the road out of Osaka. The enemy will see it and certainly use their elite troops to pursue it. We will then quickly advance our main force on horseback toward Sumisaka. They will take the water from the Uda River and use it to quench the live charcoal fires. Then they immediately move on the enemy while they do not expect it and will surely defeat them."

The emperor approved the plan and sent out a detachment to face the enemy. The enemy thought that the main force had come, and they fought back with all they had. Up to now, the imperial army had taken without fail what they assaulted and had won without fail when they fought, but soldiers on the battlefield cannot escape exhaustion. So the emperor took a moment and composed a song to ease the soldiers' minds. He sang,

> Line up the shields!
> Passing through the trees
> at Mt. Isana,
> we, fighting
> while keeping lookout,
> are hungry!
> Island birds,†
> keepers of the cormorants,
> come to our aid!

As intended, the main force crossed Sumisaka, and afterward came from behind and defeated the enemy.[26] They beheaded the enemy general E-shiki and others.

Twelfth month, fourth day. The imperial army finally attacked Naga-sune-hiko, but though they fought many battles, they could not gain victory. Then the skies suddenly darkened, and it rained ice. Next there was a strange gold-colored kite that flew to the top of the emperor's bow. The kite shone dazzlingly, like lightning, and Naga-sune-hiko's army was blinded, lost their way, and could not continue fighting. Nagasune was the original name for

---

26 Jinmu's main force avoided the primary defensive fortification at Osaka by taking the long way around over Sumisaka. Meanwhile, Jinmu himself and a smaller detachment distracted E-shiki's forces at Osaka. E-shiki's position fell when Jinmu's main force turned to attack Sumisaka from the side.

邑之本號焉。因亦以爲人名。及皇軍之得鵄瑞也、時人仍號鵄邑。今云鳥見是訛也。

　昔孔舍衞之戰、五瀬命中矢而薨。天皇銜之、常懷憤懟。至此役也、意欲窮誅。乃爲御謠之曰、

瀰都瀰都志	みつみつし
倶梅能故邏餓	くめのこらが
介耆茂等珥	かきもとに
阿波赴珥破	あはふには
介瀰羅毗苔茂苔	かみらひともと
曾廼餓毛苔	そのがもと
曾禰梅屠那藝弖	そねめつなぎて
于笞弖之夜莽務	うちてしやまむ

　又謠之曰、

瀰都々々志	みつみつし
倶梅能故邏餓	くめのこらが
介耆茂等珥	かきもとに
宇惠志破餌介瀰	うゑしはじかみ
句致弭比倶	くちびひく
和例破涴輸例儒	われはわすれず
于智弖之夜莽務	うちてしやまむ

　因復縱兵忽攻之。凡諸御謠、皆謂來目歌。此的取歌者而名之也。

　時長髄彦、乃遣行人、言於天皇曰、嘗有天神之子、乘天磐船、自天降止。號曰櫛玉饒速日命。饒速日、此云儞藝波揶卑。是娶吾妹三炊屋媛亦名長髄媛、亦名鳥見屋媛。遂有兒息。名曰可美眞手命。可美眞手、此云于魔詩莽耐。故吾以饒速日命、爲君而奉焉。夫天神之子、豈有兩種乎。奈何更稱

this village, and for this reason, it was also used as a personal name. Since the imperial army had a miraculous kite, people at the time called the village Tobi-no-mura, or Kite Village. Now it is called Tomi, a corruption.[xxvi]

Previously, at the battle of Kusae, Itsu-se was hit by an arrow and perished. The emperor was haunted by this, and was seething and bitter inside. When it came to this fight, he thus sought complete annihilation of the other side. Accordingly, he sang,

> Fiercely, fiercely,
> the young Kume
> in their millet field,
> at the base of the hedge,
> have before them a pungent garlic chive.
> Seize it by the roots and stem
> at the base.
> Strike now and end them!

Then he again sang,

> Fiercely, fiercely,
> the young Kume
> eat the Japanese pepper planted
> at the base of the hedge,
> and their mouths tingle.[27]
> I will not forget!
> Strike now and end them!

He then released the troops to suddenly attack. These songs are all called Kume songs—a name entirely based on who sang them.

At that time, Naga-sune-hiko sent a messenger to tell the emperor, "A long time ago, a child of heavenly kami rode a stone boat of heaven out of heaven and descended. He was called Kushi-tama-nigi-haya-hi.[28] He married my younger sister, Mi-kashiki-ya-hime. They had a child, called Umashi-made.[29] So I serve Nigi-haya-hi as my lord. But how can there be two lineages of children of the heavenly kami? How can you claim to be the

---

27 The Japanese pepper is of the same genus as the Sichuan pepper. Just as its numbing sensation lingers in the mouth, so Jinmu's resentment at the death of his brother lingers in his heart.
28 This kami is referred to with a shortened name in Jinmu's first speech of this book.
29 An original note adds that Mi-kashiki-ya-hime was also called Naga-sune-hime and Tomi-ya-hime.

天神子、以奪人地乎。吾心推之、未必爲信。

　天皇曰、天神子亦多耳。汝所爲君、是實天神之子者、必有表物。可相示之。長髓彦即取饒速日命之天羽々矢一隻及步靫、以奉示天皇。天皇覽之曰、事不虛也。還以所御天羽々矢一隻及步靫、賜示於長髓彦。長髓彦見其天表、益懷踧踖。然而凶器已構、其勢不得中休。而猶守迷圖、無復改意。

　饒速日命、本知天神慇懃、唯天孫是與。且見夫長髓彦稟性愎佷、不可教以天人之際、乃殺之。帥其衆而歸順焉。

　天皇素聞饒速日命、是自天降者而今果立忠效。則褒而寵之。此物部氏之遠祖也。

　己未年春二月壬辰朔辛亥、命諸將、練士卒。是時、層富縣波哆丘岬、有新城戸畔者。丘岬、此云塢介佐棄。又和珥坂下、有居勢祝者。坂下、此云瑳伽梅苔。臍見長柄丘岬、有猪祝者。此三處土蜘蛛、並恃其勇力、不肯來庭。天皇乃分遣偏師、皆誅之。又高尾張邑、有土蜘蛛。其爲人也、身短而手足長。與侏儒相類。皇軍結葛網、而掩襲殺之。因改號其邑曰葛城。

child of a heavenly kami and steal away people's lands? When I consider these matters, surely you cannot be believed."

The emperor said, "The children of the heavenly kami are many.[30] As for the lord you serve, if he is truly a child of the heavenly kami, there must be some object that proves this. Show it to me." Naga-sune-hiko then took one of Nigi-haya-hi's heavenly viper arrows and his marching quiver and presented them for the emperor to see. The emperor briefly looked at them and said, "These are not fake." In turn, he showed to Naga-sune-hiko one of the heavenly viper arrows and the marching quiver he wore. Naga-sune-hiko saw this heavenly proof and felt increasingly respectful. Despite this, his armaments were already in place, his momentum could not be halted midway, and he still harbored delusional schemes. So did not alter his intentions.

Nigi-haya-hi knew from the first that the heavenly kami were solicitous toward the heavenly grandson alone. On top of this, he saw that Naga-sune-hiko was obstinate and could not be taught the boundaries between the heavenly and the human, so he killed him, took charge of his troops, and surrendered.

The emperor heard that Nigi-haya-hi had first come down from heaven and now had acted loyally, and so he praised him and showed him favor. Nigi-haya-hi was the distant ancestor of the Mononobe.[31]

Year of the Earth Sheep [662 BCE], spring, second month, twentieth day. The emperor ordered his various generals to train soldiers. At that time, at the hilly cape of Hata in the district of Soho, there was one called Nii-ki-tobe.[xxvii] Also, at the base of Wani Hill, there was one called Kose-hafuri.[xxviii] Also, at the hilly cape of Hosomi-no-nagara, there was one called Ino-hafuri.[xxix] The earth-spider[32] rebels in these three places relied on their bravery and strength, and did not pay their respects at court. The emperor sent detachments and had them all put to death. There also were earth-spider rebels at the village of Takaohari. As for their appearance, they had short bodies but long arms and legs, like dwarves. The imperial army tied arrowroot into nets, launched a surprise attack, and killed them. Accordingly, the name of the village was changed to Kazuraki, or Climbing Vines Fort.[xxx]

---

30 This passage demonstrates that Jinmu's legitimacy does not derive from his status as a descendant of the heavenly kami.
31 A clan associated with military affairs and state ritual. Their exploits are described in great detail later in the *Chronicles*.
32 A pun on "hole dweller," which also dehumanizes this group of people.

夫磐余之地、舊名片居。片居、此云伽哆韋。亦曰片立。片立、此云伽哆哆知。逮我皇師之破虜也、大軍集而滿於其地。因改號爲磐余。或曰、天皇、往嘗嚴瓮粮、出軍西征。是時、磯城八十梟帥、於彼處屯聚居之。屯聚居、此云怡波瀰蓑。果與天皇大戰。遂爲皇師所滅。故名之曰磐余邑。又皇師立誥之處、是謂猛田。作城處、號曰城田。又賊衆戰死而僵屍、枕臂處、呼爲頬枕田。天皇以前年秋九月、潛取天香山之埴土、以造八十平瓮、躬自齋戒祭諸神。遂得安定區宇。故號取土之處、曰埴安。

　　三月辛酉朔丁卯、下令曰、自我東征、於茲六年矣。賴以皇天之威、凶徒就戮。雖邊土未清、餘妖尚梗、而中洲之地、無復風塵。誠宜恢廓皇都、規摹大壯。而今運屬屯蒙、民心朴素。巢棲穴住、習俗惟常。夫大人立制、義必隨時。苟有利民、何妨聖造。且當披拂山林、經營宮室、而恭臨寶位、以鎭元元。上則答乾靈授國之德、下則弘皇孫養正之心。然後、

The old name for the location Iware was Kataru, also Katatachi. When the imperial army had defeated the enemy, the full army gathered and completely filled this village. So its name was changed to Iware. It is also said that the emperor ate the food from the fierce clay jars, then mobilized his army westward to conquer. At the time, the many generals of Shiki mustered in that place. There ended up being a grand battle with the emperor, and ultimately the imperial army destroyed them. So the place was named Iware-no-mura, or Gathering Place Village.[xxxi] Also, the place where the emperor's troops roared is called Takeda, or Ferocious Field. The place they built their fort is called Kida, or Fort Field. Moreover, the place where the enemies fought and died, their corpses piling up as if using each other's forearms for pillows, is called Tsuramakita, or Cheek Pillow Field. The emperor, in autumn, the ninth month of the previous year, had secretly taken clay from Heavenly Mt. Kagu and used it to make eighty wide platters, purified himself for ritual worship, and venerated the various kami. In the end, he was able to subjugate the realm. So the place where he took the clay from is called Haniyasu, or Clay Subjugate.

Jinmu Founds the Yamato State

Third month, seventh day. The emperor issued an order, saying, "It has been six years since our eastern expedition. By means of the energies of the heavenly kami,[33] the enemies have been executed. Although the borderlands are not yet quelled and the remaining enemies are still powerful, in the central lands there is not even dust in the wind.[34] Truly, we should clear space for an imperial capital and build a grand palace. But the world is still young and immature, and the people are of simple mind. They dwell in nests and holes, a custom that has become ubiquitous. But after all, when a sage establishes order, then morality will certainly follow to accord with the times. If it provides even a small benefit to the people, who would hinder the sage's work? This being the case, I must clear an expanse of forest and build a palace, humbly accede to the imperial throne, and peacefully govern my subjects. To those above, I will reciprocate the virtues of the heavenly kami who bestowed this land upon me, and to those below, I shall spread the proper mindset cultivated by the heavenly grandson. Afterward, would

---

33 Referring to Jinmu's decision to circle around Sumisaka and apply the energy of Amaterasu.
34 A metaphor for troops marching.

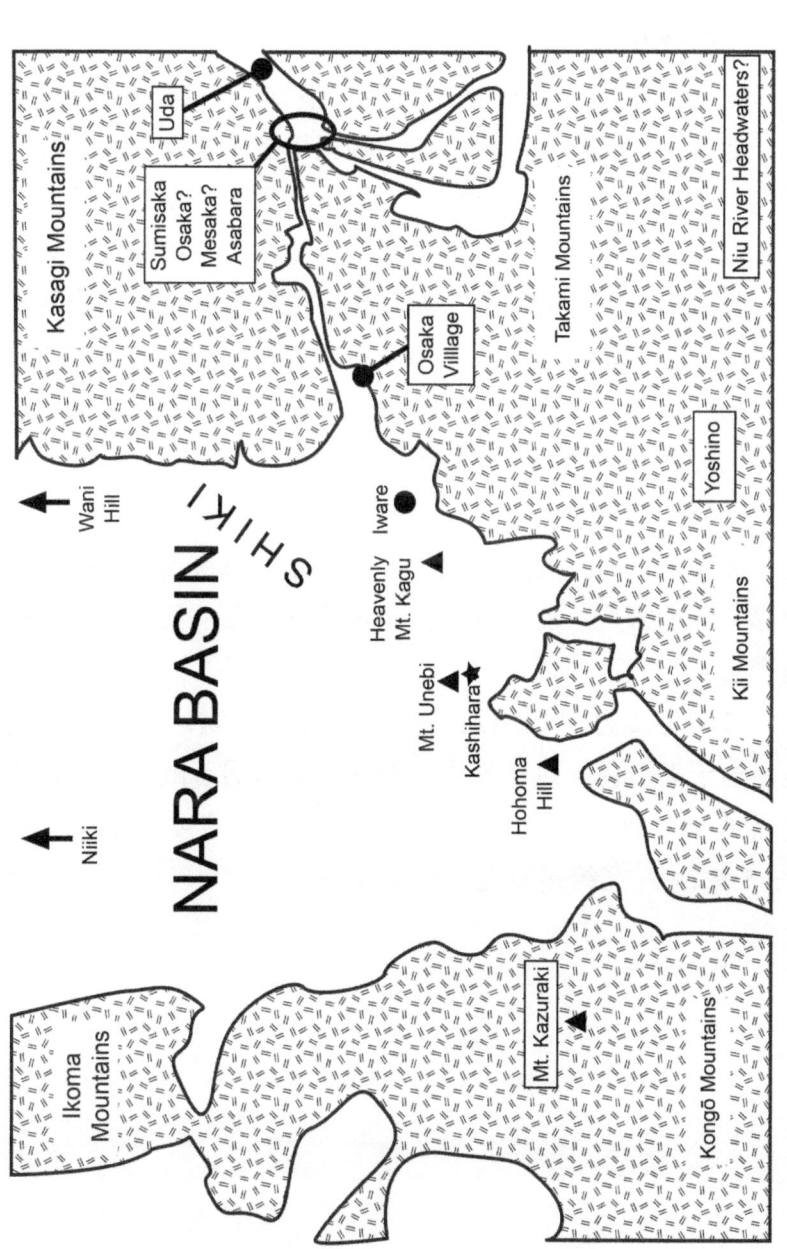

MAP 9 South Nara Basin. Jinmu's force moved in from Uda in the east to Kashihara.

兼六合以開都、掩八紘而爲宇、不亦可乎。觀夫畝傍山畝傍山、此云宇禰縻夜摩。東南橿原地者、蓋國之墺區乎。可治之。是月、即命有司、經始帝宅。

庚申年秋八月癸丑朔戊辰、天皇當立正妃。改廣求華冑。時有人奏之曰、事代主神、共三嶋溝橛耳神之女玉櫛媛所生兒、號曰媛蹈韛五十鈴媛命。是國色之秀者。天皇悅之。九月壬午朔乙巳、納媛蹈韛五十鈴媛命、以爲正妃。

辛酉年春正月庚辰朔、天皇即帝位於橿原宮。是歲爲天皇元年。尊正妃爲皇后。生皇子神八井命・神渟名川耳尊。故古語稱之曰、於畝傍之橿原也、太立宮柱於底磐之根、峻峙搏風於高天之原、而始馭天下之天皇、號曰神日本磐余彥火々出見天皇焉。

初天皇草創天基之日也、大伴氏之遠祖道臣命、帥大來目部、奉承密策、能以諷歌倒語、掃蕩妖氣。倒語之用、始起乎茲。

二年春二月甲辰朔乙巳、天皇定功行賞。賜道臣命宅地、居于築坂邑、以寵異之。亦使大來目居于畝傍山以西川邊之地。今號來目邑、此其緣也。以珍彥爲倭國造。珍彥、此云于莒毗故。又給弟猾猛田邑。因爲

it not be good for me to unify the lands in the six quarters, build a capital, and spread my dominion as a roof to the ends of the earth? Looking upon Mt. Unebi, is not the place to its southeast, Kashihara, the center of the land?[xxxii] Build the capital there." That very month he ordered government officials to begin building a palace.

Year of the Metal Monkey [661 BCE], autumn, eighth month, sixteenth day. The emperor wanted to establish an official wife, and formally searched everywhere among the aristocracy. At that time, someone addressed him, saying, "The kami Koto-shiro-nushi and the daughter of the kami Mi-shima-no-mizo-kui-mimi, Tama-kushi-hime, had a child, called Hime-tatara-i-suzu-hime.[35] She is the most beautiful in all the land. This pleased the emperor.

Ninth month, twenty-fourth day. The emperor installed Hime-tatara-i-suzu-hime as his official wife.

Year of the Metal Rooster [660 BCE], spring, first month, first day.[xxxiii] The emperor acceded to the imperial throne at Kashihara Palace. This year was set as the first of his imperial reign, and his official wife was honored as empress. She gave birth to the imperial princes Kamu-ya-i and Kamu-nu-na-kawa-mimi [Suizei].[xxxiv] Hence, there is a saying that goes, "At Kashihara in Unebi, the palace pillars were thick and planted to the depths of the bedrock, and the crossbeams of the roof rose even to the High Heavenly Plain. He thus ruled all under heaven as the first emperor." He was styled Emperor Kamu-yamato-iware-hiko-ho-ho-de-mi [Jinmu].[xxxv]

On the day when the emperor newly founded the imperial succession, the distant ancestor of the Ōtomo, Michi-no-omi, led the greater Kume and received secret orders, and by the effective application of metaphorical songs and indirect language,[36] drove off evildoers. This was the first use of indirect language.

Second year [659 BCE], spring, second month, second day. The emperor evaluated accomplishments and provided rewards. He granted Michi-no-omi land for a house, letting him dwell in Tsukisaka Village, and favored him with distinction.[xxxvi] He also made the greater Kume dwell on the land near the river to the west of Mt. Unebi. This is the reason that this land is now called Kume Village.[xxxvii] Utsu-hiko was made provincial chieftain of Yamato. He gave Takeda Village to Oto-ukashi, thereby making him the

---

35 The lineage of Hime-tatara-i-suzu-hime is given in S8.6 of the "Age of the Gods."
36 A reference to the Kume songs, which likened enemies to garlic roots, Japanese pepper, etc. Indirect language suggests code words and ciphers.

猛田縣主。是菟田主水部遠祖也。弟磯城名黑速、爲磯城縣主。復以劒根者、爲葛城國造。又頭八咫烏、亦入賞例。其苗裔、即葛野主殿縣主部是也。

四年春二月壬戌朔甲申、詔曰、我皇祖之靈也、自天降鑒、光助朕躬。今諸虜已平、海內無事。可以郊祀天神、用申大孝者也。乃立靈畤於鳥見山中、其地號曰上小野榛原・下小野榛原。用祭皇祖天神焉。

卅有一年夏四月乙酉朔、皇輿巡幸。因登腋上嗛間丘、而廻望國狀曰、姸哉乎國之獲矣。姸哉、此云鞅奈珥夜。雖内木錦之眞迹國、猶如蜻蛉之臀呫焉。由是、始有秋津洲之號也。

昔伊弉諾尊目此國曰、日本者浦安國、細戈千足國、磯輪上秀眞國。秀眞國、此云袍圖莽句儞。復大己貴大神目之曰、玉牆內國。及至饒速日命、乘天磐船、而翔行太虛也、睨是鄉而降之、故因目之、曰虛空見日本國矣。

卅有二年春正月壬子朔甲寅、立皇子神渟名川耳尊、爲皇太子。

七十有六年春三月甲午朔甲辰、天皇崩于橿原宮。時年一百廿七歲。

明年秋九月乙卯朔丙寅、葬畝傍山東北陵。

Agatanushi of Takeda. He is the distant ancestor of the Moitori of Uda.[xxxviii] Oto-shiki, whose name was Kuro-haya, was made Agatanushi of Shiki.[xxxix] Also, the one known as Tsurugi-ne was made Provincial Miyatsuko of Kazuraki.[xl] Ya-ta-garasu too was given an award. Its descendants are the Agatanushi of Kazuno.[xli]

Fourth year [657 BCE], spring, second month, twenty-third day. The emperor issued an edict, saying, "The spirits of my imperial ancestors looked down from heaven and illuminated Our body to aid us. We have now pacified the various enemies, and the realm is without incident. We must venerate the heavenly kami outside of the city and put our great filial piety into words." Then he established locations for venerating their spirits at Mt. Torimi, named those places Uetsuono-no-harihara and Shitatsuono-no-harihara, and venerated his imperial ancestors the heavenly kami.[xlii]

Thirty-first year [630 BCE], summer, fourth month, first day. The emperor went on a tour. On tour he climbed Hohoma Hill in Wakigami, looked around at the shape of the country, and said, "Ah, what a beautiful country I have obtained![xliii] Even though its interior is slender, it resembles the shape of dragonflies mating." For his reason, it was first called Akitsushima, or Dragonfly Island.[37]

In ancient times, Izanagi had named Yamato Urayasu-no-kuni, or Land of Tranquil Beaches, Kuwashihoko-no-chidaru-kuni, or Land of a Thousand Halberds, and Shiwakami-no-hotsuma-kuni, or Excellent Land of High Sea Cliffs. Also, Ō-ana-muchi called it Tamakaki-no-uchi-kuni, or Land within Jeweled Hedges. Nigi-haya-hi, riding a stone boat of heaven, flew in the sky, and when he looked down on this land, he descended here. Hence, this land was called Sora-mi-tsu-yamato, or Yamato as Seen from the Sky."

Forty-second year [619 BCE], spring, first month, first day. The emperor named the imperial prince Kamu-nu-na-kawa-mimi [Suizei] as crown prince.

Seventy-sixth year [585 BCE], spring, third month, eleventh day. The emperor expired at Kashihara Palace. At the time he was 127 years old.

The next year, autumn, ninth month, twelfth day. The emperor was buried in Ushitora Tomb on Mt. Unebi.[xliv]

---

37 Akizu means "dragonfly," which renders Akitsu-shima as "dragonfly island." The narrow, curved Yamato basin resembles this insect, which serves as a stand-in for the early Japanese state.

神渟名川耳天皇　綏靖天皇

神渟名川耳天皇、神日本磐余彦天皇第三子也。母曰媛蹈韛五十鈴媛命。事代主神之大女也。天皇風姿岐嶷。少有雄拔之氣、及壯容貌魁偉。武藝過人。而志尚沈毅。

至卌八歲、神日本磐余彦天皇崩。時神渟名川耳尊、孝性純深、悲慕無已。特留心於喪葬之事焉。其庶兄手研耳命、行年已長、久歷朝機。故亦委事而親之。然其王立操厝懷、本乖仁義。遂以諒闇之際、威福自由。苞藏禍心、圖害二弟。于時也、太歲己卯。

冬十一月、神渟名川耳尊、與兄神八井耳命、陰知其志而善防之。至於山陵事畢、乃使弓部稚彦造弓、倭鍛部天津眞浦造眞麛鏃、矢部作箭。及弓矢既成、神渟名川耳尊、欲以射殺手研耳命。會有手研耳命於片丘大窨中、獨臥于大牀。時渟名川耳尊、

Book 4
Emperors Suizei, Annei, Itoku, Kōshō, Kōan, Kōrei, Kōgen, and Kaika[i]

Treachery of Ta-gishi-mimi

Emperor Kamu-nu-na-kawa-mimi [Suizei] was the third son of Emperor Kamu-yamato-iware-hiko [Jinmu].[ii] His mother was called Hime-ta-tara-i-suzu-hime, the oldest daughter of the kami Koto-shiro-nushi. The emperor was refined in his appearance,[iii] possessed outstanding boldness from a young age, and when he blossomed into adulthood, was tall and impressive. He surpassed others in the martial arts and was ambitious, composed, and decisive.

When he was forty-eight years old, his father Emperor Kamu-yamato-iware-hiko expired.[1] In reaction, Kamu-nu-na-kawa-mimi was filled with a deep and earnest sense of filial piety, and there was no end to his sadness and longing. His mind was especially preoccupied by the funeral. His half-brother, Ta-gishi-mimi, was older and had more experience at court. For that reason, Kamu-nu-na-kawa-mimi entrusted Ta-gishi-mimi with matters of governance and had him rule directly. However, the older prince's disposition was far from humane and just. Furthermore, during the period of mourning he continued issuing rewards and punishments as he saw fit. Covertly he harbored treasonous intentions and made plans to dispose of his two younger brothers. This was the year of the Earth Rabbit [582 BCE].

Winter, eleventh month. Kamu-nu-na-kawa-mimi [Suizei] and his older brother Kamu-ya-i-mimi secretly became aware of the older prince's plan and adeptly prevented it. After their father was interred, they had Wa-ka-hiko of the bow-making hereditary guild make a bow, Ama-tsu-ma-ura[iv] of the smithing hereditary guild make fawn-slaying arrowheads, and the arrow-making hereditary guild make arrows. Once the bow and arrows were finished, Kamu-nu-na-kawa-mimi wanted to shoot and kill Ta-gishi-mimi. Fortunately, Ta-gishi-mimi was just then in a large chamber in Kataoka, lying down alone in a grand bed.[v] Kamu-nu-na-kawa-mimi said to

---

1   Suizei ruled for thirty-three years and died at eighty-four, which means that he did not take the throne until he was fifty-one. Since Jinmu died when Suizei was forty-eight, there was an unusually long three-year period with no sitting emperor.

謂神八井耳命曰、今適其時也。夫言貴密、事宜愼。故我之陰謀、本無預者。今日之事、唯吾與爾自行之耳。吾當先開窖戶。爾其射之。

因相隨進入。神渟名川耳尊、突開其戶。神八井耳命、則手脚戰慄、不能放矢。時神渟名川耳尊、掣取其兄所持弓矢、而射手硏耳命。一發中胸。再發中背、遂殺之。於是、神八井耳命、憮然自服。讓於神渟名川耳尊曰、吾是乃兄、而懦弱不能致果。今汝特挺神武、自誅元惡。宜哉乎、汝之光臨天位、以承皇祖之業。吾當爲汝輔之、奉典神祇者。是卽多臣之始祖也。

元年春正月壬申朔己卯、神渟名川耳尊、卽天皇位。都葛城、是謂高丘宮。尊皇后曰皇太后。是年也、太歲庚辰。

二年春正月、立五十鈴依媛爲皇后。一書云、磯城縣主女川派媛。一書云、春日縣主大日諸女絲織媛也。卽天皇之姨也。后生磯城津彥玉手看天皇。

四年夏四月、神八井耳命薨。卽葬于畝傍山北。

廿五年春正月壬午朔戊子、立皇子磯城津彥玉手看尊、爲皇太子。

卅三年夏五月、天皇不豫。癸酉、崩。時年八十四。

Kamu-ya-i-mimi, "Now is our chance! Keeping a secret is important, and caution is best. For that reason, I have not entrusted our secret plan to anyone else. Today, you and I alone will carry it out. First, I will open the door of the chamber, then you shoot him."

They went forward together and Kamu-nu-na-kawa-mimi quickly threw open the door. But Kamu-ya-i-mimi's hands and feet were trembling, and he could not let loose the arrow. Then Kamu-nu-na-kawa-mimi wrested away the bow and arrows from his older brother and shot Ta-gishi-mimi. The first shot hit him in the chest, the second in the back, and the last killed him. Kamu-ya-i-mimi agonized in shame and yielded to his younger brother of his own accord. Deferring to Kamu-nu-na-kawa-mimi, he said, "Though I am the elder brother, I acted cowardly and did not dare to kill our enemy. You have an exceptional godlike martial spirit, and you slew the villain all by yourself. I assent to your assuming reign as emperor and inheriting the enterprise of our imperial ancestor. I will serve as your assistant and take charge of the worship of the kami of heaven and earth." Kamu-ya-i-mimi was the first ancestor of the Omi of the Ō.[2]

Emperor Suizei

First year [581 BCE], spring, first month, eighth day. Kamu-nu-na-kawa-mimi [Suizei] acceded to the imperial throne. He built his capital in Kazuraki and called it Takaoka Palace.[vi] His mother, the empress, was honored with the title of empress dowager.[vii] This was the year of the Metal Dragon.

Second year [580 BCE], spring, first month. I-suzu-yori-hime was named empress.

<small>One text says that she was the daughter of the Agatanushi of Shiki, Kawa-mata-hime. One text says that she was the daughter of Ōhimoro, Agatanushi of Kasuga, I-tori-hime.[3]</small>

She was the emperor's aunt. The empress gave birth to Emperor Shiki-tsu-hiko-tamate-mi [Annei].

Fourth year [578 BCE], spring, fourth month. Kamu-ya-i-mimi perished. He was buried on the north side of Mt. Unebi.

Twenty-fifth year [557 BCE], spring, first month, seventh day. The imperial prince Shiki-tsu-hiko-tamate-mi [Annei] was named crown prince.[viii]

Thirty-third year [549 BCE], spring, fifth month. The emperor fell ill. On the tenth day, he expired. He was eighty-four years old.

---

2 The Ō were concentrated in present-day Tawaramoto Town, Nara Prefecture, where Kamu-ya-i-mimi is venerated at the Ō-ni-masu-mishiri-tsu-hiko Shrine. The Ō lineage group begun by Suizei's brother included Ō no Yasumaro (d. 723), author of *Ancient Matters*, and its lineage is provided in that work.
3 Original notes provide alternative accounts for the identity of empresses through Kōrei.

磯城津彦玉手看天皇 安寧天皇

　磯城津彦玉手看天皇、神渟名川耳天皇太子也。母曰五十鈴依媛命。事代主神之少女也。天皇以神渟名川耳天皇廿五年、立爲皇太子。年廿一。

　卅三年夏五月、神渟名川耳天皇崩。其年七月癸亥朔乙丑、太子即天皇位。

　元年冬十月丙戌朔丙申、葬神渟名川耳天皇於倭桃花鳥田丘上陵。尊皇后曰皇太后。是年也、太歲癸丑。

　二年遷都於片鹽。是謂浮孔宮。

　三年春正月戊寅朔壬午、立渟名底仲媛命、亦曰渟名襲媛。爲皇后。一書云、磯城縣主葉江女川津媛。一書云、大間宿禰女糸井媛。先是、后生二皇子。第一曰息石耳命。第二曰大日本彥耜友天皇。一云、生三皇子。第一曰常津彥某兄。第二曰大日本彥耜友天皇。第三曰磯城津彥命。

　十一年春正月壬戌朔、立大日本彥耜友尊、爲皇太子也。弟磯城津彥命、是猪使連之始祖也。

　卅八年冬十二月庚戌朔乙卯、天皇崩。時年五十七。

Emperor Annei

Emperor Shiki-tsu-hiko-tamate-mi [Annei] was the oldest son of Emperor Kamu-nu-na-kawa-mimi [Suizei].[ix] His mother was I-suzu-yori-hime, the younger daughter of the kami Koto-shiro-nushi.

In the twenty-fifth year of the reign of Emperor Kamu-nu-na-kawa-mimi, he was named crown prince. He was twenty-one years old.

Thirty-third year [549 BCE], spring, fifth month. Emperor Kamu-nu-na-kawa-mimi [Suizei] expired. In the same year, seventh month, third day, the crown prince acceded to the imperial throne.

First year [548 BCE], winter, tenth month, eleventh day. Emperor Kamu-nu-na-kawa-mimi was buried in Tsukita-no-oka-no-ue Tomb in Yamato.[x] The empress was honored with the title of empress dowager. This was the year of the Water Ox.

Second year [547 BCE]. The emperor moved the capital to Katashio,[4] calling his palace Ukiana Palace.[xi]

Third year [546 BCE], spring, first month, fifth day. Nu-na-soko-naka-tsu-hime was named empress.

Also called Nu-na-so-hime. One text says that she was the daughter of Hae, Agatanushi of Shiki, Kawa-tsu-hime. One text says that she was the daughter of the Sukune of Oma, Ito-i-hime.

Previously, she had given birth to two imperial princes. The first was called Oki-shi-mimi, and the second was called Emperor Ō-yama-to-hiko-suki-tomo [Itoku].[xii]

Another account says that there were three imperial princes. The first was called Oki-shi-mimi, the second Emperor Ō-yamato-hiko-suki-tomo, and the third Shiki-tsu-hiko.

Eleventh year [538 BCE], spring, first month, first day. Ō-yama-to-hiko-suki-tomo was named crown prince. His younger brother Shiki-tsu-hiko was the first ancestor of the Muraji of the Itsukai.[5]

Thirty-eighth year [511 BCE], winter, twelfth month, sixth day. The emperor expired. He was fifty-seven years old.[6]

---

4 It was customary to move the "capital," that is, the residence of the emperor, each time there was a change in reign until the first permanent capital was built at Fujiwara in 694 CE. Impurity caused by the death of the previous emperor, the convenience of relocating to the current residence of the rising emperor, and building decay have been suggested as reasons for this practice.
5 An allied miyatsuko group associated with raising hogs. In Tenmu 13.12, they are promoted to sukune.
6 As recorded, there is a ten-year miscalculation: if Annei acceded to the throne at twenty-nine, when he died in the thirty-eighth year of his reign, he would be sixty-seven, not fifty-seven as noted.

大日本彦耜友天皇　懿德天皇

大日本彦耜友天皇、磯城津彦玉手看天皇第二子也。母曰渟名底仲媛命。事代主神孫、鴨王女也。磯城津彦玉手看天皇十一年正春正月壬戌、立爲皇太子。年十六。

　卅八年冬十二月、磯城津彦玉手看天皇崩。

　元年春二月己酉朔壬子、皇太子即天皇位。秋八月丙午朔、葬磯城津彦玉手看天皇於畝傍山南御陰井上陵。九月丙子朔乙丑、尊皇后曰皇太后。是年也、太歲辛卯。

　二年春正月甲戌朔戊寅、遷都於輕地。是謂曲峽宮。二月癸卯朔癸丑、立天豐津媛命爲皇后。一云、磯城縣主葉江男弟猪手女泉媛。一云、磯城縣主太眞稚彦女飯日媛也。后、生觀松彦香殖稻天皇。一云、天皇母弟武石彦奇友背命。

　廿二年春二月丁未朔戊午、立觀松彦香殖稻尊、爲皇太子。年十八。

　卅四年秋九月甲子朔辛未、天皇崩。

觀松彦香殖稻天皇　孝昭天皇

觀松彦香殖稻天皇、大日本彦耜友天皇太子也。母皇后天豐津媛命、息石耳命之女也。天皇、以大日本彦耜友天皇廿二年春二月丁未朔戊午、立爲皇太子。卅四年秋九月、大日本彦耜友天皇崩。

Emperor Itoku

Emperor Ō-yamato-hiko-suki-tomo [Itoku] was the second son of Emperor Shiki-tsu-hiko-tamate-mi [Annei].[xiii] His mother was Nu-na-soko-naka-tsu-hime, granddaughter of the kami Koto-shiro-nushi and the daughter of the Kimi of Kamo. In the eleventh year [538 BCE], spring, first month, first day, of the reign of Emperor Shiki-tsu-hiko-tamate-mi, he was named crown prince. He was sixteen years old.

Thirty-eighth year [511 BCE], winter, twelfth month. Emperor Shiki-tsu-hiko-tamate-mi expired.[7]

First year [510 BCE], spring, second month, fourth day. The crown prince acceded to the imperial throne. Autumn, eighth month, first day. Emperor Shiki-tsu-hiko-tamate-mi was buried in Mihotoi-no-e Tomb south of Mt. Unebi. Ninth month, fourteenth day. The empress was honored with the title of empress dowager. This was the year of the Metal Rabbit.

Second year [509 BCE], spring, first month, fifth day. The emperor moved the capital to Karu,[xiv] calling his palace Magario Palace.

Second month, eleventh day. Ama-toyo-tsu-hime was named empress.

<small>Another account says that she was the daughter of the younger brother of Hae, Agatanushi of Shiki, Izumi-hime. Another account says that she was the daughter of Futo-ma-waka-hiko, Agatanushi of Shiki, Ii-hi-hime.</small>

The empress gave birth to Emperor Mima-tsu-hiko-kaeshi-ne [Kōshō].[xv]

<small>Another account says that he was the emperor's younger brother, Take-shi-hiko-kushi-tomo-se.</small>

Twenty-second year [489 BCE], spring, second month, twelfth day. Mima-tsu-hiko-kaeshi-ne was named crown prince. He was eighteen years old.

Thirty-fourth year [477 BCE], autumn, ninth month, eighth day. The emperor expired.

Emperor Kōshō

Emperor Mima-tsu-hiko-kaeshi-ne [Kōshō] was the oldest son of Emperor Ō-yamato-hiko-suki-tomo [Itoku].[xvi] His mother was Ama-toyo-tsu-hime, daughter of Oki-shi-mimi. In the twenty-second year [489 BCE], spring, second month, twelfth day, of the reign of Emperor Ō-yamato-hiko-suki-tomo, he was named crown prince.

Thirty-fourth year [477 BCE], autumn, ninth month. Emperor Ō-yamato-hiko-suki-tomo expired.

---

7   Annei's burial location, Mihotoi-no-e Tomb, is traditionally held to be in the Yoshida area of Kashihara City, Nara Prefecture.

明年冬十月戊午朔庚午、葬大日本彦耜友天皇於畝傍山南纖沙谿上陵。

元年春正月丙戌朔甲午、皇太子即天皇位。夏四月乙卯朔己未、尊皇后曰皇太后。秋七月、遷都於掖上。是謂池心宮。是年也、太歲丙寅。

廿九年春正月甲辰朔丙午、立世襲足媛爲皇后。一云、磯城縣主葉江女淳名城津媛。一云、倭國豊秋狹太媛女大井媛也。后生天足彦國押人命・日本足彦國押人天皇。

六十八年春正月丁亥朔庚子、立日本足彦國押人尊、為皇太子。年廿。天足彦國押人命、此和珥臣等始祖也。

八十三年秋八月丁巳朔辛酉、天皇崩。

日本足彦國押人天皇 孝安天皇

日本足彦國押人天皇、觀松彦香殖稻天皇第二子也。母曰世襲足媛。尾張連遠祖瀛津世襲之妹也。天皇、以觀松彦香殖稻天皇六十八年春正月、立爲皇太子。八十三年秋八月、觀松彦香殖稻天皇崩。

The next year, winter, tenth month, thirteenth day. Emperor Ō-yamato-hiko-suki-tomo was buried in Manago-no-tani-no-e Tomb south of Mt. Unebi.[xvii]

First year [475 BCE], spring, first month, ninth day. The crown prince acceded to the imperial throne.[8]

Spring, fourth month, fifth day. The empress was honored with the title of empress dowager.

Autumn, seventh month. The emperor moved the capital to Wakigami,[9] calling his palace Ikegokoro Palace.

Twenty-ninth year [447 BCE], spring, first month, third day. Yoso-tarashi-hime was named empress. The empress gave birth to Ama-tarashi-hiko-kuni-oshi-hito and Emperor Yamato-tarashi-hiko-kuni-oshi-hito [Kōan].

<small>Another account says that she was the daughter of Hae, Agatanushi of Shiki, Nunaki-tsu-hime. Another account says that she was the daughter of Toyo-aki-sada-hime of Yamato, Ō-i-hime.</small>

Sixty-eighth year [408 BCE], spring, first month, fourteenth day. Yamato-tarashi-hiko-kuni-oshi-hito was named crown prince. He was twenty years old. Ama-tarashi-hiko-kuni-oshi-hito was the first ancestor of the Omi of Wani.[xviii]

Eighty-third year [393 BCE], autumn, eighth month, fifth day. The emperor expired.

Emperor Kōan

Emperor Yamato-tarashi-hiko-kuni-oshi-hito [Kōan] was the second son of Emperor Mima-tsu-hiko-kaeshi-ne [Kōshō].[xix] His mother was Yoso-tarashi-hime, the older sister of Oki-tsu-yoso, the distant ancestor of the Muraji of Owari. In the sixty-eighth year, spring, first month of the reign of Emperor Mima-tsu-hiko-kaeshi-ne, he was named crown prince.

Eighty-third year [393 BCE], autumn, eighth month. Emperor Mima-tsu-hiko-kaeshi-ne expired.

---

8 Kōshō's accession uncharacteristically takes place over one year after the death of the previous emperor.
9 Perhaps the same Wakigami in present-day Gose City that appears in Jinmu 31.4.

元年春正月乙酉朔辛卯、皇太子即天皇位。秋八月辛巳朔、尊皇后曰皇太后。是年也、太歲己丑。

二年冬十月、遷都於室地。是謂秋津嶋宮。

廿六年春二月己丑朔壬寅、立姪押媛爲皇后。一云、磯城縣主葉江女長媛。一云、十市縣主五十坂彥女五十坂媛也。后生大日本根子彥太瓊天皇。

卅八年秋八月丙子朔己丑、葬觀松彥香殖稻天皇于掖上博多山上陵。

七十六年春正月己巳朔癸酉、立大日本根子彥太瓊尊、爲皇太子。年廿六。

百二年春正月戊戌朔丙午、天皇崩。

大日本根子彥太瓊天皇 孝靈天皇

大日本根子彥太瓊天皇、日本足彥國押人天皇太子也。母曰押媛。蓋天足彥國押人命之女乎。天皇、以日本足彥國押人天皇七十六年春正月、立爲皇太子。百二年春正月、日本足彥國押人天皇崩。秋九月甲午朔丙午、葬日本足彥國押人天皇于玉手丘上陵。冬十二月癸亥朔丙寅、皇太子遷都於黑田。是謂廬戶宮。

元年春正月壬辰朔癸卯、太子即天皇位。尊皇后曰皇太后。是年也、太歲辛未。

First year [392 BCE], spring, first month, seventh day. The crown prince acceded to the imperial throne. Autumn, eighth month. On the first day, the empress was honored with the title of empress dowager. This was the year of the Earth Ox.

Second year [391 BCE], winter, tenth month. The emperor moved the capital to Muro, calling his palace Akizushima Palace.

Twenty-sixth year [367 BCE], spring, second month, fourteenth day. The emperor's niece, Ōshi-hime, was named empress.

_{Another account says that she was the daughter of Hae, Agatanushi of Shiki, Naga-hime. Another account says that she was the daughter of I-saka-hiko, Agatanushi of Tōchi, I-saka-hime.[10]}

The empress gave birth to Emperor Ō-yamato-neko-hiko-futo-ni [Kōrei].

Thirty-eighth year [355 BCE], autumn, eighth month, fourteenth day. Emperor Mima-tsu-hiko-kaeshi-ne was buried in Waki-no-kami-no-hakata-no-yama-no-e Tomb.[xx]

Seventy-sixth year [317 BCE], spring, first month, fifth day. Ō-yamato-neko-hiko-futo-ni was named crown prince. He was twenty-six years old.[xxi]

One hundred and second year [291 BCE], spring, first month, ninth day. The emperor expired.

Emperor Kōrei

Emperor Ō-yamato-neko-hiko-futo-ni [Kōrei] was the oldest son of Emperor Yamato-tarashi-hiko-kuni-oshi-hito [Kōan].[xxii] His mother was Oshi-hime, thought to be the daughter of Ama-tarashi-hiko-kuni-oshi-hito. In the seventy-sixth year [317 BCE], spring, first month, of the reign of Emperor Yamato-tarashi-hiko-kuni-oshi-hito, he was named crown prince.

One-hundred and second year [291 BCE], spring, first month, Emperor Yamato-tarashi-hiko-kuni-oshi-hito expired.

Autumn, ninth month, thirteenth day. Emperor Yamato-tarashi-hiko-kuni-oshi-hito was buried in Tamate-no-oka-no-e Tomb.[xxiii]

Winter, twelfth month, fourth day. The crown prince moved the capital to Kuroda,[xxiv] calling his palace Ioto Palace.

First year [290 BCE], spring, first month, twelfth day. The crown prince acceded to the imperial throne. The empress was honored with the title of empress dowager. This was the year of the Metal Sheep.

---

10 Tōchi is the present-day Tōichi area of Kashihara City, Nara Prefecture.

二年春二月丙辰朔丙寅、立細媛命、爲皇后。一云、春日千乳早山香媛。一云、十市縣主等祖女眞舌媛也。后生大日本根子彦國牽天皇。

妃倭國香媛、亦名絚某姉。生倭迹々日百襲姫命・彦五十狹芹彦命亦名吉備津彦命・倭迹々稚屋姫命。

亦妃絚某弟、生彦狹嶋命・稚武彦命。弟稚武彦命、是吉備臣之始祖也。

卅六年春正月己亥朔、立彦國牽尊、爲皇太子。

七十六年春二月丙午朔癸丑、天皇崩。

大日本根子彦國牽天皇 孝元天皇

大日本根子彦國牽天皇、大日本根子彦太瓊天皇太子也。母曰細媛命。磯城縣主大目之女也。天皇、以大日本根子彦太瓊天皇卅六年春正月、立爲皇太子。年十九。

七十六年春二月、大日本根子彦太瓊天皇崩。

元年春正月辛未朔甲申、太子卽天皇位。尊皇后曰皇太后。是年也、太歲丁亥。

四年春三月甲申朔甲午、遷都於輕地。是謂境原宮。

六年秋九月戊戌朔癸卯、葬大日本根子彦太瓊天皇于片丘馬坂陵。

七年春二月丙寅朔丁卯、立欝色謎命爲皇后。后生二男

Second year [289 BCE], spring, second month, eleventh day. Hoso-hime was named empress.

<small>Another account says that she was Chi-chi-haya-yamaka-hime of Kasuga. Another account says that she was the daughter of the ancestor of the Agatanushi of Tōshi, Ma-shita-hime.</small>

The empress gave birth to Emperor Ō-yamato-neko-hiko-kuni-kuru [Kōgen].[xxv]

Imperial consort Yamato-no-kuni-ka gave birth to Yamato-to-to-hi-momo-so-bime, Hiko-i-saseri-biko, and Yamato-to-to-waka-ya-hime.[11]

Imperial consort Hae-iro-do gave birth to Hiko-sa-shima and Waka-take-hiko. The younger brother, Waka-take-hiko, was the first ancestor of the Omi of Kibi.[12]

Thirty-sixth year [255 BCE], spring, first month, first day. Hiko-kuni-kuru was named crown prince.

Seventy-sixth year [215 BCE], spring, second month, eighth day. The emperor expired.

Emperor Kōgen

Emperor Ō-yamato-neko-hiko-kuni-kuru [Kōgen] was the oldest son of Emperor Ō-yamato-neko-hiko-futo-ni [Kōrei].[xxvi] His mother was Hoso-hime, the daughter of Ōme, Agatanushi of Shiki. In the thirty-sixth year [255 BCE], spring, first month, of the reign of Emperor Ō-yamato-neko-hiko-futo-ni, he was named crown prince.

Seventy-sixth year [215 BCE], spring, second month, Emperor Ō-yamato-neko-hiko-futo-ni expired.

First year [214 BCE], spring, first month, fourteenth day. The crown prince acceded to the imperial throne. The empress was honored with the title of empress dowager. This was the year of the Fire Boar.

Fourth year [211 BCE], spring, third month, eleventh day. The emperor moved the capital to Karu, calling his palace Sakaihara Palace.

Sixth year [209 BCE], autumn, ninth month, sixth day. Emperor Ō-yamato-neko-hiko-futo-ni was buried in Kataoka-no-umasaka Tomb.[xxvii]

Seventh year [208 BCE], spring, second month, second day. Utsushi-ko-me was named empress. The empress gave birth to two boys and one

---

11 An original note adds for Yamato-no-kuni-ka, "Also called Hae-iro-ne," and for Hiko-i-saseri-biko, "Also called Kibi-tsu-hiko."
12 A regional lineage group based in Kibi, present-day Okayama Prefecture.

一女。第一曰大彦命。第二曰稚日本根子彦大日々天皇。第三曰倭迹々姫命。一云、天皇母弟少彦男心命也。

妃伊香色謎命生彦太忍信命。

次妃河內靑玉繫女埴安媛生武埴安彦命。

兄大彦命、是阿倍臣・膳臣・阿閉臣・狹々城山君・筑紫國造・越國造・伊賀臣、凡七族之始祖也。彦太忍信命、是武內宿禰之祖父也。

廿二年春正月己巳朔壬午、立稚日本根子彦大日々尊、爲皇太子。年十六。

五十七年秋九月壬申朔癸酉、大日本根子彦牽天皇崩。

稚日本根子彦大日々天皇 開化天皇

稚日本根子彦大日々天皇、大日本根子彦國牽天皇第二子也。母曰欝色謎命。穗積臣遠祖欝色雄命之妹也。天皇、以大日本根子彦國牽天皇廿二年春正月、立爲皇太子。年十六。五十七年秋九月、大日本根子彦國牽天皇崩。冬十一月辛未朔壬午、太子卽天皇位。

元年春正月庚午朔癸酉、尊皇后曰皇太后。冬十月丙申朔戊申、遷都于春日之地。春日、此云箇酒鵝。是謂率川宮。率川、此云伊社箇波。是年也、太歲甲申。

13　Who goes on to lead a rebellion in Sujin 10.
14　The lineages started by Ō-hiko were scattered across Japan. The Omi of Ahe were a powerful ancient lineage group. The Omi of the Kashiwade were an allied miyatsuko group responsible for providing and preparing court meals. The Omi of Ahe in Iga, differentiated in the original from the first lineage noted by the characters used for "Ahe," were concentrated in present-day Iga City, Mie Prefecture. The Yama-no-kimi of Sasaki were concentrated in the present-day Azuchi area of Ōmihachiman City, Shiga Prefecture. The Omi of Iga were concentrated in present-day Iga City, Mie Prefecture.
15　Who went on to serve emperors Keikō through Nintoku. His descendants are given in *Ancient Matters*. He is the ancestor of a striking twenty-seven lineage groups, twenty-five of which bore the hereditary nobility title of Omi.

girl. The first was Ō-hiko. The second was Emperor Waka-yamato-neko-hiko-ō-bibi [Kaika].^{xxviii} The third was Yamato-to-to-hime.

<small>Another account says, the emperor's younger brother was Sukuna-hiko-o-kokoro.</small>

Imperial consort I-kaga-shi-ko-me gave birth to Hiko-futo-oshi-makoto.

The next imperial consort Hani-yasu-hime was the daughter of Ao-tama-kake of Kōchi, and she gave birth to Take-hani-yasu-biko.[13]

The older child, Ō-hiko, was the ancestor the Omi of Ahe, the Omi of Kashiwade, the Omi of Ahe in Iga, the Yama-no-kimi of Sasaki, the Provincial Miyatsuko of Tsukushi, the Provincial Miyatsuko of Koshi, and the Omi of Iga.[14] ^{xxix} Hiko-futo-oshi-makoto was the grandfather of Takeuchi no Sukune.[15]

Twenty-second year [193 BCE], spring, first month, fourteenth day. Waka-yamato-neko-hiko-ō-bibi [Kaika] was named crown prince. He was sixteen years old.

Fifty-seventh year [158 BCE], autumn, ninth month, second day. Emperor Ō-yamato-neko-hiko-kuni-kuru [Kōgen] expired.

Emperor Kaika

Emperor Waka-yamato-neko-hiko-ō-bibi [Kaika] was the second child of Emperor Ō-yamato-neko-hiko-kuni-kuru [Kōgen].^{xxx} His mother was Utsushi-ko-me, the older sister of Utsushi-ko-o, the distant ancestor of the Omi of Hozumi.[16] In the twenty-second year [193 BCE], spring, first month, of the reign of Emperor Ō-yamato-neko-hiko-kuni-kuru, he was named crown prince. He was sixteen years old.

Fifty-seventh year [158 BCE], autumn, ninth month. Emperor Ō-yamato-neko-hiko-kuni-kuru expired.

Winter, eleventh month, twelfth day. The crown prince acceded to the imperial throne.[17]

First year [157 BCE], spring, first month, fourth day. The empress was honored with the title of empress dowager.

Winter, tenth month, thirteenth day. The emperor moved the capital to Kasuga,^{xxxi} calling his palace Izakawa Palace. This was the year of the Wood Monkey.

---

16 The Omi of Hozumi, descended from Kaika's uncle Utsushi-ko-o, were concentrated in the present-day Senzai area of Tenri City, Nara Prefecture. *Original Records* gives Utsushi-ko-o as the fifth-generation descendant of Nigi-haya-hi.

17 Kaika, like a selection of emperors to follow, takes the throne the same year that the previous emperor died. However, the counting of years of his reign does not begin until the new year.

五年春二月丁未朔壬子、葬大日本根子彥國牽天皇于劍池嶋上陵。

　　六年春正月辛丑朔甲寅、立伊香色謎命爲皇后。是庶母也。后生御間城入彥五十瓊殖天皇。

　　先是、天皇、納丹波竹野媛爲妃。生彥湯産隅命。亦名彥蔣簀命。次妃和珥臣遠祖姥津命之妹姥津媛生彥坐王。

　　廿八年春正月癸巳朔丁酉、立御間城入彥尊、爲皇太子。年十九。

　　六十年夏四月丙辰朔甲子、天皇崩。冬十月癸丑朔乙卯、葬于春日率川坂本陵。一云、坂上陵。時年百十五。

Fifth year [153 BCE], spring, second month, sixth day. Emperor Ō-yamato-neko-hiko-kuni-kuru was buried in Tsurugi-no-ike-no-shima-no-ue Tomb.[xxxii]

Sixth year [152 BCE], spring, first month, fourteenth day. I-kaga-shi-kome was named empress. The empress gave birth to Emperor Mi-maki-iri-biko-i-nie [Sujin].

> She was his stepmother.[18]

Previously, the emperor had taken Take-hime from Tanba as his consort. She gave birth to Hiko-yu-musu-mi. His next consort, the younger sister of Haha-tsu, the distant ancestor of the Omi of Wani, gave birth to Hiko-imasu.[19]

Twenty-eighth year [130 BCE], spring, first month, fifth day. Mi-maki-iri-biko-i-nie [Sujin] was named crown prince. He was nineteen years old.

Sixtieth year [98 BCE], summer, fourth month, ninth day. The emperor expired.

Winter, tenth month, third day. He was buried in Kasuga in Izakawa-no-sakamoto Tomb.[xxxiii]

> Another account calls it Saka-no-ue Tomb. He was 115 years old.

---

18 That is, an imperial consort of his father.
19 An original note adds that Hiko-yu-musu-mi was also called Hiko-komosu.

御間城入彥五十瓊殖天皇 崇神天皇

御間城入彥五十瓊殖天皇、稚日本根子彥大日々天皇第二子也。母曰伊香色謎命。物部氏遠祖大綜麻杵之女也。天皇年十九歲、立爲皇太子。識性聰敏。幼好雄略。既壯寬博謹愼、崇重神祇。恆有經綸天業之心焉。

六十年夏四月、稚日本根子彥大日々天皇崩。

元年春正月壬午朔甲午、皇太子即天皇位。尊皇后曰皇太后。

二月辛亥朔丙寅、立御間城姬爲皇后。先是、后生活目入彥五十狹茅天皇・彥五十狹茅命・國方姬命・千々衝倭姬命・倭彥命・五十日鶴彥命。又妃紀伊國荒河戸畔女遠津年魚眼眼妙媛、一云、大海宿禰女八坂振天某邊生豐城入彥命・豐鍬入姬命。次妃尾張大海媛、生八坂入彥命・淳名城入姬命・十市瓊入姬命。是年也、太歲甲申。

三年秋九月、遷都於磯城、是謂瑞籬宮。

Book 5
Emperor Sujin

Accession of Emperor Sujin

Emperor Mi-maki-iri-biko-i-nie [Sujin][1][i] was the second son of Emperor Waka-yamato-neko-hiko-ō-bibi [Kaika].[ii] His mother was called I-kaga-shi-ko-me. She was the daughter of Ō-heso-ki, the distant ancestor of the Mononobe.[iii] When the emperor was nineteen years old he was named crown prince. He was discerning and clever, and from a young age he was fond of grand strategies. By the time he blossomed into adulthood, he was broad-minded and prudent.[iv] He respected and revered the kami of heaven and earth, and always set his mind on the heavenly endeavor of governing the realm.

Sixtieth year [98 BCE], summer, fourth month. Emperor Waka-yamato-neko-hiko-ō-bibi expired.

First year [97 BCE], spring, first month, thirteenth day. The crown prince acceded to the imperial throne. The empress was honored with the title of empress dowager.

Second month, sixteenth day. Mi-maki-hime was named empress.[v] Previously, the empress had given birth to Emperor Ikume-iri-biko-isa-chi [Suinin],[vi] Hiko-i-sachi, Kuni-kata-hime, Chi-chi-tsuku-yamato-hime, Yamato-hiko, and Ika-tsuru-hiko.[vii] Also, his consort, the daughter of Ara-kawa-tobe from the land of Kii, Tō-tsu-ayu-me-maguwashi-hime, gave birth to Toyo-ki-iri-biko and Toyo-suki-iri-bime.[viii]

> Another account says, this consort was the daughter of the Sukune of Ōama, Yasaka-furu-ama-irobe.[ix]

His next consort, Ō-ama-hime of Owari, give birth to Ya-saka-iri-biko, Nunaki-iri-bime, and Tōchi-ni-iri-bime.[x] This was the year of the Wood Monkey.

Third year [95 BCE], autumn, ninth month. The emperor moved the capital to Shiki, calling his palace Mizukaki Palace.

---

1   Sujin means "revere divinity"; his pre-accession record includes a note that he "revered the kami of heaven and earth," and his worship of the kami, especially of the Miwa kami Ō-mono-nushi, is a prominent component of the Sujin book.

四年冬十月庚申朔壬午、詔曰、惟我皇祖、諸天皇等、光臨宸極者、豈爲一身乎。蓋所以司牧人神、經綸天下。故能世闡玄功、時流至德。今朕奉承大運、愛育黎元。何當聿遵皇祖之跡、永保無窮之祚。其群卿百僚、竭爾忠貞、共安天下。不亦可乎。
　五年、國内多疾疫、民有死亡者、且大半矣。
　六年、百姓流離。或有背叛。其勢難以德治之。是以、晨興夕惕、請罪神祇。先是、天照大神・倭大國魂二神、並祭於天皇大殿之内。然畏其神勢、共住不安。故、以天照大神、託豐鍬入姬命、祭於倭笠縫邑。仍立磯堅城神籬。神籬、此云比莽呂岐。亦以日本大國魂神、託渟名城入姬命令祭。然渟名城入姬、髮落體瘦而不能祭。
　七年春二月丁丑朔辛卯、詔曰、昔我皇祖、大啓鴻基。其後、聖業逾高、王風轉盛。不意、今當朕世、數有災害。恐朝無善政、取咎於神祇耶。蓋命神龜、以極致災之所由也。

Plague, Divination

Fourth year [94 BCE], winter, tenth month, twenty-third day. The emperor issued an edict, saying, "When my imperial ancestors, the various emperors, assumed their reigns as the polestars of the realm, was it for themselves alone? I think it was in order to provide for the people's bodies and minds and to govern all under heaven. For that reason, they made evident their profound accomplishments era after era, and in their own times, they disseminated the utmost virtue. Now We have humbly received charge of this great enterprise and provide loving nurture to the common people. How can We follow in the footsteps of our imperial ancestors and forever preserve the enduring altars of state? High government officials and other administrators, you must loyally serve and together administrate the realm in peace."

Fifth year [93 BCE]. There were many outbreaks of pestilence in the land, and more than half of the people died.

Sixth year [92 BCE]. People wandered, and there were rebels in the land. This trend was difficult to suppress with virtue. The emperor, waking early in the morning and fearful and reverent until late at night, entreated the kami of heaven and earth to say what crime had caused this calamity. Previously, the two kami Amaterasu and Yamato-ō-kuni-tama were both venerated within the imperial palace.[xi] Fearing their divine powers, however, the emperor was uneasy dwelling together with them. So he charged Toyo-suku-iri-bime[2] with venerating Amaterasu in Kasanui Village in Yamato. There he built an enclosed dwelling for the kami. Also, he charged Nunaki-iri-bime with venerating Yamato-ō-kuni-tama. However, Nunaki-iri-bime's hair fell out and her body became emaciated, so she could not perform the veneration.

Seventh year [91 BCE], spring, second month, fifteenth day. The emperor issued an edict, saying, "In antiquity, my imperial ancestor grandly initiated the foundations of the realm, and ever after, this sacred endeavor grew loftier, and the virtues facilitated by the ruler spread and flourished. But now in Our era, there have been a number of unexpected calamities. I fear that Our court's administration lacks righteous administration and that We are suffering the condemnation of the kami of heaven and earth. We must perform divination using turtle shells to discern the reason for these disasters."

---

2 Both Toyo-suku-iri-bime and Nunaki-iri-bime below were daughters of Sujin with consorts.

於是、天皇乃幸于神淺茅原、而會八十萬神、以卜問之。是時、神明憑倭迹々日百襲姫命曰、天皇、何憂國之不治也。若能敬祭我者、必當自平矣。

天皇問曰、教如此者誰神也。

答曰、我是倭國域內所居神、名爲大物主神。

時得神語隨教祭祀。然猶於事無驗。天皇乃沐浴齋戒、潔淨殿內、而祈之曰、朕禮神尚未盡耶。何不享之甚也。冀亦夢裏教之、以畢神恩。

是夜夢、有一貴人。對立殿戶、自稱大物主神曰、天皇、勿復爲愁。國之不治、是吾意也。若以吾兒大田々根子、令祭吾者、則立平矣。亦有海外之國、自當歸伏。

秋八月癸卯朔己酉、倭迹速神淺茅原目妙姫・穗積臣遠祖大水口宿禰・伊勢麻績君、三人共同夢、而奏言、昨夜夢之、有一貴人誨曰、以大田々根子命爲祭大物主大神之主、亦以市磯長尾市、爲祭倭大國魂神主、必天下太平矣。

天皇得夢辭、益歡於心。布告天下、求大田々根子、即於茅渟縣陶邑得大田々根子而貢之。天皇、即親臨于神淺茅原、會諸王卿及八十諸部、而問大田々根子曰、汝其誰子。

對曰、父曰大物主大神。母曰活玉依媛。陶津耳之女。

The emperor then went to the holy site Asajihara and assembled all the kami and inquired of them using divination.[xii] At that time, a kami possessed Kami-yamato-to-to-hi-momo-so-bime,[3] and said, "Why does the emperor bemoan the unrest in the land? If you humbly venerate me, certainly all will naturally be at peace."

The emperor asked, "What kami instructs me thus?"

The kami replied, "I am a kami who dwells in the land of Yamato, called Ō-mono-nushi."[xiii]

The emperor received the kami's words and performed ritual worship as instructed, but it had no effect. The emperor then bathed to purify himself and cleaned the interior of the palace, and then prayed, saying, "Is Our respect for the kami still not enough? Why is my uttermost supplication not received? Please, if I may exhaust all divine favor, explain this in another dream."

That night, a nobleman appeared in his dream, stood facing the palace door, and announced himself as Ō-mono-nushi, saying, "Emperor, do not despair any longer. The unrest in the land is by my design. If you make my child Ō-tata-neko venerate me, then things will immediately be at peace. Moreover, the lands across the sea[4] will also surrender of their own accord."

Autumn, eighth month, seventh day. Yamato-to-haya-kamu-asaji-hara-magu-washi-hime, the distant ancestor of the Omi of Hozumi, Ō-mina-kuchi no Sukune, and Ōmi,[5] Kimi of Ise, all had the same dream, and reported, "Last night in our dreams a nobleman appeared. He said, 'If you make Ō-tata-neko the head priest for veneration of Ō-mono-nushi and also make Naga-o-chi from Ichi-shi the head priest for veneration of Yamato-ō-kuni-tama, then certainly there will be peace in the realm.'"

The emperor heard about these dreams and was even more delighted. After the emperor widely proclaimed a search for Ō-tata-neko, he was found in Sue Village in Chinu District and presented to the emperor. The emperor himself promptly made for the holy site Asajihara, assembled the various lords and ministers and all of the hereditary guilds, and asked Ō-tata-neko, "Whose son are you?"

He replied, "My father is called Ō-mono-nushi, and my mother is called Iku-tama-yori-bime, the daughter of Sue-tsu-mimi." Another account says

3 A daughter of Emperor Kōrei.
4 Presumably referring to Mimana, on the Korean peninsula, which sends tribute in Sujin 65.
5 Meaning "hemp twiners" and referring to a hereditary guild responsible for providing rope to the Ise Grand Shrine.

亦云、奇日方天日方武茅渟祇之女也。

天皇曰、朕當榮樂。乃卜使物部連祖伊香色雄、爲神班物者、吉之。又卜便祭他神、不吉。

十一月丁卯朔己卯、命伊香色雄、而以物部八十平瓫、作祭神之物。即以大田々根子、爲祭大物主大神之主。又以長尾市、爲祭倭大國魂神之主。然後、卜祭他神、吉焉。便別祭八十萬群神。仍定天社・國社、及神地・神戸。於是、疫病始息、國内漸謐。五穀既成、百姓饒之。

八年夏四月庚子朔乙卯、以高橋邑人活日、爲大神之掌酒。掌酒、此云佐介弭苔。

冬十二月丙申朔乙卯、天皇、以大田々根子、令祭大神。是日、活日自擧神酒、獻天皇。仍歌之曰、

許能瀰枳破	このみきは
和餓瀰枳那羅孺	わがみきならず
椰磨等那殊	やまとなす
於朋望能農之能	おほものぬしの
介瀰之瀰枳	かみしみき
伊句臂佐	いくひさ
伊久臂佐。	いくひさ

如此歌之、宴于神宮。即宴竟之、諸大夫等歌之曰、

that she is the daughter of Ayashi-hi-kata-ama-tsu-hika-take-kechi-nu-tsu-mu.[xiv]

The emperor said, "We anticipate enjoying prosperity." He then divined whether to make the ancestor of the Muraji of Mononobe, I-kaga-shi-ko-o,[6] the court envoy for delivering paper streamers to the shrine. The reply was "Favorable." He also divined whether to go ahead with veneration of the other kami. The reply was "Not Favorable."

Eleventh month.[xv] The emperor ordered I-kaga-shi-ko-o to use the sacred offering vessels made by Yasote of the Mononobe, made Ō-tata-ne-ko the head priest for venerating Ō-mono-nushi, and made Naga-o-chi the head priest for venerating Yamato-ō-kuni-tama. Afterward he divined whether to venerate the other kami. The reply was "Favorable." Accordingly, he separately venerated all the various kami and established shrines to the kami of heaven and the kami of earth, as well as their lands and the people who would farm them. Thereupon the pestilence began to subside, and the land gradually became calm. The five grains ripened, and the people flourished.

Eighth year [90 BCE], summer, fourth month, sixteenth day. A man from Takahashi Village, Iku-hi, was made sake brewer for the great Miwa kami.[7]

Winter, twelfth month, twentieth day. The emperor made Ō-tata-neko venerate the great kami. On that day, Iku-hi personally consecrated sacred wine and presented it to the emperor. Then he sang,

> This sacred wine
> is not my sacred wine;
> it is the sacred wine brewed
> by Ō-mono-nushi,
> who finished creating the land of Yamato.
> May it ever flourish;
> may it ever flourish!

He thus sang, and they held a feast in the shrine.[8] Then at the end of the banquet, the various lower-ranked priests sang,

---

6 Likely a relative of Sujin's mother, I-kaga-shi-ko-me.
7 Ō-mono-nushi.
8 Presumably, the shrine that appears in the drinking party and poetic exchange at the end of this section was built for these spirits in the "Age of the Gods"; there is no discussion of a shrine being built during Sujin's reign.

宇磨佐開	うまさけ
瀰和能等能々	みわのとのの
阿佐妬珥毛	あさとにも
伊弟氐由介那	いでてゆかな
瀰和能等能渡塢	みわのとのとを

　於茲、天皇歌之曰、

宇磨佐階	うまさけ
瀰和能等能々	みわのとのの
阿佐妬珥毛	あさとにも
於辭寐羅箇禰	おしびらかね
瀰和能等能渡烏	みわのとのとを

　即開神宮門、而幸行之。所謂大田々根子、今三輪君等之始祖也。

　九年春三月甲子朔戊寅、天皇夢有神人、誨之曰以赤盾八枚・赤矛八竿、祠墨坂神。亦以黑盾八枚・黑矛八竿、祠大坂神。

　四月甲午朔己酉、依夢之教、祭墨坂神・大坂神。

　十年秋七月丙戌朔己酉、詔群卿曰、導民之本、在於教化也。今既禮神祇、災害皆耗。然遠荒人等、猶不受正朔。是未習王化耳。其選群卿、遣于四方、令知朕憲。

　九月丙戌朔甲午、以大彥命遣北陸。武渟川別遣東海。吉備津彥遣西道。

Sweet wine†
at the Miwa Shrine;
we hope to not leave its doors
until morning,
the doors of the Miwa Shrine.

At this, the emperor sang,

Sweet wine†
at the Miwa Shrine;
may you not push open its doors
until morning,
the doors of the Miwa Shrine.

Then he opened the doors of the shrine and went out. The man called Ō-tata-neko was the first ancestor of the Kimi of Miwa.

Ninth year [89 BCE], spring, third month, fifteenth day. A kami appeared in the emperor's dream. He gave instructions, saying, "Venerate the kami of Sumisaka with eight red shields and eight red halberds. Venerate the kami of Ōsaka with eight black shields and eight black halberds."

Fourth month, sixteenth day. The emperor, according to the instructions in the dream, venerated the kami of Sumisaka and Ōsaka.[9 xvi]

Rebellion of Hani-yasu-biko

Tenth year [88 BCE], autumn, seventh month, twenty-fourth day. The emperor issued an edict to the high government officials, saying, "The basis of leading the people lies in educating them. Now rites have already been performed for the kami of heaven and earth, and the disasters have all come to an end. However, people in far-away lands have not accepted the proper calendar, for they are still not accustomed to the virtues of kingly rule.[10] Select high government officials and dispatch them in all four directions, to promulgate Our rule."

Ninth month, ninth day. Ō-hiko was dispatched to the north, Take-nu-na-kawa-wake to the eastern seacoast, Kibi-tsu-hiko to the western circuit,

---

9   This worship perhaps relates the strategic positions of these sites for controlling passage east and west from the Nara Basin.

10 To accept the imperial calendar and the shared time of the empire implies surrendering to the Yamato state.

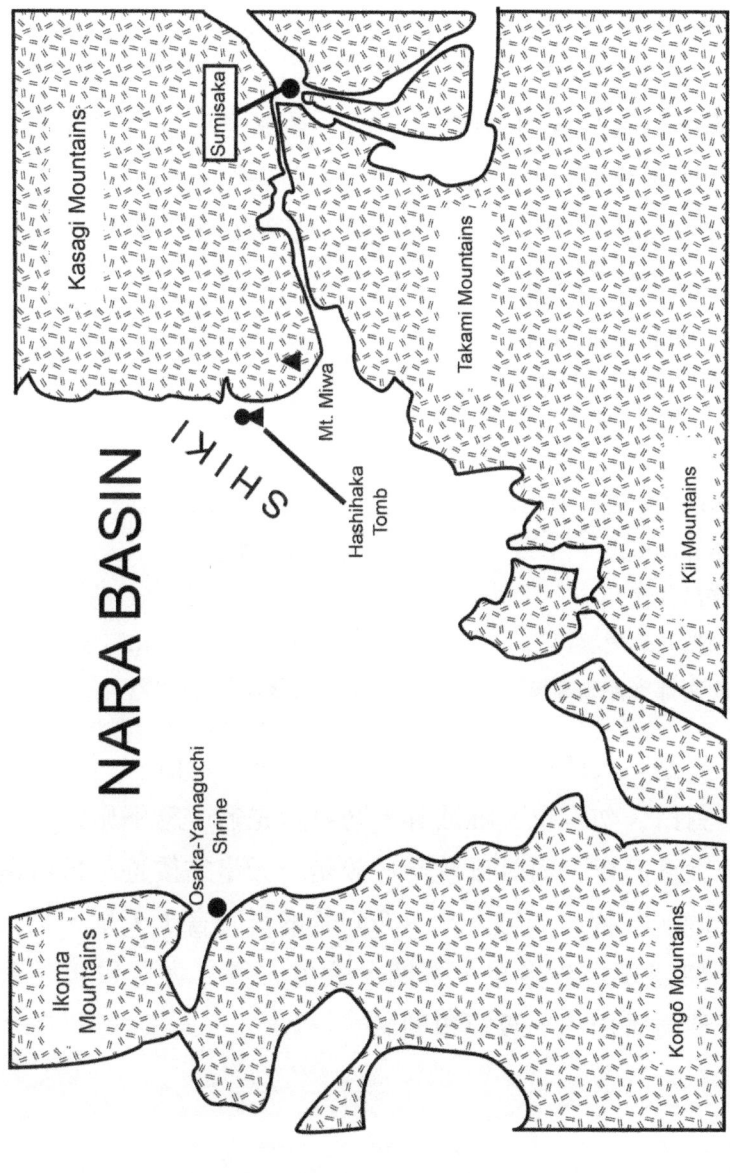

MAP 10 Sumisaka and Osaka. Sumisaka and Osaka were both positioned at strategic locations for entering the Nara Basin. Mt. Miwa overlooked Sujin's palace in Shiki. The Hashihaka Tomb, described below, holds the wife of the Miwa kami.

丹波道主命遣丹波。因以詔之曰、若有不受教者、乃舉兵伐之。既而共授印綬爲將軍。壬子、大彥命、到於和珥坂上、時有少女、歌之曰、一云、大彥命到山背平坂、時道側有童女歌之曰、

瀰磨紀異利寐胡播揶	みまきいりびこはや
飫迺餓烏塢	おのがをを
志齊務苔	しせむと
農殊末句志羅珥	ぬすまくしらに
比賣那素寐殊望	ひめなそびすも

一云、

於朋耆妬庸利	おほきとより
于介伽卑氐	うかかひて
許呂佐務苔	ころさむと
須羅句塢志羅珥	すらくをしらに
比賣那素寐須望。	ひめなそびすも

於是、大彥命異之、問童女曰、汝言何辭。

對曰、勿言也。唯歌耳。乃重詠先歌、忽不見矣。

大彥乃還、而具以狀奏。於是、天皇姑倭迹々日百襲姬命、聰明叡智、能識未然。乃知其歌怪、言于天皇、是武埴安彥將謀反之表者也。吾聞、武埴安彥之妻吾田媛、密來之、取倭香山土、裹領巾頭

and the Michinushi of Taniha to Tanba.¹¹ Then the emperor decreed, "If there are any who will not receive instruction, muster troops immediately and attack them." He bestowed upon each of them the insignia for the rank of general. On the twenty-seventh day, Ō-hiko arrived at the top of Wani Hill.¹² ˣᵛⁱⁱ

> Another account says that when Ō-hiko arrived at Hirasaka in Yamashiro, a young girl on the side of the road sang to him.

There, a girl sang to him:

Alas, Mi-maki-iri-biko!¹³
While you dally with the ladies,¹⁴
you know not that secretly
someone means to cut short
the thread of your life.

> Another account says,
> While you dally with the ladies,
> you know not even
> that someone is peeping in
> from the palace gate
> to kill you.

At this, Ō-hiko was suspicious and asked the young girl, "What are you talking about?"

She replied, "I didn't say anything. I'm just singing." Then she sang the previous song again and suddenly disappeared.

Ō-hiko promptly returned and reported this in detail. The emperor's aunt, Yamato-to-to-hi-momo-so-bime, being intelligent and wise, knew of things before they occurred. She understood the portent in the song and said to the emperor, "This is a sign that Take-hani-yasu-biko is plotting a rebellion. I hear that Take-hani-yasu-biko's wife, Ata-hime, has secretly come here, taken the soil of Mt. Kagu in Yamato, wrapped it in the hem

---

11 The north refers to the Hokurikudō northeast along the Sea of Japan. The eastern seacoast refers to the Tōkaidō, northeast along the Pacific Ocean. The west refers to the San'yōdō, westward along the Seto Inland Sea. Tanba is north of the capital and leads to the San'indō westward along the Sea of Japan.
12 The hilltop location suggests the vantage of the pass north to Yamashiro, as does Hirasaka in the note below.
13 Emperor Sujin.
14 There is no suggestion in the historical record of his reign that Sujin neglected his kingdom. Perhaps "dally" was meant as a metaphor for complacency after having appeased the kami and brought peace to the land.

而祈曰、是倭國之物實、則反之。物實、此云望能志呂。是以、知有事焉。非早圖、必後之。

於是、更留諸將軍、而議之。未幾時、武埴安彦與妻吾田媛、謀反逆、興師忽至。各分道、而夫從山背、婦從大坂、共入欲襲帝京。時天皇、遣五十狹芹彦命、擊吾田媛之師。即遮於大坂、皆大破之。殺吾田媛、悉斬其軍卒。

復遣大彦與和珥臣遠祖彦國葺、向山背、擊埴安彦。爰以忌瓮、鎮坐於和珥武鐰坂上。則率精兵、進登那羅山而軍之。時官軍屯聚、而蹢跙草木。因以號其山、曰那羅山。蹢跙、此云布瀰那羅須。更避那羅山、而進到輪韓河、與埴安彦、挾河屯之、各相挑焉。故時人改號其河、曰挑河。今謂泉河訛也。

埴安彦望之、問彦國葺曰、何由矣、汝興師來耶。

對曰、汝逆天無道。欲傾王室。故舉義兵、欲討汝逆。是天皇之命也。

於是、各爭先射。武埴安彦、先射彦國葺、不得中。後彦國葺、射埴安彦。中胸而殺焉。其軍衆脅退。則追破於河北。而斬首過半。屍骨多溢。故號其處、曰羽振苑。亦其卒怖走、屎漏于褌。乃脱甲而逃之。知不得免、叩頭曰、

of her shawl, made an invocation, saying, 'This stands for the true land of Yamato,' and then returned home.[15] Based on this, I know something is afoot. If you do not quickly make a plan, it will be too late."

In this circumstance, the emperor stayed the various generals and consulted with them. Shortly thereafter, Take-hani-yasu-biko and his wife Ata-hime plotted a rebellion, mustered troops, and suddenly attacked. Each took a different route, with the husband marching from Yamashiro and the wife marching from Ōsaka, with the intent of uniting forces and attacking the capital. The emperor dispatched I-sa-seri-biko to attack Ata-hime's forces. He prevented their advance from Ōsaka and routed them all. He killed Ata-hime and executed all of her soldiers.

Additionally, the emperor sent Ō-hiko and the distant ancestor of the Omi of Wani, Hiko-kuni-buku, to Yamashiro to attack Hani-yasu-biko. They secured consecrated vessels for ritual worship atop Takesuki Hill in Wani, then led their elite troops on a march up Mt. Nara, where they bivouacked. There the loyalist army assembled, trampling the grass and trees underfoot. For this reason, the mountain is called Mt. Nara, or Stomping Mountain. Then they departed Mt. Nara and marched to the Wakara River, where they faced Hani-yasu-biko across the water and each side challenged the other. Accordingly, people at that time changed the name to the Idomi River, or Challenge River. Now it is called the Izumi River, but this is a corruption.

Hani-yasu-biko gazed upon them and asked Hiko-kuni-buku, "For what reason have you mustered troops and come here?"

He replied, "You have gone against heaven and lack proper principles: you intend to overtake the throne. So I have marshaled the soldiers of justice and will put down your rebellion. This is what the emperor orders!"

Thereupon, the two exchanged arrows. Take-hani-yasu-biko shot first at Hiko-kuni-buku, but could not hit him. After this Hiko-kuni-buku shot Hani-yasu-biko, hit him in the chest, and killed him. Hani-yasu-biko's army cowered and fled. Then Hiko-kui-buku's force pursued and routed them north of the river. His army beheaded over half of them, and the place had an overabundance of corpses. Hence, this place is called Hafuri-sono, or Overabundant Garden. Also, Hani-yasu-biko's soldiers ran away in fear, and their feces leaked from their pants, so they removed their armor and fled. When they knew they could not escape, they kowtowed and said,

---

15 As in the Jinmu book, taking the soil from Heavenly Mt. Kagu serves as a stand-in for seizing control of Japan.

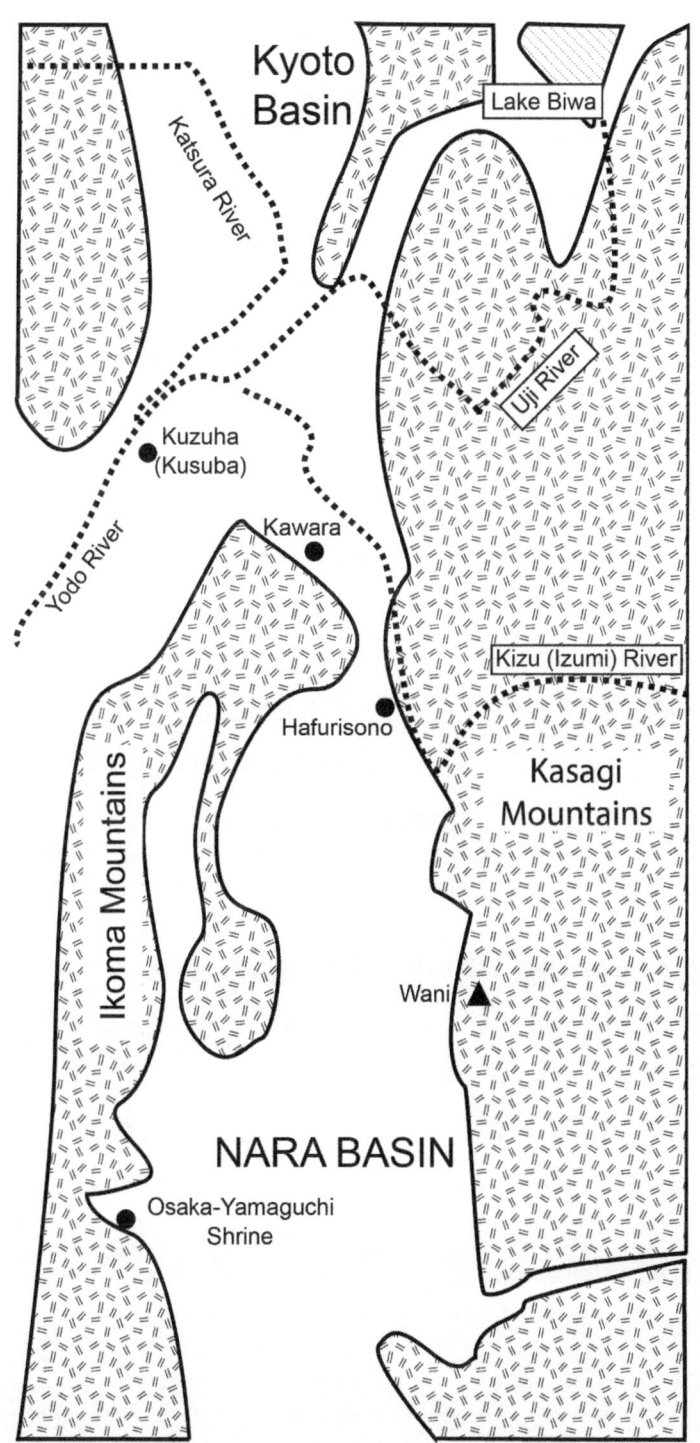

MAP 11 Revolt of Hani-yasu-biko

我君。故時人號其脱甲處、曰伽和羅。褌屎處曰屎褌。今謂樟葉訛也。又號叩頭之處、曰我君。叩頭、此云廼務。

是後、倭迹々日百襲姫命、爲大物主神之妻。然其神常晝不見、而夜來矣。

倭迹々姫命語夫曰、君常晝不見者、分明不得視其尊顏。願暫留之。明旦仰欲觀美麗之威儀。

大神對曰、言理灼然。吾明旦入汝櫛笥而居。願無驚吾形。

爰倭迹々姫命、心裏密異之。待明以見櫛笥、遂有美麗小蛇。其長大如衣紐。則驚之叫啼。

時大神有恥、忽化人形。謂其妻曰、汝不忍令羞吾。吾還令羞汝。仍踐大虛、登于御諸山。

爰倭迹々姫命仰見、而悔之急居急居。此云菟岐于。則箸撞陰而薨。乃葬於大市。故時人號其墓、謂箸墓也、是墓者、日也人作、夜也神作。故運大坂山石而造。則自山至于墓、人民相踵、以手遞傳而運焉。時人歌之曰、

飫朋佐介珥	おほさかに
菟藝廼煩例屢	つぎのぼれる
伊辭務邏塢	いしむらを
多誤辭珥固佐縻	たごしにこさば
固辭介氏務介茂	こしかてむかも

"Our lords!" So people at that time called the place where they shed their armor Kawara, Armor, and where their feces dropped from their pants, Kusobakama, Feces Pants. Now it is called Kusuba; this is a corruption. Also, people call the place where they kowtowed Akimi, Our Lords.

Legend of Hashihaka Tomb

After all this, Yamato-to-to-hi-momo-so-bime became the wife of Ō-mo-no-nushi. However, this kami always failed to appear during the day and came around only at night.

Yamato-to-to-hi-momo-so-bime said to her husband, "You always fail to appear during the day, so I cannot see your face clearly. I beg you to stay a while. Tomorrow morning, I wish to look upon your radiant and imposing appearance."

The great kami replied, "Your words shine with reason. Tomorrow morning, I will go into your comb case and stay. I ask you not to be shocked at my form."

In the back of her mind, Yamato-to-to-hi-momo-so-bime was discreetly curious at this. She waited until morning and looked in her comb case, and there was a small radiant snake inside.[xviii] Its length and thickness were that of clothing thread. She was shocked and screamed.

The great kami, ashamed, promptly changed into human form and said to his wife, "You lack composure and have brought me shame. Now I will shame you in return." Then he stepped up into the sky and climbed to Mt. Miwa.

Yamato-to-to-hi-momo-so-bime looked up in regret, then suddenly fell on her backside. When she did, a chopstick stabbed her in the vagina, and she perished. She was buried in Ōchi. Hence, people at the time called the tomb Hashihaka, or Chopstick Tomb.[xix] This tomb was made by humans in the daytime and by kami at night. Since they transported the stone from Mt. Ōsaka to build it, the humans formed a chain from the mountain to the tomb and moved the stone hand to hand. People at the time sang,

> Perhaps because they are passed from hand to hand
> we can transport
> these many stones,
> which continue to climb
> up this great hill.

冬十月乙卯朔、詔群臣曰、今反者悉伏誅。畿内無事。唯海外荒俗、騷動未止。其四道將軍等、今急發之。丙子、將軍等共發路。

十一年夏四月壬子朔己卯、四道將軍、以平戎夷之狀奏焉。是歲、異俗多歸、國內安寧。

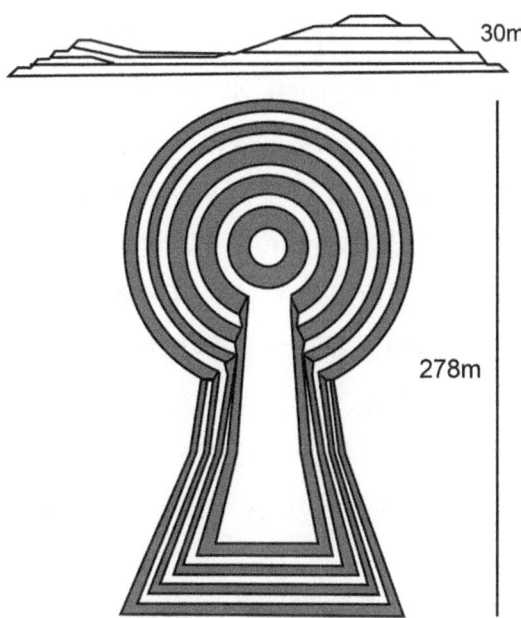

FIGURE 5 Hashihaka Tomb, Sakurai City, Nara Prefecture

Creation of Taxes, Establishment of Succession, Collection of Treasures from Izumo

Winter, tenth month, first day. The emperor decreed to the high government officials, "Now, all of the rebels have been executed, and the areas around the capital are without incident.[16] However, among the far-off provincial lands outside the capital area, noisy disruptions have not ceased. The generals for the four directions shall now depart immediately." On the twenty-second day, the generals were simultaneously dispatched to their circuits.

Eleventh year [87 BCE], summer, fourth month, twenty-eighth day. The four generals reported that they had pacified the barbarians.[17] This year, foreign peoples[18] surrendered in great numbers, and the country was at peace.

---

16 The capital area consisted of Yamato, Yamashiro, Setsu, Kōchi, and Izumi provinces, generally corresponding to present-day Nara, Kyoto, and Osaka Prefectures.
17 In the Sino-centric state system, the characters for "barbarians" specifically refer to peoples to the east and west, though the Japanese gloss is akin to "rustic."
18 People with different customs. Later they will also be characterized as speaking different languages.

十二年春三月丁丑朔丁亥、詔、朕初承天位、獲保宗廟、明有所蔽、德不能綏。是以、陰陽謬錯、寒暑失序。疫病多起、百姓蒙災。然今解罪、改過、敦禮神祇。亦垂教、而綏荒俗、舉兵以討不服。是以、官無廢事、下無逸民。教化流行、衆庶樂業。異俗重譯來。海外既歸化。宜當此時、更校人民、令知長幼之次第、及課役之先後焉。

秋九月甲辰朔己丑、始校人民、更科調役。此謂男之弭調、女之手末調也。是以、天神地祇共和享、而風雨順時、百穀用成。家給人足、天下大平矣。故稱謂御肇國天皇也。

十七年秋七月丙午朔、詔曰、船者天下之要用也。今海邊之民、由無船以甚苦步運。其令諸國、俾造船舶。冬十月、始造船舶。

卅八年春正月己卯朔戊子、天皇勅豐城命・活目尊曰、汝等二子、慈愛共齊。不知、曷爲嗣。各宜夢。朕以夢占之。

二皇子、於是、被命、淨沐而祈寐。各得夢也。會明、兄豐城命以夢辭奏于天皇曰、自登御諸山、向東而八廻弄槍、八廻擊刀。

Twelfth year [86 BCE], spring, third month, eleventh day. The emperor issued an edict, saying, "When We first assumed the heavenly rank and the maintenance of the altars of state, there were places where the brightness of our reign did not shine, and its virtue was unable to bring the people tranquility. For this reason, the system of yin and yang was in error, cold and hot lost their proper order, many pestilences occurred, and the people suffered calamities. However, now We have atoned for our crimes, corrected Our mistakes, and earnestly revere the kami of heaven and earth. Furthermore, We have provided instruction, subdued the provincials, and mustered troops to attack those who would not be ruled. Thereby, there is no impediment to court administration, and no people who can evade its coverage. Civilization has spread and the masses take joy in their productive enterprises. Foreign peoples come with many interpreters, and those overseas have surrendered. At this time, it is appropriate to conduct a census of the people and inform them of the order of old and young and the system for taxation and corvée labor."xx

Autumn, ninth month, sixteenth day. A census of the people began, and tax and labor assignments were levied. For men, it was a tax on bow nocks, and for women, a tax on handicrafts.[19] Thereby, the kami of heaven and earth were appeased, the weather conformed with the seasons, the many grains ripened, households were sufficiently provisioned, the people were amply supplied, and the realm enjoyed great peace. Hence, the emperor was styled "first emperor to rule the state."xxi

Seventeenth year [81 BCE], autumn, seventh month, first day. The emperor issued an edict, saying, "Boats are indispensable to the realm. At present the people along the coast suffer greatly when transporting things by land because they have no boats. I order the provinces to make boats." Winter, tenth month. They started building boats.

Forty-eighth year [50 BCE], spring, first month, tenth day. The emperor decreed to Toyo-ki and Iku-me, saying, "My loving kindness extends to both of you princes, and I do not know who should be made my successor. Each of you will have a dream, and We will divine it."

The two imperial princes received the order, bathed themselves, prayed, and went to sleep. Each had a dream. At dawn, the older brother Toyo-ki reported his dream vision to the emperor, saying, "Alone, I climbed to the peak of Mt. Miwa, looked to the east, thrust my halberd eight times, and swung my sword eight times.

---

19 The names of the taxes levied suggest that men would be paid in objects related to hunting and women with weaving and textiles.

弟活目尊以夢辭奏言、自登御諸山之嶺、繩絚四方、逐食粟雀。

　　則天皇相夢、謂二子曰、兄則一片向東。當治東國。弟是悉臨四方。宜繼朕位。

　　四月戊申朔丙寅、立活目尊、爲皇太子。以豊城命令治東。是上毛野君・下毛野君之始祖也。

　　六十年秋七月丙申朔己酉、詔群臣曰、武日照命一云、武夷鳥。又云、天夷鳥。從天將來神寶、藏于出雲大神宮。是欲見焉。則遣矢田部造遠祖武諸隅、一書云、一名大母隅也。而使獻。

　　當是時、出雲臣之遠祖出雲振根主于神寶。是往筑紫國、而不遇矣。其弟飯入根、則被皇命、以神寶、付弟甘美韓日狹與子鸕濡淳而貢上。

　　既而出雲振根、從筑紫還來之、聞神寶獻于朝廷、責其弟飯入根曰、數日當待。何恐之乎、輙許神寶。

　　是以、既經年月、猶懷恨忿、有殺弟之志。仍欺弟曰、頃者、於止屋淵多生菱。願共行欲見。則隨兄而往之。

　　先是、兄竊作木刀。形似眞刀。當時自佩之。弟佩眞刀。

The younger brother Iku-me reported his dream vision, saying, "Alone, I climbed to the peak of Mt. Miwa, roped off each of the four directions, and chased off the sparrows eating the millet."

Then the emperor told his two sons the meanings of their dreams, saying, "The older brother faced only the east, so he will subdue the eastern countries. The younger brother attended to all four directions, so he should succeed to Our throne."

Fourth month, nineteenth day. Iku-me was named crown prince. Toyo-ki was ordered to subdue the east. He was the first ancestor of the Kimi of Kamitsuke and Shimotsuke.[xxii]

Sixtieth year [38 BCE], autumn, seventh month, fourteenth day. The emperor issued an edict to the high government officials, saying, "The sacred treasures that Take-hina-teru brought down from heaven are stored in the Izumo Grand Shrine.[20][xxiii] I wish to see them." Accordingly, he dispatched the distant ancestor of the Yatabe allied miyatsuko, Take-moro-sumi, to present them to him.[21][xxiv]

At that time the distant ancestor of the Omi of Izumo, Izumo-furu-ne, owned the sacred treasures, but he had gone to Tsukushi and could not meet with Take-moro-sumi. Izumo-furu-ne's younger brother, Ii-iri-ne, received the emperor's order, and he entrusted the sacred treasures to his younger brother Umashi-kara-hisa and his son U-kazu-kune to be presented to the emperor.[xxv]

After Izumo-furu-ne returned from Tsukushi, he heard that the sacred treasures had been presented to the court and blamed his younger brother Ii-iri-ne, saying, "You could have waited a few days. What were you so afraid of, that you surrendered our sacred treasures so easily?"

On account of this incident, even after months and years had passed, Izumo-furu-ne still harbored anger and resentment in his heart, and so he intended to kill his younger brother. He deceived his younger brother, saying, "Around this time, there are a lot of water lilies growing in the pool at Yamuya. I want to go see them with you." So Ii-iri-ne accompanied his older brother, and they went.

Previously, the older brother had secretly made a wooden sword shaped like a real sword. He wore that sword himself, and his brother wore a real sword.

20 An original note adds, "Another account says Take-hina-tori. It is also called Ama-hina-toru."
21 An original note for Take-moro-sumi adds "One text says Ō-moro-sumi."

共到淵頭、兄謂弟曰、淵水淸冷。願欲共游沐。弟從兄言、各解佩刀、置淵邊、沐於水中。乃兄先上陸、取弟眞刀自佩。後弟驚而取兄木刀。共相擊矣。弟不得拔木刀。兄擊弟飯入根而殺之。故時人歌之曰、

椰句毛多菟	やくもたつ
伊頭毛多鷄流餓	いづもたけるが
波鷄流多知	はけるたち
菟頭邏佐波磨枳	つづらさはまき
佐微那辭珥	さみなしに
阿波禮	あはれ

於是、甘美韓日狹・鸕濡渟、參向朝廷、曲奏其狀。則遣吉備津彥與武渟河別、以誅出雲振根。故出雲臣等、畏是事、不祭大神而有間。

時丹波氷上人、名氷香戸邊、啓于皇太子活目尊曰、己子有小兒。而自然言之、玉萎鎭石。出雲人祭、眞種之甘美鏡。押羽振、甘美御神、底寶御寶主。山河之水泳御魂。靜挂甘美御神、底寶御寶主也。萎、此云毛。是非似小兒之言。若有託言乎。於是、皇太子奏于天皇。則勅之使祭。

六十二年秋七月乙卯朔丙辰、詔曰、農天下之大本也。民所恃以生也。

When they arrived together at the edge of the pool, the older brother said to the younger, "The pool is clean and cool. Let's go for a swim together." The younger brother agreed with what his brother said, and they each removed the swords they carried, placed them at the edge of the pool, and swam out into the water. Then the older brother got out first, took his brother's real sword and wore it himself. Afterward, the younger brother, shocked, took the older brother's wooden sword. They came to blows. The younger brother could not draw the wooden sword, and the older brother struck Ii-iri-ne and killed him. People at the time sang,

The scabbard of the sword worn
by the brave man of Izumo
where eight-fold clouds rise†
is adorned with much arrowroot,
but there is no blade inside. How sad![xxvi]

Then Umashi-kara-hisa and U-kazu-kune went to court and reported this affair in detail. The emperor dispatched Kibi-tsu-hiko and Take-nu-na-kawa-wake, who put Izumo-furu-ne to death. The Omi of Izumo, in dread of this affair, did not venerate the great kami of Izumo[22] for some time.

Around that time, a man called Hika-tobe from Hikami in Tanba said to the crown prince Iku-me, "My son is still a child.[xxvii] Yet he spontaneously says, 'Like a stone that sank among jeweled water lilies, this mirror, venerated by the people of Izumo, is a true and resplendent mirror. And also a respondent kami, overflowing in spirit. A jewel in the depths, an august master of the jewel. An august jewel, submerged in the mountain stream; a quietly hanging resplendent kami. A jewel in the depths, an august master of the jewel.' These do not seem to be the words of a child. Perhaps they are a divine revelation."[23] The crown prince made a report to the emperor. The emperor decreed that the great kami be worshiped.

Sixty-second year [36 BCE], autumn, seventh month, second day. The emperor issued an edict, saying, "Agriculture is the foundation of the realm and our subjects rely on it to live.[xxviii] Now there is a water shortage in

---

22 Ō-ana-muchi or Ō-kuni-nushi.
23 An examination of the treasure appears in Suinin 26.8, which suggests that it was returned in the interim, perhaps when the emperor heard about the oracle. There is debate over whether the treasure is a jewel or a mirror, but ultimately, the oracle is cryptic.

今河內狹山埴田水少。是以、其國百姓、怠於農事。其多開池溝、以寬民業。

冬十月、造依網池。

十一月、作苅坂池・反折池。一云、天皇居桑間宮、造是三池也。

六十五年秋七月、任那國、遣蘇那曷叱知、令朝貢也。任那者去筑紫國、二千餘里。北阻海以在鷄林之西南。

天皇、踐祚六十八年冬十二月戊申朔壬子、崩。時年百廿歲。明年秋八月甲辰朔甲寅、葬于山邊道上陵。

Hanita, in Sayama in Kōchi, and for that reason, the people of that land are neglecting agriculture.^xxix Dig many reservoirs and canals, and expand the livelihoods of the people." Winter, tenth month. The reservoir of Yosami was created. Eleventh month. The reservoirs of Karisaka and Sakaori were created.

> One account says that the emperor dwelt in Kuwama Palace and had three reservoirs made.

Sixty-fifth year [33 BCE], autumn, seventh month. The state of Mimana dispatched Sonagalchilchi to pay tribute at court.[24] Mimana is separated by the sea over two thousand leagues north of Tsukushi, to the southwest of Silla.[25]

The emperor expired on the fifth day of the second month, in winter, of the sixty-eighth year [30 BCE] after his accession. He was 120 years old. The following year, in autumn, on the eleventh day of the eighth month, he was buried in Yama-no-be-no-michi-no-e Tomb.^xxx

---

24 Mimana refers to states in the southern part of the Korean peninsula; here and in the Suinin book, specifically to Kŭmgwan Kaya. In the Kinmei book, the name is used to refer to the Kaya Confederacy.
25 Silla, given here as Shiraki, was a large state on the eastern side of the Korean peninsula.

活目入彥五十狹茅天皇 垂仁天皇

活目入彥五十狹茅天皇、御間城入彥五十瓊殖天皇第三子也。母皇后曰御間城姬。大彥命之女也。天皇、以御間城天皇廿九年歲次壬子春正月己亥朔、生於瑞籬宮。生而有岐嶷之姿。及壯偶儻大度。率性任眞、無所矯飾。天皇愛之、引置左右。廿四歲、因夢祥、以立爲皇太子。

六十八年冬十二月、御間城入彥五十瓊殖天皇崩。

元年春正月丁丑朔戊寅、皇太子即天皇位。

冬十月癸卯朔癸丑、葬御間城天皇於山邊道上陵。

十一月壬申朔癸酉、尊皇后曰皇太后。是年也、太歲壬辰。

二年春二月辛未朔己卯、立狹穗姬爲皇后。后生譽津別命。生而天皇愛之、常在左右、及壯而不言。

冬十月、更都於纏向。是謂珠城宮也。

是歲、任那人蘇那曷叱智請之、欲歸于國。蓋先皇之世來朝未還歟。故敦賞蘇那曷叱智、仍齎赤絹一百匹、

Book 6
Emperor Suinin

Accession of Emperor Suinin

Emperor Ikume-iri-biko-isa-chi [Suinin] was the third son of Emperor Mi-maki-iri-biko-i-nie [Sujin].[i] His mother the empress was called Mi-maki-hime. She was the daughter of Ō-hiko. The emperor was born in the twenty-ninth year [69 BCE] of the reign of Emperor Mi-maki, when Jupiter was in the mansion of the Water Rat, in spring, on the first day of the first month, in Mizuaki Palace.[1] From birth he had a refined appearance, and when he blossomed into adulthood, he was exceptionally generous. In personality, he was naturally genuine and unaffected.[ii] The emperor loved him and kept him at his side. When he was twenty-four years old,[2] on the basis of a sign in his dream, he was named crown prince.

Sixty-eighth year [30 BCE], winter, twelfth month. Emperor Mi-maki-iri-biko-i-nie expired.

First year [29 BCE], spring, first month, second day. The crown prince acceded to the imperial throne.

Winter, tenth month, eleventh day. Emperor Mi-maki was buried at Yama-no-be-no-michi-no-e Tomb.

Eleventh month, second day. The empress was honored with the title of empress dowager. The year was Water Dragon.

Second year [28 BCE], spring, second month, ninth day. Saho-hime was named empress.[iii] The empress gave birth to Homutsu-wake. When the child was born, the emperor loved him and always kept him at his side. When the child blossomed into adulthood, he could not speak.

Winter, tenth month. The emperor moved the capital to Makimuku,[iv] calling his palace Tamaki Palace.

Visitors from the Korean Peninsula

In this year, the man from Mimana, Sonagalchilchi, said that he wished to return to his land. He probably had not returned since coming to court during the reign of the previous emperor. Therefore, the emperor lavishly rewarded Sonagalchilchi and presented one hundred bolts of red silk to

---

1   Jupiter takes about 12 years to orbit the sun and was used to mark the year. It, along with the sexagenary cycle, was used in the *Chronicles* for marking time.
2   This would be twenty according to the years given in the Sujin book.

賜任那王。然新羅人遮之於道而奪焉。其二國之怨、始起於是時也。

　一云、御間城天皇之世、額有角人、乘一船、泊于越國笥飯浦。故號其處曰角鹿也。

　問之曰、何國人也。

　對曰、意富加羅國王之子、名都怒我阿羅斯等。亦名曰于斯岐阿利叱智于岐。傳聞日本國有聖皇、以歸化之。到于穴門時、其國有人。名伊都々比古。謂臣曰、吾則是國王也。除吾復無二王。故勿往他處。然臣究見其爲人、必知非王也。即更還之。不知道路。留連嶋浦。自北海廻之、經出雲國至於此間也。

　是時遇天皇崩。便留之、仕活目天皇逮于三年。天皇問都怒我阿羅斯等曰、欲歸汝國耶。對諮、甚望也。

　天皇詔阿羅斯等曰、汝不迷道必速詣之、遇先皇而仕歟。是以、改汝本國名、追負御間城天皇御名、便爲汝國名。仍以赤織絹給阿羅斯等、返于本土。故號其國謂彌摩那國、其是之緣也。於是、阿羅斯等以所給赤絹、藏于己國郡府。新羅人聞之、起兵至之、皆奪其赤絹。是二國相怨之始也。

　一云、初都怒我阿羅斯等、有國之時、黃牛負田器、將往田舍。黃牛忽失。則尋迹覓之。跡留一郡家中。

　時有一老夫曰、汝所求牛者、入於此郡家中。然郡公等曰、由牛所負物而推之、必設殺食。若其主覓至、則以物償耳、即殺食也。若問牛直欲得何物、莫望財物。便欲得郡內祭神云爾。

　俄而郡公等到之曰、牛直欲得何物。

be bestowed upon the Kokishi of Mimana.[v] However, people from Silla blocked his passage and stole the silk. The resentment between the two states first arose at this time.[vi]

It is also said, During the reign of Emperor Mi-maki, there was a man with a horn on his forehead who took a single ship and stayed at Kei Beach in Koshi Province.[vii] Accordingly, that place was named Tsunuga, "deer antler."[viii]

He was asked, "What land are you from?"

He replied, "I am a prince from Ōkara, named Tonoa Arasadŭng, also called Usagi Arijilji Kan'gi.[ix] I heard it said that there was a sage emperor in Yamato and came to pledge myself to him. When I arrived in Anato, there was a man in that land called Itsutsu-hiko, who told me, 'I am the king of this country.[x] There is no other king besides me, so do not go elsewhere.' I closely examined his temperament, however, and knew that he was certainly no king, so I set out again. I did not know the way, so I roamed the islands and beaches and circled the northern sea, passed through Izumo, and arrived here."

At that time, the emperor[3] had expired, and so he stayed and attended on Emperor Iku-me, and three years passed. The emperor asked Tonoa Arasadŭng, "Do you wish to return to your country?"

He replied, "I very much want to return."

The emperor then issued an edict to Arasadŭng, saying, "If you had not lost your way and had come here more quickly, you could have met the previous emperor and attended upon him. So change the name of your home country so that it bears the name of Emperor Mimaka; make that its name."[xi] Then he gave Arasadŭng red silk and returned him to his homeland. That country is called Mimana, and this is the reason. Arasadŭng stowed the silk that he was granted in a regional treasury of his country. The people of Silla heard of this, mustered soldiers and went there, then took all the red silk. Thus, the two countries began to hate each other.

Another account says, back when Tonoa Arasadŭng was in his own land, he loaded farming tools onto a tan-colored ox and led it to a barn in the fields, and the ox suddenly disappeared. He followed its hoof marks to search for it, and the tracks stopped at a village office.

At that time an old man said, "The ox you are searching for entered this district office. However, the district officers said, 'Based on the things loaded upon this ox, it certainly was meant to be slaughtered and eaten. If the owner comes looking for it, then we will compensate him for it.' They then killed and ate the ox. If they ask you what you want as restitution for the ox, do not seek treasure. Instead, say that you want the kami venerated in this district."

Soon after the district officials came and asked, "What do you want as restitution for the ox?"

---

3   Sujin.

對如老父之教。其所祭神、是白石也。乃以白石授牛直。因以將來置于寢中。其神石化美麗童女。於是、阿羅斯等大歡之欲合。然阿羅斯等去他處之間、童女忽失也。阿羅斯等大驚之、問己婦曰、童女何處去矣。

對曰、向東方。

則尋追求。遂遠浮海以入日本國。所求童女者、詣于難波爲比賣語曾社神。且至豐國々前郡、復爲比賣語曾社神。並二處見祭焉。

三年春三月、新羅王子天日槍來歸焉。將來物、羽太玉一箇、足高玉一箇、鵜鹿々赤石玉一箇、出石小刀一口、出石桙一枝、日鏡一面、熊神籬一具、幷七物。則藏于但馬國、常爲神物也。

一云、初天日槍、乘艇泊于播磨國、在於宍粟邑。時天皇遣三輪君祖大友主、與倭直祖長尾市於播磨而問天日槍曰、汝也誰人、且何國人也。

天日槍對曰、僕新羅國主之子也。然聞日本國有聖皇、則以己國授弟知古而化歸之。仍貢獻物、葉細珠、足高珠、鵜鹿々赤石珠、出石刀子、出石槍、日鏡、熊神籬、膽狹淺大刀、幷八物。

仍詔天日槍曰、播磨國宍粟邑、淡路島出淺邑、是二邑、汝任意居之。

時天日槍啓之曰、臣將住處、若垂天恩、聽臣情願地者、臣親歷視諸國、則合于臣心欲被給。乃聽之。

於是、天日槍自菟道河泝之、北入近江國吾名邑而暫住。復更自近江經若狹國、西到但馬國則定住處也。是以、近江國鏡村谷陶人、則天日槍之從人也。故天日槍、娶但馬國出嶋人、太耳女麻多烏、生但馬諸助也。諸助生但馬日楢杵。日楢杵生淸彥。淸彥生田道間守之。

He replied as the old man had instructed him. The kami that was venerated was a white stone. He received this white stone as restitution for the ox. He took the stone with him and placed it in his bedchamber, and the divine stone transformed into a beautiful young lady. At this, Arasadŭng was greatly pleased, and he wanted to sleep with her. However, while Arasadŭng was out, the girl suddenly disappeared. Arasadŭng was quite shocked, and he asked his wife, "Where did the young lady go?"

She replied, "She headed east."

He went in pursuit searching for her, and at last crossed the distant sea and entered the land of Yamato. The young lady that he was searching for had gone to Naniwa and became the kami of the Himegoso Shrine. Or she had gone to the district of Kunisaki in the land of Toyo and become the kami at the Himegoso Shrine. She is venerated in both these places.[xii]

Third year [27 BCE], spring, third month. A prince of Silla, Ame-no-hi-hoko, came to pledge his allegiance. The objects he brought with him were one fat-tipped magatama, one long-legged jewel, one shining red bead, one Izushi[4] short sword, one Izushi halberd, one sun-mirror, and one divine shrine dwelling; seven items in all. He stored them in the land of Tajima, treating them as divine objects.[xiii]

It is also said, At first Ame-no-hi-hoko took a ship and stayed in Shisawa Village in Harima. At that time, the emperor dispatched the ancestor of the Kimi of Miwa, Ō-tomo-nushi, and the ancestor of the Atai of Yamato, Naga-ochi, to Harima to ask Ame-no-hi-hoko, "Who are you? Where are you from?"[xiv]

Ame-no-hi-hoko answered, "I am a prince from Silla. However, I heard that in Yamato there was a sage emperor, so I bestowed my own country on my younger brother Chigo and pledge my allegiance to the emperor." Then he presented several objects: one slender-tipped magatama, one long-legged jewel, one shining red bead, one Izushi short sword, one Izushi halberd, one sun-mirror, one divine shrine dwelling, and one Isasa long sword; eight items in all.

Then the emperor decreed to Ame-no-hi-hoko, "Shisawa Village in the land of Harima and Idesa Village in the land of Awaji: dwell in these two villages as you see fit."

Ame-no-hi-hoko humbly said, "As for the place that I am to dwell, if with the blessing of the emperor, I might receive a place of my choosing, then I will personally tour the various lands and be granted a place in keeping with my heart's desire." The emperor accepted this proposal.

Then Ame-no-hi-hoko went up the Uji River to Ana Village in the north of the land of Ōmi and dwelt there briefly. Then from Omi he passed through Wakasa and went west to the land of Tajima, where he established his dwelling. Hence, the ceramists from the valley in Kagami Village in the land of Ōmi became his retainers. Ame-no-hi-hoko wed Matao, from Izushima in the land of Tajima, the daughter of Futo-mimi, and they gave birth to Tajima no Morosuke. Morosuke sired Tajima no Hinaraki. Hinaraki sired Kiyohiko. Kiyohiko sired Tajima-mori.

---

4   The name of a place in Tajima.

四年秋九月丙戌朔戊申、皇后母兄狹穗彥王謀反、欲危社稷。因伺皇后之燕居、而語之曰、汝孰愛兄與夫焉。

　　於是、皇后不知所問之意趣、輙對曰、愛兄也。

　　則誂皇后曰、夫以色事人、色衰寵緩。今天下多佳人。各遞進求寵。豈永得恃色乎。是以冀、吾登鴻祚、必與汝照臨天下。則高枕而永終百年、亦不快乎。願爲我弑天皇。仍取匕首、授皇后曰、是匕首佩于裙中、當天皇之寢、廼刺頸而弑焉。

　　皇后於是、心裏兢戰、不知所如。然視兄王之志、便不可得

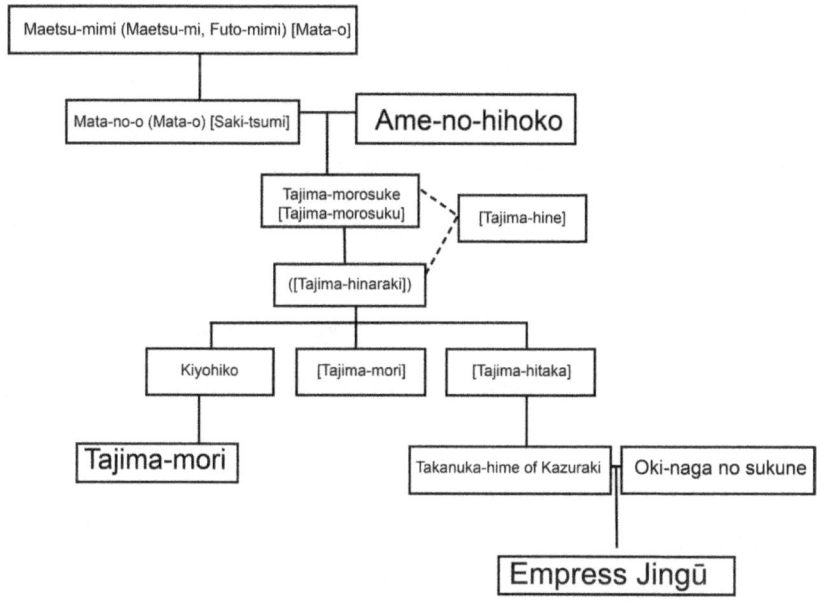

FIGURE 6 Lineage of Ame-no-hi-hoko, Tajima-mori, and Empress Jingū. Parentheses indicate elements from the *Chronicles* notes. Brackets and dashed lines indicate elements from *Ancient Matters*. Note that Tajima-mori has different lineages in these two works.

Treason of Prince Saho-biko

Fourth year [26 BCE], autumn, ninth month, twenty-third day. The empress's older brother, Saho-biko, plotted a rebellion and wanted to plunge the state into danger. To this end, he visited the empress while she was relaxing and told her, "Do you love your brother or your husband more?"

The empress knew not the reason he was asking and, without thinking replied, "I love my older brother."

Then he coaxed the empress, saying, "Those chosen to serve others based on their looks will see that affection fades when their looks wane. At present there are many beautiful women in the realm, each in turn seeking his affection. How long can you depend on your looks? My desire is to ascend to the position of emperor, after which we will without fail govern the realm together. Then we shall rest our heads on high pillows for the rest of our lives. Will that not be grand? I want you to assassinate the emperor for me." Then he took a dagger and bestowed it upon the empress, saying, "Wear this dagger inside your robe and when the emperor is sleeping, quickly stab him in the neck and assassinate him."

Thereupon the empress trembled with fear and did not know what to do. However, upon witnessing her older brother's ambitions, she could not

諫。故受其匕首、獨無所藏、以著衣中。遂有諫兄之情歟。

五年冬十月己卯朔、天皇幸來目居於高宮。時天皇枕皇后膝而晝寢。於是、皇后、既无成事。而空思之、兄王所謀、適是時也。即眼淚流之落帝面。天皇則寤之、語皇后曰、朕今日夢矣、錦色小蛇、繞于朕頸。復大雨從狹穗發而來之濡面、是何祥也。

皇后則知不得匿謀、而悚恐伏地、曲上兄王之反狀。因以奏曰、妾不能違兄王之志。亦不得背天皇之恩。告言則亡兄王。不言則傾社稷。是以、一則以懼、一則以悲。俯仰喉咽、進退而血泣。日夜懷悒、無所訴言。唯今日也、天皇枕妾膝而寢之。於是、妾一思矣、若有狂婦、成兄志者、適遇是時、不勞以成功乎。茲意未竟、眼涕自流。則擧袖拭涕、從袖溢之沾帝面。故今日夢也、必是事應焉。錦色小蛇、則授妾匕首也。大雨忽發、則妾眼淚也。

天皇謂皇后曰、是非汝罪也。即發近縣卒、命上毛野君遠祖八綱田、令擊狹穗彥。時狹穗彥興師距之。忽積稻作城。其堅不可破。此謂稻城也。

踰月不降。於是、皇后悲之曰、吾雖皇后、既亡兄王、何以面目、莅天下耶、則抱王子譽津別命、而入之於兄王稻城。

天皇更益軍衆、悉圍其城。即勅城中曰、急出皇后與皇子。然不

admonish him right away. So she received the dagger and, having nowhere to hide it, secured it in her robe. Perhaps she meant to remonstrate with her brother at a later time.

Fifth year [25 BCE], winter, tenth month, first day. The emperor toured Kume and was in Taka Palace. One time, the emperor was resting his head on the empress' lap, taking an afternoon nap. The empress, not yet having carried out the deed, suddenly thought that this would be precisely the time to go through with her brother's plan. Then her eyes teared up and the tears fell on the emperor's face. The emperor awoke and told the empress, "I just had a dream. A tiny brocade snake wrapped itself around my throat. Then a heavy rainstorm moved in from Saho and wet my face. What could this portend?"

The empress then knew she would not be able to conceal the plot, so she prostrated herself in fear and reported her brother's treason in detail. Then she addressed the emperor, saying, "I could not go against my brother's ambitions, nor can I betray my gratitude to the emperor. If I inform on my brother, then I will lose him, but if I do not speak, the altars of state will be toppled. For this reason, I have been sometimes in fear, sometimes in sadness. Looking up or down, there was bitter wailing, going forward or backward, I was choked by tears. My days and nights have been filled with despair, and so I did not give away his plan. But today, the emperor put his head on my lap and fell asleep. Because of this, I thought, in the corner of my mind, if I were an insane wife and meant to fulfill my brother's wishes, now would be the time, so wouldn't I follow through without difficulty? While I was thinking this, my tears began to flow on their own, and I raised my sleeve to wipe them away. My sleeves became saturated and dripped onto your face. The reason for your dream today is no doubt in response to these matters. The tiny brocade snake is the dagger I received, and the sudden heavy rainfall was my tears."

The emperor said to the empress, "This is not your crime." Then he promptly called up soldiers from nearby regions and ordered the distant ancestor of the Kimi of Kamitsuke, Ya-tsuna-da, to attack Saho-biko.[XV] In turn, Saho-biko mustered his army and prevented their advance, then he quickly piled up rice stalks and made a stronghold whose fortifications were too reinforced to be breached. This was called the rice fortress.

One month passed, and Saho-biko had not surrendered. At that, the empress said with regret, "Though I am the empress, with my brother being lost, how can I attend on the realm?" Then clutching Prince Homutsu-wake, she went into her brother's rice fortress.

The emperor increased the numbers of his force and completely surrounded the fortress. Then he decreed to those inside, "Release the empress and the imperial prince immediately!" However, they did not

出矣。則將軍八綱田、放火焚其城。

於焉、皇后令懷抱皇子、踰城上而出之。因以奏請曰、妾始所以逃入兄城、若有因妾子、免兄罪乎。今不得免、乃知、妾有罪。何得面縛。自經而死耳。唯妾雖死之、敢勿忘天皇之恩。願妾所掌后宮之事、宜授好仇。其丹波國有五婦人。志並貞潔。是丹波道主王之女也。道主王者、稚日本根子太日々天皇之孫、彦坐王子也。一云、彦湯産隅王之子也。當納掖庭、以盈后宮之數。

天皇聽矣。時火興城崩、軍衆悉走。狹穗彦與妹共死于城中。天皇、於是、美將軍八綱田之功、號其名謂倭日向武日向彦八綱田也。

七年秋七月己巳朔乙亥、左右奏言、當麻邑有勇悍士、曰當摩蹶速。其爲人也、強力以能毀角申鉤。恆語衆中曰、於四方求之、豈有比我力者乎。何遇強力者、而不期死生、頓得爭力焉。

天皇聞之、詔群卿曰、朕聞、當摩蹶速者、天下之力士也。若有比此人耶。

一臣進言、臣聞、出雲國有勇士。曰野見宿禰。試召是人、欲當于蹶速。即日、遣倭直祖長尾市、喚野見宿禰。

於是、野見宿禰、自出雲至。則當摩蹶速與野見宿禰令捔力。二人相對立。各舉足相蹶。則蹶折當摩蹶速之脇骨。亦蹈

let them out, and so General Ya-tsuna-da lit a fire and set the fortress ablaze.

Then the empress clutched the imperial prince to her bosom, scaled the fortress walls, and made it out. She addressed the emperor, saying, "The reason I first fled to my brother's fortress was that if he had me and the child, his crime might be pardoned. But now he cannot be pardoned, and I know that I too am guilty. How could I face you with my hands tied behind my back like a criminal? My only recourse is to hang myself. However, even if I die, I can never forget the depths of my gratitude to the emperor. I hope that the inner palace that I managed can be bestowed upon a good spouse. In the land of Tanba, there are five women, all of pure intentions. They are the daughters of the Kimi and Michinushi of Tanba.

<small>The Kimi and Michinushi of Tanba was the grandson of Emperor Waka-yamato-neko-ō-bibi, the son of Hiko-imasu. Another account says that he was the son of Hiko-yusumi.</small>

Invite them to the inner palace, so as to fill its numbers."

The emperor agreed. Then the fire surged, the fortress collapsed, and the soldiers all ran. Saho-biko and his younger sister both died in the fortress. Thereupon the emperor praised the accomplishments of General Ya-tsuna-da and renamed him Yamato-himuka-take-himuka-hiko-ya-tsuna-da.

Duel of Ke-haya and Nomi no Sukune, Maidens of Tanba, Cure of Prince Homutsu-wake

Seventh year [23 BCE], autumn, seventh month, seventh day. Those near the emperor addressed him, saying, "In Tagima Village, there is a mighty and terrible man named Tagima no Ke-haya, or the "swift kicker of Tagima." His strength is enough to break horns and straighten fishhooks.[xvi] He is always telling the crowds, "I have searched in every direction, and there seems to be no one who can match my power. I want to meet someone strong enough to engage me in a contest of strength with no regard for life or death."

The emperor heard this and decreed to the high government officials, "We hear of Tagima no Ke-haya, a strong man of the realm. Is there one who perhaps can contest him?"

One minister came forth and said, "I have heard that in the land of Izumo there is a mighty man named Nomi no Sukune. Try summoning him and having him challenge Tagima no Ke-haya." That very day, the ancestor of the Atai of Yamato, Naga-ochi, was sent to call on Nomi no Sukune.

In due course, Nomi no Sukune arrived from Izumo. So Tagima no Ke-haya and Nomi no Sukune were ordered to compete in strength. The two stood facing each other, then each raised his legs to kick each other. Nomi no Sukune kicked and broke Tagima no Ke-haya's ribs, then trampled him,

折其腰而殺之。故奪當摩蹶速之地、悉賜野見宿禰。是以其邑有腰折田之緣也。野見宿禰乃留仕焉。

　十五年春二月乙卯朔甲子、喚丹波五女、納於掖庭。第一曰日葉酢媛。第二曰淳葉田瓊入媛。第三曰眞砥野媛。第四曰薊瓊入媛。第五曰竹野媛。

　秋八月壬午朔、立日葉酢媛命爲皇后、以皇后弟之三女爲妃。唯竹野媛者、因形姿醜、返於本土。則羞其見返葛野、自墮輿而死之。故號其地謂墮國。今謂弟國訛也。

　皇后日葉酢媛命、生三男二女。第一曰五十瓊敷入彥命。第二曰大足彥尊。第三曰大中姬命。第四曰倭姬命。第五曰稚城瓊入彥命。妃淳葉田瓊入媛、生鐸石別命與膽香足姬命。次妃薊瓊入媛、生池速別命・稚淺津姬命。

　廿三年秋九月丙寅朔丁卯、詔群卿曰、譽津別王、是生年既卅、髯鬚八掬、猶泣如兒。常不言、何由矣。因有司而議之。

　冬十月乙丑朔壬申、天皇立於大殿前。譽津別皇子侍之。時有鳴鵠、度大虛。皇子仰觀鵠曰、是何物耶。

　天皇則知皇子見鵠得言而喜之。詔左右曰、誰能捕是鳥獻之。

　於是、鳥取造祖天湯河板擧奏言、臣必捕而獻。

broke his pelvis, and killed him. Thereupon the emperor confiscated Tagima no Ke-haya's lands and bestowed them entirely upon Nomi no Sukune. For this reason, this village has a place called Koshioreda, or Hip-Breaker Field. Nomi no Sukune stayed and attended court.

Fifteenth year [15 BCE], spring, second month, tenth day. The emperor summoned the five maidens of Tanba and installed them in the inner palace. The first was called Hi-basu-hime, the second Nuha-tani-iri-bime, the third Ma-tono-hime, the fourth Azami-ni-iri-bime, and the fifth Taka-no-hime.

Autumn, eighth month, first day. Hi-basu-hime was named empress. The empress's three younger sisters were named consorts. Only Taka-no-hime, because she was ugly, was sent back to her homeland. Ashamed at being so returned, she threw herself from her palanquin at Kazuno and died. Consequently, this place is called Ochikuni, or Land of Falls. Now it is called Otokuni, a corruption.[xvii]

Empress Hi-basu-hime gave birth to three boys and two girls. The first was I-ni-shiki-iri-biko. The second was Ō-tarashi-hiko.[xviii] The third was Ō-naka-tsu-hime. The fourth was Yamato-hime. The fifth was Waka-ki-ni-iri-biko. Consort Nuha-tani-iri-bime gave birth to Nu-te-shi-wake and I-ka-tarashi-hime. Next, Consort Azami-ni-iri-bime gave birth to Ike-haya-wake and Waka-asa-tsu-hime.

Twenty-third year [7 BCE], autumn, ninth month, second day. The emperor issued an edict to the high government officials, saying, "Prince Homutsu-wake is already thirty years old[5] and has long whiskers and a beard, but he still cries like a child and cannot speak normally. What is the reason for this? Confer on this with the relevant officials."

Winter, tenth month, eighth day. The emperor stood before the great palace with Imperial Prince Homutsu-wake[6] attending on him. At that time, a white swan flew through the sky. The imperial prince looked up and saw the swan and said, "What is that?"

The emperor realized that the imperial prince had seen the swan and spoken, and was greatly pleased. He proclaimed to those around him, "Who can catch that swan and present it to me?"

At this, the ancestor of the Allied Miyatsuko of Totori, Ame-no-yu-ka-wa-tana, said, "I will definitely catch it and present it to you."

---

5   This would make Homutsu-wake born in Sujin 62 and twelve years old when his mother carried him out of the fortress during Saho-biko's rebellion.
6   This is the first use of "Imperial Prince" as a formal title. Consistent usage of the title does not begin until the Keikō book.

即天皇勅湯河板舉板舉、此云拕儺日、汝獻是鳥、必敦賞矣。

時湯河板舉、遠望鵠飛之方、追尋詣出雲、而捕獲。或曰、得于但馬國。

十一月甲午朔乙未、湯河板舉獻鵠也。譽津別命弄是鵠、遂得言語。由是、以敦賞湯河板舉。則賜姓而曰鳥取造。因亦定鳥取部・鳥養部・譽津部。

廿五年春二月丁巳朔甲子、詔阿倍臣遠祖武渟川別・和珥臣遠祖彥國葺・中臣連遠祖大鹿嶋・物部連遠祖十千根・大伴連遠祖武日、五大夫曰、我先皇御間城入彥五十瓊殖天皇、惟叡作聖。欽明聰達。深執謙損、志懷沖退。綢繆機衡、禮祭神祇。剋己勤躬、日愼一日。是以人民富足、天下太平也。今當朕世、祭祀神祇、豈得有怠乎。

三月丁亥朔丙申、離天照大神於豐耜入姬命、託于倭姬命。爰倭姬命求鎭坐大神之處、而詣莵田筱幡。筱、此云佐佐。更還之入近江國、東廻美濃、到伊勢國。時、天照大神誨倭姬命曰、是神風伊勢國、則常世之浪重浪歸國也。

The emperor immediately decreed to Yu-kawa-tana, "If you present that bird, you will be richly rewarded."

Yu-kawa-tana gazed into the distance in the direction the bird had flown, pursued it to Izumo, and captured it. It is also said that he caught it in Tajima.

Eleventh month, second day. Yu-kawa-tana presented the swan to the emperor. Homutsu-wake played with the swan, and subsequently was able to speak. Hence, the emperor richly rewarded Yu-kawa-tana and gave him the title Miyatsuko of Totori. Also, because of his merit, he established the Totori, Torikai, and Homutsu hereditary guilds.[7]

Worship of Amaterasu and Yamato-no-ō-kami

Twenty-fifth year [5 BCE], spring, second month, eighth day. The emperor issued an edict to the distant ancestor of the Omi of Abe, Take-nu-kawa-wake; the distant ancestor of the Omi of Wani, Hiko-kuni-buku; the distant ancestor of the Muraji of the Nakatomi, Ō-ka-shima; the distant ancestor of the Muraji of the Mononobe, Tōchine; and the distant ancestor of the Muraji of the Ōtomo, Takehi.[8] He pronounced to these five ministers, "The emperor who preceded me, Mimaki-iri-biko-i-nie, was astute and well-versed in matters, respectful and wise about knowledgeable accomplishment, deeply modest and humble, unpretentious in ambition and goals, consolidating in administrating the court, and reverently venerating of the kami of heaven and earth. He overcame his private desires and exerted himself day after day while remaining circumspect. Because of these attributes, the people enjoyed wealth and abundance, and the realm was blessed with great peace. Now in Our own era, how could We be negligent in performing ritual worship of the kami of heaven and earth?"

Third month, tenth day. The emperor released Toyo-suku-hime from service to Amaterasu and entrusted worship of this goddess instead to Yamato-hime. Thereupon Yamato-hime searched for a place to enshrine the kami and went to Sasahata in Uda. Then she backtracked and entered the land of Ōmi, went east to Minō, and arrived in the land of Ise. At that time, Amaterasu instructed Yamato-hime, saying, "In Ise, land of the divine wind, the waves from Tokoyo come in over and over again. It is a

---

7 The Totori were charged with capturing swans, the Torikai with raising them, and the Homutsu with maintaining lands to support Prince Homutsu-wake.
8 Take-nu-kawa-wake was a general dispatched to the east in Sujin 10.9. Hiko-kuni-buku aided in putting down the rebellion of Hani-yasu-biko in Sujin 10. Tōchine will later be charged with keeping of the treasures of Izumo. Takehi will be sent with Yamato Take to attack the east in Keikō 40.7.

傍國可怜國也。欲居是國。故隨大神教、其祠立於伊勢國。因興齋宮于五十鈴川上。是謂磯宮。則天照大神始自天降之處也。

　一云、天皇以倭姬命爲御杖、貢奉於天照大神。是以倭姬命以天照大神、鎭坐於磯城嚴橿之本而祠之。然後隨神誨、取丁巳年冬十月甲子、遷于伊勢國渡遇宮。

　是時倭大神、著穗積臣遠祖大水口宿禰、而誨之曰、太初之時期曰、天照大神悉治天原。皇御孫尊、專治葦原中國之八十魂神。我親治大地官者。言已訖焉。然先皇御間城天皇、雖祭祀神祇、微細未探其源根、以粗留於枝葉。故其天皇短命也。是以、今汝御孫尊、悔先皇之不及而愼祭、則汝尊壽命延長、復天下太平矣。

　時天皇聞是言、則仰中臣連祖探湯主、而卜之。誰人以令祭大倭大神。即渟名城稚姬命食卜焉。因以命渟名城稚姬命、定神地於穴磯邑、祠於大市長岡岬。

　然是渟名城稚姬命、既身體悉瘦弱、以不能祭。是以命大倭直祖長尾市宿禰、令祭矣。

廿六年秋八月戊寅朔庚辰、天皇勅物部十千根大連曰、屢遣使者於出雲國、雖檢校其國之神寶、無分明申言者。汝親行于出雲、宜檢校定。則十千根大連、校定神寶、而分明奏言之。仍令掌神寶也。

land neighboring Yamato and is beautiful. I wish to dwell in this land." So, according to the instructions of this kami, her shrine was set in Ise, and the place for ritual worship near the Isuzu River. It is called Iso Shrine. This is where Amaterasu descended from heaven for the first time.

It is also said, The emperor named Yamato-hime as assistant to the kami and presented her to Amaterasu. Thereupon Yamato-hime enshrined her in Shiki at the base of a hallowed evergreen oak and worshipped her there. Afterward, in accordance with the kami's instructions, on the twenty-sixth year, winter, tenth month, day of the Wood Rat, she was moved to Watarai Shrine in Ise.[xix]

At that time, Yamato-no-ō-kami[9] possessed the distant ancestor of the Omi of Hozumi, Ō-mina-kuchi no Sukune, and gave instruction, saying, "At the beginning of time, we made a vow, saying, 'Amaterasu shall definitely govern the heavenly plain, the august imperial descendants shall exclusively govern the many kami enshrined in the central reed plain land, and I myself shall govern the kami of the earth.' This promise has already been fulfilled. However, the previous emperor, Emperor Mi-maki, though he venerated the kami of heaven and earth, did not seek out the origins of this practice, and stopped short at its then-present implementation. Consequently, that emperor was short-lived. For this reason, you should atone for that which the previous emperor did not achieve and carefully venerate the kami. Then your lifespan will be lengthened, and also the realm will enjoy great peace."

When the emperor heard these words, he immediately ordered the ancestor of the Muraji of the Nakatomi, Kuka-nushi, to divine who should be ordered to venerate Yamato-no-ō-kami. It turned out that he divined Nunaki-waka-hime. Thereupon the emperor commanded Nunaki-waka-hime to establish the kami's land as Anashi Village and to enshrine him at Cape Nagaoka in Ōchi.[xx]

However, Nunaki-waka-hime was weak and emaciated, and she could not perform the worship. So the emperor ordered the ancestor of the Atai of Yamato, Naga-ochi no Sukune, to venerate the kami.

Twenty-sixth year [4 BCE], autumn, eighth month, third day. The emperor decreed to the Ō-muraji Mononobe no Tōchine,[10] saying, "I frequently dispatch messengers to Izumo, and even if they inspect the divine treasure of that land, no one reports clearly. Go to Izumo yourself and inspect it properly." And so the Ō-muraji Mononobe no Tōchine inspected the treasure and made a clear report. He was then ordered to take charge of the treasure.

---

9   Presumably the same Yamato-ō-kuni-tama kami seen in Sujin 6.
10 This is the first appearance of the title and office Ō-muraji, which, along with the Ō-omi, constituted the highest echelon of the Yamato court. The Ō-muraji was primarily charged with military matters and occupied by the Ōtomo and Mononobe clans. The downfall of the Ōtomo is given in Kinmei 1.9, and that of the Mononobe in Sushun 2.7.

廿七年秋八月癸酉朔己卯、令祠官、卜兵器爲神幣、吉之。故弓矢及橫刀納諸神之社。仍更定神地・神戸、以時祠之。蓋兵器祭神祇、始興於是時也。是歲、興屯倉于來目邑。屯倉、此云彌夜氣。

廿八年冬十月丙寅朔庚午、天皇母弟倭彦命薨。

十一月丙申朔丁酉、葬倭彦命于身狹桃花鳥坂。

於是、集近習者、悉生而埋立於陵域。數日不死、晝夜泣吟。遂死而爛臰之。犬鳥聚噉焉。天皇聞此泣吟之聲、心有悲傷。詔群卿曰、夫以生所愛、令殉亡者、是甚傷矣。其雖古風之、非良何從。自今以後、議之止殉。

卅年春正月己未朔甲子、天皇詔五十瓊敷命・大足彦尊曰、汝等各言情願之物也。

兄王諮、欲得弓矢。

弟王諮、欲得皇位。

於是、天皇詔之曰、各宜隨情。則弓矢賜五十瓊敷命。仍詔大足彦尊曰、汝必繼朕位。

卅二年秋七月甲戌朔己卯、皇后日葉酢媛命一云、日葉酢根命也。薨。臨葬有日焉、天皇詔群卿曰、從死之道、前知不可。今此行之葬、奈之爲何。

Twenty-seventh year [3 BCE], autumn, eighth month, seventh day. The emperor ordered the Office of Divinities to divine on using weapons as offerings. The reply was "Favorable." For this reason, bows and arrows and swords were offered at various shrines of the kami. Furthermore, the emperor determined the lands of the kami and the people who would farm them, and the seasons in which the kami would be worshipped. This was probably the first time that weapons were used to venerate the kami of heaven and earth. In this year, Kume Village was made into an imperial estate.[11]

Prohibition of Following Others in Death

Twenty-eighth year [2 BCE], winter, tenth month, fifth day. The emperor's brother Yamato-hiko perished. Eleventh month, second day. Yamato-hiko was buried in Musa-no-tsukisaka.

At that time, his close attendants were gathered and buried alive standing around the tomb. For several days they did not die, and they cried and moaned day and night. When at last they died, they rotted and stank, and dogs and birds gathered and gnawed at them. The emperor heard their cries and moans and was saddened and pained. He decreed to the high government officials, saying, "It is exceedingly painful to make those who were cherished while the deceased was alive follow him in death. Although this custom is old, why continue to follow a wrong practice? From now on, plan to end the practice of following one's lord in death."

Thirtieth year [1 CE], spring, first month, sixth day. The emperor issued an edict to I-ni-shiki and Ō-tarashi-hiko, saying, "Each of you tell me what you desire."

The older prince said, "I want to receive a bow and arrow."

The younger prince said, "I want to receive the imperial throne."

Then the emperor decreed, "Each should receive what they want." Then he bestowed a bow and arrow upon I-ni-shiki and proclaimed to Ō-tarashi-hiko, "You shall definitely succeed Us."

Thirty-second year [3 CE], autumn, seventh month, sixth day. Empress Hibasu-hime perished. By one account, Hi-basu-ne. Many days passed while people were collected at the burial site. The emperor decreed to the high government officials, saying, "I have already determined that the custom of following others in death is wrong. For this funeral, what should we do?"

---

11 This is the first appearance of imperial estates (*miyake*), lands and people directly under the control of the court that constituted the economic backbone of the ancient Japanese state.

於是、野見宿禰進曰、夫君王陵墓、埋立生人、是不良也。豈得傳後葉乎。願今將議便事而奏之。則遣使者、喚上出雲國之土部壹佰人、自領土部等、取埴以造作人・馬及種種物形、獻于天皇曰、自今以後、以是土物更易生人、樹於陵墓、爲後葉之法則。

　天皇、於是、大喜之、詔野見宿禰曰、汝之便議、寔洽朕心。則其土物、始立于日葉酢媛命之墓。仍號是土物謂埴輪。亦名立物也。

　仍下令曰、自今以後、陵墓必樹是土物、無傷人焉。

　天皇厚賞野見宿禰之功、亦賜鍛地。即任土部職。因改本姓、謂土部臣。是土部連等、主天皇喪葬之緣也。所謂野見宿禰、是土部連等之始祖也。

　卅四年春三月乙丑朔丙寅、天皇幸山背。時左右奏言之、此國有佳人。曰綺戶邊。姿形美麗、山背大國不遲之女也。

　天皇、於茲、執矛祈之曰、必遇其佳人、道路見瑞。比至行宮、大龜出河中。天皇擧矛刺龜。忽化爲白石。謂左右曰、因此物而推之、必有驗乎。仍喚綺戶邊、納于後宮。生磐衝別命。是三尾君之始祖也。

　先是、娶山背苅幡戶邊。生三男。第一曰祖別命。第二曰五十日足彥命。第三曰膽武別命。五十日足彥命、是子石田君之始祖也。

　卅五年秋九月、遣五十瓊敷命于河內國、作高石池・茅渟池。

　冬十月、作倭狹城池及迹見池。

Then Nomi no Sukune came forward and said, "It is not good to bury people alive in the tombs of their lords. How can we pass that on to later generations? I wish to come up with an effective plan, which I will then report." He promptly dispatched messengers to summon one hundred members of the Haji-be, the ceramics hereditary guild of Izumo, and personally directed the lineage group to make clay humans, horses, and various other things. These he presented to the emperor, saying, "From now on, let these earthen objects stand in tombs in place of the living, and make this the law for the future."

The emperor was greatly pleased by this and proclaimed to Nomi no Sukune, "Your effective plan truly accords with Our intentions." Hence, these earthen objects first stood in the tomb of Hibasu-hime. These earthen objects were called *haniwa*, or clay circles, and also *tatemono*, or standing objects.

The emperor then ordered, "From this day forth, you must stand haniwa in tombs and not injure anyone."

The emperor richly rewarded Nomi no Sukune for this achievement, presented him with land for kilns, appointed him director of the Haji, and changed his title of nobility to Omi of the Haji. It is for this reason that the Muraji of the Haji are in charge of imperial funerals. The one called Nomi no Sukune became the first ancestor of the Muraji of the Haji.

Thirty-fourth year [5 CE], spring, third month, second day. The emperor toured Yamashiro. At that time, those at his side addressed him, saying, "There is in this land a beautiful woman called Kanihata-tobe with a radiant countenance. She is the daughter of Ōkuni-fuchi of Yamato."

Then and there, the emperor grabbed his halberd and made an oath, saying, "If I am to meet this beauty, may there be a portent on the road." When he reached his temporary palace, a large turtle came out of the river. The emperor took his halberd and stabbed the turtle, and it instantly transformed into a white rock. Then he told those at his side, "I surmise from this that I will assuredly see my oath fulfilled." Then he summoned Kanihata-tobe to the inner palace. She gave birth to Iwai-tsuku-wake, first ancestor of the Kimi of Mio.

Previously, the emperor had wed Karihata-tobe of Yamashiro, and she gave birth to three sons. The first was Ō-chi-wake. The second was I-ka-tarashi-hiko. The third was I-take-wake. The son of I-ka-tarashi-hiko was the first ancestor of the Kimi of Ishida.

Thirty-fifth year [6 CE], autumn, ninth month. The emperor dispatched I-ni-shiki to the land of Kōchi and had him build Takashi Reservoir and Chinu Reservoir.

Winter, tenth month. The emperor also had him build Yamato-no-saki Reservoir and Tomi Reservoir.

是歲、令諸國多開池溝。數八百之。以農爲事。因是、百姓富寬、天下大平矣。

卅七年春正月戊寅朔、立大足彥尊、爲皇太子。

卅九年冬十月、五十瓊敷命、居於茅渟菟砥川上宮、作劒一千口。因名其劒、謂川上部。亦名曰裸伴。裸伴、此云阿箇播娜我等母。藏于石上神宮也。是後、命五十瓊敷命、俾主石上神宮之神寶。

一云、五十瓊敷皇子、居于茅渟菟砥河上。而喚鍛名河上、作大刀一千口。是時、楯部・倭文部・神弓削部・神矢作部・大穴磯部・泊橿部・玉作部・神刑部・日置部・大刀佩部、幷十箇品部、賜五十瓊敷皇子。其一千口大刀者、藏于忍坂邑。然後、從忍坂移之、藏于石上神宮。是時、神乞之言、春日臣族、名市河令治。因以命市河令治。是今物部首之始祖也。

八十七年春二月丁亥朔辛卯、五十瓊敷命、謂妹大中姬曰、我老也。不能掌神寶。自今以後、必汝主焉。

大中姬命辭曰、吾手弱女人也。何能登天神庫耶。神庫、此云保玖羅。

五十瓊敷命曰、神庫雖高、我能爲神庫造梯。豈煩登庫乎。故諺曰、天之神庫隨樹梯之、此其緣也。然遂大中姬命、授物部十千根大連而令治。故物部連等、至于今治石上神寶、是其緣也。

That year, the emperor ordered the various lands of his realm to dig a great number of irrigation ditches, over eight hundred in all. Because he took agriculture to be an important matter, the people were rich, and the realm enjoyed great peace.

Thirty-seventh year [8 CE], spring, first month, first day. Ō-tarashi-hiko was named crown prince.

Divine Treasures in Isonokami and Chinu

Thirty-ninth year [10 CE], tenth month. I-ni-shiki, who dwelt at a shine at the headwaters of the Uto River in Chinu, made one thousand swords. So the swords were called Kawakami-no-tomo. They were also called Aka-hadaka-tomo. They were used as offerings for the Isonokami Shrine. After this, the emperor ordered I-ni-shiki to manage the divine treasures of the Isonokami Shrine.

> It is also said, Imperial Prince I-ni-shiki[12] was at the headwaters of the Uto River in Chinu and summoned a smith named Kawakami, and the smith made one thousand swords. At that time, the hereditary guilds for shield makers, mulberry and hemp dyers and weavers, bowyers, fletchers, miners, masons, jewelers, Oshisaka weapon stewards, lantern makers, and large sword wearers, all together ten hereditary guilds, were bestowed upon Imperial Prince I-ni-shiki. The one thousand swords were stored in Oshisaka Village. Later, they were moved from Oshisaka to storage at Isonokami Shrine. At that time, the kami requested that the lineage group Omi of Kasuga be renamed Ichikawa. So the emperor ordered it renamed Ichikawa. This lineage group are the first ancestors of the Obito of the Mononobe.

Eighty-seventh year [58 CE], spring, second month, fifth day. I-ni-shiki said to his younger sister Ō-naka-tsu-hime, "I am old and cannot manage the divine treasures. From now on, you must do it."

Ō-naka-tsu-hime declined, saying, "I am a feeble woman; how can I climb up to the divine storage room?"

I-ni-shiki said, "Although the divine storage room is high, I will make a divine storage-room ladder. How can you have trouble then?" Hence the proverb goes, "Follow the ladder to the divine storage room of the kami,"[13] and this is the reason. Eventually, Ō-naka-tsu-hime bestowed this task upon the Ō-muraji Mononobe no Tō-chinu. For this reason, even now the Muraji of the Mononobe manage the divine treasures of Isonokami.

---

12 The use of "Imperial Prince" here suggests source material from a later period than that of the main narrative.
13 This proverb suggests that success depends on following guidance and/or a prescribed route.

昔丹波國桑田村有人。名曰甕襲。則甕襲家有犬。名曰足往。是犬咋山獸名牟士那而殺之。則獸腹有八尺瓊勾玉。因以獻之。是玉今有石上神宮也。

　八十八年秋七月己酉朔戊午、詔群卿曰、朕聞、新羅王子天日槍、初來之時、將來寶物、今有但馬。元爲國人見貴、則爲神寶也。朕欲見其寶物。

　即日、遣使者、詔天日槍之曾孫清彥而令獻。於是、清彥被勅、乃自捧神寶而獻之。羽太玉一箇・足高玉一箇・鵜鹿鹿赤石玉一箇・日鏡一面・熊神籬一具。唯有小刀一。名曰出石。則清彥忽以爲非獻刀子、仍匿袍中、而自佩之。

　天皇未知匿小刀之情、欲寵清彥而召之賜酒於御所。時刀子從袍中出而顯之。天皇見之、親問清彥曰、爾袍中刀子者、何刀子也。

　爰清彥知不得匿刀子而呈言、所獻神寶之類也。

　則天皇謂清彥曰、其神寶之、豈得離類乎。乃出而獻焉。皆藏於神府。然後、開寶府而視之、小刀自失。則使問清彥曰、爾所獻刀子忽失矣。若至汝所乎。

　清彥答曰、昨夕、刀子自然至於臣家。乃明旦失焉。天皇則惶之、且更勿覓。是後、出石刀子、自然至于淡路嶋。其嶋人謂神、而爲刀子立祠。是於今所祠也。

　昔有一人乘艇而泊于但馬國。因問曰、汝何國人也。

　對曰、新羅王子、名曰天日槍。則留于但馬、娶其國前津耳一云、前津見。一云、太耳。女、

In ancient times, in Kuwada Village, Tanba Prefecture, there was a man called Mikaso. At Mikaso's house, there was a dog named Ayuki. This dog bit a wild animal named Mujina in the mountains and killed it. In the belly of the beast was an eight shaftment magatama, which was presented to the court. The jewel is now in the Isonokami Shrine.

Eighty-eighth year [59 CE], autumn, seventh month, tenth day. The emperor issued an edict to the high government officials, saying, "We hear that when the Prince of Silla, Ame-no-hi-hoko, first came to court, he brought treasures now stored in Tajima. They have been valued by the people of that land from the beginning and are divine. I would like to see these treasures."

That day he dispatched a messenger, who pronounced his edict to the great-grandson of Ame-no-hi-hoko, Kiyohiko, ordering that the treasures be presented to him. Kiyohiko yielded to the decree and presented them to the emperor himself. There was one fat-tipped magatama, one long-legged jewel, one shining red bead, one sun-mirror, and one divine shrine dwelling. Only in the case of the short sword called Izushi did Kiyohiko suddenly decide not to present the blade and instead hid it inside of his clothing, wearing it himself.

The emperor did not know about the hidden short sword and wanted to show Kiyohiko favor. So he summoned him and bestowed wine upon him. At that time, the dagger stuck out of his clothes and was revealed. The emperor saw it and asked Kiyohiko himself, "What is this blade in your clothing?"

Kiyohiko knew that he could not hide the blade, and candidly said, "It is one of the heavenly treasures that I presented."

Then the emperor said to Kiyohiko, "Why is this heavenly treasure separated from the others?" Kiyohiko took it out and presented it to the emperor, and all of the treasures were placed in divine storage. Later, however, he opened the door to the treasure storage and looked inside, and the small sword was gone. The emperor then sent a message to Kiyohiko, asking, "The short sword that you presented has gone missing; maybe it made its way to your place?"

Kiyohiko replied, saying, "Last night the blade came to my house of its own accord. In the morning it was gone." The emperor was disturbed by this and no longer looked for it any further. After this, the short sword Izushi went on its own to Awaji, and the people there called it a kami and built a shrine for it. It is still venerated at present.

In ancient times there was a man who came on a small boat and stayed in the land of Tajima. He was asked, "What land are you from?"

He replied, "I am a prince of Silla, called Ame-no-hihoko." He stayed in Tajima and wed the daughter of Mae-tsu-mimi from that land, Ma-

麻挓能烏。生但馬諸助。是淸彥之祖父也。

九十年春二月庚子朔、天皇命田道間守、遣常世國、令求非時香菓。香菓、此云箇倶能未。今謂橘是也。

九十九年秋七月戊午朔、天皇崩於纏向宮。時年百卅歲。

冬十二月癸卯朔壬子、葬於菅原伏見陵。

明年春三月辛未朔壬午、田道間守、至自常世國。則齎物也、非時香菓八竿八縵焉。田道間守、於是、泣悲歎之曰、受命天朝、遠往絶域。萬里蹈浪、遙度弱水。是常世國、則神仙祕區、俗非所臻。是以、往來之間、自經十年。豈期、獨凌峻瀾、更向本土乎。然賴聖帝之神靈、僅得還來。今天皇既崩。不得復命。臣雖生之、亦何益矣。乃向天皇之陵、叫哭而自死之。

群臣聞皆流涙也。田道間守、是三宅連之始祖也。

tano-o, and she gave birth to Tajima Morosuke.[14] This was Kiyohiko's grandfather.

Ninetieth year [61 CE], spring, second month, first day. The emperor ordered that Tajima-mori be dispatched to the Land of Tokoyo to search for the everlasting kaku fruit, which is now called the tachibana.[15]

Ninety-ninth year [70 CE], autumn, seventh month, fourteenth day. The emperor expired in Makimuku Palace. He was 140 years old.[16][xxi]

Winter, twelfth month, tenth day. The emperor was buried in Sugawara-no-Fushimi Tomb.

Next year, spring, third month, twelfth day. Tajima-mori arrived from the Land of Tokoyo. He brought back with him the everlasting kaku fruit, eight branches with fruit only and eight with the leaves still attached. Tajima-mori wept in sadness and grieved, saying, "I received the order of the emperor and went to a distant land. I rose over a myriad leagues of waves and crossed faraway rivers. In the Land of Tokoyo the divines and sages dwell hidden, and normal people cannot go there. For this reason, ten years passed while I came and went. How could I have expected to cross the high waves alone and return again to my homeland? However, thanks to the ethereal blessings of the sage emperor, I could just make it back. Now the emperor has expired, and I cannot make my report to him. What use is it for me to keep living?" Then he faced the emperor's tomb, shouted a bereaved cry, and died.

The high government officials heard this, and all shed tears. Tajima-mori was the first ancestor of the Muraji of Miyake.

---

14 An original note adds two names for Matano-o's father: "He is also called, Maetsumi. And he is also called, Futomimi."
15 In modern Japanese, this is a kind of mandarin orange, but it is unclear what kind of citrus is referred to in this entry. Citrus fruits were thought to be associated with long life or immortality.
16 Based on the entry for his birth in the Sujin Book, Suinin would have been 139 years old at his death. In *Ancient Matters*, he was 153 years old when he died.

大足彦忍代別天皇 景行天皇

大足彦忍代別天皇、活目入彦五十狹茅天皇第三子也。母皇后曰日葉洲媛命。丹波道主王之女也。活目入彦五十狹茅天皇卅七年、立爲皇太子。時年廿一。

九十九年春二月、活目入彦五十狹茅天皇崩。

元年秋七月己巳朔己卯、太子即天皇位。因以改元。是年也、太歲辛未。

二年春三月丙寅朔戊辰、立播磨稻日大郎姫一云、稻日稚郎姫。郎姫、此云異羅菟咩爲皇后。后生二男。第一曰大碓皇子。第二曰小碓尊。一書云、皇后生三男。其第三曰稚倭根子皇子。其大碓皇子・小碓尊、一日同胞而雙生。天皇異之、則誥於碓。故因號其二王曰、大碓・小碓也。是小碓尊、亦名日本童男。童男、此云烏具奈。亦曰日本武尊。幼有雄略之氣。及壯容貌魁偉。身長一丈、力能扛鼎焉。

三年春二月庚寅朔、卜幸于紀伊國、將祭祀群神

---

1 The relationship between Keikō's father, Suinin, and his maternal relatives is given in Suinin 5.10.
2 By these figures, he would have been 84 at his accession and would have died at 143. Later, he is recorded as dying at 106.
3 In the Suinin book, his death is given as autumn, seventh month, fourteenth day.
4 Before Keikō, only Annei and Kaika had acceded to the throne in a month other than the first, and they both acceded to the throne the same year that their predecessor died. Then, the first year of their reigns was counted from the first month of the following year. Keikō acceded in the seventh month in the year after his predecessor died. His reign is counted from with the first month of that year, even though he did not take the throne until the seventh month. Because of this irregularity, the compilers included this sentence.

Book 7
Emperors Keikō and Seimu

Accession and Children of Emperor Keikō

Emperor Ō-tarashi-hiko-oshiro-wake [Keikō] was the third child of Emperor Ikume-iri-biko-isa-chi [Suinin].[i] His mother the empress was called Hibasu-hime. She was the daughter of the Michinushi of Tanba.[1] He was named crown prince in the thirty-seventh year [8 CE] of the reign of Emperor Ikume-iri-biko-isa-chi. At the time, he was twenty-one years old.[2]

Ninety-ninth year [70 CE], spring, second month. Emperor Ikume-iri-biko-isa-chi expired.[3]

First year [71 CE], autumn, seventh month, eleventh day. The crown prince acceded to the imperial throne. Accordingly, this was counted as the first year of his reign.[4] This was the year of the Metal Sheep.

Second year [72 CE], spring, third month, third day.[5] Ō-iratsume of Inabi in Harima was named empress.[6][ii] The empress gave birth to two sons. The first was called Imperial Prince Ō-usu, and the second was called Imperial Prince O-usu.[iii]

<small>One text says that she gave birth to three sons. The third son was called Imperial Prince Waka-yamato-neko.</small>

Ō-usu and O-usu were twins born on the same day and from the same placenta. The emperor thought it strange and shouted at the mortar and pestle. Accordingly, the two princes were called Ō-usu, or Big Mortar, and O-usu, or Little Mortar. O-usu was also called Yamato Oguna, and also Yamato Take.[7] From a young age he was given to grand strategies, and when he blossomed into adulthood, he was tall and impressive. He was almost ten feet tall, and strong enough to lift a three-legged bronze cauldron.[iv]

Third year [73 CE], spring, second month, first day. The emperor divined whether to tour the land of Kii and venerate the numerous kami of heaven

---

5 The date is incorrectly recorded. Commentaries correct this error on the basis of the Kitano Manuscript.
6 An original note adds, "Another account says Waka-iratsume of Inabi."
7 Oguna means "young man." Yamato Oguna refers to his later conquest of the land of Yamato. The original includes the title "mikoto," using a character normally reserved for legitimate successors to the throne, a unique praise of his accomplishments, and recognition that his son would go on to inherit the throne. Since the late nineteenth century, he has been called "Yamato Takeru," but "takeru" is used in the *Chronicles* to refer to enemies of the state.

祇、而不吉。乃車駕止之。遣屋主忍男武雄心命一云、武猪心令祭。爰屋主忍男武雄心命、詣之居于阿備柏原、而祭祀神祇、仍住九年。則娶紀直遠祖菟道彦之女影媛、生武內宿禰。

四年春二月甲寅朔甲子、天皇幸美濃。左右奏言之、茲國有佳人。曰弟媛。容姿端正。八坂入彥皇子之女也。天皇欲得爲妃、幸弟媛之家。弟媛聞乘輿車駕、則隱竹林。於是、天皇權令弟媛至、而居于泳宮之。泳宮、此云區玖利能彌挪。鯉魚浮池、朝夕臨視而戲遊。時弟媛欲見其鯉魚遊、而密來臨池。天皇則留而通之。

爰弟媛以爲、夫婦之道、古今達則也。然於吾而不便。則請天皇曰、妾性不欲交接之道。今不勝皇命之威、暫納帷幕之中。然意所不快。亦形姿穢陋。久之不堪陪於掖庭。唯有妾姉。名曰八坂入媛。容姿麗美。志亦貞潔。宜納後宮。

天皇聽之。仍喚八坂入媛爲妃。生七男六女。第一曰稚足彥天皇。第二曰五百城入彥皇子。第三曰忍之別皇子。第四曰稚倭根子皇子。第五曰大酢別皇子。第六曰渟熨斗皇女。第七曰渟名城皇女。第八曰五百城入姬皇女。第九曰

---

8 Later noted as the father of Takeuchi no Sukune. In the Kōgen book, Kōgen's son Hiko-fu-to-oshi-makoto is given as the grandfather of Takeuchi no Sukune, which would make Yanushi-oshi-o-take-o-kokoro Kōgen's grandson.
9 An original note adds, "Another account says Take-i-kokoro."

and earth there, but the result was "Not Favorable." Hence he cancelled the tour and dispatched Yanushi-oshi-o-take-o-kokoro[8] with orders to venerate them.[9] Thus Yanushi-oshi-o-take-o-kokoro went there and dwelt in Kashiwahara in Abi and venerated the kami of heaven and earth.[v] He lived there for nine years and wed Kage-hime, the daughter of the distant ancestor of the Atai of Ki, Uji-hiko.[10] She gave birth to Takeuchi no Sukune.[11]

Fourth year [74 CE], spring, second month, eleventh day. The emperor toured Mino. Those in close service to him told him, "There is a beautiful woman in this land called Oto-hime. Her face is radiant, and she is the daughter of Yasaka-no-iri-biko.[12] The emperor wanted to make her a consort, and so he progressed to her house. Oto-hime heard that the emperor himself had come and quickly hid in the bamboo forest. In this circumstance, the emperor formed a plan to make Oto-hime come to him. He dwelt in Kukuri Palace, released koi into the lake, and from morning to night diverted himself by watching them.[vi] Oto-hime wanted to see the koi playing and secretly came to the pond. The emperor immediately detained her and had carnal relations with her.

Afterward, Oto-hime thought, The nature of marriage has been the same from the past to the present, but I do not find it suitable. Then she made a proposal to the emperor, saying, "I have never been interested in sexual relations between men and women. At present, being unable to prevail over the authority of the emperor's orders, I for the moment have attended on your bedchamber. But I am unhappy at heart. Also, my appearance is disgraceful. I cannot bear to serve in the inner palace for long. However, I have an older sister, called Yasaka-iri-bime. She is of fair face and pure heart. Please take her into the inner palace.

The emperor agreed to this. Then he made Yasaka-iri-bime his consort. She gave birth to seven boys and six girls.[vii] The first was called Emperor Waka-tarashi-hiko [Seimu].[viii] The second was called Imperial Prince Ioki-no-iri-biko. The third was called Imperial Prince Oshi-wake. The fourth was called Imperial Prince Waka-yamato-neko. The fifth was called Imperial Prince Ō-su-wake. The sixth was called Imperial Princess Nunoshi. The seventh was called Imperial Princess Nunaki. The eighth was called Imperial Princess Ioki-no-iri-bime. The ninth was called Imperial Princess

---

10 The Atai of Ki were powerful lineage group in the southern part of Wakayama City, Wakayama Prefecture. In *Ancient Matters*, Uji-hiko is identified as the Provincial Miyatsuko of Ki.
11 Takeuchi no Sukune goes on to serve five generations of emperors, from Keikō to Nintoku, as Greater Minister. He is also known as Takeshiuchi no Sukune.
12 A son of Sujin.

䗲依姫皇女。第十曰五十狹城入彥皇子。第十一曰吉備兄彥皇子。第十二曰高城入姫皇女。第十三曰弟姫皇女。

又妃三尾氏磐城別之妹水齒郎媛、生五百野皇女。

次妃五十河媛、生神櫛皇子・稻背入彥皇子。其兄神櫛皇子、是讚岐國造之始祖也。弟稻背入彥皇子、是播磨別之始祖也。

次妃阿倍氏木事之女高田媛、生武國凝別皇子。是伊豫國御村別之始祖也。

次妃日向髮長大田根、生日向襲津彥皇子。是阿牟君之始祖也。

次妃襲武媛、生國乳別皇子與國背別皇子一云、宮道別皇子。・豐戶別皇子。其兄國乳別皇子、是水沼別之始祖也。弟豐戶別皇子、是火國別之始祖也。

夫天皇之男女、前後幷八十子。然除日本武尊・稚足彥天皇・五百城入彥皇子外、七十餘子、皆封國郡、各如其國。故當今時謂諸國之別者、即其別王之苗裔焉。

是月、天皇聞美濃國造、名神骨之女、兄名兄遠子、弟名弟遠子、並有國色、則遣大碓命、使察其婦女之容姿。時大碓命、便密通而不復命。由是、恨大碓命。

Kagoyori-hime. The tenth was called Imperial Prince Isaki-no-iri-biko. The eleventh was called Imperial Prince Kibi-no-ehiko. The twelfth was called Imperial Princess Takaki-no-iri-bime. The thirteenth was called Imperial Princess Oto-hime.

Also, Consort Mizu-ha-no-iratsume, the younger sister of Iwaki-wake of the Mio lineage group, gave birth to Imperial Princess Iono.

Next, Consort Ikawa-hime gave birth to Imperial Prince Kamu-kushi and Imperial Prince Inase-no-iri-biko. The older brother, Kamu-kushi, was the first ancestor of the provincial chieftains of Sanuki Province. The younger brother, Inase-no-iri-biko, was the first ancestor of the Wake of Harima.

Next, Consort Takata-hime, daughter of Kogoto of the Abe lineage group, gave birth to Imperial Prince Take-kuni-kori-wake. He was the first ancestor of the Mimura Wake of Iyo Province.

Next, Consort Kami-naga-ō-tane of Himuka gave birth to Imperial Prince Hi-muka-no-so-tsu-hiko. He was the first ancestor of the Kimi of Amu.

Next, Consort So-no-take-hime gave birth to Imperial Prince Kuni-chi-wake, Imperial Prince Kuni-so-wake, and Imperial Prince Toyo-to-wake.[13] The eldest brother, Imperial Prince Kuni-chi-wake, was the first ancestor of the Wake of Minuma. The youngest brother, Imperial Prince Toyo-to-wake, was the first ancestor of the Wake of Hi Province.

The sons and daughters of the emperor, from beginning to end, numbered eighty. However, except for Yamato Take, Waka-tarashi-hiko [Seimu], and Ioki-no-iri-biko, the other seventy-odd children were all enfeoffed in the provinces and districts, each of them to their respective lands.[ix] Hence, in the present, those called Wake[14] in the various provinces, are the descendants of these divided princes.

That month the emperor heard that the daughters of the Provincial Miyatsuko of Mino, Kamuhone, the older E-tōko and the younger Oto-tōko, were both very beautiful. He promptly dispatched Ō-usu with orders to examine the appearance of these women. At that time, Ō-usu secretly had affairs with the women and did not report back.[15] For this reason, the emperor resented Ō-usu.

---

13 An original note for Kuni-so-wake adds, "Another account says Imperial Prince Miya-ji-wake."
14 A title meaning "divided," which appears frequently in the names of powerful lineage groups, especially of provincial miyatsuko. Perhaps the titles were given to these groups by the imperial court.
15 Ō-usu would be only two years old. This is one of numerous examples suggesting that the chronology was a later addition to the story.

冬十一月庚辰朔、乘輿自美濃還。則更都於纏向。是謂日代宮。

十二年秋七月、熊襲反之不朝貢。八月乙未朔己酉、幸筑紫。九月甲子朔戊辰、到周芳娑麼。時天皇南望之、詔群卿曰、於南方烟氣多起。必賊將在。則留之、先遣多臣祖武諸木・國前臣祖菟名手・物部君祖夏花、令察其狀。

爰有女人、曰神夏磯媛。其徒衆甚多。一國之魁帥也。聆天皇之使者至、則拔磯津山之賢木、以上枝挂八握劒、中枝挂八咫鏡、下枝挂八尺瓊、亦素幡樹于船舳、參向而啓之曰、願無下兵。我之屬類、必不有違者。今將歸德矣。唯有殘賊者。一曰鼻垂。妄假名號、山谷響聚、屯結於菟狹川上。二曰耳垂。殘賊貪婪、屢略人民。是居於御木、此云開。川上。三曰麻剝。潛聚徒黨、居於高羽川上。四曰土折猪折。隱住於緑野川上、獨恃山川之險、以多掠人民。是四人也、其所據並要害之地。故各領眷屬、爲一處之長也。皆曰、不從皇命。願急擊之。勿失。

於是、武諸木等、先誘麻剝之徒。仍賜赤衣・褌及種々奇物、兼令撝不服之三人。乃率己衆而參來。悉捕誅之。天皇遂幸筑紫、到豐前國長峽縣、興行宮而居。故號其處曰京也。

Winter, eleventh month, first day. The emperor returned from Mino. He set his capital in Makimuku, with his court at Hishiro Palace.

Revolt of the Kumaso, Tour of Tsukushi

Twelfth year [82 CE], autumn, seventh month. The Kumaso rebelled and did not submit tribute.[x] Eighth month, fifteenth day. The emperor toured Tsukushi.[xi] Ninth month, fifth day. The emperor arrived at Saba in Suwa.[xii] At that time, the emperor looked far off to the south and issued an edict to the high government officials, saying, "Smoke rises from many places to the south. Rebels are definitely camped there." While staying there, he first sent the ancestor of the Omi of the Ō, Takemoroki; the ancestor of the Omi of Kunisaki, Unate; and the ancestor of the Kimi of the Mononobe, Natsuhana, with orders to observe the situation.[xiii]

There was a woman called Kamu-natsu-so-hime. Her followers were numerous, and she was the chieftain of an entire land. She heard that the messengers of the emperor had come and promptly uprooted a sakaki tree from Mt. Shitsu, hung an eight-hand sword from its upper branches, an eight-shaftment mirror from its middle branches, and an eight-span jewel from its lower branches. Also she hoisted a white flag at the bow of her ship. She came and humbly said, "Please do not deploy your troops. Among my cohort there are definitely none who would defy imperial rule, and I now surrender. However, some rebels remain. The first is called Hanatari, and he falsely claims the title of emperor. His assembled forces rumble in the mountains and valleys, and are concentrated at the headwaters of the Usa River.[xiv] The second is called Mimitari. He is cruel and greedy, and he steals from the people. He dwells at the headwaters of the Mike River.[xv] The third is called Asahagi. He secretly assembles conspirators, and dwells at the headwaters of the Takaha River.[xvi] The fourth is called Tsuchi-ori-i-ori. He lives alone, in secret, at the headwaters of the Midorino River, and relying on the steepness of the mountains and rivers, he pilfers many things from the people. These four rebels each occupies a strategic position, and so each rules his own gang as chief of that place. All say, 'We do not follow imperial orders.' I beseech you, attack them quickly, and do not lose this opportunity."

Thereupon Takemoroki and the others first disingenuously invited Asahagi's followers and presented them with red robes and pants and various other rare things. At the same time, they summoned the other three rebels who would not submit. Then they came leading their forces, and completely captured and executed the rebel forces. The emperor at last came to Tsukushi, arriving at the district of Nagao in the land of Toyo-no-michi, and he built a temporary palace and dwelt there. Hence, this place was called Miyako, or Capital.[xvii]

冬十月、到碩田國。其地形廣大亦麗。因名碩田也。碩田、此云於保岐陀。到速見邑。有女人。曰速津媛。爲一處之長。其聞天皇車駕、而自奉迎之諮言、茲山有大石窟。曰鼠石窟。有二土蜘蛛。住其石窟。一曰青。二曰白。又於直入縣禰疑野、有三土蜘蛛。一曰打猨。二曰八田。三曰國摩侶。是五人、並其爲人強力、亦衆類多之。皆曰、不從皇命。若強喚者、興兵距焉。

天皇惡之、不得進行。即留于來田見邑、權興宮室而居之。仍與群臣議之曰、今多動兵衆、以討土蜘蛛。若其畏我兵勢、將隱山野、必爲後愁。則採海石榴樹、作椎爲兵。因簡猛卒、授兵椎、以穿山排草、襲石室土蜘蛛、而破于稻葉川上、悉殺其黨。血流至踝。故時人其作海石榴椎之處、曰海石榴市。亦血流之處、曰血田也。

復將討打猨、侄度禰疑山。時賊虜之矢、横自山射之。流於官軍前如雨。天皇更返城原、而卜於水上。便勒兵、先擊八田於禰疑野而破。爰打猨謂不可勝、而請服。然不聽矣。皆自投澗谷而死之。

天皇初將討賊、次于柏峽大野。其野有石。長六尺、廣三尺、厚一尺五寸。天皇祈之曰、朕得滅土蜘蛛者、將蹶茲石、如柏葉而擧焉。因蹶之。則如柏上於大虛。故號其石、曰蹈石也。

Winter, tenth month. The emperor arrived in the land of Ōkita.[xviii] This land was spacious and beautiful, and for this reason was called Ōkita, or Large Paddy. The emperor went to Hayami Village, where there was a woman called Haya-tsu-hime.[xix] She was the chief of that place. She heard about the emperor's tour and went herself to offer him greetings and seek his opinion, saying, "There is a large cave in this mountain, called Nezumi Cave. There are two earth spiders[16] who live in this cave. The first is called Ao, the second is called Shiro. Also, in Negino, Naoiri District, there are three earth spiders.[xx] The first is called Uchisaru, the second is called Yata, and the third is called Kunimaro. These five rebels are powerful, and their followers are many. All say, 'We do not follow imperial orders.' If you summon them by force, they will muster their troops and resist."

The emperor detested this, but he could not proceed. He stayed in Kutami Village, where he erected a provisional palace, and dwelt there.[xxi] Then he conferred with the high government officials, saying, "I presently want to mobilize a large number of troops and strike the earth spiders. If they fear the martial spirit of my troops and hide in the mountains and fields, then we definitely will regret it later." He took a camellia tree and made a rod for a weapon. Then he chose a brave soldier and bestowed the rod upon him, and he dug into the mountain and cleared away the grass. He attacked the earth spiders of the stone cave, and routed them at the headwaters of the Inaba River.[xxii] He killed all of the gang, and blood flowed up to the ankle. So people at that time called the place where the rod was made Tsubakichi, or Camellia Rod, and the place where blood flowed Chida, or Blood Field.

To attack Uchisaru, the emperor promptly crossed Mt. Negi. At that time, the rebels fired arrows from the mountainsides, which coursed before the army like rain. The emperor retreated to Kihara and performed divination near the river.[xxiii] Then, taking control of the army, he went first to attack Yata in Negino and defeated him. At this juncture, Uchisaru thought that it would be impossible to achieve victory and tried to surrender. However, the emperor would not permit it, and enemy rebels threw themselves into the river valley and died.

When the emperor was first going to attack the rebels, he camped in a large field in Kashiwao. In the field was a rock six spans long, three spans wide, and one span five inches thick. The emperor made an oath, saying, "If We can defeat the earth spiders, when I kick this rock, it will fly up like the leaf of an oak tree." Then he kicked it and it rose into the sky like the leaf of an oak tree. Hence, this rock is called Homishi, or Stepping Rock.

---

16 An earth spider is a hole dweller, a term that also dehumanizes this group of people.

是時、禱神、則志我神・直入物部神・直入中臣神三神矣。

十一月、到日向國、起行宮以居之。是謂高屋宮。

十二月癸巳朔丁酉、議討熊襲。於是、天皇詔群卿曰、朕聞之、襲國有厚鹿文・迮鹿文者。是兩人熊襲之渠帥者也。衆類甚多。是謂熊襲八十梟帥。其鋒不可當焉。少興師則不堪滅賊。多動兵、是百姓之害。何不假鋒刃之威、坐平其國。

時有一臣。進曰、熊襲梟帥有二女。兄曰市乾鹿文。乾、此云賦。弟曰市鹿文。容既端正。心且雄武。宜示重幣以擕納麾下。因以伺其消息、犯不意之處、則會不血刃、賊必自敗。天

皇詔、可也。

於是、示幣欺其二女、而納幕下。天皇則通市乾鹿文而陽寵。時市乾鹿文、奏于天皇曰、無愁熊襲之不服。妾有良謀。即令從一二兵於己。

而返家以多設醇酒、令飲己父。乃醉而寐之。市乾鹿文、密斷父弦。爰從兵一人、進殺熊襲梟帥。天皇則惡其不孝之甚、而誅市乾鹿文。仍以弟市鹿文、賜於火國造。

十三年夏五月、悉平襲國。因以居於高屋宮、已六年也。於是其國有佳人。曰御刀媛。御刀、此云彌波迦志。則召爲妃。生豐國別皇子。是日向國造之始祖也。

Upon this, he prayed to the three kami Shiga, Nao-iri-no-mononobe, and Nao-iri-no-naka-omi.

Eleventh month. The emperor arrived in the land of Himuka. He built a temporary palace and dwelt there. It was called Takaya Palace.[xxiv]

Twelfth month, fifth day. The emperor held a conference on attacking the Kumaso. Hence he decreed to the high government officials, saying, "This is what we hear: In the land of So there are two people called Atsukaya and Sakaya. They are the chieftains of the Kumaso.[xxv] Their followers are quite numerous, and they are together called the 'many braves of Kumaso.' Their military force cannot be resisted. If I muster a small army, I will not be able to defeat the rebels. If I mobilize many troops, it will harm the people. Is there not some way to avoid using military force and still pacify that land without stirring from my seat?"

One of his vassals said, "The braves of Kumaso include two women. The oldest is called Ichifukaya, and the younger is called Ichikaya. Their faces are radiant, and in their hearts they have the courage of warriors. Please give them valuable gifts, and invite them into the command tent. Then you can inquire about the situation and advance somewhere unexpected, and without bloodying your blade, the rebels will without doubt be defeated of their own accord."

The emperor proclaimed, "So be it."

The emperor gave gifts to the two women and so deceived them, and they came into his tent. The emperor immediately had carnal relations with Ichifukaya and showed her great favor. At that time, Ichifukaya said to the emperor, "Do not worry about the insubordination of the Kumaso. I have a good idea. Lend me one or two soldiers."

Then returning to her home, she prepared a great amount of strong wine and made her father drink it. He got drunk and fell asleep. Ichifukaya secretly cut her father's bowstring, then one of the soldiers following her came forth and killed the Kumaso chieftain. The emperor despised this unfilial act of hers and executed Ichifukaya. Her younger sister, Ichikaya, was bestowed upon the Provincial Miyatsuko of Hi.

Thirteenth year [83 CE], summer, fifth month. The emperor completely pacified the land of So. He lived in Takaya Palace for six years.[17] In this land there was a beautiful woman called Mi-hakashi-hime. The emperor summoned her to be an imperial consort, and she gave birth to Imperial Prince Toyo-kuni-wake. He was the first ancestor of the Provincial Miyatsuko of Himuka.

---

17 Keikō returns to the capital in year eighteen. He built Takaya Palace in year twelve.

十七年春三月戊戌朔己酉、幸子湯縣、遊于丹裳小野。時東望之、謂左右曰、是國也直向於日出方。故號其國曰日向也。是日、陟野中大石、憶京都而歌之曰、

波辭枳豫辭	はしきよし
和藝幣能伽多由	わぎへのかたゆ
區毛位多知區暮	くもゐたちくも
夜摩苔波	やまとは
區珥能摩倍邏摩	くにのまほらま
多々儺豆久	たたなづく
阿烏伽枳	あをかき
夜摩許莽例屢	やまこもれる
夜摩苔之于屢破試	やまとしうるはし
異能知能	いのちの
摩曾祁務比苔破	まそけむひとは
多々瀰許莽	たたみこも
幣愚利能夜摩能	へぐりのやまの
志邏伽之餓延塢	しらかしがえを
于受珥左勢	うずにさせ
許能固	このこ

是謂思邦歌也。

十八年春三月、天皇將向京、以巡狩筑紫國。始到夷守。是時、於石瀨河邊人衆聚集。於是、天皇遙望之、詔左右曰、其集者何人也。若賊乎。乃遣兄夷守・弟夷守二人令覘。

乃弟夷守、還來而諮之曰、諸縣君泉媛、依獻大御食、而其族會之。

夏四月壬戌朔甲子、到熊縣。其處有熊津彥者。兄弟二人。天皇先使徵兄熊。

Seventeenth year [87 CE], spring, third month, twelfth day. The emperor toured Koyu District and enjoyed himself in Nimo-no-ono.[xxvi] At that time, he looked far off to the east and said to those in close service, "This land directly faces the rising sun." Hence, this land is called Himuka, or Sun-Facing." On that day, the emperor climbed up a great stone in the field, remembered the capital,[18] and sang,

> From the direction
> of my beloved home,
> the clouds rise.
>
> Yamato is
> a great land,
> surrounded by mountains,
> like lush layers
> of verdant hedges.
> Beautiful Yamato.
>
> Those of you
> who still have life,
> decorate your hair
> with a twig of white oak
> from the many layers
> of the Heguri mountains,[xxvii]
> you young ones.[xxviii]

This is called a Kunishinobi song, a song of missing home.

Eighteenth year [88 CE], spring, third month. The emperor was going to head to the capital, but first did some hunting in Tsukushi. He first arrived in Hinamori.[xxix] At that time, a group of people were assembled near the Iwase River.[xxx] The emperor gazed upon them from afar and said to those in close service, "Who are these assembled people? Perhaps they are rebels?" Then he dispatched Ehinamori and Otohinamori to find out.

Otohinamori returned and reported, "Izumi-hime, Kimi of Moroagata,[19] has prepared a great feast for the emperor, and so her clan has gathered."

Summer, fourth month, third day. The emperor arrived in Kuma District.[xxxi] There were two brothers together called the "Lords of Kuma." The emperor first sent a messenger to summon the older Kuma brother,

---

18 Here referring to Hishiro Palace back in Yamato.
19 A powerful lineage group in the southwest of present-day Miyazaki Prefecture.

則從使詣之。因徵弟熊。而不來、故遣兵誅之。

　壬申、自海路泊於葦北小嶋而進食。時召山部阿弭古之祖小左、令進冷水。適是時、嶋中無水。不知所爲。則仰之祈于天神地祇。忽寒泉從崖傍涌出。乃酌以獻焉。故號其嶋曰水嶋也。其泉猶今在水嶋崖也。

　五月壬辰朔、從葦北發船到火國。於是、日沒也。夜冥不知著岸。遙視火光。天皇詔挾杪者曰、直指火處。因指火往之。即得著岸。天皇問其火光之處曰、何謂邑也。

　國人對曰、是八代縣豐村。

　亦尋其火、是誰人之火也。然不得主。茲知、非人火。故名其國曰火國也。

　六月辛酉朔癸亥、自高來縣、渡玉杵名邑。時殺其處之土蜘蛛津頰焉。

　丙子、到阿蘇國。其國也郊原曠遠、不見人居。天皇曰、是國有人乎。

　時有二神、曰阿蘇都彥・阿蘇都媛。忽化人以遊詣之曰、吾二人在。何無人耶。故號其國曰阿蘇。

　秋七月辛卯朔甲午、到筑紫後國御木、居於高田行

KEIKŌ 18 [88 CE]

and he immediately followed the messenger and came. Then he summoned the younger Kuma brother, but he did not come. Therefore, he dispatched soldiers to execute him.

Eleventh day. The emperor went by sea and stopped at a small island in Ashikita to have a meal.[xxxii] At that time, he summoned the ancestor of the Abiko of Yamabe,[20] Ohidari, and had him present cold water. Just at that time, there was no water on the island. Not knowing what to do, Ohidari looked up and prayed to the kami of heaven and earth. Then suddenly a cold spring issued out from the side of a cliff. He ladled this water and presented it to the emperor. Consequently, this island is called Mizushima, or Water Island. There is this spring is even now at the cliff on Mizushima.[xxxiii]

Fifth month, first day. The emperor departed Ashikita by boat and arrived at the land of Hi,[21] when the sun was going down. The night was dark, and he could not get the boat to the shoreline. Far off he saw the light of a fire. The emperor proclaimed to the steersman, "Head straight for the fire." By heading for the fire, they quickly reached the shoreline. The emperor asked at the place where he saw the firelight, "What village is this?"

Someone from that land answered, "This is Toyo Village in Yatsushiro District."[xxxiv]

Then he inquired about the fire, saying, "Whose fire is that?" But the owner could not be found. By this he knew that the fire was not manmade. So this land was called the land of Hi, or Fire.[xxxv]

Sixth month, third day. The emperor crossed from Takaku District to Tamakina Village.[22] At that time, he killed Tsutsura, the earth spider of that region.

Sixteenth day. The emperor arrived in the land of Aso.[xxxvi] The open spaces in this land were expansive and distant, but he saw no people dwelling there. The emperor said, "Is there anyone in this land?"

At that time, two kami called Aso-tsu-hiko and Aso-tsu-hime suddenly transformed into humans and sauntered up, saying, "We two are here. Why would there be no people here?" Consequently, that land is called Aso.

Autumn, seventh month, fourth day. The emperor arrived in Mike, in the land of Michinoshiri, in Tsukushi, and dwelt in the temporary Takada

---

20 A hereditary guild charged with mountain and forest management. Abiko likely reflects their status as an allied lineage group.
21 Here referring to a single geographical area at the mouth of the Kuma River near present-day Yatsushiro Bay, not to the provinces of Hizen and Higo, which later use the same moniker.
22 Takaku District refers to the Shimabara Peninsula in Nagasaki Prefecture, to which the emperor has crossed in going west from Yatsushiro. Tamakina is present-day Tamana District in Kumamoto Prefecture, which means that he has now crossed back by sea going northeast.

宮。時有僵樹、長九百七十丈焉。百寮蹈其樹而往來。時人歌曰、

阿佐志毛能	あさしもの
瀰概能佐烏麼志	みけのさをばし
魔幣菟耆瀰	まへつきみ
伊和哆羅秀暮	いわたらすも
瀰開能佐烏麼志	みけのさをばし

爰天皇問之曰、是何樹也。

有一老夫曰、是樹者歷木也。嘗未僵之先、當朝日暉、則隱杵嶋山。當夕日暉、亦覆阿蘇山也。

天皇曰、是樹者神木。故是國宜號御木國。

丁酉、到八女縣。則越藤山、以南望粟岬。詔之曰、其山峯岫重疊、且美麗之甚。若神有其山乎。

時水沼縣主猨大海奏言、有女神。名曰、八女津媛。常居山中。故八女國之名、由此而起也。

八月、到的邑而進食。是日、膳夫等遺盞。故時人號其忘盞處曰浮羽。今謂的者訛也。昔筑紫俗號盞曰浮羽。

十九年秋九月甲申朔癸卯、天皇至自日向。

廿年春二月辛巳朔甲申、遣五百野皇女、令祭天照大神。

廿五年秋七月庚辰朔壬午、遣武內宿禰、

Palace.ˣˣˣᵛⁱⁱ At that time, there was a fallen tree, 9,700 feet long, and local officials came and went treading across this tree. People at the time sang,

> Swiftly vanishing morning frost†
> on the log bridge
> of Mike.
> The government officials
> traverse it,
> the log bridge of Mike.

Then the emperor asked, "What tree is this?"

One old man said, "This is the Kunugi tree. A long time ago, before it fell, when struck by the rays of the morning sun, it shadowed Mt. Kishima, and when struck by the rays of the evening sun, it hid Mt. Aso."ˣˣˣᵛⁱⁱⁱ

The emperor said, "This is a divine tree. So let this land be called land of the Mike, or August Tree.

Seventh day. The emperor arrived in Yame District and crossed Mt. Fuji.ˣˣˣⁱˣ He gazed south to Awa Promontory and proclaimed, "The crests of this mountain form many layers, and it is very beautiful. Is there perhaps a kami in this mountain?"

At that time, the Agatanushi of Minuma,[23] Saruōmi, said, "There is such a kami. She is called Yame-tsu-hime, and she lives ever inside the mountain." This is the origin of the name for the land of Yame.ˣˡ

Eighth month. The emperor arrived in Ikuha Village and took his meal. Then he said, "My cooks have forgotten my cup." So people at the time called the place where the cup was forgotten Ukiha. Now it is called Ikuha, but this is a corruption.ˣˡⁱ In antiquity, according to the custom of Tsukushi, a cup was called "ukiha."

Return of the Emperor, Dispatch of Yamato Take

Nineteenth year [89 CE], autumn, ninth month, twentieth day. The emperor returned from Himuka.

Twentieth year [90 CE], spring, second month, fourth day. The emperor dispatched Imperial Princess Iono[24] to venerate Amaterasu.

Twenty-fifth year [95 CE], autumn, seventh month, third day. The emperor dispatched Takeuchi no Sukune to investigate the geography of the

---

23 A powerful lineage group in that area. Their ancestry is linked to Keikō through Saruōmi's son Kuni-chi-wake.
24 Keikō's daughter by Consort Mizu-ha-no-iratsume.

MAP 12 Keikō's tour of Tsukushi

令察北陸及東方諸國之地形、且百姓之消息也。

廿七年春二月辛丑朔壬子、武內宿禰自東國還之奏言、東夷之中、有日高見國。其國人男女、並椎結文身、爲人勇悍。是總曰蝦夷。亦土地沃壤而曠之。擊可取也。

秋八月、熊襲亦反之、侵邊境不止。

冬十月丁酉朔己酉、遣日本武尊、令擊熊襲。時年十六。於是、日本武尊曰、吾得善射者欲與行。其何處有善射者焉。

或者啓之曰、美濃國有善射者。曰弟彥公。於是、日本武尊、遣葛城人宮戶彥、喚弟彥公。故弟彥公、便率石占横立及尾張田子之稻置・乳近之稻置而來。則從日本武尊而行之。

十二月、到於熊襲國。因以、伺其消息及地形之嶮易。時熊襲有魁帥者。名取石鹿文。亦曰川上梟帥。悉集親族而欲宴。

於是日本武尊、解髮作童女姿、以密伺川上梟帥之宴時。仍佩劒裙裏、入於川上梟帥之宴室、居女人之中。川上梟帥、感其童女之容姿、則携手同席、擧坏令飲而戲弄。于時也更深人闌。川上梟帥且被酒。於是日本武尊抽裙中之劒、

Hokuriku region and the various lands of Azuma and the circumstances of the peoples therein.[xlii]

Twenty-seventh year [97 CE], spring, second month, twelfth day. Take-uchi no Sukune returned from the land of Azuma and reported, "Among the eastern barbarians, there is the land of Hidakami.[25] The people of that land, both men and women, tie their hair up in the shape of a mallet and tattoo themselves. Their disposition is ferocious and wild. As a whole, they are called the Emishi.[26] The land there is fertile and spacious. We should attack and take it."

Autumn, eighth month. The Kumaso rebelled again, and their attacks on the borders did not cease.

Winter, tenth month, thirteenth day. The emperor dispatched Yamato Take with orders to attack the Kumaso. At the time, he was sixteen years old.[27] Yamato Take said, "I wish to find someone skilled at archery and go together with him. Where is someone skilled at archery?"

Someone respectfully said, "In the land of Mino there is a skilled archer called Otohiko no Kimi." Yamato Take then dispatched someone from Kazuraki, Miyatohiko, to summon Otohiko no Kimi. Otohiko no Kimi promptly came leading Yokotachi of Ishiura and the Inaki of Tago and Chichika in Owari.[xliii] They accompanied Yamato Take and set out.

Twelfth month. They arrived in the land of the Kumaso. Once there, they considered its features and the steep and flat areas of its terrain. At that time, there was a chieftain in Kumaso named Torishi-kaya, also called Kawakami Takeru.[xliv] He had assembled all of his relatives and meant to hold a banquet for them.

Yamato Take untied his hair and did it up in the style of a young girl, then covertly inquired about the time of Kawakami Takeru's banquet. He wore a sword inside of his clothing and entered Kawakami Takeru's banquet room, staying among the women. Kawakami Takeru was interested in the girl's looks, and he took her hand without delay and brought her to his own seat, raised his cup and had her drink, and made merry. In time the night grew late and the people thinned out, and Kawakami Takeru at last was drunk. Thereupon Yamato Take drew the sword from his clothing

---

25 In the entry for year forty, after conquering the northeast, Yamato Take goes from Hidakami southwest through Hitachi Province to Kai Province, making Hidakami somewhere northeast of Hitachi Province. A number of conflicting theories offer more precision.
26 One group of the more general category of eastern barbarians. Wars between the Yamato court and the Emishi continued through the entire eighth century.
27 Were this the case, he would have been born in Keikō 12; however, his birth is described in Keikō 2.

刺川上梟帥之胸。未及之死、川上梟帥叩頭曰、且待之。吾有所言。時日本武尊、留劔待之。川上梟帥啓之曰、汝尊誰人也。

對曰、吾是大足彦天皇之子也、名日本童男也。

川上梟帥、亦啓之曰、吾是國中之強力者也。是以、當時諸人、不勝我之威力、而無不從者。吾多遇武力矣、未有若皇子者。是以、賤賊陋口以奉尊號。若聽乎。

曰、聽之。

即啓曰、自今以後、號皇子應稱日本武皇子。言訖乃通胸而殺之。故至于今、稱曰日本武尊。是其緣也。

然後、遣弟彦等、悉斬其黨類、無餘噍。既而從海路還倭、到吉備以渡穴海。其處有惡神。則殺之。亦比至難波、殺柏濟之惡神。濟、此云和多利。

廿八年春二月乙丑朔、日本武尊、奏平熊襲之狀曰、臣頼天皇之神靈、以兵一擧、頓誅熊襲之魁帥者、悉平其國。是以、西洲既謐。百姓無事。唯吉備穴濟神、及難波柏濟神、皆有害心、以放毒氣、令苦路人。並爲禍害之藪。故悉殺其惡神、並開水陸之徑。天皇、於是、美日本武之功而異愛。

卅年夏六月、東夷多叛、邊境騷動。

and stabbed Kawakami Takeru in the chest. Before he died, Kawakami Takeru bowed his head and said, "Wait a moment. I have something to say." Yamato Take stayed his sword and waited for him. Kawakami Takeru humbly addressed him, saying, "What lord are you?"[28]

He replied, "I am the son of Emperor Ō-tarashi-hiko, called Yamato Oguna."

Kawakami Takeru addressed him again, saying, "I am the strongest in this land. Consequently, up until now no one has been able to overcome my power, and I have been without match. I have met many valiant warriors, but none like you, prince. If the mouth of this lowly rebel offered up a title for you, would you permit it?"

He said, "So be it."

He then addressed him, saying, "From now on, this prince ought to be called Yamato Take,[29] or Brave of Yamato. When he finished speaking, Yamato Take thrust the sword through his chest and killed him. For this reason, even now he is called Yamato Take.

Afterward, he sent out Otohiko and the others, who put the rest of the band to death, leaving not one alive. Right away he followed the sea route to return to Yamato. When he arrived at Kibi, he passed through the Ana Sea.[xlv] In this place there was an evil kami, and he promptly killed it. When he arrived in Naniwa, he also killed the evil kami of Kashiwa Crossing.[xlvi]

Twenty-eighth year [98 CE], spring, second month, first day. Yamato Take reported how he had pacified the Kumaso, saying, "I relied on the divine power of the emperor, mustered troops all at once, single-mindedly killed the Kumaso chieftain, and completely pacified that land. By this means, the western lands are fully tranquil, and the people live without incident. However, the kami of the Ana Channel in Kibi and of the Kashiwa Channel in Naniwa both had injurious intentions, and they released poison gas that caused suffering to those using the route. Both were sites of disaster. So I killed both evil kami and opened up the land and sea passages. Thereupon, the emperor praised Yamato Take's gallantry and showed him especial favor.[xlvii]

Fortieth year [110 CE], summer, sixth month. The eastern barbarians rebelled in great numbers and caused disruptions in the borderlands.

---

28 The words for "humbly addressed" and "you" here are reserved for speech to the emperor, empress, or crown prince. Although Yamato Take has not been named crown prince, the honorifics used in the *Chronicles* treat him as such.
29 The text calls him Yamato Take from the beginning, but this is the point in the narrative when he gets the name. The *Chronicles* has called him Yamato Take anachronistically up to this point.

秋七月癸未朔戊戌、天皇詔群卿曰、今東國不安、暴神多起。亦蝦夷悉叛、屢略人民。遣誰人以平其亂。

　群臣皆不知誰遣也。日本武尊奏言、臣則先勞西征。是役必大碓皇子之事矣。時大碓皇子愕然之、逃隱草中。

　則遣使者召來。爰天皇責曰、汝不欲矣、豈強遣耶。何未對賊、以豫懼甚焉。因此、遂封美濃。仍如封地。是身毛津君・守君、凡二族之始祖也。

　於是、日本武尊、雄誥之曰、熊襲既平、未經幾年、今更東夷叛之。何日逮于大平矣。臣雖勞之、頓平其亂。

　則天皇持斧鉞、以授日本武尊曰、朕聞、其東夷也、識性暴強。凌犯爲宗。村之無長、邑之勿首。各貪封堺、並相盜略。亦山有邪神。郊有姦鬼。遮衢塞徑。多令苦人。其東夷之中、蝦夷是尤強焉。男女交居、父子無別。冬則宿穴、夏則住樔。衣毛飲血、昆弟相疑。登山如飛禽、行草如走獸。承恩則忘。見怨必報。是以、

Autumn, seventh month, sixteenth day. The emperor decreed to the high government officials, "Now there is unrest in the lands to the east, and many violent kami are active. The Emishi are in complete revolt and are repeatedly plundering the people. By whose dispatch might this rebellion be pacified?"

None of the high government officials knew whom to dispatch. Then Yamato Take addressed the emperor, saying, "I first labored to subjugate the west. Certainly this is a task for Ō-usu." Ō-usu was shocked and fled to hide in the grass.

So the emperor sent a messenger to summon him, and blamed him, saying, "How could you be dispatched by force to do something you do not wish to do? You have yet to face the rebels. Why are you so afraid at the outset?" In the end, the emperor enfeoffed Ō-usu in Mino and had him rule that land. Ō-usu was the first ancestor of two clans: the Kimi of Mugetsu and the Kimi of Mori.[30]

At this, Yamato Take valiantly roared, saying, "Though not even a few years have passed since I pacified the Kumaso,[31] now the eastern barbarians are in rebellion. When will there be peace? Even though this task is arduous for me, I will earnestly pacify this rebellion."

The emperor took an axe and halberd and bestowed them upon Yamato Take, saying,

> We hear that the eastern barbarians are of fierce temperament, concerned only with invasion. Their villages have no chief, their hamlets have no leader. Each seeks to expand his boundaries, and they fight and plunder each other. In their mountains are perverse kami, and in the fields wicked demons, kami and demons who barricade the highways and block off the roads, making much hardship for the people. Among the eastern barbarians, the Emishi are especially strong. The men and women consort together, and paternal relations are not distinct. In the winter they stay in holes, and in the summer, they live in nests. They are clothed in hides and drink blood. Even brothers suspect one another. When they climb mountains, they fly like birds, and when they pass through the grass, they run like dogs. They forget past kindnesses, but always revenge grudges. Accordingly, they hide

---

30 The Mugetsu were a powerful lineage group in the Muge District of Mino Province, present-day Seki City and Mino City. The Mori were also a powerful lineage group in Mino Province.
31 Thirteen years have passed.

箭藏頭髻、刀佩衣中。或聚黨類、而犯邊堺。或伺農桑、以略人民。擊則隱草。追則入山。故往古以來、未染王化。

今朕察汝爲人也、身體長大、容姿端正。力能扛鼎。猛如雷電。所向無前、所攻必勝。即知之、形則我子、實則神人。寔是、天愍朕不叡、且國不平、令經綸天業、不絶宗廟乎。亦是天下則汝天下也。是位則汝位也。願深謀遠慮、探姦伺變、示之以威、懷之以德、不煩兵甲、自令臣隷。即巧言而調暴神、振武以攘姦鬼。

於是、日本武尊、乃受斧鉞、以再拜奏之曰、嘗西征之年、賴皇靈之威、提三尺劔、擊熊襲國。未經浹辰、賊首伏罪。今亦賴神祇之靈、借天皇之威、往臨其境、示以德教、猶有不服、即擧兵擊。仍重再拜之。

天皇則命吉備武彥與大伴武日連、令從日本武尊。亦以七掬脛爲膳夫。

冬十月壬子朔癸丑、日本武尊發路之。戊午、抂道拜伊勢神宮。

arrows in their hair and swords in their clothing. Sometimes they assemble in bands and attack the borders, sometimes they consider the timing of agriculture and sericulture and pillage the people. When attacked, they immediately hide in the grass, and when pursued, they hastily make for the mountains. Consequently, from ancient times until now, they are still unaffected by our kingly influence.

Now, as We look upon your physique, you are tall and of radiant face, strong enough to lift a three-legged bronze cauldron, and of valiant spirit like thunder and lightning. No enemy can occupy the direction you face, and victory is certain wherever you attack. Hence, I knew: in form you are my son, but in fact you are truly divine. Could it really be that heaven pities Our failures of discernment and the lack of proper governance, and orders the unification of the realm so that the imperial succession never ceases to worship the altars of state? Also, this realm is your realm, and this office is your office. I want you to make deep plans and consider farsighted possibilities to seek out the wicked and investigate the traitorous. Show them by means of authority, and persuade them by means of virtue. Do not resort to force of arms; make them become vassals of their own accord. Use clever words to appease the rampaging kami, and brandish your bravery to drive away the wicked demons."[xlviii]

Thereupon Yamato Take received the halberd, bowed twice, and addressed the emperor, saying, "During the year that I subjugated the west, I relied on the authority of imperial blessing, raised my three-span sword, and attacked the land of the Kumaso.[xlix] Before even a few days passed, the enemy leader received his punishment. Now again, depending on the blessings of the kami of heaven and earth and borrowing the authority of the emperor, I will go to the borderlands and demonstrate civilizing influence through virtue. If they still do not surrender, then I will immediately muster soldiers and attack." He again bowed twice.

The emperor then ordered Takehiko of Kibi and Takehi, Muraji of the Ōtomo, to accompany Yamato Take.[32] Also he also made Nana-tsuka-hagi the cook for Yamato Take.

Winter, tenth month, second day. Yamato Take departed by road. Seventh day. He diverted from the route to worship at Ise Grand Shrine. Then

---

32 Takehiko of Kibi is the father of Anato-no-takehime of Kibi, a consort Yamato Take marries in Keikō 51. Ōtomo no Takehi is one of the five ministers receiving an edict from Suin'n in Suinin 25; 115 years have since passed.

仍辭于倭姬命曰、今被天皇之命、而東征將誅諸叛者。故辭之。

於是、倭姬命取草薙劒、授日本武尊曰、愼之。莫怠也。

是歲、日本武尊初至駿河。其處賊陽從之欺曰、是野也、麋鹿甚多。氣如朝霧、足如茂林。臨而應狩。

日本武尊信其言、入野中而覓獸。賊有殺王之情王謂日本武尊也。放火燒其野。王知被欺、則以燧出火之、向燒而得免。一云、王所佩劒叢雲自抽之、薙攘王之傍草。因是、得免。故號其劒曰草薙也。叢雲、此云茂羅玖毛。

王曰、殆被欺。則悉焚其賊衆而滅之。故號其處曰燒津。亦進相摸、欲往上總。望海高言曰、是小海耳。可立跳渡。

乃至于海中、暴風忽起、王船漂蕩、而不可渡。時有從王之妾。曰弟橘媛、穗積氏忍山宿禰之女也。啓王曰、今風起浪泌、王船欲沒。是必海神心也。願賤妾之身、贖王之命而入海。言訖乃披瀾入之。暴風即止。船得著岸。故時人號其海、曰馳水也。

爰日本武尊、則從上總轉、入陸奧國。時大鏡懸於王

he bade farewell to Yamato-hime,[33] saying, "I have now received the emperor's orders and go to the east to put the rebels to death. Thus, I depart."

Yamato-hime then took the sword Kusa-nagi[34] and bestowed it upon Yamato Take, saying, "Be cautious, and do not be negligent."

That year, Yamato Take first arrived in Suruga. The rebels in that place lied, tricking him by saying, "In the fields there are many large stags, so many that their breath is like morning dew and their legs like a thick forest. Go out and hunt them."

Yamato Take believed what they said and went into the field to hunt for game. The rebels, wanting to kill the prince, set fire to the field. The prince is Yamato Take.[35]

The prince, knowing that he had been tricked, immediately took out his flint and set a backfire, and thus was able to escape.

> Another account says that the sword the prince wore, Mura-kumo, drew itself of its own accord and cut down the grass around the prince, and so he was able to escape. Hence, this sword was called Kusa-nagi or Grass Mower.

The prince said, "I was nearly deceived." Then he promptly set fire to the rebel band, utterly destroying them. As a result, this place is called Yakitsu, or Burned.[l] His forces then proceeded to Sagami and wanted to go on to Kamitsufusa. Gazing upon the sea, the prince intoned, "This sea is so tiny that I could dash across."[li]

When he put out to sea, a violent wind suddenly rose, and the prince's boat was taken by the current, so he could not cross. At this time, the consort accompanying him was called Oto-tachibana-hime. She was the daughter of Oyama no Sukune of the Hozumi lineage group.[lii] She said to the prince, "Now there are high winds and rough waves, and the prince's boat is going to founder. This is definitely the will of Wata-tsu-mi, the sea kami. May I substitute my lowly body for your life by casting myself into the sea." When she finished speaking, she parted the waves and entered the water. The violent winds immediately stopped, and the boat was able to make it to shore. Hence, people at that time called this sea Hashiru-mizu, or Dash Waters.[liii]

Yamato Take then continued to Kamitsufusa and shifted to enter the land of Michinoku.[liv] At that time, they hung a large mirror from the prince's

---

33 Keikō's sister and thus Yamato Take's aunt.
34 Found by Susano-o inside the eight-headed serpent in S8 of the "Age of the Gods." In S9.1 the sword is given to Ninigi when he descends from heaven. The sword is not mentioned when the Ise Grand Shrine to Amaterasu is built, but seemingly it was relocated to Ise at that time.
35 The text begins calling him "prince" at this point.

船、從海路廻於葦浦。横渡玉浦、至蝦夷境。蝦夷賊首嶋津神・國津神等、屯於竹水門而欲距。然遙視王船、豫怖其威勢、而心裏知之不可勝、悉捨弓矢、望拜之曰、仰視君容、秀於人倫。若神之乎。欲知姓名。

王對之曰、吾是現人神之子也。於是、蝦夷等悉慄、則褰裳披浪、自扶王船而着岸。仍面縛服罪。故免其罪。因以、俘其首帥、而令從身也。蝦夷既平、自日高見國還之、西南歷常陸、至甲斐國、居于酒折宮。時擧燭而進食。是夜、以歌之問侍者曰、

珥比麼利	にひばり
菟玖波塢須擬氏	つくはをすぎて
異玖用伽禰菟流	いくよかねつる

諸侍者不能答言。時有秉燭者。續王歌之末、而歌曰、

伽餓奈倍氏	かがなべて
用珥波虛々能用	よにはここのよ
比珥波苔塢伽塢	ひにはとをかを

即美秉燭人之聰而敦賞。則居是宮、以靫部賜大伴連之遠祖武日也。

boat, and followed the sea route around to Ashiura, crossed Tamanoura, and arrived at the borders of the Emishi.^lv

The Emishi leaders—Shimatsukami, Kunitsukami, and others—had camped at the port of Taka and meant to repel the attack.^lvi However, when they saw the prince's boat from afar, they at once became fearful of his ferocity and knew in the depths of their hearts that they could not win. They completely discarded their bows and arrows and bowed from afar, saying, "As we look up upon your figure, we see that you are superior to humans. Might you be a kami? We wish to learn your name."

The prince then replied, saying, "I am the child of a kami made manifest." Thereupon the Emishi all trembled, tied up the legs of their clothing, parted the waves, and helped bring the prince's boat to shore. Then they bound their own hands behind their backs and surrendered, and so he pardoned their crimes. At that point the leader was made a prisoner of war and made to attend on the prince. The Emishi were totally pacified, so Yamato Take returned from the land of Hidakami. He passed through Hitachi, going southwest, and arrived in the land of Kai, where he stayed at Sakaori Palace.^lvii Then he lit a torch and had a meal. That night, he used a poem to question his retainers, saying,

> Since passing Tsukuba
> and Niibari,
> how many nights have we slept?^lviii

His various retainers could not reply. At that time, there was a torch bearer who continued the prince's poem, saying,

> Counting them up,
> nine nights
> and ten days.

The prince praised the intelligence of the torch bearer and richly rewarded him.[36] While staying in this palace, he gave the Yugei-no-tomo[37] lineage group to Takehi, the distant ancestor of the Muraji of the Ōtomo.

---

36 It is unusual that the torch bearer is praised for merely counting, and it is similarly unusual that the other retainers were unable to answer. One possibility is that Yamato Take's praise is for being able to come up with a reply in verse on the spot; another is that the torch bearer understood some unspoken nuance of the query.

37 Yugei means "quiver-bearers"; a powerful lineage group from the periphery united or led by the Ōtomo.

於是、日本武尊曰、蝦夷凶首、咸伏其辜。唯信濃國・越國、頗未從化。則自甲斐北、轉歷武藏・上野、西逮于碓日坂。時日本武尊、每有顧弟橘媛之情。故登碓日嶺、而東南望之三歎曰、吾嬬者耶。嬬、此云菟摩。

故因號山東諸國、曰吾嬬國也。於是、分道、遣吉備武彥於越國、令監察其地形嶮易及人民順不。

則日本武尊、進入信濃。是國也、山高谷幽、翠嶺萬重。人倚杖而難升。巖嶮磴紆、長峯數千、馬頓轡而不進。然日本武尊、披烟凌霧、遙徑大山。

既逮于峯、而飢之。食於山中。山神令苦王、以化白鹿、立於王前。王異之、以一箇蒜彈白鹿。則中眼而殺之。爰王忽失道、不知所出。時白狗自來、有導王之狀。隨狗而行之、得出美濃。吉備武彥、自越出而遇之。先是、度信濃坂者、多得神氣、以瘻臥。但從殺白鹿之後、蹈是山者、嚼蒜塗人及牛馬。自不中神氣也。

日本武尊、更還於尾張、即娶尾張氏之女宮簀媛、而淹留踰月。於是、聞近江五十葺山有荒神、即解劒置於宮簀媛家、而徒行之。

至膽吹山、山神化大蛇當道。爰日本武尊、不知主神化蛇之謂、是大蛇必荒神之使也。既得殺主神、其使者豈足求乎。因跨蛇猶行。

時山神之興雲零冰。峯霧谷曀、無復可行之路。

At this, Yamato Take said, "The evil leaders of the Emishi have surrendered for their crimes. Only the lands of Shinano and Koshi still do not follow the kingly way."[lix] Then from Kai he went around north, passed through Musashi and Kamitsukeno, and headed west to Usui Hill.[lx] Around this time, Yamato Take was always longing for Oto-tachibana-hime. So he climbed to the peak of Usui, gazed to the southeast, and sighed three times, saying, "Alas, my wife!" Consequently, the various lands east of this mountain were called Azuma, or My Wife.

Here the road parted, and so he dispatched Takehiko of Kibi to Koshi with orders to investigate the steep and flat areas of its terrain and whether or not the people had fallen in line.

Yamato Take proceeded to enter Shinano. The mountains of this land were tall and its valleys deep, with layer upon layer of verdant ridges, making it difficult for people to climb even with a staff. The peaks were steep and the passes tortuous, and the high summits numbered in the thousands, and the horses balked and would not proceed. However, Yamato Take parted the fog and passed through the mists, crossing the distant, grand mountains.

Having reached the summit, he was hungry in the mountains. The kami of the mountain wanted to torment the prince, and so it transformed into a white deer and stood in front of the prince. The prince thought it strange, and so he threw a bulb of garlic at the deer and hit it in the eye, killing it. Then the prince lost his way and did not know how to get out. At that point, a white dog came forth of its own accord to lead the prince. Walking along following the dog, he came out in Mino. Takehiko of Kibi left Koshi on his own and met him there. Before this, when people crossed through Shinano Pass, many of them collapsed from illness due to the poison gas of the kami.[lxi] After the prince killed the white deer, those who crossed this mountain were unaffected by the kami's gas if they chewed garlic and spread it on human, ox, and horse.

Yamato Take returned again to Owari, where he wed Miyazu-hime, a daughter of the Owari lineage group, and he stayed there at length, into the next month.[lxii] Then he heard that there was a kami rampaging in Ōmi at Mt. Ibuki, and so he unsheathed his sword and placed it in Miyazu-hime's home and went out on foot.[lxiii]

When he arrived at Mt. Ibuki, the mountain kami transformed into a giant snake and blocked the road. Yamato Take, not knowing whether the kami itself had changed into a snake, said, "This giant snake is no doubt a messenger of the rampaging kami. If I am to kill the kami itself, why should I concern myself with its messenger?" He then straddled over the snake and continued on.

The mountain kami generated clouds and made it rain. The peak was covered in fog, the valleys were darkened, and there was no road on which

乃捷遑不知其所跋渉。然凌霧強行。方僅得出。猶失意如醉。因居山下之泉側、乃飲其水而醒之。故號其泉、曰居醒泉也。

　日本武尊、於是、始有痛身。然稍起之、還於尾張。爰不入宮簀媛之家、便移伊勢、而到尾津。

　昔日本武尊、向東之歳、停尾津濱而進食。是時、解一劒置於松下。遂忘而去。今至於此、是劒猶存、故歌曰、

烏波利珥	をはりに
多陀珥霧伽幣流	ただにむかへる
比苔菟麻菟阿波例	ひとつまつあはれ
比等菟麻菟	ひとつまつ
比苔珥阿利勢麼	ひとにありせば
岐農岐勢摩之塢	きぬきせましを
多知波開摩之塢	たちはけましを

　逮于能褒野、而痛甚之。則以所俘蝦夷等、獻於神宮。因遣吉備武彦、奏之於天皇曰、臣受命天朝、遠征東夷。則被神恩、賴皇威、而叛者伏罪、荒神自調。是以、卷甲戢戈、愷悌還之。冀曷日曷時、復命天朝。然天命忽至、隙駟難停。是以、獨臥曠野。無誰語之。豈惜身亡。唯愁不面。既而崩于能褒野、時年卅。

to continue further. Being at a loss, Yamato Take did not know where to step or cross. Nonetheless, he passed through the mists, forced his way ahead, and could just barely make it out. However, he was dazed as if he were drunk. So he stopped at the base of a mountain near a spring, and when he drank its water, he came to his senses. Hence, this spring is called Isame, or Awakening Place.[lxiv]

There Yamato Take first began to feel pain. However, he at last got up and returned to Owari. Yet he did not go to Miyazu-hime's house, and instead went on to Ise, and then to Otsu.[lxv]

Much earlier, in the year that he set out for the east, Yamato Take had stayed at the beach in Otsu and had a meal. At that time, he drew one of his swords and placed it at the base of a pine tree. Then, forgetting about it, he departed. Now, when he came back, the sword was still there. So he sang,

> Oh solitary pine,
> directly facing
> Owari.
> Solitary pine,
> were you a man,
> I would clothe you in a robe
> and equip you with a sword.[38]

He went on to Nobono, and his illness got worse.[lxvi] He presented the Emishi that he had captured to Ise Shrine. Then he dispatched Takehiko of Kibi to report to the emperor, saying, "I received the order of the heavenly court to conquer the distant eastern barbarians. Then, receiving the blessings of the kami and relying on the authority of the emperor, I punished the rebels for their crimes, and the rampaging kami were appeased as a matter of course. Having done this, I wrapped up my armor and surrendered my halberd and returned without cares. I wished someday to report back to the heavenly court. However, the lifespan allotted to me by heaven has suddenly run out, and my time cannot be stayed any more than a cart by a crack in the road. And so I lie down alone in this wasteland, with no one to speak to. Why should I regret my death? I lament only that we cannot meet again." Then he expired in Nobono. He was thirty years old.[39]

---

38 The poem suggests Yamato Take's desire to return to Owari, where Miyazu-hime awaits him. The *Ancient Matters* version of the poem adds the opening line "On Cape Otsu."
39 If Yamato Take was sixteen in the tenth month of Keikō 27, as the end of this section gives the year Keikō 43, Yamato Take should be thirty-two years old when he died. One theory is that the character for "2" was mistakenly dropped; another is that the affairs of Keikō 43 refer only the construction of Yamato Take's tomb.

天皇聞之、寢不安席。食不甘味。晝夜喉咽、泣悲摽擗。因以、大歎之曰、我子小碓王、昔熊襲叛之日、未及總角、久煩征伐、既而恆在左右、補朕不及。然東夷騷動、勿使討者。忍愛以入賊境。一日之無不顧。是以、朝夕進退、佇待還日。何禍兮、何罪兮、不意之間、倐亡我子。自今以後、與誰人之、經綸鴻業耶。即詔群卿命百寮、仍葬於伊勢國能褒野陵。

時日本武尊化白鳥、從陵出之、指倭國而飛之。群臣等、因以、開其棺櫬而視之、明衣空留、而屍骨無之。於是、遣使者

---

40 Disappearance of the corpse suggests the doings of a Daoist transcendent, as for example in the *Biographies of Transcendents* (*Liexian zhuan* 列仙傳).

MAP 13 Eastern travels of Yamato Take

When the emperor heard this, he could not sleep soundly and food had lost its flavor. Day and night he wailed and cried in sadness, beating his breast. Then he said, with great lament, "My son, Imperial Prince O-usu, long ago in the days when the Kumaso rebelled, was still not of age to tie up his hair, yet he labored long in conquest. In no time at all, he was constantly at my side, compensating for Our inadequacies. However, the eastern barbarians revolted, and there was no one to send to attack them. Concealing my love, I sent him to dwell in the rebel frontier, but there was not one day that I did not miss him. Because of this, the days and nights came and went while I anxiously awaited his return. What a disaster, what a crime! All of a sudden, I have lost my son. From now on, with whom will I govern this heavenly endeavor?" Then he decreed to the high government officials, ordering the local officials to bury him in Nobono Tomb in the land of Ise.

At that time, Yamato Take transformed into a swan, exited the tomb, pointed toward the land of Yamato, and flew there. The high government officials went and opened the coffin and looked inside, but only a clean, empty robe occupied it, and there was no corpse.[40] Messengers were dispatched

追尋白鳥。則停於倭琴彈原。仍於其處造陵焉。白鳥更飛至河內、留舊市邑。亦其處作陵。故時人號是三陵、曰白鳥陵。然遂高翔上天。徒葬衣冠。因欲錄功名、即定武部也。是歲也、天皇踐祚卌三年焉。

　五十一年春正月壬午朔戊子、招群卿而宴數日矣。時皇子稚足彥尊・武內宿禰、不參赴于宴庭。天皇召之問其故。因以、奏之曰、其宴樂之日、群卿百寮、必情在戲遊、不存國家。若有狂生、而伺牆閣之隙乎。故侍門下備非常。

　時天皇謂之曰、灼然。灼然、此云以椰知擧。則異寵焉。

　秋八月己酉朔壬子、立稚足彥尊、爲皇太子。是日、命武內宿禰、爲棟梁之臣。

　初日本武尊所佩草薙橫刀、是今在尾張國年魚市郡熱田社也。於是、所獻神宮蝦夷等、晝夜喧譁、出入無禮。時倭姬命曰、是蝦夷等、不可近於神宮。則進上於朝庭。仍令安置御諸山傍。未經幾時、悉伐神山樹、叫呼隣里、而脅人民。

　天皇聞之、詔群卿曰、其置神山傍之蝦夷、是本有獸心、

to follow and search for the swan, which had stopped in Yamato, in the field of Kotohiki.^lxvii This being so, a tomb was built in this place. The swan then flew to Kōchi and stopped in Furuichi Village.^lxviii And another tomb was built there. Accordingly, people at the time called these three tombs Shiratori no Misasagi, or Swan Tombs. In the end, however, the swan flew up into heaven, and so they buried only his clothing and cap. Wanting to commemorate his meritorious service, the emperor established the Take lineage group. This was the forty-third year [113 CE] since the emperor first acceded to the imperial endeavor.

Naming of Crown Prince, Death of Emperor Keikō

Fifty-first year [121 CE], spring, first month, seventh day. The emperor summoned the high government officials to a feast that lasted several days.[41] During this time, Imperial Prince Waka-tarashi-hiko [Seimu] and Takeuchi no Sukune did not come to the feast courtyard. The emperor summoned them and asked the reason. They addressed him, saying, "During the days of this feast, the high government officials and local officials are given over to fun and amusement and do not consider matters of state. What if some madman were to look in through a gap in the palace gate? We stationed ourselves inside in case of emergency."

The emperor said to them, "Brilliant!" He especially favored the two.

Autumn, eighth month, fourth day. Waka-tarashi-hiko [Seimu] was named crown prince.[42] That day, the emperor appointed Takeuchi no Sukune as the leader of all his vassals.

At first, the broad-blade sword Kusa-nagi[43] worn by Yamato Take was at the Atsuta Shrine in Ayuchi District in the land of Owari.^lxix The Emishi who had been presented to the Ise Shrine were noisy and disruptive day and night and disrespectful with their comings and goings. And so Yamato-hime said, "These Emishi cannot be allowed near the shrine," and she presented them to the court. As a result, they were ordered to reside near Mt. Mimoro. In no time at all, they had cut down all of the trees on the sacred mountain, clamored about in the villages, and threatened the residents.

The emperor heard about this and decreed to the high government officials, "The Emishi settled near Mt. Mimoro have the hearts of beasts,

---

41 The Aouma no Sechie 白馬節會 (Festival of the White Horse) normally took place on the seventh day of the first month; this is the first mention of a celebration on this date in the *Chronicles*.
42 The pre-accession record for Seimu claims that he was named crown prince in Keikō 46.
43 This is the only place that Kusa-nagi is referred to as a broadsword.

難住中國。故隨其情願、令班邦畿之外。是今播磨・讚岐・伊勢・安藝・阿波、凡五國佐伯部之祖也。

初日本武尊、娶兩道入姬皇女爲妃、生稻依別王。次足仲彥天皇。次布忍入姬命。次稚武王。其兄稻依別王、是犬上君・武部君、凡二族之始祖也。又妃吉備武彥之女吉備穴戶武媛、生武卵王與十城別王。其兄武卵王、是讚岐綾君之始祖也、弟十城別王、是伊豫別君之始祖也。次妃穗積氏忍山宿禰之女弟橘媛、生稚武彥王。

五十二年夏五月甲辰朔丁未、皇后播磨太郎姬薨。

秋七月癸卯朔己酉、立八坂入媛命爲皇后。

五十三年秋八月丁卯朔、天皇詔群卿曰、朕顧愛子、何日止乎。冀欲巡狩小碓王所平之國。是月、乘輿幸伊勢、轉入東海。

冬十月、至上總國、從海路渡淡水門。是時、聞覺賀鳥之聲。欲見其鳥形、尋而出海中。仍得白蛤。於是、膳臣遠祖名磐鹿六鴈、以蒲爲手繦、白蛤爲膾而進之。故美六鴈臣之功、而賜膳大伴部。

十二月、從東國還之、居伊勢也。是謂綺宮。

---

44 Such details of consorts and descendants are usually given only for emperors. The pre-accession record for Chūai notes that Futaji-no-iri-bime was the daughter of Suinin.
45 An allied lineage group managed by the Kimi of Takebe.
46 A powerful lineage group in Sanuki Province, present-day Ayauta District.

and it is difficult to have them living in the central lands. Therefore, in accordance with their desires, I order them dispersed among distant lands." They are the ancestors of what is now the Saeki lineage group of the five provinces of Harima, Sanuki, Ise, Aki, and Awa.[lxx]

Previously, Yamato Take took Imperial Princess Futaji-no-iri-bime as his consort, and she gave birth to Prince Ina-yori-wake, Emperor Tarashi-naka-tsu-hiko [Chūai],[lxxi] Nuno-shi-iri-bime, and then Prince Waka-take.[44] The older brother, Prince Ina-yori-wake, was the first ancestor of the Kimi of Inukami and of Takebe.[45][lxxii] Another consort was the daughter of Takehiko of Kibi, Anato-no-takehime of Kibi. She gave birth to Prince Take-kaigo and Prince Tō-ki-wake. The older brother, Prince Take-kaigo, was the first ancestor of the Kimi of Aya in Sanuki.[46] The younger brother, Prince Tō-ki-wake, was the first ancestor of the Kimi of Wake in Iyo.[47] Another consort was the daughter of Oshiyama no Sukune of the Hozumi lineage group, Oto-tachibana-hime. She gave birth to Prince Waka-take-hiko.

Fifty-second year [122 CE], summer, fifth month, fourth day. Empress Ō-iratsume of Harima perished.[48]

Autumn, seventh month, seventh day. Yasaka-iri-bime was named empress.[49]

Fifty-third year [123 CE], autumn, eighth month, first day. The emperor issued an edict to the high government officials, saying, "Our longing for the son We loved, when will it stop? We wish to take a tour of the lands pacified by O-usu." That month, the imperial palanquin went to Ise, and from there, eastward to the sea.

Winter, tenth month. The emperor arrived in Kamitsufusa, then went by sea across to the port of Awa.[lxxiii] At that time, he heard the cry of an osprey and, wanting to see the bird, pursued it to sea. By doing so, he got a white clam. On this occasion, the distant ancestor of the Omi of the Kashiwade, called Iwa-kamu-tsu-kari,[50] used a cattail to tie up his sleeves, thinly sliced the clam, and presented it to the emperor. As a reward for this feat, the Kashiwade Ōtomo[51] lineage group was bestowed upon him.

Twelfth month. The emperor returned from the eastern countries and dwelt in Ise. The place was called Kanihata Palace.[lxxiv]

---

47 Perhaps a powerful lineage group in Iyo Province. In *Ancient Matters*, the Kimi of Aya in Sanuki have the same lineage as the Kimi of Wake in Ise; perhaps that text confused Iyo and Ise.
48 In Keikō 2, her name is given as Ō-iratsume of Inabi in Harima.
49 Yasaka-no-iri-bime first appears in Keikō 4.
50 In the Kōgen book, Ō-hiko is given as the ancestor of the Omi of Kashiwade.
51 Perhaps a group of Kashiwade, or cooks, managed by, or serving, the Muraji of the Ōtomo.

五十四年秋九月辛卯朔己酉、自伊勢還、於倭居纏向宮。

　　五十五年春二月戊子朔壬辰、以彥狹嶋王、拜東山道十五國都督。是豐城命之孫也。然到春日穴咋邑、臥病而薨之。是時、東國百姓、悲其王不至、竊盜王尸、葬於上野國。

　　五十六年秋八月、詔御諸別王曰、汝父彥狹嶋王、不得向任所而早薨。故汝專領東國。

　　是以、御諸別王、承天皇命、且欲成父業。則行治之、早得善政。時蝦夷騷動。即舉兵而擊焉。時蝦夷首帥足振邊・大羽振邊・遠津闇男邊等、叩頭而來之。頓首受罪、盡獻其地。因以、免降者、而誅不服。是以東久之無事焉。由是、其子孫、於今有東國。

　　五十七年秋九月、造坂手池。即竹蒔其堤上。

　　冬十月、令諸國興田部屯倉。

　　五十八年春二月辛丑朔辛亥、幸近江國、居志賀三歲。是謂高穴穗宮。

　　六十年冬十一月乙酉朔辛卯、天皇崩於高穴穗宮、時年一百六歲。

52　The office of "head" is of Chinese origin. The fifteen provinces of the east are not specified, and eastern Japan was usually conceived of as being comprised of nine provinces.
53　Toyoki was a son of Sujin ordered to rule the east in Sujin 48, and is given as the ancestor of the Kimi of Kamitsukeno and Shimotsukeno. In Suinin 5, the general Ya-tsuna-da is given as the ancestor of the Kimi of Kamitsukeno, which means that Hiko-sashima could

Fifty-fourth year [124 CE], autumn, ninth month, nineteenth day. The emperor returned to Yamato from Ise and dwelt in Makimuku Palace.

Fifty-fifth year [125 CE], spring, second month, fifth day. Prince Hiko-sashima was appointed commander-in-chief of the fifteen lands east of the eastern mountain region.[52] He was the grandson of Toyoki.[53] However, when he arrived at Anakui Village in Kasuga, he fell ill and perished.[lxxv] At that time, the people of the eastern lands were saddened that the prince would not be coming, and so they secretly stole the prince's body and buried him in Kamitsukeno.

Fifty-sixth year [126 CE], autumn, eighth month. The emperor decreed to Mimoro-wake, saying, "Your father, Hiko-sashima, could not attend to his posting and died before his time. Therefore, you must go and rule the eastern lands."

Upon this, Mimoro-wake received the emperor's order and, furthermore, wanted to complete his father's undertaking. So he went and governed and quickly instituted good administration. At that time, the Emishi revolted. He promptly mustered troops and attacked. The Emishi leaders Ashifuribe, Ōhafuribe, and Tōtsukuraobe came forth bowing their heads. They put their faces to the ground and received their punishment and presented all of their lands to him. Thereupon, he forgave those who surrendered and put to death those who resisted. Consequently, the eastern lands were without incident for a long time. For this reason, Mimoro-wake's descendants are now in the eastern lands.

Fifty-seventh year [127 CE], autumn, ninth month. The government built Sakate Reservoir. Bamboo was planted on the dike.[lxxvi]

Winter, tenth month. The emperor ordered the various lands to establish Tabe imperial fiefs.[lxxvii]

Fifty-eighth year [128 CE], spring, second month, eleventh day. The emperor toured the land of Ōmi and dwelt in Shiga for three years. His place of residence was called Taka-anaho Palace.[lxxviii]

Sixtieth year [130 CE], winter, eleventh month, seventh day. The emperor expired in Taka-anaho Palace. He was 106 years old.[54]

---

    be Ya-tsuna-da's son. However, Ya-tsuna-da is not identified as a prince. Hiko-sashima's name is perhaps taken from the Sashima District in present-day Ibaraki Prefecture.

54 This would mean that he ascended the throne at age forty-seven and was born in Suinin 54, which contradicts the year given when he was named crown prince, Suinin 37. Following the earlier note that gives his age as twenty-one when being named crown prince, Keikō would be 143 at the time of his death.

稚足彦天皇 成務天皇

稚足彦天皇、大足彦忍代別天皇第四子也。母皇后曰八坂入姬命。八坂入彦皇子之女也。大足彦天皇卅六年、立爲太子。年廿四。

六十年冬十一月、大足彦天皇崩。

元年春正月甲申朔戊子、皇太子卽位。是年也、太歲辛未。

二年冬十一月癸酉朔壬午、葬大足彦天皇於倭國之山邊道上陵。尊皇后曰皇太后。

三年春正月癸酉朔己卯、以武內宿禰爲大臣也。初天皇與武內宿禰同日生之。故有異寵焉。

四年春二月丙寅朔、詔之曰、我先皇大足彦天皇、聰明神武、膺籙受圖。洽天順人、撥賊反正。德侔覆燾。道協造化。是以、普天率土、莫不王臣。稟氣懷靈、何非得處。今朕嗣踐寶祚。夙夜兢惕。然黎元蠢爾、不悛野心。是國郡無君長、縣邑無首渠者焉。自今以後、國郡立長、縣邑置首。卽取當國之幹了者、任其國郡之首長、是爲中區之蕃屛也。

55 The two characters used for "lady" (hime) distinguish between daughters and granddaughters or later descendants of emperors up to the Seimu book, at which point the distinction is lost.
56 In the Keikō book, Seimu is named crown prince in Keikō 51.

Accession of Emperor Seimu

Emperor Waka-tarashi-hiko [Seimu] was the fourth child of Emperor Ō-tarashi-hiko-oshiro-wake [Keikō].[lxxix] His mother was Yasaka-iri-bime, the daughter of Yasaka-iri-biko.[55]

In the forty-sixth year [116 CE] of the reign Emperor Ō-tarashi-hiko-oshiro-wake, he was named crown prince.[56] He was twenty-four years old.

Sixtieth year [130 CE], winter, eleventh month. Emperor Ō-tarashi-hiko-oshiro-wake expired.

First year [131 CE], spring, first month, fifth day. The crown prince acceded to the imperial throne. This was the year of the Metal Sheep.

Second year [132 CE], winter, eleventh month, tenth day. Emperor Ō-tarashi-hiko-oshiro-wake was buried in Yama-no-be-no-michi-no-e Tomb.[lxxx] The empress was honored with the title of empress dowager.

Third year [133 CE], spring, fifth month, seventh day. Takeuchi no Sukune was named Greater Minister.[57] Previously, the emperor and Takeuchi no Sukune had been born on the same day.[58] So he was especially favored.

Fourth year [134 CE], spring, second month, first day. The emperor issued an edict, saying, "Our previous Emperor Ō-tarashi-hiko-oshiro-wake [Keikō] was brilliantly intelligent and divinely brave. He succeeded to the throne and received its mandate. His reign corresponded with the will of heaven and followed the hearts of men, and he drove out the rebels and returned them to propriety. His virtue equaled that of heaven and earth, and his manner facilitated the creation of all things. So even to the ends of heaven and earth, there were none who did not serve as his vassals. How could the people not dwell in peace? Now We have succeeded him in ruling this heavenly endeavor, and day and night We are wary and cautious. However, the people squirm under our rule and will not reform their untamed hearts. The lands and regions have no lords nor heads, and localities and villages have no chieftains. From now on, in the lands and regions leaders will be established, and in localities and villages chieftains will be placed. Accordingly, take superior people from the relevant lands and appoint them as lords and heads of provinces and domains.[lxxxi] Thereby, a protective barrier will be formed around the central regions."[lxxxii]

---

57 The position of Greater Minister (Ō-imichi, Ōmachikimi) should be distinguished from that of Ō-omi, which uses the same characters. The title here is an extension of the status "leader of all his vassals," which Takeuchi no Sukune received in Keikō 51. Note that the lineage groups that later succeeded to Ō-omi—the Heguri, Kose, and Soga—traced their lineage to Takeuchi no Sukune.

58 Likely referring to the same day of the month, or days with the same stem-branch combination.

五年秋九月、令諸國、以國郡立造長、縣邑置稻置。並賜楯矛以爲表。則隔山河而分國縣、隨阡陌以定邑里。因以東西爲日縱、南北爲日橫。山陽曰影面。山陰曰背面。是以、百姓安居。天下無事焉。
　　卅八年春三月庚辰朔、立甥足仲彦尊、爲皇太子。
　　六十年夏六月己巳朔己卯、天皇崩。時年一百七歳。

Fifth year [135 CE], autumn, ninth month. The emperor ordered the various provinces to establish lords in provinces and chieftains in districts and villages. He also bestowed upon them a shield and halberd as a marker of rank. According to the divisions established by mountains and rivers, he divided up the provinces, and based on the cardinal directions, he established the villages.[59] So east and west followed the path of the sun, the north and south is perpendicular to the path of the sun, the side of the mountains struck by the sun was south, and the side of the mountains in the shadows was north. Thereby the people dwelt in peace, and the realm was without incident.

Forty-eighth year [178 CE], spring, third month, first day. The emperor's nephew Tarashi-naka-tsu-hiko [Chūai] was named crown prince.[60]

Sixtieth year [190 CE], summer, sixth month, eleventh day. The emperor expired. He was 107 years old.[61]

---

59 This carries out the edict of the previous year, the first time that regional administration was implemented across the entire Yamato state.
60 Tarashi-naka-tsu-hiko was the son of Yamato Take, Seimu's half-brother.
61 According to his pre-accession record, Seimu was named crown prince in Keikō 46 at age twenty-four, so he should be ninety-eight years old at his death.

足仲彦天皇 仲哀天皇

足仲彦天皇、日本武尊第二子也。母皇后曰兩道入姬命。活目入彦五十狹茅天皇之女也。天皇容姿端正。身長十尺。稚足彦天皇卌八年、立爲太子。時年卅一。稚足彦天皇無男。故立爲嗣。

六十年、天皇崩。明年秋九月壬辰朔丁酉、葬于倭國狹城盾列陵。盾列、此云多々那美。

元年春正月庚寅朔庚子、太子即天皇位。

秋九月丙戌朔、尊母皇后曰皇太后。

冬十一月乙酉朔、詔群臣曰、朕未逮于弱冠、而父王既崩之。乃神靈化白鳥而上天。仰望之情、一日勿息。是以、冀獲白鳥、養之於陵域之池、因以、覩其鳥、欲慰顧情。則令諸國、俾貢白鳥。

閏十一月乙卯朔戊午、越國貢白鳥四隻。於是、送鳥使人、宿菟道河邊。時蘆髮蒲見別王、視其白鳥、而問之曰、何處將去白鳥也。

Book 8
Emperor Chūai

Accession of Emperor Chūai, Burial of Yamato Take

Emperor Tarashi-naka-tsu-hiko [Chūai] was the second child of Yamato Take.^i His mother the empress was called Futa-ji-no-iri-bime.¹ She was the daughter of Emperor Ikume-iri-biko-isa-chi [Suinin]. The emperor had a beautiful face and was almost ten feet tall. He was named crown prince in the forty-eighth year [178 CE] of the reign of Emperor Waka-tarashi-hiko.

At that time, he was thirty-one years old.

Emperor Waka-tarashi-hiko [Seimu] had no sons. So Tarashi-naka-tsu-hiko was named successor.^ii

Sixtieth year [190 CE]. The emperor expired. In the next year [191 CE], autumn, ninth month, sixth day, he was buried in Saki no Tatanami Tomb, Yamato Province.^iii

First year [192 CE], spring, first month, eleventh day. The crown prince acceded to the imperial throne.

Autumn, ninth month, first day. The empress was honored with the title of empress dowager.

Winter, eleventh month, first day. The emperor decreed to the high government officials, saying, "Before We reached twenty years of age, Our father had already expired,² and his spirit turned into a swan and went up to heaven. My feelings of longing do not abate for even one day. For this reason, I wish to capture swans and raise them in the moat around his tomb. Then my looking upon the swans will comfort my feelings of grief." He then ordered the various provinces to present him with swans.

Intercalary eleventh month, fourth day.³ Koshi Province presented four swans.^iv The messenger who brought them stayed near the Uji River. At that time, Prince Ashi-kami-no-kamami-wake saw the swans and asked, "Where are you taking the swans?"

---

1   Although he never acceded to the throne, Yamato Take and his empress Futa-ji-no-iri-bime are treated in the text as though they were equal to ruling sovereigns.
2   If Chūai was thirty-one when he became crown prince in the forty-eighth year of Seimu, that would mean that he was not born for thirty-six years after the death of his father Yamato Take.
3   The Chinese lunisolar calendar added leap months, about seven every nineteen years, to keep the lunar calendar and the solar calendar relatively aligned. This is the first appearance of an intercalary month in the *Chronicles*.

越人答曰、天皇戀父王、而將養狎。故貢之。

則蒲見別王、謂越人曰、雖白鳥而燒之則爲黑鳥。仍強之奪白鳥而將去。爰越人參赴之請焉。天皇、於是、惡蒲見別王无禮於先王、乃遣兵卒而誅矣。蒲見別王、則天皇之異母弟也。時人曰、父是天也。兄亦君也。其慢天違君、何得免誅耶。是年也、太歲壬申。

二年春正月甲寅朔甲子、立氣長足姬尊爲皇后。

先是、娶叔父彥人大兄之女大中姬爲妃。生麛坂皇子・忍熊皇子。

次娶來熊田造祖大酒主之女弟媛、生譽屋別皇子。

二月癸未朔戊子、幸角鹿。即興行宮而居之。是謂笥飯宮。即月、定淡路屯倉。

三月癸丑朔丁卯、天皇巡狩南國、於是、留皇后及百寮、而從駕二三卿大夫及官人數百、而輕行之。至紀伊國、而居于德勒津宮。當是時、熊襲叛之不朝貢。天皇、於是、將討熊襲國。則自德勒津發之、浮海而幸穴門。即日、使遣角鹿、勅皇后曰、便從其津發之、逢於穴門。

夏六月辛巳朔庚寅、天皇泊于豐浦津。且皇后從角鹿發而行之、到渟田門、食於船上。時海鯽魚、多聚船傍。皇后以酒灑鯽魚。鯽魚即醉而浮之。時海人多獲其魚而歡曰、聖王所賞之魚焉。

The person from Koshi replied, "The emperor loved his father the prince and wants to raise them. Therefore we will present them to him."

Prince Kamami-wake said to the person from Koshi, "Even a swan turns black when roasted." Then he forcibly stole the swans and took them away. The person from Koshi presented himself at court and reported what had happened. The emperor despised Prince Kamami-wake's disrespect for the departed prince and promptly dispatched soldiers to kill him. Prince Kamami-wake was the emperor's paternal younger half-brother. People at the time said, "His father was heaven, and his older brother is lord. By his action he insulted heaven and defied his lord, how could he escape execution?" This year was that of Water Monkey.

Second year [193 CE], spring, first month, eleventh day. Okinaga-tarashi-hime [Jingū] was named empress.[v]

Previously the emperor had wed O-naka-tsu-hime, daughter of his uncle Hiko-hito-ōe, and made her his consort. She gave birth to Imperial Prince Kagosaka and Imperial Prince Oshikuma.[4]

Next, he wed Oto-hime, daughter of the ancestor of the Miyatsuko of Kukumata, Osaka-nushi. She gave birth to Imperial Prince Homuya-wake.

Second month, sixth day. The emperor went to Tsunuga. There he built a temporary palace and dwelt therein, calling it Kehi Palace.[vi] That month he established the imperial fief of Awaji.

Revolt of the Kumaso

Third month, fifteenth day. The emperor did an inspection tour of the southern provinces. The empress and the public officials stayed behind, but two or three high government officials and several hundred bureaucrats, travelling lightly, accompanied him. The emperor arrived in Kii Province and stayed in Tokorotsu Palace.[vii] At that time, the Kumaso revolted and would not present tribute. The emperor, in response, wanted to attack the land of the Kumaso. He promptly departed Tokorotsu and went by boat to Anato. The same day, he dispatched a messenger to Tsunuga with a decree for the empress, saying, "Leave that port immediately and meet me at Anato."[viii]

Summer, sixth month, tenth day. The emperor stayed at the harbor of Toyura.[ix] The empress departed from Tsunuga, arrived at the port of Nuta, and ate aboard the ship.[x] At that time a great number of seabream collected alongside the ship, and the empress poured wine on them. The seabream quickly became drunk and floated. At that point, the fishers caught them in great numbers, and said happily, "These fish are the gift of a sage king."

---

4   Kagosaka and Oshikuma later lead a revolt after Chūai's death, detailed in the pre-accession record of Jingū.

故其處之魚、至于六月、常傾浮如醉、其是之緣也。

秋七月辛亥朔乙卯、皇后泊豐浦津。是日、皇后得如意珠於海中。

九月、興宮室于穴門而居之、是謂穴門豐浦宮。

八年春正月己卯朔壬午、幸筑紫。時岡縣主祖熊鰐、聞天皇之車駕、豫拔取五百枝賢木、以立九尋船之舳、而上枝掛白銅鏡、中枝掛十握劒、下枝掛八尺瓊、參迎于周芳沙麼之浦。而獻魚鹽地。因以奏言、自穴門至向津野大濟爲東門、以名籠屋大濟爲西門。限沒利嶋・阿閉嶋爲御筥、割柴嶋爲御鼠。御鼠、此云彌那陪。以逆見海爲鹽地。既而導海路。自山鹿岬廻之入岡浦。

到水門、御船不得進。則問熊鰐曰、朕聞、汝熊鰐者、有明心以參來。何船不進。

熊鰐奏之曰、御船所以不得進者、非臣罪。是浦口有男女二神。男神曰大倉主。女神曰菟夫羅媛。必是神之心歟。

天皇則禱祈之、以挾秒者倭國菟田人伊賀彥爲祝令祭。則船得進。

皇后別船、自洞海洞、此云久岐。入之。潮涸不得進。時熊鰐更還之、自洞奉迎皇后。則見御船不進、惶懼之、忽作魚沼・鳥池、悉聚魚鳥。皇后看是魚鳥之遊、而忿心稍解。及潮滿即泊于岡津。

又筑紫伊覩縣主祖五十迹手、聞天皇之行、拔取五百枝賢木、立于船之舳艫、上枝掛八尺瓊、中枝掛白銅鏡、

For this reason, in the sixth month, the fish of this place always open and close their mouths as though drunk.

Autumn, seventh month, fifth day. The empress stayed at the harbor of Toyura. On that day, the empress got a wish-fulfilling pearl from the sea.

Ninth month. The emperor built a palace in Anato and dwelt there, calling it Anato no Toyura Palace.[xi]

Eighth year [199 CE], spring, first month, fourth day. The emperor went to Tsukushi. At that time, the ancestor of the Agatanushi of Oka, Wani, heard of the emperor's procession, so he preemptively uprooted a many-branched sakaki tree and placed it at the prow of a nine-fathom ship.[xii] He hung from its upper branches an alloy mirror, hung from its middle branches a ten-hand sword, hung from its lower branches an eight-shaftment jewel, and awaited the emperor at Saba Harbor in Suwa.[xiii] He presented to the emperor a location for collecting salt and catching fish. Then he addressed the emperor, saying, "From Anato to the great crossing of Mukatsuno is the eastern gate, and to the great crossing of Nagoya the western gate.[xiv] Up to the islands of Motori and Ahe shall be the august basket, and up to Shiba Island shall be the august pot, and the Sakami Sea is the land of salt."[xv] Then he guided the emperor and his retinue along the sea route. They went around Cape Yamaka to Oka Harbor.[xvi]

When they reached the harbor, the imperial ship could no longer proceed. The emperor thus asked Wani, "We hear that you, Wani, came to greet us with pure intentions. Why, then, can the ships not proceed?"

Wani addressed the emperor, saying, "The reason the ship cannot go forward is not because of any crime I have committed. Near the mouth of this harbor there are two kami, one male and one female. The male kami is called Ōkura-nushi, and the female kami is called Tsubura-hime. Surely this is the will of these kami."

The emperor immediately prayed, and made the captain, a man from Uda in Yamato, Igahiko, serve as priest and made him worship these kami. Thereupon the ships could proceed.

The empress came on a separate ship and set out from the Kuki Sea.[xvii] However, the tide was out, and she could not proceed. At this time, Wani returned and went to meet the empress at Kuki, but seeing that the ship could not proceed, he was afraid. He quickly made a pond for fish and pond for birds and stocked them completely with fish and birds. The empress saw the fish and the birds at play, and the anger in her heart was gradually put at ease. When the tide came, she went on to stay at Oka Harbor.

Also, the ancestor of the Agatanushi of Ito in Tsukushi, Itote, heard of the emperor's coming, so he uprooted a many-branched sakaki tree and placed it at the prow of his ship.[xviii] He hung from its upper branches an eight-shaftment jewel, from its middle branches an alloy mirror, and from

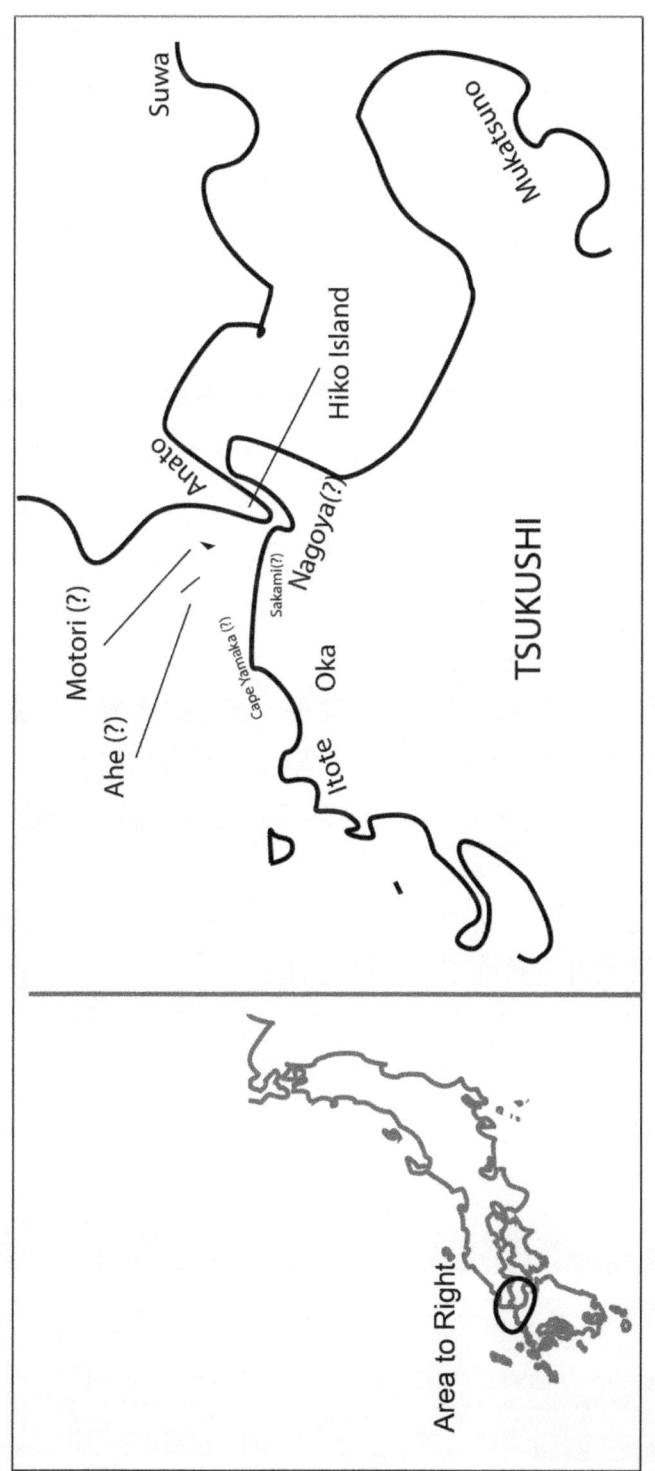

MAP 14 Place-names in Chūai 8

下枝掛十握劒、参迎于穴門引嶋而獻之。因以奏言、臣敢所以獻是物者、天皇如八尺瓊之勾、以曲妙御宇、且如白銅鏡、以分明看行山川海原、乃提是十握劒、平天下矣。

天皇即美五十迹手、曰伊蘇志。故時人號五十迹手之本土、曰伊蘇國。今謂伊覩者訛也。

己亥、到儺縣、因以居橿日宮。

秋九月乙亥朔己卯、詔群臣以議討熊襲。時有神、託皇后而誨曰、天皇何憂熊襲之不服。是膂宍之空國也。豈足舉兵伐乎。愈茲國而有寶國、譬如處女之睩、有向津國_{睩、此云麻用弭枳}。眼炎之金・銀・彩色、多在其國。是謂栲衾新羅國焉。若能祭吾者、則曾不血刃、其國必自服矣。復熊襲爲服。其祭之、以天皇之御船、及穴門直踐立所獻之水田、名大田、是等物爲幣也。

天皇聞神言、有疑之情。便登高岳、遙望之大海、曠遠而不見國。於是、天皇對神曰、朕周望之、有海無國。豈於大虛有國乎。誰神徒誘朕。復我皇祖諸天皇等、盡祭神祇。豈有遺神耶。

時神亦託皇后曰、如天津水影、押伏而我所見國、何謂無國、以誹謗我言。其汝王之、如此言、

its lower branches a ten-hand sword. He came to meet the emperor at Hiko Island and presented these things.[xix] In doing so, he addressed the emperor, saying, "The reason I dare to present these things to the emperor is this: like the bend in an eight-shaftment jewel, may you bend the heavens into line, and like looking into an alloy mirror, may you clearly look upon the mountains, rivers, seas, and fields, and bringing down this ten-hand sword, may you pacify the realm."

The emperor then praised Itote saying, "Isoshi!"[5] So people at the time called Itote's homeland the land of Iso. Now it is called Ito, a corruption.

On the twenty-first day, the emperor arrived in the district of Naga and stayed in Kashihi Palace.[xx]

Divine Instruction to Conquer Korea, Death of the Emperor

Autumn, ninth month, fifth day. The emperor decreed to the high government officials, making them hold conference on whether to attack the Kumaso. At that time, there was a kami who, using the empress as a medium, said, "Emperor, why do you worry about the insubordination of the Kumaso? It is an empty, barren land. How could it be worth mustering troops to attack it? There is a land of treasure that exceeds the Kumaso land. That land is like the drawn eyebrow of a lady.[6] It is a land opposite our harbors. There is so much gold, silver, and bright fabrics that it makes one's eyes burn. That land is called Taku-busuma Shiraki. If you venerate me well, then without bloodying your sword at all, that land will surrender all on its own. The Kumaso too will be made to surrender. All I ask for veneration is the emperor's ship, and the paddy field named Ota presented by Homutachi, the Agatanushi of Anato, to be used as offerings."

The emperor heard the kami's words, but harbored doubts. So he climbed to the top of a tall hill and gazed afar over the great sea, but far and wide he saw no land. Thereupon the emperor replied to the kami, saying, "We have looked all around: there is no land, only sea. How could there be a great land when seen from the sky? What kami is this who mischievously tricks me? My imperial ancestors, the past emperors, completely venerated all the kami of heaven and earth. How could there be a kami that has not been venerated?"

The kami again spoke through the empress, saying, "How can you say there is no land—the land that I look down upon and see like a shadow on the water—and doubt my words? You, king, having thus spoken, because in

---

5   Meaning devoted.
6   Perhaps referring to the curved eastern coast of the Korean peninsula as seen from the sea.

而遂不信者、汝不得其國。唯今皇后始之有胎。其子有獲焉。

然天皇猶不信、以強擊熊襲。不得勝而還之。

九年春二月癸卯朔丁未、天皇忽有痛身、而明日崩。時年五十二。即知、不用神言而早崩。一云、天皇親伐熊襲、中賊矢而崩也。於是、皇后及大臣武內宿禰、匿天皇之喪、不令知天下。則皇后詔大臣及中臣烏賊津連・大三輪大友主君・物部膽咋連・大伴武以連曰、今天下、未知天皇之崩。若百姓知之、有懈怠者乎。

則命四大夫、領百寮令守宮中。竊收天皇之屍、付武內宿禰、以從海路遷穴門。而殯于豐浦宮、爲无火殯斂。无火殯斂、此謂褒那之阿餓利。甲子、大臣武內宿禰、自穴門還之、復奏於皇后。是年、由新羅役、以不得葬天皇也。

the end you do not believe, will not obtain this land. However, the empress now has become pregnant, and that child will obtain it."

Nevertheless, the emperor still did not believe, and attacked the Kumaso on his own. He was unable to win victory and returned.

Ninth year [200 CE], spring, second month, fifth day. The emperor suddenly fell ill, and on the next day, he expired.

> At the time, he was fifty-two years old.[7] As for his death, because he did not heed the words of the kami, he expired at a young age. It is also said that the emperor attacked the Kumaso himself, and that he was hit by an enemy arrow and expired.[8]

The empress and Greater Minister Takeuchi no Sukune concealed the emperor's temporary burial, and did not let it be known in the realm. Then the empress decreed to Greater Minister Takeuchi no Sukune as well as to Ikatsu, Muraji of the Nakatomi; Ōtomonushi, Kimi of Ōmiwa; Ikui, Muraji of the Mononobe; and Takemotsu, Muraji of the Ōtomo; saying, "At present, the realm does not know that the emperor has expired. If the people knew, they might become indolent."[xxi]

She ordered these four high government officials to lead the public officials in guarding the interior of the palace. She then secretly packed up the emperor's corpse and bestowed it upon Takeuchi no Sukune, who returned to Anato by sea. There he held the temporary burial at Toyura Palace, but did so without lighting any fires. On the twenty-second day, Greater Minister Takeuchi no Sukune returned from Anato by himself and made his report to the empress. The same year, because of the Silla campaign, they could not bury the emperor.

---

7   Chūai is earlier said to have become crown prince at thirty-one. Seimu died twelve years after, and Chūai then died nine years later, meaning he should have been fifty-three. The writer of the note failed to count one year, 191 CE, in which there was no sitting emperor.
8   In some manuscripts the note does not begin until "It is also said," and the earlier text appears in full-size.

氣長足姬尊 神功皇后

氣長足姬尊、稚日本根子彥大日々天皇之曾孫、氣長宿禰王之女也。母曰葛城高顙媛。足仲彥天皇二年、立爲皇后。幼而聰明叡智。貌容壯麗。父王異焉。

九年春二月、足仲彥天皇崩於筑紫橿日宮。時皇后傷天皇不從神敎而早崩、以爲、知所祟之神、欲求財寶國。是以、命群臣及百寮、以解罪改過、更造齋宮於小山田邑。

三月壬申朔、皇后選吉日、入齋宮、親爲神主。則命武內宿禰令撫琴。喚中臣烏賊津使主、爲審神者。因以千繒高繒、置琴頭尾、而請曰、先日敎天皇者誰神也。願欲知其名。

逮于七日七夜、乃答曰、神風伊勢國之百傳度逢縣之拆鈴五十鈴宮所居神、名撞賢木嚴之御魂天疎向津媛命焉。

亦問之除是神復有神乎。

答曰、幡荻穗出吾也、於尾田吾田節之淡郡所居神之有也。

問、亦有耶。

答曰、於天事代於虛事代玉籤入彥嚴之事代主神有之也。

問、亦有耶。

答曰、有無之不知焉。

於是、審神者曰、今不答而更後有言乎。

Book 9
Empress Jingū

The Silla Campaign

Okinaga-tarashi-hime [Jingū] was the great-grandchild of Emperor Wa-ka-yamato-neko-hiko-ō-bibi [Kaika].[i] Her mother was Takanuka-hime of Kazuraki. In the second year of the reign of Emperor Tarashi-naka-tsu-hiko [Chūai], she was named empress. From a young age, she was astute and intelligent, and she was very beautiful.[ii] Her father[1] thought it strange.

Ninth year [200 CE], spring, second month. Emperor Tarashi-naka-tsu-hiko expired in Kashihi Palace in Tsukushi. At that time, the empress grieved that the emperor had not followed the instructions of the kami and died an early death. She wished to discover the identity of the kami who smote him, and to seek out the land of treasure. So she ordered the high government officials and public officials to purge evils and correct mistakes and, furthermore, made them construct a palace for ritual worship in Oyamada Village.[iii]

Third month. On the first day, the empress selected an auspicious day, entered the palace for ritual worship, and acted herself as the head priest. She ordered Takeuchi no Sukune to play the zither and summoned Ikatsu, Omi of the Nakatomi, to act as the interpreter.[iv] She placed many woven offerings upon the head and tail of the zither and said, "Who is the kami that instructed the emperor the other day? I want to know its name."

Seven days and seven nights passed, and she[2] replied, "The kami[v] who dwells in the shrine at Isuzu, in the Watarai District of Ise Province.[vi] She is called Tsuki-sakaki-itsu-no-mitama-ama-sakaru-muka-tsu-hime."[vii]

The empress then asked, "Are there any kami besides this one?"

She replied, "I who have appeared before you like swaying ears of rice dwell in Agatafushi in Oda, in Awa District."[viii]

The empress then asked again, "Are there any others?"

She replied, "There is the kami Ame-ni-koto-shiro-sora-ni-koto-shiro-tama-kushi-iri-biko-itsu-no-koto-shiro."[ix]

Then the empress asked again, "Are there any others?"

She replied, "I don't know if there are any others or not."

Thereupon the interpreter said, "Now you have no reply, but is there anything further you have to say?"

---

1 Okinaga no Sukune.
2 Here "she" is Jingū. Since she is the head priest and medium, she is actually talking to herself.

則對曰、於日向國橘小門之水底所居、而水葉稚之出居神、名表筒男・中筒男・底筒男神之有也。

問、亦有耶。

答曰、有無之不知焉。

遂不言且有神矣。時得神語、隨教而祭。然後、遣吉備臣祖鴨別、令撃熊襲國。未經浹辰、而自服焉。

且荷持田村荷持、此云能登利。有羽白熊鷲者。其爲人强健。亦身有翼、能飛以高翔。是以、不從皇命。每略盜人民。

戊子、皇后欲撃熊鷲、而自橿日宮遷于松峽宮。時飄風忽起、御笠墮風。故時人號其處曰御笠也。辛卯、至層增岐野、即擧兵撃羽白熊鷲而滅之。謂左右曰、取得熊鷲。我心則安。故號其處曰安也。

丙申、轉至山門縣、則誅土蜘蛛田油津媛。時田油津媛之兄夏羽、興軍而迎來。然聞其妹被誅而逃之。

夏四月壬寅朔甲辰、北到火前國松浦縣、而進食於玉嶋里小河之側。於是、皇后勾針爲鉤、取粒爲餌、抽取裳縷爲緡、登河中石上、而投鉤祈之曰、朕西欲求財國。若有成事者、河魚飮鉤。因以擧竿、乃獲細鱗魚。時皇后曰、希見物也。希見、此云梅豆邏志。

故時人號其處、曰梅豆羅國。今謂松浦訛焉。是以、其國女人、每當四月上旬、以鉤投河中、

She replied, "Dwelling in the depths at Tachibana in Odo in Himuka Province, budding youthfully like water grass, are the kami named Uwa-tsu-tsu-no-o, Naka-tsu-tsu-no-o, and Soko-tsu-tsu-no-o.[x]

The empress asked, "Are there any others?"

She replied, "I don't know if there are any others or not."

In the end, the kami did not say if there were any other kami. Having received the words of the kami, the empress knew that they were venerated in accordance with their instructions. Afterward, the ancestor of the Omi of Kibi, Kamo-no-wake, was dispatched to attack the Kumaso.[3] Before much time had passed, they surrendered of their own accord.

Also, in Notorita Village, there was a man called Hashiro Kumawashi.[xi] He was strong and powerful in constitution, and he had wings enabling him to fly high in the sky. On account of these traits, he was insubordinate to the empress and was always stealing from the people.

On the seventeenth day, the empress wanted to attack Kumawashi and moved from Kashihi Palace to Matsuo Palace.[xii] At that time a cyclone suddenly struck, and the empress's hat was blown away. So people at the time called this place Mikasa, or August Hat.[xiii] On the twentieth day, the empress reached Sosokino, mustered troops, attacked Hashiro Kumawashi, and defeated him.[xiv] Then she said to those in close service, "We were able to take Kumawashi, and my heart is at peace." Accordingly, this place is called Yasu, or Peace.[xv]

On the twenty-fifth day, the empress moved to Yamato District and put to death the earth spider rebel Tabura-tsu-hime.[xvi] At that time the older brother of Tabura-tsu-hime, Natsuha, raised an army and came to meet the empress, but when he heard that his sister had been put to death, he fled.

Summer, fourth month, third day. The empress arrived in Matsura District in the northern part of Hizen Province and took her meal near Ogawa in Tamashima Village.[xvii] There the empress bent a wire and made a fishhook, used a bit of rice flour as bait, took a thread from her skirt for a line, and climbed atop a rock in the river. She cast the hook and prayed, saying, "We wish to seek the jewel country in the west.[4] If this is to be, may the fish of the river bite my hook." Then she lifted out her rod, and she had caught an ayu sweetfish. Then the empress said, "How mysterious this is!"

So people at the time called this place the land of Mezura, or the land of the Mysterious. Now it is called Matsura, a corruption. For this reason, the women of this land, in the first ten days of the fourth month, cast hooks

---

3 In Ōjin 22, Kamo-no-wake is identified as the younger brother of Mito-no-wake, also of Kibi, and as the Omi of Kasa.
4 Silla.

捕年魚、於今不絶。唯男夫雖釣、以不能獲魚。

　既而皇后、則識神教有驗、更祭祀神祇、躬欲西征。爰定神田而佃之。時引儺河水、欲潤神田、而掘溝。及于迹驚岡、大磐塞之、不得穿溝。皇后召武內宿禰、捧劒鏡令禱祈神祇、而求通溝。則當時、雷電霹靂、蹴裂其磐、令通水。故時人號其溝曰裂田溝也。

　皇后還詣橿日浦、解髮臨海曰、吾被神祇之教、賴皇祖之靈、浮渉滄海、躬欲西征。是以、令頭滌海水。若有驗者、髮自分爲兩。即入海洗之、髮自分也。

　皇后便結分髮而爲髻。因以、謂群臣曰、夫興師動衆、國之大事。安危成敗、必在於斯。今有所征伐。以事付群臣。若事不成者、罪有於群臣。是甚傷焉。吾婦女之、加以不肖。然暫假男貌、强起雄略。上蒙神祇之靈、下藉群臣之助、振兵甲而度嶮浪、整艫船以求財土。若事就者、群臣共有功。事不就者、吾獨有罪、既有此意。其共議之。

　群臣皆曰、皇后爲天下、計所以安宗廟社稷。且罪不及于臣下。頓首奉詔。

　秋九月庚午朔己卯、令諸國、集船舶練兵甲。

into the river and catch ayu sweetfish. This custom continues to the present. Even if the men try to fish, however, they cannot catch anything.

The empress knew that her catch was a validation of the instructions of the kami, and she went on to worship the kami of heaven and earth and planned to go herself to the west and conquer that land. she established fields to provide offerings to the kami. Then she drew water from the Na River and wanted to irrigate the field, so she dug a ditch.[xviii] When she reached Todoroki Hill, a large boulder was blocking her, and she was unable to continue digging the ditch.[xix] The empress summoned Takeuchi no Sukune, and he held up a sword and mirror and prayed to the kami of heaven and earth asking for the ditch to be passed through. At just that moment there was a flash of lightning that shattered the boulder and made the water pass through. Accordingly, people at the time called this ditch Sakuta no Unade, or Splitting-Field Ditch.

The empress went back to the harbor at Kashihi, unfastened her hair, and looked at the sea, saying, "I have received the instructions of the kami, and so relying on the blessings of my imperial ancestors, I myself will cross the blue seas to conquer the west. I hereby dip my head into the waters, and if there be good prospects, my hair will naturally part in two." Then she went into the sea and rinsed her hair, and it naturally parted.

The empress tied up the two tresses of her hair and made them into buns.[5] Then she told the high government officials, "Mustering an army and mobilizing the people is a great matter of state. Safety and peril, success and failure, entirely depend on it. Now we are about to attack. If I entrusted the high government officials with these matters and we were unsuccessful, then the blame would fall on the officials. This would be truly unfortunate. I am a woman. Moreover, I am inexperienced. For the time being, however, I will take on the appearance of a man and plan brave stratagems. Covered above by the blessings of the heavenly and earthly kami, and supported from below by the high government officials, I shall lead our troops and cross the high waves, array our fleet, and seek out the land of treasure. If this endeavor succeeds, the glory will be shared with the high government officials. If it fails, then it shall be my transgression alone. I have already made up my mind. Let us hold counsel together."[xx]

The high government officials all said, "On behalf of the realm and for the stability of its altars of state, the empress has made this plan. Furthermore, no blame will extend to us. Kowtowing, we shall receive your edicts."[xxi]

Autumn, ninth month, tenth day. The empress ordered the various provinces to collect ships and train soldiers. At that time, it was difficult to

---

5 Restyling her hair like an adult male.

時軍卒難集。皇后曰、必神心焉、則立大三輪社以奉刀矛矣。軍衆自聚。於是、使吾瓮海人烏摩呂、出於西海、令察有國耶。還曰、國不見也。

又遣磯鹿海人名草而令視。數日還之曰、西北有山。帶雲橫絚。蓋有國乎。

爰卜吉日、而臨發有日。時皇后親執斧鉞、令三軍曰、金鼓無節、旌旗錯亂、則士卒不整。貪財多欲、懷私內顧、必爲敵所虜。其敵少而勿輕。敵強而無屈。則奸暴勿聽。自服勿殺。遂戰勝者必有賞。背走者自有罪。

既而、神有誨曰、和魂服王身而守壽命。荒魂爲先鋒而導師船。和魂、此云珥岐瀰多摩。荒魂、此云阿邏瀰多摩。即得神教、而拜禮之。因以依網吾彥男垂見爲祭神主。

于時也、適當皇后之開胎。皇后則取石插腰、而祈之曰、事竟還日、產於茲土。其石今在于伊都縣道邊。既而則擧荒魂、爲軍先鋒、請和魂、爲王船鎭。

冬十月己亥朔辛丑、從和珥津發之。時飛廉起風、陽侯擧浪、海中大魚、悉浮扶船。則大風順吹、帆舶隨波。不勞櫓楫、

assemble troops. The empress said, "It must be the will of the kami." Then she promptly built a shrine to the Miwa kami and presented a sword and a halberd to it, and the troops came together all on their own.[xxii] Then she dispatched the fisherman from Ahe, Omaro, along the western sea route to observe whether there was land there.[xxiii] He came back and reported, "I could not see any land."

Again, she then dispatched a fisherman from Shika, Nagusa, to look.[xxiv] After many days he returned and said, "There is a mountain to the northwest, as well as a belt of clouds stretching across the sky. There probably is land there."

Then she divined an auspicious day, but there were still several days before the army would embark. At that time, the empress herself took her axe and halberd and ordered the whole of the army, saying, "If the drums lose their rhythm and the banners are in disarray, then our forces will not be properly arrayed. If you greedily seek treasure and think only of yourself and your wife and mistresses, then you no doubt will be captured by the enemy. Though the enemy be few, do not underestimate them, and even if the enemy is strong, do not falter. The taking of women by force is not permitted. Do not kill those who surrender. Those who fight victoriously will certainly be rewarded, and those who flee will be punished as a matter of course."[xxv]

Later there were instructions from the kami, which said, "Spirits of peace shall accompany the king[6] and protect his life; spirits of violence shall go first and lead the armada.[7] Receiving the instructions of the kami, the empress made offerings to them. Otarumi, Abiko of Yosami, was made the principal for their ritual worship.[xxvi]

At that time, the empress was about to give birth. The empress took a rock and thrust it up into her loins and prayed, saying, "When this is over, on the day I return, may I give birth here." This rock is now on the side of the road in Ito District.[xxvii] Shortly thereafter the spirits of violence were invited to become the army's vanguard, and the spirits of peace were asked to guard the king's ship.

Winter, tenth month, third day. The empress left the port of Wani.[xxviii] At that time, the kami of the winds caused strong gales, and the kami of the seas raised high waves, but the great fish of the ocean all floated up to support the boats. A powerful tailwind blew, and the sailboats went along with the waves. Even without the labor of rudder or oars, they soon

---

6   Namely, Jingū.
7   These, along with the spirits of fortune and spirits of discernment, seen in S8.6 of the "Age of the Gods," are the component spirits of a kami.

便到新羅。時隨船潮浪、遠逮國中。即知、天神地祇悉助歟。

新羅王、於是、戰々慄々厝身無所。則集諸人曰、新羅之建國以來、未嘗聞海水凌國。若天運盡之、國爲海乎。是言未訖之間、船師滿海、旌旗耀日。鼓吹起聲、山川悉振。

新羅王遙望以爲、非常之兵、將滅己國。讋焉失志。乃今醒之曰、吾聞、東有神國。謂日本。亦有聖王。謂天皇。必其國之神兵也。豈可舉兵以距乎、即素旆而自服。素組以面縛。封圖籍、降於王船之前。因以、叩頭之曰、從今以後、長與乾坤、伏爲飼部。其不乾船柁、而春秋獻馬梳及馬鞭。復不煩海遠、以每年貢男女之調。則重誓之曰、非東日更出西、且除阿利那禮河返以之逆流、及河石昇爲星辰、而殊闕春秋之朝、怠廢梳鞭之貢、天神地祇共討焉。

時或曰、欲誅新羅王。

於是、皇后曰、初承神教、將授金銀之國。又號令三軍曰、勿殺自服。今既獲財國。亦人自降服。殺之不祥、乃解其縛爲飼部。遂入其國中、封重寶府庫、收圖籍文書。即以皇后所杖矛、樹於新羅王門、爲後葉之印。故其矛今猶樹于新羅王之門也。

reached Silla. The waves carrying the boats spilled far into the interior of the land. Thereby it was known that all the kami of heaven and earth were aiding them.

The King of Silla shuddered in fear and had no recourse. He assembled his various peoples and said, "Since the state of Silla was founded, never have I heard of the seawater rising to flow inland. Perhaps the movements of the heavens have ended, and our land will become sea." Before he had finished his words, the armada filled the sea before him, and its banners dazzled in the sunshine. The drums and flutes raised their voices, and the mountains and rivers all trembled.

The King of Silla saw this from afar and thought that this unimaginable force must be intent on overthrowing his state, and so he lost hope and despaired. Then suddenly he returned to his senses and said, "I have heard that to the east there is a divine land called Yamato, and also that it has a sage-king called emperor. For sure, these are the divine soldiers of that land. How can I raise arms and resist them?" He promptly raised a white flag and surrendered himself, and with a white plait tied his own hands behind his back, sealed the land's plot and survey registers, and presented them to the king's ship.[xxix] Then he kowtowed and said, "From now on, as long as heaven and earth endure, we surrender to being your stable grooms. Without letting the rudders of our ships go dry, we shall, every spring and autumn, present horse combs and horse whips. Without being bothered by the distance across the sea, we shall, every year, send men and women as tribute." Then he further swore, "Unless the sun rises not in the east but instead in the west, unless the Arinare River reverses its flow, unless the stones of the rivers rise up to become stars, should we be lacking in our spring and autumn attendance to your court or neglect our tribute of combs and whips, let all the kami of heaven and earth punish us."[xxx]

At that time, some people said, "Put the Silla king to death."

Then the empress said, "Previously I received instruction from the kami that the land of gold and silver was to be bestowed upon us, and I ordered the three armies, saying, 'Do not kill those who surrender of their own accord.' Now we already possess the land of treasure, and its people surrendered of their own accord. Killing them would be inauspicious."[xxxi] The empress released his bonds and made him her stable groom,[8] then at last went inland, placed many treasures in storehouses, and collected the land's plot and survey registers. She stood the halberd she held at the gate of the King of Silla as a marker for future generations. Hence, this halberd stands even now at the gate of the King of Silla.

---

8   Jingū's sparing the king's life is recalled in the Kinmei book. However, in the alternative account that follows, the king is put to death.

爰新羅王波沙寐錦、即以微叱己知波珍干岐爲質、仍齎金銀彩色及綾・羅・縑絹、載于八十艘船、令從官軍。是以、新羅王、常以八十船之調貢于日本國、其是之緣也。

於是、高麗・百濟二國王、聞新羅收圖籍、降於日本國、密令伺其軍勢。則知不可勝、自來于營外、叩頭而款曰、從今以後、永稱西蕃、不絶朝貢。故因以、定内官家屯倉。是所謂之三韓也。皇后從新羅還之。

十二月戊戌朔辛亥、生譽田天皇於筑紫。故時人號其産處曰宇瀰也。

一云、足仲彦天皇、居筑紫橿日宮。是有神、託沙麼縣主祖内避高國避高松屋種、以誨天皇曰、御孫尊也、若欲得寶國耶、將現授之。便復曰、琴將來以進于皇后。則隨神言、而皇后撫琴。於是、神託皇后、以誨之曰、今御孫尊所望之國、譬如鹿角。以無實國也。其今御孫尊所御之船及穴戸直踐立所貢之水田、名大田爲幣、能祭我者、則如美女之睩、而金銀多之、眼炎國以授御孫尊。

時天皇對神曰、其雖神何謾語耶。何處將有國。且朕所乘船、既奉於神、朕乘曷船。然未知誰神。願欲知其名。

時神稱其名曰、表筒雄・中筒雄・底筒雄。如是稱三神名、且重曰、吾名向匱男聞襲大歷五御魂速狹騰尊也。

時天皇謂皇后曰、聞惡事之言坐婦人乎。何言速狹騰也。

---

9   Alternatively, Hasa-mukimu and Mishikochi-hatori-kanki. Hasa-mukimu is the legendary fifth king of Silla, Pasa isagŭm. "Mukimu" is the same title as Korean "isagŭm," for "king." Mishikochi-hatori is Misahŭn, son of Naemul isagŭm, fifteenth king of Silla (d. 402, r. 356–402). Mishikochi's name appears again later in the narrative, spelled differently but with the same pronunciation.

The King of Silla, P'asa-maegŭm, made Mijilgiji-p'ajin-kan'gi[9] a hostage. Then he came bearing gold, silver, bright cloth, patterned silk, thin silk, and tightly woven silk, loaded them onto eighty ships, and sent them with the armada.[xxxii] For this reason, the King of Silla always uses eighty ships for sending tribute to Yamato.[10]

The kings of the two states of Koguryŏ and Paekche heard that Silla had presented its maps and registers and had surrendered to Yamato.[xxxiii] They secretly inquired into the power of its army and knew that they could not win. They came of their own accord to the exterior of the empress' encampment, kowtowed, and sincerely said, "From now on, we will forever be called the western vassal states, and will never fail in our tribute." Accordingly, the states were established as imperial estates called the Three Han.[11] The empress then returned from Silla.

Twelfth month, fourteenth day. The empress gave birth to Emperor Homuta [Ōjin] in Tsukushi. Henceforth, people at the time called the place of his birth Umi, or Birth.[xxxiv]

Another account says, Emperor Tarashi-naka-tsu-hiko [Chūai] was in Kashihi Palace in Tsukushi.[xxxv] There were kami there, and they took possession of the ancestor of the Agatanushi of Saba, Utsu-hiko-kuni-hiko-matsuyatane, and instructed the emperor, saying, "August descendant, if you wish to gain the land of treasure, then verily I will bestow it upon you."[xxxvi] Then they said, "Bring a zither and present it to the empress." He did as the kami said, and the empress played the zither. Then the kami possessed the empress and instructed her, saying, "Now the land desired by the august descendant is like the antler of a deer. It is barren. If you give us the ship that the august descendant is now aboard and the paddy field called Ōta presented by Homutachi of Atai District as an offering, and perform ritual worship, then we will bestow upon the august descendant a land that, like the eyebrow of a beautiful girl, is rich in gold and silver and dazzles the eye."

The emperor replied to the kami, "Though you be kami, why do you deceive me? Where is there land? And if We present Our boat to the kami, which boat should We ride in? Furthermore, I still do not know what kami you are. I want to know your names."

The kami then said their names, "Uwa-tsu-tsu-no-o, Naka-tsu-tsu-no-o, Soko-tsu-tsu-no-o," which were the names of three kami. Then one added, "My name is Muka-hi-tsu-o-mo-o-so-ō-itsu-no-mitama-haya-sa-agari."[12]

The emperor said to the empress, "Are you a wife who speaks of unpropitious things? Why do you say haya-sa-agari?"[13]

---

10 Nintoku 17 and Ingyō 42 refer to eighty ships coming, but "eighty" likely means simply many ships.
11 Derived from the names of the Korean confederacies of Pyŏnhan, Chinhan, and Mahan. These three confederacies developed into the states of Paekche, Kaya, and Silla.
12 It is not clear what kami this is; it could be any of the kami that appear in this episode.
13 Meaning "quickly perish."

於是、神謂天皇曰、汝王如是不信、必不得其國。唯今皇后懷姙之子、蓋有獲歟。是夜天皇忽病發以崩之。然後、皇后隨神教而祭。

則皇后爲男束裝、征新羅。時神留導之。由是隨船浪之、遠及于新羅國中。於是、新羅王宇流助富利智干、參迎跪之、取王船即叩頭曰、臣自今以後、於日本國所居神御子、爲內官家、無絶朝貢。

一云、禽獲新羅王、詣于海邊、拔王臏筋、令匍匐石上。俄而斬之、埋沙中。則留一人、爲新羅宰而還之。

然後、新羅王妻、不知埋夫屍之地、獨有誘宰之情。乃誂宰曰、汝當令識埋王屍之處、必敦報之。且吾爲汝妻。

於是、宰信誘言、密告埋屍之處。則王妻與國人、共議之殺宰。更出王屍葬於他處。乃時取宰屍、埋于王墓土底、以擧王櫬、窆其上曰、尊卑次第、固當如此。

於是、天皇聞之、重發震忿、大起軍衆、欲頓滅新羅。是以、軍船滿海而詣之。是時、新羅國人悉懼、不知所如。則相集共議之、殺王妻以謝罪。

於是、從軍神表筒男・中筒男・底筒男三神、誨皇后曰、我荒魂、令祭於穴門山田邑也。

時穴門直之祖踐立・津守連之祖田裳見宿禰、啓于皇后曰、神欲居之地、必宜奉定。則以踐立、爲祭荒魂之神主。仍祠立於穴門山田邑。

Then the kami told the emperor, "Since you do not believe this, king, you shall never obtain that land. However, perhaps the child now carried by the empress can obtain it." That night the emperor suddenly fell ill and expired. Afterward, however, the empress performed ritual worship according to the kami's instructions.

Then the empress clothed herself as a man and attacked Silla. At that time, the kami guided them. Owing to this guidance, the ship followed the waves, spilling far into the interior of the land of Silla. The King of Silla, Uryuyujoburi-chigan,[14] went out to meet them, genuflected, and grasped the king's ship, then kowtowed and said, "From now on, I shall manage an imperial estate and will present tribute without ceasing to the august children of the kami that dwell in the land of Yamato."

Another account says, The empress captured the King of Silla, led him to the seaside, kneecapped him, and made him crawl to the top of a rock.[xxxvii] Shortly thereafter she killed him and buried him in the sand. Then she stationed one of her men there, made him administrator of Silla, and returned home.

Afterward, however, the wife of the King of Silla did not know where her husband's body was buried and planned to trick the administrator. And so she tempted him, saying, "If you truthfully tell me where the king's body is buried, you will certainly be richly rewarded. Also, I will become your wife."

The administrator believed her deception and secretly told her where the body was buried. Then the king's wife and the people of that land conferred together and killed the administrator, exhumed the king's body, and entombed it in another location. At the time, they took the administrator's body and buried it under the king's grave, raised up the king's coffin, and buried him on top, saying, "The original order of honored and despised should be thus."

The emperor[15] heard this and was furious, marshaled a great army, and wanted to destroy Silla completely. The armada, filling the sea, arrived. At that time, the people of Silla were filled with fear and did not know what to do. They gathered together to confer and killed the king's wife to atone for their crimes.

Then the three kami that had led the army, Uwa-tsu-tsu-no-o, Naka-tsu-tsu-no-o, and Soko-tsu-tsu-no-o, instructed the empress, saying, "Perform ritual worship of our spirits of violence in Yamada Village in Anato."[xxxviii]

At that time, the ancestor of the Atai of Anato, Homutachi, and the ancestor of the Muraji of Tsumori, Tamomi no Sukune, said to the empress, "The land that the kami wish to dwell in should definitely be defined and presented to them."[xxxix] Then Homutachi was made the principal for ritual worship of the spirits of violence. Thereupon a shrine was built in Yamada Village in Anato.

---

14 Or Uru-sohorichika, perhaps Sŏk Uro, a son of the legendary King Naehae of Silla (r. 196–230), with "sohori(chi)ka" referring to an alternative name, sŏbalhan, for the first Silla Bone Rank of ibŏlch'an.
15 There is no sitting emperor at this time. Presumably, this is Jingū.

爰伐新羅之明年春二月、皇后領群卿及百寮、移于穴門豐浦宮。即收天皇之喪、從海路以向京。

　　時麛坂王・忍熊王、聞天皇崩、亦皇后西征、幷皇子新生、而密謀之曰、今皇后有子。群臣皆從焉。必共議之立幼主。吾等何以兄從弟乎。

　　乃詳爲天皇作陵、詣播磨興山陵於赤石。仍編船絚于淡路嶋、運其嶋石

MAP 15 Korea, Three Kingdoms Period, ca. 5th century

Treason of Kagosaka and Oshikuma

In the spring, second month after the year after Silla was attacked, the empress led the high government officials and public officials and moved to Toyura Palace in Anato. There she collected the emperor's remains from the temporary grave and made for the capital by sea.[xl]

At that time, Prince Kagosaka and Prince Oshikuma heard that the emperor had expired, that the empress had conquered the west, and that a new imperial prince had been born.[16] They secretly plotted, saying, "Now the empress has a child. The high government officials all follow her. Clearly, they plan to make him a child emperor. But how can we older brothers, serve the younger?"

And so, pretending to create a tomb for the emperor, they went to Harima to build a mountain tomb in Akashi. They tied their ships together, spanning the distance to Awaji, and transported the stones from that

---

16 The two princes are brothers. Their genealogy is given in the Chūai book.

而造之。則每人令取兵、而待皇后。

　於是、犬上君祖倉見別與吉師祖五十狹茅宿禰、共隷于麛坂王。因以、爲將軍令興東國兵。時麛坂王・忍熊王、共出菟餓野、而祈狩之日、祈狩、此云于氣比餓利。若有成事、必獲良獸也。二王各居假㢈。赤猪忽出之登假㢈、咋麛坂王而殺焉。軍士悉慄也。

　忍熊王謂倉見別曰、是事大怪也。於此不可待敵。則引軍更返、屯於住吉。

　時皇后聞忍熊王起師以待之、命武內宿禰、懷皇子橫出南海、泊于紀伊水門。皇后之船、直指難波。

　于時、皇后之船、廻於海中、以不能進。更還務古水門而卜之。

　於是、天照大神誨之曰、我之荒魂、不可近皇后。當居御心廣田國。即以山背根子之女葉山媛令祭。

　亦稚日女尊誨之曰、吾欲居活田長峽國。因以海上五十狹茅令祭。

　亦事代主尊誨之曰、祠吾于御心長田國。則以葉山媛之弟長媛令祭。

　亦表筒男・中筒男・底筒男三神誨之曰、吾和魂宜居大津渟中倉之長峽。便因看往來船。

island to build it. Then they ordered the people to take up arms and await the empress.[17]

The ancestor of the Kimi of Inukami, Kuramiwake, and the ancestor of the Kishi, Isachi no Sukune, both served Prince Kagosaka.[18] Accordingly, as his generals, they were made to muster troops from the lands to the east. At that time, Prince Kagosaka and Prince Oshikuma went to Togano and, making a hunting oath, said, "If we get good game, this endeavor will surely succeed!"[xli] The two princes each stayed in their respective hunting towers. A red boar suddenly came out, climbed one of the hunting towers, and fatally bit Prince Kagosaka. The soldiers all trembled in fear.

Prince Oshikuma told Kuramiwake, "This was a significant omen. We should not wait here for the enemy." He then had his army withdraw to camp in Suminoe.[xlii]

The empress heard that Prince Oshikuma had raised an army and was waiting for her. So she ordered Takeuchi no Sukune to take the imperial prince to his bosom, take the sea route to the south, and anchor in the harbor of Ki Province. The empress's boat made straight for Naniwa.

Later, the empress's boat was going in circles in the ocean and was not able to proceed. She went back to the port at Muko and performed divination.[xliii]

When doing so, Amaterasu instructed her, "My spirit of violence should not draw near to the empress. It should dwell in the land of Hirota." The daughter of Neko of Yamashiro, Hayama-hime, was made to perform ritual worship.[xliv]

Then Waka-hiru-me instructed her, saying, "I wish to dwell in Ikuta, in the land of Nagao." Therefore, Unagamino-isachi was made to perform ritual worship.

Then Koto-shiro-nushi instructed her, saying, "Worship me in the land of Nagata." Then the younger sister of Hayama-hime, Naga-hime, was made to perform ritual worship.

Then the three kami Uwa-tsu-tsu-no-o, Naka-tsu-tsu-no-o, and Soko-tsu-tsu-no-o instructed her, "Our spirits of peace should dwell at the great harbor in Nagao in Nunakura in Ōtsu. From there we can watch over the ships coming and going."[xlv]

---

17 An example of using construction of a tomb to muster troops appears in Tenmu 1.5. Tying the boats together aided in transporting stone, but also served as a blockade.
18 The Inukami appear in the Keikō book; Kuramiwake appears here alone. Kishi is used as both a title of nobility and a lineage name; it is often associated with people involved in foreign relations. "Kishi" may derive from the fourteenth rank of the Silla Bone Rank system, *kilsa*.

於是、隨神教以鎭坐焉。則平得度海。

忍熊王復引軍退之、到菟道而軍之。皇后南詣紀伊國、會太子於日高。以議及群臣、遂欲攻忍熊王、更遷小竹宮。小竹、此云芝努。

適是時也、晝暗如夜、已經多日。時人曰、常夜行之也。

皇后問紀直祖豐耳曰、是怪何由矣。

時有一老父曰、傳聞、如是怪謂阿豆那比之罪也。

問何謂也。

對曰、二社祝者、共合葬歟。

因以、令推問巷里、有一人曰、小竹祝與天野祝、共爲善友。小竹祝逢病而死之。天野祝血泣曰、吾也生爲交友。何死之無同穴乎、則伏屍側而自死、仍合葬焉。蓋是之乎。

乃開墓視之實也。故更改棺櫬、各異處以埋之。則日暉炳爛、日夜有別。

三月丙申朔庚子、命武內宿禰・和珥臣祖武振熊、率數萬衆、令擊忍熊王。

爰武內宿禰等、選精兵從山背出之。至菟道以屯河北。忍熊王出營欲戰。時有熊之凝者。爲忍熊王軍之先鋒。熊之凝者、葛野城首之祖也。一云、多吳吉師之遠祖也。則欲勸己衆、因以、高唱之歌曰、

Thereupon the kami were enshrined as they had instructed. Then the empress could cross the sea peacefully. Prince Oshikuma again withdrew his army, arrived in Uji, and made camp.^xlvi The empress went south to Ki Province and met the crown prince in Hidaka.[19] ^xlvii She held conference with the high government ministers and, in order to attack Prince Oshikuma at last, moved on to Shino Palace.^xlviii

Around that time, the daytime sky became as dark as night, and this continued for many days. People at the time said, "It seems like it is always night."

The empress asked the ancestor of the Atai of Ki,[20] Toyomimi, saying, "What is the reason for this omen?"

At that time, an old man said, "From what I've heard, this kind of omen is from the crime called 'azunahi.'"

She asked him, "What do you mean?"

He replied, "The priests of two different shrines may have been buried together."

She investigated the hamlets and villages, and there was one person who said, "The priests from Shino Shrine and Amano Shrine were fast friends, but the priest from Shino fell ill and died.^xlix Then the priest from Amano Shrine cried profusely and said, 'I was his fast friend when he was alive. Why should we not share the same hole in death?' Then he lay down beside the corpse and died himself. Hence, they were buried together. This is probably where they were buried."

They opened the tomb and looked in, and it was so. So they made a new coffin and buried each of them in a different place. Then the sun shone, and day and night were separated.

Third month, fifth day. The empress ordered Takeuchi no Sukune and the ancestor of the Omi of Wani, Takefurukuma, to lead an army of tens of thousands and attack Prince Oshikuma.^l

Takeuchi no Sukune and others selected elite troops and led them out of Yamashiro. They arrived in Uji and camped to the north of the river. Prince Oshikuma decamped and intended to give battle. At that time, a person called Kumanokori[21] was in the vanguard of Prince Oshikuma's army.

Kumanokori was the ancestor of the Obito of Kazuno of Ki. Another account says that he was the distant ancestor of the Kishi of Tago.^li

Wanting to raise the spirits of his troops, he sang in a high voice:

---

19 Ōjin was not named crown prince until Jingū 3; here, use of the title is anachronistic.
20 The Atai of Ki appear in Keikō 3.
21 He does not appear elsewhere.

烏智箇多能	をちかたの
阿邏々麻菟麼邏	あららまつばら
摩菟麼邏珥	まつばらに
和多利喩祇氐	わたりゆきて
菟區喩彌珥	つくゆみに
末利椰塢多具陪	まりやをたぐへ
宇摩比等破	うまひとは
于摩譬苔奴知野	うまひとどちや
伊徒姑播茂	いとこはも
伊徒姑奴池	いとこどち
伊裝阿波那	いざあはな
和例波	われは
多摩岐波屢	たまきはる
于池能阿層餓	うちのあそが
波邏濃知波	はらぬちは
異佐誤阿例椰	いさごあれや
伊裝阿波那	いざあはな
和例波	われは

　時武內宿禰、令三軍悉令椎結。因以號令曰、各以儲弦藏于髮中、且佩木刀。既而乃擧皇后之命、誘忍熊王曰、吾勿貪天下。唯懷幼王從君王者也。豈有距戰耶。願共絕弦捨兵、與連和焉。然則、君王登天業、以安席高枕、專制萬機。則顯令軍中、悉斷弦解刀、投於河水。

　忍熊王信其誘言、悉令軍衆、解兵投於河水、而斷弦。爰武內宿禰、令三軍出儲弦更張、以佩眞刀。度河而進之。

　忍熊王知被欺、謂倉見別・五十狹茅宿禰曰、吾既被欺。今無儲兵。豈可得戰乎。曳兵稍退。武內宿禰出精兵而追之。適遇

To the pine grove,
the sparse pine grove
in the distance,
across the river.
To your zelkova bows
string whistling arrows,
nobles
with other nobles,
good friends
with other good friends,
we are together.
Is the belly
of Takeuchi no Ason
stopped up with sand?[22]
Let us fight,
and so we shall.

At that time, Takeuchi no Sukune ordered his whole army to tie up their hair. Then he ordered them, "Each of you, hide spare bowstrings in your hair, and wear wooden swords." Once they had done this, he pronounced the empress' orders. Then he deceived Prince Oshikuma, saying, "I do not desire the realm. I only wish to take the young prince to my bosom and serve him as my lord. Why do we fight and impede each other? I want to cut our bowstrings and throw down our swords and have peace with each other. If we do so, you, my lord, can ascend to the heavenly succession, be at rest on the august throne, spread your pillow on high, and take sole control of the vast machinery of governance." Then he openly issued orders to his army for them to cut their bowstrings and to draw their swords and throw them in the river.

Prince Oshikuma believed these deceptive words and ordered his army to draw their weapons and throw them in the river, and to cut their bowstrings. Then Takeuchi no Sukune ordered his army to take out their spare bowstrings and string their bows, and to put on their real swords. They crossed the river and advanced.

Prince Oshikuma saw that he had been tricked, and he told Kuramiwake and Isachi no Sukune, "I have been tricked. We have no spare weapons. How can we fight?" He withdrew his troops and fled. Takeuchi no Sukune released his elite troops to pursue them. They met Prince Oshikuma's army

---

22 Takeuchi no Ason is Takeuchi no Sukune. Oshikuma perhaps means to suggest that like sand scattered by the wind, so his forces will scatter those of Takeuchi.

于逢坂以破。故號其處曰、逢坂也。軍衆走之。及于狹々浪栗林而多斬。於是、血流溢栗林。故惡是事、至于今、其栗林之菓不進御所也。忍熊王逃無所入。則喚五十狹茅宿禰、而歌之曰、

伊裝阿藝	いざあぎ
伊佐智須區禰	いさちすくね
多摩枳波屢	たまきはる
于知能阿曾餓	うちのあそが
勾夫菟智能	くぶつちの
伊多氏於破孺破	いたておはずは
珥倍迺利能	にほどりの
介豆岐齊奈	かづきせな

則共沈瀨田濟而死之。于時、武內宿禰歌之曰、

阿布彌能彌	あふみのみ
齊多能和多利珥	せたのわたりに
伽豆區苔利	かづくとり
梅珥志彌曳泥麼	めにしみえねば
異枳廼倍呂之茂	いきどほろしも

於是、探其屍而不得也。然後、數日之出於菟道河、武內宿禰亦歌曰、

阿布瀰能瀰	あふみのみ
齊多能和多利珥	せたのわたりに
介豆區苔利	かづくとり
多那伽瀰須疑氏	たなかみすぎて
于泥珥等邏倍菟	うぢにとらへつ

and routed them at Ōsaka.^lii So that place is called Ōsaka, or Meeting Hill. The enemy soldiers fled. The army caught up to them at Kurusu in Sasanami and executed many of them.^liii A stream of blood flooded Kurusu. So in disgust of this place, even at present, the tree nuts of Kurusu are not presented to the emperor. Prince Oshikuma had no place to run and hide. He called Isachi no Sukune to his side and sang:^liv

> Well, my lord,
> Isachi Sukune,
> rather than suffer
> the bulb-pommeled sword
> of Takeuchi no Ason,
> let us dive
> like the grebe.

Then together they plunged in at the crossing at Seta and died. At that time Takeuchi no Sukune sang:

> I am irritated
> because the grebe dove
> out of sight
> at the crossing at Seta
> on Ōmi Sea.^lv

Men searched for the bodies, but could not find them. However, a few days later, they came out at the Uji River. Then Takeuchi no Sukune sang again:

> At the crossing at Seta
> on the sea of Ōmi,
> the diving bird
> overshot Tanakami
> and was caught at Uji.^lvi

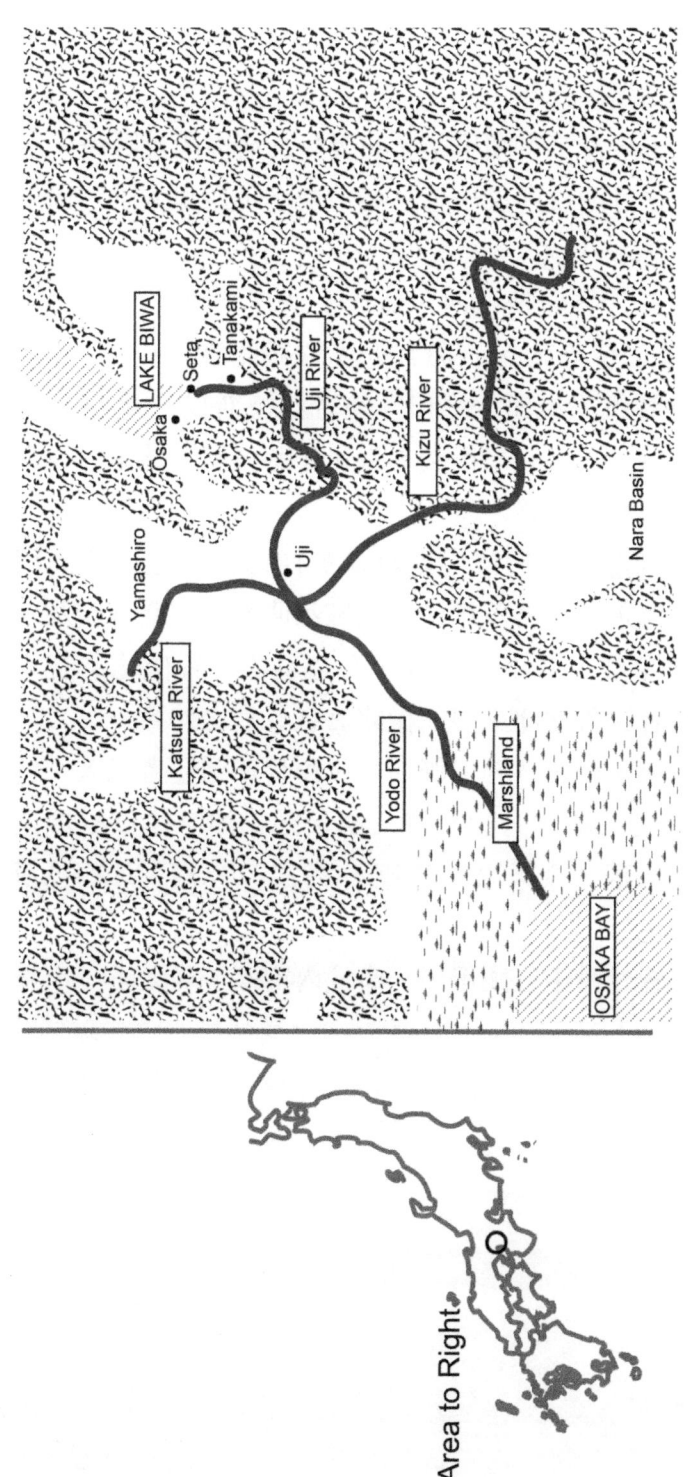

MAP 16 Treason of Kagosaka and Oshikuma

冬十月癸亥朔甲子、群臣尊皇后曰皇太后。是年也、太歳辛巳。則爲攝政元年。

　二年冬十一月丁亥朔甲午、葬天皇於河內國長野陵。

　三年春正月丙戌朔戊子、立譽田別皇子爲皇太子、因以都於磐余。是謂若櫻宮。

　五年春三月癸卯朔己酉、新羅王遣汙禮斯伐・毛麻利叱智・富羅母智等朝貢。仍有返先質微叱許智伐旱之情。是以、誂許智伐旱、而給之曰、使者汙禮斯伐・毛麻利叱智等、告臣曰、我王以坐臣久不還、而悉沒妻子爲孥。冀蹔還本土、知虛實而請焉。

　皇太后則聽之。因以、副葛城襲津彥而遣之。共到對馬、宿于鉏海水門。時新羅使者毛麻利叱智等、竊分船及水手、載微叱旱岐、令逃於新羅。乃造蒭靈、置微叱許智之床、詳爲病者、告襲津彥曰、微叱許智忽病之將死。

　襲津彥使人令看病者。既知欺、而捉新羅使者三人、納檻中、以火焚而殺。乃詣新羅、次于蹈鞴津、拔草羅城還之。是時俘人等、今桑原・佐糜・高宮・忍海、凡四邑漢人等之始祖也。

　十三年春二月丁巳朔甲子、命武內宿禰、從太子、令拜

Naming of the Crown Prince, Friction with Silla, Friendship with Paekche

Winter, tenth month, second day. The high government officials honored the empress with the title of empress dowager. This was the year of the Metal Snake. It was made the first year of her regency [201 CE].

Second year [202 CE], winter, eleventh month, eighth day. The emperor was buried in Nagano Tomb, Kōchi Province.[lvii]

Third year [203 CE], spring, first month, third day. Imperial prince Homuta-wake [Ōjin] was named crown prince. So a capital was built in Iware.[23]

Fifth year [205 CE], spring, third month, seventh day. The King of Silla dispatched Oryesabŏl, Momarijilji, and Puramoji to present tribute to the court.[lviii] In doing so, he also intended to get back Mijirhŏji-pŏrhan, who had previously been taken hostage. The king had them call upon Hŏji-pŏrhan, whom he made say, deceitfully, "The messengers Oryesabŏl, Momarijilji, and others told me, 'Because you have not returned for a long time, our king has confiscated your wife and children and made them all into slaves.' I wish to return to my homeland for a bit to learn if this is true or false."

The empress dowager allowed it and thereby dispatched Sotsuhiko of Kazuraki to accompany him.[lix] Together they arrived in Tsushima and stayed in the port at the sea of Sahi.[lx] At that time, the Silla envoys Momarijilji and the others secretly hired a ship and sailors and loaded Mijirhŏji onto it, and he escaped to Silla. Then they made a straw doll, placed it in Mijirhŏji's bed, and lied that he was sick. They told Sotsuhiko, "Mijirhŏji suddenly fell ill and may die."

Sotsuhiko sent a messenger to check in on the sick man. Thereby he knew that he had been deceived. He captured the three Silla envoys, put them in a cage, and burned them to death. Then he went to Silla, laid anchor at Tatara Port, sacked Sawara Fortress, and returned.[lxi] The prisoners captured around this time were the first descendants of the Ayahito[24] of the four villages of Kuhahara, Sabi, Takamiya, and Oshinumi.[lxii]

Thirteenth year [213 CE], spring, second month, eighth day. The empress ordered Takeuchi no Sukune to accompany the crown prince and worship

---

23 An original note adds, "It was called Wakasakura Palace." It is unusual for the palace name to take the form of a note. The same palace name appears in the main text in Jingū 69. A palace of the same name is used by Richū.

24 "Ayahito" refers to immigrant lineages. The characters suggest that they were from China, but the moniker was used to include peoples from the Korean peninsula as well. These immigrant lineage groups were often associated with advanced technology and the production of goods.

角鹿笥飯大神。癸酉、太子至自角鹿。是日皇太后宴太子於大殿。皇太后擧觴以壽于太子、因以歌曰、

虚能彌企破	このみきは
和餓彌企那羅儒	わがみきならず
區之能伽彌	くしのかみ
等虚豫珥伊廠輸	とこよにいます
伊破多々須	いはたたす
周玖那彌伽未能	すくなみかみの
等豫保枳	とよほき
保枳茂苔陪之	ほきもとほし
訶武保枳	かむほき
保枳玖流保之	ほきくるほし
摩菟利虚辭彌企層	まつりこしみきそ
阿佐孺塢齊	あさずをせ
佐佐	ささ

武內宿禰爲太子答歌之曰、

許能彌企塢	このみきを
伽彌鷄武比等破	かみけむひとは
曽能菟豆彌	そのつづみ
于輸珥多氐々	うすにたてて
于多比菟々	うたひつつ
伽彌鷄梅伽墓	かみけめかも
許能彌企能	このみきの
阿椰珥	あやに
于多娜濃芝	うただぬし
作沙	ささ

卅九年、是年也太歲己未。魏志云、明帝景初三年六月、倭女王遣大夫難斗米等、詣郡、求詣天子

the great kami Kehi in Tsunuga.[lxiii] On the seventeenth day, the crown prince returned from Tsunuga. On that day, the empress dowager threw a grand banquet for the crown prince in the great hall. The empress dowager raised her cup to wish the crown prince a long life and sang,

> This august wine
> is not my august wine.
> The master of sacred wine
> who dwells in Tokoyo
> standing upon a rock,
> Sukuna-biko-na,
> with lavish celebration
> made it while dancing in jubilation,
> with divine celebration,
> made it while losing himself in jubilation.
> He presented us with
> this august wine.
> Drink every drop.
> Hurrah![lxiv]

Takeuchi no Sukune answered for the crown prince, singing,

> The people who made
> this august wine,
> perhaps when they made it,
> sang,
> banging their mortars
> like drums:
> This august wine
> is really
> delicious.
> Hurrah![25]

Thirty-ninth year [239 CE], the year of the Earth Sheep.

The *History of Wei* says, In the sixth month of the third year of Jingchu, during the reign of Emperor Ming, the Queen of Wa dispatched senior minister Nan Doumi and others, and they arrived at Daifang Commandery, where they sought to go to the emperor and present

---

25 In antiquity, people likely made wine by chewing rice, spitting it out, and then grinding it with mortars. The saliva in the mash would encourage fermentation.

朝獻。太守鄧夏遣吏將送詣京都也。

　卅年。魏志云、正始元年、遣建忠校尉梯携等、奉詔書印綬、詣倭國也。

　卅三年。魏志云、正始四年、倭王復遣使大夫伊聲者掖耶約等八人上獻。

　卅六年春三月乙亥朔、遣斯摩宿禰于卓淳國。斯麻宿禰者、不知何姓人也。於是、卓淳王末錦旱岐、告斯摩宿禰曰、甲子年七月中、百濟人久氐・彌州流・莫古三人、到於我土曰、百濟王、聞東方有日本貴國、而遣臣等、令朝其貴國。故求道路、以至于斯土。若能教臣等、令通道路、則我王必深德君王。時謂久氐等曰、本聞東有貴國。然未曾有通、不知其道。唯海遠浪嶮。則乘大船、僅可得通。若雖有路津、何以得達耶。於是、久氐等曰、然即當今不得通也。不若、更還之備船舶、而後通矣。仍曰、若有貴國使人來、必應告吾國。如此乃還。

　爰斯摩宿禰即以傔人爾波移與卓淳人過古二人、遣于百濟國、慰勞其王。

tribute to the court.^lxv The governor, Deng Xia, dispatched messengers to accompany them, and they went to the capital city.²⁶

Fortieth year [240 CE].

The *History of Wei* says, In the first year of the new government,²⁷ Imperial Guard Captain Ti Xi and others were dispatched, with written edicts and a seal, to go to the land of Wa.^lxvi

Forty-third year [243 CE].

The *History of Wei* says, In the fourth year of the new government, the King of Wa again dispatched government officials—senior minister Iseisha, Yayayaku, and others, eight people in all—to present tribute.^lxvii

Forty-sixth year [246 CE], spring third month, first day. Shima no Sukune²⁸ was dispatched to the land of Tokujun.

It is unknown what title of nobility was held by Shima no Sukune.

Thereupon, the King of Tokujun, Malgŭm-han'gi,²⁹ told Shima no Sukune, "In the year of the Wood Rat [244 CE], in the middle of the seventh month, three men from Paekche came to our land: Kujŏ, Mijuryu, and Makko.³⁰ They said, 'The King of Paekche heard that to the east is the enlightened land of Yamato, and so he dispatched us to attend the court of that enlightened land. Therefore, we seek the route that will see us to that land. If you instruct us and allow us to pass through, our king would certainly be deeply delighted with your lordship.' At that time, I told Kujŏ and the others, 'Previously I heard that there is an enlightened land in the east. However, as we still have never gone there, we do not know the way. But it is far across the sea, and the waves are rough, so only by taking a large ship can we get there. Even if there were ports along the way, we probably could not make it without one.' In response, Kujŏ and the others said, 'In that case, right now we cannot get through. But we will return and prepare a ship and try to get through later.' Then he added, 'If an envoy from the enlightened land comes, definitely tell our country about it.' Upon saying these things, they left."

Then Shima no Sukune dispatched his retainer, Nihaya, and a man of Tokujun called Kwago to Paekche to show appreciation to the king.³¹

---

26 The governor was the commander of Daifang. The *History of Wei* in the *History of the Three Kingdoms* gives his name as Liu Xia. The capital was the Cao Wei capital of Luoyang.
27 That of Cao Fang.
28 "Shima" appears later in the narrative with a different spelling, but the same vernacular Japanese pronunciation.
29 Makimu-kanki.
30 Tokujun was a Kaya Confederacy state located in present-day Daegu City. Makimu is perhaps Mukimu (Kr. "isakŭm" for "king," used above); the characters Ma and Mu are very similar.
31 Neither Nihaya nor Kwago appear elsewhere.

時百濟肖古王、深之歡喜、而厚遇焉。仍以五色綵絹各一匹、及角弓箭、幷鐵鋌卌枚、幣爾波移。便復開寶藏、以示諸珍異曰、吾國多有是珍寶。欲貢貴國、不知道路。有志無從。然猶今付使者、尋貢獻耳。

於是、爾波移奉事而還、告志摩宿禰。便自卓淳還之也。

卌七年夏四月、百濟王使久氐・彌州流・莫古、令朝貢。時新羅國調使、與久氐共詣。於是、皇太后・太子譽田別尊、大歡喜之曰、先王所望國人、今來朝之。痛哉、不逮于天皇矣。群臣皆莫不流涕。仍檢校二國之貢物。於是、新羅貢物者、珍異甚多。百濟貢物者、少賤不良。

便問久氐等曰、百濟貢物、不及新羅、奈之何。

對曰、臣等失道、至沙比新羅。則新羅人捕臣等禁囹圄。經三月而欲殺。時久氐等、向天而呪詛之。新羅人怖其呪詛而不殺。則奪我貢物因以、爲己國之貢物。以新羅賤物、相易爲臣國之貢物。謂臣等曰、若誤此辭者、及于還日、當殺汝等。故久氐等恐怖從耳。是以、僅得達于天朝。

時皇太后・譽田別尊、責新羅使者、因以、祈天神曰、當遣誰人於百濟、將檢事之虛實。當遣誰人於新羅、將推問其罪。

便天神誨之曰、令武內宿禰行議。因以千熊長彥爲使者、當如所願。

King Ch'ogo of Paekche was deeply pleased and warmly welcomed them.[32] Thereupon he gave Nihaya five bolts of silk, each of a different color, a horn bow and arrows, and forty iron bars. He then opened up his treasure storehouse, pointed to various rare items, and said, "In my land we have many rare treasures. Though I wanted to send tribute to the enlightened country, I did not know how. I had the intention, but could not realize it. However, now I will send messengers and present tribute."

Nihaya took this message, returned, and told Shima no Sukune. Afterward Shima no Sukune came back from Tokujun.

Forty-seventh year [247 CE], spring, fourth month. The King of Paekche sent Kujŏ, Mijuryu, and Makko to present tribute to the imperial court. An envoy bearing tribute from Silla also came with Kujŏ. The empress dowager and Crown Prince Homuta-wake [Ōjin] were greatly pleased and said, "People from the lands desired by the previous lord have now come to court. How sad that they could not meet the emperor!" Among the high government officials, everyone shed tears. Then they inspected the tribute from the two countries. The tribute from Silla had very many rare and peculiar things. The tribute from Paekche was scant, mean, and no good.

Kujŏ and the others were asked, "The tribute from Paekche does not compare with that of Silla. Why is this?"

Kujŏ replied, "We lost our way and arrived at Sahi, in Silla. The people from Silla captured us and locked us up in cells. Three months passed, and they were going to kill us. At that time, Kujŏ and the rest of us looked to heaven and laid down a curse. The people from Silla were afraid that we had laid down a curse, and did not kill us. Then they stole our tribute and made it that of their own land. They took mean items from Silla and replaced items from Paekche. Hence, they became tribute from our country. Then they told us, 'If you divulge this, when the day comes for you to return, you will be killed.' So Kujŏ and the rest of us were afraid and could only follow orders. By doing so, we were barely able to arrive here at the heavenly court."

At this time, the empress dowager and Homuta-wake [Ōjin] blamed the Silla envoy and prayed to the kami of heaven, saying, "Who should be sent to Paekche to investigate the truth of this matter? And who should be sent to Silla to interrogate them about this crime?"

The heavenly kami instructed them, saying, "Have Takeuchi no Sukune draw up a plan. Then if you make Chikuma-nagahiko the messenger, things will turn out as you desire."

---

32 King Ch'ogo is King Kŭnch'ogo (r. 346–375).

千熊長彦者、分明不知其姓人。一云、武藏國人。今是額田部槻本首等之始祖也。百濟記云職麻那々加比跪者、蓋是歟也。
　　於是、遣千熊長彦于新羅、責以濫百濟之獻物。
　　卅九年春三月、以荒田別・鹿我別爲將軍。則與久氐等、共勒兵而度之、至卓淳國、將襲新羅。時或曰、兵衆少之、不可破新羅。更復、奉上沙白・蓋盧、請增軍士。即命木羅斤資・沙々奴跪是二人不知其姓人也。但木羅斤資者、百濟將也。領精兵、與沙白・蓋盧共遣之、俱集于卓淳、擊新羅而破之。因以平定比自㶱・南加羅・喙國・安羅・多羅・卓淳・加羅、七國。
　　仍移兵、西廻至古爰津、屠南蠻忱彌多禮、以賜百濟。於是、其王肖古及王子貴須、亦領軍來會。時比利・辟中・布彌支・半古四邑自然降服。是以、百濟王父子及荒田別・木羅斤資等、共會意流村。今云州流須祇。相見欣感。厚禮送遣之。
　　唯千熊長彦與百濟王、至于百濟國、登辟支山盟之。復登古沙山、共居磐石上。時百濟王盟之曰、若敷草爲坐、恐見火燒。且取木爲坐、

It is not clearly known what title of nobility Chikuma-nagahiko held. According to one account, he was from Musashi Province and was the first ancestor of the Obito of Nukatabe no Tsukimoto. According to the *Record of Paekche*, there was a man called Chingma-nanagabigwe; this is probably him.[lxviii]

Thereupon, Chikuma-nagahiko was dispatched to Silla to reproach the people of Silla for switching out the tribute from Paekche.

Forty-ninth year [249 CE], spring, third month. Arata-wake and Kaga-wake were named generals. Then with Kujŏ and the others, they outfitted soldiers and crossed the sea, arriving in the country of Tokujun with the intention of attacking Silla. At that time someone said, "Our troops are too few in number to defeat Silla." So they sent Sahaku and Kōro to the empress to ask her to increase the number of troops. Mongna Kŭnja[33] and Sasanako were ordered to lead spirited troops and were dispatched along with Sahaku and Kōro.

The personal names of these two people are not known, but Mokura Konshi was a general of Paekche.[34]

They assembled in Tokujun, attacked Silla, and defeated it. They then conquered the seven states of Hishiho, Arihishino-kara, Tokuno-kuni, Ara, Tara, Tokujun, and Kara.[lxix]

Then they moved the troops, circling around westward, and arrived at the harbor of Kokei. They slaughtered the southern barbarians of Tomutare and bestowed that land upon Paekche.[lxx] Thereupon King Ch'ogo and Prince Kwisu[35] again came leading their army to meet them. At that time, the four villages of Hiri, Hechu, Homuki, and Hanko all surrendered of their own accord.[lxxi] Then the Kings of Paekche, father and son, met together with Arata-wake, Mongna Kŭnja, and others in Orusuki. This place is now called Tsurusuki.[lxxii]

Delighted to see each other, they cordially exchanged formalities and then saw the others on their way.

Only Chikuma-nagahiko and the King of Paekche arrived in the state of Paekche, climbed Mt. Hekino, and made an oath. They then climbed Mt. Kosa and sat together atop a boulder.[lxxiii] At that time, the King of Paekche swore, saying, "If we spread grass for our seats, there is a chance that it could catch fire and burn. If we take wood to make a seat, it could

---

33 Mokura Konshi.
34 The two people referred to are Mokura Konshi and Sasanako. The Moku lineage group, presumably the same as the Mokura lineage group here, appears in several *Chronicles* entries and in the "Eastern Barbarians" book of the *History of the Sui Dynasty* as one of the eight great lineage groups of Paekche. Ōjin 25 claims that Mokura Konshi married a woman of Silla when he attacked it, giving birth to Moku Manchi.
35 Kŭn'gusu, son of King Kŭnch'ogo and fourteenth king of Paekche (r. 375–384).

恐爲水流。故居磐石而盟者、示長遠之不朽者也。是以、自今以後、千秋萬歲、無絶無窮。常稱西蕃、春秋朝貢。則將千熊長彥、至都下厚加禮遇。亦副久氐等而送之。

　五十年春二月、荒田別等還之。

　夏五月、千熊長彥・久氐等、至自百濟。於是、皇太后歡之問久氐曰、海西諸韓、既賜汝國。今何事以頻復來也。

　久氐等奏曰、天朝鴻澤、遠及弊邑。吾王歡喜踊躍、不任于心。故因還使、以致至誠。雖逮萬世、何年非朝。

　皇太后勅云、善哉汝言。是朕懷也。增賜多沙城、爲往還路驛。

　五十一年春三月、百濟王亦遣久氐朝貢。於是、皇太后語太子及武內宿禰曰、朕所交親百濟國者、是天所致。非由人故。玩好珍物、先所未有。不闕歲時、常來貢獻。朕省此款、每用喜焉。如朕存時、敦加恩惠。

　即年、以千熊長彥、副久氐等遣百濟國。因以、垂大恩曰、朕從神所驗、始開道路。平定海西、以賜百濟。今復厚結好、永寵賞之。

　是時、百濟王父子、並顙致地、啓曰、貴國鴻恩、重於天地。何日何時、敢有忘哉。聖王在上、明如日月。今臣在下、固如山岳。永爲西蕃、終無貳心。

be washed away by water. Therefore, seated on this boulder, showing that for eternity our oath will never rot, we swear that from now and ever after, through one thousand autumns and ten thousand years, without limit and without end, we will always be called the western territories and will pay tribute in spring and fall." Then, leading Chikuma-nagahiko, he arrived in the capital and cordially exchanged formalities. He had Kujŏ and the others accompany him home.

Fiftieth year [250 CE], spring, second month. Arata-wake and the others returned.

Summer, fifth month. Chikuma-nagahiko, Kujŏ, and the others returned from Paekche. The empress dowager was pleased and asked Kujŏ, "The various lands of Kara to the west across the sea have already been bestowed upon your country. Why do you now come again so frequently?"

Then Kujŏ and the others addressed her, saying, "The vast grace of the imperial court has extended to our faraway, lowly village. Our king dances with delight and cannot restrain his feelings. Hence, by means of a return envoy, he demonstrates his sincerity. Though myriad ages may pass, will there ever be a year when we fail to attend court?"

The empress dowager then decreed, "What felicitous things you say! We absolutely agree." Tasa Fortress was then bestowed upon Paekche as a post station for going back and forth.[lxxiv]

Fifty-first year [251 CE], spring, third month. The King of Paekche again dispatched Kujŏ (Kutei) to the imperial court with tribute. At this, the empress dowager told the crown prince and Takeuchi no Sukune, "The state of Paekche, with whom We have friendly relations, was granted to us by heaven, and not because of anything anyone has done. The novelties and rare treasures in their tribute are things we previously lacked in our land. They never miss a year and always come with tribute. When We reflect on this, We are always pleased. As long as We are alive, continue to show them deep favor."

The same year, Chikuma-nagahiko, accompanying Kujŏ and the others, was dispatched to Paekche. Accordingly, the empress gave them great consideration, saying, "We followed the signs of the kami, and from there first discovered the route, conquered the lands west of the sea, and bestowed them upon Paekche. Now again we secure our deep friendship, forever granting deep favor."

At that time the Kings of Paekche, father and son, kowtowed and humbly said, "The vast grace of the enlightened land is weightier than heaven and earth. Is there any day, any hour, when we could forget such grace? The sage king is above, and her brightness shines like the sun and moon. We are below, resolute like mountain peaks, forever the western territories, without duplicity to the end."

五十二年秋九月丁卯朔丙子、久氐等從千熊長彥詣之。則獻七枝刀一口・七子鏡一面・及種々重寶。仍啓曰、臣國以西有水。源出自谷那鐵山。其邈七日行之不及。當飲是水、便取是山鐵、以永奉聖朝。乃謂孫枕流王曰、今我所通、海東貴國、是天所啓。是以、垂天恩、割海西而賜我。由是、國基永固。汝當善脩和好、聚歛土物、奉貢不絶、雖死何恨。自是後、毎年相續朝貢焉。

　五十五年、百濟肖古王薨。

　五十六年、百濟王子貴須立爲王。

　六十二年、新羅不朝。即年、遣襲津彥擊新羅。

　百濟記云、壬午年、新羅不奉貴國。貴國遣沙至比跪令討之。新羅人莊飾美女二人、迎誘於津。沙至比跪、受其美女、反伐加羅國。加羅國王己本旱岐、及兒百久至・阿首至・國沙利・伊羅麻酒・爾汶至等、將其人民、來奔百濟。百濟厚遇之。

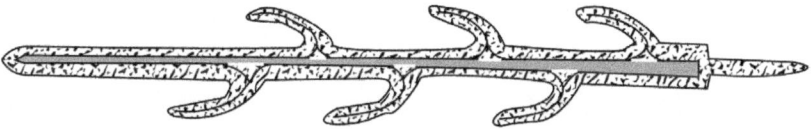

FIGURE 7 Seven-branched sword, Isonokami Shrine

Fifty-second year [252 CE], autumn, ninth month, tenth day. Kujŏ and the others, following Chikuma-nagahiko, went to court. There they presented as tribute a seven-branched sword,[36] a seven-faceted mirror, and various treasures. Then they humbly said, "In the west of our country is a river. Its source is Mt. Kane, or Iron Mountain, in Kokuna.[lxxv] It is so far away that you cannot reach it even after seven days of travel. We drank this water, harvested the iron from this mountain, and shall forever present it to the sage court." Then he told his grandson Prince Ch'imnyu,[37] "Now, the place we have passed through to, the enlightened land across the sea to the east, was founded by heaven. Hence, they pass down heavenly grace, and have divided up the lands west of the sea and bestowed them upon us. By doing so, the foundations of our state shall be forever solid. You too must maintain good friendship, gather the things of our country, and pay tribute without ceasing. Then even if you die, there will be nothing to regret." Thereafter, every year tribute came to court.

Fifty-fifth year [255 CE]. The King of Paekche, Ch'ogo, perished.[38]

Fifty-sixth year [256 CE]. The Prince of Paekche, Kwisu, was crowned king.

Sixty-second year [262 CE]. Silla did not present tribute. That year, the empress dispatched Sotsuhiko to attack Silla. According to the *Record of Paekche*, in the year of the Water Horse [262 or 382 CE], Silla did not present tribute to the enlightened country. The enlightened country dispatched Sajibigwe[39] to attack. The people of Silla adorned two beautiful women, who met him at port and seduced him. Sajibigwe received these women and instead attacked the land of Kara.[40] The King of Kara, Kibon Han'gi, and his sons Paekkujŏ, Asuji, Kuksari, Iramaju, Imunji, and others, led their people and fled to Paekche, where they were warmly received.

36 A seven-branched sword of Korean origin is held by the Isonokami Shrine in Nara Prefecture and is often associated with this entry. The inscription on the sword itself indicates that it was given by a prince of Paekche to the King of Wa (Japan), without explicitly indicating a hierarchical relationship in either direction.
37 Prince Tomuru, fifteenth King of Paekche (r. 384–385) and son of Kŭn'gusu.
38 King Kŭnch'ogo died in 375 CE, 120 years after 255, which means that the 60-year calendar cycle used here is aligned, despite the disparity in the Western calendar dates.
39 Sajibigwe is Sotsuhiko from the entries for Jingū 5 and Jingū 62.
40 "Kara" here refers to the state of Taegaya.

加羅國王妹既殿至、向大倭啓云、天皇遣沙至比跪、以討新羅。而納新羅美女、捨而不討。反滅我國。兄弟人民、皆爲流沈。不任憂思。故、以來啓。天皇大怒、即遣木羅斤資、領兵衆來集加羅、復其社稷。

　一云、沙至比跪、知天皇怒、不敢公還。乃自竄伏。其妹有幸於皇宮者。比跪密遣使人、問天皇怒解不。妹乃託夢言、今夜夢見沙至比跪。

　天皇大怒云、比跪何敢來。妹以皇言報之。比跪知不免、入石穴而死也。

　六十四年、百濟國貴須王薨。王子枕流王立爲王。

　六十五年、百濟枕流王薨。王子阿花年少。叔父辰斯奪立爲王。

The younger sister of the King of Kara, Kijŏnji, made for Yamato[41] and humbly said, "The emperor dispatched Sajibigwe to attack Silla. However, he married women from Silla, disregarded his orders, and did not attack. Instead, he overthrew our state. My siblings and the people have all become wanderers. I cannot bear my feelings of sadness, and so have come to respectfully report this to you." The emperor was greatly angered and immediately dispatched Mongna Kŭnja with orders to lead his troops and assemble at Kara, to restore that state.

According to one version, Sajibigwe knew of the emperor's anger and did not dare to return openly. So he went into hiding. His younger sister was in service to the imperial court. Pigwe[42] secretly sent a messenger to her to ask whether or not the emperor's anger had abated. The younger sister made use of a dream, saying, "Last night I saw Sajibigwe in a dream."

The emperor was greatly angered and said, "Pigwe! Why did he dare to come back?" The sister reported the emperor's words. Pigwe, knowing that he had not been forgiven, went into a hole in a rock and died.

Sixty-fourth year [264 CE]. The King of Paekche, Kwisu, perished. Prince Ch'imnyu was crowned king.

Sixty-fifth year [265 CE]. The King of Paekche, Ch'imnyu, perished. Prince Ahwa was a child, so his uncle, Chinsa, usurped the throne.[43]

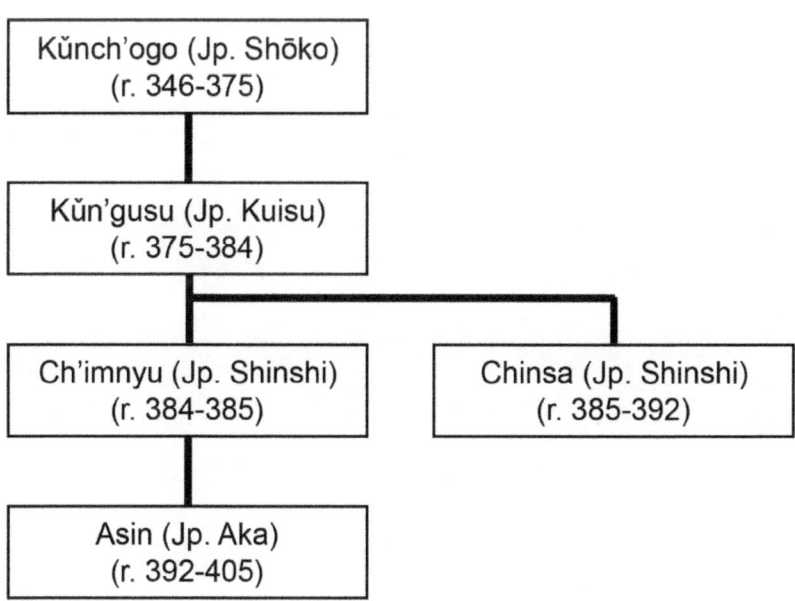

FIGURE 8   Kings of Paekche mentioned in the Jingū book

---

41 "Yamato" here refers to the Yamato State, Japan.
42 That is, Sajibigwe.
43 Prince Ahwa is Asin, seventeenth King of Paekche (r. 392–405), and Chinsa is the sixteenth King of Paekche (r. 385–392). The conflict between Chinsa and Asin does not appear in the *Samguk sagi*.

六十六年。

是年、晉武帝泰初二年。晉起居注云、武帝泰初二年十月、倭女王遣重譯貢獻。

六十九年夏四月辛酉朔丁丑、皇太后崩於稚櫻宮。時年一百歲。冬十月戊午朔壬申、葬狹城盾列陵。是日、追尊皇太后、曰氣長足姬尊。是年也、太歲己丑。

Sixty-sixth year [266 CE].

This year was the second year of Taishi during the reign of Emperor Wu of Jin.[44] According to *Notes on the Emperor's Doings* of Jin, "In the second year, tenth month of Taishi during the reign of Emperor Wu, the Queen of Wa sent layers of interpreters and tribute."[45]

Sixty-ninth year [269 CE], spring, fourth month, seventeenth day. The empress dowager expired in Wakasakura Palace.

At the time she was one hundred years old.

Winter, tenth month, fifteenth day. The empress was buried in Sakino-tatanami Tomb.[lxxvi] On this day, the empress dowager was honored with the posthumous name of Okinaga-tarashi-hime [Jingū]. This was the year of the Wood Ox.

---

44 The first emperor of the Jin Dynasty (r. 266–290 CE).
45 *Notes on the Emperor's Doings* was a diary-style record of the day-to-day actions of Chinese sovereigns. The compilers of the *Chronicles*, in this note, sought to associate Jingū with the Queen of Wa, Pimiko. Layers of interpreters were required because of the many interim languages used to facilitate communication.

譽田天皇　應神天皇

譽田天皇、足仲彥天皇第四子也。母曰氣長足姬尊。天皇、以皇后討新羅之年、歲次庚辰冬十二月、生於筑紫之蚊田。幼而聰達。玄監深遠。動容進止。聖表有異焉。皇太后攝政之三年、立爲皇太子。時年三。

初天皇在孕、而天神地祇授三韓。既產之、宍生腕上。其形如鞆。是肖皇太后爲雄裝之負鞆。肖、此云阿叡。故稱其名、謂譽田天皇。

上古時俗、號鞆謂褒武多焉。一云、初天皇爲太子、行于越國、拜祭角鹿笥飯大神。時大神與太子名相易。故號大神曰去來紗別神。太子名譽田別尊。然則可謂大神本名譽田別神、太子元名去來紗別尊。然無所見也、未詳。

攝政六十九年夏四月、皇太后崩。時年百歲。

元年春正月丁亥朔、皇太子即位。是年也、太歲庚寅。

二年春三月庚戌朔壬子、立仲姬爲皇后。后生荒田皇女・大鷦鷯天皇・根鳥皇子。

Book 10
Emperor Ōjin

Accession of Emperor Ōjin, Empress and Children

Emperor Homuta [Ōjin] was the fourth son of Emperor Tarashi-naka-tsu-hiko [Chūai].[i] His mother was called Okinaga-tarashi-hime [Jingū]. In the year when the empress attacked Silla, that of the Metal Dragon [201 CE], winter, twelfth month, the emperor was born in Kada in Tsukushi.[ii] He was intelligent from a young age and could perceive things deeply and from a distance. In his manner and bearing, he had the miraculous appearance of a sage.[iii] In the third year of the empress dowager's regency, he was named crown prince.

> At the time he was three years old.[1]

Originally, when the emperor was in the womb, the kami of heaven and earth[2] bestowed upon him the Three Han of Korea.[3] When he was born, the flesh of his upper arm bulged in the shape of an elbow pad. It recalled the time when the empress dowager put on male armor and wore an elbow pad. Accordingly, this feature was styled as his name, and he was called Emperor Homuta.

> In ancient times days, elbow-pads were called "homuta." Another account says, When the emperor first became crown prince, he went to Koshi Province and worshiped the great kami Tsunuga of Kehi. At that time, the great kami and the crown prince exchanged names. So the great kami was called Izasa-wake, and the crown prince was named Homuta-wake. Hence, the great kami's original name was Homuta-wake, and the crown prince's original name was Izasa-wake. However, this is not seen elsewhere, and remains unclear.[iv]

In the sixty-ninth year of her regency [269 CE], summer, fourth month, the empress dowager expired.

> At the time, she was one hundred years old.

First year [270 CE], spring, first month, first day. The crown prince acceded to the throne. This was the year of the Metal Tiger.

Second year [271 CE], spring, third month, third day.[v] Naka-tsu-hime was named empress.[vi] The empress gave birth to Imperial Princess Arata-hime, Emperor Ōsazaki [Nintoku], and Imperial Prince Netori.[vii]

---

1   If he was born in Chūai 9, he would have been four.
2   These kami are not referred to in the entry from Chūai 8, alluded to here.
3   Paekche, Silla, and Koguryŏ.

先是、天皇以皇后姉高城入姬爲妃、生額田大中彥皇子・大山守皇子・去來眞稚皇子・大原皇女・澇來田皇女。
　又妃皇后弟々姬、生阿倍皇女・淡路御原皇女・紀之菟野皇女。
　次妃和珥臣祖日觸使主之女宮主宅媛、生菟道稚郎子皇子・矢田皇女・雌鳥皇女。
　次妃宅媛之弟小甂小甂、此云烏儺謎。媛、生菟道稚郎姬皇女。
　次妃河派仲彥女弟媛、生稚野毛二派皇子。派、此云摩多。
　次妃櫻井田部連男鉏之妹糸媛、生隼總別皇子。
　次妃日向泉長媛、生大葉枝皇子・小葉枝皇子。
　凡是天皇、男女幷廿王也。根鳥皇子、是大田君之始祖也。大山守皇子、是土形君・榛原君、凡二族之始祖也。去來眞稚皇子、是深河別之始祖也。
　三年冬十月辛未朔癸酉、東蝦夷悉朝貢。卽役蝦夷而作厩坂道。
　十一月、處々海人、訕哅之不從命。訕哅、此云佐麼賣玖。則遣阿曇連祖大濱宿禰、平其訕哅。因爲海人之宰。故俗人諺曰、佐麼阿摩者、其是緣也。
　是歲、百濟辰斯王立之、失禮於貴國天皇。故

Previously, the emperor had taken the empress's older sister Takaki-no-iri-bime as his consort. She gave birth to Imperial Prince Nukata-no-ō-naka-tsu-hiko, Imperial Prince Ō-yama-mori, Imperial Prince Iza-no-ma-waka, Imperial Princess Ō-hara, and Imperial Princess Ko-muku-ta.

Another consort, the empress' younger sister Oto-hime, gave birth to Imperial Princess Ahe, Imperial Princess Awaji-no-mi-hara, and Imperial Princess Kino-uno.[viii]

His next consort was Miya-nushi-yaka-hime,[4] daughter of the ancestor of the Omi of Wani, Hifure-no-omi.[ix] She gave birth to Imperial Prince Uji-no-waki-iratsuko, Imperial Princess Yata, and Imperial Princess Metori.[5]

His next consort was the younger sister of Princess Yaka, O-nabe-hime. She gave birth to Imperial Princess Uji-no-waki-iratsume.

His next consort was the daughter of Kawa-mata-naka-tsu-hiko, Oto-hime.[x] She gave birth to Imperial Prince Waka-nuke-futa-mata.

His next consort was Ito-hime, the younger sister of the Muraji of Sakurai-tabe, Osai.[xi] She gave birth to Imperial Prince Hayabusa-wake.

His next consort was Princess Naga-hime of Izumi in Himuka.[xii] She gave birth to Imperial Prince Ōhae and Imperial Prince Ohae.

Altogether the Emperor had twenty royal children.[6] Imperial prince Netori became the first ancestor of the Kimi of Ōta.[xiii] Imperial prince Ō-yama-mori was the first ancestor of two clans: the Kimi of Hijikata and the Kimi of Harihara.[xiv] Imperial prince Iza-no-ma-waka was the first ancestor of the Wake of Fukakawa.[xv]

Foreign Relations

Third year [272 CE], winter, tenth month, third day. The Emishi of Azuma presented tribute to the court. Then they were set to work on the road of Umayasaka.[xvi]

Eleventh month. The fishing peoples of several places revolted and refused to follow orders. Thereupon, the ancestor of the Muraji of Azumi, Ōhama no Sukune, was dispatched to pacify this rebellion. He thereby became the steward of these fishing peoples. The proverb repeated by the common people Saba-ama originates from this event.[7]

The same year, King Chinsa became King of Paekche, but failed to observe proprieties to the emperor of the enlightened land. For this reason,

---

4   Princess Yaka.
5   Princess Yata will become empress to Emperor Nintoku. Princess Metori later appears in Nintoku 42.
6   Only nineteen children are listed here.
7   Saba-ama means "noisy fishers." One interpretation is that the fisherman spoke a different language or distinct dialect.

遣紀角宿禰・羽田矢代宿禰・石川宿禰・木菟宿禰、噴讓其无禮狀。由是、百濟國殺辰斯王以謝之。紀角宿禰等、便立阿花爲王而歸。

五年秋八月庚寅朔壬寅、令諸國、定海人及山守部。

冬十月、科伊豆國、令造船。長十丈。船既成之。試浮于海、便輕泛疾行如馳。故名其船曰枯野。由船輕疾名枯野、是義違焉。若謂輕野、後人訛歟。

六年春二月、天皇幸近江國、至菟道野上而歌之曰、

知麼能	ちばの
伽豆怒塢彌例麼	かづのをみれば
茂々智儀蘆	ももちだる
夜珥波母彌喩	やにはもみゆ
區珥能朋母彌喩	くにのほもみゆ

七年秋九月、高麗人・百濟人・任那人・新羅人、並來朝。時命武內宿禰、領諸韓人等作池。因以、名池號韓人池。

八年春三月、百濟人來朝。百濟記云、阿花王立无禮於貴國。故奪我枕彌多禮、及峴南・支侵・谷那・東韓之地。是以、遣王子直支于天朝、以脩先王之好也。

the emperor dispatched Tsuno no Sukune of Ki, Hata no Yashiro no Sukune, Ishikawa no Sukune, and Tsuku no Sukune to reproach him for his lack of manners.[xvii] In turn, the state of Paekche killed King Chinsa and apologized. Then Tsuno no Sukune of Ki and the others set up Ahwa as King of Paekche and returned.[8]

Fifth year [274 CE], autumn, eighth month, thirteenth day. The emperor ordered the various provinces to establish hereditary guilds of fishers and mountain wardens.

Winter, tenth month. Izu Province was ordered to make a boat thirty meters in length. After the boat was finished, it was tested at sea. It floated easily and moved quickly, as if it could run. Accordingly, it was named Karano.

Where it says that "the boat was light and swift, and so was called Karano," the meaning is incorrect. Perhaps it was called "Karuno," or "light one," and later people corrupted the term.

Sixth year [275 CE], spring, second month. The emperor toured Ōmi Province. When he drew near to Uji Field, he sang:[xviii]

When I survey
the fields of arrowroot,
I also see
many rich households,
And also see
the peerlessness of this land.

Seventh year [276 CE], autumn, ninth month. People from Koguryŏ, Paekche, Mimana, and Silla all attended court. At that time, the emperor ordered Takeuchi no Sukune to lead the various Koreans with him and make a reservoir. The reservoir was called Karahito no Ike, or Reservoir of the Koreans.[xix]

Eighth year [277 CE], spring, third month. People from Paekche attended court.

According to the *Record of Paekche*, King Ahwa took the throne but lacked propriety toward the enlightened land. Consequently, our land of Tomutare, as well as the lands of Kennamu, Shishimu, Kokuna, and Tōkan, were stolen away.[xx] Therefore, Prince Chikchi[9] was dispatched to the heavenly court to restore the friendship of past kings.

---

8   The accession of King Asin of Paekche, here called Ahwa (Jp. Aka), was in 392 CE, hence the same sexagenary cycle year as 272 CE. The character used for the "ka" of "Aka" closely resembles that of "sin" of "Asin" and is probably a mistake.
9   Later King Chŏnji of Paekche (r. 405–420 CE). *Samguk sagi* similarly notes that Chŏnji went to Wa (Japan).

九年夏四月、遣武內宿禰於筑紫、以監察百姓。時武內宿禰弟甘美內宿禰、欲廢兄、即讒言于天皇、武內宿禰、常有望天下之情。今聞、在筑紫而密謀之曰、獨裂筑紫、招三韓令朝於己、遂將有天下。於是、天皇則遣使、以令殺武內宿禰。

時武內宿禰歎之曰、吾元無貳心、以忠事君。今何禍矣、無罪而死耶。

於是、有壹伎直祖眞根子者。其爲人能似武內宿禰之形。獨惜武內宿禰無罪而空死、便語武內宿禰曰、今大臣以忠事君。既無黑心。天下共知。願密避之、參赴于朝、親辨無罪、而後死不晚也。且時人每云、僕形似大臣。故今我代大臣而死之、以明大臣之丹心、則伏劒自死焉。

時武內宿禰、獨大悲之、竊避筑紫、浮海以從南海廻之、泊於紀水門。僅得逮朝、乃辨無罪。

天皇則推問武內宿禰與甘美內宿禰。於是、二人各堅執而爭之。是非難決。天皇勅之、令請神祇探湯、是以、武內宿禰與甘美內宿禰、共出于磯城川湄、爲探湯。武內宿禰勝之、便執橫刀、以毆仆甘美內宿禰、遂欲殺矣。天皇勅之令釋。仍賜紀伊直等之祖也。

Plot against Takeuchi no Sukune, Courtship of Princess Kami-naga

Ninth year [278 CE], summer, fourth month. The emperor dispatched Takeuchi no Sukune to Tsukushi to observe its people. At that time Takeuchi no Sukune's younger brother, Umashiuchi no Sukune, wished to get rid of his brother and laid false charges on him, telling the emperor, "Takeuchi no Sukune has always had a mind to take over the realm for himself.[xxi] Now I hear that he is in Tsukushi secretly planning treason, saying, 'I will divide Tsukushi from the rest of the state and invite the Korean kingdoms to attend my court, and in time I will possess the entire realm.'" Upon hearing this, the emperor dispatched a messenger to kill Takeuchi no Sukune.

Takeuchi no Sukune said with a sigh, "From the start I have had no duplicitous intentions and have served my lord loyally. What travesty of justice is this whereby the guiltless must die?"

There was a man, the ancestor of the Atai of Iki, Maneko,[xxii] who in appearance looked very similar to Takeuchi no Sukune. Of his own volition, he lamented that the guiltless Takeuchi no Sukune had to die a meaningless death, and so he told Takeuchi no Sukune, "Now the Greater Minister serves our lord loyally, and all the realm knows that he has no impure intentions. I wish for you to secretly escape and attend on the court and prove that you are without offense. If you are killed afterward, it will not be too late. People these days always tell me, 'You look just like the Greater Minister.' Therefore, I will die now in place of the Greater Minister so that the Greater Minister can clearly demonstrate his pure intentions." He then used his sword to kill himself.

Takeuchi no Sukune, greatly saddened, secretly escaped from Tsukushi. He took a boat around the sea to the south and stayed in the port of Ki.[10] Barely making it to the court, he then petitioned that he was without guilt.

The emperor then interrogated Takeuchi no Sukune and Umashiuchi no Sukune, but each adamantly argued their cases, so it was difficult to decide who was right and who was wrong. The emperor decreed that they beseech the kami of heaven and earth and perform a trial by boiling water.[11] And so Takeuchi no Sukune and Umashiuchi no Sukune went out to the banks of the Shiki River and performed a trial by boiling water. Takeuchi no Sukune was victorious. Then he drew his broad-blade sword and felled Umashiuchi no Sukune and was about to kill him. But the emperor decreed that he be pardoned and turned him over to the ancestors of the Atai of Ki.[12]

---

10 Also used in Jingū 1.
11 Both suitors would pray and then immerse their hands in boiling water. The person seriously injured by the boiling water would be held as in the wrong.
12 Meaning that he was made into a manservant. In Keikō 3, Takeuchi no Sukune's mother, Kage-hime, is given as the distant ancestor of the Atai of Ki.

十一年冬十月、作劒池・輕池・鹿垣池・厩坂池。

是歲、有人奏之曰、日向國有孃子。名髮長媛。即諸縣君牛諸井之女也。是國色之秀者。天皇悅之、心裏欲覓。

十三年春三月、天皇遣專使、以徵髮長媛。

秋九月中、髮長媛、至自日向。便安置於桑津邑。爰皇子大鷦鷯尊、及見髮長媛、感其形之美麗、常有戀情。

於是、天皇知大鷦鷯尊感髮長媛而欲配。是以、天皇宴于後宮之日、始喚髮長媛、因以、上坐於宴席。時携大鷦鷯尊、以指髮長媛、乃歌之曰、

伊奘阿藝	いざあぎ
怒珥比蘆菟湄珥	のにひるつみに
比蘆菟瀰珥	ひるつみに
和餓喩區瀰智珥	わがゆくみちに
伽遇破志	かぐはし
波那多智麼那	はなたちばな
辭豆曳羅波	しづえらは
比等未那等利	ひとみなとり
保菟曳波	ほつえは
等利委餓羅辭	とりゐがらし
瀰菟遇利	みつぐりの
那伽菟曳能	なかつえの
府保語茂利	ふほごもり
阿伽例蘆塢等咩	あかれるをとめ
伊奘佐伽麼曳那	いざさかばえな

於是、大鷦鷯尊、蒙御歌、便知得賜髮長媛、而大悅之、報歌曰、

| 瀰豆多摩蘆 | みづたまる |
| 豫佐瀰能伊戒珥 | よさみのいけに |

Eleventh year [280 CE], winter, tenth month. The emperor built Tsurugi, Karu, Kanokaki, and Umayasaka Reservoirs.[xxiii]

That year, someone addressed the emperor, saying, "A woman in Himuka Province named Kami-naga-hime, the daughter of the Kimi of Morogata, Ushi-moroi,[13] is the most beautiful in all the land." The emperor was pleased to hear this and, in the back of his mind, desired to seek her out.

Thirteenth year [282 CE], spring, third month. The emperor dispatched a special messenger to summon Kami-naga-hime.

Autumn, ninth month, middle week.[14] Kami-naga-hime departed from Himuka and arrived at Kuhatsu Village.[xxiv] There it came to pass that Imperial Prince Ōsazaki [Nintoku] saw Kami-naga-hime, admired her great beauty, and incessantly longed for her.

The emperor knew that Ōsazaki admired Kami-naga-hime and wanted to join the two of them. So on a day when the emperor held a banquet in the inner palace, he first summoned Kami-naga-hime and had her sit in a chair. Then he sent for Ōsazaki, pointed at Kami-naga-hime, and sang:

Come, my lord,
to pick spring onions in the field,
to pick spring onions.
Upon the road we travel are
fragrantly†
flowering tachibana orange blossoms.
Those on the lower branches
have all been taken by people,
those on the upper branches,
scattered by the nesting birds.
Blushing maiden,
plump like the buds
on the middle branches,
come into bloom!

Receiving this august song, Ōsazaki knew that Kami-naga-hime was to be bestowed upon him. He was greatly pleased and sang in reply:

I knew not the length
of the water shield I reel in

13 Kami-naga-hime (long-haired lady) could refer to her appearance, or it could be a place-name. Kami-naga-ō-tane of Himuka is one of Keikō's consorts listed in Keikō 4. Morogata appears in the Keikō book. Ushimoroi appears later as simply Ushi and in the Nintoku book as Ushimoro.

14 The traditional month was made up of three ten-day weeks.

奴那波區利	ぬなはくり
破陪鶏區辭羅珥	はへけくしらに
委遇比菟區	ゐぐひつく
伽破摩多曳能	かはまたえの
比辭餓羅能	ひしがらの
佐辭鶏區辭羅珥	さしけくしらに
阿餓許居呂辭	あがこころし
伊夜于古珥辭氏	いやうこにして

　大鷦鷯尊、與髮長媛既得交懽懃、獨對髮長媛歌之曰、

彌知能之利	みちのしり
古破儾塢等綿塢、	こはだをとめを
伽未能語等	かみのごと
枳虛曳之介廼	きこえしかど
阿比摩區羅摩區	あひまくらまく

　又歌之曰、

彌知能之利	みちのしり
古波儾塢等綿	こはだをとめ
阿羅素破儒	あらそはず
泥辭區塢之敍	ねしくをしぞ
于蘆波辭彌茂布	うるはしみもふ

一云、日向諸縣君牛、仕于朝庭、年既耆耈之不能仕。仍致仕退於本土。則貢上己女髮長媛。始至播磨。時天皇幸淡路嶋、而遊獵之。於是、天皇西望之、數十麋鹿、浮海來之。便入于播磨鹿子水門。天皇謂左右曰、其何麋鹿也。泛巨海多來。

爰左右共視而奇、則遣使令察。使者至見、皆人也。唯以著角鹿皮、爲衣服耳。問曰、誰人也。

對曰、諸縣君牛、是年耆之、雖致仕、不得忘朝。故以己女髮長媛而貢上矣。天皇悅之、即喚令從御船。

是以、時人號其著岸之處、曰鹿子水門也。凡水手曰鹿子、蓋始起于是時也。

upon Yosami Reservoir.
I knew not the height
of the water caltrop planted
on the banks of the river.
How foolish
my perception was!

After Ōsazaki and Kami-naga-hime consummated their relationship, they were very intimate with each other. When they were alone, he faced Kami-naga-hime and sang:

Though I had heard
of the striking beauty
of the maiden
from faraway Kohada in Himuka,
now I lie entwined.

Then he sang again:

The maiden
from faraway Kohada in Himuka,
slept with me
without resisting.
How splendid she is!

Another account says, Ushi, Kimi of Morogata in Himuka, served the imperial court. When he became very advanced in age and could no longer serve, he withdrew and returned to his homeland. Then he presented his daughter, Kami-naga-hime. At first she went to Harima. At that time the emperor was touring Awaji and hunting. Then the emperor, gazing to the west, saw dozens of large stags floating toward him on the sea. They went on into Kako Harbor in Harima.[xxv] The emperor said to those in close service, "What large stags are these, that come floating in such numbers upon the great sea?"

Those in close service looked with him and thought the situation strange, and promptly dispatched messengers to investigate. When the messengers went and looked, the stags all turned out to be human. However, they used deer hides with antlers attached as clothing. The emperor asked, "Who are you all?"

One replied, "Ushi, Kimi of Morogata. I aged and withdrew, but I could not forget the court. So I present my daughter, Kami-naga-hime." The emperor was pleased and immediately summoned her and made her accompany him on his ship.

On account of this incident, people at the time called the place where they came ashore Kako Harbor, or Fawn Harbor.[xxvi] As for the practice of calling sailors "kako," this is probably the first instance.

十四年春二月、百濟王貢縫衣工女。曰眞毛津、是今來目衣縫之始祖也。

是歲、弓月君自百濟來歸。因以奏之曰、臣領己國之人夫百廿縣而歸化。然因新羅人之拒、皆留加羅國。爰遣葛城襲津彥、而召弓月之人夫於加羅。然經三年而襲津彥不來焉。

十五年秋八月壬戌朔丁卯、百濟王遣阿直伎、貢良馬二匹。即養於輕坂上廐。因以阿直岐令掌飼。故號其養馬之處、曰廐坂也。阿直岐亦能讀經典。即太子菟道稚郎子師焉。於是天皇問阿直岐曰、如勝汝博士亦有耶。

對曰、有王仁者。是秀也。

時遣上毛野君祖、荒田別・巫別於百濟、仍徵王仁也。其阿直岐者、阿直岐史之始祖也。

十六年春二月、王仁來之。則太子菟道稚郎子師之。習諸典籍於王仁。莫不通達。所謂王仁者、是書首等之始祖也。

是歲、百濟阿花王薨。天皇召直支王謂之曰、汝返於國以嗣位。仍且賜東韓之地而遣之。東韓者、甘羅城・高難城・爾林城是也。

八月、遣平群木菟宿禰・的戶田宿禰於加羅。仍授精兵詔之曰、襲津彥久之不還。必由新羅之拒而滯之。汝等急往之擊新羅、披其道路。於是、木菟宿禰等進

Arrival of Wani and Other Immigrants, Longing for E-hime

Fourteenth year [283 CE], spring, second month. The King of Paekche presented the emperor with a silk stitcher named Chinmojin, the first ancestor of the silk stitchers of Kume.[15]

This year, the Kimi of Yutsuki came from Paekche.[xxvii] He addressed the emperor, saying, "I have come to pledge myself to you, leading the people from 120 districts of my own land. However, because Silla is preventing them from coming, they are all stuck in the land of Kara."[16] At this the emperor dispatched Sotsuhiko of Kazuraki to summon Yutsuki's people from Kara. However, three years passed and Sotsuhiko did not return.

Fifteenth year [284 CE], autumn, eighth month, sixth day. The King of Paekche dispatched Ajikki to present two good horses.[xxviii] They were raised in the stables atop Karu Hill. Henceforth Ajikki was put in charge of raising them. The place where these horses were raised was called Umayasaka, or Horse Hill. Ajikki was also a good reader of the Confucian Classics. And so he was made tutor to Crown Prince Uji-no-waki-iratsuko.[17] Then the emperor asked Ajikki, saying, "Are there scholars superior to you?"

He replied, "One called Wangin is superior."[xxix]

At that time, the emperor dispatched the ancestors of the Kimi of Kamitsukeno, Arata-wake, and Kamunaki-wake, to Paekche, to summon Wangin. Ajikki was the first ancestor of the Fubito of Achiki.[xxx]

Sixteenth year [285 CE], spring, second month. Wangin came. He was made tutor of Crown Prince Uji-no-waki-iratsuko, who learned various writings from Wangin, a scholar well versed in everything. Wangin was the first ancestor of the Obito of Fumi.[xxxi]

That year, King Ahwa of Paekche perished.[xxxii] The emperor summoned King Chikchi and told him, "Return to your land and succeed to the throne." Then he bestowed upon him the lands of Tōkan and sent him off.

The lands of Tōkan were the fortresses Kamura, Konan, and Nirimu.[xxxiii]

Eighth month. The emperor dispatched Tsuku no Sukune of Heguri and Toda no Sukune of Ikuha to Kara.[xxxiv] The emperor gave them choice soldiers and decreed, "Sotsuhiko has not come back for a long time. Silla is no doubt preventing his return. Go quickly and attack Silla and unblock his passage." Then Tsuku no Sukune and the others marched with the choice

---

15 Neither Chinmojin nor the silk stitchers are seen elsewhere. Other textile workers arrive in Ōjin 37 and 41, and in Yūryaku 14.
16 The "land of Kara" usually indicates the entire region of Mimana, but here perhaps refers more narrowly to Koryŏng Kaya.
17 The entry naming Uji-no-waki-iratsuko as crown prince does not appear until Ōjin 40.

精兵、莅于新羅之境。新羅王愕之服其罪。乃率弓月之人夫、與襲津彦共來焉。

十九年冬十月戊戌朔、幸吉野宮。時國樔人來朝之。因以醴酒、獻于天皇、而歌之曰、

伽辭能輔珥	かしのふに
豫區周塢菟區利	よくすをつくり
豫區周珥	よくすに
伽綿蘆淤朋瀰枳	かめるおほみき
宇摩羅珥	うまらに
枳虛之茂知塢勢	きこしもちをせ
磨呂俄智	まろがち

歌之既訖、則打口以仰咲。今國樔獻土毛之日、歌訖即擊口仰咲者、蓋上古之遺則也。

夫國樔者、其爲人甚淳朴也。每取山菓食。亦煮蝦蟇爲上味。名曰毛瀰。其土自京東南之、隔山而居于吉野河上。峯嶮谷深、道路狹巘。故雖不遠於京、本希朝來。然自此之後、屢參赴以獻土毛。其土毛者、栗・菌及年魚之類焉。

廿年秋九月、倭漢直祖阿知使主、其子都加使主、並率己之黨類十七縣、而來歸焉。

soldiers up to the border of Silla. The King of Silla, full of fear, admitted his crime. They led the people of Yutsuki and came back together with Sotsuhiko.

Nineteenth year [288 CE], winter, tenth month, first day. The emperor toured Yoshino Palace.[xxxv] At that time, the people of Kuzu came to court.[18] They presented wine to the emperor and sang:

> Where the live oaks grow
> we make a wide mortar.
> Please drink
> and enjoy
> the great august wine mashed
> in the wide mortar,
> dear sire.

When their song was finished, they struck their mouths, lifted their heads, and laughed. Even at present, on the day that the Kuzu people present the products of their land, when their song is finished they strike their mouths, lift their heads, and laugh. This is probably in imitation of ancient customs.

As for Kuzu, its people are of a simple character. They often eat the tree fruit of the mountains, and they boil frog and deliciously season it, for a dish called "momi." The land is southeast of the capital, separated from the capital by mountains, near the headwaters of the Yoshino River. Its peaks are steep, its valleys deep, and its roads very narrow. For this reason, even though it is not far from the capital, it was originally rare for its people to come to court. However, since that time, they frequently visit and present the products of their land, like chestnuts, mushrooms, and a variety of sweetfish.

Twentieth year [289 CE], autumn, ninth month. The ancestor of the Atai of Aya in Yamato, Achi no Omi, and his son, Tsuka no Omi, came together leading their people from seventeen districts and pledged allegiance to the court.[19]

---

18 The Kuzu, called Kunisu in *Ancient Matters,* dwelt in the region near the headwaters of the Yoshino River.
19 The Atai of Aya in Yamato resided in the southern part of the Nara Basin and were associated with writing and literate administration. They were promoted to muraji in Tenmu 11 and imiki in Tenmu 14. *New Selected Records* assigns them Chinese origins. Tsuka later appears in Yūryaku 7.

廿二年春三月甲申朔戊子、天皇幸難波、居於大隅宮。丁酉、登高臺而遠望。時妃兄媛侍之。望西以大歎。兄媛者、吉備臣祖御友別之妹也。於是、天皇問兄媛曰、何爾歎之甚也。

對曰、近日、妾有戀父母之情。便因西望而自歎矣。冀暫還之、得省親歟。

爰天皇愛兄媛篤温凊之情、則謂之曰、爾不視二親、既經多年。還欲定省、於理灼然。則聽之、仍喚淡路御原之海人八十人爲水手、送于吉備。

夏四月、兄媛自大津發船而往之。天皇居高臺、望兄媛之船以歌曰、

阿波旎辭摩	あはぢしま
異椰敷多那羅弭	いやふたならび
阿豆枳辭摩	あづきしま
異椰敷多那羅弭	いやふたならび
豫呂辭枳辭摩之魔	よろしきしましま
儾伽多佐例阿羅智之	たかたされあらちし
吉備那流伊慕塢	きびなるいもを
阿比瀰菟流慕能	あひみつるもの

秋九月辛巳朔丙戌、天皇狩于淡路嶋。是嶋者横海、在難波之西。峯巖紛錯、陵谷相續。芳草薈蔚、長瀾潺湲。亦麋鹿・鳧・鴈、多在其嶋。故乘輿屢遊之。天皇便自淡路轉、以幸吉備、遊于小豆嶋。庚寅、亦移居於葉田葉田、此云簸娜。葦守宮。

時御友別參赴之。則以其兄弟子孫爲膳夫而奉饗焉。天皇、於是、看御友別謹惶侍奉之狀、而有悅情。因以割吉備國、封其子等也。則分川嶋縣、封長子稻速別。是下道臣之始祖也。次以上道縣、封中子仲彥。

ŌJIN 22 [291 CE]

Twenty-second year [291 CE], spring, third month, fifth day. The emperor toured Naniwa and stayed in Ōsumi Palace.[xxxvi] On the fourteenth day, he climbed a high terrace and gazed into the distance. At that time, his consort E-hime was attending him. She gazed to the west and heaved a heavy sigh.

> E-hime was the younger sister of the ancestor of the Omi of Kibi, Mitomo-wake.[xxxvii]

The emperor asked E-hime, "Why do you sigh so heavly?"

She replied, "These days, I miss my father and mother. Just now when I gazed off to the west, I suddenly sighed. Please let me return for a time so that I can visit my parents."

The emperor admired E-hime's warm feelings for her parents and said to her, "Many years have passed since you have seen your parents. Wanting to visit them is only natural." Then he permitted it. Accordingly, he summoned eighty fisherman from Mihara in Awaji, made them sailors, and sent them to Kibi.

Summer, fourth month. E-hime left Ōtsu by boat.[xxxviii] The emperor, on his high terrace, gazed out at E-hime's ship, and sang,

> The island of Awaji
> is paired well;
> the island of Azuki
> is paired well.
> These islands are well matched!
> Who has gone off far away?
> My darling from Kibi,
> oh how I long for her!

Autumn, ninth month, sixth day. The emperor went hunting on the island of Awaji. This island stretches across the sea to the west of Naniwa. It has intricate mountain peaks and crags, and its hills and valleys continue on and on. Its grasses bloom thickly, and the torrents of its rapids rumble as they flow. Deer, ducks, and geese are plentiful on the island. For these reasons, the emperor visited it frequently. The emperor went on around Awaji and toured Kibi, visiting Azuki Island. On the tenth day, he moved to Ashimori Palace in Hada.[xxxix]

At that time Mitomo-wake came. He had his siblings, children, and grandchildren serve as cooks and provide the emperor's meal. The emperor saw how humbly Mitomo-wake attended to his duties and was pleased. So he divided up the land of Kibi and enfeoffed Mitomo-wake's sons.[xl] His oldest son, Inahaya-wake, was enfeoffed in the division of Kawashima District; he was the first ancestor of the Omi of Shimotsumichi.[xli] His middle son, Naka-tsu-hiko, was enfeoffed in Kamitsumichi District; he was the first

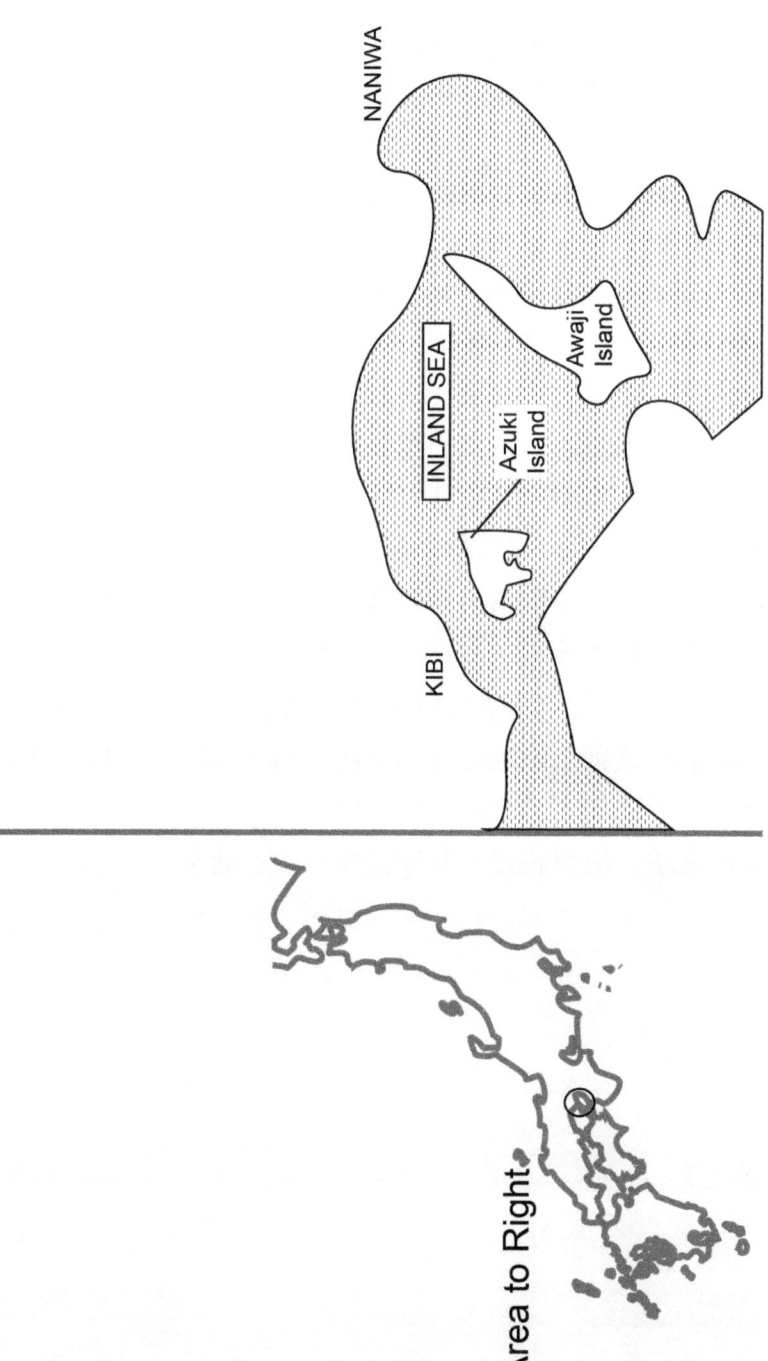

MAP 17 Awaji and Azuki Islands

是上道臣・香屋臣之始祖也。次以三野縣封弟彥、是三野臣之始祖也。復以波區藝縣、封御友別弟鴨別。是笠臣之始祖也。即以苑縣、封兄浦凝別。是苑臣之始祖也。即以織部、賜兄媛。是以、其子孫、於今在于吉備國。是其緣也。

廿五年、百濟直支王薨。即子久爾辛立爲王。王年幼、木滿致執國政。與王母相婬、多行無禮。天皇聞而召之。

<small>百濟記云、木滿致者、是木羅斤資、討新羅時、娶其國婦、而所生也。以其父功、專於任那。來入我國、往還貴國。承制天朝、執我國政。權重當世。然天朝聞其暴召之。</small>

廿八年秋九月、高麗王遣使朝貢。因以上表。其表曰、高麗王教日本國也。時太子菟道稚郞子讀其表、怒之責高麗之使、以表狀無禮、則破其表。

卅一年秋八月、詔群卿曰、官船名枯野者、伊豆國所貢之船也。是朽之不堪用。然久爲官用、功不可忘。何其船名勿絶、而得傳後葉焉。

群卿便被詔、以令有司、取其船材、爲薪而燒鹽。於是、得五百籠鹽。則施之周賜諸國。因令造船。是以、諸國一時貢上五百船。悉集於武庫水門。

當是時、新羅調使、共宿武庫。爰於新羅

ancestor of the Omi of Kamitsumichi and the Omi of Kaya.[xlii] His youngest son, Oto-hiko, was enfeoffed in Mino District; he was the first ancestor of the Omi of Mino.[xliii] Also Mitomo-wake's younger brother, Kamo-wake, was enfeoffed in Hakugi District; he was the first ancestor of the Omi of Kasa.[xliv] Mitomo-wake's older brother, Urakori-wake, was enfeoffed in Sono District; he was the first ancestor of the Omi of Sono.[xlv] The Hatori hereditary guild of weavers was bestowed upon E-hime. This is why her descendants are now in the land of Kibi.

Twenty-fifth year [294 CE]. King Chikchi of Paekche died.[xlvi] His son Kuisin became king. The king was young, and so Mok Manch'i took control of the state's administration.[xlvii] He became intimate with the king's mother, and there were multiple instances of discourtesy. The emperor heard this and recalled him.

> According to the *Record of Paekche*, Mok Manch'i was born when Mongna Kŭnja attacked Silla, and he married a woman from that land. Because of his father's service, he had absolute power in Mimana. He came to our land and went back and forth to the enlightened land. He received a mandate from the imperial court to take control of our state's administration. His authority was like that of a sovereign. However, the court heard of his tyranny and recalled him.

Twenty-eighth year [297 CE], autumn, ninth month. The King of Koguryŏ dispatched a messenger with tribute. He also presented a manifest. This manifest said, "The King of Koguryŏ instructs the land of Yamato." When Crown Prince Uji-no-waki-iratsuko read it, he was angered, and while censuring the messenger of Koguryŏ because the tone of the address lacked propriety, he tore up the manifest.

Thirty-first year [300 CE], autumn, eighth month. The emperor decreed to the high government officials, saying, "The command ship called Karano presented by Izu Province has rotted and can no longer be used. However, as it was in official use for a long time, its service should not be forgotten. How can we pass on the boat's name in unbroken fashion to future generations?"

The high government officials received this edict and ordered the administrators to take the wood from the boat and use it as firewood for roasting salt. Upon doing so, they got five hundred baskets of salt. These they donated to all the surrounding lands. Also, they had the surrounding lands make boats. In all, the various lands together presented five hundred boats. These were assembled in Muko Harbor.[20]

At just that time, some tributary emissaries from Silla were staying together at Muko. Suddenly, the place where the people from Silla were

---

20 Muko Harbor appears in Jingū 1 and Jingū 41.

停忽失火。即引之及于聚船。而多船見焚。由是、責新羅人。新羅王聞之、讋然大驚、乃貢能匠者。是猪名部等之始祖也。

　　初枯野船、爲鹽薪燒之日、有餘燼。則奇其不燒而獻之。天皇異以令作琴。其音鏗鏘而遠聆。是時天皇歌之曰、

訶羅怒烏	からのを
之襃珥椰枳	しほにやき
之餓阿摩離	しがあまり
虛等珥菟句離	ことにつくり
訶枳譬句椰	かきひくや
由羅能斗能	ゆらのとの
斗那訶能異句離珥	となかのいくりに
敷例多菟	ふれたつ
那豆能紀能	なづのきの
佐椰佐椰	さやさや

　　卅七年春二月戊午朔、遣阿知使主・都加使主於吳、令求縫工女。爰阿知使主等、渡高麗國、欲達于吳。則至高麗、更不知道路。乞知道者於高麗。高麗王乃副久禮波・久禮志、二人、爲導者。由是、得通吳。吳王、於是、與工女兄媛・弟媛・吳織・穴織、四婦女。

　　卅九年春二月、百濟直支王、遣其妹新齊都媛以令仕。爰新齊都媛、率七婦女、而來歸焉。

staying caught fire, and it spread to where the boats were gathered. Many of the boats were burned. The emperor blamed the people from Silla. When the King of Silla heard this, he was fearful and shocked, and so he presented a skilled carpenter to the court. He was the first descendant of the Ina hereditary guild.[21]

Back when the surrounding lands used the boat Karano as firewood for roasting salt, there was some firewood among the cinders leftover. Thinking it strange that it had not burned, it was presented to the emperor. The emperor was curious and made it into a zither. Its sound was clear and could be heard from a distance. At that time, the emperor sang,

Karano
was burnt for salt,
and with what remained
was made a zither.
When I pluck it,
the sound reverberates,
like the seaweed
brushing up against
the underwater stones
at Yura Harbor.

Thirty-seventh year [306 CE], spring, second month, first day. The emperor dispatched Achi no Omi and Tsuka no Omi to Wu to search for a seamstress.[22] Achi no Omi and the others crossed into Koguryŏ, seeking to reach Wu. But while they reached Koguryŏ, they did not know the way beyond there. They asked for a guide from Koguryŏ. The King of Koguryŏ then sent two people, Kuryep'a and Kuryeji, to accompany them as guides. Thanks to the guides, they were able to reach Wu. The King of Wu gave them four seamstresses: E-hime, Oto-hime, Kure-hatori, and Ana-hatori.[23]

Thirty-ninth year [308 CE], spring, second month. King Chikchi of Paekche sent his younger sister Shinjedo-wŏn to attend on the emperor.[24] Shinjedo-wŏn, leading seven other ladies, pledged her allegiance to the court.

---

21 Ina District appears in Nintoku 38, referring to the present-day northeastern region of Nigasaki City, Hyōgo Prefecture. A carpenter with the name Inabe appears in Yūryaku 13.
22 This entry pairs with that for Ōjin 41. A similar mission to Wu to search for skilled labor appears in Yūryaku 12 and 14. Wu refers to the Jiangnan area of China. Adding 120 years to this entry for two sexagenary cycles would place this incident in the Liu Song Dynasty. The *History of the Liu Song* records diplomatic exchanges with the Five Kings of Wa.
23 Yūryaku 14 has Kure-hatori, Aya-hatori, and the seamstresses E-hime and Oto-hime.
24 Shisetsu-hime does not appear elsewhere. An Iketsu-hime appears in Yūryaku 2.

卅年春正月辛丑朔戊申、天皇召大山守命・大鷦鷯尊、問之曰、汝等者愛子耶。

對言、甚愛也。

亦問之、長與少孰尤焉。

大山守命對言、不逮于長子。

於是天皇、有不悅之色、時大鷦鷯尊、預察天皇之色、以對言、長者多經寒暑、既爲成人。更無悒矣。唯少子者、未知其成不。是以、少子甚憐之。

天皇大悅曰、汝言寔合朕之心。

是時、天皇常有立菟道稚郎子、爲太子之情。然欲知二皇子之意。故發是問。是以、不悅大山守命之對言也。甲子、立菟道稚郎子爲嗣。即日、任大山守命、令掌山川林野。以大鷦鷯尊、爲太子輔之、令知國事。

卅一年春二月甲午朔戊申、天皇崩于明宮。時年一百一十歲。一云、崩于大隅宮。

是月、阿知使主等、自吳至筑紫。時胸形大神、有乞工女等。故以兄媛奉於胸形大神。是則今在筑紫國、御使君之祖也。既而率其三婦女、以至津國及于武庫、而天皇崩之。不及。即獻于大鷦鷯尊。是女人等之後、今吳衣縫・蚊屋衣縫是也。

Naming of the Crown Prince, Death of the Emperor

Fortieth year [309 CE], spring, first month, eighth day. The emperor summoned Ō-yama-mori and Ōsazaki [Nintoku] and asked them, "Are you two fond of your children?"

They replied, "Very fond."

Then he asked them again, "Between the older and the younger, which is superior?"

Ō-yama-mori replied, "None can match the older."

At this, the emperor's displeasure was evident on his face. Ōsazaki, observing the emperor's reaction, replied, "The older has passed many summers and winters and is already an adult, so I am not anxious about him. As for the younger, however, it is still unknown if he will reach adulthood, so I worry greatly."

Then the emperor said with great pleasure, "Your words match Our heart."

At that time, the emperor had been wanting to name Uji-no-waki-iratsuko as crown prince. However, he wanted to know the feelings of these two imperial princes, so he made this inquiry. He was not pleased with the reply of Ō-yama-mori. On the twenty-fourth day, Uji-no-waki-iratsuko was named his successor. The same day, Ō-yama-mori was charged with administration of the mountains, rivers, woods, and fields. Ōsazaki [Nintoku] was made assistant to the crown prince and ordered to direct matters of state.

Forty-first year [310 CE], spring, second month, fifteenth day. The emperor expired in Akira Palace.[xlviii] At that time, he was 110 years old.[25]

> According to one account, he expired at Ōsumi Palace.[26]

That month, Achi no Omi and the others arrived in Tsukushi from Wu. At that time, the great kami of Munakata wanted seamstresses. Accordingly, E-hime was offered to the great kami of Munakata, and now being in the land of Tsukushi, she became the ancestor of the Kimi of Mitsukai.[27] After this, Achi no Omi and the others led the other three women, and they arrived in Tsu Province, but by the time they arrived at Muko Harbor, the emperor had expired. They were not in time, and so they presented the other three women to Ōsazaki. The descendants of these women are now the seamstresses of Kure and Kaya.

---

25 In *Ancient Matters*, Ōjin was 130 when he died. According to the chronology of the *Chronicles*, he should be 111.
26 In Naniwa.
27 The Kimi of Mitsukai is not seen elsewhere. Munakata appears in S6 of the "Age of the Gods."

大鷦鷯天皇　仁徳天皇

大鷦鷯天皇、譽田天皇之第四子也。母曰仲姬命。五百城入彥皇子之孫也。天皇幼而聰明叡智。貌容美麗。及壯仁寬慈惠。

　卌一年春二月、譽田天皇崩。時太子菟道稚郎子、讓位于大鷦鷯尊、未即帝位。仍諮大鷦鷯尊、夫君天下、以治萬民者、蓋之如天、容之如地。上有驩心、以使百姓。

Book 11
Emperor Nintoku

Disputes over the Throne

Emperor Ōsazaki [Nintoku] was the fourth child of Emperor Homuta [Ōjin].[i] His mother was called Naka-tsu-hime, the granddaughter of Imperial Prince Ioki-iri-biko.[1] From a young age, he was astute and intelligent, and he was quite handsome.[ii] When he blossomed into adulthood, he was gracious and charitable.[iii]

In spring of the forty-first year [310 CE], second month, of his reign, Emperor Homuta expired. At that time, Crown Prince Uji-no-waki-iratsuko deferred to Ōsazaki and did not accede to the imperial throne himself. On this he conferred with Ōsazaki, saying, "The lord of the realm who rules the myriad peoples must embrace them like the heavens and receive them like the earth. By possessing a joyful heart above, he makes use of the people.

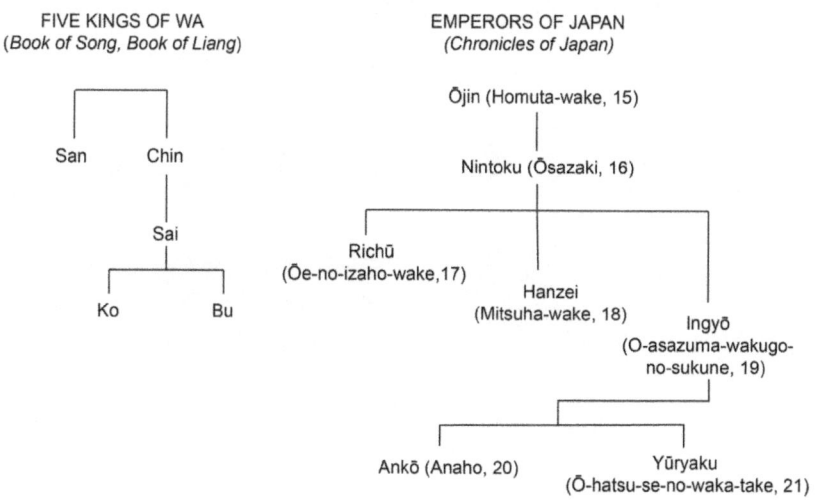

FIGURE 9 Five kings of Wa

---

1 Ioki-iri-biko appears as a son of Keikō in Keikō 4. The Ōjin book of *Ancient Matters* gives Naka-tsu-hime's father as Homuta-no-ma-waka.

百姓欣然、天下安矣。今我也弟之。且文獻不足。何敢繼嗣位、登天業乎。大王者風姿岐嶷。仁孝遠聆、以齒且長。足爲天下之君。其先帝立我爲太子、豈有能才乎。唯愛之者也。亦奉宗廟社稷重事也。僕之不佞、不足以稱。夫昆上而季下、聖君而愚臣、古今之常典焉。願王勿疑、須即帝位。我則爲臣之助耳。

大鷦鷯尊對言、先皇謂、皇位者一日之不可空。故預選明德、立王爲貳。祚之以嗣、授之以民。崇其寵章、令聞於國。我雖不賢、豈棄先帝之命、輒從弟王之願乎。固辭不承、各相讓之。

是時、額田大中彥皇子、將掌倭屯田及屯倉、而謂其屯田司出雲臣之祖淤宇宿禰曰、是屯田者、自本山守地。是以、今吾將治矣。爾之不可掌。時淤宇宿禰啓于太子。

太子謂之曰、汝便啓大鷦鷯尊。

2 This is the first appearance of the title "Great King" in the *Chronicles*. It has been suggested that around this time Japanese rulers began to be called by this title, which would be used until the late seventh century, when it was replaced by "Emperor." The description of Nintoku's appearance is also used for Suizei and Tenmu.
3 According to Ōjin 2, Imperial Prince Nukata-no-ō-naka-tsu-hiko is the son of Ōjin and his consort Takaki-no-iri-bime, and is thus a full brother of Ō-yama-mori. He later appears as a loyal subject in Nintoku 62.

The people rejoice, and the realm is at peace.[iv] Now, I am the younger brother and as yet insufficiently educated.[v] How could I dare to succeed as heir to the throne and assume this heavenly endeavor? Great King, your appearance is refined, your benevolence and filial piety far-reaching, and your remaining lifespan still long.[2] You are worthy of being lord of this realm. Indeed, the previous emperor named me crown prince, but was it because I have any talent?[vi] He simply adored me. Furthermore, serving the altars of state is a serious matter, and I am incompetent and unworthy. [vii] The older sibling is above and the younger below; the sage is lord and the fool his vassal. In the past and present, this has always been the rule. I wish you, my king, to have no doubt and to ascend the imperial throne. I as your vassal will only provide aid to you."

Then Ōsazaki [Nintoku] replied to him, saying, "The previous emperor said, 'The imperial throne cannot be left empty for even a day.'[viii] Hence, he preemptively chose the brightest individual and named him as the next king. You were given his blessing as heir, and the people were bestowed upon you. This esteem, a sign of his affection, he made known in the realm.[ix] Being immature myself, how could I disregard the order of the previous emperor and so casually go along with my younger brother's request?" He thus firmly rejected and would not sanction the order to take the throne, and in this fashion each of them deferred to the other.

During this time, Imperial Prince Nukata-no-ō-naka-tsu-hiko[3] was plotting to take command of the imperial rice paddies and imperial estates of Yamato. But the steward of these imperial rice paddies, the ancestor of the Omi of Izumo, Ō no Sukune, said to him, "These imperial rice paddies were originally the land of the mountain wardens.[4] So I will rule them now. You shall have no command here." Ō no Sukune reported all this to the crown prince.[5]

The crown prince told him, "Quickly go report this to Ōsazaki."

---

4   Ō no Sukune does not appear elsewhere in the *Chronicles or Ancient Matters*. Ō is a place-name in Izumo associated with the Kumano Grand Shrine and is seen in Saimei 5, which suggests that he was a Provincial Miyatsuko of Izumo. A hereditary guild of mountain wardens was created in Ōjin 5, but it is unclear if this statement refers to that group or to the Imperial Prince Ō-yama-mori, whose name means "Great Mountain Warden."
5   Ō-yama-mori's revolt also appears in *Ancient Matters*, but without this earlier violation by Nukata-no-ō-naka-tsu-hiko. It has been suggested that the two brothers have been conflated.

於是、淤宇宿禰啓大鷦鷯尊曰、臣所任屯田者、大中彦皇子距不令治。

　大鷦鷯尊、問倭直祖麻呂曰、倭屯田者、元謂山守地、是如何。

　對言、臣之不知。唯臣弟吾子籠知也。

　適是時、吾子籠遣於韓國而未還。爰大鷦鷯尊、謂淤宇曰、爾躬往於韓國、以喚吾子籠。其兼日夜而急往。乃差淡路之海人八十爲水手。爰淤宇往于韓國、即率吾子籠而來之。

　因問倭屯田。對言、傳聞之、於纏向玉城宮御宇天皇之世、科太子大足彦尊、定倭屯田也。是時、勅旨、凡倭屯田者、每御宇帝皇之屯田也。其雖帝皇之子、非御宇者、不得掌矣。是謂、山守地非之也。

　時大鷦鷯尊、遣吾子籠於額田大中彦皇子、而令知狀。大中彦皇子、更無如何焉。乃知其惡、而赦之勿罪。

　然後、大山守皇子、每恨先帝廢之非立、而重有是怨。則謀之曰、我殺太子、遂登帝位。

6　The Atai of Yamato appears in the Jinmu, Sujin, and Suinin books. An alternative account in Suinin 3 gives Nagaochi as the ancestor of the Atai of Yamato.

7　Agoko would later be dispatched to Tōtōmi Province in Nintoku 62 and would participate in a rebellion in the pre-accession record of Richū. Agoko escaped by presenting his sister to the emperor, which began a tradition of the Atai of Yamato presenting women to the throne.

Ō no Sukune reported to Ōsazaki, "I cannot govern the imperial estate with which I have been charged because Imperial Prince Ō-naka-tsu-hiko is preventing it."

Ōsazaki asked the ancestor of the Atai of Yamato,[6] Maro, "It has been said that the imperial rice paddies in Yamato were originally the land of the mountain wardens. Is this the case?"

He replied, "I do not know. Only my younger brother, Agoko,[7] would know." At that time, Agoko had been dispatched to Korea and had not yet returned.

Ōsazaki [Nintoku] then told Ō, "Go personally to Korea and summon Agoko. Go quickly, by day and by night." Then he immediately gave him eighty fishermen from Awaji to serve as sailors.[8] Ō went to Korea and promptly came back with Agoko.

Thereupon they asked him about the imperial rice paddies of Yamato. He replied, "What I have heard passed down is that in the time of the reign of the emperor who ruled the realm from Tamaki Palace in Makimuku, Crown Prince Ō-tarashi-hiko was enjoined to establish the imperial rice paddies of Yamato.[9] At that time, the emperor decreed, 'The imperial rice paddies of Yamato shall always be an imperial estate of the emperor of the realm. Even a child of the emperor, if they do not rule the realm, cannot take command of them.' As for it being the land of the mountain wardens, that is not true."

At that time, Ōsazaki dispatched Agoko to Imperial Prince Nukata-no-ō-naka-tsu-hiko to notify him of the situation. Imperial Prince Ō-naka-tsu-hiko could not say anything more. Ōsazaki thus knew of his evil intentions, but forgave him without punishing him.

A while later, Imperial Prince Ō-yama-mori, who had always resented that the previous emperor had cast him aside and not named him crown prince, begrudged his situation even further.[10] So he plotted, saying, "I will kill the crown prince and then ascend the imperial throne."

---

8   Fishermen from Awaji are used as sailors also in Ōjin 22.
9   No such pronouncement appears in the book for Suinin, the emperor in question here.
10 One interpretation for "even further" is that the earlier entry confused Nukata-no-ō-naka-tsu-hiko with Ō-yama-mori, and that it was the latter prince who attempted to usurp the imperial estates of Yamato.

爰大鷦鷯尊、預聞其謀、密告太子、備兵令守。時太子設兵待之。大山守皇子、不知其備兵、獨領數百兵士、夜半、發而行之。會明、詣菟道、將渡河。

時太子服布袍取檝櫓、密接度子、以載大山守皇子而濟。至于河中、誂度子、蹈船而傾。於是、大山守皇子、墮河而沒。更浮流之歌曰、

知破揶臂苔	ちはやひと
于旋能和多利珥	うぢのわたりに
佐烏刀利珥	さをとりに
破揶鶏務臂苔辭	はやけむひとし
和餓毛胡珥虛務	わがもこにこむ

然伏兵多起、不得著岸。遂沈而死焉。令求其屍、泛於考羅濟。時太子視其屍、歌之曰、

智破揶臂等	ちはやひと
于旋能和多利珥	うぢのわたりに
和多利涅珥	わたりでに
多氐屢	たてる
阿豆瑳由瀰摩由瀰	あづさゆみまゆみ
伊枳羅牟苔	いきらむと
虛々呂破望閉耐	こころはもへど
伊斗羅牟苔	いとらむと
虛々呂破望閉耐	こころはもへど
望苔弊破	もとへは
枳瀰烏於望臂涅	きみをおもひで
須慧幣破	すゑへは
伊暮烏於望比涅	いもをおもひで
伊羅那鶏區	いらなけく
曾虛珥於望比	そこにおもひ
伽那志鶏區	かなしけく
虛々珥於望臂	ここにおもひ
伊枳羅儒層區屢	いきらずそくる
阿豆瑳由瀰摩由瀰	あづさゆみまゆみ

Ōsazaki [Nintoku] came to hear of this plan in advance. He secretly told the crown prince and prepared troops to protect him. In turn, the crown prince arrayed the troops and waited. Imperial Prince Ō-yama-mori did not know that troops had been stationed and took lead of only few hundred of his own soldiers and set out at night. When dawn broke, he had reached Uji and was just about to cross the river.

At that time, the crown prince wore hempen clothing and, having secretly mixed in with the boat people, had taken the helm. He loaded Imperial Prince Ō-yama-mori aboard and began the crossing. When they reached the middle of the river, he ordered the boat people to step on the gunwale and capsize the boat. Imperial Prince Ō-yama-mori fell into the river, bobbing up and down, and as he was carried along, he sang,

> Dear people,
> skillfully piloting boats
> at the crossing at Uji,
> quickly, dear people,
> come to my aid![x]

However, a large number of soldiers who had been hiding appeared, and he could not reach shore. In the end, he drowned. When his body was ordered found, it had floated to the crossing at Kawara.[xi] At that time, the crown prince looked upon the body and sang,

> Dear spindle tree,
> standing
> at the crossing at Uji,
> at the crossing place,
> though in my heart I think
> of cutting you down,
> though in my heart I think
> of taking you away,
> at your roots,
> I remember you, my lord,
> at your branches,
> I remember your beloved.
> Thinking of this,
> I grieve;
> thinking of that,
> I am saddened.
> And so I return without cutting you down,
> dear spindle tree.[xii]

乃葬于那羅山。既而興宮室於菟道、而居之。猶由讓位於大鷦鷯尊、以久不即皇位。

爰皇位空之、既經三載。時有海人、齎鮮魚之苞苴、獻于菟道宮也。太子令海人曰、我非天皇、乃返之令進難波。大鷦鷯尊亦返、以令獻菟道。於是、海人之苞苴、鯘於往還。更返之、取他鮮魚而獻焉、讓如前日。鮮魚亦鯘。海人苦於屢還、乃棄鮮魚而哭。故諺曰、有海人耶、因己物以泣、其是之緣也。

太子曰、我知不可奪兄王之志。豈久生之、煩天下乎、乃自死焉。

時大鷦鷯尊、聞太子薨以驚之、從難波馳之、到菟道宮。爰太子薨之經三日。時大鷦鷯尊、摽擗叩哭、不知所如。乃解髮跨屍、以三乎曰、我弟皇子。

乃應時而活。自起以居。爰大鷦鷯尊、語太子曰、悲兮、惜兮。何所以歟自逝之。若死者有知、先帝何謂我乎。

乃太子啓兄王曰、天命也。誰能留焉。若有向天皇之御所、具奏兄王聖之、且有讓矣。然聖王聞我死、以急馳遠路。豈得無勞乎。

He was buried at Mt. Nara.^xiii The crown prince built a palace in Uji and dwelt there. However, because he had deferred the throne to Ōsazaki [Nintoku], much time passed without his acceding to the imperial throne.

And so the imperial throne was unoccupied for three years. At that time, there was a fisherman who wanted to use fresh fish as an offering, and so presented fish at Uji Palace. The crown prince ordered the fisherman, saying, "I am not the emperor," and made the fisherman go back to Naniwa to present the fish there.[11] Ōsazaki too sent the fish back, making the fisherman present the gift at Uji. With all the coming and going, the fisherman's offering went bad. The fisherman returned and caught more fresh fish to take and present. But the two brothers deferred to each other just as on the previous day, and the fresh fish again went bad. The fisherman, taxed with all the going back and forth, threw the fish away and wept. This is the origin of the proverb, "Even a fisherman can be brought to tears because of his possessions."

The crown prince said, "I know that I cannot take away my older brother's resolve. The longer I live, the more peril for the realm." Then he killed himself.^xiv

When Ōsazaki [Nintoku] heard that the crown prince had perished, he was shocked and rushed from Naniwa to Uji Palace. By then three days had passed since the crown prince had perished. Ōsazaki beat his breast, cried out, and did not know what to do. Then he untied his hair, straddled the corpse, and called out three times, "My brother the prince!"[12]

Suddenly, he came back to life and sat up by himself. Ōsazaki told the crown prince, "What sadness! What remorse! Why did you kill yourself? If the dead could know things, what would the previous emperor think of me?"

Then the crown prince told his older brother, "This lifespan was allotted to me by heaven. Who can stay its course? If I go to the place where the emperor is, I will address him saying that my older brother, being a sage, deferred the throne over and over again. Sage-king, when you heard of my death, you quickly rushed across a great distance. How could I not show my appreciation?"

---

11 Uji-no-waki-iratsuko at Uji and Ōsazaki at Naniwa recalls the Akira Palace and Ōsumi Palace used by Emperor Ōjin, the former being in Uji and the latter in Naniwa.
12 These are perhaps practices for summoning spirits.

乃進同母妹八田皇女曰、雖不足納采、僅充掖庭之數。乃且伏棺而薨。於是、大鷦鷯尊素服、爲之發哀哭之甚慟。仍葬於菟道山上。

元年春正月丁丑朔己卯、大鷦鷯尊即天皇位。尊皇后曰皇太后。都難波。是謂高津宮。即宮垣室屋弗堊色也。桷梁柱楹弗藻飾也。茅茨之蓋弗割齊也。此不以私曲之故、留耕績之時者也。

初天皇生日、木菟入于產殿。明旦、譽田天皇、喚大臣武內宿禰語之曰、是何瑞也。

大臣對言、吉祥也。復當昨日、臣妻產時、鷦鷯入于產屋。是亦異焉。

爰天皇曰、今朕之子與大臣之子、同日共產。並有瑞。是天之表焉。以爲、取其鳥名、各相易名子、爲後葉之契也。則取鷦鷯名、以名太子、曰大鷦鷯皇子。取木菟名、號大臣之子、曰木菟宿禰。是平群臣之始祖也。是年也、太歲癸酉。

二年春三月辛未朔戊寅、立磐之媛命爲皇后。皇后生大兄去來穗別天皇・住吉仲皇子・瑞齒別天皇・雄朝津間稚子宿禰天皇。

又妃日向髮長媛、生大草香皇子・幡梭皇女。

Then he presented his younger sister by the same mother, Imperial Princess Yata,[13] and said, "She may not be worthy of marriage, but please have her among those in the inner palace." Then he laid back down in the coffin and perished. At that, Ōsazaki put on bleached hempen clothing and grieved, wailing and lamenting. They buried him atop Mt. Uji.[xv]

Accession, Empress and Children, Virtuous Works

First year [313 CE], spring, first month, third day.[14] Ōsazaki [Nintoku] acceded to the imperial throne. The empress[15] was honored with the title of empress dowager. The capital, called Takatsu Palace, was at Naniwa.[xvi] The palace outer walls and buildings were not painted, its rafters, trusses, joists, and columns not decorated, and the thatch on its roof untrimmed.[xvii] This was because the emperor did not wish to pause agricultural work on behalf of himself.

Back when the emperor was born, a horned owl entered the birthing chamber. The next morning, Emperor Homuta [Ōjin] summoned Greater Minister Takeuchi no Sukune and said, "What sort of sign is this?"

The greater minister replied, "It is a good sign. My wife as well was giving birth, and a wren entered the birthing chamber. This too is strange."

At this, the emperor said, "Now, then, Our son and the greater minister's son were born on the same day. Taken together, this is a sign, a portent from heaven. In consideration of the matter, let us take the names of these birds and exchange them to name our respective children, as a sign to future generations." Then, using the name of the wren he named the crown prince Imperial Prince Ōsazaki. Using the name of the horned owl, he named the greater minister's child Tsuku no Sukune. He was the first ancestor of the Omi of Heguri. This was the year of the Water Chicken.

Second year [314 CE], spring, third month, eighth day. Imperial Princess Iwa-no-hime was named empress.[xviii] She gave birth to Emperor Ōe-no-iza-ho-wake [Richū], Imperial Prince Nakatsu of Suminoe, Emperor Mitsu-ha-wake [Hanzei],[xix] and Emperor O-asazuma-wakugo-no-sukune [Ingyō].[xx]

His consort, Kami-naga-hime of Himuka, gave birth to Imperial Prince Ō-kusaka and Imperial Princess Hatabi.[xxi]

---

13 Imperial Princess Yata first appears in Ōjin 2. She is named empress in Nintoku 38 after the death of the previous empress, with whom Nintoku fought when he tried to name Yata as consort in Nintoku 22.
14 Ōjin died in 310. The year 313 corresponds with the three years that the throne was empty because of Ōsazaki and Uji-no-waki-iratsuko deferring to each other.
15 Naka-tsu-hime, empress of Ōjin.

四年春二月己未朔甲子、詔群臣曰、朕登高臺、以遠望之、烟氣不起於域中。以爲、百姓既貧、而家無炊者。朕聞、古聖王之世、人々誦詠德之音、每家有康哉之歌。今朕臨億兆、於茲三年。頌音不聆。炊烟轉疎。即知、五穀不登、百姓窮乏也。封畿之內、尚有不給者。況乎畿外諸國耶。

　　三月己丑朔己酉、詔曰、自今以後、至于三年、悉除課役、以息百姓之苦。是日始之、黼衣絓履、不弊盡不更爲也。溫飯煖羹、不酸餧不易也。削心約志、以從事乎無爲。是以、

NINTOKU 4 [316 CE]

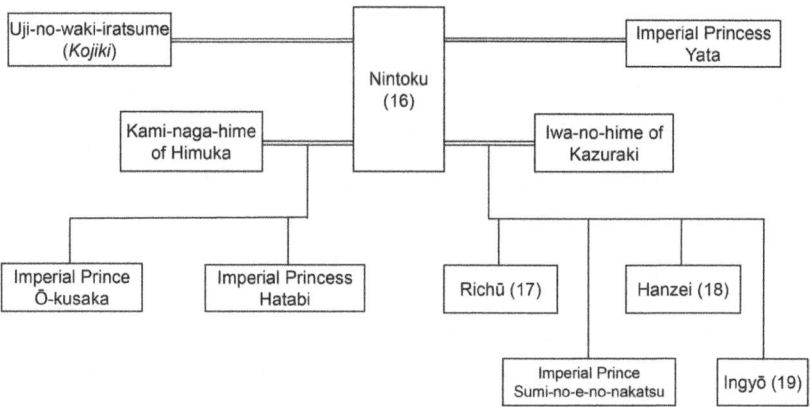

FIGURE 10 Children of Nintoku

Fourth year [316 CE], spring, second month, sixth day. The emperor decreed to the high government officials, "We climbed a high terrace and gazed into the distance, and no smoke rose from within the land.[xxii] In view of this, it seems that the people are so poor that they are not cooking in their houses. We hear that in days of old, in the age of sage-kings, the people raised their voices with hymns of virtue, and every household sang of peace.[xxiii] Now We have looked upon the multitudes for three years, but hear no such voices singing. The smoke of cooking fires is becoming more and more scarce. Hence, I know that the five grains are not growing, and the people are impoverished. Even the regions near the capital still lack adequate provisions; this circumstance is surely more severe in the distant provinces."

Third month, twenty-first day. The emperor decreed, "From now on, until three years have passed, corvée labor[16] shall be completely suspended in order to relieve the hardships of the people." From this day, the emperor's clothing and shoes were not replaced until they were tattered and thoroughly used up, and his rice and soup was not cooked anew until they became spoiled and sour. He suppressed his desires and restrained his intentions, letting matters run their course without intervening.[xxiv] Because of this

---

16 The word used here also refers to taxation, but the gloss emphasizes corvée. The system for assessing taxation and corvée labor was specified in the Civil and Penal Codes (Ritsuryō 律令), adopted in Japan in the late seventh century.

宮垣崩而不造、茅茨壞以不葺。風雨入隙、而沾衣被。星辰漏壞、而露床蓐。是後、風雨順時、五穀豐穰。三稔之間、百姓富寬。頌德既滿、炊烟亦繁。

七年夏四月辛未朔、天皇居臺上而遠望之、烟氣多起。是日、語皇后曰、朕既富矣。更無愁焉。

皇后對諮、何謂富矣。

天皇曰、烟氣滿國。百姓自富歟。

皇后且言、宮垣壞而不得脩。殿屋破之衣被露。何謂富乎。

天皇曰、其天之立君、是爲百姓。然則君以百姓爲本。是以、古聖王者、一人飢寒、顧之責身。今百姓貧之、則朕貧也。百姓富之、則朕富也。未之有百姓富之君貧矣。

秋八月己巳朔丁丑、爲大兄去來穗別皇子、定壬生部。亦爲皇后、定葛城部。

九月、諸國悉請之曰、課役並免、既經三年。因此、以宮殿朽壞、府庫已空。今黔首富饒、而不拾遺。是以、里無鰥寡、

policy, though the palace outer wall crumbled, it was not repaired, and though the thatch reeds of the roof came apart, they were not mended. The wind and the rain came in through the cracks and soaked his clothing and bedding. Starlight leaked in and bathed his bed and sleeping mat. Afterward, the wind and rain followed their season, and the five grains grew in abundance. During these three years, the people enjoyed bumper crops, songs of virtue filled the land, and the smoke of cooking fires was thick.

Seventh year [319 CE], summer, fourth month, first day. The emperor was atop his terrace gazing into the distance, where much smoke was rising. That day, he told the empress, "We are prosperous. Can there be anything further to worry about?"

Then the empress replied, conferring with him, "How can you say that you are prosperous?"

The emperor said, "The land is full of smoke. The people have become prosperous as a matter of course."

Then the empress told him, "The palace wall has crumbled and cannot be repaired. The palace is in ruins, and your clothing and bedding is wet with dew. How can you say that you are prosperous?"

The emperor said, "Indeed, Heaven institutes the position of ruler, for the people.[xxv] Accordingly, the ruler takes the people as the foundation. For this reason, the sage-kings of old reflected on such matters and blamed themselves if even one single person was hungry or cold. Now, if the people are poor, then We are poor. If the people are prosperous, then We are prosperous. There has never yet been a case where the people were prosperous and the ruler poor."

Autumn, eighth month, ninth day. The emperor established the Mibu hereditary guild[17] for Imperial Prince Ōeno-izaho-wake. He also established the Kazuraki hereditary guild[18] for the empress.

Ninth month. The various provinces all entreated the emperor, saying, "Since we became exempted from corvée labor, three years have passed. Because of this, the imperial palace has decayed, and the treasury is empty. Now the people are well off and prosperous, and do not even bother to collect dropped objects.[xxvi] In the villages there are no widows or wid-

---

17 Perhaps the same as the Wakasakura hereditary guild seen in Richū 3. The pre-accession record of Richū claims that he was born in Nintoku 17. A note in Richū 6 giving Richū's age when he died would make Nintoku 24. However, neither year accords with this entry.
18 The name perhaps derives from the father of the empress, Sotsuhiko of Kazuraki. A longer entry establishing more groups is given in *Ancient Matters*.

家有餘儲。若當此時、非貢税調、以脩理宮室者、懼之、其獲罪于天乎。然猶忍之不聽矣。

十年冬十月、甫科課役、以構造宮室。於是、百姓之不領、而扶老携幼、運材負簣。不問日夜、竭力競作。是以、未經幾時、而宮室悉成。故於今稱聖帝也。

十一年夏四月戊寅朔甲午、詔群臣曰、今朕視是國者、郊澤曠遠、而田圃少乏。且河水橫逝、以流末不駛。聊逢霖雨、海潮逆上、而巷里乘船、道路亦泥。故群臣共視之、決橫源而通海、塞逆流以全田宅。

冬十月、掘宮北之郊原、引南水以入西海。因以號其水曰堀江。又將防北河之澇、以築茨田堤。是時、有兩處之築而乃壞之難塞。時天皇夢、有神誨之曰、武藏人強頸・河內人茨田連衫子衫子、此云莒呂母能古。二人、以祭於河伯、必獲塞。則覓二人而得之。因以、禱于河神。

爰強頸泣悲之、没水而死。乃其堤成焉。唯衫子取全匏兩箇、臨于難塞水。乃取兩箇匏、投於水中、請之曰、河神崇之、以吾爲幣。是以、今吾來也。必欲得我者、沈是匏而不令泛。則吾知眞神、親入水中。若不得沈匏者、自知僞神。何徒亡吾身。

於是、飄風忽起、引匏没水。匏轉浪上而不沈。則渝々汎以遠流。

owers, and households have savings in reserve. If at this time we do not present our taxes and labor, or do not repair the palace, we fear, indeed, the punishment of heaven." However, the emperor continued to weather his hardships and would not permit them to do these things.

Tenth year [322 CE], winter, tenth month. Corvée labor was at that time reinstated, and the palace rebuilt. The people acted without orders, helping the elderly, taking children by the hand, transporting materials and baskets on their backs. With no concern for day or night, they exhausted themselves, contending with each other to build. Thereby, in little time the palace was completely finished. Even up to the present, Nintoku is still praised as a sage-emperor.

Eleventh year [323 CE], summer, fourth month, seventeenth day. The emperor decreed to the high government officials, "Now when We look upon this land, We see that the plains and marshlands are vast, but the paddies and fields are few. Also, river water spreads out over the land and the current is not swift. When we meet with a long spell of rain, seawater flows back upstream, and the hamlets and villages take to boats, while roads become covered in mud. Therefore, high government officials, look upon this together, dig channels for the spreading seawater to pass through, prevent it from flowing upstream, and safeguard the paddies and residences."

Winter, tenth month. The plains north of the palace were dug out, and the river from the south was redirected so that it emptied into the sea to the west. Hence, this river was named Horie, "dug river."[xxvii] Also, to prevent flooding of the northern river, the people built Mamuta Dyke.[xxviii] At that time, two places were difficult to block up, as the construction there immediately broke down. Then the emperor had a dream in which a kami instructed him, saying, "If Kowakubi of Musashi and Koromonoko of Kōchi, Muraji of Mamuta[xxix] venerate the kami of the river, then it certainly can be blocked off."[xxx] The emperor then searched for the two men and found them. Thereupon, they were ritually offered to the river kami.

At that point, Kowakubi cried in sadness, entered the river, and died. Immediately, the dyke there was finished. However, Koromonoko took two whole bottle gourds and faced the river at the place where it was difficult to block up. He quickly took both gourds, threw them into the river, and made an oath, saying, "Kami of the river, by your curse I am to become an offering.[xxxi] Now I have come. If you must have me, sink these two flasks and do not let them float. Then I will know that you are a true kami and shall myself enter into the river. If you cannot sink the two gourds, I will know that you are in fact a false kami. Why should I lose my life in vain?"

Then a whirlwind suddenly rose up and pulled the gourds down into the river. But the gourds were tossed about atop the waves and did not sink. Dancing on the rush of the swift current, they were carried far away.

是以、衫子雖不死、而其堤且成也。是因衫子之幹、其身非亡耳。故時人號其兩處、曰強頸斷間・衫子斷間也。

是歲、新羅人朝貢、則勞於是役。

十二年秋七月辛未朔癸酉、高麗國貢鐵盾・鐵的。

八月庚子朔己酉、饗高麗客於朝。是日、集群臣及百寮、令射高麗所獻之鐵盾的。諸人不得射通的。唯的臣祖盾人宿禰、射鐵的而通焉。時高麗客等見之、畏其射之勝工、共起以拜朝。

明日、美盾人宿禰、而賜名曰的戸田宿禰。同日、小泊瀬造祖宿禰臣、賜名曰賢遺臣。賢遺、此云左舸能莒里。

冬十月、掘大溝於山背栗隈縣以潤田。是以、其百姓毎年豐之。

十三年秋九月、始立茨田屯倉。因定春米部。

冬十月、造和珥池。是月、築橫野堤。

十四年冬十一月、爲橋於猪甘津。即號其處曰小橋也。

是歲、作大道置於京中。自南門直指之、至丹比邑。又掘大溝

---

19 A similar entry is given in Ōjin 7.
20 Abbreviated to Toda no Sukune later in Nintoku 17. Ikuha-no-toda appears earlier in Ōjin 16. Norinaga suggests that the name change was mistakenly recorded in reverse, with Tatahito ("Shield man") being the name given after he pierced the iron shields with an arrow.

By means of this stratagem, Koromonoko did not die, but the dyke was still completed, and owing to Koromonoko's ingenuity, his life was spared. Accordingly, people at the time named these two places Kowakunibi Gap and Koromonoko Gap.[xxxii]

That year, the people of Silla presented tribute and served in this corvée labor.[19]

Twelfth year [324 CE], autumn, seventh month, third day. The land of Koguryŏ presented iron shields and iron targets.

Eighth month, tenth day. The emperor held a banquet for the guests from Koguryŏ at court. On that day, the high government officials and public servants gathered and shot arrows at the metal shields and targets presented by Koguryŏ. Of all those who shot, none could pierce the targets except the ancestor of the Omi of Ikuha, Tatahito no Sukune, who shot through the iron target.[xxxiii] The guests from Koguryŏ saw this, were amazed at his superior bowmanship, and rose and bowed to the emperor.

The next day, the emperor praised Tatahito no Sukune and bestowed upon him a new name, Ikuha-no-toda no Sukune.[20] On the same day, the emperor bestowed upon the ancestor of the chieftains of Ohatsuse, Sukune no Omi, a new name, Omi of Sakanokori.[21]

Winter, tenth month. A great ditch was dug in Kurukuma District of Yamashiro to irrigate the rice paddies.[xxxiv] Thereby, people there always had a bountiful harvest.

Thirteenth year [325 CE], autumn, ninth month. The emperor first created the imperial estate of Mamuta. And for that estate he established the Tsukishine hereditary guild.[22]

Winter, tenth month. Wani Reservoir was created.[23] The same month, Yokono Dyke was constructed.[xxxv]

Fourteenth year [326 CE], winter, eleventh month. A bridge was built at Ikai Harbor.[xxxvi] Accordingly, this place was named Obashi, or Small Bridge.[xxxvii]

That year, a great road was made in the capital.[xxxviii] It went straight south from the palace gate to Tajihi Village.[xxxix] Also, a great ditch was

---

21 Ohatsuse is a name for Emperor Buretsu. What Sukune no Omi did to earn this honor is unclear.
22 Tsukishine means "rice polishing." This was presumably the occupation of this group. The Muraji of Tsukishine, who directed this group, was promoted to sukune in Tenmu 13.
23 Wani Reservoir was also created in Suiko 21.11, though that reservoir appears to have been in Yamato Province, and this one was in Yamashiro Province.

於感玖。乃引石河水、而潤上鈴鹿・下鈴鹿・上豐浦・下豐浦四處郊原、以墾之得四萬餘頃之田。故其處百姓、寬饒之無凶年之患。

　　十六年秋七月戊寅朔、天皇以宮人桑田玖賀媛、示近習舍人等曰、朕欲愛是婦女、苦皇后之妬、不能合、以經多年。何徒妨其盛年乎。仍以歌問之曰、

瀰儺曾虛赴	みなそこふ
於瀰能烏苔咩烏	おみのをとめを
多例揶始儺播務	たれやしなはむ

　　於是、播磨國造祖速待、獨進之歌曰、

瀰箇始報	みかしほ
破利摩波揶摩智	はりまはやまち
以播區娜輸	いはくだす
伽之古俱等望	かしこくとも
阿例揶始儺破務	あれやしなはむ

　　即日、以玖賀媛賜速待。
　　明日之夕、速待詣于玖賀媛之家。而玖賀媛不和。乃強近帳內。時玖賀媛曰、妾之寡婦以終年。何能爲君之妻乎。
　　於是、天皇欲遂速待之志、以玖賀媛、副速待、送遣

dug in Komuku.^xl Immediately drawing the water from the Ishi River, the four plains of Kami-tsu-suzuka, Shimo-tsu-suzuka, Kami-tsu-toyura, and Shimo-tsu-toyura were irrigated, and forty thousand square rods[24] of rice paddies reclaimed.^xli Consequently, the people there were well off and prosperous, and had no fear of poor harvest years.

Marital Troubles

Sixteenth year [328 CE], autumn, seventh month, first day. The emperor showed the maidservant Kuga-hime[25] of Kuwata to his nearby servants and said, "We wish to favor this woman, but being troubled by the jealousy of the empress, cannot join with her, and so many years have passed.^xlii How can we prevent her best years from coming to naught?" Then he asked them, singing,

> This maiden, my vassal,
> deep in the waters,†
> who will look after her?^xliii

At this point, the ancestor of the Provincial Miyatsuko of Harima, Hayamachi, alone came forth and sang,^xliv

> Hayamachi of Harima,
> where the tide is fierce†
> with fear and reverence
> that could crush boulders,†
> I shall look after her.

That day, the emperor bestowed Kuga-hime upon Hayamachi.

The next evening, Hayamachi went to Kuga-hime's house. However, Kuga-hime was not disposed toward him, and so he came near her bedchamber by force. Thereupon Kuga-hime said, "I am a widow, and my years have passed. How could I become my lord's wife?"

At this point, the emperor, wishing to see Hayamachi's intentions through, made Kuga-hime accompany Hayamachi and sent them both to

---

24 A unit of measure (Jp. shiro) used in China to refer to the size of a field that would yield one bushel of rice. Because yields depend on many factors, the precise amount of land can vary.

25 Maidservant is a technical term referring specifically to women who worked in the inner palace. This episode is not in *Ancient Matters*.

於桑田。則玖賀媛、發病死于道中。故於今有玖賀媛之墓也。

十七年、新羅不朝貢。

秋九月、遣的臣祖砥田宿禰・小泊瀬造祖賢遺臣而問闕貢之事。於是、新羅人懼之乃貢獻。調絹一千四百六十匹、及種々雜物、幷八十艘。

廿二年春正月、天皇語皇后曰、納八田皇女將爲妃。時皇后不聽。爰天皇歌、以乞於皇后曰、

于磨臂苔能	うまひとの
多菟屢虛等太氏	たつることだて
于磋由豆流	うさゆづる
多由磨菟餓務珥	たゆまつがむに
奈羅陪氏毛餓望	ならべてもがも

　皇后答歌曰、

虛呂望虛曾	ころもこそ
赴多弊茂豫者	ふたへもよき
瑳用廼虛烏	さよどこを
那羅陪務者瀰破	ならべむきみは
箇辭古耆呂介茂	かしこきろかも

　天皇又歌曰、

於辭氏屢	おしてる
那珥破能瑳耆能	なにはのさきの
那羅弭破莽	ならびはま
那羅陪務苔虛層	ならべむとこそ
曾能古破阿利鷄梅	そのこはありけめ

Kuwata. Suddenly, Kuga-hime fell ill and died en route. Consequently, Kuga-hime's grave is still along the route even now.

Seventeenth year [329 CE]. Silla did not send tribute.

Autumn, ninth month. The emperor dispatched the ancestor of the Omi of Ikuha, Toda no Sukune, and the ancestor of the Miyatsuko of Ohatsuse, Sakanori no Omi, to inquire into the matter of the missing tribute. Thereupon the people of Silla were afraid and immediately presented it. It consisted of 1,460 bolts of silk and various rare items, all together eighty ships' worth.

Twenty-second year [334 CE], spring, first month. The emperor told the empress, "I have taken Imperial Princess Yata into the inner palace and am about to name her consort." The empress would not hear of it. At this, the emperor beseeched the empress, singing,

> Those of good breeding
> clearly signal their resolutions.
> Spare bowstrings
> are strung when a string breaks.
> So I wish to line her up.[26]

The empress sang in reply:

> It is well enough to double
> one's robes,
> but how terrible
> is the lord with a lineup
> for his bed.

The emperor again sang:

> Like adjacent beaches
> at Cape Naniwa,
> warmed by the sun,†
> it is her understanding,
> that she would be thus lined up.

---

26 Nintoku implies that he intends to see Yata only when the empress is unavailable.

皇后答歌曰、

那菟務始能　　　　　なつむしの
譬務始能虛呂望　　　ひむしのころも
赴多弊耆氐　　　　　ふたへきて
箇區瀰夜儺利破　　　かくみやだりは
阿珥豫區望阿羅儒　　あによくもあらず

天皇又歌曰、

阿佐豆磨能　　　　　あさづまの
避介能烏瑳介烏　　　ひかのをさかを
介多那耆珥　　　　　かたなきに
瀰致喩區茂能茂　　　みちゆくものも
多遇譬氐序豫枳　　　たぐひてぞよき

　皇后、遂謂不聽、故默之亦不答言。
　卅年秋九月乙卯朔乙丑、皇后遊行紀國、到熊野岬、即取其處之御綱葉葉、此云箇始婆。而還。於是、天皇伺皇后不在、而娶八田皇女、納於宮中。時皇后到難波濟、聞天皇合八田皇女、而大恨之。則其所採御綱葉投於海、而不著岸。故時人號散葉之海、曰葉濟也。爰天皇不知皇后忿不著岸。親幸大津、待皇后之船。而歌曰、

那珥波譬苔　　　　　なにはひと
須儒赴泥苔羅齊　　　すずふねとらせ
許辭那豆瀰　　　　　こしなづみ
曾能赴尼苔羅齊　　　そのふねとらせ
於朋瀰赴泥苔禮　　　おほみふねとれ

The empress sang in reply:

> It is not good
> for a summer silkworm
> to make a double-layered
> cocoon
> and tuck her away within.

The emperor again sang:

> It would be better to accompany
> those who walk,[27]
> crying in heartbreak,
> through the small hills of Hika
> in Asazuma.[xlv]

The empress, ultimately unwilling to hear of this, was silent and did not reply.

Thirtieth year [342 CE], autumn, ninth month, eleventh day. The empress journeyed to Ki Province, arrived at Cape Kumano, took leaves of a tri-leaf oak[28] from there, and started back.[xlvi] The emperor, who had been waiting for the empress's absence, summoned Imperial Princess Yata and installed her inside the palace. By the time the empress had reached Naniwa Harbor, she heard that the emperor had coupled with Imperial Princess Yata and greatly resented him.[xlvii] She threw the leaves of the tri-leaf oak that she had harvested into the sea and did not come ashore. Accordingly, people at the time named the place where the leaves had been scattered Kashiwa no Watari, or Oak Crossing. The emperor did not know that the empress was angry and had not returned to shore, and he went himself to Ōtsu to wait for the empress's boat. Then he sang,

> Boat people of Naniwa,
> bring in the bell-adorned boat.[29]
> Wade in to your waist
> and bring in that boat,
> the great august boat.

---

27 It is unclear whether "those" refers to Yata or Iwa-no-hime.
28 *Dendropanax trifidus*, which has a leaf with three distinct peaks, used for presenting offerings to kami.
29 The command ship.

時皇后、不泊于大津、更引之沶江、自山背廻而向倭。明日、天皇遣舍人鳥山、令還皇后。乃歌之曰、

夜莾之呂珥	やましろに
伊辭鷄苔利夜莾	いしけとりやま
伊辭鷄之鷄	いしけしけ
阿餓茂赴菟摩珥	あがもふつまに
伊辭枳阿波牟伽茂	いしきあはむかも

皇后、不還猶行之。至山背河而歌曰、

菟藝泥赴	つぎねふ
揶莾之呂餓波烏	やましろがはを
箇破能朋利	かはのぼり
涴餓能朋例麼	わがのぼれば
箇波區莾珥	かはくまに
多知瑳介踰屢	たちさかゆる
毛々多羅儒	ももたらず
揶素麼能紀破	やそばのきは
於朋耆瀰呂介茂	おほきみろかも

即越那羅山、望葛城歌之曰、

菟藝泥赴	つぎねふ
揶莾之呂餓波烏	やましろがはを
瀰揶能朋利	みやのぼり
和餓能朋例麼	わがのぼれば
阿烏珥豫辭	あをによし
儺羅烏輸疑	ならをすぎ
烏陀氏	をだて
夜莾苔烏輸疑	やまとをすぎ
和餓瀰餓朋辭區珥	わがみがほしくには
箇豆羅紀多伽瀰揶	かづらきたかみや
和藝弊能阿多利	わぎへのあたり

更還山背、興宮室於筒城岡南而居之。

The empress did not berth at Ōtsu, but rather had the boat pulled upstream, went around Yamashiro, and then made for Yamato. The next day, the emperor dispatched his servant Toriyama to make the empress come back.^{xlviii} Then he sang,

> To Yamashiro
> pursue her, Toriyama!
> Pursue, pursue!
> Pursue, for I wish to meet
> the wife for whom I long.

The empress did not return, and instead went on ahead. She arrived at the Yamashiro River and sang,^{xlix}

> I travel up
> the Yamashiro River
> with its increasing peaks,†
> and as I travel up,
> the lushly leaved trees,
> not reaching one hundred,†
> stand grandly blooming
> in the recesses of the river,
> like my great lord.

Then she crossed Mt. Nara, gazed upon Kazuraki, and sang,

> Traveling up past the palace
> on the Yamashiro River,
> the mountain peaks get taller†
> as I travel up.
> I pass Mt. Nara,
> of quality malachite,†
> I pass Yamato,
> of small shields.†
> The land I wish to see
> is Takamiya in Kazuraki,
> near my home.

Then she returned to Yamashiro, had a palace built south of Tsutsuki Hill, and dwelt there.^l

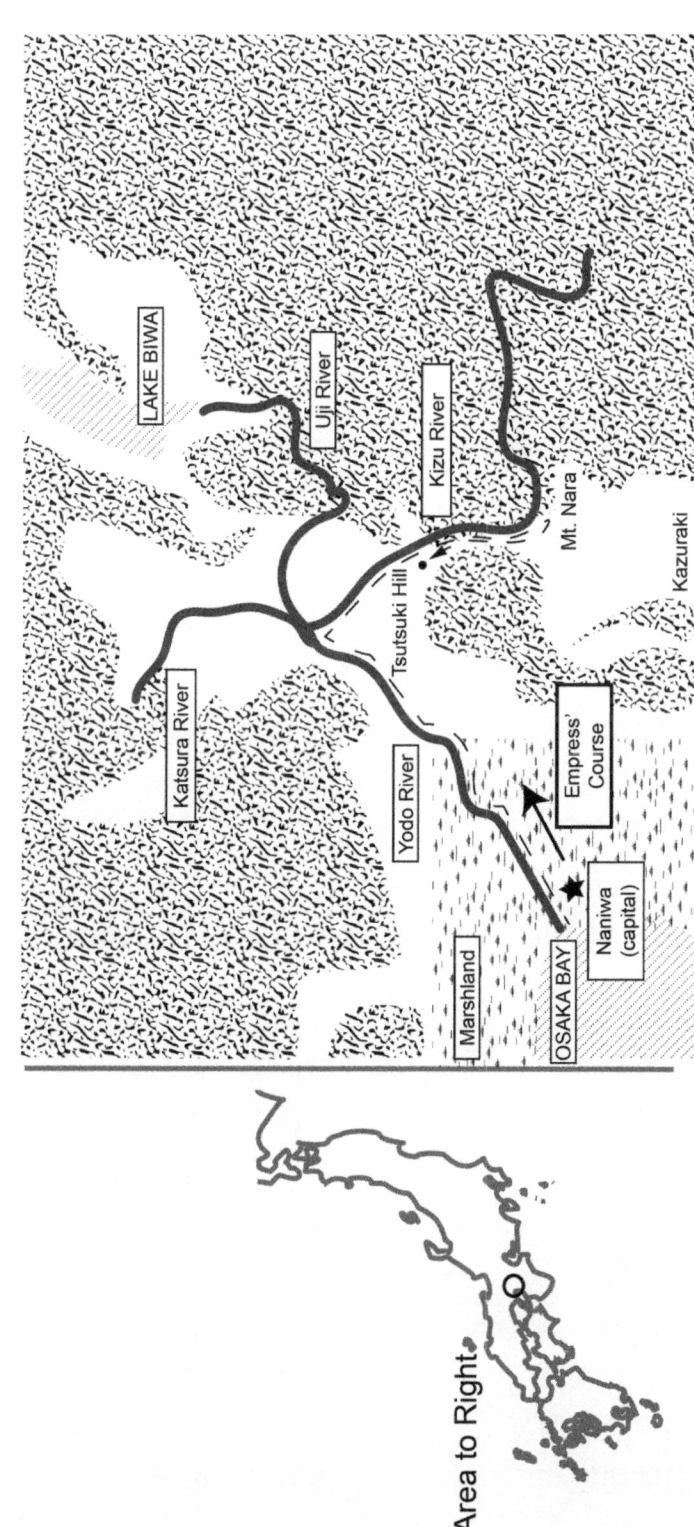

MAP 18 Course of Empress Iwa-no-hime

冬十月甲申朔、遣的臣祖口持臣喚皇后。一云、和珥臣祖口子臣。爰口持臣、至筒城宮、雖謁皇后、而默之不答。時口持臣、沾雪雨、以經日夜、伏于皇后殿前而不避。

於是、口持臣之妹國依媛、仕于皇后。適是時、侍皇后之側。見其兄沾雨、而流涕之歌曰、

揶莽辭呂能	やましろの
菟々紀能瀰揶珥	つつきのみやに
茂能莽烏輸	ものまをす
和餓齊烏瀰例麼	わがせをみれば
那瀰多遇摩辭茂	なみたぐましも

時皇后謂國依媛曰、何爾泣之。

對言、今伏庭請謁者、妾兄也。沾雨不避。猶伏將謁。是以、泣悲耳。

時皇后謂之曰、告汝兄令速還。吾遂不返焉。口持則返之、復奏于天皇。

十一月甲寅朔庚申、天皇浮江幸山背。時桑枝沿水而流之。天皇視桑枝歌之曰、

菟怒瑳破赴	つのさはふ
以破能臂謎餓	いはのひめが
飫朋呂伽珥	おほろかに
枳許瑳怒	きこさぬ
于羅遇破能紀	うらぐはのき
豫屢麻志枳	よるましじき
箇破能區莽愚莽	かはのくまぐま
豫呂朋譽喩玖伽茂	よろほひゆくかも
于羅愚破能紀	うらぐはのき

NINTOKU 30 [342 CE]

Winter, tenth month, first day. The emperor dispatched the ancestor of the Omi of Ikuha, Kuchimochi no Omi, to summon the empress.[li]

By one account, it was the ancestor of the Omi of Wani, Kuchiko no Omi.

Kuchimochi no Omi arrived at Tsutsuki Palace, but even though he sought an audience with the empress, she was silent and did not reply. In time, Kuchimochi no Omi, though soaked by the rain, spent many days and nights prostrate before the empress's hall and would not leave.

At that time, Kuchimochi no Omi's younger sister, Kuniyori-hime, was in the service of the empress.[lii] One time, while attending on the empress, she saw her brother soaked by the rain. In tears, she sang,

> When I see my older brother,
> seeking an audience
> at Tsutsuki Palace
> in Yamashiro,
> I shed tears.

Then the empress said to Kuniyori-hime, "Why do you cry?"

She replied, "The one now prostrate in the courtyard seeking an audience is my older brother. Though soaked by the rain, he has not withdrawn and still lies prostrate seeking an audience. For this reason I cry in sadness."

At that time the empress said to her, "Tell your older brother to quickly return from whence he came. I will not go back." Kuchimochi then returned and reported to the emperor.

Eleventh month, seventh day. The emperor went by riverboat to Yamashiro. There was a branch of a mulberry tree drifting along with the current. The emperor saw the branch and sang,

> Iwa-no-hime
> of many vines†
> has gone lukewarm
> and will not hear me,
> my splendid mulberry branch.
> Not drawing near to any place,
> you are carried by
> the nooks and crannies of the river,
> my splendid mulberry branch!

明日、乘輿詣于筒城宮、喚皇后。皇后不肯參見。時天皇歌曰、

　　菟藝埿赴　　　　　　つぎねふ
　　揶摩之呂謎能　　　　やましろめの
　　許久波茂知　　　　　こくはもち
　　于智辭於朋埿　　　　うちしおほね
　　佐和佐和珥　　　　　さわさわに
　　儺餓伊弊齊虛曾　　　ながいへせこそ
　　于知和多須　　　　　うちわたす
　　椰餓波曳儺須　　　　やがはえなす
　　企以利摩韋區例　　　きいりまるくれ

　亦歌曰、

　　菟藝埿赴　　　　　　つぎねふ
　　夜莽之呂謎能　　　　やましろめの
　　許玖波茂知　　　　　こくはもち
　　于智辭於朋埿　　　　うちしおほね
　　埿士漏能　　　　　　ねじろの
　　辭漏多娜武枳　　　　しろただむき
　　摩箇儒鷄麼虛曾　　　まかずけばこそ
　　辭羅儒等茂伊波梅　　しらずともいはめ

　時皇后令奏言、陛下納八田皇女爲妃。其不欲副皇女而爲后、遂不奉見。乃車駕還宮。天皇於是、恨皇后大忿。而猶有戀思。

　卅一年春正月癸丑朔丁卯、立大兄去來穗別尊、爲皇太子。

　卅五年夏六月、皇后磐之媛命、薨於筒城宮。

　卅七年冬十一月甲戌朔乙酉、葬皇后於乃羅山。

　卅八年春正月癸酉朔戊寅、立八田皇女爲皇后。

The next day, he took his carriage to Tsutsuki Palace and summoned the empress. The empress, however, did not come to see him. At the time, the emperor sang,

> Like the rustling
> of the daikon,
> dug by the woman of Yamashiro,
> with its increasing peaks,†
> holding wooden spades—
> such is your caviling!
> So I have come with great numbers,
> like the lushly growing mulberry
> that I spy over there.

And he sang again:

> Like the pure white
> of the daikon,
> dug by the woman of Yamashiro,
> with its increasing peaks†
> holding a wooden spade—
> such are your white arms!
> Had they not been wrapped around me,
> could I not say that I did not know you?

At that time the empress addressed the emperor, saying, "My liege has taken in Imperial Princess Yata and made her consort. I do not wish to be empress alongside this Imperial Princess." In the end, she would not see him. And so the emperor's carriage returned to the palace. The emperor resented the empress' great anger. However, he still had feelings of longing for her.

Thirty-first year [343 CE], spring, first month, fifteenth day. Ōeno-izaho-wake was named crown prince.

Thirty-fifth year [347 CE], summer, sixth month. Empress Iwa-no-hime perished at Tsutsuki Palace.

Thirty-seventh year [349 CE], winter, eleventh month, twelfth day. The empress was buried at Mt. Nara.[liii]

Empress Yata and Princess Metori

Thirty-eighth year [350 CE], spring, first month, sixth day. Imperial Princess Yata was named empress.

秋七月、天皇與皇后、居高臺而避暑。時每夜、自菟餓野、有聞鹿鳴。其聲寥亮而悲之。共起可怜之情。及月盡、以鹿鳴不聆、爰天皇語皇后曰、當是夕、而鹿不鳴。其何由焉。

明日、猪名縣佐伯部獻苞苴。天皇令膳夫以問曰、其苞苴何物也。

對言牡鹿也。

問之何處鹿也。

曰、菟餓野。

時天皇以爲、是苞苴者、必其鳴鹿也。因語皇后曰、朕比有懷抱、聞鹿聲而慰之。今推佐伯部獲鹿之日夜及山野、即當鳴鹿。其人雖不知朕之愛、以適逢獮獲、猶不得已而有恨。故、佐伯部不欲近於皇居。乃令有司、移鄉于安藝渟田。此今渟田佐伯部之祖也。

俗曰、昔有一人、往菟餓、宿于野中。時二鹿臥傍。將及鷄鳴、牝鹿謂牡鹿曰、吾今夜夢之、白霜多降之覆吾身。是何祥焉。

牝鹿答曰、汝之出行、必爲人見射而死。即以白鹽塗其身、如霜素之應也。時宿人心裏異之。未及昧爽、有獵人、以射牡鹿而殺。是以、時人諺曰、鳴牡鹿矣、隨相夢也。

卅年春二月、納雌鳥皇女欲爲妃、以隼別皇子爲媒。時隼別皇子密親娶、而久之不復命。於是、天皇不知有夫、而親臨雌鳥皇女之殿。時爲皇女織縑女人等歌之曰、

Autumn, seventh month. The emperor and the empress were atop a high terrace to escape the heat. At that time, every night they heard the cries of the deer from Togano.^liv Their calls were sonorous and saddening. Both of them were roused to feelings of deep compassion. At the end of the month, the cries of the deer could no longer be heard. Then the emperor said to the empress, "Tonight there are no deer cries. Why is this?"

The next day, Saekibe[30] of Ina District presented the emperor with an offering.^lv The emperor asked his cook, "What have you presented here?"

He replied, "It's deer."

Then he asked, "Deer from where?"

He replied, "From Togano."

The emperor thought this offering was no doubt the deer that had been crying, and so he told the empress, "Our worries these days had been soothed by hearing the calls of the deer. Judging from the time and the mountain where Saekibe hunted, I suspect he shot the deer that cried. Even though this man did not know that I liked this deer and hunted it by chance, I still cannot help but resent him. So I do not want Saekibe near the palace." Then he ordered an administrator to relocate him to Nuta in Agi.^lvi He is now the ancestor of the Saekibe of Nuta.

The common people say, "A long time ago, there was one man who went to Toga and stayed in a field. At that time, two deer lay down at his side. When the cock cried, the buck told the doe, 'I had a dream last night that a thick white frost fell, covering my body. What does it mean?' Then the doe answered, 'It is a portent that when you go out, you shall be shot by a human and die. Then your body will be painted white with salt, like the white of the frost.' The man in the field felt something strange in the back of his mind. At dawn, a hunter shot the buck and killed it. Based on this story, people at the time created a proverb that went, 'Though it was not a deer that cried, it was just like the dream.'"^lvii

Fortieth year [352 CE], spring, second month. The emperor wanted to install Imperial Princess Metori as his consort and used Imperial Prince Hayabusa-wake as the intermediary.[31] Imperial Prince Hayabusa-wake secretly married her himself and did not report back for a long time. Then the emperor, not knowing that she had a husband, personally visited her sleeping chambers. At that time, the weaver women for the imperial princess sang,

---

30 The Saeki hereditary guild (Saekibe) was established at various locations, was often comprised of Emishi, and performed military and security duties.
31 Metori is Yata's younger sister. Hayabusa-wake is Nintoku's half-brother.

比佐箇多能	ひさかたの
阿梅箇儺麼多	あめかなばた
謎廼利餓	めどりが
於瑠箇儺麼多	おるかなばた
波揶步佐和氣能	はやぶさわけの
瀰於須譬鵝泥	みおすひがね

爰天皇知隼別皇子密婚、而恨之。然重皇后之言、亦敦友于之義、而忍之勿罪。俄而隼別皇子、枕皇女之膝以臥。乃語之曰、孰捷鷦鷯與隼焉。

曰、隼捷也。

乃皇子曰、是我所先也。

天皇聞是言、更亦起恨。時隼別皇子之舍人等歌曰、

破夜步佐波	はやぶさは
阿梅珥能朋利	あめにのぼり
等弭箇慨梨	とびかけり
伊菟岐餓宇倍能	いつきがうへの
娑弉岐等羅佐泥	さざきとらさね

天皇聞是歌、而勃然大怒之曰、朕以私恨、不欲失親、忍之也。何豐矣私事將及于社稷、則欲殺隼別皇子。

時皇子率雌鳥皇女、欲納伊勢神宮而馳。於是、天皇聞隼別皇子逃走、即遣吉備品遲部雄鯽・播磨佐伯直阿俄能胡曰、追之所逮即殺。

The heavenly metal loom
of the hen weaves,
this metal loom,
the outer garments
of Lord Falcon.³²

Thereupon, the emperor knew Imperial Prince Hayabusa-wake had secretly married her, and he resented him. However, out of concern for what the empress might say, and out of respect for the principle of good family relations, he endured it and did not punish him.

A while later, Imperial Prince Hayabusa-wake was resting his head upon the Imperial Princess's lap. Then he said to her, "Which is faster, the wren or the falcon?"

"The falcon," she said.

Then the imperial prince said, "That is why I arrived first."

When the emperor heard of these words, his resentment was again aroused, this time even further. At that time, Imperial Prince Hayabusa-wake's servants sang,

The falcon
climbs to heaven
and soars.
Catch the wren
up in the grove!

The emperor heard this song and was even more enraged, and said, "We did not want to lose a family member because of a personal grudge and so endured it. By what shortcoming do my personal matters extend to the state?" Thus he planned to kill Imperial Prince Hayabusa-wake.

The imperial prince, leading Imperial Princess Metori, quickly fled, intending to enter the Ise Shrine.^lviii The emperor heard that Imperial Prince Hayabusa-wake had escaped and dispatched Ofuna of Homuchibe in Kibi and Aganoko, Atai of the Saeki of Harima, saying, "Pursue and overtake them, then kill them."³³

---

32 Hayabusa means falcon.
33 Homuchibe is perhaps the Homutsube established in Suinin 23. The Saeki of Harima also appear in Keikō 51.

爰皇后奏言、雌鳥皇女、寔當重罪。然其殺之日、不欲露皇女身。

乃因勅雄鯽等、莫取皇女所齎之足玉手玉。

雄鯽等、追之至菟田、迫於素珥山。時隱草中僅得免。急走而越山。於是、皇子歌曰、

破始多氏能	はしたての
佐餓始枳揶摩茂	さがしきやまも
和藝毛古等	わぎもこと
赴駄利古喩例麼	ふたこゆれば
揶須武志呂箇茂	やすむしろかも

爰雄鯽等知免、以急追及于伊勢蔣代野而殺之。時雄鯽等、探皇女之玉、自裳中得之。乃以二王屍、埋于廬杵河邊、而復命。

皇后令問雄鯽等曰、若見皇女之玉乎。

對言、不見也。

是歲、當新嘗之月、以宴會日、賜酒於內外命婦等。於是、近江山君稚守山妻與采女磐坂媛、二女之手、有纏良珠。

NINTOKU 40 [352 CE]

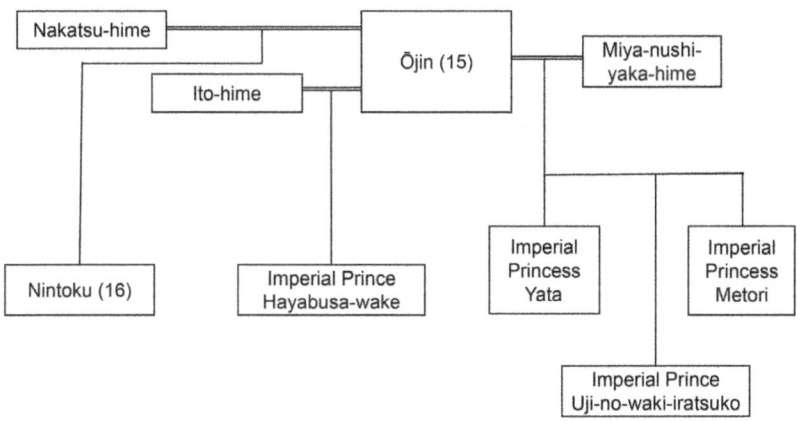

FIGURE 11 Nintoku, Metori, and Hayabusa-wake

Then the empress addressed the emperor, saying, "Imperial Princess Metori has truly committed a grave crime. However, on the day she is killed, I do not want her corpse to be exposed."

So he decreed to Ofuna and the others, "Do not take the imperial princess's hand and foot jewelry."

Ofuna and the others pursued them, arriving in Uda, and they approached Mt. Soni.[lix] At that time the two were hiding in the grass and just able to escape. They quickly fled and crossed the mountains. Then the imperial prince sang,

> They're like climbing a ladder,
> these steep mountains!
> Upon crossing them with my wife,
> we will be as comfortable as if sitting on a mat.

Ofuna and the others knew how they had escaped and quickly went to Komoshiro in Ise, where they caught up to them and killed them.[lx] Then Ofuna and the others searched for the imperial princess's jewels and took them from within her clothes. They buried the two royal corpses near the Ioki River and reported back to the emperor.[lxi]

The empress then asked Ofuna and the others, "Did you see the imperial princess's jewels?"

They replied, "We saw none."

That year, in the month of the feast of first rice, on the banquet day, wine was given to the princesses and high-ranking ladies. Then the wife of the Kimi of Ōmi no Yama, Wakamori-yama, and the inner palace lady Iwasaka-hime both had beautiful pearls wrapped around their hands.[lxii]

皇后見其珠、既似雌鳥皇女之珠、則疑之、命有司、推問其玉所得之由。對言、佐伯直阿俄能胡妻之玉也。

仍推鞫阿俄能胡。對曰、誅皇女之日、探而取之。即將殺阿俄能胡。於是阿俄能胡、乃獻己之私地、請贖死。故納其地赦死罪。是以、號其地曰玉代。

卌一年春三月、遣紀角宿禰於百濟、始分國郡壃場、具錄鄉土所出。是時、百濟王之族酒君无禮。由是、紀角宿禰訶責百濟王。時百濟王悚之、以鐵鎖縛酒君、附襲津彥而進上。爰酒君來之、則逃匿于石川錦織首許呂斯之家。則欺之曰、天皇既赦臣罪。故寄汝而活焉。久之天皇遂赦其罪。

卌三年秋九月庚子朔、依網屯倉阿弭古、捕異鳥、獻於天皇曰、臣每張網捕鳥、未曾得是鳥之類。故奇而獻之。

天皇召酒君、示鳥曰、是何鳥矣。

The empress saw the pearls and thought that they were identical to the jewels of Imperial Princess Metori, and so had suspicions. She ordered an administrator to investigate where they got the jewels. They replied, "These jewels belong to the wife of the Atai of Saeki, Aganoko."

Thus, Aganoko was accused, and he replied, "On the day we killed the imperial princess, I found them and took them." When the emperor was about to have Aganoko killed, Aganoko presented his private land and asked that he not be killed. The emperor, claiming this land, then commutated his death sentence. For this reason, that land is called Tamate, or Jewelry Exchange.

War Abroad, Strange Omens, Death of the Emperor

Forty-first year [353 CE], spring, third month. The emperor dispatched Tsuno no Sukune of Ki to Paekche to divide the land into provinces and districts for the first time and to record in detail the products of each region.[34] At that time, a relative of the king of Paekche, Sake no Kimi, did not observe proper formalities.[35] Consequently, Tsuno no Sukune of Ki reprimanded the king of Paekche.[36] The king of Paekche respectfully obeyed, bound Sake no Kimi in iron chains, and then sent him with Sotsuhiko to be presented to the emperor. Sake no Kimi then fled to hide in the household of Koroshi, Obito of the brocade weavers of Ishikawa, whom he deceived by saying, "The emperor has already pardoned my crime. So I wish to turn to you for my livelihood."[lxiii] After a long while, the emperor at last pardoned his crime.

Forty-third year [355 CE], autumn, ninth month, first day. Abiko of the imperial estate of Yosami caught a strange bird.[lxiv] He presented it to the emperor, saying, "I have many times strung up nets and caught birds, but never before have I caught a bird like this. Therefore, thinking it wonderful, I present it to you."

The emperor summoned Sake no Kimi and showed him the bird, saying, "What bird is this?"

---

34 A similar edict was issued in Taika 1.7 (645 CE) for Mimana. Tsuno no Sukune of Ki was dispatched with three other sons of Takeuchi no Sukune to censure Paekche for disrespect in Ōjin 3.
35 Sake no Kimi's lineage is unclear. He appears as a progenitor in *New Selected Records*. Older manuscripts of the *Chronicles* identify him as a relative of the Paekche king, but some later ones change the word "relative" to "descendant."
36 It is not clear which king is meant here.

酒君對言此鳥之類、多在百濟。得馴而能從人。亦捷飛之掠諸鳥。百濟俗號此鳥曰俱知。是今時鷹也。

　　乃授酒君令養馴。未幾時而得馴。酒君則以韋緡著其足、以小鈴著其尾、居腕上、獻于天皇。

　　是日、幸百舌鳥野而遊獵。時雌雉多起。乃放鷹令捕。忽獲數十雉。

　　是月、甫定鷹甘部。故時人號其養鷹之處、曰鷹甘邑也。

　　五十年春三月壬辰朔丙申、河內人奏言、於茨田堤鴈產之。即日、遣使令視。曰、既實也。天皇、於是、歌以問武內宿禰曰、

多莾耆破屢	たまきはる
宇知能阿曾	うちのあそ
儺虛曾破	なこそは
豫能等保臂等	よのとほひと
儺虛曾波	なこそは
區珥能那餓臂等	くにのながひと
阿耆豆辭莾	あきづしま
揶莾等能區珥々	やまとのくにに
箇利古武等	かりこむと
儺波企箇輸揶	なはきかすや

　　武內宿禰答歌曰、

夜輸瀰始之	やすみしし
和我於朋枳瀰波	わがおほきみは
于陪儺于陪儺	うべなうべな

Sake no Kimi replied, saying, "There are many birds like this in Paekche. If you tame it, it will follow human directions. It flies swiftly and can catch various other birds. People in Paekche call this bird a 'kuchi.'"

Now it is called a *taka*, or hawk.

Thus the emperor bestowed this bird upon Sake no Kimi and made him care for it. After not many hours, he was able to tame it. Sake no Kimi tied a soft leather cord to its leg and a small bell to its tail, placed it on his arm, and presented it to the emperor.

That day, the emperor went to Mozuno to hunt.[lxv] At that time, many female pheasants came out. The emperor then released the hawk to catch them, and soon enough it had caught many dozens of them.

That month, the emperor first established the Takakai hereditary guild.[lxvi] Accordingly, people at the time named the place where they raised the hawks Takakai Village, or Village of the Hawk Raisers."

Fiftieth year [362 CE], spring, third month, fifth day. The people of Kōchi Province addressed the emperor, saying, "At Mamuta Dyke, a goose hatched young."[37][lxvii]

That day, the emperor dispatched a messenger to see. He said, "It is true."

The emperor, upon hearing this, sang to ask Takeuchi no Sukune,

Uchi no Ason,
it is you
who are from a far-off age,
it is you
who are longest-lived in our land.
In the land of Yamato
of autumn harvests,†
have you ever heard
of a goose hatching?

Takeuchi no Sukune answered, singing,

My great king
ruler of all,†
naturally, naturally,

---

37 As a migrating bird, the goose would normally lay eggs outside of Japan. The occurrence of an improbable event demonstrates the virtue of Nintoku's reign.

和例烏斗波輪儺	われをとはすな
阿企菟辭摩	あきづしま
揶莽等能倶珥々	やまとのくにに
箇利古武等	かりこむと
和例破枳箇儒	われはきかず

　五十三年、新羅不朝貢。

　夏五月、遣上毛野君祖竹葉瀨、令問其闕貢。是道路之間獲白鹿。乃還之獻于天皇。更改日而行。俄且重遣竹葉瀨之弟田道。則詔之曰、若新羅距者、擧兵擊之。仍授精兵。新羅起兵而距之。爰新羅人、日々挑戰。田道固塞而不出。

　時新羅軍卒一人、有放于營外。則掠俘之。因問消息。對曰、有強力者。曰百衝。輕捷猛幹。毎爲軍右前鋒。故伺之擊左則敗也。

　時新羅空左備右。於是、田道、連精騎擊其左。新羅軍潰之。因縱兵乘之、殺數百人。即虜四邑之人民以歸焉。

　五十五年、蝦夷叛之。遣田道令擊。則爲蝦夷所敗、以死于伊峙水門。時有從者、取得田道之手纏、與其妻。乃抱手纏而縊死。時人聞之流涕矣。是後、蝦夷亦襲之

you ask me.
In the land of Yamato,
land of autumn harvests,†
I have never heard
of a goose hatching.

Fifty-third year [365 CE]. Silla did not send tribute to court.

Summer, fifth month. The emperor dispatched the ancestor of the Kimi of Kamitsuke, Takahase, to inquire into the missing tribute. On his way there, he hunted and killed a white deer.[38] And so he returned and presented it to the emperor. After some days passed, he went again. After a little time, the emperor also dispatched Takahase's younger brother, Taji. He decreed to him, "If Silla prevents your passage, muster troops and attack."[39] Then he bestowed upon him spirited troops. Silla raised soldiers and blocked his passage. The people of Silla challenged them in battle day after day. Taji hardened his defense at strategic points and did not go on to attack.

At that time, one of the leaders of the Silla army went outside their military encampment. He was captured and interrogated about Silla's military situation. He said, "There is a powerful soldier called Paekch'ung. He is light and swift, brave and strong. He is always in the vanguard on the right side of the army. So if you wait for your chance and attack the left side, then we will be defeated."

At one point, the left side of the Silla force was totally vulnerable, while the right was reinforced. In response, Taji gathered his choice cavalry to attack the left side. The Silla army was crushed. Taji sent forth his troops, pressing his advantage, and several hundred soldiers of the enemy were killed. Then he took the people of four villages captive and led them on his return.

Fifty-fifth year [367 CE]. The Emishi rebelled. The emperor dispatched Taji to attack them. He was defeated by the Emishi and died at Ishi Port.[lxviii] At that time, his followers took Taji's arm guards and gave them to his wife. She cradled the arm guards and hanged herself. When people at the time heard this, they wept. Later the Emishi attacked again and

---

38 The appearance of white animals was considered an auspicious sign and proof of the virtue of the ruler.
39 The attacks on Silla and the Emishi below by Takahase and Taji, along with those in Suinin 5, Ōjin 15, Ankan 1, and Jomei 9, record the exploits of the Kamitsuke lineage group. Both brothers appear in *New Selected Records*.

略人民。因以、掘田道墓。則有大蛇、發瞋目自墓出以咋。蝦夷悉被蛇毒、而多死亡。唯一二人得免耳。故時人云、田道雖既亡、遂報讎。何死人之無知耶。

五十八年夏五月、當荒陵松林之南道、忽生兩歷木。挾路而末合。

冬十月、吳國・高麗國、並朝貢。

六十年冬十月、差白鳥陵守等充役丁。時天皇親臨役所。爰陵守目杵、忽化白鹿以走。於是、天皇詔之曰、是陵自本空。故欲除其陵守、而甫差役丁。今視是怪者、甚懼之。無動陵守者。則且、授土師連等。

六十二年夏五月、遠江國司表上言、有大樹、自大井河流之、停于河曲。其大十圍、本壹以末兩。時遣倭直吾子籠令造船。而自南海運之、將來于難波津、以充御船也。

是歲、額田大中彥皇子、獵于鬪雞。時皇子自山上望之、瞻野中、有物。其形如廬。乃遣使者令視、還來之曰、窟也。

因喚鬪雞稻置大山主、問之曰、有其野中者何窨矣。

pillaged the people. In the process, they dug up Taji's tomb. Then a giant snake with stern eyes came out of the tomb and bit them. The Emishi all suffered from the snake's venom, and many of them died. Only one or two of them were able to escape. Hence, people at the time said, "Though Taji was already dead, in the end he had his revenge. How can we say that the dead know nothing?"

Fifty-eighth year [370 CE], summer, fifth month. On the road south of the pine grove of Arahaka, two sawtooth oaks suddenly grew.[lxix] They straddled the road, with their branches meeting above it.

Winter, tenth month. The states of Wu and Koguryŏ each presented tribute to court.

Sixtieth year [372 CE], winter, tenth month. The emperor assigned the keepers of the Shiratori tombs[40] to perform labor. At one time, the emperor personally went to where they working, in order to observe. The tomb keeper Meki suddenly turned into a white deer and ran off.[lxx] At this, the emperor decreed, "These tombs have always been empty. Hence, I wanted to end their assignment as tomb keepers and assign them to labor for the first time. Now that I have seen this ill portent, I am deeply afraid. Do not transfer the tomb keepers." Then, on top of this, he bestowed upon them the title Muraji of the Haji.

Sixty-second year [374 CE], summer, fifth month. The Governor[41] of Tōtōmi Province addressed the emperor, saying, "There is a great tree that floated down the Ōi River and is now stuck at a bend. Its circumference is ten yards. At its base it is one, but it then branches into two. In time the emperor dispatched the Atai of Yamato, Agoko, to make a boat. He took it around the sea to the south, came to Naniwa Harbor, and assigned it to be the emperor's ship.

That year, Imperial Prince Nukata-no-ō-naka-tsu-hiko went hunting in Tsuke.[lxxi] At that time, the imperial prince looked afar from atop a mountain and, peering at the fields, saw something. It was shaped like a hermitage. He promptly dispatched a messenger to take a look. The messenger came back and said, "It is a shed."

He then called the Inaki of Tsuke, Ō-yama-nushi, and asked him, "That structure out in the field, what manner of shed is it?"

---

40 These tombs appear in Keikō 40 as three burial sites associated with Yamato Take, who, upon his death, changed into a white bird and flew away.
41 This is the first appearance of the word "governor," a position created in the late seventh century.

啓之曰、氷室也。

皇子曰、其藏如何。亦奚用焉。

曰、掘土丈餘。以草蓋其上。敦敷茅荻、取氷以置其上。既經夏月而不泮。其用之、即當熱月、漬水酒以用也。

皇子則將來其氷、獻于御所。天皇歡之。自是以後、每當季冬、必藏氷。至于春分、始散氷也。

六十五年、飛驒國有一人。曰宿儺。其爲人、壹體有兩面。面各相背。頂合無項。各有手足。其有膝而無膕踵。力多以輕捷。左右佩劒、四手並用弓矢。是以、不隨皇命。掠略人民爲樂。於是、遣和珥臣祖難波根子武振熊而誅之。

六十七年冬十月庚辰朔甲申、幸河內石津原、以定陵地。丁酉、始築陵。是日、有鹿、忽起野中、走之入役民之中而仆死。時異其忽死、以探其痍。即百舌鳥、自耳出之飛去。因視耳中、悉咋割剝。故號其處、曰百舌鳥耳原者、其是之緣也。

是歲、於吉備中國川嶋河派、有大虯令苦人。時路人觸其處而行、必被其毒、以多死亡。

於是、笠臣祖縣守、爲人勇悍而強力。臨派淵、以三全瓠投

Ō-yama-nushi reported to him, "It is an ice shed."[lxxii]

The imperial prince said, "What do you store in it? What do you use it for?"

He said, "It is about ten feet deep in the earth and is covered with grass. We thickly spread pampas grass, place the ice, and place grass on top of it. Even when summer has passed, the ice does not disappear. As for its use, during the hot months, we use the ice to cool our water and wine."

The imperial prince came with some of the ice and presented it to the emperor. The emperor was pleased. From then on, every winter without fail they stored ice. Upon reaching the spring equinox, they began distributing it.

Sixty-fifth year [377 CE], there was a man in Hida Province called Sukuna. His body was such that he had one trunk and two sides.[42] The sides were back-to-back with each other. They came together at the head, but had no backside. Each side had its own arms and legs, and he had knees, but no backs to his knees. He was very strong, light, and swift. He wore swords on both left and right sides, and with each of his four hands could use a bow and arrows. Because of this, he did not follow the emperor. He pillaged the people and enjoyed doing so. The emperor dispatched the ancestor of the Omi of Wani, the Neko of Naniwa, Take-furu-kuma, to put him to death.[43]

Sixty-seventh year [379 CE], winter, tenth month, fifth day. The emperor went to Ishitsunohara in Kōchi and determined the place for his tomb.[lxxiii] On the eighteenth day, laborers started building the tomb. On that day, a deer suddenly came out from the fields, ran among the laborers, fell over, and died. Being suspicious of its sudden death, the people searched it for a wound. Then a shrike came out of its ear and flew away. They looked inside the ear, and it was completely bitten apart and torn up. So they named that place Mozuno-mimihara, or Ear Field of the Shrike.

That year, in Central Kibi Province at the fork of the Kawashima River, there was a giant water snake causing trouble for the people.[lxxiv] Travelers at that time who went by that place were without fail exposed to the venom, and many of them died.

Now, the ancestor of the Omi of Kasa, Agatamori,[44] was valiant and strong in body. He looked upon the depths, threw three whole bottle gourds

---

42 The appearance of a individual with a different physique augured some major change in the polity. In this case, it precedes Imperial Prince Sumi-no-e-no-nakatsu's revolt.
43 Take-furu-kuma, ancestor of the Omi of Wani, appears earlier in Jingū 1.3, where he defeats a rebellion. The additional title Neko of Naniwa appears in the *Ancient Matters* version of that campaign.
44 The first ancestor of the Omi of Kasa was Kamo-wake, younger brother of the ancestor of the Omi of Kibi, Mitomo-wake. Agatamori is not seen elsewhere.

水曰、汝屢吐毒、令苦路人。余殺汝虬。汝沈是瓠、則余避之。不能沈者、仍斬汝身。

時水虬化鹿、以引入瓠。瓠不沈。即舉劒入水斬虬。更求虬之黨類、乃諸虬族、滿淵底之岫穴。悉斬之。河水變血。故號其水、曰縣守淵也。

當此時、妖氣稍動、叛者一二始起。於是、天皇夙興夜寐、輕賦薄斂、以寬民萌、布德施惠、以振困窮。弔死問疾、以養孤孀。是以、政令流行、天下太平、廿餘年無事矣。

八十七年春正月戊子朔癸卯、天皇崩。

冬十月癸未朔己丑、葬于百舌鳥野陵。

into the river, and said, "You frequently spew venom and cause trouble for travelers. I am going to kill you. If you can sink those gourds, then I will flee. If you cannot sink them, then I will kill you immediately."

At that time, the water snake changed into a deer and pulled on the gourds. The gourds did not sink. Then Agatamori raised his sword, went into the water, and killed the snake. He searched for other snakes. Various kinds of snakes filled a hole in the depths. He killed them all, and the waters of the river changed to blood. Accordingly, this river was called Agatamori-no-fuchi, or Depths of Agatamori.

At just this time, an air of disaster was circulating, and one or two rebels began to appear. In response, the emperor woke up early in the morning and went to bed late at night, lowered taxes and lightened collections, was lenient on the people, spread virtue and disseminated grace, and succored the impoverished and those in need. He mourned for the dead, inquired about the sick, and took care of widows and widowers. By doing so, his rule flowed outward, and the realm experienced great peace.[lxxv] For over twenty years, nothing happened.

Eighty-seventh year [399 CE], spring, first month, sixteenth day. The emperor expired.[lxxvi]

Winter, tenth month, seventh day. The emperor was buried in Mozuno Tomb.[lxxvii]

去來穗別天皇 履中天皇

去來穗別天皇、大鷦鷯天皇太子也。去來、此云伊弉。母曰磐之媛命。葛城襲津彥女也。大鷦鷯天皇卅一年春正月、立爲皇太子。時年十五。

八十七年春正月、大鷦鷯天皇崩。太子自諒闇出之、未即尊位之間、以羽田矢代宿禰之女黑媛欲爲妃。納采既訖、遣住吉仲皇子、而告吉日。時仲皇子冒太子名、以奸黑媛。是夜、仲皇子忘手鈴於黑媛之家而歸焉。明日之夜、太子不知仲皇子自奸而到之。乃入室開帳、居於玉床。時床頭有鈴音。太子異之、問黑媛曰、何鈴也。

對曰、昨夜之非太子所齎鈴乎。何更問妾。太子自知仲皇子冒名以奸黑媛、則默之避也。爰仲皇子畏有事、將殺太子。密興兵、圍太子宮。

時平群木菟宿禰・物部大前宿禰・漢直祖阿知使主、三人、啓於太子。太子不信。一云、太子醉以不起。

Book 12
Emperors Richū and Hanzei

Revolt of Imperial Prince Nakatsu

Emperor Izaho-wake [Richū][i] was the oldest child of Emperor Ōsazaki [Nintoku].[ii] His mother was called Iwa-no-hime, the daughter of Sotsuhiko of Kazuraki. In the thirty-first year [343 CE], spring, first month, of Emperor Ōsazaki's reign, he was named crown prince.

> At that time, he was fifteen years old.[1]

Eighty-seventh year [399 CE], spring, first month. Emperor Ōsazaki expired. When the crown prince emerged from the mourning period, and while he had still not acceded to the venerable throne, he wanted to make the daughter of Hata no Yashiro no Sukune, Kuro-hime,[2] his consort. After the marriage arrangements had been settled, he sent Imperial Prince Nakatsu of Suminoe to report the arranged lucky day. At that time, Imperial Prince Nakatsu assumed the crown prince's name and violated Kuro-hime.[iii] That night, Imperial Prince Nakatsu forgot his hand bell at Kuro-hime's house and returned home. The next night, the crown prince went there without knowing that Imperial Prince Nakatsu had violated her. He went into her bedroom, opened the curtain and got on the bedding. When he did, there was the sound of a bell from the head of the bed. The crown prince thought it strange and asked Kuro-hime, "What is that bell?"

She replied, "Is it not the bell that the crown prince had last night? Why would you ask me this?" The crown prince then knew that Imperial Prince Nakatsu had used his name and violated Kuro-hime, but he remained silent and left. At this point, Imperial Prince Nakatsu feared that something had happened, and so he planned to kill the crown prince. He secretly mustered troops and surrounded the crown prince's palace.

At that time, three men—Tsuku no Sukune of Heguri, Mononobe no Ōmae no Sukune, and the ancestor of the Atai of Aya, Achi no Omi—reported this to the crown prince.[iv] The crown prince did not believe them.

> According to another account, the crown prince was drunk and could not be roused.

---

1   The year given here would mean that Richū was born in Nintoku 17, but in Nintoku 7, Nintoku establishes the Mibu hereditary guild on behalf of Richū, which would make him twenty-five years of age at least when named crown prince. The note at his death gives his age as seventy. This would mean he was born in Nintoku 24, and so was eight years old when named crown prince.
2   The entry in Richū 1.7 gives her father as Ashita no Sukune.

故三人扶太子、令乘馬而逃之。一云大前宿禰、抱太子而乘馬。仲皇子不知太子不在、而焚太子宮。通夜火不滅。太子到河内國埴生坂而醒之。顧望難波、見火光而大驚。則急馳之、自大坂向倭。至于飛鳥山、遇少女於山口。問之曰、此山有人乎。

對曰、執兵者多滿山中。宜廻自當摩徑踰之。太子、於是、以爲、聆少女言、而得免難、則歌之曰、

於朋佐箇珥	おほさかに
阿布夜烏等謎烏	あふやをとめを
瀰知度沛麼	みちとへば
哆駄珥破能邏孺	ただにはのらず
哆嗜摩知烏能流	たぎまちをのる

則更還之、發當縣兵、令從身、自龍田山踰之。

時有數十人執兵追來。太子遠望之曰、其彼來者誰人也。何步行急之。若賊人乎。因隱山中而待之。

近則遣一人、問曰、曷人。且何處往矣。

對曰、淡路野嶋之海人也。阿曇連濱子一云、阿曇連黑友。爲仲皇子、令追太子。於是、出伏兵圍之。悉得捕。

Then the three men saved the crown prince by putting him on a horse and escaping.

<small>According to another account, Ōmae no Sukune carried the crown prince and put him on a horse.</small>

Imperial Prince Nakatsu did not know where the crown prince was and set fire to the crown prince's palace.[v] Through the night, the fire did not go out. The crown prince arrived in Haniu Hill in Kōchi Province and woke up.[vi] He looked back over Naniwa, saw the light of a fire and was greatly shocked. Then he raced his horse from Ōsaka toward Yamato.[vii] He arrived at Mt. Asuka and met a maiden at the mouth of the mountain pass.[viii] He asked her, "Are there people on this mountain?"

She replied, "The mountain is overrun by many people armed with weapons. Please go around and cross using the pass from Tagima.[ix] The crown prince, upon hearing the maiden's words, thought that he could escape from danger, and then he sang,

When I asked the way
of the maiden I met
at Ōsaka,
she said not to go straight,
but to go through Tagima.

Then he returned back the way he had come, mustered the troops of that district, drafted them into his service, and crossed in from Mt. Tatsuta.[x]

At that time, dozens of people, armed with weapons, came chasing after them. The crown prince gazed far off and said, "Who are those people coming? Why are they coming in such a hurry? Perhaps they are enemies?" So they hid on the mountain to await them.

When they drew near, they sent one person to ask them, "Who are you, and where are you going?"

They replied, "We are fishermen from Noshima in Awaji.[xi] By the order of the Muraji of Azumi,[3] Hamako, we were ordered to pursue the crown prince for Imperial Prince Nakatsu."[4] Then the hidden soldiers came out and surrounded them. They captured them all.

---

3 In charge of fishermen.
4 An original note adds, "According to another account, he was called Muraji of Azumi, Kurotomo."

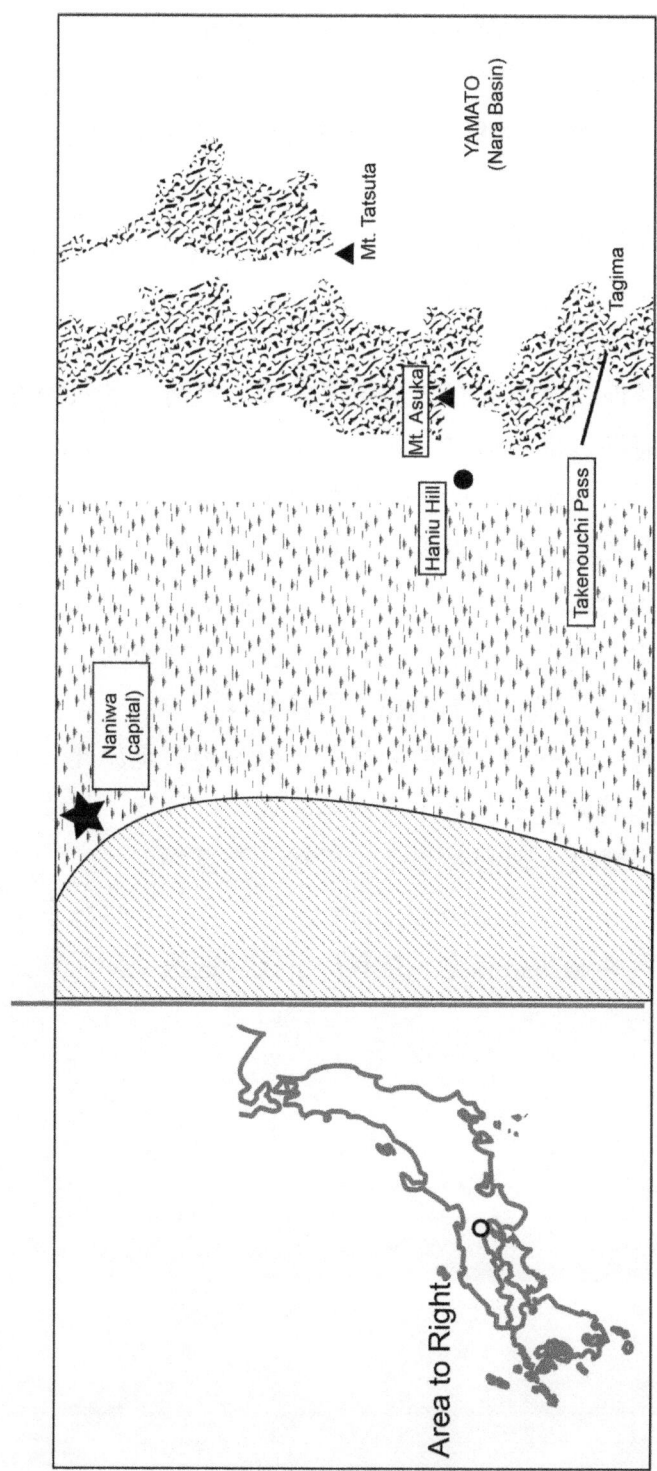

MAP 19 Escape of Richū

當是時、倭直吾子籠、素好仲皇子。預知其謀、密聚精兵數百於攪食栗林、爲仲皇子、將拒太子。時太子不知兵塞、而出山行數里。兵衆多塞、不得進行。乃遣使者、問曰、誰人也。

對曰、倭直吾子籠也。

便還問使者曰、誰使焉。

曰、皇太子之使。

時吾子籠憚其軍衆多在、乃謂使者曰、傳聞、皇太子有非常之事。將助以備兵待之。

然太子疑其心欲殺。則吾子籠愕之、獻己妹日之媛。仍請赦死罪。乃免之。其倭直等貢采女、蓋始于此時歟。

太子便居於石上振神宮。於是、瑞齒別皇子、知太子不在、尋之追詣。然太子疑弟王之心而不喚。時瑞齒別皇子令謁曰、僕無黑心。唯愁太子不在、而參赴耳。

爰太子傳告弟王曰、我畏仲皇子之逆、獨避至於此。何且非疑汝耶。其仲皇子在之、獨猶爲我病。遂欲除。故汝寔勿異心、更返難波、而殺仲皇子。然後、乃見焉。

瑞齒別皇子啓太子曰、大人何憂之甚也。今仲皇子無道、群臣及百姓、共惡怨之。復其門下人、皆叛

At just this time, the Atai of Yamato, Agoko, had been on good terms with Imperial Prince Nakatsu.[xii] He knew beforehand about this plot and secretly gathered several hundred spirited troops at Kakihami in Kurusu.[xiii] On behalf of Imperial Prince Nakatsu, he meant to cut off the crown prince. The troops were blocking him in great numbers, and he was not able to proceed. Then he dispatched a messenger, who asked, "Who are you?"

They replied, "We are with Agoko, Atai of Yamato." Then they in turn asked the messenger, "Whose messenger are you?"

He said, "I am the messenger of the crown prince."

At that time, Agoko hesitated because of the size of the army, and so he told the messenger, "I have heard that the crown prince is dealing with an unexpected issue. To aid him, I have prepared soldiers and await him."

However, the crown prince doubted his intentions and intended to kill him. Then Agoko was afraid and presented his younger sister, Hi-hime, and thus begged to be pardoned of the death penalty. He was spared. This was probably the first time that the Atai of Yamato presented an inner palace lady.[5]

The crown prince then dwelt in Furunokami Palace[6] in Isonokami. Imperial Prince Mitsu-ha-wake [Hanzei] thus knew that the crown prince was not in residence, and so sought him and came in pursuit. However, the crown prince doubted his younger brother's intentions and did not summon him. At that time, Imperial Prince Mitsu-ha-wake ordered an intermediary to have an audience and say, "I have no corrupt intentions. I was just worried because the crown prince was absent and so have come before him."

The crown prince then sent word to his younger brother, saying to him, "I feared Imperial Prince Nakatsu's betrayal and so fled alone to this place. How could I also doubt you? Indeed, Imperial Prince Nakatsu's existence is still my sole concern, and I wish to be rid of him. So if you truly do not have contrary intentions, go back to Naniwa and kill Imperial Prince Nakatsu. After that I will see you."

Then Imperial Prince Mitsu-ha-wake addressed the crown prince, saying, "My lord, why do you worry so much? Presently Imperial Prince Nakatsu lacks proper principles, and the high government officials and people all detest and resent him. Even his own retainers resist him and take him

---

5 An inner palace lady from Yamato also appears in Yūryaku 2. In the same entry, Agoko is titled Provincial Miyatsuko of Yamato.
6 Isonokami Shrine.

爲賊。獨居之無與誰議。臣雖知其逆、未受太子命之。故獨慷慨之耳。今既被命。豈難於殺仲皇子乎。唯獨懼之、既殺仲皇子、猶且疑臣歟。冀見得忠直者、欲明臣之不欺。太子則副木菟宿禰而遣焉。

爰瑞齒別皇子歎之曰、今太子與仲皇子並兄也。誰從矣、誰乖矣。然亡無道、就有道、其誰疑我。則詣于難波、伺仲皇子之消息。仲皇子思太子已逃亡、而無備。

時有近習隼人。曰刺領巾。瑞齒別皇子、陰喚刺領巾、而誂之曰、爲我殺皇子。吾必敦報汝。乃脫錦衣褌與之。刺領巾恃其誂言、獨執矛、以伺仲皇子入厠而刺殺。即隷于瑞齒別皇子。

於是木菟宿禰、啓於瑞齒別皇子曰、刺領巾爲人殺己君。其爲我雖有大功、於己君無慈之甚矣。豈得生乎。乃殺刺領巾。即日向倭也。夜半臻於石上而復命。於是、喚弟王以敦寵、仍賜村合屯倉。

是日、捉阿曇連濱子。

元年春二月壬午朔、皇太子即位於磐余稚櫻宮。

as an enemy. He is isolated and does not confer with anyone. Even though I knew of his treason, I had not received an order from the crown prince. So I was simply enraged and upset. Now that I have received your orders, what could be so difficult about killing Imperial Prince Nakatsu? My only worry is that even after I have killed Imperial Prince Nakatsu, will you still doubt me? I want someone loyal to openly see my actions, to make it clear that I am not deceiving you." The crown prince then sent Tsuku no Sukune to go with him.[xiv]

Imperial Prince Mitsu-ha-wake [Hanzei] wept, saying, "Now the crown prince and Imperial Prince Nakatsu are both my elder brothers. Whom should I follow, and whom should I oppose? However, if I defeat the one who is not following the proper way and follow the one who is, who indeed will doubt me?"[xv] He then went to Naniwa and looked into Imperial Prince Nakatsu's situation. Imperial Prince Nakatsu thought that the crown prince had escaped and had not made any preparations.

At that time, there was nearby a Hayahito servant called Sashihire.[7] Imperial Prince Mitsu-ha-wake secretly summoned Sashihire and enticed him, saying, "Kill the imperial prince for me. I will certainly repay you greatly." Then he took off his embroidered robe and pants and gave them to him. Sashihire trusted these enticing words, took up a halberd, waited for Imperial Prince Nakatsu to go to the toilet, then stabbed him to death. Then he promptly returned to Imperial Prince Mitsu-ha-wake.

Tsuku no Sukune addressed Imperial Prince Mitsu-ha-wake [Hanzei], saying, "Sashihire killed his own lord for another. Even if this was a great deed for us, to his lord it was most lacking in affection. How can he be allowed to live?" He then killed Sashihire.[xvi]

That day they made for Yamato. At night they reached Isonokami and reported back.[xvii] Thereupon the emperor summoned his younger brother and favored him greatly, bestowing upon him the imperial estate Murahase.[xviii] That day they caught the Muraji of Azumi, Hamako.

Reign of Emperor Richū

First year [400 CE], spring, second month, first day. The crown prince acceded to the throne at Iware-no-wakasakura Palace.[xix]

---

7 The Hayahito or Hayato were an ethnic group from southern Kyushu often employed as guards of the imperial family. See S10 in the "Age of the Gods." In *Ancient Matters* his name is given as Sobakari.

夏四月辛巳朔丁酉、召阿雲連濱子、詔之曰、汝與仲皇子共謀逆、將傾國家。罪當于死。然垂大恩、而免死科墨。即日黥之。因此、時人曰阿曇目。亦免從濱子野嶋海人等之罪、役於倭蔣代屯倉。

秋七月己酉朔壬子、立葦田宿禰之女黑媛爲皇妃、妃生磐坂市邊押羽皇子・御馬皇子・青海皇女。一曰、飯豐皇女。

次妃幡梭皇女、生中磯皇女。是年也、太歲庚子。

二年春正月丙午朔己酉、立瑞齒別皇子爲儲君。

冬十月、都於磐余。當是時、平群木菟宿禰・蘇賀滿智宿禰・物部伊莒弗大連・圓圓、此云豆夫羅。大使主、共執國事。十一月、作磐余池。

三年冬十一月丙寅朔辛未、天皇泛兩枝船于磐余市磯池。與皇妃各分乘而遊宴。膳臣余磯獻酒。時櫻花落于御盞。天皇異之、則召物部長眞膽連、詔之曰、是花也、非時而來。其何處之花矣。汝自可求。

於是、長眞膽連、獨尋花、獲于掖上室山、而獻之。天皇歡其希有、即爲宮名。故謂磐余稚櫻宮。其此之緣也。是日、改長眞膽連之本姓、曰稚櫻部造。

Summer, fourth month, seventeenth day. The emperor summoned the Muraji of Azumi, Hamako, and proclaimed, "You plotted treason together with Prince Nakatsu and tried to overthrow the state. This crime warrants death. However, I will show immense mercy. You will be spared death and punished with a tattoo." That day, he was tattooed near the eye. So people at the time called him Azumime.[8] Also, the emperor pardoned the crimes of the fishermen of Noshima who had followed Hamako and made them work on the imperial estate of Komoshiro in Yamato.

Autumn, seventh month, fourth day. The daughter of Ashita no Sukune, Kuro-hime, was named empress-consort.[9] She gave birth to Imperial Prince Iwasaka-no-ichi-no-he-no-oshiha,[10] Imperial Prince Mima, and Imperial Princess Aomi.[11]

His next consort was Imperial Princess Hatabi. She gave birth to Imperial Princess Nakashi. This was the year of the Metal Rat.

Second year [401 CE], spring, first month, fourth day. Imperial Prince Mitsu-ha-wake [Hanzei] was named crown prince.

Winter, tenth month. The capital was built in Iware. At that time, Tsuku no Sukune of Heguri, Machi no Sukune of Soga, the Ō-muraji Mononobe no Ikofu, and Tsubura no Ōmi together carried out matters of state.[xx]

Eleventh month. They made Iware Reservoir.[xxi]

Third year [402 CE], winter, eleventh month, sixth day. The emperor launched the double-forked boat[12] in Ichishi Reservoir of Iware. The imperial consort rode separately, and they had a banquet. The Omi of Kashiwade, Areshi, presented wine, and at the time, a cherry blossom fell into the cup.[xxii] The emperor, thinking it strange, summoned Nagamai, Muraji of the Mononobe, and decreed to him, "This flower, though out of season, has come to me.[xxiii] Where is it from? Go and personally search for it yourself."

Muraji Nagamai personally sought out the origins of the flower and found it at Mt. Wakinokami-no-muro, and presented it.[xxiv] The emperor was delighted at this rarity and took it as his palace name. For this reason, the palace was called Wakasakura Palace of Iware. That day, he elevated Muraji Nagamai from his original title of nobility, calling him Miyatsuko

---

8   "Tattoo Eye."
9   The title of empress-consort is used for only one person in the *Chronicles*, perhaps to distinguish Kuro-hime from Kusaka-no-hatabi, who is named empress in Richū 6. In *Ancient Matters*, she is given as the daughter of Sotsuhiko of Kazuraki.
10 The father of emperors Kenzō and Ninken.
11 An original note adds, "According to one account, she was called Imperial Princess Ii-doyo."
12 The origin of which is given in Nintoku 62.5.

又號膳臣余磯、曰稚櫻部臣。

　四年秋八月辛卯朔戊戌、始之於諸國置國史。記言事達四方志。

　冬十月、堀石上溝。

　五年春三月戊午朔、於筑紫所居三神、見于宮中、言、何奪我民矣。吾今慚汝。於是、禱而不祠。

　秋九月乙酉朔壬寅、天皇狩于淡路嶋。是日、河內飼部等從駕執轡。先是、飼部之黥皆未差。時居嶋伊奘諾神、託祝曰、不堪血臭矣。

　因以、卜之。兆云、惡飼部等黥之氣。故自是以後、頓絕以不黥飼部而止之。

　癸卯、有如風之聲、呼於大虛曰、劒刀太子王也。亦呼之曰、鳥往來羽田之汝妹者、羽狹丹葬立往。汝妹、此云儺邇毛。亦曰、狹名來田蔣津之命、羽狹丹葬立往也。

　俄而使者忽來曰、皇妃薨。天皇大驚之、便命駕而歸焉。

　丙午、自淡路至。

　冬十月甲寅朔甲子、葬皇妃。既而天皇、悔之不治神崇、而亡皇妃、更求其咎。或者曰、車持君行於筑紫國、而悉校

of the Wakasakurabe, and also named the Omi of Kashiwade, Areshi, Omi of Wakasakurabe.[xxv]

Fourth year [403 CE], autumn, eighth month, eighth day. The emperor assigned scribes to the various provinces for the first time, making them record their legends and events and send word about their states of affairs.[xxvi]

Winter, tenth month. Isonokami Canal was dug.[xxvii]

Fifth year [404 CE], spring, third month, first day. Three kami who dwell in Tsukushi appeared in the palace and said, "Why do you steal away our people? Now we will shame you."[13] Thereupon the emperor prayed, but did not perform veneration.

Autumn, ninth month, eighteenth day. The emperor was hunting in Awaji. On that day the horse stewards[14] of Kōchi attended on him, and one took in hand the bit of the emperor's horse. Prior to this, the tattoo near the eye of the horse steward had not completely healed. And so at that time, the kami Izanagi, who dwelt on the island,[15] possessed a priest and said, "I cannot endure the stench of blood."

The emperor performed divination, and the signs said, "The kami dislikes the smell of the horse steward's tattoo." So from this time onward, the administration completely ceased the tattooing of stewards.

Nineteenth day. A voice in the sky, like the wind, called, saying, "Crown prince of sword and blade."[16] Then it called again, saying, "Your beloved from Hata,[17] from whence the birds come and go, was buried at Hasa and departed."[xxviii] Again it spoke, saying, "Sana-kita-komotsu[18] was buried at Hasa and departed."

Suddenly, a messenger came quickly and said, "The empress-consort has perished." The emperor, greatly shocked, promptly ordered his horse readied and returned.

Twenty-second day. The emperor arrived back from Awaji.

Winter, tenth month, eleventh day. The empress-consort was buried. In turn, the emperor regretted that he did not placate the kami's wrath and lost the empress-consort. He sought out the fault anew. One person said, "The kimi of the palanquin bearers went to Tsukushi, took control of the

---

13 The three kami are from the Munakata Shrines in Kyushu, which appear in S6 of the "Age of the Gods." This narrative does not appear in *Ancient Matters*. The theft they refer to is described in Richū 5.10.
14 A hereditary guild (Umakai) associated with the care of horses.
15 Izanagi dwelt on Awaji according to S6 of the "Age of the Gods."
16 The significance of this title is unclear, but it appears to designate Richū.
17 Imperial Consort Kuro-hime, the daughter of Yashiro no Sukune of Hata.
18 Presumably a title for Kuro-hime.

車持部、兼取充神者。必是罪矣。
　天皇則喚車持君、以推問之。事既得實焉。因以、數之曰、爾雖車持君、縱檢校天子之百姓、罪一也。既分寄于神車持部、兼奪取之。罪二也。
　則負惡解除・善解除、而出於長渚崎、令秡禊。既而詔之曰、自今以後、不得掌筑紫之車持部。乃悉收以更分之、奉於三神。
　六年春正月癸未朔戊子、立草香幡梭皇女爲皇后。
　辛亥、始建藏職。因定藏部。
　二月癸丑朔、喚鯽魚磯別王之女太姬郎姬・高鶴郎姬、納於後宮、並爲嬪。於是、二嬪恆歎之曰、悲哉、吾兄王、何處去耶。
　天皇聞其歎而問之曰、汝何歎息也。
　對曰、妾兄鷲住王、爲人強力輕捷。由是、獨馳越八尋屋而遊行。既經多日、不得面言。故歎耳。
　天皇悅其強力以喚之。不參來。
　亦重使而召。猶不參來。恆居於住吉邑。自是以後、廢以不求。

19　The palanquin bearers (Kuruma-mochi) built palanquins for the emperor. The kimi of the palanquin bearers was promoted to ason in Tenmu 13. *New Selected Records* gives their lineage as descended from Toyo-ki-iri-hiko, a son of Emperor Sujin. As used here, "take control" refers also to performing an inspection and determining what goods or services will be performed at the order of the kimi. A number of palanquin bearers were assigned service to the kami. The kimi took direct control of this subgroup, which angered the kami.

palanquin bearers hereditary guild, and claimed the people of the Kamu hereditary guild.[19] Surely, this is the crime."

The emperor then summoned the kimi of the palanquin bearers and interrogated him. All that was said was true. So he reprimanded the kimi, saying, "Though you are kimi of the palanquin bearers, you took control of my subjects as it suited you. That is the first crime. Then, you stole away the members of the palanquin bearers hereditary guild that had been assigned to the kami. That is the second crime."

Then he sentenced him with expiation of evil and expiation of good,[20] sent him to Cape Nagasu, and ordered him to perform ritual cleansing there. Then he decreed, "From now on, you cannot administer the palanquin bearers hereditary guild of Tsukushi." He then drafted all of the bearers into service and allotted them anew to the three kami.

Sixth year [405 CE], spring, first month, sixth day. Imperial Princess Kusaka-no-hatabi was named empress.

Twenty-ninth day. The emperor created the Office of the Exchequer and established its hereditary guild.[xxix]

Second month, first day. The two daughters of Prince Funashi-wake, Futo-hime-no-iratsume and Taka-tsuru-no-iratsume, were summoned and installed in the inner palace, and named third-degree consorts.[21][xxx] In this circumstance, the two consorts were always grieving, saying, "How sad! Where has our older brother the prince gone?"

The emperor heard this sigh and asked them, "Why do you grieve?"

They said, "Our older brother Prince Washi-sumi is strong and agile.[xxxi] For account of this, he went out alone, racing from our grand house. Already many days have passed, and we have not seen his face or spoken. Hence, we grieve."

The emperor was delighted to hear of his strength and summoned him, but he did not come.

Then, again he sent messengers to invite him, but still he did not come. Again and again he sent messengers to summon him, but still he did not come. He remained in Suminoe Village. After a while, the emperor stopped summoning him. He is the first ancestor of the two lineage

---

20 A religious ceremony in which the offender must donate certain objects to atone for his crimes, upon which two types of "expiation" (*harae*), sometimes translated as "purification," would be performed.
21 The Civil and Penal Codes divided the emperor's partners into empress, consorts, secondary consorts, and tertiary consorts based on rank. Here the classification scheme is being anachronistically applied to the harem in Richū's reign.

是讚岐國造・阿波國脚咋別、凡二族之始祖也。

　三月壬午朔丙申、天皇玉體不悆、水土弗調。崩于稚櫻宮。時年七十。

　冬十月己酉朔壬子、葬百舌鳥耳原陵。

瑞齒別天皇 反正天皇
瑞齒別天皇、去來穗別天皇同母弟也。去來穗別天皇二年、立爲皇太子。

　天皇初生于淡路宮。生而齒如一骨。容姿美麗。於是有井。曰瑞井。則汲之洗太子。時多遲花、有于井中。因爲太子名也。多遲花者、今虎杖花也。故稱謂多遲比瑞齒別天皇。

　六年春三月、去來穗別天皇崩。

　元年春正月丁丑朔戊寅、儲君即天皇位。

　秋八月甲辰朔己酉、立大宅臣祖木事之女津野媛、爲皇夫人。生香火姫皇女・圓皇女。又、納夫人弟々媛、生財皇女與高部皇子。

　冬十月、都於河內丹比。是謂柴籬宮。當是時、風雨順時、五穀成熟、人民富饒。天下太平。是年也、太歲丙午。

　五年春正月甲申朔丙午、天皇崩于正寢。

groups of the Provincial Miyatsuko of Sanuki and the Ashikui-wake of Awa Province.[xxxii]

Third month, fifteenth day. The emperor fell ill and was unwell. He expired in Wakasakura Palace.

At that time he was seventy years old.[xxxiii]

Winter, tenth month, fourth day. The emperor was buried in Mozu-no-mimi-hara Tomb.[xxxiv]

Reign of Emperor Hanzei

Emperor Mitsu-ha-wake [Hanzei] was the younger brother of Emperor Izaho-wake [Richū] by the same mother.[xxxv] He was named crown prince in the second year of Emperor Izaho-wake's reign.

The emperor was the first born in Awaji Palace.[xxxvi] When he was born, his teeth were so straight that they were as if forming a single bone, and he was very attractive.[xxxvii] The palace had a well called the well of Mitsu.[xxxviii] Servants drew water from the well and washed the young prince with it. At that time, a *tajihi* flower[22] fell into the well. The crown prince was thereby named. The *tajihi* flower is now called the *itadori* flower.[xxxix] Hence, the emperor was titled Emperor Tajihi-no-mitsu-ha-wake.

Sixth year [405 CE], spring, third month. Emperor Izaho-wake expired.

First year [406 CE], spring, first month, second day. The crown prince acceded to the heavenly imperial throne.

Autumn, eighth month, sixth day. Tsuno-hime, daughter of Kogoto, ancestor of the Omi of Ōyake, was named empress-consort, second degree.[xl] She gave birth to Imperial Princess Kahi and Imperial Princess Tsubura. Also, the empress-consort's younger sister Oto-hime gave birth to Imperial Princess Takara and Imperial Prince Takabe.[xli]

Winter, tenth month. The capital was built in Tajihi in Kōchi. The emperor's palace was called Shibakaki Palace.[xlii] Around this time, wind and rain were in their proper seasons and the five grains grew to fruition.[xliii] The people were prosperous, and the realm was at peace. This was the year of the Fire Horse.

Fifth year [410 CE], spring, first month, twenty-third day. The emperor expired in his bedchamber.[xliv]

---

22 *Fallopia japonica*, Japanese knotweed.

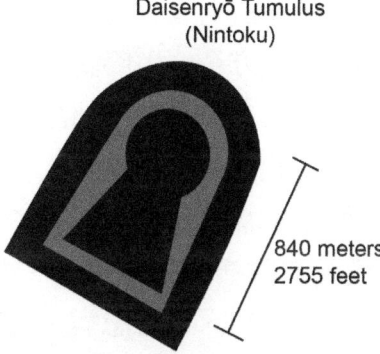
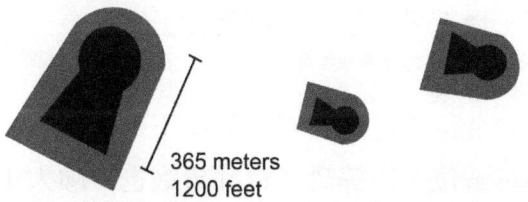

FIGURE 12 Mozu Tombs Cluster, Sakai City, Osaka Prefecture

雄朝津間稚子宿禰天皇 允恭天皇

雄朝津間稚子宿禰天皇、瑞齒別天皇同母弟也。天皇自岐嶷至於總角、仁惠儉下。及壯篤病、容止不便。

五年春正月、瑞齒別天皇崩。

爰群卿議之曰、方今、大鷦鷯天皇之子、雄朝津間稚子宿禰皇子、與大草香皇子。然雄朝津間稚子宿禰皇子、長之仁孝。即選吉日、跪上天皇之璽。

雄朝津間稚子宿禰皇子謝曰、我之不天。久離篤疾、不能步行。且我既欲除病、獨非奏言、而密破身治病、猶勿差。由是、先皇責之曰、汝雖患病、縱破身。不孝孰甚於茲矣。其長生之、遂不得繼業。亦我兄二天皇、愚我而輕之。群卿共所知。夫天下者大器也。帝位者鴻業也。且民之父母、斯則聖賢之職。豈下愚之任乎。更選賢王宜立矣、寡人弗敢當。

群臣再拜言、夫帝位不可以久曠。天命不可以謙距。今大王留時逆衆、不正號位、臣等恐、百姓望絶也。願大王雖勞、猶即天皇位。

Book 13
Emperors Ingyō and Ankō

Accession of Emperor Ingyō

Emperor O-asazuma-wakugo-no-sukune [Ingyō] was the younger brother of Emperor Mitsu-ha-wake [Hanzei] by the same mother.[i] From a young age until his hair was tied as a youth, he was clever, as well as gracious and unassuming.[ii] When he blossomed into adulthood, he became seriously ill, and his health was not sound.

Fifth year [410 CE], spring, first month. Emperor Mitsu-ha-wake expired.

Thereupon, the high government officials consulted one another and said, "Right now, the children of Emperor Ōsazaki [Nintoku] are Imperial Prince O-asazuma-wakugo-no-sukune and Imperial Prince Ō-kusaka. Moreover, Imperial Prince O-asazuma-wakugo-no-sukune is the elder, and he is benevolent and filial."[iii] They then chose an auspicious day and humbly presented him with the imperial seal.[iv]

Imperial Prince O-asazuma-wakugo-no-sukune declined, saying, "By some misfortune, I have been seriously ill for a long time and am unable to walk. Also, I previously meant to rid myself of this illness, and so without saying anything to the emperor, I secretly did harm to myself in order to cure the sickness, but my condition did not improve one bit. On account of this, the previous emperor reprimanded me, saying, 'Though it was because you were sick, you caused harm to yourself of your own will. Of unfilial acts, is there any greater than this? Even if you live a long life, you cannot succeed to the throne.' Also, my two older brothers, the emperors, thought me foolish and regarded me lightly. All this the high government officials know. Now, the realm is like a grand vessel, and the imperial throne a great endeavor.[v] Being father and mother to the people is the occupation of a wise sage. How could a lowly fool assume this post? You should choose a wise prince to accede. In all humility, I could never dare."

Then the high government officials again bowed and said, "The imperial throne cannot long be left empty. Heaven's mandate cannot be deferred or obstructed. Now the prince is spending time going against the will of the masses, and if title and throne are not rectified, we fear that the hopes of the people will die out.[vi] We wish the prince, despite the trouble, to accede to the heavenly imperial throne."

雄朝津間稚子宿禰皇子曰、奉宗廟社稷重事也。寡人篤疾。不足以稱。猶辭而不聽。

於是、群臣皆固請曰、臣伏計之、大王奉皇祖宗廟、最宜稱。雖天下萬民、皆以爲宜。願大王聽之。

元年冬十有二月、妃忍坂大中姫命、苦群臣之憂吟、而親執洗手水、進于皇子前。仍啓之曰、大王辭而不即位。位空之、既經年月。群臣百寮、愁之不知所爲。願大王從群望、強即帝位。

然皇子不欲聽、而背居不言。於是、大中姫命惶之、不知退而侍之、經四五剋。當于此時、季冬之節、風亦烈寒。大中姫所捧鋺水、溢而腕凝。不堪寒以將死。皇子顧之驚、則扶起謂之曰、嗣位重事。不得輙就。是以、於今不從。然今群臣之請、事理灼然。何遂謝耶。

爰大中姫命仰歡、則謂群卿曰、皇子將聽群臣之請。今當上天皇璽符。於是、群臣大喜、即日、捧天皇之璽符、再拜上焉。

皇子曰、群卿共爲天下請寡人。寡人何敢遂辭、乃即帝位。是年也、太歲壬子。

Imperial Prince O-asazuma-wakugo-no-sukune [Ingyō] said, "Attending to the altars of state is an important affair. In all humility, I am seriously ill and thus am unfit for the title." He then refused and would hear no more.

At this point, the high government officials all tenaciously entreated him, saying, "In our humble opinion, the prince is the most appropriate person to attend to the altars of the state of your imperial ancestors. They many people of the realm all think so as well. We wish the prince to hear us out."[vii]

First year [412 CE], winter, twelfth month. Consort Oshi-saka-no-ō-naka-tsu-hime was troubled by the anxious grieving of the high government officials, took up the hand-washing water herself, and went before the imperial prince.[viii] Then she addressed him, saying, "The prince has refused to accede to the throne, which stands empty, and already much time has passed. The high government officials and public servants are distressed and do not know what should be done. I wish the prince to go along with the wishes of the masses and do whatever it takes to accede to the throne."

However, the imperial prince did not want to hear of it, and he turned his back to her and did not speak. At this, Oshi-saka-no-ō-naka-tsu-hime, in her humility, did not know whether she could withdraw, and so waited while four or five quarters of an hour passed.

It was the last month of the year, and the wind was fierce and cold. The water in the vessel that Ō-naka-tsu-hime was holding spilled over and froze to her arms. She could not withstand the cold and was about to die. The imperial prince turned around, was shocked, and got up to help her, saying, "Succeeding to the throne is an important affair, and I cannot do it casually. Accordingly, I have not given in up to now. However, now what the high government officials ask shines with the light of reason. How can I in the end decline?"

At this turn of events, Ō-naka-tsu-hime looked up in joy, then told the high government officials, "The imperial prince will now hear out the request of the high government officials. You should now present him with the imperial seal." So the high government officials were all greatly gladdened, and that very day, they presented the imperial seal and again bowed.

The imperial prince said, "The high government officials together have made a request of my humble self on behalf of the realm. In all humility, how could I dare to refuse them to the last?"[ix] Then he acceded to the imperial throne. This was the year of the Water Rat.[1]

---

1 Normally, there would be an entry giving the location of the palace and capital here. The Ingyō book of *Ancient Matters* gives the palace as Tōtsu-asuka Palace. It is unknown whether this refers to the Asuka in Kōchi Province (Osaka) or the Asuka in Yamato Province.

二年春二月丙申朔己酉、立忍坂大中姬爲皇后。是日、爲皇后定刑部。皇后生木梨輕皇子・名形大娘皇女・境黑彥皇子・穴穗天皇・輕大娘皇女・八釣白彥皇子・大泊瀬稚武天皇・但馬橘大娘皇女・酒見皇女。

初皇后隨母在家、獨遊苑中。

時鬭鶏國造、從傍徑行之。乘馬而莅籠、謂皇后、嘲之曰、能作園乎、汝者也。汝、此云那鼻苔也。且曰、壓乞、戸母、其蘭一莖焉。壓乞、此云異提。戸母、此云覩自。

皇后則採一根蘭、與於乘馬者。因以、問曰、何用求蘭耶。

乘馬者對曰、行山撥蠛也。蠛、此云摩愚那岐。

時皇后結之意裏、乘馬者辭无禮、卽謂之曰、首也、余不忘矣。

是後、皇后登祚之年、覓乘馬乞蘭者、而數昔日之罪以欲殺。

爰乞蘭者、顙搶地叩頭曰、臣之罪實當萬死。然當其日、不知貴者。於是、皇后赦死刑、貶其姓謂稻置。

三年春正月辛酉朔、遣使、求良醫於新羅。

秋八月、醫至自新羅。則令治天皇病。未經幾時、病已差也。天皇歡之、厚賞醫以歸于國。

Second year [413 CE], spring, second month, fourteenth day. Oshi-saka-no-ō-naka-tsu-hime was named empress. On this day, on behalf of the empress, the emperor established the Oshisaka hereditary guild.² The empress gave birth to Imperial Prince Kinashi-no-karu, Imperial Princess Nagata-no-ō-iratsume, Imperial Prince Sakai-no-kuro-hiko, Emperor Anaho [Ankō],ˣ Imperial Princess Karu-no-ō-iratsume, Imperial Prince Yatsuri-no-shiro-hiko, Emperor Ō-hatsuse-no-waka-take [Yūryaku],ˣⁱ Imperial Princess Tajima-no-tachibana-no-ō-iratsume, and Imperial Princess Sakami.ˣⁱⁱ

Previously, when the empress was living in her mother's house, she took a stroll alone in the garden.

At that time, the Provincial Miyatsuko of Tsuge came along the way next to the garden. From atop his horse he looked over the hedge, and told the empress, sneering, "You have made this garden well." Then he said, "Hey, housemaid! Give me one of those leeks."

The empress then picked a leek and gave it to the man on the horse. "Why do you want a leek?" she asked him.

The man on the horse replied, "For a trip to the mountains, to chase off the gnats."

At the time, the empress, in the depths of her heart, begrudged the rudeness of the horse-rider's words, and so she told him, "You, I will not forget."

Afterward, in the year that she took the throne³ as empress, she sought out the horse rider who had asked for a leek, accused him of his crime from the distant past, and meant to kill him.

The man who had asked for the leek kowtowed, saying, "My crime is truly deserving of death. However, on that day, I did not know that you were a noble." The empress commuted his death penalty and lowered his title of nobility to Inaki.⁴

Third year [414 CE], spring, first month, first day. The emperor dispatched a messenger to seek a good doctor in Silla.

Autumn, eighth month. The doctor arrived from Silla. He was ordered to treat the emperor's illness. After not even a few hours had passed, he completely cured the disease. The emperor was pleased, generously rewarded the doctor, and returned him to his land.

---

2 *Ancient Matters* specifies that this group was created to preserve the name of the empress. In Suinin 39, there is an Oshisaka weapons steward hereditary guild. The group was widely distributed throughout Japan.
3 The word used for "took the throne" would usually be restricted to the emperor.
4 The Inaki of Tsuke appears in Nintoku 62. That title of nobility is anachronistically applied here.

四年秋九月辛巳朔己丑、詔曰、上古之治、人民得所、姓名勿錯。今朕踐祚、於茲四年矣。上下相爭、百姓不安。或誤失己姓。或故認高氏。其不至於治者、蓋由是也。朕雖不賢、豈非正其錯乎。群臣議定奏之。

　　群臣皆言、陛下舉失正枉、而定氏姓者、臣等冒死。奏可。

　　戊申、詔曰、群卿百寮及諸國造等皆各言、或帝皇之裔、或異之天降。然三才顯分以來、多歷萬歲。是以、一氏蕃息、更爲萬姓。難知其實。故諸氏姓人等、沐浴齊戒、各爲盟神探湯。

　　則於味橿丘之辭禍戸䄃、坐探湯瓮、而引諸人令赴曰、得實則全。偽者必害。盟神探湯、此云區訶陀智。或泥納釜煮沸、攘手探湯泥。或燒斧火色、置于掌。於是、諸人各著木綿手繦、而赴釜探湯。則得實者自全、不得實者皆傷。是以、故詐者愕然之、豫退無進。自是之後、氏姓自定、更無詐人。

Fourth year [415 CE], autumn, ninth month, ninth day. The emperor decreed, "In ancient times, governance meant that the people had their place, and there was no mistaking titles of nobility. Now We have assumed the throne, and four years have passed. Those above and those below fight with each other, and the people are in a state of unrest. In some cases, there was a mistake, and lineage groups have lost their titles. In other cases, they have deliberately assumed the status of a higher lineage group. Perhaps this is why my administration has not gone well. Though We are not wise, how could We not correct this mistake? High government officials, take counsel and inform me of your resolution."

Then the high government officials all said, "Sovereign, to restore what was lost and straighten what is crooked, if you establish a system of titles of nobility, we will risk our lives to see it through." At that, the emperor permitted it.

On the twenty-eighth day, the emperor decreed, "High government officials, public servants, provincial miyatsuko, and so on, all say, 'In our case, we are of imperial stock,' or 'In our case, there was a miraculous descent from heaven.' However, since the three talents manifested and separated from each other, many tens of thousands years have passed. On account of this, for one lineage group, there are myriad titles of nobility, and it is difficult to know the truth. So, let one person from each lineage group and title of nobility bathe and perform religious abstentions, and then let each perform trial by boiling water."[xiii]

So, on Koto-no-magahe Slope at Umakashi Hill, jars for the trial of boiling water were set up, and various people were brought there and told, "Those who are truthful shall be unharmed. Those who lie will undoubtedly suffer injury."[xiv]

In some cases, a clump of clay was put into a pot, and the water was boiled. Then, with sleeves rolled up, the person grabbed for the clay. In some cases, an axe was heated red and placed in the person's palm.

Thereupon, the various people wore sashes made of mulberry bark, went to the pot, and performed the trial by boiling water. Those who were truthful were, of course, unharmed, and those who were not truthful were burned. In these circumstance, those who had deliberately been false were shocked, and instead of coming forward, they fled before performing the trial. Thereafter, the lineage group titles of nobility were settled of their own accord, and no one falsified them further.

五年秋七月丙子朔己丑、地震。先是、命葛城襲津彥之孫玉田宿禰、主瑞齒別天皇之殯。則當地震夕、遣尾張連吾襲、察殯宮之消息。時諸人悉聚無闕。唯玉田宿禰無之也。吾襲奏言、殯宮大夫玉田宿禰、非見殯所。則亦遣吾襲於葛城、令視玉田宿禰。
　　是日、玉田宿禰、方集男女、而酒宴焉。吾襲舉狀、具告玉田宿禰。宿禰則畏有事、以馬一匹、授吾襲爲禮幣。乃密遮吾襲、而殺于道路。即逃隱武內宿禰之墓域。
　　天皇聞之、喚玉田宿禰。玉田宿禰疑之、甲服襖中、而參赴。甲端自衣中出之。天皇分明欲知其狀、乃令小墾田采女、賜酒于玉田宿禰。爰采女分明瞻衣中有鎧、而具奏于天皇。天皇設兵將殺。玉田宿禰、乃密逃出而匿家。天皇更發卒、圍玉田家、而捕之乃誅。
　　冬十有一月甲戌朔甲申、葬瑞齒別天皇于耳原陵。
　　七年冬十二月壬戌朔、讌于新室。天皇親之撫琴。皇后起儛。儛既終而、不言禮事。當時風俗、於宴會、

Fifth year [416 CE], autumn, seventh month, fourteenth day. There was an earthquake. Before this, the emperor had ordered the grandson of Sotsuhiko of Kazuraki, Tamata no Sukune, to oversee the temporary burial of Emperor Mitsu-ha-wake [Hanzei].⁵ On the night of the earthquake, the emperor dispatched the Muraji of Owari, Aso, to investigate the status of the temporary burial palace. At that time, the various people all assembled, and no one was absent except for Tamata no Sukune. Aso reported to the emperor, "I did not see the director of the temporary burial palace, Tamata no Sukune, there." And so the emperor dispatched Aso to Kazuraki to see Tamata no Sukune.

That day, Tamata no Sukune had assembled men and women and was having a banquet. Aso presented the matters, telling Tamata no Sukune in detail. Sukune was concerned that something was afoot and gave Aso a horse as a matter of courtesy. Then he secretly intercepted Aso and killed him on the road. Next he fled and hid in the tomb of Takeuchi no Sukune.ˣᵛ

The emperor heard of this and summoned Tamata no Sukune. Sukune was suspicious and wore armor under his clothing when he came to have an audience with the emperor. The edge of his armor stuck out from inside his clothing. The emperor, knowing the situation, then had an inner palace lady from Oharida bestow wine upon Tamata no Sukune.ˣᵛⁱ The inner palace lady clearly saw that there was armor underneath his clothing and reported to the emperor in detail. The emperor marshaled troops and meant to kill him. Tamata no Sukune then secretly fled and hid in his own house. The emperor further mustered his army, surrounded Tamata's house, caught him, and executed him.

Winter, eleventh month, eleventh day. Emperor Mitsu-ha-wake was buried in Miminohara Tomb.ˣᵛⁱⁱ

Affair with Oto-hime

Seventh year [418 CE], winter, twelfth month, first day. There was a banquet in Niimuro.⁶ The emperor himself played the zither, and the empress stood and danced. When the dance was finished, she did not speak the words of the ritual. For people at that time, when a banquet was held, and when

---

5   In a note in Yūryaku 7, Tamata no Sukune is given as the son of Sotsuhiko. Since Hanzei had died five years earlier, this entry seems unusually late for the temporary burial. Presumably, this delay was caused by the delay in Ingyō's assuming the throne.
6   One interpretation is that this was a ritual for the new palace. Niimuro means "new building." The episode that follows with Oto-hime is not in *Ancient Matters*.

儛者儛終、則自對座長曰、奉娘子也。

時天皇謂皇后曰、何失常禮也。

皇后惶之、復起儛。儛竟言、奉娘子。

天皇即問皇后曰、所奉娘子者誰也。欲知姓字。

皇后不獲已而奏言、妾弟、名弟姬焉。弟姬容姿絶妙無比。其艷色徹衣而晃之。是以、時人號曰衣通郎姬也。

天皇之志、存于衣通郎姬。故強皇后而令進。皇后知之、不輙言禮事。爰天皇歡喜、則明日、遣使者喚弟姬。

時弟姬隨母、以在於近江坂田。弟姬畏皇后之情、而不參向。又重七喚。猶固辭以不至。於是、天皇不悅。而復勅一舍人中臣烏賊津使主曰、皇后所進之娘子弟姬、喚而不來。汝自往之、召將弟姬以來、必敦賞矣。

爰烏賊津使主、承命退之。糒裹裀中、到坂田。伏于弟姬庭中言、天皇命以召之。

弟姬對曰、豈非懼天皇之命。唯不欲傷皇后之志耳。妾雖身亡、不參赴。

時烏賊津使主對言、臣既被天皇命、必召率來矣。若不將來、

the dancer finished her dance, she would face the person in the head seat and say, "I offer a girl."

The emperor told the empress, "Why have you dispensed with the usual ritual?"

The empress was concerned, and so she again stood and danced. When the dance was finished, she said, "I offer a girl."

The emperor then asked the empress, "Who is the girl you offer? I want to know her name."

The empress reluctantly addressed him, saying, "My younger sister, called Oto-hime." Oto-hime was beautiful beyond compare, and her luster shone through her clothing. Accordingly, people at the time called her So-tōshi-no-iratsume.[7][xviii]

The emperor's heart had been set on So-tōshi-no-iratsume. Thus he had forced the empress to present her to him. The empress knew this, and so did not readily speak the ritual words. Upon her doing so, the emperor was pleased and promptly the next day dispatched a messenger to summon Oto-hime.

At that time, Oto-hime was living with her mother at Sakata in Ōmi.[xix] Oto-hime was anxious about how the empress would feel and did not come. The emperor summoned her seven times, over and over again. She still firmly refused to go. At this, the emperor was displeased. He then again ordered a servant, Ikatsu, Omi of the Nakatomi,[8] "The woman presented to me by the empress, Oto-hime, does not come though I summon her. Go yourself and call for her, and if she comes, I will without fail richly reward you."

Omi Ikatsu received the order and departed. He wrapped emergency rations of dried rice cakes up inside his clothing and went to Sakata. He prostrated himself in Oto-hime's courtyard and said, "The emperor orders me to summon you."

Oto-hime replied, "How could I not humbly follow the emperor's order? I wish only not to go against the empress's sentiments. Even if it means death, I will not go."

Omi Ikatsu then replied, "I have already received the emperor's order and must summon you and bring you to him. If I do not bring you, then I

---

7   "Clothing piercing lady."
8   Ikatsu also appears in Chūai 9.2 and the pre-accession record of Jingū, though these books are quite separated in years from Ingyō 7.

必罪之。故返被極刑、寧伏庭而死耳。仍經七日、伏於庭中。與飲食而不湌。密食懷中之糒。

於是、弟姬以爲、妾因皇后之嫉、既拒天皇命。且亡君之忠臣、是亦妾罪、則從烏賊津使主而來之。到倭春日、食于櫟井上、弟姬親賜酒于使主、慰其意。使主、即日至京。留弟姬於倭直吾子籠之家、復命天皇。天皇大歡之、美烏賊津使主而敦寵焉。

然皇后之色不平。是以、勿近宮中、則別構殿屋於藤原而居也。適產大泊瀬天皇之夕、天皇始幸藤原宮。皇后聞之恨曰、妾初自結髮、陪於後宮、既經多年。甚哉、天皇也、今妾產之、死生相半。何故、當今夕、必幸藤原、乃自出之、燒產殿而將死。

天皇聞之、大驚曰、朕過也、因慰喩皇后之意焉。

八年春二月幸于藤原、密察衣通郎姬之消息。是夕、衣通郎姬、戀天皇而獨居。其不知天皇之臨、而歌曰、

和餓勢故餓	わがせこが
勾倍枳豫臂奈利	くべきよひなり
佐瑳餓泥能	ささがねの
區茂能於虛奈比	くものおこなひ
虛豫比辭流辭毛	こよひしるしも

will certainly be charged with a crime. Rather than returning to be killed, I would rather die lying prostrate in your courtyard." Seven days thus passed with him lying in the courtyard. Though he was given food and water, he did not eat it. He surreptitiously ate the dried rice cakes from his pockets.

Thereupon Oto-hime thought, "I have already refused the emperor's order on account of the empress's jealousy. If my lord were further to lose his loyal servant, this would also be my transgression." She then went, following Omi Ikatsu. They arrived at Kasuga in Yamato and ate at Ichii Well.[xx] Oto-hime herself served wine to the Omi, in order to comfort his mind. The Omi, that day, arrived in the capital. He left Oto-hime in the house of Agoko, Agatanushi of Yamato,[9] and reported to the emperor. The emperor was greatly pleased, praised Omi Ikatsu, and richly favored him.

However, the empress did not think well of the matter. On account of this, Oto-hime could not come near the inner palace, and so a separate residence was built for her at Fujihara, where she dwelt. On the night that she gave birth to Emperor Ō-hatsuse [Yūryaku], the emperor went to Fujihara for the first time. The empress heard of this and resented him, saying, "I have dwelt in the inner palace since I first tied up my hair, and now many years have passed. How awful, my emperor, that now, when I am giving birth, halfway between life and death, even on this night you must go to Fujihara." Then she departed on her own, set fire to the parturition chamber, and was on the verge of death.

The emperor heard this, was greatly shocked, and said, "We were wrong," thereby comforting the empress's heart with his words.

Eighth year [419 CE], spring, second month. The emperor went to Fujihara.[xxi] In secret, he observed the condition of So-tōshi-no-iratsume. That night, So-tōshi-no-iratsume, dwelling alone, longed for the emperor. Not knowing that the emperor was there, she sang,

'Tis twilight, when my beloved
is supposed to come.
The spider's movement
is striking this evening.[10]

---

9 Agoko also appears in the pre-accession record of Nintoku, in Nintoku 62.5, and in Yūryaku 2.12. The unusually long span of years suggests an artificial lengthening of the historical record.

10 The appearance of a spider spinning its web was thought to portend the appearance of a late-night visitor.

天皇聆是歌、則有感情。而歌之曰、

佐瑳羅餓多	ささらがた
邇之枳能臂毛弘	にしきのひもを
等枳舍氣帝	ときさけて
阿麻哆絆泥受邇	あまたはねずに
多儀比等用能未	ただひとよのみ

　明旦、天皇見井傍櫻華、而歌之曰、

波那具波辭	はなぐはし
佐區羅能梅涅	さくらのめで
許等梅涅麼	ことめでば
波椰區波梅涅孺	はやくはめでず
和我梅豆留古羅	わがめづるこら

　皇后聞之、且大恨也。於是、衣通郎姬奏言妾、常近王宮、而晝夜相續、欲覩陛下之威儀。然皇后則妾之姊也。因妾以恆恨陛下。亦爲妾苦。是以、冀離王居、而欲遠居。若皇后嫉意少息歟。

　天皇則更興造宮室於河内茅渟、而衣通郎姬令居。因此、以屢遊獵于日根野。

　九年春二月、幸茅渟宮。

　秋八月、幸茅渟。

　冬十月、幸茅渟。

　十年春正月、幸茅渟。於是皇后奏言、妾如毫毛、非嫉弟姬。然恐陛下屢幸於茅渟。是百姓之苦歟。仰願宜除車駕之數也。是後、希有之幸焉。

The emperor heard this song, was touched in heart, and so sang,

Untie
the delicate
patterned brocade string.
If not to sleep together for many nights,
then even for only one night.

The next morning, the emperor saw the cherry blossoms near the well and sang,

Beautiful as a flower†
The joy of the cherry blossoms!
If it be the same joy,
better we join quickly,
my joyous darling.

The empress heard this and was again vexed. Thereupon So-tōshi-no-iratsume addressed the emperor, saying, "I am always near the king's palace, and both day and night wish to see the striking figure of my lord. However, the empress is my older sister. Because of me, she is always vexed, and also because of me, she suffers. So I wish to depart the king's palace and dwell at a distance. Perhaps doing so will abate the empress's jealous feelings a bit."

The emperor then immediately built a palace in Kōchi, in Chinu, and So-tōshi-no-iratsume dwelt there.[xxii] For this reason, the emperor frequently went hunting in Hineno.[xxiii]

Ninth year [420 CE], spring, second month. The emperor went to Chinu Palace.

Autumn, eighth month. The emperor went to Chinu.

Winter, tenth month. The emperor went to Chinu.

Tenth year [421 CE], spring, first month. The emperor went to Chinu. In response the empress addressed the emperor, saying, "I am not jealous of Oto-hime in the least. However, I fear that my lord's frequent visits to Chinu are causing suffering for the people. I wish you would reduce the frequency of your travels there." After that, he rarely went there.

十一年春三月癸卯朔丙午、幸於茅渟宮。衣通郎姫歌之曰、

等虛辭陪邇	とこしへに
枳彌母阿閇椰毛	きみもあへやも
異舎儺等利	いさなとり
宇彌能波摩毛能	うみのはまもの
余留等枳等枳弘	よるときときを

時天皇謂衣通郎姫曰、是歌不可聆他人。皇后聞必大恨。故時人號濱藻、謂奈能利曾毛也。

先是、衣通郎姫居于藤原宮。時天皇詔大伴室屋連曰、朕頃得美麗孃子。是皇后母弟也。朕心異愛之。冀其名欲傳于後葉奈何。

室屋連依勅而奏可。則科諸國造等、爲衣通郎姫、定藤原部。

十四年秋九月癸丑朔甲子、天皇獵于淡路嶋。時麋鹿・猨・猪、莫々紛々、盈于山谷。焱起蠅散。然終日、以不獲一獸。

於是、獵止以更卜矣。嶋神祟之曰、不得獸者、是我之心也。赤石海底、有眞珠。其珠祠於我、則悉當得獸。

爰更集處々之白水郎、以令探赤石海底。海深不能至底。唯有一海人。曰男狹磯。

Eleventh year [422 CE], spring, third month, fourth day. The emperor went to Chinu Palace. So-tōshi-no-iratsume sang,

Continually
does my lord meet me? No ...
The seaweed on the beach
only comes from time to time.

At that time, the emperor told So-tōshi-no-iratsume, "Do not let anyone else hear this song. If the empress hears it, she will most certainly be greatly vexed." Therefore, people at the time named the seaweed Nanoriso-mo.[11]

Previously, So-tōshi-no-iratsume was in Fujihara Palace. At that time, the emperor decreed to Muraji Ōtomo no Muroya, "We recently obtained a beautiful woman.[xxiv] She is the younger sister of the empress. In Our heart, she is especially beloved. I wish for her name to passed down to future generations. What say you?"

In response to this decree, Muraji Muroya addressed the emperor, and the decree was thus approved. So the various provincial miyatsuko were ordered, on behalf of So-tōshi-no-iratsume, to establish Fujihara hereditary guilds.[12]

The Pearl of Akaishi, Death of the Emperor

Fourteenth year [425 CE], autumn, ninth month, twelfth day. The emperor went hunting on Awaji Island. At that time, there were throngs of large stags, monkeys, and wild boar, as plentiful as grass, filling the mountains and valleys. They rose up like flames and scattered like flies. However, at the end of the day, the emperor could not get quarry of even one animal.

In this circumstance, he stopped the hunt and performed divination. The kami of the island said, "It is by my design that you got no quarry. In the depths of the sea at Akashi there is a pearl.[xxv] If you venerate me with it, you will get all the game you want."

Upon this, the emperor assembled fishermen from various places and made them search the depths of the sea at Akashi. The sea was deep, and most could reach its depths. Yet there was one fisherman called Osashi from

---

11 An attested name for Sargassum seaweed, meaning "do-not-tell seaweed."
12 The guild was promoted to muraji in Tenmu 12.9.

是阿波國長邑之海人也。勝於諸白水郎也。是腰繋繩入海底、差須臾之出曰、於海底有大蝮、其處光也。

諸人皆曰、嶋神所請之珠、殆有是蝮腹乎。亦入而探之。爰男狹磯、抱大蝮而泛出之。乃息絶、以死浪上。既而下繩測海深、六十尋。則割蝮。實眞珠有腹中。其大如桃子。乃祠嶋神而獵之。多獲獸也。唯悲男狹磯入海死之、則作墓厚葬。其墓猶今存之。

廿三年春三月甲午朔庚子、立木梨輕皇子爲太子。容姿佳麗。見者自感。同母妹輕大娘皇女、亦艷妙也。太子恆念合大娘皇女。畏有罪而默之。然感情既盛、殆將至死。爰以爲、徒空死者、雖有刑、何得忍乎。遂竊通。乃悒懷少息。因以歌之曰、

阿資臂紀能	あしひきの
椰摩娜烏菟勾利	やまだをつくり
椰摩娜箇彌	やまだかみ
斯哆媚烏和之勢	したびをわしせ
志哆那企貳	したなきに
和餓儺勾菟摩	わがなくつま
箇哆儺企貳	かたなきに
和餓儺勾菟摩	わがなくつま
去鐏去曾	こぞこそ
椰主區泮娜布例	やすくはだふれ

Naga Village in Awa Province, who was better than the other fishermen.[xxvi] He tied a rope around his waist and went into the depths of the sea. After some time he came out and said, "There is a giant abalone in the depths of the sea, and that place shines."

Everyone said, "The pearl spoken of by the island kami is likely in the stomach of that abalone." He went in again and searched. This time, Osashi embraced the giant abalone and came up to the surface. Then he was out of breath and died atop the waves. When they lowered a rope to measure the depth of the sea there, it was sixty fathoms. They then split open the abalone, and indeed there was a pearl as big as a peach in its belly. And so the emperor venerated the kami of the island and went hunting. He got much game. Yet he was saddened that Osashi went into the sea and died, and so he built a tomb and buried him with honors. That tomb still exists even now.

Twenty-third year [434 CE], spring, third month, seventh day. Kinashi-no-karu was named crown prince. He was attractive in appearance, and those who saw him were naturally quite taken. His younger sister by the same mother, Karu-no-ō-iratsume, was also quite beautiful. The crown prince had always wanted to marry Ō-iratsume, but he feared it was a crime and so kept silent.[13] However, the depth of his feelings swelled to the point where he was about to die. At that point he thought, "Rather than suffer an empty death in vain, though it is a crime, what is to be gained by holding back?" And so, in the end, he secretly joined with her. Then his raging passions abated somewhat. Thereby he sang,

> I build a rice paddy in the mountains.
> The mountain is high,
> so I run an irrigation canal underground.
> I cry in secret.
> Oh wife, for whom I cry,
> I am on the verge of tears,
> oh wife, for whom I cry,
> may tonight be the night
> that you caress my skin.

---

13 In ancient Japan, marriage between half-siblings was permitted, but not between full siblings.

廿四年夏六月、御膳羹汁、凝以作氷。天皇異之、卜其所由。卜者曰、有內亂。蓋親々相姦乎。

時有人曰、木梨輕太子、姦同母妹輕大娘皇女。因以、推問焉。辭既實也。太子是爲儲君、不得加刑。則移大娘皇女於伊豫。于時太子歌之曰、

於裒企彌烏	おほきみを
志摩珥波夫利	しまにはぶり
布儺阿摩利	ふなあまり
異餓幣利去牟鋤	いがへりこむぞ
和餓哆々瀰由梅	わがたたみゆめ
去等烏許曾	ことをこそ
哆多瀰等異泮梅	たたみといはめ
和餓菟摩烏由梅	わがつまをゆめ

又歌之曰、

阿摩儀霧	あまだむ
箇留惋等賣	かるをとめ
異哆儺介縻	いたなかば
臂等資利奴陪瀰	ひとしりぬべみ
幡舍能夜摩能	はさのやまの
波刀能	はとの
資哆儺企邇奈勾	したなきになく

卅二年春正月乙亥朔戊子、天皇崩。時年若干。

於是、新羅王聞天皇既崩、而驚愁之。貢上調船八十艘、及種々樂人八十。是泊對馬而大哭。到筑紫亦大哭。泊于難波津、則皆素

Twenty-fourth year [435 CE], summer, sixth month. The soup served to the emperor froze into ice. The emperor thought it strange and divined the reason. The diviner said, "There is chaos in your household, probably sex between full siblings."

At that time someone said, "Crown Prince Kinashi-no-karu had sex with his little sister by the same mother, Imperial Princess Karu-no-ō-iratsume." Thereupon, the matter was investigated, and that person's words turned out to be true. Since he would be the succeeding ruler, the crown prince could not be punished. So the emperor relocated Imperial Princess Karu-no-ō-iratsume to Iyo.^xxvii At that time, the crown prince sang,

Even were my great lord[14]
to be banished to an island,
she would certainly return.
Keep the tatami clean.
Speaking of which,
speaking of tatami,
keep clean, my wife.

Then he sang again:

Maiden of Karu,
if I cry loudly,
people will probably notice,
and so like a dove from Mt. Hasa,
I cry in subdued tones.

Forty-second year [453 CE], spring, first month, fourteenth day. The emperor expired. At the time he was rather old.[15]

When the King of Silla heard that the emperor had expired, he was shocked and grieved. He sent eighty tribute ships and presented eighty people of various schools of song and dance. When they were anchored in Tsushima, they cried loudly. When they reached Tsukushi, they again cried loudly. When they anchored in Naniwa, all of them put on bleached

---

14 "My lord" can refer to either a male or a female. Kinashi-no-karu uses it to refer to Karu-no-ō-iratsume.
15 *Ancient Matters* records Ingyō's death as occurring in the first month, fifteenth day, of the year Wood Horse, at the age of seventy-eight. The date is only one day off, but the *Chronicles* gives Wood Horse as the first year of Ankō's reign.

服之。悉捧御調、且張種々樂器、自難波至于京、或哭泣、或儛歌。遂參會於殯宮也。

　冬十一月、新羅弔使等、喪禮既闋而還之。爰新羅人、恆愛京城傍耳成山・畝傍山。則到琴引坂、顧之曰、宇泥咩巴椰、彌々巴椰。是未習風俗之言語。故訛畝傍山、謂宇泥咩、訛耳成山、謂瀰々耳。

　時倭飼部、從新羅人、聞是辭、而疑之以爲、新羅人通釆女耳。乃返之啓于大泊瀨皇子。

　皇子則悉禁固新羅使者、而推問。時新羅使者啓之曰、無犯釆女。唯愛京傍之兩山而言耳。則知虛言、皆原之。於是、新羅人大恨、更減貢上之物色及船數。

　冬十月庚午朔己卯、葬天皇於河內長野原陵。

穴穗天皇 安康天皇

穴穗天皇、雄朝津間稚子宿禰天皇第二子也。一云、第三子也。母曰忍坂大中姬命。稚淳毛二岐皇子之女也。

　卌二年春正月、天皇崩。

hempen clothing, then they all took up the tribute and prepared their various instruments, and from Naniwa until they reached the capital, they sometimes wailed and cried, and sometimes danced and sang. At last they came to the temporary burial palace.

Winter, eleventh month. The funeral messengers from Silla finished the rites of mourning and were going to return. By then, the people from Silla were completely taken by Mt. Miminashi and Mt. Unebi near the capital.[xxviii] When they reached Kotohiki Slope, they looked back and said, "Ah, Uneme! Ah, Mimi!"[xxix] Being unaccustomed to the language used by people in this land, they corrupted Mt. Unebi and called it "Uneme" and corrupted Mt. Miminashi and said only "Mimi."

At that time, a member of the horse stewards hereditary guild, the Umakai-be of Yamato, was accompanying the people from Silla. He heard these words and had doubts about these people, thinking, "The people from Silla had intercourse with an inner palace lady, an uneme. And so he went back and reported this to Imperial Prince Ō-hatsuse [Yūryaku].

The imperial prince promptly detained all of the messengers from Silla and investigated. When interrogated, the messengers from Silla said, "We have violated no inner palace lady. We just spoke of our love for the two mountains near the capital." Thus it was known that the horse steward had spoken incorrectly, and all of the messengers were forgiven. However, the people from Silla were greatly resentful and reduced the variety of tribute goods and the number of tribute ships.

Winter, tenth month, tenth day. The emperor was buried in Naga-no-no-hara Tomb in Kōchi.[xxx]

Reign of Emperor Ankō

Emperor Anaho [Ankō] was the second son of Emperor O-asazuma-waku-go-no-sukune [Ingyō].

<small>According to one account, he was the third son.[xxxi]</small>

His mother was Oshi-saka-no-ō-naka-tsu-hime, the daughter of Imperial Prince Waka-nuke-futa-mata.

Forty-second year [453 CE], spring, first month. The emperor expired.

冬十月葬禮畢之。是時、太子行暴虐、淫于婦女。國人謗之。群臣不從。悉隷穴穗皇子。爰太子欲襲穴穗皇子、而密設兵。穴穗皇子、復興兵將戰。故穴穗括箭・輕括箭、始起于此時也。
　時太子知群臣不從、百姓乖違、乃出之、匿物部大前宿禰之家。穴穗皇子、聞則圍之。大前宿禰、出門而迎之。穴穗皇子歌之曰、

　　於朋摩弊　　　　　　おほまへ
　　烏摩弊輸區泥餓　　　をまへすくねが
　　訶那杜加礙　　　　　かなとかげ
　　訶區多智豫羅泥　　　かくたちよらね
　　阿梅多知夜梅牟　　　あめたちやめむ

　　　大前宿禰答歌之曰、
　　瀰椰比等能　　　　　みやひとの
　　阿由臂能古輸孺　　　あゆひのこすず
　　於智珥岐等　　　　　おちにきと
　　瀰椰比等々豫牟　　　みやひととよむ
　　佐杜弭等茂由梅　　　さとびともゆめ

　乃啓皇子曰、願勿害太子。臣將議。由是、太子自死于大前宿禰之家。一云、流伊豫國。
　十二月己巳朔壬午、穴穗皇子、即天皇位、尊皇后曰

ANKŌ PA [453 CE]   471

Winter, tenth month. Burial rites were completed. At that time, the crown prince had committed an atrocity, having been in an obscene relationship with a woman. The people of the land slandered him, and the high government officials did not follow him; they completely supported Imperial Prince Anaho. Such being the case, the crown prince wanted to attack Imperial Prince Anaho and secretly marshaled troops. Imperial Prince Anaho also mustered troops to fight. In preparation for battle, Anaho-style and Karu-style arrows were first created at this time.[16]

At that time, the crown prince knew that the high government officials did not follow him and that the people rebelled against him, and so he went out and hid in the house of Mononobe no Ōmae no Sukune. Imperial Prince Anaho heard about this and surrounded the place. Ōmae no Sukune came out of the gate to meet him. Imperial Prince Anaho sang,

> In the shade of the gate
> of Ōmae no Sukune,
> of Omae,[17]
> come here and stand like this.
> Let us stand and wait out the rain.

Ōmae no Sukune sang in reply:

> A bell tied to the garter
> of a courtier
> has fallen,
> and the courtiers are in a state of uproar.
> Village people, restrain yourselves.

Then he addressed the imperial prince, saying, "I wish for you not to kill the crown prince. I will counsel him." Because of this, the crown prince died of his own accord in the house of Ōmae no Sukune.

According to one account, he was banished to Iyo Province.[xxxii]

Twelfth month, fourteenth day. Imperial Prince Anaho [Ankō] acceded to the imperial throne. The empress was honored with the title of empress

---

16 *Ancient Matters* specifies that Anaho-style arrowheads used iron and Karu-style arrowheads used copper or bronze.
17 *Ancient Matters* gives a double-name Ōmae Omae Sukune, which matches the song here. That suggests that whoever composed the song in the *Chronicles* was cognizant of the name give in *Ancient Matters*. Norinaga suggests that Ōmae Omae refers to two brothers, lit. "Greater Mae" and "Lesser Mae."

皇太后。則遷都于石上。是謂穴穂宮。

　當是時、大泊瀬皇子、欲聘瑞齒別天皇之女等。女名不見諸記。於是、皇女等皆對曰、君王恆暴強也。儵忽忿起、則朝見者夕被殺。夕見者朝被殺。今妾等顔色不秀。加以、情性拙之。若威儀言語、如毫毛不似王意、豈爲親乎。是以、不能奉命。遂遁以不聽矣。

　元年春二月戊辰朔、天皇爲大泊瀬皇子、欲聘大草香皇子妹幡梭皇女。則遣坂本臣祖根使主、請於大草香皇子曰、願得幡梭皇女、以欲配大泊瀬皇子。

　爰大草香皇子對言、僕頃患重病、不得愈。譬如物積船以待潮者。然死之命也。何足惜乎。但以妹幡梭皇女之孤、而不能易死耳。今陛下不嫌其醜、將滿荇菜之數。是甚之大恩也。何辭命辱。故欲呈丹心、捧私寶名押木珠縵、一云、立縵。又云、磐木縵。附所使臣根使主、而敢奉獻。願物雖輕賤、納爲信契。

dowager. The capital was moved to Isonokami, and the palace called Anaho Palace.[xxxiii]

At just that time, Imperial Prince Ō-hatsuse [Yūryaku] wanted to propose to the daughters of Emperor Mitsu-ha-wake [Hanzei].

The names of the girls are not to be found in the various records.[xxxiv]

But the imperial princesses all replied, saying, "Our lord is always violent and terrifying. When he suddenly becomes angry, the person he saw in the morning will be killed in the evening, and the person he saw in the evening will be killed in the morning. Now, our own beauty is not surpassing, nor are we adept. If our words or actions, even in the slightest, do not accord with the prince's desires, how could he ever open his heart to us? On account of this, we cannot comply with this order." In the end, they fled and would not receive him.

First year [454 CE], spring, second month, first day. The emperor wanted the younger sister of Imperial Prince Ō-kusaka, Imperial Princess Hatabi, for Imperial Prince Ō-hatsuse.[18] So he then dispatched the ancestor of the Omi of Sakamoto,[19] Ne no Omi, and asked Imperial Prince Ō-kusaka, saying, "I want to arrange for Imperial Princess Hatabi to marry Imperial Prince Ō-hatsuse."

Imperial Prince Ō-kusaka replied, saying, "These days I have been very ill and have been unable to recover. It is like loading cargo onto a ship and waiting for the tide. However, dying is one with living. So why should I have any regrets? Yet because I will orphan my younger sister Imperial Princess Hatabi, I cannot die freely. Now, my lord, not being repelled by her ugliness, would add her to the flowers of the inner palace. This is an exceedingly great blessing. How could anyone refuse such a gracious order? So, in an effort to show my loyalty, I present my treasure, a jeweled crown in the shape of a tree branch, and send it with your messenger, making so bold as to present it to you.

According to one account, it was in the shape of a climbing vine. Another account says that it was in the shape of a vine on rocks and trees.

I wish that this thing, though it is humble and inconsequential, be received as a sign of our agreement."

---

18 All children of Nintoku. See Nintoku 2.3.
19 A powerful regional lineage group concentrated in the present-day Sakamoto area of Izumi City, Osaka Prefecture. In Tenmu 13.11, they are promoted to ason.

於是、根使主見押木珠縵、感其麗美、以爲盜爲己寶。則詐之奏天皇曰、大草香皇子者不奉命、乃謂臣曰、其雖同族、豈以吾妹、得爲妻耶。既而留縵、入己而不獻。

　於是、天皇信根使主之讒言。則大怒之、起兵圍大草香皇子之家、而殺之。是時、難波吉師日香蛟父子、並仕于大草香皇子。共傷其君无罪而死之、則父抱王頸、二子各執王足、而唱曰、吾君无罪以死之、悲乎。我父子三人、生事之、死不殉、是不臣矣。即自刎之、死於皇尸側。軍衆悉流涕。爰取大草香皇子之妻中蒂姬、納于宮中。因爲妃。復遂喚幡梭皇女、配大泊瀬皇子。是年也、太歲甲午。

　二年春正月癸巳朔己酉、立中蒂姬命爲皇后。甚寵也。初中蒂姬命、生眉輪王於大草香皇子。乃依母以得免罪。常養宮中。

　三年秋八月甲申朔壬辰、天皇爲眉輪王見弒。辭具在大泊瀬天皇紀。三年後、乃葬菅原伏見陵。

Ne no Omi saw the jeweled crown in the shape of a tree branch and was touched by its beauty. So he thought to steal it and make it a treasure of his own.[xxxv] Hence, when addressed the emperor, he lied, saying, "Imperial Prince Ō-kusaka would not accept your order. He told me, 'Being in the same family, how can I make my younger sister into his wife?'"[xxxvi] He kept the crown for himself and did not present it.

The emperor believed the slanderous words of Ne no Omi. Greatly angered, he mustered troops, surrounded the house of Imperial Prince Ō-kusaka, and killed him. At that time, the father Hikaka, Kishi of Naniwa,[20] and his sons were all in service to Imperial Prince Ō-kusaka. They were grievously upset that their lord had died without committing any crime, and so the father held the prince's head, and his two sons each held one of the prince's legs, and they moaned together: "How sad! Our master died though he had committed no crime. We three, father and sons, served him in life, and so if we do not follow him in death, we are not worthy to be his servants." They then cut their own throats and died next to the imperial prince's corpse. The army all shed tears. Thereupon, the emperor took Imperial Prince Ō-kusaka's wife, Naka-shi-hime,[21] and installed her in the inner palace, making her a consort. Also, in the end, he summoned Imperial Princess Hatabi and arranged for her to marry Imperial Prince Ō-hatsu-se [Yūryaku]. This was the year of the Wood Horse.

Second year [455 CE], spring, first month, seventeenth day. Naka-shi-hime was named empress. The emperor exceedingly favored her. Previously, Naka-shi-hime had given birth to Prince Mayowa by Imperial Prince Ō-kusaka. Because of his mother, he escaped punishment, and he was raised in the palace.

Third year [456 CE], autumn, eighth month, ninth day. The emperor was killed by Prince Mayowa.

This is told in detail in the "Annals of Emperor Ō-hatsuse."

After three years, the emperor was buried in Sugawara-no-fushimi Tomb.[xxxvii]

---

20 Later given as the Muraji of Naniwa and the Imiki of Naniwa.
21 A daughter of Richū.

大泊瀨幼武天皇 雄略天皇

　大泊瀨幼武天皇、雄朝嬬稚子宿禰天皇第五子也。天皇産而、神光滿殿。長而伉健過人。
　　三年八月、穴穗天皇、意將沐浴。幸于山宮。遂登樓兮遊目。因命酒兮肆宴。爾乃情盤樂極、間以言談、顧謂皇后去來穗別天皇女曰中蒂姬皇女。更名長田大娘皇女也。大鷦鷯天皇子大草香皇子、娶長田皇女、生眉輪王也。於後、穴穗天皇用根臣讒、殺大草香皇子、而立中蒂姬皇女爲皇后。語在穴穗天皇紀也。曰、吾妹稱妻爲妹、蓋古之俗乎。汝雖親昵、朕畏眉輪王。眉輪王、幼年遊戲樓下、悉聞所談。
　　既而穴穗天皇、枕皇后膝、晝醉眠臥。於是眉輪王、伺其熟睡、而刺殺之。
　　是日、大舍人闕姓字也驟言於天皇曰、穴穗天皇、爲眉輪王見殺。天皇大驚、卽猜兄等、被甲帶刀、率兵自將、逼問八釣白彥皇子。皇子見其欲害、嘿坐不語。天皇乃拔刀而斬。更逼問坂合黑彥皇子。皇子亦

1　In the Japanese vernacular of the period in which the *Chronicles* was written, the sinograph for "sister" could mean either "sister" or "wife."
2　The distinctions between a chief servant and other types of palace servants are given in the Civil and Penal Codes. This servant is here anachronistically categorized since he was attending on the emperor, a restricted duty.

Book 14
Emperor Yūryaku

Murders of Ankō and Rivals of Yūryaku

Emperor Ō-hatsuse-no-waka-take [Yūryaku] was the fifth son of Emperor Ō-asazuma-wakugo-no-sukune [Ingyō].^i When the emperor was born, a divine light filled the palace.^ii When he grew up, his strength exceeded that of other men.

Third year [456 CE], eighth month. Emperor Anaho [Ankō] wanted to bathe and went to a mountain palace. Eventually, he climbed up the tower and enjoyed the view. Thereby he issued an order for wine and held a banquet, where he became flushed with drink. At this he was feeling relaxed and at the height of pleasure. At that moment, he wished to make conversation and turned back toward the empress.

<small>The daughter of Emperor Izaho-wake [Richū] was called Imperial Princess Nakashi-hime. Another name for her was Imperial Princess Nagata-no-ō-iratsume. The son of Emperor Ōsazaki [Nintoku], Imperial Prince Ō-kusaka, married Imperial Princess Nagata, and she gave birth to Prince Mayowa. Later, Emperor Anaho, on the basis of slander by Ne no Omi, killed Imperial Prince Ō-kusaka and named Imperial Princess Nakashi-hime empress. These events are given in the Anaho book.</small>

He told her, "My wife, (Calling one's wife "sister" is perhaps an old custom.¹) although you are quite comfortable and familiar, We fear Prince Mayowa." Prince Mayowa was young and was playing around at the base of the tower, and heard all of this conversation.^iii

Later, the Emperor Anaho [Ankō] was resting his head upon the empress's lap and, having been drinking that afternoon, fell asleep. Prince Mayowa, realizing that the emperor was sound asleep, stabbed and killed him.^iv A chief servant ran and told the emperor [Yūryaku], "Emperor Anaho has been killed by Prince Mayowa."²

<small>The title of nobility of the chief servant is not given.</small>

The emperor, greatly shocked, suspected his brothers. So he put on armor and girded his sword, mustered troops and took command of them himself. Then he interrogated Imperial Prince Yatsuri-no-shiro-hiko.³ ^v The imperial prince saw that he was going to be killed, and so kept silent and said nothing. The emperor then drew his sword and cut him down. Then he interrogated Imperial Prince Sakai-no-kuro.⁴ ^vi The imperial prince also

---

3 The fourth son of Ingyō, Yūryaku's full brother.
4 The second son of Ingyō, Yūryaku's full brother.

知將害、嘿坐不語。天皇忿怒彌盛。乃復幷爲欲殺眉輪王、案劾所由。眉輪王曰、臣元不求天位。唯報父仇而已。

坂合黑彥皇子、深恐所疑、竊語眉輪王。遂共得間、而出逃入圓大臣宅。

天皇使々乞之。大臣以使報曰、蓋聞、人臣有事、逃入王室。未見君王隱匿臣舍。方今坂合黑彥皇子與眉輪王、深恃臣心、來臣之舍。詎忍送歟。由是、天皇復益興兵、圍大臣宅。

大臣出立於庭、索脚帶。時大臣妻、持來脚帶、愴矣傷懷而歌曰、

飫瀰能古簸	おみのこは
多倍能波伽摩嗚	たへのはかまを
那々陛嗚絁	ななへをし
儞播儞陀々始諦	にはにたたして
阿遙比那陀須暮	あよひなだすも

大臣裝束已畢、進軍門跪拜曰、臣雖被戮、莫敢聽命。古人有云、匹夫之志、難可奪、方屬乎臣。伏願、大王奉獻臣女韓媛與葛城宅七區、請以贖罪。天皇不許、縱火燔宅。

於是、大臣與黑彥皇子眉輪王、俱被燔死。時坂合部連

knew that he was going to be killed, and so kept silent and said nothing. The emperor, overflowing with rage, was also going to kill Prince Mayowa as well. He asked him why he had done it. Prince Mayowa said, "From the start, I never sought the imperial throne. I wanted only to avenge my father."

Imperial Prince Sakai-no-kuro was afraid of the emperor's deep suspicion of him and secretly told Prince Mayowa about it. In the end, together they seized a moment when no one was around and went out, escaping to the house of the Ō-omi Tsubura.[vii]

The emperor sent a messenger to make inquiry. The Ō-omi, via the messenger, reported back to the emperor, saying, "I have heard of a vassal who in some circumstance might flee to the manor of his lord. But I have yet to see a lord who hides himself in the house of his vassal. At present, Imperial Prince Sakai-no-kuro and Prince Mayowa have placed their trust deep in my heart and come to my house. How can I bear to render them to you?" Upon this, the emperor mustered even more troops and surrounded the house of the Ō-omi.

The Ō-omi came out and stood in the courtyard and asked for his garters. At that time, the Ō-omi's wife brought them, and in heart-rending sadness, sang,

> The minister, my husband,
> puts on many layers
> of trousers made from mulberry bark.
> Standing in the courtyard,
> he ties his garters.[5]

The Ō-omi finished dressing himself, came out of the gate, and prostrated himself, saying, "Though it be a crime, I cannot comply with your order. There is a saying among the people of old: 'It is difficult to steal away the will of even a common man.'[viii] Truly, this is how it is with me. I prostrate myself and ask my lord that I may present to you my daughter, Kara-hime, and seven of my residences in Kazuraki, and seek forgiveness for this crime."[ix] The emperor would not permit it, and so he lit a fire and burned down the house.

As a result, the Ō-omi, Imperial Prince Sakai-no-kuro, and Prince Mayowa were together burned to death. At the time, the Muraji of the Sakai-

---

5 Wearing multiple layers of clothing and tying up one's cuffs suggests preparing for battle.

贄宿禰、抱皇子屍而見燔死。其舍人等、闕名。收取所燒、遂難擇骨。盛之一棺、合葬新漢擬本南丘。擬字未詳。蓋是槻乎。

　冬十月癸未朔、天皇、恨穴穗天皇曾欲以市邊押磐皇子、傅國而遙付囑後事、乃使人於市邊押磐皇子、陽期狡獵、勸遊郊野曰、近江狹々城山君韓帒言、今於近江來田綿蚊屋野、猪鹿多有。其戴角類枯樹末。其聚脚如弱木株。呼吸氣息、似於朝霧。願與皇子、孟冬作陰之月、寒風肅殺之晨、將逍遙於郊野、聊娛情以騁射。市邊押磐皇子、乃隨馳獵。

　於是、大泊瀨天皇、彎弓驟馬、而陽呼曰猪有、即射殺市邊押磐皇子。

　皇子帳內佐伯部賣輪、更名仲手子。抱屍駭惋、不解所由。反側呼號、往還頭脚。天皇尚誅之。

　是月、御馬皇子、以曾善三輪君身狹故、思欲遣慮而往。不意、道逢邀軍、於三輪磐井側逆戰。不久被捉。臨刑指井而詛曰、此水者百姓唯得飲焉。王者獨不能飲矣。

6　The duties of the border hereditary guild (sakaai-be, sakai-be) are unclear. Perhaps they were involved with determining administrative units, or were responsible for providing for Sakai-no-kuro's upbringing. *New Selected Records* gives them as descendants of Nie, eighth-generation descendant of Ho-no-akari. The Muraji of the Sakai was promoted to sukune in Tenmu 13.12.
7　Yūryaku's cousin and the oldest son of Richū.

be,[6] Nie no Sukune, held the imperial prince's corpse in his arms and was killed by the flames. The servants collected the burnt remains, but in the end could not separate the bones.

> The names of the servants are not given.

They gathered the bones in one coffin and buried them together at the hill south of Tsukimoto in Imakinoaya.[x]

> The reading of the character used for "tsuki" is still not clear, but it is probably "tsuki."

Winter, tenth month, first day. The emperor resented that previously, Emperor Anaho [Ankō] had wanted to pass rule of the land to Imperial Prince Ichi-no-he-no-oshiwa[7] and to entrust to him matters of the future. So he sent a messenger to Imperial Prince Ichi-no-he-no-oshiwa, who falsely promised to go on a hunt together. He invited the latter out to the fields, saying, "The Kimi of Sasaki Mountain in Ōmi, Karafukuro, told me, 'Right now at Kayano, in Kutawata of Ōmi, there are many wild boar and deer.[xi] Their tusks and antlers rise up like the branches of dead trees, their legs clump together like bushes, and their breath issues forth like morning fog.' I want to go with the imperial prince during the brisk tenth month, when the chill of the wind remains slight, find diversion in the fields, and lightly amuse ourselves with some mounted shooting." Imperial Prince Ichi-no-he-no-oshiwa by and by joined him for the hunt.

Emperor Ō-hatsuse-no-waka-take [Yūryaku] drew his bow, galloped his horse, and falsely called out, "A boar!" Then he shot Imperial Prince Ichi-no-he-no-oshiwa dead.

The imperial prince's servant, Uruwa of the Saeki hereditary guild, held the corpse in his arms, panted in panic, and did not know what to do.[8] He writhed in agony and cried out the imperial prince's name, and paced back and forth beside the corpse. The emperor killed him too.

That month, Imperial Prince Mima,[9] since he had previously been on good terms with Musa, Kimi of Miwa, went to confide in him his feelings. Unexpectedly, he met with an ambushing force, and they fought near Iwa Well in Miwa.[xii] After a short while, he was captured. As he was about to be put to death, he pointed at the well and cursed it, saying, "This water can be drunk only by the people. No lord can drink from it."

---

8   An original note adds, "Another name for Uruwa was Nakachiko." This name appears later in the Kenzō and Ninken books. His posting is glossed as "servant," but the characters refer to a servant who worked for a prince of the blood.
9   Ichi-no-he-no-oshiwa's full brother.

十一月壬子朔甲子、天皇命有司、設壇於泊瀨朝倉、即天皇位。遂定宮焉。以平群臣眞鳥爲大臣。以大伴連室屋・物部連目爲大連。

元年春三月庚戌朔壬子、立草香幡梭姫皇女爲皇后。更名橘姫皇女。

是月、立三妃。元妃葛城圓大臣女曰韓媛。生白髮武廣國押稚日本根子天皇與稚足姫皇女。更名栲幡娘姫皇女。是皇女侍伊勢大神祠。

10 Perhaps the son of Tsuku no Sukune.
11 From the late fifth century to the early seventh century, the two titles of Ō-omi and Ō-muraji were given to the highest appointed officials in the Yamato state. In the *Chronicles*, Ō-omi is used for Takeuchi no Sukune in Seimu 1.5, but its meaning in reference to a specific office emerged around the time mentioned here. The Ō-omi came from the most powerful omi lineages: Kazuraki, Soga, Heguri, and Kose, whose names originate

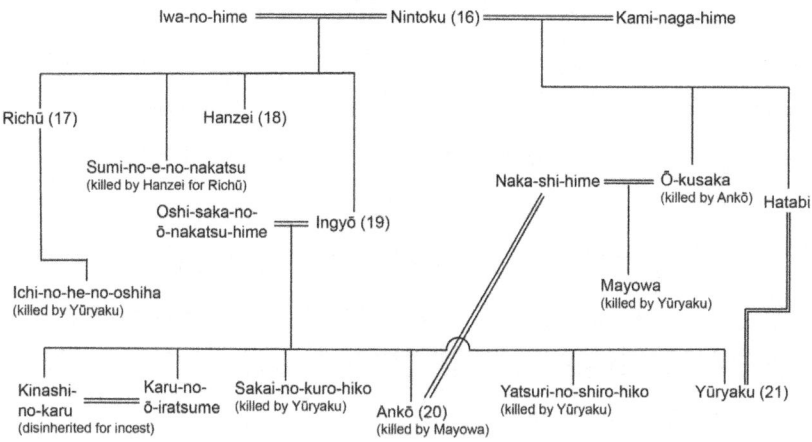

FIGURE 13 Assassinations leading to accession of Yūryaku

Accession of Emperor Yūryaku

Eleventh month, thirteenth day. The emperor ordered the officials to build a dais in Asakura at Hatsuse and there acceded to the imperial throne.[xiii] Then he established his palace. The Omi of Heguri, Matori,[10] was named Ō-omi. The Muraji of the Ōtomo, Muroya, and the Muraji of the Mononobe, Me, were named Ō-muraji.[11]

First year [457 CE], spring, third month, third day. Imperial Princess Kusaka-no-hatabi-hime was named empress.[12]

That month, three consorts were established. The first was the daughter of Ō-omi Tsubura of Kazuraki, Kara-hime. She gave birth to Emperor Shiraka-no-take-hiro-kuni-oshi-waka-yamato-neko [Seinei] and Imperial Princess Waka-tarashi-hime.[13] This imperial princess serves at the shrine for the great kami of Ise.[xiv]

---

from place-names in the Nara Basin and who in lore are all descended from Takeuchi no Sukune. The Ō-muraji came from the Ōtomo and Mononobe muraji lineage groups and were allied miyatsuko associated with performing military duties for the Yamato court. This is the first appearance of the title Ō-muraji in the *Chronicles*.

12 An original note adds, "Another name was Imperial Princess Tachibana-hime." She was the daughter of Nintoku and the younger sister of Imperial Prince Ō-kusaka.

13 An original note adds, "Another name was Imperial Princess Taku-hata-hime."

次有吉備上道臣女稚媛。一本云、吉備窪屋臣女。生二男。長曰磐城皇子。少曰星川稚宮皇子。見下文。次有春日和珥臣深目女。曰童女君。生春日大娘皇女。更名高橋皇女。

童女君者本是采女。天皇與一夜而脈。遂生女子。天皇疑不養。

及女子行步、天皇御大殿。物部目大連侍焉。女子過庭。目大連顧謂群臣曰、麗哉、女子。古人有云。娜毗騰耶幡麼珥。此古語未詳。徐步清庭者、言誰女子。

天皇曰、何故問耶。

目大連對曰、臣觀女子行步、容儀能似天皇。

天皇曰、見此者咸言、如卿所噵。然朕與一宵而脈。產女殊常、由是生疑。

大連曰、然則一宵喚幾廻乎。

天皇曰、七廻喚之。

大連曰、此娘子、以清身意奉與一宵。安輒生疑、嫌他有潔。臣聞、易產腹者、以褌觸體、即便懷脈。況與終宵而、妄生疑也。天皇命大連、以女子爲皇女、以母爲妃。是年也、大歲丁酉。

14 Kuboya is not seen elsewhere. There was a Kuboya District in Okayama Prefecture, present-day Tsukubo District.
15 The note refers to Hoshi-kawa's rebellion. Hoshi-kawa may refer to a place in present-day Tenri City.

Next was the daughter of the Omi of Kamitsumichi of Kibi, Waka-hime.

<small>According to one account, she was the daughter of the Omi of Kuboya of Kibi.¹⁴</small>

She gave birth to two sons. The older was called Imperial Prince Iwaki. The younger was called Imperial Prince Hoshi-kawa-no-waka-miya.

<small>Seen below.¹⁵</small>

Next was the daughter of Fukame, Omi of the Kasuga Wani, called Omina-gimi.^XV She gave birth to Imperial Princess Kasuga-no-ō-iratsume.¹⁶

Omina-gimi was originally an inner palace lady.¹⁷ The emperor was with her for one night, and she became pregnant, later giving birth to a girl. The emperor had doubts and did not raise the girl.

When the girl could walk, the emperor moved her to the palace. Ō-muraji Mononobe no Me was attending on him when the girl passed by the courtyard. Ō-omi Me turned to the high government officials and told them, "How beautiful that girl is. People of old would say, 'Na hito ya haha ni.' (The meaning of this old phrase is still unclear.) Whose child is that calmly walking in the pristine courtyard?"

The emperor said, "Why do you ask?"

Ō-muraji Me replied, saying, "When I saw that girl walk, her gait resembled that of the emperor."

The emperor said, "People who see her all say the same as you. However, I was with her mother for just one night, and then she became pregnant. Such being the case, her giving birth to the girl was unusual, so I have my doubts."

The Ō-muraji said, "Yet in that one night, how many times did you summon her?"

The emperor said, "I summoned her seven times."

The Ō-muraji said, "This noble lady was of pure body and mind, and served the emperor, staying with him for one night. How can you so easily doubt and bear ill will toward one of pure body? I hear that for those who are easy to impregnate, if you brush against them with your pants, they will be with child. How can you wildly cast doubt upon one with whom you were with all night?" The emperor ordered the Ō-muraji to name the girl an imperial princess and her mother a consort. This was the year of the Fire Chicken.

---

16 An original note adds, "Another name was Imperial Princess Takahashi." She would be empress to Ninken. Takahashi is a place-name in Yamato, like Wani and Kasuga.

17 Inner palace ladies were often from regional elites. Thus Omina-gimi is exceptional in that she is from the Yamato-based Omi of the Kasuga Wani.

二年秋七月、百濟池津媛、違天皇將幸、婬於石河楯。舊本云、石河股合首祖楯。天皇大怒、詔大伴室屋大連、使來目部張夫婦四支於木、置假庪上、以火燒死。百濟新撰云、己巳年、蓋鹵王立。天皇遣阿禮奴跪、來索女郎。百濟莊飾慕尼夫人女、曰適稽女郎。貢進於天皇。

冬十月辛未朔癸酉、幸于吉野宮。丙子、幸御馬瀬。命虞人縱獵。凌重巘赴長莽。未及移影、獮什七八。每獵大獲。鳥獸將盡。遂旋憩乎林泉。相羊乎藪澤、息行夫展車馬。問群臣曰、獵場之樂、使膳夫割鮮。何與自割。群臣忽莫能對。於是、天皇大怒、拔刀斬御者大津馬飼。

是日、車駕至自吉野宮。國內居民、咸皆振怖。由是、皇太后與皇后、聞之大懼。使倭采女日媛擧酒迎進。天皇見采女面貌端麗、形容温雅、乃和顏悅色曰、朕豈不欲覩汝妍咲、乃相携手、入於後宮。

Hunts in Yoshino and Kazuraki

Second year [458 CE], autumn, seventh month. Ike-tsu-hime of Paekche, whom the emperor had meant to summon for himself, defied him and had intercourse with Ishikawa no Tate.

_{According to older writings, the ancestor of the Obito of Komura in Ishikawa was called Tate.¹⁸}

The emperor was greatly enraged and decreed to Ō-muraji Ōtomo no Muroya to use the Kume hereditary guild to place her atop a raised observation platform, bind her four limbs to trees, and light a fire to roast her to death.

_{According to the *New Compiled Records of Paekche*, in the year of the Earth Snake [429 or 489 CE], King Kaero became king of Paekche. The emperor dispatched Arenako, who went seeking a lady. Paekche made up the daughter of Madam Muni, called Lady Chiyakukei. She was presented to the emperor.[xvi]}

Winter, tenth month, third day. The emperor went to Yoshino Palace. On the sixth day, he went to Mimase. He gave orders to the mountain game wardens and hunted as he pleased.[xvii] He climbed layers of peaks and passed through tall grassy fields, and before the shadows stirred at sunset, he got seven or eight out of ten of his quarries. Every time he hunted, he got a lot of game, and he tried to exhaust the supply of birds and beasts. At last he came around to a spring in a grove and rested. He walked along the thickets and by the waters, made his hunting attendants rest, and checked on the carriage horses. He asked the high government officials, "The joy of hunting is making the cooks prepare fresh food, but why don't we prepare it ourselves?" The high government officials could not promptly reply. At that, the emperor was greatly enraged, loosed his sword, and cut down an attendant, the horse steward of Ōtsu.[xviii]

That day the emperor came back from Yoshino Palace. The people of the land all trembled in fear. The empress dowager and the empress too, who had heard of the incident, were afraid, and sent an inner palace lady from Yamato, Hi-no-hime, to serve him wine and greet him.¹⁹ The emperor saw that the inner palace lady shone with beauty, and her figure radiated dignity. He said, "How could We not wish to look upon your beautiful smile?" Then they joined hands and she was placed in the inner palace.

---

18 In Nintoku 41.3, a relative of the King of Paekche hides with the Obito of the brocade weavers of Ishikawa. This entry is evidence that there is a strong connection between the Paekche royal family and the Ishikawa lineage group.

19 The empress dowager is Yūryaku's mother, Oshi-saka-no-ō-naka-tsu-hime, and the empress is Kusaka-no-hatabi-hime. Hi-no-hime, a younger sister of Agoko, Provincial Miyatsuko of Yamato, is presented to Richū in the pre-accession record of Richū.

語皇太后曰、今日遊獵、大獲禽獸。欲與群臣割鮮野饗、歷問群臣、莫能有對。故朕嚊焉。
　皇太后知斯詔情、奉慰天皇曰、群臣不悟陛下因遊獵場、置宍人部、降問群臣。群臣嘿然、理、且難對。今貢未晚。以我爲初。膳臣長野、能作宍膾。願以此貢。
　天皇跪禮而受曰、善哉。鄙人所云、貴相知心、此之謂也。
　皇太后觀天皇悅、歡喜盈懷。更欲貢人曰、我之厨人菟田御戸部眞鋒田高天、以此二人、請將加貢、爲宍人部。
　自茲以後、大倭國造吾子籠宿禰、貢狹穗子鳥別、爲宍人部。臣連伴造國造又隨續貢。
　是月、置史戸・河上舍人部。天皇、以心爲師。誤殺人衆。天下誹謗言、大惡天皇也。唯所愛寵、史部身狹村主靑・檜隈民使博德等。
　三年夏四月、阿閉臣國見、更名磯特牛。譖栲幡皇女與湯人廬城部連武彥曰、武彥奸皇女而使任身。湯人、此云臾衞。

The emperor told the empress dowager, "During today's hunt, I got many birds and beasts. I wanted to prepare fresh food with the high government officials and have an outdoor banquet, but when I asked all the high government officials about the idea, not one could respond to me. Therefore, We were angry."

The empress dowager understood the sense of this pronouncement and consoled the emperor, saying, "The high government officials did not understand that they were being asked about setting up an hereditary guild of butchers[20] where my lord was hunting. It is only natural that the high government officials kept silent, for it was difficult for them to respond. But now it is not too late to present one. I will start. The Omi of my cooks, Nagano, is skilled at preparing fresh food.[xix] I wish to present him to you."

The emperor bowed and received him, saying, "Wonderful! Perhaps this is what the common people mean when they say 'The nobility know each other's minds.'"

The empress dowager saw that the emperor was pleased, and her bosom was filled with gladness. Again intending to present people, she said, "I also present, from my kitchen staff, Uda no Mitobe and Masakita Takame, and ask that they be made part of the hereditary guild of butchers."[xx]

After this, Agoko no Sukune, the provincial chieftain of Yamato, presented Kotori-wake of Saho for the hereditary guild of butchers.[xxi] Accordingly, the omi, muraji, allied miyatsuko, and provincial miyatsuko[21] all presented people.

That month, the hereditary guilds of scribes and of servants from Kawakami were set up.[xxii] The emperor, acting on impulse, killed many people by mistake. He showed favor only to the Suguri of Musa, Ao, and the Tami no Tsukai of Hinokuma, Hakatoko, from the hereditary guild of scribes.[xxiii]

Third year [459 CE], summer, fourth month. Omi of Ahe, Kunimi, defamed Imperial Princess Takuhata and the Muraji of the Ioki hereditary guild of bath attendants, Takehiko, saying, "Takehiko raped the imperial princess and impregnated her."[22]

Another name for Kunimi was Shikotohi.

---

20 The Shishi-be also appears in the original note at the end of Yūryaku 7. Perhaps this group focused on meat and poultry, in contrast to the Kashiwade or cooks, who may have focused on fish.
21 This phrase appears here for the first time and is used in the *Chronicles* to refer to the constituent powerful lineage groups that formed the Yamato Court.
22 Kunimi is not seen elsewhere. Imperial Princess Taku-hata is an alternative name for Waka-tarashi-hime, according to the note in Yūryaku 1.3. Yūryaku's daughter by his consort Kara-hime, she served at the Ise Grand Shrine. Takehiko is not seen elsewhere. The Ioki hereditary guild appears across Japan.

武彥之父枳莒喩、聞此流言、恐禍及身。誘率武彥於廬城河、僞使鸕鷀沒水捕魚、因其不意而打殺之。

天皇聞遣使者、案問皇女。皇女對言、妾不識也。俄而皇女齋持神鏡、詣於五十鈴河上、伺人不行、埋鏡經死。

天皇疑皇女不在、恆使闇夜東西求覓。乃於河上虹見如蛇、四五丈者。掘虹起處、而獲神鏡。移行未遠、得皇女屍。割而觀之、腹中有物如水。水中有石。

枳莒喩、由斯、得雪子罪。還悔殺子、報殺國見。逃匿石上神宮。

四年春二月、天皇射獵於葛城山。忽見長人。來望丹谷。面貌容儀、相似天皇。天皇知是神、猶故問曰、何處公也。

長人對曰、現人之神。先稱王諱。然後應噵。

天皇答曰、朕是幼武尊也。

長人次稱曰、僕是一事主神也。

遂與盤于遊田、驅逐一鹿、相辭發箭、竝轡馳騁。言詞恭恪、有若逢仙。於是、日晚田罷。

23 Kikoyu, Muraji of the Ioki hereditary guild, appears later in Ankan 1.12. That may not be the same person.
24 Early commentators suggested that this mirror was the divine mirror venerated at the Ise Shrine.
25 Commentators disagree about whether it was Kikoyu or Kunimi who hid; the text is ambiguous.

Takehiko's father, Kikoyu,[23] heard this rumor and feared the disaster would spread to himself. He summoned Takehiko and led him to the Ioki River, then deceived him, pretending to be like a cormorant diving into the river to catch fish. Thereby catching him unawares, he struck and killed him.[xxiv]

The emperor heard about this and dispatched a messenger to interrogate the imperial princess. The imperial princess replied, "I don't know anything." Soon thereafter, the imperial princess took a divine mirror,[24] went to the area of the Isuzu River, waited for a time when no one was around, buried the mirror, and hanged herself.

The emperor had doubts about the disappearance of the imperial princess and had her searched for everywhere in the dark of night. Then near the Isuzu River they saw a rainbow that looked like a snake, forty or fifty feet long. They dug at the source of the rainbow and obtained the divine mirror. Not far off, they found the imperial princess's corpse. When they opened her up, there was something like water in her belly. Inside the water was a stone.

Hence, Kikoyu was able to atone for his son's crime. Yet he regretted killing his son, and in revenge planned to kill Kunimi, who fled and hid in Isonokami Shrine.[25]

Fourth year [460 CE], spring, second month. The emperor went hunting at Mt. Kazuraki. Suddenly, he saw a tall person. The emperor came, and they gazed at each other across the gorge. The person's face and figure resembled those of the emperor.[xxv] The emperor, though he knew this was a kami, still thus asked them, "What lord are you?"

The tall one answered, "I am a kami made manifest.[26] First the prince should say his name, then I shall speak afterward."

The emperor replied, saying, "We are Wakatake no mikoto."

The tall one then addressed him, saying, "I am Hito-koto-nushi no kami."[xxvi]

Eventually, they came to enjoy hunting together. When chasing a single deer, each deferred the first shot to the other. They raced their horses bit alongside bit.[xxvii] Their words were deferential and respectful, as when two sages meet one another. Thus day passed into night, and the

---

26 This expression is used in the *Chronicles* to refer to the emperor, for example, by Yamato Take in Keikō 40.

神侍送天皇、至來目水。是時、百姓咸言、有德天皇也。

秋八月辛卯朔戊申、行幸吉野宮。庚戌、幸于河上小野。命虞人駈獸。欲躬射而待。虻疾飛來、嚙天皇臂。於是、蜻蛉忽然飛來、噛虻將去。天皇嘉厥有心、詔群臣曰、爲朕讃蜻蛉歌賦之。

群臣莫能敢賦者。天皇乃口號曰、

野麼等能	やまとの
嗚武羅能陀該儞	をむらのたけに
之々符須登	ししふすと
拕例柯	たれか
擧能居登	このこと
飫裒磨陛儞麻嗚須	おほまへにまをす
一本、以飫裒磨陛儞麼嗚須、易飫裒枳彌儞麻嗚須。	あるふみに、おほまへにまをすをもちて、おほきみにまをすにかふ
飫裒枳瀰簸	おほきみは
贼據嗚枳舸斯題	そこをきかして
柂磨々枳能	たままきの
阿娛羅儞陀々伺	あぐらにたたし
一本、以陀々伺、易伊麻伺也。	あるふみに、たたしをもちて、いましにかふ
施都魔枳能	しつまきの
阿娛羅儞陀々伺	あぐらにたたし
斯々魔都登	ししまつと
倭我伊麻西麼	わがいませば
佐謂麻都登	さるまつと
倭我陀々西麼	わがたたせば
陀俱符羅爾	たくぶらに
阿武柯枳都枳	あむかきつき
曾能阿武嗚	そのあむを
婀枳豆波野俱譬	あきづはやくひ
波賦武志謀	はふむしも
飫裒枳瀰儞磨都羅符	おほきみにまつらふ
儺我柯陀播	ながかたは
於柯武	おかむ
婀岐豆斯麻野麻登	あきづしまやまと
一本、以婆賦武志謀以下、易舸矩能御等、儺儞於婆武登、蘇羅瀰豆、野麼等能矩儞嗚、婀岐豆斯麻登以符。	あるふみに、はふむしもよりしもをもちて、かくのごと なにおはむ とそらみつ やまとのくにを あきづしまといふにかふ

hunt ended. The kami saw the emperor off, and they came to the Kume River.[xxviii] There the people all said, "What a virtuous emperor."

Autumn, eighth month, eighteenth day. The emperor went to Yoshino Palace. On the twentieth day, the emperor went to the small field at Kawakami.[xxix] He ordered the mountain wardens to chase out some game. He waited to shoot his arrow. Suddenly, a gadfly quickly flew over and bit the emperor's elbow. Thereupon a dragonfly flew over, bit the gadfly, and flew off with it. The emperor was pleased by this considerate action and decreed to the high government officials, "Compose Us a song praising the dragonfly."

The high government officials did not have anyone skilled at composing songs. So the emperor sang to himself:

> On Mt. Omura
> in Yamato,
> the deer and boar are lying down.
> Who thus
> addresses their sovereign?
> (One version says "great lord" instead of "sovereign.")
> Hearing this,
> the great lord—
> sitting on a chair,
> (One version says "seated" instead of "sitting.")
> bedecked with jewels;
> sitting on a chair,
> bedecked with cloths of Yamato—
> says, "Wait on the deer and boar."
> I prepare myself,
> saying "Wait on the boar."
> I rise,
> when on the flesh of my arm
> a gadfly bites me.
> A dragonfly swiftly eats
> the gadfly.
> Even the crawling insects
> serve the great lord.
> I will leave you
> something to be remembered by,
> Yamato, island of the dragonfly.[xxx]

因讚蜻蛉、名此地爲蜻蛉野。

五年春二月、天皇狡獵于葛城山。靈鳥忽來。其大如雀。尾長曳地。而且鳴曰、努力々々。

俄而見逐嗔猪、從草中暴出逐人。獵徒緣樹大懼。天皇詔舍人曰、猛獸逢人則止。宜逆射而且刺。舍人性儒弱、緣樹失色、五情無主。嗔猪直來、欲噬天皇。天皇用弓刺止、擧脚踏殺。於是、田罷、欲斬舍人。舍人臨刑、而作歌曰、

野須瀰斯志	やすみしし
倭我飫袁枳瀰能	わがおほきみの
阿蘇麼斯志	あそばしし
斯斯能	ししの
宇拖枳舸斯固瀰	うたきかしこみ
倭我尼导能袁利志	わがにげのぼりし
阿理嗚能宇倍能	ありをのうへの
婆利我曳陀	はりがえだ
阿西嗚	あせを

皇后聞悲、興感止之。詔曰、皇后不與天皇、而顧舍人。

對曰、國人皆謂陛下、安野而好獸。無乃不可乎。今陛下以嗔猪故、而斬舍人。陛下譬無異於豺狼也。

天皇乃與皇后上車歸。呼萬歳曰、樂哉。人皆

He thus praised the dragonfly. Accordingly, that place was named Akizu-no-ono, or Small Field of the Dragonfly."[xxxi]

Fifth year [461 CE], spring, second month.[xxxii] The emperor was hunting at Mt. Kazuraki when a mysterious bird suddenly appeared. Its size was like that of a sparrow. It had a long tail that dragged on the ground. It also cried, "On your guard! On your guard!"

All of a sudden, a wild boar that they had been pursuing unexpectedly came out of the grass and chased people. The hunting retinue climbed trees and were sorely afraid. The emperor decreed to his servants, "A raging beast stops when it meets a human. Shoot at it! Stab it!" The servants were cowardly and weak in demeanor. They climbed the trees and blanched in fear, losing all control of their senses. The boar came straight at the emperor and tried to bite him. The emperor thrust his bow to bring it to a halt, lifted his leg, and stomped, killing it. When the hunt was over, he wanted to kill the servants. The servants, facing punishment, made a song, saying,

> Afraid of the growl of the wild boar
> during the hunt
> of our great lord,
> we climbed to escape,
> into the branches of the alder tree
> atop the hill.
> Oh, you![27]

Then the empress heard this and was sad, and being moved, wanted to bring an end to the hunt. The emperor proclaimed, "The empress is not with the emperor on this, but is concerned about the servants."[xxxiii]

She replied, saying, "The people of the land all say about our liege, 'He enjoys the hunt and loves the boar.' Is this not dreadful? Now my liege is going to kill his servants because of a wild boar. My liege, are you then no different from a wolf?"

The emperor then got in his carriage with the empress and returned home. To the cry of "Banzai!" the emperor said, "How amusing! The people

---

27 The poem appears to be praising the tree, to whom the final line of the poem is addressed, for saving the servants from the boar.

獵禽獸。朕獵得善言而歸。

　　夏四月、百濟加須利君、蓋鹵王也。飛聞池津媛之所燔殺、適稽女郎也。而籌議曰、昔貢女人爲采女。而既無禮、失我國名。自今以後、不合貢女。乃告其弟軍君崑支君也。曰、汝宜往日本以事天皇。

　　軍君對曰、上君之命不可奉違。願賜君婦、而後奉遣。

　　加須利君、則以孕婦、嫁與軍君曰、我之孕婦、既當產月。若於路產、冀載一船、隨至何處、速令送國。遂與辭訣、奉遣於朝。

　　六月丙戌朔、孕婦果如加須利君言、於筑紫各羅嶋產兒。仍名此兒曰嶋君。於是。軍君、即以一船、送嶋君於國。是爲武寧王。百濟人呼此嶋曰主嶋也。

　　秋七月、軍君入京。既而有五子。百濟新撰云、辛丑年、蓋鹵王遣弟昆支君、向大倭、侍天王。以脩兄王之好也。

　　六年春二月壬子朔乙卯、天皇遊乎泊瀨小野。觀山野之體勢、慨然興感歌曰、

have all hunted birds and beasts. We have hunted and have gotten some good words. And now We return."

Summer, fourth month. Kasuri no Kishi of Paekche heard the news that Ike-tsu-hime had been burned to death, and took counsel, saying, "Of old, we presented women as inner palace ladies.

<small>Kasuri[28] no Kishi is King Kaero and Iketsu-hime is Lady Chŏkkye.</small>

However, this is insulting, and our state has lost face. From now on, we should not present women." Then he told to his younger brother the Konikishi, "Go to Yamato and serve the emperor."

<small>The Konikishi is the Koniki.[29]</small>

The Konikishi replied, "I cannot go against my lord's orders. I wish my lord to bestow upon me one of his ladies; send her later."

Kasuri no Kishi accordingly took one of his pregnant ladies, made her marry the Konikishi, and said, "My lady is pregnant and is already at the month when she will give birth. If she gives birth en route, I want you to put them in one boat and, from wherever you have arrived, quickly send them back to our land." At last they took their leave from each other, and he came to serve in the court.

Sixth month, first day. The pregnant lady, just as Kasuri no Kishi had said, gave birth to a child in Tsukushi at Kakara Island.[xxxiv] So this child was named Sema-kishi. The Konikishi put them on the same boat and returned Sema-kishi to their land. This child is King Muryŏng.[xxxv] The people of Paekche all called this island Nirimu-sema, or King Island.

Autumn, seventh month. The Konikishi entered the capital. After some time, he had five sons.

<small>According to the *New Compiled Records of Paekche*, in the year of the Metal Ox [461 CE], King Kaero dispatched his younger brother the Koniki-kishi, who went to Yamato and served the heavenly king. Thereby he earned the favor of his elder the king.[xxxvi]</small>

Sixth year [462 CE], spring, second month, fourth day. The emperor was recreating at a small field in Hatsuse. Looking upon the mountain scenery, he was deeply moved and sang,

---

28 Perhaps a transliteration of Kaero or of Kaero's birth name, Kyŏngsa.
29 Both are royal titles of Paekche.

舉暮利矩能	こもりくの
播都制能野麼播	はつせのやまは
伊底挓智能	いでたちの
與慮斯企野麼	よろしきやま
和斯里底能	わしりでの
與盧斯企夜磨能	よろしきやまの
據暮利矩能	こもりくの
播都制能夜麼播	はつせのやまは
阿野儞于羅虞波斯	あやにうらぐはし
阿野儞于羅虞波斯	あやにうらぐはし

於是、名小野、曰道小野。

三月辛巳朔丁亥、天皇欲使后妃親桑、以勸蠶事。爰命螺蠃螺蠃、人名也。此云須我屢。聚國内蠶。於是、螺蠃、誤聚嬰兒、奉獻天皇。天皇大咲、賜嬰兒於螺蠃曰、汝宜自養。螺蠃即養嬰兒於宮墻下。仍賜姓、爲少子部連。

夏四月、吳國遣使貢獻也。

七年秋七月甲戌朔丙子、天皇詔少子部連螺蠃曰、朕欲見三諸岳神之形。或云、此山之神爲大物主神也。或云、菟田墨坂神也。汝膂力過人。自行捉來。

螺蠃答曰、試往捉之。乃登三諸岳、捉取大蛇、奉示天皇。天皇不齋戒。其雷虺々、目精赫々。天皇畏、蔽目不見、

> The mountains of Hatsuse
> are excellent mountains,
> standing straight.
> They are excellent mountains,
> running along.
> The mountains of Hatsuse
> are truly beautiful,
> truly beautiful.[xxxvii]

Thereupon, he named the small field Michi-no-ono, or Small Field of the Way."[xxxviii]

Third month, seventh day. The emperor wanted the empress and his consorts to personally plant mulberry trees and encourage sericulture. Thus, he ordered Sugaru[xxxix] to collect silkworms from across the land.

> Sugaru is a personal name.

Being so ordered, Sugaru mistakenly collected children and presented them to the emperor. The emperor laughed heartily and bestowed the children upon Sugaru, saying, "Raise them yourself." Sugaru then raised them near the palace hedge. Accordingly, a title of nobility was bestowed upon him: Muraji of the Chihisako-be.[30][xl]

Summer, fourth month. The state of Wu dispatched messengers with tribute.[31]

Treason in Japan, War in Korea

Seventh year [463 CE], autumn, seventh month, third day. The emperor proclaimed to Sugaru, Muraji of the Chihisako-be, saying, "We wish to see the form of the kami of Mimoro Hill. You are stronger than most people. Go yourself, catch it, and come back."[xli]

> According to one account, the kami of this mountain was the kami Ō-mono-nushi. By another, it was the kami Sumisaka of Uda.

Sugaru replied, saying, "I shall attempt to catch it." He then climbed Mimoro Hill, caught a great snake,[32] and showed it to the emperor. The emperor had not performed ritual abstinence. The snake made thunder crash, and its eyes glistened. The emperor, afraid, closed his eyes, did not look,

---

30 Small-children hereditary guild.
31 Diplomatic relations with Wu or the southern dynasties of the Northern and Southern Dynasties Period appear in Ōjin 37.2, Nintoku 58.10, and later in Yūryaku 8.2, 10.9, 12.4, and 14.1. Chinese records suggest increased diplomatic relations with Wa during the fifth century.
32 In Sujin 10, the kami Ō-mono-nushi manifests as a snake.

却入殿中。使放於岳。仍改賜名爲雷。

八月、官者吉備弓削部虛空、取急歸家。吉備下道臣前津屋、或本云、國造吉備臣山。留使虛空。經月不肯聽上京都。天皇遣身毛君大夫召焉。虛空被召來言、前津屋、以小女爲天皇人、以大女爲己人、競令相鬭。見幼女勝、即拔刀而殺。復以小雄鷄、呼爲天皇鷄、拔毛剪翼、以大雄鷄、呼爲己鷄、著鈴・金距、競令鬭之。見禿鷄勝、亦拔刀而殺。天皇聞是語、遣物部兵士卅人、誅殺前津屋幷族七十人。

是歲、吉備上道臣田狹、侍於殿側、盛稱稚媛於朋友曰、天下麗人、莫若吾婦。茂矣綽矣、諸好備矣。曄矣溫矣、種相足矣。鉛花弗御、蘭澤無加。曠世罕儔。當時獨秀者也。

天皇、傾耳遙聽、而心悅焉。便欲自求稚媛爲女御。拜田狹、爲任那國司。俄而、天皇幸稚媛。

田狹臣娶稚媛、而生兄君・弟君。別本云、田狹臣婦名毛媛者。葛城襲津彦子、玉田宿禰之女也。天皇聞體貌閑麗、殺夫自幸焉。

YŪRYAKU 7 [463 CE]

and hid inside the palace. He had the snake released on the hill. Thereby he bestowed the new name Ikazuchi upon it.[33]

Eighth month. The palace servant Ōzora of the Yuge hereditary guild of Kibi suddenly returned home.[xlii] The Omi of Shimotsumichi of Kibi, Sakitsuya, detained Ōzora and made the latter work for him.

> According to one account, it was the Provincial Miyatsuko and Omi of Kibi, Yama.

Months passed, but there was no indication that he would be allowed to return to the capital. The emperor dispatched the Kimi of Muketsu, Masurao,[34] to summon him. Ōzora was summoned and came, saying, "Sakitsuya had a young girl represent the emperor's people and a grown woman represent his own people and made them fight with each other. When he saw the young girl win, he drew his sword and killed her. In addition, he took a small rooster, plucked its feathers, clipped its wings, and called it the emperor's chicken. He took a large rooster, attached a bell and metal spur, and called it his own chicken. Then he made them fight. When he saw the plucked chicken win, he again drew his sword and killed it." When the emperor heard about this, he dispatched thirty soldiers from the Mononobe, and they put Sakitsuya and seventy of his family to death.

That year, the Omi of Kamitsumichi in Kibi, Tasa, attended at the palace.[xliii] He frequently praised Waka-hime to his friends, saying, "Of all the beauties in the realm, none compare with my wife. There is an effortlessness to her beauty, and she is endowed with every favorable quality. She is radiant and warm, and perfect in every way. She does not use face powder, nor put on any makeup. In all the wide world, few are like her. These days she is a singular exception."[xliv]

The emperor perked up his ears and heard this from afar and was pleased at heart. Then he sought Waka-hime for himself, wishing to make her his consort. He gave orders to Tasa, making him the provincial governor of Mimana. After some time, he summoned Waka-hime.

Tasa no Omi married Waka-hime, and she gave birth to E-kimi and Oto-kimi.

> According to another book, Tasa no Omi's wife, named Ke-hime, was the daughter of Tamata no Sukune, who was the son of Sotsuhiko of Kazuraki. The emperor heard that she was very beautiful, killed her husband, and took her for himself.[xlv]

---

33 It is unclear whether it is Sugaru or the hill that is renamed. *New Selected Records* refers to an Ikazuchi of the Chihisako-be, which would suggest that it was Sugaru.
34 The characters for Masurao mean "minister official," so this could be a title instead of a name.

田狹既之任所、聞天皇之幸其婦、思欲求援而入新羅。

于時、新羅不事中國。天皇詔田狹臣子弟君與吉備海部直赤尾曰、汝宜往罰新羅。

於是、西漢才伎歡因知利在側。乃進而奏曰、巧於奴者、多在韓國。可召而使。

天皇詔群臣曰、然則宜以歡因知利、副弟君等、取道於百濟、幷下勅書、令獻巧者。

於是、弟君銜命、率衆、行到百濟、而入其國。國神化爲老女、忽然逢路。弟君就訪國之遠近。老女報言、復行一日、而後可到。

弟君自思路遠、不伐而還。集聚百濟所貢今來才伎於大嶋中、託稱候風、淹留數月。

任那國司田狹臣、乃喜弟君不伐而還、密使人於百濟、戒弟君曰、汝之領項、有何牢錮而伐人乎。傳聞、天皇幸吾婦、遂有兒息。兒息已見上文。今恐、禍及於身、可蹻足待。吾兒汝者、跨據百濟、勿使通於日本。

吾者據有任那、亦勿通於日本。

Tasa had already gone to his assigned post, heard that the emperor had summoned his wife, and thought to go to Silla to seek aid.

At the time, Silla was not serving the emperor.[xlvi] The emperor then decreed to the son of Tasa no Omi, Oto-kimi, and to Akao, Atai of the fishing people of Kibi, saying, "Go to Silla and punish them."[35]

At that time, Kan'in Chiri of the artisans of the Aya of Kōchi was at the emperor's side.[36] Addressing the emperor, he suggested, "There are many people in the land of Kara more talented than I.[37] You should summon them and put them to work."

Then the emperor decreed to the high government officials, "If that is so, Kan'in Chiri shall accompany Oto-kimi and the others. Take the road through Paekche, and also hand down a written proclamation demanding the presentation of talented individuals."

Oto-kimi received the order and, leading a multitude, departed. They arrived in Paekche and entered that land. The kami of that land transformed into an old woman and unexpectedly met them on the road. Oto-kimi asked how far or close they were to the land to which they wanted to go. The old woman reported, "If you continue for one more day, you should soon arrive."

Oto-kimi himself thought that the way was distant and returned without attacking. The newly arrived artisans presented by Paekche were assembled at Ōshima.[xlvii] Saying that they were waiting for favorable winds, they stayed for some time, counting the months.

The Provincial Governor of Mimana, Tasa no Omi, was delighted that Oto-kimi had returned without attacking. He secretly sent a person to Paekche to admonish Oto-kimi, saying, "How firm your neck must be, that you can attack others! I hear that the emperor summoned my wife, and that they went on to have children.

The children[38] are seen in the passage above.

What I now fear is that disaster will spread to me personally, and I am on tiptoe, waiting. You, my child, plant yourself in Paekche and have no correspondence with Yamato. I will hold Mimana and also not correspond with Yamato."

---

35 Akao is not seen elsewhere. The Atai of the fishing people of Kibi appears again in Bidatsu 2.5 and 12.7 in reference to dealing with people from abroad.
36 Kan'in Chiri is not seen elsewhere. The artisans of the Aya of Kōchi were of continental lineage and managed by the Aya no Uji or Aya lineage group.
37 Kara refers to the southern Korean states of Paekche, Silla, and the Kaya Confederacy.
38 Imperial Prince Iwaki and Imperial Prince Hoshi-kawa-no-waka-miya, given in Yūryaku 1.3.

弟君之婦樟媛、國家情深、君臣義切。忠踰白日、節冠青松。惡斯謀叛、盜殺其夫、隱埋室內、乃與海部直赤尾將百濟所獻手末才伎、在於大嶋。天皇聞弟君不在、遣日鷹吉士堅磐固安錢、堅磐、此云柯陀之波。使共復命。遂即安置於倭國吾礪廣津廣津、此云比盧岐頭。邑。而病死者衆。

由是、天皇詔大伴大連室屋、命東漢直掬、以新漢陶部高貴・鞍部堅貴・畫部因斯羅我・錦部定安那錦・譯語卯安那等、遷居于上桃原・下桃原・眞神原三所。或本云、吉備臣弟君、還自百濟、獻漢手人部・衣縫部・宍人部。

八年春二月、遣身狹村主靑・檜隈民使博德使於吳國。自天皇即位、至于是歲、新羅國背誕、苞苴不入、於今八年。而大懼中國之心、脩好於高麗。由是、高麗王、遣精兵一百人守新羅。有頃、高麗軍士一人、取假歸國。時以新羅人爲典馬。典馬、此云于麻柯比。而顧謂之曰、汝國爲吾國所破非久矣。一本云、汝國果成吾土非久矣。

The wife of Oto-kimi, Kusu-hime, had deep appreciation for the state and absolutely followed the principle of lord-vassal relations.[xlviii] Her loyalty was clearer than the bright sun, and her integrity more constant than the green pine. She despised this treason against the emperor,[39] and so secretly killed her husband and concealed his body by burying it under the house. With Akao, Atai of the fisherpeople, she led the artisans presented by Paekche and stayed in Ōshima. The emperor heard that Oto-kimi was absent and dispatched the Kishi of Hitaka, Katashiwa and Koanzen,[40] and made them both report back. In the end, they were settled in Hirokitsu Village in Ato in the land of Yamato.[xlix] Many of them fell ill and died.

On account of this, the emperor decreed to Ō-muraji Ōtomo no Muroya that he order the Atai of the Aya of Yamato, Tsuka, to relocate the newly arrived artisans of Aya—Kōki of the Sue-style ceramics hereditary guild, Kenki of the saddle-makers hereditary guild, Inshiraga of the painters hereditary guild, Jōannakomi of the brocade weaving hereditary guild, and Myōanna of the interpreters—to three places: Kami-tsu-momohara, Shimo-tsu-momohara, and Makami-no-hara.[l]

According to another book, the Omi of Kimi, Oto-kimi, returned from Paekche and presented the occupational lineage groups of the artisans of Aya,[41] the cloth-weavers, and the butchers.

Eighth year [464 CE], spring, second month. The emperor dispatched the Suguri of Musa, Ao, and the Tami no Tsukai of Hinokuma, Hakatoko,[42] to Wu. Since the emperor had acceded to the imperial throne until this year, Silla was defiant and deceptive, and it was now eight years since they had presented tribute. However, greatly fearing the feelings of the emperor, they developed good relations with Koguryŏ. On account of these good relations, the King of Koguryŏ dispatched one hundred elite troops to Silla for protection. After some time, one of Koguryŏ's soldiers returned to his own country for a bit. At that time, a person from Silla was charged with the care of his horse. The soldier secretly told him, "It will not be long before your state is defeated by my state."[li]

According to one book, "It will not be long until your state ends up becoming our land."

---

39 The Civil and Penal Codes distinguishes between treason against the state and treason against the emperor. Here the word choice indicates the latter.
40 This could be one individual. Commentators are divided on how to parse this collection of personal names, place-names, and titles.
41 It is not clear what services this group performed, but likely earthenware leatherwork, artwork, or weaving—crafts generally associated with immigrant lineage groups.
42 From the hereditary guild of scribes. See Yūryaku 2.10.

其典馬聞之、陽患其腹、退而在後。遂逃入國、說其所語。於是、新羅王、乃知高麗僞守、遣使馳告國人曰、人殺家內所養雞之雄者。國人知意、盡殺國內所有高麗人。惟有遺高麗一人、乘間得脫、逃入其國、皆具爲說之。

　高麗王卽發軍兵、屯聚筑足流城。或本云、都久斯岐城。遂歌儛興樂。於是、新羅王、夜聞高麗軍四面歌儛、知賊盡入新羅地。乃使人於任那王曰、高麗王征伐我國。當此之時、若綴旒然。國之危殆、過於累卵。命之脩短、太所不計。伏請救於日本府行軍元帥等。由是、任那王勸膳臣斑鳩 斑鳩、此云伊柯屢餓。・吉備臣小梨・難波吉士赤目子、往救新羅。

　膳臣等、未至營止。高麗諸將、未與膳臣等相戰皆怖。膳臣等乃自力勞軍。令軍中、促爲攻具、急進攻之。與高麗相守十餘日。乃夜鑿險、爲地道、悉過輜車、設奇兵。會明、高麗謂膳臣等爲遁也。悉軍來追。乃縱奇兵、步騎夾攻、大破之。二國之怨、自此而生。

The horse steward heard this and pretended to have a stomach ailment, and so delayed his return. Then the steward escaped to his own land and explained what he had been told. Thereupon, the King of Silla knew that Koguryŏ only pretended to protect Silla and dispatched messengers to race to the people of his land and tell them, "Of the chickens in your household, kill the roosters."[lii] The people of the land knew what this meant and killed all of the men of Koguryŏ in their land. Only one man from Koguryŏ avoided this fate and was able to flee by riding for some time. He escaped to his land and told of everything in detail.

The King of Koguryŏ mustered his army, and they camped at Tsukusokuru Fortress.[43] There they danced to music and raised their voices in song. At night the King of Silla heard the Koguryŏ army singing and dancing in all four directions and knew that his enemy had completely infiltrated the land of Silla.[liii] He dispatched someone to the King of Mimana to say, "The King of Koguryŏ[44] attacks our land. At this moment, we are hung up like a pennant, and the danger to our state exceeds that of a stack of eggs.[liv] It is difficult to measure how much life we have left. I humbly beg for aid from the military officers of the Japanese administration."[45] So the King of Mimana appealed to the Omi of Kashiwade, Ikaruga; the Omi of Kibi, Onashi; and the Kishi of Naniwa, Akameko, and they went to save Silla.[lv]

Before they had arrived, the Omi of Kashiwade and the others made camp and stopped.[lvi] The various generals of Koguryŏ had not yet fought against the Omi of Kashiwade and the others, and they were all afraid. The Omi of Kashiwade and the others made efforts to rally their army. They ordered the entire army to quickly prepare for an attack, then suddenly advanced to make battle. For more than ten days, they were at a standoff with Koguryŏ. At night, they dug underground tunnels at places where the terrain was steep, put all of their equipment and rations in them, and set up soldiers in hiding. At dawn, Koguryŏ thought that the Omi of Kashiwade and the others were fleeing and sent every last one of their troops to pursue them. Then they released the hidden soldiers in a pincer formation with both infantry and cavalry, leading to a great defeat of Koguryŏ. The enmity between the two countries arose from this incident.

---

43 An original note adds, "According to one book, Tsukishiki Fortress." Present-day Taegu City.
44 It is not clear what king or which state in the Kaya Confederacy is meant.
45 This is the first appearance of this phrase with reference to the Korean peninsula. At this time, the name "Japan" did not yet exist, nor was there any semblance of a united Mimana government, which suggests an anachronistic and exaggerated imagining of Yamato influence on the peninsula in the fifth century on the part of the compilers of the *Chronicles*.

言二國者、高麗新羅也。

膳臣等謂新羅曰、汝以至弱、當至強。官軍不救、必爲所乘。將成人地、殆於此役。自今以後、豈背天朝也。

九年春二月甲子朔、遣凡河內直香賜與采女、祠胸方神。香賜既至壇所香賜、此云舸拕夫。及將行事、奸其采女。天皇聞之曰、祠神祈福、可不愼歟。乃遣難波日鷹吉士將誅之。時香賜退逃亡不在。天皇復遣弓削連豐穗、普求國郡縣、遂於三嶋郡藍原、執而斬焉。

三月、天皇欲親伐新羅。神戒天皇曰、無往也。

天皇由是、不果行。乃勅紀小弓宿禰・蘇我韓子宿禰・大伴談連談、此云箇陀利。・小鹿火宿禰等曰、新羅自居西土。累葉稱臣。朝聘無違。貢職允濟。逮乎朕之王天下、投身對馬之外、竄跡匝羅之表、阻高麗之貢、吞百濟之城。況復朝聘既闕、貢職莫脩。狼子野心、飽飛、飢附。以汝四卿、拜爲大將。宜以王師薄伐、天罰襲行。

於是、紀小弓宿禰、使大伴室屋大連、憂陳於天皇曰、臣雖拙弱、敬奉勅矣。但今、臣婦命過之際。

The two countries are Koguryŏ and Silla.

Then the Omi of Kashiwade told Silla, "Though you are an extremely weak state, you went to war with an extremely strong one. If our army had not saved you, you certainly would have been overrun. From this conflict you might have become part of someone else's land. From now on, how can you defy the imperial court?"

Ninth year [465 CE], spring, second month, first day. The Atai of Ōshikōchi, Katabu, and an inner palace lady were dispatched to venerate the kami of Munakata.[lvii] Katabu had already reached the shrine and was about to perform the ceremony when he raped the inner palace lady. The emperor heard of this and said, "When venerating the kami and praying for good fortune, you must be respectful." Then he dispatched the Kishi of Hitaka in Naniwa to put him to death. At that time, Katabu escaped and could not be found anywhere. The emperor further dispatched the Muraji of the Yuge,[46] Toyoho, who sought him in every province and district, and eventually caught and killed him at Ainohara in Mishima District.[lviii]

Third month. The emperor wished to attack Silla himself. A kami warned the emperor, "Do not go."[lix]

The emperor, on account of this warning, ended up not going. He decreed to Oyumi no Sukune of Ki, Karako no Sukune of Soga, Katari, Muraji of the Ōtomo, and Okahi no Sukune,[47] "Since the state of Silla was formed in the west, it has been subservient generation after generation. Never has it gone contrary to Our court. Its tribute has always been presented in full. When We came to be lord of the realm, they invested in their own interests outside of Tsushima, hid the traces of their misdeeds outside of Sora, blocked the tribute from coming from Koguryŏ, and swallowed up the forts of Paekche. Moreover, their attendance at court has been lacking, and their tribute has not been paid. They have the wild heart of a wolf cub, running off when sated and returning when hungry.[lx] You four government ministers are appointed commanding generals. Take the royal army and attack them, respectfully rendering heavenly retribution upon them."[lxi]

Thereupon, Oyumi no Sukune of Ki had Ō-muraji Ōtomo no Muroya convey his grief to the emperor and say, "Though I am a coward, I humbly receive this imperial decree. However, at present, my wife has just passed

---

46 The Muraji of the Yuge oversaw the bowyer hereditary guild (yuge-be). They were promoted to sukune in Tenmu 13.12.
47 Oyumi no Sukune is unclear. Later he is claimed to have a connection to Ōtomo no Muroya, but the nature of that connection is also unclear. Soga no Karako is the son of Soga no Manchi. Ōtomo no Katari is the son of Ōtomo no Muroya and father of Ōtomo no Kanamura. Okahi no Sukune is not seen elsewhere; perhaps he is the son or relative of Oyumi no Sukune.

莫能視養臣者。公冀將此事具陳天皇。於是、大伴室屋大連、具爲陳之。天皇聞悲頬歎、以吉備上道采女大海、賜於紀小弓宿禰、爲隨身視養。遂推轂以遣焉。

紀小弓宿禰等、即入新羅、行屠傍郡。行屠、並行並擊。新羅王、夜聞官軍四面鼓聲、知盡得喙地、與數百騎亂走。是以、大敗。小弓宿禰、追斬敵將陣中。喙地悉定、遺衆不下。紀小弓宿禰亦收兵、與大伴談連等會。兵復大振、與遺衆戰。是夕、大伴談連及紀岡前來目連、皆力鬪而死。

談連從人同姓津麻呂、後入軍中、尋覓其主。從軍不見出問曰、吾主大伴公、何處在也。

人告之曰、汝主等果爲敵手所殺。指示屍處。

津麻呂聞之、踏叱曰、主既已陷。何用獨全。因復赴敵、同時殞命。有頃、遺衆自退。官軍亦隨而却。大將軍紀小弓宿禰、值病而薨。

夏五月、紀大磐宿禰、聞父既薨、乃向新羅、執小鹿火宿禰所掌兵馬・船官及諸小官、

away. There is no one who can see to my care. My lord, I wish you to convey this matter in detail to the emperor." Accordingly, Ō-muraji Ōtomo no Muroya conveyed the message in detail. The emperor heard this and sighed in sadness, then bestowed upon Oyumi no Sukune of Ki the inner palace woman from Kamitsumichi in Kibi, Ōshiama.[lxii] She was made to accompany him and see to his care. Then at last the emperor deployed his generals and dispatched them.

Oyumi no Sukune of Ki and the others then went to Silla. They moved forward attacking from district to neighboring district.

"Moved forward" means "moved forward in a line formation and attacked."

The King of Silla, at night, heard the imperial army sounding drums in all four directions and knew they had completely taken the land of Toku.[lxiii] Several hundred mounted soldiers fled in disarray, and owing to this, Silla suffered a major defeat. Oyumi no Sukune of Ki pursued the enemy general into his army and cut him down. The land of Toku was completely taken, but the remaining enemies would not surrender. Oyumi no Sukune of Ki collected his troops and met with Katari, Muraji of the Ōtomo, and the others. They again greatly rallied the troops and gave battle to the enemy remnants. That night, Katari, Muraji of the Ōtomo and the Muraji of the Kume of Okazaki in Ki both fought valiantly and died.[lxiv]

A man called Tsumaro, from the retinue of Muraji Katari with the same title of nobility, later went through the army searching for his master.[lxv] When he could not find him in the army, he asked, "Where is my master Lord Ōtomo?"

Someone told him, "Your master ended up being killed at the hands of the enemy." That person directed him to the location of the corpse.

Tsumaro heard this, stomped his feet, and cried, saying, "My master has already fallen. What use is it for me to live on alone?" He went back into enemy lines and lost his life in the same way. After some time, the remaining enemies retreated on their own. The imperial army also withdrew in turn. The great battle general Oyumi no Sukune of Ki got sick and perished.

Summer, fifth month. Ōiwa no Sukune of Ki[48] heard that his father had already perished and promptly made for Silla. He took control of the troops and horses, fleet command, and various junior officers that had been under

---

48 Son of Oyumi no Sukune of Ki. Ōiwa is perhaps the same as the Oiwa no Sukune of Ki seen in Kenzō 3, who leads a campaign in the Korean peninsula.

專用威命。於是、小鹿火宿禰、深怨乎大磐宿禰。乃詐告於韓子宿禰曰、大磐宿禰、謂僕曰、我當復執韓子宿禰所掌之官不久也。願固守之。由是、韓子宿禰與大磐宿禰有隙。

於是、百濟王、聞日本諸將、緣小事有隙。乃使人於韓子宿禰等曰、欲觀國堺。請、垂降臨。

是以、韓子宿禰等、並轡而往。及至於河、大磐宿禰、飮馬於河。是時、韓子宿禰、從後而射大磐宿禰鞍几後橋。大磐宿禰愕然反視、射墮韓子宿禰。於中流而死。是三臣由前相競、行亂於道、不及百濟王宮而却還矣。

於是、采女大海、從小弓宿禰喪、到來日本。遂憂諮於大伴室屋大連曰、妾不知葬所。願占良地。大連即爲奏之。

天皇勅大連曰、大將軍紀小弓宿禰、龍驤虎視、旁眺八維。掩討逆節、折衝四海。然則身勞萬里、命墜三韓。宜致哀矜、充視葬者。又汝大伴卿與紀卿等、同國近隣之人、由來尚矣。

於是、大連奉勅、使土師連小鳥、作冢墓於田身輪邑、而葬之也。由是、大海欣悅、不能自默、以韓奴室・兄麻呂・弟麻呂・御倉・小倉・針六口送大連。吉備上道蚊嶋田邑家人部是也。

the command of Okahi no Sukune, monopolizing authority. At this, Okahi no Sukune deeply resented Ōiwa no Sukune of Ki, and so he lied to Karako no Sukune, saying, "Ōiwa no Sukune told me, 'It will not be long before I also take control of the officers under the command of Karako no Sukune.' I suggest that you harden your defenses." This caused a rift between Karako no Sukune and Ōiwa no Sukune of Ki.

The king of Paekche heard that there was a rift between the various generals of Yamato because of some trifling issue. So he sent someone to Karako no Sukune, saying, "I wish to show you the borderlands. I beg that you deign to accompany me."

Thereby Karako no Sukune and the others lined up the bits of their horses and went. When they reached the river, Ōiwa no Sukune let his horse drink from the river. At that time, Karako no Sukune shot the back part of Ōiwa no Sukune of Ki's saddle from behind. Ōiwa no Sukune of Ki was shocked, turned around, and shot down Karako no Sukune. He died in the river. These three vassals were in competition with each other from the first and created chaos during the journey. They returned without ever reaching the palace of the king of Paekche.

The inner palace lady Ōshiama came back to Yamato for the funeral of Oyumi no Sukune of Ki. In sadness, she ended up saying to Ō-muraji Ōtomo no Muroya, "I do not know where to bury him. Please divine a good location." The Ō-muraji spoke about this with the emperor.

The emperor decreed to the Ō-muraji, "The great general Oyumi no Sukune of Ki raised his head like a dragon and looked about like a tiger, surveying all eight directions.[lxvi] He attacked the traitors and destroyed enemies on all four seas. He thus labored ten thousand leagues away and lost his life in the three states of Korea. To carry out the mourning, we should appoint a funeral director. Also, you Ōtomo officials are from the same province and are neighbors to the Ki officials, and you have a long-standing connection."[lxvii]

The Ō-muraji received the decree and sent the Muraji of the Haji, Otori, to make a tomb in Tamuwa Village and to bury him there.[lxviii] Ōshiama was delighted and could not keep silent. She sent six slaves from Korea—Noshil, Hyŏngmaryŏ, Chemaryŏ, Ŏch'ang, Soch'ang, and Ch'im—to the Ō-muraji. They form the hereditary guild of household servants[49] of Kashimada Village in Kamitsumichi in Kibi.

---

49 Household servants were one of five categories of indentured servants under the Civil and Penal Codes, but members of hereditary guilds were of higher social status than these, which makes the meaning of "hereditary guild of household servants" (*yakahito-be*) unclear. This group may be connected to the household hereditary guild (*yaka-be*), created in Tenji 3.2.

別小鹿火宿禰、從紀小弓宿禰喪來。時獨留角國。使倭子連連、未詳何姓人。奉八咫鏡於大伴大連、而祈請曰、僕不堪共紀卿奉事天朝。故請、留住角國。是以、大連爲奏於天皇、使留居于角國。是角臣等、初居角國。而名角臣、自此始也。

秋七月壬辰朔、河內國言飛鳥戶郡人・田邊史伯孫女者、古市郡人・書首加龍之妻也。伯孫、聞女産兒、往賀聟家而月夜還、於蓬蔂丘譽田陵下蓬蔂、此云伊致寐姑、逢騎赤駿者、其馬時濩略而龍翥、欻聳擢而鴻驚、異體峯生、殊相逸發。

伯孫、就視而心欲之、乃鞭所乘驄馬、齊頭並轡、爾乃、赤駿超攄絶於埃塵、驅騖迅於滅沒。於是、驄馬後而怠足、不可復追。其乘駿者、知伯孫所欲、仍停換馬、相辭取別。伯孫、得駿甚歡、驟而入廐、解鞍秣馬眠之。其明旦、赤駿變爲土馬。伯孫心異之、還覓譽田陵、乃見驄馬在於土馬之間、取代而置所換土馬也。

Separately, Okahi no Sukune came for the funeral of Oyumi no Sukune of Ki. At that time, he stopped by himself in the land of Tsu.[lxix] He had the Muraji of Yamato go present an eight-shaftment mirror to Ō-muraji Ōtomo and pray, entreating him, "I cannot bear to attend on the emperor along with the officials from Ki.

<small>The lineage group of the muraji is still not precisely known.</small>

Therefore, I beg you to let me stay in the land of Tsu." The Ō-muraji reported this to the emperor, who made him dwell in the land of Tsu. The title Omi of Tsu[50] began with this decree of the emperor's.

Miscellaneous Deeds

Autumn, seventh month, first day. Kōchi Province reported, "In Asukabe District, the daughter of the Fubito of Tanabe, Hakuson, is the wife of a man from Furuichi District, Karyō, Obito of the Fumi.[lxx] Hakuson heard that his daughter had given birth to a son and went to celebrate at his son-in-law's house, returning home during the moonlit night. At the base of Homuta Tomb on Ichibiko Hill, he met someone riding a sorrel horse.[lxxi] At times, the horse, writhing like a dragon, flew, or all of a sudden took off like a startled giant bird.[lxxii] Its strange body was shaped like a mountain peak, and its unusual form towered over all else.

Hakuson came near and looked, and desired to make the horse his own. He put the whip to the dapple grey horse he rode, going head-to-head and bit-to-bit with the other horse. The sorrel took off, leaving only dust. It raced so fast, it was as if it had vanished entirely. The dapple grey was slow and fell behind, unable to keep up. The person riding the superior horse thus knew that Hakuson desired the sorrel, and so stopped and exchanged horses with him. Then they departed from each other and went their separate ways. Hakuson was exceedingly delighted that he had obtained the superior horse and galloped into his stable. He removed the saddle, gave it fodder, and went to sleep. The next morning, the sorrel had changed into a clay horse.[51] Hakuson thought this was strange, and when he went back to Homuta Tomb to investigate, he saw his dapple grey amongst the sorrel clay horses. He took it back and in exchange placed the clay horse there.

---

50 Also called Omi of Tsunu and Omi of Tsuno. The Kōgen book of *Ancient Matters* notes that Tsu no Sukune of Ki was the ancestor of this Omi, the Omi of Ki, and the Omi of Sakamoto. All three were promoted to ason in Tenmu 13.11.
51 Clay figurines or haniwa are commonly excavated from Tomb-period tombs. An origin story for haniwa appears in Suinin 32.7. The reddish brown of the sorrel horse matches that of the fired clay figurines.

十年秋九月乙酉朔戊子、身狹村主靑等、將吳所獻二鵝、到於筑紫。是鵝爲水間君犬所囓死。別本云、是鵝、爲筑紫嶺縣主泥麻呂犬所囓死。由是、水間君恐怖憂愁、不能自默、獻鴻十隻與養鳥人、請以贖罪。天皇許焉。

冬十月乙卯朔辛酉、以水間君所獻養鳥人等、安置於輕村・磐余村、二所。

十一年夏五月辛亥朔、近江國栗太郡言、白鸕鷀居于谷上濱。因詔置川瀨舍人。

秋七月、有從百濟國逃化來者。自稱名曰貴信。又稱貴信吳國人也。磐余吳琴彈壇手屋形麻呂等、是其後也。

冬十月、鳥官之禽、爲菟田人狗所囓死。天皇瞋、黥面而爲鳥養部。

於是、信濃國直丁與武藏國直丁侍宿、相謂曰、嗟乎、我國積鳥之高、同於小墓。旦暮而食、尚有其餘。今天皇由一鳥之故、而黥人面。太無道理。惡行之主也。

天皇聞而使聚積之。直丁等不能忽備。仍詔爲鳥養部。

Tenth year [466 CE], autumn, ninth month, fourth day. Ao, Suguri of Musa, and the others[52] arrived in Tsukushi with two geese presented by Wu. The geese were bitten by the dog of the Kimi of Minuma and died.

<small>According to another book, they were bitten by the dog of Nemaro, Agatanushi of Mine in Tsukushi, and died.[lxxiii]</small>

On account of this, the Kimi of Minuma was afraid and could not keep silent. He presented ten swans and bird keepers, seeking atonement for his crime. The emperor forgave him.

Winter, tenth month, seventh day. The bird keepers presented by the Kimi of Minima were settled in two locations: Karu Village and Iware Village.

Eleventh year [467 CE], summer, fifth month, first day. Kurumoto District in Ōmi Province reported, "There is a white cormorant on the Tanakami Beach."[lxxiv] So the emperor issued an edict establishing the servants of Kawase.[lxxv]

Autumn, seventh month. A man who fled Paekche came. He stated his name as Kuishin.[lxxvi] It is also said that he was from Wu. Yakatamaro of Sakate and other Wu zither players that live in Iware are his descendants.[lxxvii]

Winter, tenth month. A bird from the bird-keeping office was bitten by the dog of someone from Uda and died. The emperor was angry, had his face tattooed, and made him part of the bird-keeping hereditary guild.[53]

With this development, the conscripted watchmen[54] of Shinano and Musashi provinces on night watch said to themselves, "Alas, were you to stack them up, the height of the birds in our provinces would be the same as that of a small tomb.[lxxviii] Even if you ate them morning and night, they would still be in excess. Now on account of one bird, the emperor has tattooed someone's face. This is highly improper. He is an evil lord."

The emperor heard this and made them stack up the birds to see. The conscripted watchmen could not complete their task quickly enough. Hence, the emperor issued an edict making them part of the bird-keeping hereditary guild.

---

52 Including Tami no Tsukai of Hinokuma, Hakatoko, who was dispatched with Ao to Wu in Yūryaku 8.2.
53 The free peoples of the bird-keeping office (*tori no tsukasa*) should be distinguished from the bird-keeping hereditary guild (*torikai-be*). The latter was established in Suinin 23.11.
54 Yohoro were people conscripted for public service. The conscripted watchmen (*tsukae no yohoro*) performed surveillance and guard duties.

十二年夏四月丙子朔己卯、身狹村主靑與檜隈民使博德、出使于吳。

冬十月癸酉朔壬午、天皇命木工鬪鶏御田、一本云猪名部御田、蓋誤也。始起樓閣。於是、御田登樓、疾走四面、有若飛行。時有伊勢采女、仰觀樓上、怪彼疾行、顚仆於庭、覆所擎饌。饌者、御膳之物也。天皇便疑御田奸其采女、自念將刑、而付物部。

時秦酒公侍坐。欲以琴聲、使悟於天皇。横琴彈曰、

柯武柯噬能	かむかぜの
伊制能	いせの
伊制能奴能	いせののの
娑柯曳鳴	さかえを
伊裒甫流柯枳底	いほふるかきて
志我都矩屢麻泥爾	しがつくるまでに
飫裒枳瀰爾	おほきみに
柯拕倶	かたく
都柯陪麻都羅武騰	つかへまつらむと
倭我伊能致謀	わがいのちも
那我俱母鵝騰	ながくもがと
伊比志拕倶彌皤夜	いひしたくみはや
阿拕羅陀倶彌皤夜	あたらたくみはや

於是、天皇悟琴聲、而赦其罪。

十三年春三月、狹穗彦玄孫齒田根命、竊奸采女山邊小嶋子。天皇聞、以齒田根命、收付於物部目大連、而使責讓。齒田根命、以馬八匹・大刀八口、被除罪過。既而歌曰、

Twelfth year [468 CE], summer, fourth month, fourth day. Ao, Suguri of Musa, and Hakatoko, Tami no Tsukai of Hinokuma, were sent to Wu.

Winter, tenth month, tenth day. The emperor ordered a carpenter, Mita of Tsuke, to build a pavilion.[lxxix]

> According to one book, he is Mita of Inabe. This is probably an error.

Mita climbed the pavilion and ran about its four sides as if he were flying. At that time, an inner palace lady from Ise looked up at the pavilion, saw him, and startled by his quick movements, passed out in the courtyard and spilled the imperial meal she was carrying.[55] The emperor suspected that Mita had violated this inner palace lady and planned to kill him. He turned him over to the Mononobe.

At that time, Sake no Kimi of the Hada[56] was attending on the emperor. Using the sound of the zither, he wished to make the emperor realize what had happened. He placed the zither and strummed it, singing,

> Until the five hundred dangling
> blossoming tree branches
> in Ise
> the fields of Ise,
> until they die,
> may I steadfastly
> serve my lord,
> and may my lifespan
> be so long.
> Alas, for the carpenter who thus spoke!
> How regrettable for that carpenter!

At this point, because of the sound of the zither, the emperor realized what had happened, and he forgave the crime.

Thirteenth year [469 CE], spring, third month. The great-grandson of Saho-biko, Hatane, secretly raped an inner palace lady, Yamabe no Koshima-ko.[57][lxxx] The emperor heard of this and turned Hatane over to Ō-muraji Mononobe no Me to have him censured. Hatane expiated his crime with eight horses and eight swords, after which he sang,

---

55 An original note clarifies the meaning of the character used for "imperial meal," perhaps because this character originally meant only "food" and not "food and drink presented to the emperor."
56 In Yūryaku 15, Hada is given as Sake, Miyatsuko of the Hada. In *New Selected Records*, he is Sake, Kimi of Hada.
57 Saho-biko plotted treason against Suinin with his sister Saho-hime in Suinin 4 and 5. Hatane and Yamabe no Koshima-ko are not seen elsewhere.

耶麼能謎能	やまのべの
故思麼古喩衞爾	こしまこゆゑに
比登涅羅賦	ひとでらふ
宇麼能耶都擬播	うまのやつぎは
嗚思稽矩謀那欺	をしけくもなし

　目大連聞而奏之。天皇使齒田根命、資財露置於餌香市邊橘本之土。遂以餌香長野邑、賜物部目大連。

　秋八月、播磨國御井隈人文石小麻呂、有力強心、肆行暴虐。路中抄劫、不使通行。又斷商客艠舮、悉以奪取。兼違國法、不輸租賦。於是、天皇遣春日小野臣大樹、領敢死士一百、並持火炬、圍宅而燒。時自火炎中、白狗暴出、逐大樹臣。其大如馬。大樹臣神色不變、拔刀斬之、即化爲文石小麻呂。

　秋九月、木工韋那部眞根、以石爲質、揮斧斵材。終日斵之、不誤傷刃。天皇遊詣其所、而怪問曰、恆不誤中石耶。

　眞根答曰、竟不誤矣。

　乃喚集采女、使脫衣裙、而著犢鼻、露所相撲。於是、眞根暫停、仰視而斵。不覺手誤傷刃。天皇因嘖讓曰、何處奴。不畏朕、用不貞心、妄輙輕答。仍付物部、使刑於野。

> For Koshima-ko
> of Yamabe,
> losing eight horses
> flaunted by others
> is not regrettable in the least.

Ō-muraji Me heard this and reported it to the emperor. The emperor made Hatane place his objects of worth[58] out in the open at the base of a Tachibana orange tree near Eka Market.[lxxxi] Consequently, Nagano Village in Eka was bestowed upon Ō-muraji Mononobe no Me.[lxxxii]

Autumn, eighth month. In Miikuma, Harima Province, there was a man, Ayashi no Omaro, who was very powerful and strong-willed.[lxxxiii] He engaged in violent atrocities as he liked. He robbed people on the road and did not let them pass. He also intercepted merchant ships and plundered everything from them. On top of this, he ran afoul of the laws of the land and did not tender his taxes and duties. In response, the emperor dispatched the Omi of Kasuga-no-ono, Ōki,[59] in charge of one hundred valiant soldiers. They carried torches, surrounded his house, and set fire to it. At that time, a white dog suddenly burst out from the flames and chased after Omi Ōki. The dog was as big as a horse. Omi Ōki, with no change in spirit or countenance, drew his sword and cut it down. Then it transformed into Ayashi no Omaro.

Autumn, ninth month. The carpenter Mane of the Ina hereditary guild[60] was using a stone as a block and chopping wood with a hand axe. Though he chopped all day, he never missed and damaged the blade. The emperor, having gone out to that place, suspected something and asked him, "Have you ever missed and hit the rock?"

Mane replied, "I never miss."

Then the emperor summoned and assembled the inner palace ladies, had them take off their clothes, put on loincloths, and wrestle each other out in the open.[lxxxiv] Mane paused for a moment, then looked up while he chopped. His hands accidentally failed him, and he damaged the blade. The emperor then censured him, saying, "Who do you think you are, that you should not fear Us and reply lightly with such an improper mindset?" Then he turned him over to the Mononobe to be executed in the field.

---

58 The Civil and Penal Codes specifies these are assets aside from land, assets such as animals, slaves, rice, etc.
59 Ōki is not seen elsewhere. The Omi of both Kasuga and Ono were descended from the Wani.
60 Mane is not seen elsewhere. The Ina hereditary guild, descending from a woodworker from Silla, appears in Ōjin 31.8.

爰有同伴巧者、歎惜眞根、而作歌曰、

婀拕羅斯枳	あたらしき
偉儺謎能陀倶彌	ゐなべのたくみ
柯該志須彌儺播	かけしすみなは
旨我那稽麼	しがなけば
拕例柯々該武預	たれかかけむよ
婀拕羅須彌儺播	あたらすみなは

天皇聞是歌、反生悔惜、唱然頰歎曰、幾失人哉。乃以赦使、乘於甲斐黑駒、馳詣刑所、止而赦之。用解徽纏、復作歌曰、

農播拕磨能	ぬばたまの
柯彼能矩盧古磨	かひのくろこま
矩羅枳制播	くらきせば
伊能致志儺磨志	いのちしなまし
柯彼能倶盧古磨	かひのくろこま
一本換伊能致志儺磨志、而云伊志歌孺阿羅麻志也。	あるふみに、いのちしなましにかへて、いしかずあらまし」といふ

十四年春正月丙寅朔戊寅、身狹村主靑等、共吳國使、將吳所獻手末才伎、漢織・吳織及衣縫兄媛・弟媛等、泊於住吉津。是月、爲吳客道、通磯齒津路。名吳坂。

三月、命臣連迎吳使。卽安置吳人於檜隈野。因名吳原。以衣縫兄媛、奉大三輪神。以弟媛爲漢衣縫部也。漢織・吳織衣縫、是飛鳥衣縫部・伊勢衣縫之先也。

Another carpenter sighed and grieved for Mane. He composed a song, singing,

> How grievous
> is the charcoal line[61]
> strung by the carpenter of Inabe!
> If he were not here,
> who would string it,
> the grievous charcoal line.

The emperor heard this song and was moved to grief. Sighing and lamenting, he said, "How many have been lost!" Then he sent a messenger to pardon Mane, who mounted a black horse from Kai and raced to the place of execution to stop it and pardon him. Accordingly, his bonds were loosened. The carpenter again made a song, singing,

> Black horse of Kai,
> had you worn a saddle,
> his life would have ended,
> black horse of Kai.
> (In one book, 'his life would have ended' is instead 'you might have been too late.')[lxxxv]

Messengers from Wu, Treason of Ne no Omi

Fourteenth year [470 CE], spring, first month, thirteenth day. Ao, Suguri of Musa, and the others, along with the messengers from Wu and the skilled artisans presented by Wu—including the weavers of Aya, the weavers of Kure, and the tailors E-hime, Oto-hime, and others—stayed in the harbor at Sumi-no-e. That month a road was made for the guests from Wu. Called Kure-saka, or Wu Slope, it passed through Shihatsu-no-michi.[lxxxvi]

Third month. The emperor ordered the omi and muraji to welcome the messengers from Wu. He then settled the people from Wu in the fields of Hinokuma. Hence, these fields were called Kure-hara, or Wu Fields.[lxxxvii] The tailor E-hime was given presented to the kami of Ōmiwa. Oto-hime was made a member of the tailor hereditary guild of Aya. The tailors and weavers of Aya and the weavers of Kure are the ancestors of the tailor hereditary guilds of Asuka and Ise.[lxxxviii]

---

61 Similar to a chalk line, allowing carpenters to mark straight lines.

夏四月甲午朔、天皇欲設吳人、歷問群臣曰、其共食者誰好乎。

群臣僉曰、根使主可。

天皇、即命根使主爲共食者。遂於石上高拔原、饗吳人。時密遣舍人、視察裝飾。舍人復命曰、根使主所著玉縵、太貴最好。又衆人云、前迎使時、又亦著之。

於是、天皇欲自見、命臣連、裝如饗之時、引見殿前。皇后仰天歔欷、啼泣傷哀。天皇問曰、何由泣耶。

皇后避床而對曰、此玉縵者、昔妾兄大草香皇子、奉穴穗天皇勅、進妾於陛下時、爲妾所獻之物也。故致疑於根使主、不覺涕垂哀泣矣。

天皇聞驚大怒。深責根使主。根使主對言、死罪々々、實臣之愆。

詔曰、根使主、自今以後、子々孫々八十聯綿、莫預群臣之例。乃將欲斬之。

根使主逃匿、至於日根、造稻城而待戰。遂爲官軍見殺。天皇命有司、二分子孫、一分爲大草香部民、以封皇后。一分賜茅渟縣主爲負囊者。即求難波吉士日香々子孫、賜姓爲

YŪRYAKU 14 [470 CE]

Summer, fourth month, first day. The emperor wanted to have a reception for the people from Wu and asked the high government officials, each in turn, "Who would be best to have eat together with them?"

The high government officials all said, "Ne no Omi would be best."

Accordingly, the emperor ordered Ne no Omi to eat together with them. They held a reception for the people from Wu in Takanuki Field in Isonokami.[lxxxix] At that time, the emperor secretly dispatched a servant to observe their jewelry and accessories. The servant reported back, "The jeweled hair ornament worn by Ne no Omi was exceptional and quite lovely. Also, the people there all said, 'He also wore it before, when he greeted the messengers.'"

The emperor wanted to see it himself, and he ordered the omi and muraji to dress as they had at the reception and held an audience with them in front of the palace. The empress looked up to heaven, distressed, and sighed and shed tears. The emperor asked her, "Why do you cry?"

The empress came down[62] and replied, "A long time ago, this jeweled hair ornament was presented on my behalf, when my older brother Imperial Prince Ō-kusaka received an order from Emperor Anaho [Ankō] and presented me to you. I suspected Ne no Omi and, without thinking, began to cry and became distressed."[63]

The emperor heard this and was shocked and greatly angered. He harshly censured Ne no Omi. Ne no Omi replied, saying, "I humbly beg your pardon. This crime is truly my doing."

Then the emperor decreed, "Ne no Omi, from now on, your children and your children's children cannot be entrusted with high government office for eighty generations." Then he was going to cut him down.

Ne no Omi escaped and hid. Reaching Hine, he built a fort and awaited the battle.[xc] In the end, he was killed by the imperial army. The emperor ordered his officials to split the descendants of Ne no Omi into two groups. One group became the hereditary guild of Ō-kusaka, and they were apportioned to the empress.[xci] One group was bestowed upon the Agatanushi of Chinu to serve as porters. Then he sought out the descendants of the Kishi of Naniwa, Hikaka, and bestowed upon them the title of nobility Kishi of

---

62 Presumably, the emperor and empress were sitting on a dais, from which she descended to reply.
63 This episode continues the episode in Ankō 1.2, in which Ne no Omi slanders Ō-kusaka and steals the accessory.

大草香部吉士。其日香々等語、在穴穗天皇紀。

　事平之後、小根使主、小根使主、根使主子。夜臥謂人曰、天皇城不堅。我父城堅。

　天皇傳聞是語、使人見根使主宅。實如其言。故收殺之。根使主之後爲坂本臣、自是始焉。

　十五年、秦民分散臣連等、各隨欲駈使。勿委秦造。由是、秦造酒甚以爲憂、而仕於天皇。天皇愛寵之。詔聚秦民、賜於秦酒公。公仍領率百八十種勝、奉獻庸調絹縑、充積朝庭。因賜姓曰禹豆麻佐。一云、禹豆母利麻佐、皆盈積之貌也。

　十六年秋七月、詔、宜桑國縣殖桑。又散遷秦民、使獻庸調。

　冬十月、詔、聚漢部、定其伴造者。賜姓曰直。一云、賜、漢使主等、賜姓曰直。

the hereditary guild of Ō-kusaka. Matters related to Hikaka and others are detailed in the "Annals of Emperor Anaho."

After things had calmed down, One no Omi told someone laying down that night, "The emperor's fortress is not fortified.^{xcii} My father's fortress is fortified."

<small>One no Omi was the son of Ne no Omi.</small>

Down the line, the emperor heard of this matter and sent men to look at the house of Ne no Omi. It was as was said. So they captured and killed him [Ne no Omi]. The tradition of the descendants of Ne no Omi becoming the Omi of Sakamoto began from this time hence.^{xciii}

Fifteenth year [471 CE]. The people of Hada were divided up among the omi and muraji, who each put them to work as they pleased and they did not entrust them to the Miyatsuko of Hada.^{xciv} On account of this, Sake, Miyatsuko of the Hada, was exceedingly troubled and brought the issue to the emperor. The emperor showed him special favor. He decreed that the people of Hada be assembled, and then he bestowed them upon Kimi Sake of the Hada. This lord thereby came to lead the *suguri* of many kinds of crafters, and he presented rough and fine silk as his taxes and duties, which accumulated in piles at court.[64] For this reason, the emperor bestowed upon him a new title of nobility, Utsumasa.[65]

<small>According to one account, Utsu-mori-masa, meaning "everything in overflowing piles."</small>

Sixteenth year [472 CE], autumn, seventh month. The emperor decreed that mulberry trees be planted in suitable provinces and districts. Also, he scattered and moved the people of Hada around, and forced them to pay their taxes and duties.

Winter, tenth month. The emperor decreed that the Aya hereditary guild[66] be assembled and an allied chieftain for it be established. He bestowed upon it the title of nobility Atai.

<small>According to one account, the title of Atai was bestowed upon the Omi of Aya.[67]</small>

---

64 The precise role of *suguri* is unclear, but it appears to refer to a lower-tier administrator. The vernacular reading is disputed. "Suguri" appears in Yūryaku 2.10, with the characters "village master" and is probably of Korean linguistic origin. Another reading might render the translation "Utsumasa of many kinds of crafters," referring to the new title bestowed upon Sake in the following sentence.
65 This title may be connected to the place-name Uzumasa, in present-day Ukyō Ward, Kyoto City.
66 In Ōjin 20.9, the ancestor of this lineage group arrives in Yamato leading people from seventeen regions on the continent.
67 Many provincial miyatsuko held the title of nobility of omi. The Aya of various regions maintained this title into the Tenmu era. The note was added to clarify the recipient of the title.

十七年春三月丁丑朔戊寅、詔土師連等、使進應盛朝夕御膳清器者。於是、土師連祖吾笥、仍進攝津國來狹々村、山背國內村・俯見村、伊勢國藤形村及丹波・但馬・因幡私民部。名曰贄土師部。

十八年秋八月己亥朔戊申、遣物部菟代宿禰・物部目連、以伐伊勢朝日郎。朝日郎、聞官軍至、即逆戰於伊賀青墓。自矜能射、謂官軍曰、朝日郎手、誰人可中也。其所發箭、穿二重甲。官軍皆懼。菟代宿禰、不敢進擊。相持二日一夜。

於是、物部目連、自執大刀、使筑紫聞物部大斧手、執楯叱於軍中、俱進。朝日郎乃遙見、而射穿大斧手楯二重甲。幷入身肉一寸。大斧手以楯翳物部目連。目連即獲朝日郎斬之。

由是、菟代宿禰、羞愧不克、七日不服命。天皇問侍臣曰、菟代宿禰、何不服命。

爰有讚岐田蟲別、進而奏曰、菟代宿禰怯也、二日一夜之間、不能擒執朝日郎。而物部目連、率筑紫聞物部大斧手、獲斬朝日郎矣。天皇聞之怒。輒奪菟代宿禰所有猪名部、賜物部目連。

Seventeenth year [473 CE], spring, third month, second day. The emperor decreed to the Muraji of the Haji[68] that they present people to him for making clean, pure dishware fit for the piles of food at his morning and evening meals. Thereupon, Ake, ancestor of the Muraji of the Haji, presented the people of Kusasa Village in Tsu Province, Uchi and Fushimi Villages in Yamashiro Province, Fujikata Village in Ise Province, and people from his own private hereditary guilds in Tanba, Tajima, and Inaba Provinces. They were named the imperial dishware and ceramics hereditary guild.[xcv]

Eighteenth year [474 CE], autumn, eighth month, tenth day. The emperor dispatched Sukune Mononobe no Ushiro and Muraji Mononobe no Me to attack Asake no Iratsuko of Ise.[xcvi] Asake no Iratsuko heard that the imperial army had arrived and waited to give battle at Aohaka in Iga.[xcvii] Proud of his own ability with the bow, he told the imperial army, "Who will accept the challenge to oppose Asake no Iratsuko?" The arrow that he fired pierced through two layers of armor. Everyone in the imperial army was afraid. Sukune Ushiro did not dare to advance and attack, and so each force waited for the other to initiate hostilities for two days and one night.

Thereupon, Muraji Mononobe no Me took his sword, made Mononobe no Ō-onote of Kiku in Tsukushi take a shield, issued a great shout from within the force, and together they advanced.[xcviii] Asake no Iratsuko saw this from afar and shot through Ō-onote's shield and two layers of armor, and about an inch into his flesh. Ō-onote used the shield to cover Muraji Mononobe no Me. Muraji Me then caught Asake no Iratsuko and cut him down.

Hence, Sukune Ushiro was ashamed that he could not overcome the enemy, and for seven days he did not report back. The emperor asked his attending ministers, "Why does Sukune Ushiro not report back?"

At this point, one in attendance, Tamushi-no-wake of Sanuki, came forth and addressed the emperor, saying, "Sukune Ushiro, in his cowardice, could not catch Asake no Iratsuko for two days and one night. However, Muraji Mononobe no Me led Mononobe no Ō-onote of Kiku in Tsukushi and caught and cut down Asake no Iratsuko." The emperor heard this and was angry. He then confiscated the boar-keepers hereditary guild[69] held by Sukune Ushiro and bestowed it upon Muraji Mononobe no Me.

---

68 The Muraji of the Haji, who appears in S6 of the "Age of the Gods," descended from Ama-no-hohi.
69 The Muraji of the boar-keepers hereditary guild (I-tsukai-be) appears in Annei 11. Some manuscripts render this guild I-na-be, also likely a boar-keeping hereditary guild, and *New Selected Records* identifies the miyatsuko in charge of this group as of the Isonokami lineage group, which is of the same lineage as the Mononobe.

十九年春三月丙寅朔戊寅、詔置穴穗部。

廿年冬、高麗王、大發軍兵、伐盡百濟。爰有小許遺衆、聚居倉下。兵糧既盡、憂泣茲深。於是、高麗諸將、言於王曰、百濟心許非常、臣每見之、不覺自失。恐更蔓生。請遂除之。

王曰、不可矣。寡人聞、百濟國者爲日本國之官家、所由來遠久矣。又其王入仕天皇。四隣之所共識也。遂止之。

百濟記云、蓋鹵王乙卯年冬、狛大軍來、攻大城七日七夜。王城降陷、遂失尉禮。國王及大后、王子等、皆沒敵手。

廿一年春三月、天皇聞百濟爲高麗所破、以久麻那利賜汶洲王、救興其國。時人皆云、百濟國、雖屬既亡、聚憂倉下、實賴於天皇、更造其國。汶洲王蓋鹵王母弟也。日本舊記云、以久麻那利、賜末多王。蓋是誤也。久麻那利者、任那國下哆呼唎縣之別邑也。

廿二年春正月己酉朔、以白髮皇子爲皇太子。

70　The Miyatsuko of the Anaho, who managed this group, was promoted to muraji in Tenmu 12.9. The Anaho appear to have been concentrated in Shimōsa Province. The passage could be read to suggest that it was around the late fifth century that these areas fell under control of the Yamato state.

71　Both the *Samguk sagi* and the citation from the *Record of Paekche* in the following note give the year of this successful campaign by King Changsu of Koguryŏ as 475 CE. Perhaps

Nineteenth year [475 CE], spring, third month, thirteenth day. The emperor decreed that the Anaho hereditary guild[70] be established.

War in Korea, Urashima Taro, Death of the Emperor

Twentieth year [476 CE], winter. The king of Koguryŏ marshaled a great army, attacked and annihilated Paekche.[71] At that point, a few remnants of the defeated force gathered at Hesuoto.[xcix] Their rations were already exhausted, and their despair at this turn of events ran deep. Thereupon, the various generals of Koguryŏ reported to their king, "The spirits of those from Paekche are unnatural. Whenever we see them, we are unexpectedly at a loss. But we expect that Paekche will rise and spread again. We beg you to pursue and eliminate them."[c]

The king said, "We cannot. I have heard that the state of Paekche has a long history as an imperial estate of Yamato. Also, their king has gone to Yamato and served the emperor. Neighboring lands are all aware of this." In the end they stopped.

> The *Record of Paekche* says, In the winter of the year Wood Rabbit during the reign of King Kaero [475 CE], a great army from Koguryŏ came and attacked the great stronghold for seven days and seven nights. The king's fortress fell, and in the end, Ire was lost. The king, queen, and royal children all fell into the hands of the enemy.[ci]

Twenty-first year [477 CE], spring, third month. The emperor heard that Paekche had been defeated by Koguryŏ. He bestowed Kumunari upon King Munju to rescue and reestablish that state.[cii] People at the time all said, "The state of Paekche and its people were already lost, and they gathered at Kusuoto and mourned that fact, but truly by the blessing of the emperor, their state rose again."

> King Munju was the younger brother of King Kaero's mother. The *Old Record of Japan*[72] says, The emperor bestowed Komunari upon King Mata. However, this is probably in error. Kusumori was a freestanding village in the Aroshitakori District of the state of Mimana.[73][ciii]

Twenty-second year [478 CE], spring, first month, first day. Imperial Prince Shiraka was named crown prince.

---

the compilers modified the date in the *Chronicles* to create a narrative from the entries from 476 CE to 479 CE that presents historical Yamato authority on the peninsula as the eighth-century compilers would like to imagine it having been.

72 *Nihon kuki*. This text is no longer extant.
73 An alternative reading of the note would give "Munju was the younger brother of King Kaero by the same mother."

秋七月、丹波國餘社郡管川人瑞江浦嶋子、乘舟而釣。遂得大龜。便化爲女。於是、浦嶋子感以爲婦。相逐入海。到蓬萊山、歷覩仙衆。語在別卷。

　廿三年夏四月、百濟文斤王薨。天王、以昆支王五子中、第二末多王、幼年聰明、勅喚內裏。親撫頭面、誠勅慇懃、使王其國。仍賜兵器、幷遣筑紫國軍士五百人、衞送於國。是爲東城王。

　是歲、百濟調賦、益於常例。筑紫安致臣・馬飼臣等、率船師以擊高麗。

　秋七月辛丑朔、天皇寢疾不預。詔、賞罰支度、事無巨細、並付皇太子。

　八月庚午朔丙子、天皇疾彌甚。與百寮辭訣、並握手歔欷。崩于大殿。

　遺詔於大伴室屋大連與東漢掬直曰、方今區宇一家、煙火萬里。百姓乂安、四夷賓服。此又天意、欲寧區夏。所以小心勵己、日愼一日、蓋爲百姓故也。臣・連・伴造、每日朝參、

Autumn, seventh month. A man named Mizu-no-e no Urashima-no-ko from Tsutsukawa, Yoza District, Tanba Province, went fishing in a boat. Eventually he caught a great turtle. It suddenly transformed into a woman. Urashima-no-ko was taken with her, and he made her his wife. He followed her and entered the sea. They arrived at the Land of Tokoyo and toured with the sages. This story is in another book.^{civ}

Twenty-third year [479 CE], summer, fourth month. King Mun'gŭn[74] of Paekche perished. The heavenly king decreed that of the five sons of King Konki, the second child, King Malta, who was bright from a young age, be summoned to the palace.[75] The king himself patted him on the head, courteously admonished him, and made him the next king of that state. He bestowed upon him troops and dispatched him with five hundred people from the army of the land of Tsukushi, who protected him and escorted him to his land. He was King Tongsŏng.

That year, the tribute of Paekche was higher than usual. The Omi of Achi, Muraji of the Umakai, and others of Tsukushi led a fleet to attack Koguryŏ.^{cv}

Autumn, seventh month. On the first day, the emperor became sick. He decreed that rewards, punishments, and financial matters, no matter how big or small, be left to the crown prince.^{civ}

Eighth month, seventh day. The emperor's sickness grew worse. He bade farewell to the administrators, taking each of their hands and grieving with them. Then he expired in the palace.[76]

In his final proclamation to Ō-muraji Ōtomo no Muroya and the Atai of Tsuka of the Aya of Yamato, he said, "Truly, the realm under heaven is now like one household, and smoke from cooking fires rises even ten thousand leagues away. The people are at peace, and the barbarians in all four directions are in submission. This is indeed because the will of heaven desired for all the land to be tranquil. I believe that the reason that I, though having little willpower, was encouraged day after day to act in moderation, was because I acted on behalf of the people. The omi, muraji, allied miyatsuko, and provincial miyatsuko attended every day at court, the

---

74 Presumably, King Samgŭn (r. 477–479 CE).
75 "Heavenly King" is glossed "emperor," but is an unusual construction. Perhaps it was "Great King" in the original source. Konki is the Konkishi who comes to stay in Yamato and has five sons (Yūryaku 5.4 to 5.7). King Malta is King Tongsŏng (r. 479–501 CE).
76 *Ancient Matters* gives his age at death as 124 and the year as that of the Earth Snake [489 CE]. The Ingyō book notes his birth in Ingyō 7.12 [418 CE], which makes him sixty-one in 479.

國司・郡司、隨時朝集。何不罄竭心府、誠勅懇懃。義乃君臣、情兼父子。庶藉臣連智力、內外歡心、欲令普天之下、永保安樂。不謂、邁疾彌留、至於大漸。此乃人生常分。何足言及。但朝野衣冠、未得鮮麗。教化政刑、猶未盡善。興言念此、唯以留恨。今年踰若干。不復稱夭。筋力精神、一時勞竭。如此之事、本非爲身。止欲安養百姓、所以致此。人生子孫、誰不屬念。既爲天下、事須割情。

今星川王、心懷悖惡、行闕友于。古人有言、知臣莫若君。知子莫若父。縱使星川得志、共治國家、必當戮辱、遍於臣連、酷毒流於民庶。夫惡子孫、已爲百姓所憚。好子孫、足堪負荷大業。此雖朕家事、理不容隱。大連等、民部廣大、充盈於國。皇太子、地居儲君上嗣、仁孝著聞。以其行業、堪成朕志。以此、共治天下、朕雖瞑目、何所復恨。

provincial governors and district governors[77] fell into line and assembled at court as needed. How could I not pour out the last bit of my heart and courteously admonish? The principle is that of lord and vassal, to which is added the feeling of father and sons. I wish that the omi and muraji, by the power of their wisdom, be joyful both inside and out, and I want them to preserve the realm in peace and tranquility for a long time to come. I never thought that my illness would worsen, and that I would proceed to the land of death. But this is a normal part of human life. What can I say? However, I have not yet been able to make clear prescriptions for caps and clothing in court and countryside, nor to complete the spread of civilization, government, and law.[cvii] When I reflect on this and put it into words, I am full of regret. Now I am no longer young, nor can I say that my life was short. My strength and spirit were expended in a flash. These things I do not say on my own behalf. I say them because I want only to make the people safe and civilized. Who alive does not invest his heart in his descendants? You must exhaust your hearts in matters of the realm.

Prince Hoshikawa now harbors contrarian evil in his heart, and his actions lack the accord of a brother.[78] There is a saying from people of old. 'No one knows the vassal better than the lord. No one knows the child better than the father.'[cviii] Should Hoshikawa achieve his ambition and rule over the state, truly it would lead to disgrace that would spread to the omi and muraji, and diffuse poison among the people. Indeed, bad descendants are loathed by the people, while good descendants are capable of carrying the burden of great endeavors. Though this is a matter of Our own house, proper principle demands that We should not conceal it. The Ō-muraji have vast holdings of private hereditary guilds; the land is full of them. The crown prince is in place to succeed to the throne, and I hear he demonstrates benevolence and filial piety. Judging by his actions, he is capable of bringing Our ambitions to fruition. In light of this, if you rule the realm together with him, though Our eyes will be closed forever, how could there be anything to regret?"

---

77 These offices were not established until the Taika Reforms in 645 CE.
78 Hoshikawa is Yūryaku's son by Waka-hime of Kibi. Here he is not referred to as an imperial prince.

一本云、星川王、腹悪心毚、天下著聞。不幸朕崩之後、當害皇太子。汝等民部甚多。努力相助。勿令侮慢也。

是時、征新羅將軍吉備臣尾代、行至吉備國過家。後所率五百蝦夷等、聞天皇崩、乃相謂之曰、領制吾國天皇既崩。時不可失也。乃相聚結、侵寇傍郡。於是、尾代從家來、會蝦夷於娑婆水門、合戰而射。蝦夷等、或踊或伏。能避脫箭。終不可射。是以、尾代空彈弓弦。於海濱上、射死踊伏者二隊。二簶之箭既盡。即喚船人索箭。船人恐而自退。尾代乃立弓執末而歌曰、

瀰致儞阿賦耶	みちにあふや
嗚之慮能古	をしろのこ
阿母儞擧曽	あもにこそ
枳擧曳儒阿羅毎	きこえずあらめ
矩儞々播	くにには
枳擧曳底那	きこえてな

唱訖自斬數人。更追至丹波國浦掛水門、盡逼殺之。一本云、追至浦掛、遣人盡殺之。

YŪRYAKU 23 [479 CE]

> According to one book, Throughout the realm one hears that Prince Hoshikawa is of evil humor and coarse spirit. Unfortunately, after We expire, he will certainly cause harm to the crown prince. You all have many private occupational lineage groups. Make an effort to help the latter, and do not underestimate the former.

At that time, the Omi of Kibi, Oshiro, the general who led the army in the attack on Silla, arrived in Kibi Province and went to his house.^{cix} Behind him were five hundred Emishi whom he had taken command of, and when they heard that the emperor had expired, they said to one another, "The emperor who took over our land has expired. We cannot lose this moment."[79] Then they assembled and invaded the neighboring district. Thereupon, Oshiro came out of his house, met them at Saba Port, and fought with them, shooting arrows.^{cx} The Emishi, now jumping, now ducking, skillfully avoided the arrows. In the end, he could not shoot them. This being the case, Oshiro, strummed his bowstring without an arrow in it. Then near the seashore, he shot dead two companies of the Emishi who had been jumping and ducking.[80] He went through two quivers of arrows, then called the boatmen, seeking more arrows. The boatmen were afraid and fled. Oshiro then stood his bow vertically, grabbed the tip of it, and sang,

> Oshiro
> met them en route.
> They may not hear of this
> in heaven,
> but in my land
> I want everyone to know it.

After he finished singing, he cut down many people on his own. Then he pursued them and, arriving at Urakake Harbor in Tanba Province, he attacked and killed them all.

> According to one book, he pursued them and arrived at Urakake, then his soldiers killed them all.

---

79 Use of foreign fighters as bodyguards is attested, but the Emishi made up the Saeki hereditary guild, and there is no instance of them being used as sailors or being deployed abroad.

80 Strumming a bowstring was a common practice for dispersing evil spirits.

白髮武廣國押稚日本根子天皇 清寧天皇

白髮武廣國押稚日本根子天皇、大泊瀬幼武天皇第三子也。母曰葛城韓媛。天皇生而白髮、長而愛民。大泊瀬天皇、於諸子中、特所靈異。廿二年、立爲皇太子。廿三年八月、大泊瀬天皇崩。吉備稚媛、陰謂幼子星川皇子曰、欲登天下之位、先取大藏之官。

　長子磐城皇子、聽母夫人教其幼子之語曰、皇太子雖是我弟、安可欺乎。不可爲也。星川皇子、不聽、輒隨母夫人之意。遂取大藏官。鑠閉外門、式備乎難。權勢自由、費用官物。

　於是、大伴室屋大連、言於東漢掬直曰、大泊瀬天皇之遺詔、今將至矣。宜從遺詔、奉皇太子。乃發軍士圍繞大藏。自外拒閉、縱火燔殺。是時、吉備稚媛・磐城皇子異父兄々君・城丘前來目闕名。隨星川皇子、而被燔殺焉。

　惟河內三野縣主小根、慄然振怖、避火逃出。抱草香部吉士漢彥脚、因使祈生於大伴室屋大連曰、奴縣主小根、事星川皇子者信。

Book 15
Emperors Seinei, Kenzō, and Ninken

Rebellion of Prince Hoshikawa, Reign of Emperor Seinei

Emperor Shiraka-no-take-hiro-kuni-oshi-waka-yamato-neko [Seinei][i] was the third son of Emperor Ō-hatsuse-no-waka-take [Yūryaku]. [ii] His mother was called Kara-hime of Kazuraki.[1] The emperor was born with white hair. When he grew up, he loved his people. Of all the sons of Emperor Ō-hatsuse, he was especially outstanding. In the twenty-second year [478 CE], he was named crown prince. In the twenty-third year [479 CE], eighth month, Emperor Ō-hatsuse expired. Waka-hime of Kibi secretly told the younger Imperial Prince Hoshikawa, "If you wish to ascend to the highest rank in the realm, first take the Office of the Treasury."[iii]

Her older son, Imperial Prince Iwaki, heard the advice given by his mother the consort to the young child and said, "Although the crown prince is my younger brother, how can we deceive him?[iv] This cannot come to pass." Imperial Prince Hoshikawa did not listen and rashly followed the plans laid down by his mother. Hence, he took the Office of the Treasury, chained its outer gate shut, and thereby prepared himself for conflict.[v] He used his authority as he desired and spent office resources.

The Ō-muraji Ōtomo no Muroya told Tsuka, Atai of the Aya of Yamato, "As foreseen in the final edict of Emperor Ō-hatsue, so has it now come to pass. We must follow the final edict and serve the crown prince." Then he deployed the army and surrounded the treasury. He tightly blocked off egress, set it on fire, and burned those inside to death. At that time, followers Imperial Prince Hoshikawa—Waka-hime of Kibi; E-kimi, half-brother of Imperial Prince Iwaki; and Okasaki no Kume of Ki—were killed in the fire.[2]

The name of Okasaki no Kume of Ki is not given.

The Agatanushi of Mino in Kōchi, Oné, trembling in fear, escaped the fire by fleeing outside.[vi] He embraced the legs of Ayahiko, Kishi of Kusakabe, and pleaded for his life to the Ō-muraji Ōtomo no Muroya, saying, "It is true that I, Agatanushi Oné, served Imperial Prince Hoshikawa.[vii]

---

1   Daughter of Ō-omi Tsubura of Kazuraki.
2   E-kimi was the son of Waka-hime by her first husband, Tasa, Omi of Kamitsumichi of Kibi. A Muraji of the Kume of Okazaki in Ki appears in Yūryaku 9.3, though he dies in battle on the Korean peninsula.

而無有背於皇太子。乞、降洪恩、救賜他命。漢彦乃具爲啓於大伴大連、不入刑類。

小根仍使漢彦啓於大連曰、大伴大連、我君、降大慈愍、促短之命、既續延長、獲觀日色。輒以難波來目邑大井戸田十町、送於大連。又以田地、與于漢彦、以報其恩。

是月、吉備上道臣等、聞朝作亂、思救其腹所生星川皇子、率船師卅艘、來浮於海。既而聞被燔殺、自海而歸。天皇即遣使、嘖讓於上道臣等、而奪其所領山部。

冬十月己巳朔壬申、大伴室屋大連、率臣連等、奉璽於皇太子。

元年春正月戊戌朔壬子、命有司、設壇場於磐余甕栗、陟天皇位。遂定宮焉。尊葛城韓媛、爲皇太夫人。以大伴室屋大連爲大連、平群眞鳥大臣爲大臣、並如故。臣連伴造等、各依職位焉。

冬十月癸巳朔辛丑、葬大泊瀬天皇于丹比高鷲原陵。于時、隼人晝夜哀號陵側。與食不喫。七日而死。有司造墓陵北、以禮葬之。是年也、太歳庚申。

However, I did not defy the crown prince. I beg you to bestow mercy upon me and spare my life." Ayahiko told all this to Ō-muraji Ōtomo, and the man was not put to death.

Then Oné, through Ayahiko, addressed the Ō-muraji, saying, "My lord Ō-muraji Ōtomo has bestowed upon me great benevolence, my shortened lifespan has been extended, and I can now see the color of the sun."[viii] Then he gave ten hectares of rice paddies from the Kume village Ōie in Naniwa to the Ō-muraji.[ix] Also he gave rice paddies to Ayahiko to repay this act of mercy.

That month, the Omi of Kamitsumichi in Kibi and others heard that there had been a rebellion at court. Thinking to rescue the child borne from that belly, Imperial Prince Hoshikawa, they led an armada of forty ships and came by sea.[3] When they heard that he had already been killed by fire, they returned to the sea. The emperor then dispatched a messenger to censure the Omi of Kamitsumichi and take away the mountain hereditary guilds that he ruled.[4]

Winter, tenth month, fourth day. The Ō-muraji Ōtomo no Muroya led the omi and muraji and presented the imperial signet to the crown prince.

First year [480 CE], spring, first month, fifteenth day. The emperor ordered the administration to build a dais in Mikakuri of Iware, where he acceded to the imperial throne.[x] Then he established his palace. Kara-hime of Kazuraki was honored with the title of empress dowager. The Ō-muraji Ōtomo no Muroya was made Ō-muraji, and the Ō-omi Heguri no Matori was made Ō-omi, each as he was before. The omi, muraji, and allied miyatsuko served according to their respective offices and ranks.

Winter, tenth month, ninth day. They buried Emperor Ō-hatsuse [Yūryaku] at Tajihi-no-taka-washi-no-hara Tomb.[xi] At that time, the Hayahito[5] howled at the tomb day and night. Though food was given to them, they did not eat, and they died in seven days. The administration made a gravesite for them north of the tomb, where they were ceremoniously interred. The year was that of the Metal Monkey.

---

3 The Omi of Kamitsumichi in Kibi are the relatives of Waka-hime and thus maternal relations of Hoshikawa.
4 Shiraka (Seinei) is at this point still only the crown prince, not the emperor. In Ōjin 5.8, the Yama hereditary guild is established in various provinces, but this is the first instance where it is suggested that the Omi of Kamitsumichi in Kibi was in charge of these groups. Their command is given to Odate in Kenzō 1.4.
5 The Hayahito or Hayato first appear in S10 of the "Age of the Gods." They also appear in close service to Emperor Richū in the pre-accession account of Richū.

二年春二月、天皇、恨無子、乃遣大伴室屋大連於諸國、置白髪部舍人・白髪部膳夫・白髪部靫負。冀垂遺跡令觀於後。

冬十一月、依大嘗供奉之料、遣於播磨國司、山部連先祖伊豫來目部小楯、於赤石郡縮見屯倉首忍海部造細目新室、見市邊押磐皇子々億計・弘計、畏敬兼抱、思奉爲君。奉養甚謹、以私供給。便起柴宮、權奉安置。乘驛馳奏。天皇愕然驚歎、良以愴懷曰、懿哉、悅哉、天垂博愛、賜以兩兒。是月、使小楯持節、將左右舍人、至赤石奉迎。語在弘計天皇紀。

三年春正月丙辰朔、小楯等、奉億計・弘計、到攝津國。使臣連持節、以王靑蓋車、迎入宮中。

夏四月乙酉朔辛卯、以億計王爲皇太子。以弘計王爲皇子。

秋七月、飯豐皇女、於角刺宮、與夫初交。謂人曰、一知女道。又安可異。終不願交於男。此曰有夫、未詳也。

九月壬子朔癸丑、遣臣連、巡省風俗。

6　The inaugural feast of first rice was attached special significance. The office of provisional governor did not exist at this time, and the name of Odate's office varies between the *Chronicles*, *Ancient Matters*, and the *Gazetteer of Harima Province*. The Yama-be, or mountain hereditary guild, was charged with maintenance of mountain areas, including presenting their products to the court. Odate later became Muraji of these groups, in Kenzō 1.4. The Muraji of the Yamabe was promoted to sukune in Tenmu 13.12.

SEINEI 2 [481 CE]

Second year [481 CE], second month. The emperor lamented that he had no children. He dispatched Ō-muraji Ōtomo no Muroya to the various provinces and established the servants, cooks, and bath attendants of the Shiraka [Seinei] hereditary guild. He wished to establish a legacy that would be seen in future ages.[xii]

Winter, eleventh month. To get goods for the inaugural feast of first rice, the emperor dispatched the ancestor of the Muraji of Yamabe, Odate of the Kume hereditary guild of Iyo, to Harima.[6] At the newly built house of Hosome, Miyatsuko of the Oshinumi hereditary guild and Obito of the imperial estate at Shijimi in the district of Akashi, he saw the sons of Imperial Prince Ichi-no-he-no-oshiwa, Oke [Ninken] and Woke [Kenzō].[7][xiii] He reverently took them in his arms and thought to take them as his lords. He was exceptionally courteous in seeing to their upbringing and presented his own private possessions to them.[xiv] Then he erected a simple brushwood palace for them as a temporary dwelling. He raced by swift horse and reported to the emperor.[xv] The emperor was shocked and disconsolate, but at length he was moved and said, "How wonderful, how joyous! Heaven has bestowed a great blessing and given me two children." That month, the emperor sent Odate, bearing a token of authority and leading servants for close service to Akashi, to meet and escort the princes.[xvi] This is told in the "Record of Emperor Woke."

Third year [482 CE], spring, first month, first day. Odate and the others accompanied Oke and Woke, and they arrived in Tsu Province.[xvii] The emperor made the omi and muraji bear tokens of authority, and using a blue palanquin, they escorted the princes into the palace.[xviii]

Summer, fourth month, seventh day. Prince Oke [Ninken] was named crown prince. Prince Woke [Kenzō] was named imperial prince.

Autumn, seventh month. Imperial Princess Iidoyo had her first sexual experience at Tsu-no-sashi Palace.[xix] She told people, "I have only recently learned the way of womanhood, but it seems that nothing has changed. I do not wish to have sex with men."

It is still not clear whether she had a husband.

Ninth month, second day. The omi and muraji were dispatched to make an inspection of the circumstances of the people.[xx]

---

7 The two sons of Imperial Prince Ichi-no-he-no-oshiwa, who later become emperors Ninken and Kenzō, bear Japanese names that are both romanized as "Oke" in the present-day Hepburn system of romanization. In this particular case, I use the historical romanization to distinguish the two brothers. Thus, I romanize 弘計 as "Woke," while 億計 remains as "Oke."

冬十月壬午朔乙酉、詔、犬馬器翫、不得獻上。

十一月辛亥朔戊辰、宴臣連於大庭。賜綿帛。皆任其自取、盡力而出。

是月、海表諸蕃、並遣使進調。

四年春正月庚戌朔丙辰、宴海表諸蕃使者於朝堂。賜物各有差。

夏閏五月、大酺五日。

秋八月丁未朔癸丑、天皇親錄囚徒。是日、蝦夷・隼人並内附。

九月丙子朔、天皇、御射殿。詔百寮及海表使者射。賜物各有差。

五年春正月甲戌朔己丑、天皇崩于宮。時年若干。

冬十一月庚午朔戊寅、葬于河內坂門原陵。

弘計天皇 顯宗天皇
弘計天皇更名來目稚子。大兄去來穗別天皇孫也。市邊押磐皇子子也。母曰荑媛。荑、此云波曳。

譜第曰、市邊押磐皇子、娶蟻臣女荑媛。遂生三男二女、其一曰居夏姬。其二曰億計王。更名嶋稚子。更名大石尊。其三曰弘計王。更名來目稚子。其四曰飯豐女王。亦名忍海部女王。其五曰橘王。一本以飯豐女王。列敍於億計王之上。蟻臣者葦田宿禰子也。

---

8   The *Record of Gods and Sovereigns* (*Jinnō shōtōki* 神皇正統記, mid. 14th cent.) gives his age as thirty-nine, the *Water Mirror* (*Mizu kagami* 水鏡, late 12th cent.) as forty-one, and the *Record of Imperial Reigns* (*Kōdaiki* 皇代記) as forty-two.
9   An original note adds, "He was also called Kume-no-wakugo."

Winter, tenth month, fourth day. The emperor decreed, "Dogs, horses, and playthings may not be presented to the throne."[xxi]

Eleventh month, eighteenth day. The emperor held a banquet for the omi and muraji in the great courtyard. He bestowed cotton and silk upon them. They all took as much as they could carry and departed.[xxii]

This month, the various territories across the sea dispatched emissaries who presented tribute.

Fourth year [483 CE], spring, first month, seventh day. The emperor held a banquet in the court hall for the emissaries from the various territories across the sea, bestowing distinct gifts upon each of them.[xxiii]

Summer, intercalary fifth month. There was feasting and heavy drinking for five days.[xxiv]

Autumn, eighth month, seventh day. The emperor personally investigated the cases of prisoners.[xxv] That day, the Emishi and Hayahito both paid homage.

Ninth month, first day. The emperor went out to the archery hall. He decreed that the public officials and the emissaries from across the sea should shoot. And he bestowed distinct gifts upon them.[xxvi]

Fifth year [484 CE], spring, first month, sixteenth day. The emperor expired in the palace. At the time he was not that old.[8]

Winter, eleventh month, ninth day. The emperor was buried in Kōchi-no-sakato-no-hara Tomb.[xxvii]

Discovery of the Royal Heirs

Emperor Woke [Kenzō] was the grandson of Emperor Ōe-no-izaho-wake [Richū].[9][xxviii] He was the son of Imperial Prince Ichi-no-he-no-oshiwa. His mother was called Hae-hime.

> The *Record of Successions to Titles of Nobility* says, "Imperial Prince Ichi-no-he-no-oshiwa married the daughter of the Omi of Ari, Hae-hime.[10] She gave birth to three sons and two daughters. The first was called I-natsu-hime.[xxix] The second was called Prince Oke [Ninken]. Another name for him was Shima-no-wakugo.[xxx] Yet another name for him was Ōshi.[xxxi] The third was called Prince Woke [Kenzō]. Another name for him was Kume-no-wakugo. The fourth was called Princess Iidoyo. Another name for her was Princess Oshi-numibe.[xxxii] The fifth was called Prince Tachibana.[xxxiii] According to one account, Princess Iidoyo was born before Prince Oke. The Omi of Ari was the son of Ashida no Sukune."

---

10 The *Record of Successions to Titles of Nobility*, while not extant, was presumably a genealogical register. It may be a variant of *Annals of the Kings and Emperors*, cited in Kinmei 2.3. The Omi of Ari is given later as the son of Ashida no Sukune. The Richū book of *Ancient Matters* gives Ashida no Sukune as a son of Sotsuhiko of Kazuraki, and Richū marries Kuro-hime, a daughter of Ashida no Sukune. This would mean that Ichi-no-he-no-oshiwa married his aunt.

天皇久居邊裔、悉知百姓憂苦。恆見枉屈、若納四體溝隍。布德施惠、政令流行。邮貧養孀、天下親附。
　穴穗天皇三年十月、天皇父市邊押磐皇子及帳內佐伯部仲子、於蚊屋野、爲大泊瀬天皇見殺。因埋同穴。於是、天皇與億計王、聞父見射、恐懼皆逃亡自匿。帳內日下部連使主使主日下部連之名也。使主、此云於瀰。與吾田彦吾田彦、使主之子也。竊奉天皇與億計王、避難於丹波國余社郡。

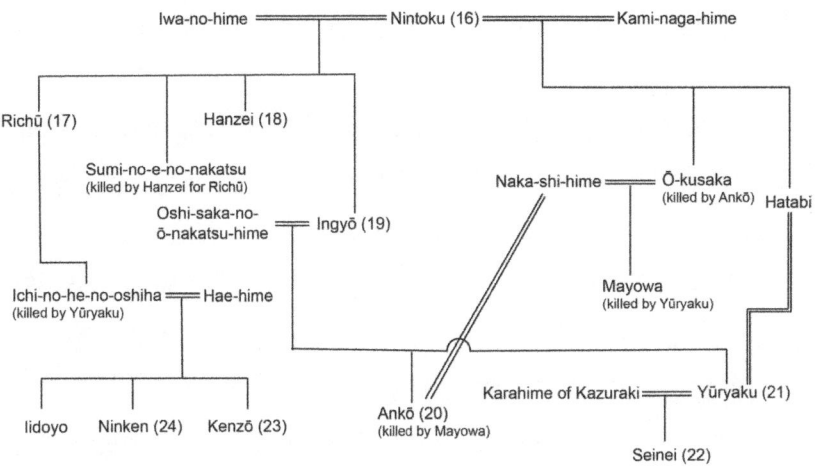

FIGURE 14 Lineage of Iidoyo, Kenzō, and Ninken

The emperor dwelt for a long time in the borderlands and thoroughly knew the troubles and hardships of the people. Frequently seeing their bent backs made him feel as if his own limbs had been thrown into a ditch. He spread virtue and effected grace, and his governance was effectively carried out.[xxxiv] He took pity on the impoverished and provided for widows, and kindly attended to the realm.

In the third year [456 CE], tenth month, of the reign of Emperor Anaho [Ankō], the emperor's father, Imperial Prince Ichi-no-he-no-oshiwa and his servant Saekibe no Nakachiko[11] were in Kayano, where they were killed by Emperor Ō-hatsuse [Yūryaku]. Hence, they were buried in the same hole. When the emperor and Prince Oke [Ninken] heard that their father had been shot, they were sorely afraid, and fled and hid themselves.[xxxv] The servant and Muraji of the Kusakabe, Omi, and Atahiko secretly attended on the emperor and Prince Oke, and they escaped disaster by going to the district of Yoza in Taniwa Province.

<small>Omi was the name of the Muraji of the Kusakabe. Atahiko was the son of Omi.</small>

---

11 Known as Uruwa in the Yūryaku book, with Nakachiko provided in an original note as an alternative name.

使主遂改名字、曰田疾來。尚恐見誅、從茲遁入播磨縮見山石室、而自經死。

天皇尚不識使主所之。勸兄億計王、向播磨國赤石郡、俱改字曰丹波小子。就仕於縮見屯倉首。縮見屯倉首、忍海部造細目也。吾田彥、至此不離、固執臣禮。

白髮天皇二年冬十一月。播磨國司山部連先祖伊豫來目部小楯、於赤石郡、親辨新嘗供物。一云、巡行郡縣、收斂田租也。適會縮見屯倉首、縱賞新室、以夜繼晝。

爾乃、天皇謂兄億計王曰、避亂於斯、年踰數紀。顯名著貴、方屬今宵。

億計王惻然歎曰、其自導揚見害、孰與全身免厄也歟。

天皇曰、吾是去來穗別天皇之孫。而困事於人飼牧牛馬、豈若顯名被害也歟。遂與億計王、相抱涕泣。不能自禁。

億計王曰、然則非弟、誰能激揚大節、可以顯著。

天皇固辭曰、僕不才。豈敢宣揚德業。

億計王曰、弟英才賢德。爰無以過。如是相讓再三。

而果使天皇、自許稱述、俱就室外、居乎下風。屯倉首命居竈傍、左右秉燭。

夜深酒酣、次第儛訖。屯倉首語小楯曰、僕見

Omi went on to change his name to Tatoku, but still fearing that he would be put to death, he fled to Iwaya at Mt. Shijimi in Harima Province and hanged himself.[xxxvi]

The emperor, not knowing where Omi had gone, urged his older brother Prince Oke to make for Akashi District in Harima Province. They both changed their names to those of young boys from Taniwa. When they arrived, they served the Obito of the imperial estate at Shijimi.

<small>The Obito of the imperial estate at Shijimi was Hosome, Miyatsuko of the Oshinumi occupational lineage group.</small>

Up to this time, Atahiko never left the two and steadfastly served them.

In the second year [481 CE], winter, eleventh month, of the reign of Emperor Shiraka [Seinei], the governor of Harima Province and ancestor of the Muraji of the mountain hereditary guild, Odate of the Kume hereditary guild of Iyo, was in Akashi District himself to handle the offerings for the feast of first rice.

<small>According to one account, he was touring the districts and provinces and collecting the rice levies.</small>

Just then he met the Obito of the imperial estate at Shijimi, who was holding a banquet for his new house that went through the night and continued to the next day.

Then the emperor told his older brother Prince Oke [Ninken], "Since we fled disaster up to here, many years have passed. If we are ever to reveal our names and announce our royalty, it must be tonight."

Distressed, Prince Oke said, "Should we pronounce ourselves for who we are and risk being killed, or instead keep ourselves safe?"

The emperor said, "We are the grandsons of Emperor Izaho-wake [Richū]. Now, however, we suffer as the servants of another man, raising his cows and horses. So what if we reveal our names and are killed?" Then he embraced Prince Oke, and they cried, unable to stop their tears.

Prince Oke said, "That being the case, who could speak to this matter and reveal the truth better than my younger brother?"

The emperor firmly refused, saying, "Lacking talent, how can I pretend to speak of great deeds?"

Prince Oke said, "My younger brother is talented and clever. No one can match him."

In this fashion, each deferred to the other over and over. And so at last, it was decided that the emperor himself would make the statement. The two of them reached the door of the house and sat at the end of the table. The Obito of the imperial estate ordered them to sit next to the hearth and shine the light here and there.

The night deepened, and drinking continued unabated. In turn the dances came to an end. The Obito of the imperial estate told Odate, "When I look

此秉燭者、貴人而賤己、先人而後己。恭敬撙節。退讓以明禮。撙者猶趁也。相從也。止也。可謂君子。

於是、小楯撫絃、命秉燭者曰、起儛。

於是兄弟相讓、久而不起、小楯嘖之曰、何爲太遲。速起儛之。億計王起儛既了。天皇次起、自整衣帶、爲室壽曰、

築立稚室葛根	つきたつるわかむろかづね
築立柱者	つきたつるはしらは
此家長御心之鎭也	このいへのきみのみこころのしづまりなり
取擧棟梁者	とりあぐるむねうつはりは
此家長御心之林也	このいへのきみのみこころのはやしなり
取置椽橑者	とりおけるはへきは
此家長御心之齊也	このいへのきみのみこころのととのほりなり
取置蘆葦者	とりおけるえつりは
此家長御心之平也	このいへのきみのみこころのたひらかなるなり
蘆葦、此云哀都利。葦音之潤反。	蘆葦、此おばえつりと云ふ。葦音の音、之潤の反。
取結繩葛者	
此家長御壽之堅也	
取葺草葉者	とりゆへるつなかづらは
此家長御富之餘也	このいへのきみのみこころのみいのちのかたまりなり
出雲者新墾	
新墾之十握稻、	とりふけるかやは
於淺甕	このいへのきみのみこころのみとみのあまりなり
釀酒	
美飮喫哉美飮喫哉、	いづもはにひはり
此云于魔羅儞烏野羅甫屢柯倭。	にひはりのとつかしねを あさらけに
吾子等子者、男子之通稱也。	かめるおほみき
脚日木此傍山	うまらにをやはふるかわ美飮喫哉、此おばうまらにをやはふるかわと云ふ。
牡鹿之角牡鹿、此云左鳥子加。	わがこども子は、男子の通稱也。あしひきのこのかたやまに
擧而吾儛者	さをしかのつの牡鹿、此をばさをしかと云ふ。
旨酒餌香市	
不以直買	ささげてわがまひすれば
手掌憀亮手掌憀亮、此云陀那則擧謀耶羅々儞。	うまさけゑかのいちに あたひもてかはぬ たなそこもやららに手掌憀亮、此おばたなそこもやららにと云ふ。
拍上賜	うちあげたまひつ
吾常世等	わがとこよたち

at the two shining the light, they exalt others while lowering themselves, let others go first and then proceed after, are deferent and follow principle. They are worthy of being called gentlemen."[12][xxxvii]

At this, Odate strummed the zither and ordered the ones shining the light, "Stand and dance."

Then the brothers each deferred to each other, and neither stood for some time. Odate scolded them, saying, "Why do you tarry in excess? Quickly stand up and dance!" Then Prince Oke [Ninken] rose and performed a dance to completion. The emperor stood next, adjusted his clothes and belt, and said the blessing for the new house:

> May the creeping vines of this newly built house, the newly constructed pillars, stabilize the heart of the master of this house. May the raised ridge beams acclaim the heart of the master of this house. May the orderly rafters guide the heart of the master of this house. May the sheathing placed under the roof thatch keep the master of this house levelheaded. May the tied ropes and vines resolutely maintain the lifespan of the master of this house. May the woven thatch bring abundant bounty to the master of this house. From a newly claimed field, from a newly claimed field like Izumo, may you take ten bushels of rice, brew it in a shallow pot, and drink that sake with contented joy. My boys, when I dance holding up the antlers of a stag from this mountainside, I'm saying that this delicious sake cannot be bought for any price at Eka Market. Keep the rhythm of the hand-clapping crisp, my old fellows.

---

12 An original note clarifies the meanings of "following principle."

壽畢乃赴節歌曰、

伊儺武斯蘆	いなむしろ
呵簸泝比野儺擬	かはそひやなぎ
寐逗喩凱磨	みづゆけば
儺弭企於巳陀智	なびきおきたち
曾能泥播宇世儒	そのねはうせず

小楯謂之曰、可怜。願復聞之。

天皇遂作殊儛。

殊儛、古謂之立出儛。立出、此云陀豆々。儛狀者乍起乍居而儛之。

詡之曰、

倭者彼	やまとは
々茅原	そそちはら
淺茅原	あさちはら
弟日	おとひ
僕是也	やつこらま

小楯由是、深奇異焉。更使唱之、天皇詡之曰、

石上	いそのかみ
振之神榲榲、此云須擬	ふるのかむすぎ榲、此おばす
伐本	ぎと云ふ
截末伐本截末、此云譜登岐利須	もときり
衞於茲婆羅比。	するおしはらひ伐本截末、此
於市邊宮	おばもときりするおしはらひと云
治天下	ふ
天萬國萬押磐尊御裔	いちのへのみやに
僕是也	あめのしたしらしし
	あめよろづくによろづおし
	はのみことのみあなすゑ
	やつこらま

When the blessing was finished, he then sang a song in keeping with the rhythm:

Though the willow on the riverbank
may bend or raise its branches
as the water flows by,
its roots are never lost.

Odate told him, "How intriguing. I want to hear more."
The emperor then performed a Tatsuzu dance.

A Tatsuzu dance was originally called a "Tatsu-zu" dance, using the characters "stand" and "exit." The dance is performed now standing up, now sitting down.

Then he raised his voice and sang,

Yamato is
a rustling field of cogon grass.
A prince
of this cogon grass field,
I am.

At this point, Odate became deeply suspicious. He made him sing again. The emperor raised his voice and sang,

The divine cedar at Furu
in Isonokami!
Its roots were cut
and its branches swept away.
An august descendant
of Ame-yorozu-kuni-yorozu-oshiwa
who ruled the realm
from Ichi-no-he Palace,
I am.

小楯大驚、離席悵然再拜、承事供給、率屬欽伏、於是、悉發郡民造宮。不日權奉安置。

　　乃詣京都、求迎二王。白髮天皇、聞憙咨歎曰、朕無子也。可以爲嗣、與大臣大連、定策禁中。仍使播磨國司來目部小楯、持節、將左右舍人、至赤石奉迎。

　　白髮天皇三年春正月。天皇隨億計王、到攝津國。使臣連持節、以王靑蓋車、迎入宮中。

　　夏四月、立億計王爲皇太子、立天皇爲皇子。

　　五年春正月、白髮天皇崩。

　　是月、皇太子億計王與天皇讓位。久而不處。由是、天皇姉飯豐靑皇女、於忍海角刺宮、臨朝秉政。自稱忍海飯豐靑尊。當世詞人歌曰、

野麻登陛儞	やまとへに
瀰我保指母能婆	みがほしものは
於尸農瀰能	おしぬみの
莒能陀哿紀儺屢	このたかきなる
都奴娑之能瀰野	つのさしのみや

Odate, greatly shocked, left his seat and, distressed, repeatedly bowed. He submitted himself, presented what he had collected, and led his people in reverentially serving the two. Then he roused all of the people in the district, and they built a palace. Before one day had passed, the princes could dwell in it temporarily.

Odate reported back to the capital and requested to escort the two princes. Emperor Shiraka [Seinei] heard this, sighed with great delight, and said, "We have no children. So they shall succeed Us." He held conference in the palace with the Ō-omi and the Ō-muraji. Thereupon he made the Governor of Harima Province, Odate of the Kume hereditary guild, bear a token of authority and lead servants for close service, to Akashi to meet and escort the princes.

In the third year [482 CE], spring, first month, of the reign of Emperor Shiraka, the emperor [Woke], along with Prince Oke, arrived in Tsu Province. The omi and muraji, made by the emperor to bear tokens of authority and using a blue palanquin, escorted the princes into the palace.

Summer, fourth month. Prince Oke [Ninken] was named crown prince, and the emperor [Woke] named Imperial Prince.

Administration of Princess Iidoyo, Accession of Emperor Kenzō

Fifth year [484 CE], spring, first month. Emperor Shiraka [Seinei] expired.

That month, since Crown Prince Oke and the emperor [Woke, Kenzō] kept deferring the throne to each other, for a long time it was unoccupied. For this reason, the emperor's older sister, Imperial Princess Iidoyo-no-ao, attended to the administration of the court from Oshinumi-no-tsu-no-sashi Palace. She styled herself the Honorable Iidoyo-no-ao of Oshinumi.[13] The bards of that time sang,

> What I wish to see
> in the Yamato area
> is Tsu-no-sashi Palace,
> the high fort at
> Oshinumi.

---

13 The addition of "Honorable" (*mikoto*) to Iidoyo's name, a title usually reserved for emperors, as well as the use below of "expired" and her burial in an imperial tomb (*misazaki*), suggest that the compilers of the *Chronicles* regarded her as equivalent to an emperor in status. Only Iidoyo and Yamato Take warranted this honor. Some historical materials, such as the *Brief History of Fūsō* (*Fusō ryakki* 扶桑略記, late 12th cent.), count Iidoyo in the succession of emperors.

冬十一月、飯豐靑尊崩。葬葛城埴口丘陵。

十二月、百官大會。皇太子億計、取天皇之璽、置之天皇之坐。再拜從諸臣之位曰、此天子之位、有功者可以處之。著貴蒙迎、皆弟之謀也。以天下讓天皇。

天皇顧讓以弟、莫敢即位。又奉白髮天皇、先欲傳兄、立皇太子、前後固辭曰、日月出矣、而爝火不息。其於光也、不亦難乎。時雨降矣、而猶浸灌。不亦勞乎。所貴爲人弟者、奉兄、謀逃脫難、照德解紛、而無

處也。即有處者、非弟恭之義。弘計不忍處也。兄友弟恭、不易之典。聞諸古老。安自獨輕。

皇太子億計曰、白髮天皇、以吾兄之故、擧天下之事、而先屬我。我其羞之。惟大王、首建利遁。聞之者歎息。彰顯帝孫、見之者殞涕。憫々摺紳、忻荷戴天之慶。哀々黔首、悅逢履地之恩。是以、克固四維、永隆萬葉。功隣造物、淸猷映世。超哉、邈矣、粤無得而稱。雖是曰兄、豈先處乎。非功而據、咎悔必至。吾聞、天皇不可以久曠。天命不可以謙拒。大王以社稷爲計、百姓爲心。發言慷慨、至于流涕。

Winter, eleventh month. The Honorable Iidoyo-no-ao expired.[14] She was buried in Hanikuchi-no-oka Tomb in Kazuraki.[xxxviii]

Twelfth month. All the officials convened in a great meeting. Crown Prince Oke [Ninken] took the imperial signet and sat in the imperial seat. He bowed and then went to where the high government officials were and said, "The rank of emperor should be occupied by one who is valiant. That my royal status was revealed, and that I was escorted here, was all the doing plan of my younger brother." Then he deferred in assuming the realm to the emperor.

The emperor in turn deferred, saying that as he was the younger brother, he did not dare succeed to the throne. Also, Emperor Shiraka [Seinei] had wanted the older brother to succeed first and named him crown prince, and so from beginning to end, he firmly declined, saying, "When the sun or moon comes out but you do not cease making lighting lamps, is setting up those lights not acting contrary to the natural light? When timely rain falls but you still irrigate the fields, is it not wasted labor? The reasons for esteeming a model younger brother are: service to his older brother, planning to avoid difficulties, resolving conflicts in ways that reflect virtue, and not occupying his proper place. Hence, to take his place would go against the principles by which a younger brother is to be esteemed. I, Woke [Kenzō], cannot bear to be in such a position. The older brother takes care of the younger, and the younger brother respects the older: this is the unchanging rule. Such is what I hear from the elders. How could I alone make light of these principles?"[xxxix]

Crown Prince Oke said, "Emperor Shiraka first charged me with the matters of the realm because I am the older brother. How ashamed I am at this! Thinking on matters, it was you, my prince, who first effected our escape, and those who hear of it sigh in admiration. When you revealed that we are descended from an emperor, those who witnessed shed tears. Accordingly, anxious public officials will gladly shoulder the burden of living under heaven, and pitiful commoners will consider themselves fortunate to set foot on this earth. Therefore, fortify well the four directions and prosper long, for a myriad generations.[xl] Your meritorious deeds are close to the creation itself, and your genuine designs clear to the world. How preeminent; how outstanding! The marvel of it all cannot be expressed in words. Though I am called the elder brother, how could I first assume this position? Were I to occupy it without merit, my doing so would certainly lead to blame and regret. I hear that the emperorship should not be empty

---

14 *Water Mirror* gives her age as 45.

天皇於是、知終不處、不逆兄意、乃聽。而不即御坐。世嘉其能以實讓曰、宜哉、兄弟怡々、天下歸德。篤於親族、則民興仁。

　　元年春正月己巳朔、大臣・大連等奏言、皇太子億計、聖德明茂、奉讓天下。陛下正統。當奉鴻緖、爲郊廟主、承續祖無窮之烈、上當天心、下厭民望。而不肯踐祚。遂令金銀蕃國群僚、遠近莫不失望。天命有屬。皇太子推讓。聖德彌盛、

　　福祚孔章。在孺而勤、謙恭慈順。宜奉兄命、承統大業。

　　制曰、可。乃召公卿百僚於近飛鳥八釣宮、即天皇位。百官陪位者、皆忻々焉。

for long, nor should heaven's mandate be deferred or refused. My great lord, make the state and its households according to your designs, and keep the people in your heart."[xli] He was so impassioned while speaking that he was brought to tears.

The emperor, at this point, had not intended to occupy the throne, but he could not go against his older brother's wishes, and so he considered the matter. However, he did not succeed to the throne. People at the time heard of the sincerity with which the two deferred to each other and praised them, saying, "How excellent! When older and younger brothers are happily in harmony, the realm will enjoy virtue. When families are in accord, the people will be moved to benevolence."

First year [485 CE], spring, first month, first day. The Ō-omi and the Ō-muraji addressed the emperor, saying, "Crown Prince Oke [Ninken] is clearly the pinnacle of sagacious virtue, and he has deferred the realm to you. Our liege, you must succeed to the throne. Receive the heavenly endeavor, become the master of the realm, and continue the boundless achievements of your ancestors. Above, pay heed to the intentions of heaven, and below, grant the wishes of the people. However, should you reject governing the heavenly endeavor, then as a result, the high government officials of the tributary nations of gold and silver, those both far and near, cannot but lose their hopes. The heavenly mandate must be followed. The crown prince deferred the throne. Your sagacious virtue is ever at its peak, and your blessings remarkably pronounced. You labored when you were young, humbly, respectfully, and graciously following. Accept your older brother's order and succeed to the great endeavor."[xlii]

The emperor decreed, "So be it." Then he summoned the high government officials and public servants to Yatsuri Palace in Chika-tsu-asuka and acceded to the imperial throne.[xliii] The functionaries of the government offices were all pleased.

或本云、弘計天皇之宮、有二所焉。一宮於小郊、二宮於池野。又或本云、宮於甕栗。

是月、立皇后難波小野王。赦天下。難波小野王、雄朝津間稚子宿禰天皇曾孫、磐城王孫、丘稚子王之女也。

二月戊戌朔壬寅、詔曰、先王遭離多難、殞命荒郊。朕在幼年、亡逃自匿。狎遇求迎、升纂大業。廣求御骨、莫能知者。詔畢、與皇太子億計、泣哭憤惋、不能自勝。

是月、召聚耆宿、天皇親歷問。有一老嫗進曰、置目知御骨埋處。請以奉示。置目老嫗名也。近江國狹々城山君祖倭帒宿禰妹、名曰置目。見下文。於是、天皇與皇太子億計、將老嫗婦、幸于近江國來田絮蚊屋野中、掘出而見、果如婦語。臨穴哀號、言深更慟。自古以來、莫如斯酷。仲子之尸、交橫御骨、莫能別者。

爰有磐坂皇子之乳母。奏曰、仲子者上齒墮落。以斯可別。於是、雖由乳母、相別髑髏、而竟難別四支諸骨。由是、

According to one account, Emperor Woke [Kenzō] had palaces in two locations. One was at Ono, and the other was at Ikeno. Also, according to another account, he built a palace in Mikakuri.[15]

That month, Ono of Naniwa was named empress. An amnesty was issued for the realm.

Ono of Naniwa was the great-granddaughter of Emperor O-asazuma-wakugo-no-sukune, the granddaughter of Prince Iwaki, and the daughter of Prince Oka-no-wakugo.[16]

Resolution of the Murder of the Emperor's Father, Death of the Emperor

Second month, fifth day. The emperor proclaimed, "The late prince[17] met with many misfortunes and lost his life in the wilds. We were then young, and fled and hid Ourself. By chance, We were found and brought here, and have since succeeded to the great endeavor. Though We have searched widely for his august remains, no one knows precisely where they are." When he completed this proclamation, he and Crown Prince Oke [Ninken] uncontrollably wailed in grief.

That month, the emperor assembled the elderly and personally asked them about the matter individually. An old woman came forth and said, "Okime knows where the august remains are buried. Ask and I will show you where."

Okime was the old woman's name. Okime was the name of the younger sister of the ancestor of the Kimi of Sasaki-no-yama in Ōmi, Yamato-fukuro no Sukune. It is seen in the text below.

The emperor and Crown Prince Oke led the old woman and went to Kayano in Kutawata in Ōmi Province. When they exhumed him and looked, it was as the old woman had said. They looked at the hole and wailed with a sadness arising from the depths of their hearts. And again they lamented. Since ancient times, never was there anything as heart-rending as this. The remains of Nakachiko were mixed in with those of the august deceased, and no one could properly separate them.

The wet nurse of Imperial Prince Iwasaka was then in attendance. She addressed the emperor, "Nakachiko's upper teeth had fallen out. Thereby you can separate the two." They distinguished the skulls based on what the wet nurse said, but it was difficult to separate the trunks and limbs. So the

---

15 Mikakuri was the location of Seinei's palace.
16 Iwaki does not appear in the Ingyō book, and Oka-no-wakugo is unclear. In Yūryaku 1.3, his consort Waka-hime of Kibi has a son named Imperial Prince Iwaki.
17 Ichi-no-he-no-oshiwa.

仍於蚊屋野中、造起雙陵、相似如一。葬儀無異。詔老嫗置目、居于宮傍近處。優崇賜㕮、使無乏少。

是月、詔曰、老嫗伶俜羸弱、不便行步。宜張繩引紐、扶而出入。繩端懸鐸、無勞謁者。入則鳴之。朕知汝到。

於是、老嫗奉詔、鳴鐸而進。天皇遙聞鐸聲、歌曰、

阿佐膩簸囉	あさぢはら
嗚贈禰嗚須擬	をそねをすぎ
謨謀逗拕甫	ももづたふ
奴底喩羅倶慕與	ぬてゆらくもよ
於岐毎倶羅之慕	おきめくらしも

三月上巳、幸後苑、曲水宴。

夏四月丁酉朔丁未、詔曰、凡人主之所以勸民者、惟授官也。國之所以興者、惟賞功也。夫前播磨國司來目部小楯、更名磐楯。求迎擧朕。厥功茂焉。所志願勿難言。

小楯謝曰、山官宿所願。乃拜山官、改賜姓山部連氏。以吉備臣爲副、以山守部爲民。哀善顯功、

emperor erected at Kayano a pair of tombs, each like the other. Nor was there any difference in the funeral ceremonies. The emperor decreed to the old woman Okime that she live nearby the palace. He humbly showed her favor and ensured that she lived without poverty.

That month the emperor proclaimed, "Old woman, you are tottering and frail, and walking is not easy for you. A rope will be strung for you, and by grasping onto it, you may come and go. At the end of the rope shall be attached a bell, so no one will need announce you. When you enter, ring the bell, and We will know you have come."

The old woman received the proclamation, rang the bell, and came forth. The emperor heard the sound of the bell from far away and sang,

> Across the barren land
> and sparse cogon grass field,
> like post-station chimes,
> the bell tolls.
> It seems Okime has come.

Third month, third day. The emperor went to the imperial courtyard and hosted a winding-stream banquet.[18]

Summer, fourth month, eleventh day. The emperor proclaimed, "In general, the means by which the ruler encourages the people is by bestowing authority. The means by which the state prospers is by rewarding achievement.[xliv] The previous Governor of Harima Province, Odate of the Kume hereditary guild, sought Us out and welcomed Us.[19] His achievements are great. Speak your desires, and do not hold back."

Odate thankfully said, "I have always wished to administer the mountains." Thereby he was named Administrator of the Mountains, and the new title of nobility Muraji of the Yamabe was bestowed upon him. The Omi of Kibi was made his second-in-command, and the Yamamori hereditary guild were made his people. His good deeds were praised and his achievements

---

18 This is the first of three winding-stream banquets held during Kenzō's reign. Afterward there is no record of such an event until Monmu 5.3 in the *Continued Chronicles of Japan*.
19 An original note adds, "He was also called Iwatate."

酬恩答厚。寵愛殊絶、富莫能儔。

五月、狹々城山君韓帒宿禰、事連謀殺皇子押磐。臨誅叩頭言詞極哀。天皇不忍加戮、充陵戸兼守山。削除籍帳、隸山部連。惟倭帒宿禰、因妹置目之功、仍賜本姓狹々城山君氏。

六月、幸避暑殿、奏樂。會群臣、設以酒食。是年也、太歲乙丑。

二年春三月上巳、幸後苑曲水宴。

是時、喜集公卿大夫・臣連國造伴造、爲宴。群臣頻稱萬歲。

秋八月己未朔、天皇謂皇太子億計曰、吾父先王無罪。而大泊瀨天皇射殺、棄骨郊野、至今未獲。憤歎盈懷。臥泣、行號、志雪讎恥。吾聞、父之讎不與共戴天、兄弟之讎不反兵。交遊之讎不同國。夫匹夫之子、居父母之讎、寢苫枕干不仕。不與共國。遇諸市朝、不反兵而便鬪。況吾立爲天子、二年于今矣。願壞其陵、攘骨投散。今以此報、不亦孝乎。

clear, and in return for the favor shown to him, he responded graciously. The imperial favor shown to him was exceptional, and no one could match his riches.

Fifth month. The Kimi of Sasaki-no-yama, Kara-fukuro no Sukune, was charged with plotting to murder Imperial Prince Oshiwa. When he was about to be put to death he kowtowed, and his words were extremely moving. The emperor could not bear to kill him, and so tasked him with maintaining the tombs, as well as serving as steward of the mountain. His genealogy was removed from the official registers,[20] and he was made to serve the Muraji of the Yamabe. Because of the meritorious deeds of his younger sister Okime, Yamato-fukuro no Sukune was granted his former title of nobility, Kimi of Sasaki-no-yama.

Sixth month. The emperor went to his summer palace and had music played. He gathered the high government officials and held a banquet. This was the year of the Wood Ox.

Second year [486 CE], spring, third month, third day. The emperor went to the imperial courtyard and hosted a winding-stream banquet.

At that time, he gladly assembled the high government officials, omi, muraji, provincial miyatsuko, and allied miyatsuko, and hosted a banquet. The high government officials repeatedly wished him a long reign.

Autumn, eighth month, first day. The emperor told Crown Prince Oke [Ninken], "Our father the late prince was innocent. However, Emperor Ō-hatsuse [Yūryaku] shot him dead and discarded his corpse in a field, and even now we have not recovered it. Resentment and grief fill my bosom. I weep in my sleep and cry while awake, and desire to clear away this shame. I have heard, 'Do not share the same heaven as the enemy of thy father. Do not be remiss in arming yourself if there be enemies of thy brothers. Do not dwell in the same land as the enemies of thy friends.'[xlv] The child of a commoner, if there are enemies of their father or mother, will sleep on straw matting and make his shield his pillow. He will not live in the same land, and if they might chance upon him in the market or in public, will ensure he does not have to return home for weapons and so can immediately give fight. Yet since I became the emperor, two years have passed. I wish to destroy Emperor Ō-hatsuse's tomb, rend his corpse asunder, and scatter the pieces. Now, if I revenge myself in this way, is it not also filial piety?"

---

20 Meaning that his family was reduced to commoner status, though this punishment is anachronistic, since the Civil and Penal Codes had not yet been implemented.

皇太子億計、歔欷不能答、乃諫曰、不可。大泊瀬天皇、正統萬機、臨照天下。華夷欣仰、天皇之身也。吾父先王、雖是天皇之子、遭遇迍邅、不登天位。以此觀之、尊卑惟別。而忍壞陵墓、誰人主以奉天之靈。其不可毀、一也。又天皇與億計、曾不蒙遇白髮天皇厚寵殊恩、豈臨寶位。大泊瀬天皇、白髮天皇之父也。億計聞諸老賢。老賢曰、言無不訓、德無不報。有恩不報、敗俗之深者也。陛下饗國、德行廣聞於天下。而毀陵、翻見於華裔、億計恐、其不可以莅國子民也。其不可毀、二也。

　天皇曰、善哉。令罷役。

　九月、置目老困、乞還曰、氣力衰邁、老耄虛羸。要假扶繩、不能進步。願歸桑梓、以送厥終。

　天皇聞惋痛、賜物千段。逆傷岐路、重感難期。乃賜歌曰、

於岐每慕與	おきめもよ
阿甫瀰能於岐毎	あふみのおきめ
阿須用利簸	あすよりは
瀰野磨我倶利底	みやまがくりて
彌曳孺哿謨阿羅牟	みえずかもあらむ

Crown Prince Oke was sobbing and could not reply. He then remonstrated with the emperor, saying, "You cannot. Emperor Ō-hatsuse [Yūryaku] rightly carried on the imperial line and attended on the realm. Both noble and commoner gladly respect the authority of the emperor. Our father, the late prince, though he was the son of an emperor, met with disaster and did not rise to the imperial throne. In view of this consideration, their respective social positions were different. If you can bear to destroy his tomb, who will serve the spirit of heaven as a lord? This is the first reason that you cannot destroy it. Furthermore, had you, the emperor, and Oke, myself, not met by chance with the courteous favor and exceptional grace of Emperor Shiraka, how could you have attained the precious throne? Emperor Ō-hatsuse was the father of Emperor Shiraka [Seinei]. I, Oke, have been listening to the elder wise ones. They say, 'No utterance is without retaliation. No action is without repayment.[xlvi] Not returning a favor is a deep affront to society.'[xlvii] My liege, you rule the state, and your actions are widely known in the realm. If you destroy the tomb, showing yourself as such to the noble and commoner, I, Oke, fear that on account of this, you would be unable to rule the state and cultivate its people. This is the second reason that you cannot destroy it."

The emperor said, "Well said," and ended the effort.

Ninth month. Okime was troubled with old age and begged leave to return, saying, "My vitality has declined too much, and I have weakened in my dotage. Even if I hold onto the rope, I cannot walk.[xlviii] I wish to return to my homeland and there spend the last of my life."

The emperor heard this and was saddened, and he bestowed upon her one thousand bolts of cloth. He grieved that their paths were diverging and mourned that it was unlikely that they would meet again. Then he bestowed upon her a song that went,

Okime,
Okime of Ōmi!
From tomorrow
you will be hidden by the mountains,
and I will likely be unable to see you.

冬十月戊午朔癸亥、宴群臣。是時、天下安平、民無徭役。歲比登稔、百姓殷富。稻斛銀錢一文。馬被野。

三年春二月丁巳朔、阿閉臣事代銜命、出使于任那。於是、月神著人謂之曰、我祖高皇産靈、有預鎔造天地之功。宜以民地、奉我月神。若依請獻我、當福慶。事代由是、還京具奏。奉以歌荒樔田歌荒樔田者、在山背國葛野郡也。壹伎縣主先祖押見宿禰侍祠。

三月上巳、幸後苑、曲水宴。

夏四月丙辰朔庚申、日神著人、謂阿閉臣事代曰、以磐余田、獻我祖高皇産靈。事代便奏。依神乞獻田十四町。對馬下縣直侍祠。戊辰、置福草部。庚辰、天皇崩于八釣宮。

是歲、紀生磐宿禰、跨據任那、交通高麗。將西王三韓、整脩宮府、自稱神聖。用任那左魯・那奇他甲背等計、殺百濟適莫爾解於爾林。爾林、高麗地也。

Winter, tenth month, sixth day. The emperor held a banquet for the high government officials. At the time, the realm was at peace, and the people did not have corvée labor duties. The harvest was bountiful this year and the people were well off. A bushel of rice sold for one silver coin, and horses were plentiful in the fields.[xlix]

Third year [487 CE], spring, second month, first day. The Omi of Ahe,[21] Kotoshiro, received an imperial order and was sent to Mimana as a messenger. At that time, the kami of the moon possessed a person and told him, "My ancestor Taka-mi-musuhi molded heaven and earth. Offer people and land to me, the moon god. If you present them to me as I ask, you will experience good fortune and joy." Kotoshiro returned to the capital and reported this to the emperor in detail. The emperor used as offering the rice paddies of Uta-arasu.

> The rice paddies of Uta-arasu are in the Kadono District of Yamashiro Province.

The distant ancestor of the Agatanushi of Iki, Oshimi no Sukune, attended to the veneration of the kami.[l]

Third month, third day. The emperor went to the imperial courtyard and hosted a winding-stream banquet.

Summer, fourth month, fifth day. The kami of the sun possessed a person and told the Omi of Ahe, Kotoshiro, "Present the rice paddies of Iware to my ancestor Taka-mi-musuhi." Kotoshiro promptly reported this to the emperor. In accordance with the request of the kami, the emperor presented fourteen hectares of rice fields. The Atai of Shimotsu District in Tsushima attended to the veneration of the kami.[li] Thirteenth day. The emperor established the Sakikusa hereditary guild.

Twenty-fifth day. The emperor expired at Yatsuri Palace.[22]

That year, Oiwa no Sukune of Ki crossed through Mimana and established communication with Koguryŏ. Out west, in an effort to become the ruler of the three kingdoms of Korea, he set up a palace administration and declared himself to be a kami.[lii] Using plans by Chwaro and Nagit'a-gappae of Mimana, he killed Chŏng-mag-ihae at Nirimu.[liii]

> Nirimu is a place in Koguryŏ.

---

21 The Kōgen book gives Kōgen's son Ō-hiko as the first ancestor of the Omi of Ahe.
22 *Ancient Matters* claims that Kenzō ruled for eight years and died at thirty-eight.

築帶山城、距守東道。斷運糧津、令軍飢困。百濟王大怒、遣領軍古爾解・內頭莫古解等、率衆趣于帶山攻。

於是、生磐宿禰、進軍逆擊。膽氣益壯、所向皆破。以一當百。俄而兵盡力竭。知事不濟、自任那歸。由是、百濟國殺佐魯・那奇他甲背等三百餘人。

億計天皇 仁賢天皇

億計天皇、諱大脚。更名大爲。自餘諸天皇、不言諱字。而至此天皇、獨自書者、據舊本耳。字嶋郎。弘計天皇同母兄也。幼而聰穎、才敏多識。壯而仁惠、謙恕温慈。及穴穗天皇崩、避難於丹波國余社郡。

白髮天皇元年冬十一月、播磨國司山部連小楯、詣京求迎。白髮天皇、尋遣小楯、持節、將左右舍人、至赤石奉迎。二年夏四月、遂立億計天皇、爲皇太子。事具弘計天皇紀也。五年、白髮天皇崩。天皇以天下讓弘計天皇。爲皇太子、如故。

He built the fortress of Shitoro-moro, blocking off and fortifying the way to Yamato.[liv] He cut off the ports used for transporting provisions and threatened the army with starvation. The King of Paekche, greatly angered, dispatched General Koihae and Interior Ministry Head Makkohae to lead an army to Shitoro-moro and attack it.[23]

Oiwa no Sukune advanced his army and counterattacked. Overflowing with fighting spirit, they broke through wherever they turned. Each soldier was worth one hundred.[lv] But in time, the troops were exhausted, and knowing that they could not finish things, they returned from Mimana. Owing to this turn of events, the King of Paekche killed over three hundred people, including Chwaro and Nagit'a-gappae.

Reign of Emperor Ninken

Emperor Oke [Ninken] had Ōshi as his real name.[lvi]

He was also called Ōsu.[lvii] The real names of the other various emperors are not given. However, that it is recorded for this emperor is only on account of an old record.

His courtesy name was Shima-no-iratsuko. He was the older brother of Emperor Woke [Kenzō] by the same mother. When he was young, he was exceptionally bright, and being intelligent, he knew many things. When he blossomed into adulthood, he was gracious, humble, and merciful.[lviii] When Emperor Anaho [Ankō] expired, he fled to Yoza District, Taniwa Province.

In the first year [480 CE], winter, eleventh month, of the reign of Emperor Shiraka, Odate, Governor of Harima Province and Muraji of the Yamabe, came to the capital, then sought out and welcomed the emperor. Emperor Shiraka had Odate, bearing a token of authority and leading servants for close service, escort him to Akashi.

In the second year [481 CE], summer, fourth month,[24] Emperor Oke [Ninken] was named crown prince.

This matter is recorded in detail in the "Annals of Emperor Woke."

In the fifth year [484 CE], Emperor Shiraka [Seinei] expired. The emperor [Oke, Ninken] deferred the realm to Emperor Woke [Kenzō]. He was named crown prince, as before.

---

23 The Paekche army was divided into five corps, each with its own general. It is not clear which corps is referred to here. Koni (Kr. Koi) is the name of Paekche's eighth king and appears to be used as a last name. A Koi Mannyŏn appears in Kaero 21.9 in the *Samguk sagi*. Makkohae does not appear elsewhere.

24 In the Seinei book, his being named crown prince takes place in the third year, summer, fourth month.

事具弘計天皇紀也。

三年夏四月、弘計天皇崩。

元年春正月辛巳朔乙酉、皇太子、於石上廣高宮、即天皇位。或本云、億計天皇之宮、有二所焉。一宮於川村、二宮於縮見高野。其殿柱至今未朽。

二月辛亥朔壬子、立前妃春日大娘皇女爲皇后。春日大娘皇女、大泊瀬天皇、娶和珥臣深目之女童女君所生也。遂産一男六女。其一曰高橋大娘皇女。其二曰朝嬬皇女。其三曰手白香皇女。其四曰樟氷皇女。其五曰橘皇女。其六曰小泊瀬稚鷦鷯天皇。及有天下、都泊瀬列城。其七曰眞稚皇女。一本、以樟氷皇女列于第三、以手白香皇女列于第四、爲異焉。

次和珥臣日爪女糠君娘、生一女。是爲春日山田皇女。一本云、和珥臣日觸女大糠娘、生一女。是爲山田大娘皇女。更名赤見皇女。文雖稍異、其實一也。

冬十月丁未朔己酉、葬弘計天皇于傍丘磐杯丘陵。是歲也、太歲戊辰。

二年秋九月、難波小野皇后、恐宿不敬自死。

This details of this matter are in the "Annals of Emperor Woke."

In the third year [487 CE], summer, fourth month of his reign, Emperor Woke expired.

First year [488 CE], spring, first month, fifth day. The crown prince succeeded to the imperial throne at Isonokami-no-hirotaka Palace.[25]

> One book says, Emperor Oke had two palaces. One was in Kawamura, and the second palace was in Shijimi-no-takano. A pillar from that palace still has not rotted.

Second month, second day. His former consort, Imperial Princess Kasuga-no-ō-iratsume, was named empress.

> Kasuga-no-ō-iratsume was born of the marriage of Emperor Ō-hatsuse [Yūryaku] to Omina-gimi, the daughter of the Omi of Wani, Fukame.

She gave birth to one son and six daughters. The first was called Imperial Princess Takahashi-no-ō-iratsume.[lix] The second was called Imperial Princess Asazuma.[lx] The third was called Imperial Princess Tashiraka.[lxi] The fourth was called Imperial Princess Kusubi.[lxii] The fifth was called Imperial Princess Tachibana.[lxiii] The sixth was called Emperor O-hatsuse-no-waka-sazaki [Buretsu]. He went on to rule the realm and built his capital at Namiki in Hatsuse. The seventh was called Imperial Princess Mawaka.[lxiv]

> One difference, according to one source, is that Imperial Princess Kusubi was third and Imperial Princess Tashiraka was fourth.

Next, the daughter of Hitsume, Omi of Wani, Arakimi-no-iratsume, gave birth to one daughter.[26] She was Imperial Princess Kasuga-no-yamada.

> One source says, the daughter of Hifure, Omi of Wani, Ō-ara-no-iratsume, gave birth to one daughter. She was Imperial Princess Yamada-no-ō-iratsume. Another name for her was Imperial Princess Akami. Though the records differ, there is only one truth.

Winter, tenth month, third day. Emperor Woke [Kenzō] was buried at Kataoka-no-iwatsuki-no-oka Tomb.[lxv] This was the year of the Earth Dragon.

Second year [489 CE], autumn, ninth month. Empress Ono of Naniwa, on account of fear born of previous disrespectful behavior, killed herself.

---

25 Isonokami is the present-day Isonokami area of Tenri City, Nara Prefecture.
26 In Kinmei 2.3, Kinmei takes as his consort the daughter of Hitsume, Omi of Kasuga, Arako, and she gives birth to Imperial Princess Kasuga-no-yamada and Imperial Prince Tachibana-no-maro. However, Kasuga-no-yamada is empress to Ankan, making the genealogy here more probable. In *Ancient Matters*, she is given as Nuka-no-wakugo.

弘計天皇時、皇太子億計侍宴、取瓜將喫、無刀子。弘計天皇、親執刀子、命其夫人小野傳進、夫人就前、立置刀子於瓜盤。是日、更酌酒、立喚皇太子。緣斯不敬、恐誅自死。

三年春二月己巳朔、置石上部舍人。

四年夏五月、的臣蚊嶋・穗瓮君瓮、此云倍。有罪、皆下獄死。

五年春二月丁亥朔辛卯、普求國郡散亡佐伯部。以佐伯部仲子之後、爲佐伯造。佐伯部仲子、事見弘計天皇紀。

六年秋九月己酉朔壬子、遣日鷹吉士、使高麗、召巧手者。

是秋、日鷹吉士、被遣使後、有女人、居于難波御津、哭之曰、於母亦兄、於吾亦兄。弱草吾夫何怜矣。言於母亦兄、於吾亦兄、此云於慕尼慕是、阿例尼慕是。言吾夫何怜矣、此云阿我圖摩播耶。言弱草、謂古者以弱草喩夫婦。故以弱草爲夫。哭聲甚哀、令人斷腸。

菱城邑人鹿父鹿父、人名也。俗、呼父爲柯曾。聞而向前曰、何哭之哀、甚若此乎。

女人答曰、秋葱之轉雙雙、重也。納、可思惟矣。

鹿父曰、諾。即知所言矣。

有同伴者、不悟其意、問曰、何以知乎。

答曰、難波玉作部鯽魚女言鯽魚女、此云浮儺謎。嫁於韓白水郎暎言韓白水郎暎、此云柯羅摩能波陀該。暎耕麥田之也。

During the reign of Emperor Woke, Crown Prince Oke [Ninken] was in attendance at a banquet. He took a gourd and meant to eat it but had no knife. Emperor Woke took his own knife and ordered his wife Ono to pass it to him. She came forth and placed the knife on the plate with the melon while standing. On that day, she also poured wine, and she called upon the crown prince while standing. Because of that disrespectful behavior, she feared being put to death and killed herself.

Third year [490 CE], spring, second month, first day. The emperor established the servants of the Isonokami hereditary guild.

Fourth year [491 CE], summer, fifth month. Kashima, the Omi of Ikuha, and Hohe no Kimi committed a crime, were imprisoned, and died.[lxvi]

Fifth year [492 CE], spring, second month, fifth day. The emperor searched for the Saeki hereditary guild, which, in flight, had been scattered to every district and province. The descendants of Nakachiko of the Saeki hereditary guild were made Miyatsuko of the Saeki.

The matter of Nakachiko of the Saeki is seen in the "Annals of Emperor Woke [Kenzō]."

Sixth year [493 CE], autumn, ninth month, fourth day. The emperor dispatched the Kishi of Hitaka on an embassy to Koguryŏ to summon skilled workers.

That autumn, after the Kishi of Hitaka had been dispatched on his embassy, a woman who lived in Mitsu in Naniwa cried out, "An older brother to my mother, and an older brother to me. Alas, for Wakakusa, my husband."

In antiquity, 'wakakusa' was a metaphor for husband and wife.

Her crying was exceedingly sad and made people heartbroken.

Kakaso, a man from Hishiki Village, heard her and faced her, saying, "Why are your cries so exceedingly sad?"[lxvii]

Kakaso is a personal name. People also customarily called their father 'kaso.'

The woman replied, "Think of how the autumn onion has two layers."

Then Kakaso said, "I see." He understood her words.

He had a friend who did not understand the meaning and asked, "How do you know what she means?"

He said, "Funame of the Tamasuri hereditary guild of Naniwa married Karama-no-hatake."[lxviii]

Hatake refers to a field where barley is grown.

生哭女。哭女言哭女、此云儺倶謎。嫁於住道人山杵、生飽田女。韓白水郎暯與其女哭女、曽既倶死。住道人山杵、上奸玉作部鯽魚女、生麁寸。麁寸娶飽田女。於是、麁寸從日鷹吉士、發向高麗。由是、其妻飽田女、徘徊顧戀、失緒傷心。哭聲尤切、令人腸斷。

玉作部鯽魚女與韓白水郎暯、爲夫婦生哭女。住道人山杵娶哭女、生飽田女。山杵妻父韓白水郎暯與其妻哭女、曽既倶死。住道人山杵、上奸妻母玉作部鯽魚女、生麁寸。麁寸娶飽田女。或本云、玉作部鯽魚女、共前夫韓白水郎暯、生哭女。更共後夫住道人山杵、生麁寸。則哭女與麁寸、異父兄弟之故、哭女之女飽田女、呼

麁寸、曰於母亦兄也。哭女嫁於山杵、生飽田女。山杵又淫鯽魚女、生麁寸。則飽田女與麁寸、異母兄弟之故、飽田女呼夫麁寸、曰於吾亦兄也。古者不言兄弟長幼、女以男稱兄。男以女稱妹。故云於母亦兄、於吾亦兄耳。

是歳、日鷹吉士、還自高麗、獻工匠須流枳・奴流枳等。今大倭國山邊郡額田邑熟皮高麗、是其後也。

七年春正月丁未朔己酉、立小泊瀬稚鷦鷯尊、爲皇太子。

八年冬十月、百姓言是時、國中無事、吏稱其官。海內歸仁、民安其業。

是歳、五穀登衍、蠶麥善收。遠近清平、戶口滋殖焉。

十一年秋八月庚戌朔丁巳、天皇崩于正寢。

冬十月己酉朔癸丑、葬堺生坂本陵。

They gave birth to Nakume. Nakume married a man from Sumuchi, Yamaki, and gave birth to Akutame.^lxix Karama-no-hatake and his daughter Nakume had already passed away. Yamaki, the man from Sumuchi, raped Funame of the Tamasuri hereditary guild, and she gave birth to Araki. Araki married Akutame. Then Araki, as a follower of the Kishi of Hitaka, departed for Koguryŏ. Thereby his wife, Akutame, uneasy and yearning, despaired and was brokenhearted. The sound of her cries was exceedingly piercing and made people think of heartbreak.

> Funame of the Tamasuri hereditary guild and Karama-no-hatake became husband and wife and gave birth to Nakume. The man of Sumuchi, Yamaki, married Nakume, and she gave birth to Akutame. The father of Yamaki's wife, Karama-no-hatake, and his daughter Nakume, both died. Then the man of Sumuchi, Yamaki, raped his wife's mother, Funame of the Tamasuri hereditary guild, and she gave birth to Araki. Araki married Akutame. In one book it says, Funame of the Tamasuri hereditary guild, with Karama-no-hatake, first gave birth to Nakume. Then afterward, with the man of Sumuchi, Yamaki, she gave birth to Araki. Nakume and Araki are siblings by different fathers. So Nakume's daughter Akutame referred to Araki by saying, "He is the older brother of my mother." Nakume married Yamaki, and she gave birth to Akutame. Yamaki also had improper relations with Funame, and she gave birth to Araki. Hence, Akutame and Araki are siblings of different mothers. So Akutame called her husband Araki "older brother." In antiquity, there were no words to distinguish older and younger siblings, and women called their husbands using the word for brother, and men called their wives using the word for sister. That is why she said, "He is a brother to my mother, and a brother to me."

That year, the Kishi of Hitaka returned from Koguryŏ and presented the skilled workers Suryuji and Noryuji.^lxx The Kawaoshi-no-koma[27] of Nukata Village in Yamabe District, Yamato Province, are their descendants.^lxxi

Seventh year [494 CE], spring, first month, third day. Ō-hatsuse-no-waka-sazaki [Buretsu] was named crown prince.

Eighth year [495 CE], winter, tenth month. The people said, "These days, nothing untoward is happening within the country. Administrators are named to the appropriate administrative units, benevolence is spreading in the realm, and the people feel secure in their labor."

That year the five grains were abundant, and silkworms and barley enjoyed good harvests. Near and far there was peace, and the number of households increased.^lxxii

Eleventh year [498 CE], autumn, eighth month, eighth day. The emperor expired in his bedchamber.[28]

Winter, tenth month, fifth day. The emperor was buried at Haniu-no-sakamoto Tomb.^lxxiii

---

27 Leather makers. Koma refers to their origins in Koguryŏ.
28 *Water Mirror* gives his age as fifty.

小泊瀨稚鷦鷯天皇 武烈天皇

小泊瀨稚鷦鷯天皇、億計天皇太子也。母曰春日大娘皇后。億計天皇七年、立爲皇太子。長好刑理。法令分明。日晏坐朝、幽枉必達。斷獄得情。又頻造諸惡。不修一善。凡諸酷刑、無不親覽。國內居人、咸皆震怖。

十一年八月、億計天皇崩。大臣平群眞鳥臣、專擅國政、欲王日本。陽爲太子營宮。了即自居。觸事驕慢、都無臣節。

於是、太子思欲聘物部麁鹿火大連女影媛、遣媒人、向影媛宅期會。影媛會奸眞鳥大臣男鮪。鮪、此云茲寐。恐違太子所期、報曰、妾望、奉待海柘榴市巷。

由是、太子欲往期處。遣近侍舍人、就平群大臣宅、奉太子命、求索官馬。

大臣戲言陽進曰、官馬爲誰飼養、隨命而已、久之不進。太子懷恨、忍不發顏。果之所期、立歌場衆、歌場、此云宇多我岐。執影媛袖、躑躅從容。

Book 16
Emperor Buretsu

Fall of Heguri no Matori, Accession of Emperor Buretsu

Emperor O-hatsuse-no-waka-sazaki [Buretsu] was the oldest son of Emperor Oke [Ninken].[i] His mother was called Empress Kasuga-no-ō-iratsume.[1] In the seventh year of Emperor Oke [494 CE], he was named crown prince. When he grew up, he enjoyed punishing criminals and judging right from wrong. He was discerning in matters of law and held court until the sun set, making every effort to see through concealed transgressions and discerning the truth of matters when deciding suits.[ii] He also frequently committed various evil deeds and did not preside over even a single good action. When cruel punishments were carried out, there were none that he did not watch personally. The people of the land all trembled in fear of him.

In the eighth month in the eleventh year of his reign [498 CE], Emperor Oke expired. The Ō-omi, Matori, Omi of Heguri, despotically monopolized the administration as he liked and wished to become King of Yamato. Deceivingly, he built a palace for the crown prince, but when it was completed, he dwelt in it himself. In dealing with matters, he was haughty and disdainful, and he was not at all the model of a good vassal.

The crown prince, seeking to court Kage-hime, the daughter of the Ō-muraji Mononobe no Arakai, dispatched a messenger to the house of Kage-hime to set up a meeting. Kage-hime had previously been violated by Shibi, the son of Ō-omi Matori.[iii] She feared to refuse to set up a meeting with the crown prince, and reported back to him, "I will await you on the street at Tsubaki Market."[iv]

When the crown prince was about to go to the promised place, he dispatched a nearby servant to the house of the Omi of Heguri to present him with an order requesting official horses.

The Ō-omi jokingly pretended to present them, saying, "For whom are the official horses kept? It shall be as you order." But for a long time he did not present them. The crown prince was offended at heart, but endured and did not let it show on his face. When at last he went to the promised place, he stood among those people who courted each other with song, took Kage-hime's sleeve, and sauntered about with her here and there.

---

1   A note in the Ninken book gives Ō-iratsume as a daughter of Yūryaku and Omina-gimi, the daughter of Fukame, Omi of Wani.

俄而鮪臣來、排太子與影媛間立。由是、太子放影媛袖、移廻向前、立直當鮪。歌曰、

之裒世能	しほせの
儺嗚理嗚彌黎麼	なをりをみれば
阿蘇寐俱屢	あそびくる
思寐我簸多泥儞	しびがはたでに
都摩陀氏理彌喩	つまたてりみゆ
一本、以之裒世易彌儺斗	あるふみに、しほせをもちてみなとにかふ

鮪答歌曰、

飫瀰能古能	おみのこの
耶陛耶賀羅賀枳	やへやからかき
瑜屢世登耶瀰古	ゆるせとやみこ

太子歌曰、

飫裒陀撆嗚	おほたちを
多黎播枳多撆氏	たれはきたちて
農賀儒登慕	ぬかずとも
須衞婆陀志氏謀	すゑはたしても
阿波夢登茹於謀賦	あはむとぞおもふ

鮪臣答歌曰、

飫裒枳瀰能	おほきみの
耶陛能矩瀰賀枳	やへのくみかき
賀々梅騰謀	かかめども
儺嗚阿摩之耳彌	なをあましじみ
賀々農俱彌柯枳	かかぬくみかき

Shortly thereafter, Omi Shibi came and pushed apart the crown prince and Kage-hime. The crown prince let go of Kage-hime's sleeve, turned around, came forth, and stood directly in front of Shibi. Then he sang,

> Looking upon the waves breaking
> on the fast-moving shallows,
> alongside the tuna[2]
> that has come to play,
> I see my wife standing.
> (One version has "at the harbor" instead of "on the fast-moving shallows.")

Then Shibi sang in reply,

> Say you, Prince, to loosen her
> from within the Korean-style hedges
> of the son of the Omi?

The crown prince sang,

> I stand wearing
> my large sword.
> Though I draw it not,
> in the end,
> by this sword I will win her.

The Omi Shibi replied, singing,

> Though you mean to build
> a multilayer hedge
> fit for a great lord,
> you have no one to enclose,
> and you build no hedge.

---

[2] Shibi's name means "tuna."

太子歌曰、

於彌能姑能	おみのこの
耶賦能之魔柯枳	やふのしばかき
始陀騰余瀰	したとよみ
那爲我與鼇據魔	なるがよりこば
耶黎夢之魔柯枳	やれむしばかき
一本、以耶賦能之魔柯枳易耶陛哿羅哿枳	あるふみにやふのしばかきをもちてやへからかきにかふ

太子贈影媛歌曰、

擧騰我瀰儞	ことがみに
枳謂屢箇皚比謎	きるるかげひめ
拕摩儺羅磨	たまならば
婀我裒屢柁摩能	あがほるたまの
婀波寐之羅陀魔	あはびしらたま

鮪臣爲影媛答歌曰、

於裒枳瀰能	おほきみの
瀰於寐能之都波拕	みおびのしつはた
夢須寐陀黎	むすびたれ
陀黎耶始比登謀	たれやしひとも
阿避於謀婆儺俱儞	あひおもはなくに

太子甫知鮪曾得影媛。悉覺父子無敬之狀、赫然大怒。此夜、速向大伴金村連宅、會兵計策。大伴連、將數千兵、徼之於路、戮鮪臣於乃樂山。

The crown prince sang,

> Many-sided is the brushwood hedge
> of the son of the Omi,
> yet should the earth quake
> and its base move,
> the brushwood hedge will break.
> (One version has "Many-sided is the brushwood hedge" instead of "Many-sided is the Korean-style hedge.")

Then the crown prince bestowed upon Kage-hime a song:

> Kami, to the strummed zither,
> come like a shadow, Kage-hime.[3]
> Were you a jewel,
> you would be the jewel I most desire,
> the white pearl of an abalone.

The Omi Shibi sang a reply on behalf of Kage-hime:

> Though the august paper mulberry sash
> of the great lord
> be tied so as to dangle,
> no matter to whom it might be,
> I have no intention of hanging back.

The crown prince then knew that Shibi had previously had Kage-hime. Completely realizing the rude actions of father and son, the crown prince flushed and was greatly angered. That night, he quickly went to the house of the Muraji Ōtomo no Kanamura,[4] assembled soldiers, and made a plan.[v] Muraji Ōtomo led several thousand troops and waylaid him on the road, killing Omi Shibi at Mt. Nara.

---

3   The song uses Kage-hime's name (shadow lady) as a pun.
4   The Ōtomo were a powerful lineage group that led the Kume, and who traced their lineage to the kami Ame-no-oshi-hi. They were associated with war and security. Along with the Muraji of Saeki, they were promoted to sukune in Tenmu 13.12. Kanamura is the grandson of Muroya and the son of Katari, and served as Ō-muraji for the five reigns from Buretsu to Kinmei.

一本云、鮪宿影媛舍、即夜被戮。是時、影媛逐行戮處、見是戮已。驚惶失所、悲涙盈目。遂作歌曰、

伊須能箇瀰	いすのかみ
賦屢嗚須擬底	ふるをすぎて
擧慕摩矩羅	こもまくら
柁箇播志須擬	たかはしすぎ
慕能娑幡儞	ものさはに
於裒野該須擬	おほやけすぎ
播屢比	はるひ
箇須我嗚須擬	かすがをすぎ
逗摩御暮屢	つまごもる
嗚佐裒嗚須擬	をさほをすぎ
抌摩該儞播	たまけには
伊比佐倍母理	いひさへもり
抌摩暮比儞	たまもひに
瀰逗佐倍母理	みづさへもり
儺岐曽裒遲喩倶謀	なきそほちゆくも
柯㝵比謎阿婆例	かげひめあはれ

於是、影媛收埋既畢、臨欲還家、悲鯁而言、苦哉。今日、失我愛夫。即便灑涕愴矣、纏心歌曰、

婀嗚儞與志	あをによし
乃樂能婆娑摩儞	ならのはさまに
斯々貳暮能	ししじもの
瀰逗矩陛御暮梨	みづくへごもり
瀰儺曾々矩	みなそそく
思痲能和倶吾嗚	しびのわくごを
阿娑理逗那偉能古	あさりづなるのこ

冬十一月戊寅朔戊子、大伴金村連謂太子曰、眞鳥賊、可擊。請討之。

According to one source, Shibi stayed at the residence of Kage-hime and was killed that night.

At that time, Kage-hime followed him to the place where he was killed, and upon seeing his remains, was shocked and afraid, losing herself as her eyes overflowed with tears. At length she made a song:

From Isonokami,
she passes Furu,
she passes Takahashi,
she passes Ōyake,
she passes Kasuga,
she passes Osao.
Rice overflows
in the beautiful funerary bowl,
water overflows,
in the beautiful funerary cup.
She goes, drenched in tears.
Ah, Kage-hime!

Then, when the burial was completely finished, Kage-hime was about to return home, and choked with tears, she said, "How heartbreaking! Today, I lost my beloved husband."[vi] Drenched in tears, she felt her heart was tied in knots, and she sang,

In the valley of Mt. Nara,
with creatures like deer and boar,
the young lad Shibi
is tucked away, wet at the water's edge
and soaked by the water.
Do not disturb him in your rummaging, young boars!

Winter, eleventh month, eleventh day. Muraji Ōtomo no Kanamura told the crown prince, "We should strike our enemy Matori. If you ask, I will attack."

太子曰、天下將亂。非希世之雄、不能濟也。能安之者、其在連乎。即與定謀。於是、大伴大連、率兵自將、圍大臣宅。縱火燔之。所拕雲靡。

眞鳥大臣、恨事不濟、知身難免。計窮望絶。廣指鹽詛。遂被殺戮。及其子弟。

詛時唯忘角鹿海鹽、不以爲詛。由是、角鹿之鹽、爲天皇所食、餘海之鹽、爲天皇所忌。

十二月、大伴金村連、平定賊訖、反政太子。請上尊號曰、今億計天皇子、唯有陛下。億兆欣歸、曾無與二。又賴皇天翼戴、淨除凶黨。英略雄斷、以盛天威天祿。日本必有主。主日本者、非陛下而誰。伏願、陛下仰答靈祇、弘宣景命、光宅日本。誕受銀鄉。

於是、太子命有司、設壇場於泊瀬列城、陟天皇位。遂定都焉。是日、以大伴金村連爲大連。

元年春三月丁丑朔戊寅、立春日娘子爲皇后。

The crown prince said, "The realm is in chaos. Should a supremely valiant one not appear in the world, there is no one who can save it. Is not the Muraji the only one who can bring peace?"[vii] Together, they immediately settled on a plan of attack. Ō-muraji Ōtomo[5] then led the troops personally as their general and surrounded the house of the Ō-omi. He set it on fire and burned it. Under his command, his forces moved like clouds.

Ō-omi Matori, resentful that what he desired would not come to pass, realized that he himself could not escape.[viii] His schemes were at an end, and his hopes were cut off.[ix] He spread salt widely around and cursed it. Then he was killed, along with his family.

When he cast the curse, he forgot only the salt from the sea at Tsunuga and did not curse it. For this reason, salt from Tsunuga is used for the emperor's meals, while the salt from other seas is avoided.

Twelfth month. Muraji Ōtomo no Kanamura finished pacifying the enemy and returned the administration to the crown prince. He asked to present the crown prince with his august title, saying, "Now you, son of Emperor Oke [Kenzō], are the only liege lord. There is certainly no one else to whom the multitudes pledge their allegiance. Also, owing to the support given by the power of heaven, you have swept away the brigands. By your superior planning and valiant decisions, imperial authority and the imperial throne are at their height. There must be a ruler in Yamato, and for the ruler of Yamato, if not my liege, then who could it be? I humbly request my liege to look up and respond to the kami of heaven and earth, to widely proclaim the great mandate, shine upon Yamato as ruler, and receive the great lands of treasure."[x]

Thereupon, the crown prince ordered the administration to build a dais at Namiki in Hatuse, where he acceded to the imperial throne.[xi] There he established his capital. That day, Muraji Ōtomo no Kanamura was named Ō-muraji.

Succession Conflicts in Paekche, Reign of Emperor Buretsu

First year [499 CE], spring, third month, second day. Kasuga-no-iratsume was named empress.

---

5   Kanamura is not promoted to Ō-muraji until the following month.

未詳娘子父。是年也、太歲己卯。

二年秋九月、刳孕婦之腹而觀其胎。

三年冬十月、解人指甲、使掘暑預。

十一月、詔大伴室屋大連、發信濃國男丁、作城像於水派邑。仍曰城上也。

是月、百濟意多郎卒。葬於高田丘上。

四年夏四月、拔人頭髮、使昇樹巓。斫倒樹本、落死昇者爲快。

是歲、百濟末多王無道、暴虐百姓。國人遂除、而立嶋王。是爲武寧王。

百濟新撰云、末多王無道、暴虐百姓。國人共除。武寧王立。諱斯麻王。是琨支王子之子。則末多王異母兄也。琨支向倭。時至筑紫嶋、生斯麻王。自嶋還送、不至於京、產於嶋。故因名焉。今各羅海中有主嶋。王所產嶋。故百濟人號爲主嶋。今案、嶋王是蓋鹵王之子也。末多王、是琨支王之子也。此曰異母兄、未詳也。

五年夏六月、使人伏入塘楲。流出於外、持三刃矛刺殺、爲快。

六年秋九月乙巳朔、詔曰、傳國之機、立子爲貴。朕無繼嗣。何以傳名。且依天皇舊例、

---

6 Muroya is probably an error for his grandson, Kanamura. A Mimata Palace appears in Yomei 2.4.
7 Takada Hill is perhaps the Okazaki area of Yamatotakada City, Nara Prefecture.

The details of her father are still unknown.

This was the year of the Earth Rabbit.

Second year [500 CE], autumn, ninth month. The emperor cut open the belly of a pregnant woman and examined the fetus.[xii]

Third year [501 CE], winter, tenth month. The emperor removed a man's fingernails and made him dig up yams.

Eleventh month. The emperor decreed to Ō-muraji Ōtomo no Muroya, "Levy the corvée laborers of Shinano Province to make a fortress in Mimata Village."[6] Hence, it was called Kinoe, or Upper Fortress.[xiii]

That month, Ŭidarang of Paekche died.[xiv] He was buried atop Takada Hill.[7]

Fourth year [502 CE], summer, fourth month. The emperor pulled out the hair of a man's head and made him climb into the branches of a tree. Then he took pleasure in cutting the tree down at its base so that the man who had climbed it fell to his death.

That year, King Malta of Paekche was wicked and committed atrocities against his people. The people of that land eventually deposed him and installed King Sema. This was King Munyŏng.[xv]

> According to the *Newly Compiled Record of Paekche*, King Malta was wicked and committed atrocities against the people. The people of that country collectively deposed him and installed King Munyŏng. His real name was King Sama. He was the child of Prince Konji. That is to say, he was the half-brother of King Malta. Konji came to Yamato. At that time, when he reached the island of Tsukushi, he gave birth to King Sama. He returned home from the island and did not reach the capital. Sema was born on an island. Hence, he was so named. In the present-day sea of Kakara is the island Nirimu-sema. This is island where the king was born. So the people of Paekche named it "Nirimu-sema," or Ruler Island.[8] We now surmise that King Sema was the son of King Kaero. King Malta was the son of King Konji.[9] As for why they were called half-brothers, the details are still unclear.

Fifth year [503 CE], summer, sixth month. The emperor made men lie down in the drainage canal of a reservoir. He took pleasure in stabbing them with a trident he held as they washed away.

Sixth year [504 CE], autumn, ninth month, first day. The emperor decreed, "For the administration to pass on rule of the state, it is important to name an heir. We have no successor, so how can my name be passed on? For the time being, according to past precedent of other emperors, I

---

8 Use of "nirimu" as a title of respect is preserved in modern Korean "nim." *The Chronicles* uses two sets of characters for Munyŏng's name. One set glosses the character for island (Jp. *shima*) as "sema." This suggests that "sema" is a Paekche word for island and links Munyŏng's name to his birth on an island. Another set spells "Shima" phonetically in Japanese, romanized here in modern Korean as "Sama."
9 Malta's lineage as son of King Kaero is given in Yūryaku 5.4 and 5.6.

置小泊瀨舍人、使爲代號、萬歲難忘者也。

冬十月、百濟國遣麻那君進調。天皇以爲、百濟歷年不脩貢職。留而不放。

七年春二月、使人昇樹、以弓射墜而咲。

夏四月、百濟王遣期我君進調。別表曰、前進調使麻那者、非百濟國主之骨族也。故謹遣斯我、奉事於朝。遂有子、曰法師君。是倭君之先也。

八年春三月、使女躶形、坐平板上、牽馬就前遊牝。觀女不淨、沾濕者殺。不濕者沒爲官婢。以此爲樂。及是時、穿池起苑、以盛禽獸。而好田獵、走狗試馬。出入不時。不避大風甚雨。衣溫而忘百姓之寒。食美而忘天下之飢。大進侏儒倡優、爲爛漫之樂、設奇偉之戲、縱靡々之聲。日夜常與宮人沈湎于酒、以錦繡爲席。衣以綾紈者衆。

冬十二月壬辰朔己亥、天皇崩于列城宮。

will establish the guild of Servants of O-hatsuse [Buretsu], and by taking my name, it will not be forgotten for all eternity."

Winter, tenth month. Paekche dispatched Lord Mana[10] to present tribute. Thinking that Paekche had not tendered tribute for many years, the emperor held, and would not release, him.

Seventh year [505 CE], spring, second month. The emperor made a man climb a tree, shot him down with a bow and arrow, and laughed.

Summer, fourth month. The King of Paekche dispatched Lord Saa to present tribute.[xvi] Separately, he presented a manifest, saying, "The messenger previously dispatched with tribute, Mana, is of no relation to the rulers of Paekche. Therefore, I humbly dispatch Saa to serve the court." Eventually he had a son, called Monk Kun. He is the first ancestor of the Kimi of Yamato.[xvii]

Eighth year [506 CE], spring, third month. The emperor made women strip naked and sat them upon a flat board.[xviii] Then he led horses before them and made them breed. When he then inspected the women's genitals, those who were wet were killed. Those who were dry were pressed into administrative slavery. This he enjoyed. Around that time, he had a pond dug and a garden made, and it overflowed with birds and beasts. Since the emperor enjoyed hunting, he ran dogs and raced horses. He went in and out regardless of the season, not even avoiding times of high wind or heavy rain. In the warmth of his own clothing, he forgot the chill of his people. At his sumptuous feasts, he forgot the famine in the realm. He assembled dwarves and actors to perform obscene music and put on outrageous plays, and he indulged as he liked in their dissolute songs. Day and night he and his courtiers drowned in wine, sitting atop cushions of embroidered brocade. He had numerous garments of twill weave and unbleached silk.

Winter, twelfth month, eighth day. The emperor expired at Namiki Palace.

---

10 Mana appears again in Keitai 23.3 as a general.

Appendix 1
Glossary of Kami in the *Chronicles*

Kami are listed according to their names as given in *Ancient Matters*, as this is the most common moniker for secondary scholarship. Alternative names that appear in the *Chronicles* will direct the reader to the appropriate *Ancient Matters* entry. Kami that do not appear in *Ancient Matters* are given by their names in the *Chronicles*. References to kami appearing in *Izumo no kuni fudoki*, *Harima no kuni fudoki*, *Kogo shūi*, and *Sendai kuji hongi* are also provided. However, this list is not a comprehensive list of kami appearing in texts other than the *Chronicles*.

Kami names are followed by their literal translation in parentheses. For kami that appear in *Ancient Matters*, transliterations of kami names from the Philippi translation of *Kojiki* are provided to identify Old Japanese vowels. The translations of kami names from the Heldt translation *An Account of Ancient Matters* are also provided on account of their high literary quality. For detailed entries on kami in *Ancient Matters*, see the Glossary of Personal Names in the Heldt translation. In Japanese, see the "Koten bunka gaku" online database hosted by Kokugakuin University.

Below is a list of abbreviations:

K1–3	*Kojiki*, Books 1–3
S1–S11	*Nihon shoki*, "Age of the Gods," Sections 1–11
Jinmu PA	*Nihon shoki*, pre-accession narrative of Jinmu
IFD	*Izumo no kuni fudoki*
HFD	*Harima no kuni fudoki*
KGSI	*Kogo shūi*
SK	*Sendai kuji hongi*

Aka-tsutsu (red earth) – produced by Izanagi during his ablution after his escape from Yomi
  Aka-tsutsu 赤土命 (S5.10)

Aki-gui-no-ushi (open bite) – produced from Izanagi's pants during his ablution after his escape from Yomi
  Aki-gui-no-ushi-no-kami 飽咋之宇斯能神 (K1, Aki-gupi-nö-ushi-nö-kamï, Master Filled Full), Aki-kui-no-kami 開囓神 (S5.6), Aki-kui-no-kami 開囓神 (SK), Aki-gui-no-ushi-no-kami 飽咋之宇斯能神 (SK)

Aki-kui – See **Aki-gui-no-ushi**

Aji-shiki-taka-hiko-ne (gathering plow high lord) – earthly kami and friend of Ame-waka-hiko

Aji-shiki-taka-hiko-ne-no-kami 阿遲志貴高日子根神 (K1, Adi-sikï-taka-pikone-nö-kamï, Lofty Little Lad of Fine Plows), Aji-suki-taka-hiko-no-kami 阿遲鉏高日子神 (K1), Aji-suki-taka-hiko-ne-no-kami 阿遲鉏高日子根神 (K1), Kamo-no-ō-kami 迦毛之大御神 (K1, Kami-nö-opo-mi-kamï, Great and Mighty Spirit of Wild Ducks), Aji-suki-taka-hiko-ne-no-kami 味耜高彦根神 (S9, S9.1), Aji-soki-taka-hiko-ne 阿泥素企多伽避顧禰 (S9.1), Aji-suki-taka-hiko-no-mikoto 阿遲須枳高日子命 (IFD), Aji-suki-taka-hiko-ne-no-mikoto-no-kami 阿遲須伎高日古尼命神 (HFD)

Aji-suki-taka-hiko-ne – See **Aji-shiki-taka-hiko-ne**

Ama-no-ho-akari – See **Ame-no-ho-akari**, **Ho-no-akari**

Ama-no-akaru-tama – See **Tama-no-oya**

Ama-no-fuki-ne (heavenly thatch root, perhaps) – a descendant of Susano-o

Ama-no-fuki-ne-no-kami 天之葺根神 (S8.4)

Ama-no-hi-washi (unclear) – a producer of barkcloth and cotton, associated with some Inbe lineages

Ama-no-hi-washi 天日鷲 (S7.2, S9.2)

Ama-no-ho-hi (heavenly superior divine spirit) – See **Ame-no-ho-hi**

Ama-no-kagami (heavenly mirror) – one of the first kami

Ama-no-kagami-no-mikoto 天鏡尊 (S2.2), Ame-ai-no-mikoto 天合尊 (SK)

Ama-no-kagase-o – See **Kagase-o**

Ama-no-kako-yama (alternatively read Ama-no-kagu-yama; name of a mountain in Nara Prefecture) – child of Ama-no-ho-no-akari, ancestor of the Muraji of Owari

Ama-no-kako-yama 天香山 (S9.6)

Ama-no-kise – See **Ninigi**

Ama-no-koyane – See **Ame-no-koyane**

Ama-no-kuma-hito (heavenly offering presenter person) – sent by Amaterasu to investigate the body of Uke-mochi

Ama-no-kuma-hito 天熊人 (S5.11)

Ama-no-kuni-tama – See **Ama-tsu-kuni-tama**

Ama-no-mi-naka-nushi – See **Ame-no-mi-naka-nushi**

Ama-no-nigi-shi-kuni-no-nigi-shi-ama-tsu-hiko-ho-no-ninigi – See **Ninigi**

Ama-no-nuka-do (unclear) – ancestor of the mirror-makers

Ama-no-nuka-do 天糠戸 (S7.2), Ama-no-nuka-do 天抜戸 (S7.3)

Ama-no-ō-mimi – See **Oshi-ho-mimi**

Ama-no-oshi-hi – See **Ame-no-oshi-hi**

Ama-no-oshi-ho-mimi – See **Oshi-ho-mimi**

Ama-no-oshi-ho-ne – See **Oshi-ho-mimi**

Ama-no-osu-kami – See **Jinmu**

APPENDIX 1   595

Ama-no-sagu-me (heavenly seeking woman) – a servant of Ame-waka-hiko
Ama-no-sagu-me 天佐具売 (K1, Ama-nö-sagu-me, Spy Woman of Heaven), Ama-no-sagu-me 天探女 (S9, S9.1), Ama-no-sagu-me 天探女 (SK)

Ama-no-ta-jikara-o – See **Ame-no-ta-jikara-o**

Ama-no-tane (heavenly seed) – an ancestor of the Nakatomi and descendant of Ame-no-koyane
Ama-no-tane-no-mikoto 天種子命 (Jinmu PA)

Ama-no-toko-tachi – See **Ame-no-toko-tachi**

Ama-no-uzu-me-no-mikoto – See **Ame-no-uzu-me**

Ama-no-yorozu (heavenly myriad) – one of the first kami
Ama-no-yorozu-no-mikoto 天万尊 (S2.2)

Ama-no-yosa-tsura (heavenly good creeping plant, perhaps) – one of the first kami
Ama-no-yosa-tsura 天吉葛 (S5.3)

Ama-terasu (heaven shining) – sun goddess and progenitor of the imperial clan, worshipped at the Ise Grand Shrine
Ama-terasu-ō-mikami 天照大御神 (K1, Ama-terasu-opo-mi-kamï, Heaven Shining), Ama-terasu-ō-mikami 天照大神 (K1), Hi-no-kami 日神 (S5, S6.1, S6.3, S7.2, S7.3, Jinmu PA), Ō-hiru-me-no-muchi 大日孁貴 (S5), Ama-terasu-ō-mikami 天照大神 (S5, S5.6, S5.11, S6, S6.2, S7, S9, S9.1, S9.2, Jinmu PA, Sujin 6, Suinin 25.3, Keikō 25.2, Jingū PA), Tsuki-sakaki-itsu-no-mitama-ama-sakaru-muka-tsu-hime 撞賢木厳之御魂天疎向津媛命 (Jingū PA), Ama-terasu-ō-hiru-me (heaven shining great sun woman) 天照大孁尊 (S5), Ō-hiru-me (great sun woman) 大日孁尊 (S5.1, Jinmu PA), Ama-terasu-ō-mikami 天照大神 (HFD), Hi-no-kami 日神 (KGSI), Ama-terasu-ō-mikami 天照大神 (KGSI), Ama-terasu-ō-mikami 天照太神 (SK), Ama-terasu-ō-mikami 天照大御神 (SK)

Ama-teru-kuni-teru-hiko-ho-no-akari – See **Ame-no-ho-akari**

Ama-tsu-hiko-hiko-ho-no-ninigi – See **Ninigi**

Ama-tsu-hiko-ne (heavenly lord) – child of Amaterasu and Susano-o, brother of Oshi-ho-mimi
Ama-tsu-hiko-ne-no-mikoto 天津彦根命 (K1, Ama-tu-pikone-nö-mikötö, Little Lad of Heaven), Ama-tsu-hiko-ne-no-mikoto 天津彦根命 (S6, S6.1, S6.2, S6.3, S7.3), Ama-tsu-hiko-ne-no-mikoto 天津彦根命 (SK)

Ama-tsu-hiko-ne-ho-no-nigi-ne – See **Ninigi**

Ama-tsu-kume (heavenly Kume) – ancestor of the military Kume hereditary guild
Ama-tsu-kume-no-mikoto 天津久米命 (K1, Ama-tu-kumë-nö-mikötö, Fighter of Heaven), Ame-kushi-tsu-ō-kume (heaven mystical great Kume) – 天櫛津大来目 (S9.4)

Ama-tsu-kuni-tama (heavenly land spirit) – father of Ame-waka-hiko
Ama-tsu-kuni-tama-no-kami 天津国玉神 (K1, Ama-tu-kuni-tama-nö-kamï, Land Soul of Heaven), Ama-no-kuni-tama 天国玉 (S9), Ama-tsu-kuni-tama-no-kami 天津国玉神 (SK)

Ama-tsu-mika-hoshi – See **Kagase-o**

Ame-kuni-nigishi-hiko-ho-no-ninigi – See **Ninigi**

Ame-kushi-tsu-ō-kume – See **Ama-tsu-kume**

Ame-ma-hitotsu (heavenly one eye) – 天目一箇神 (S9.2). See also **Ame-no-mi-kage**

Ame-ni-koto-shiro-sora-ni-koto-shiro-tama-kushi-iri-biko-itsu-no-koto-shiro – See **Koto-shiro-nushi**

Ame-no-hata-ori-me (heavenly loom weaving woman) – a weaver goddess, perhaps a younger sister or daughter of Ama-terasu

Ame-no-hata-ori-me 天服織女 (K1, Weaver Woman of Heaven), Waka-hiru-me (Young sun woman) 稚日女尊 (S7.1, Jingū PA)

Ame-no-ho-akari (heavenly rice ear redness) – a brother of Ninigi, associated with Nigi-haya-hi in later sources

Ame-no-ho-akari 天火明命 (K1, Amë-nö-po-akari-nö-mikötö, Ruddy Rice Ears of Heaven), Ama-no-ho-no-akari 天火明命 (S9.6), Ama-teru-kuni-teru-hiko-ho-no-akari 天照国照彦火明命 (S9.8), Ama-teru-kuni-teru-hiko-ama-no-ho-akari-kushi-tama-nigi-haya-hi (天照国照彦天火明櫛玉饒速日尊, SK. See also **Nigi-haya-hi**, **ho-no-akari**). Ama-no-wake-ama-no-ho-no-akari 天別天火明命 (SK)

Ame-no-ho-hi (heavenly superior divine spirit, among other meanings) – a brother of Oshi-ho-mimi sent to pacify the central reed plain land, son-in-law and head priest for worship of Ō-kuni-nushi, progenitor of the Provincial Miyatsuko of Izumo

Ame-no-ho-hi-no-mikoto 天之菩卑能命 (K1, Amë-nö-po-pi-nö-kamï, Majestic Rice Ears of Heaven), Ame-no-ho-hi-no-mikoto 天菩比命 (K1), Ame-no-ho-hi-no-kami 天菩比神 (K1), Ama-no-ho-hi-no-mikoto 天穂日命 (S6, S6.1, S6.2, S6.3, S7.3, S9, S9.2), Ama-no-ho-hi-no-mikoto 天乃夫比命 (IFD), Ama-no-ho-hi-no-mikoto 天穂日命 (SK)

Ame-no-koyane (unclear) – a god associated with ritual worship who helps lure Amaterasu out of the heavenly rock cave, progenitor of the Nakatomi lineage group

(K1, 天児屋命 Amë-nö-ko-yane-nö-mikötö Little Roof of Heaven), Ame-no-koyane 天児屋命 (S7, S7.2, S7.3, S9.1, S9.2), Ama-no-koyane 天児屋命 (KGSI), Ama-no-koyane 天児屋命 (SK), Ama-no-koyane 天児屋根命 (SK)

Ame-no-mi-naka-nushi (heavenly august central master) – one of the first kami 天之御中主神 (K1, Amë-nö-mi-naka-nusi-nö-kamï, Master Mighty Center of Heaven), Ame-no-mi-naka-nushi-no-kami 天御中主神 (K1), Ama-no-mi-naka-nushi-no-mikoto 天御中主尊 (S1.4), Ama-no-mi-naka-nushi-no-kami 天御中主神 (KGSI), Ama-no-mi-naka-nushi-no-mikoto 天御中主尊 (SK)

APPENDIX 1   597

Ame-no-mi-kage (heavenly august shadow) – father-in-law to Kaika
Ame-no-mi-kage-no-kami 天之御影神 (K2, Amë-nö-mi-kagë-no-kami, Mighty Shade of Heaven), Ame-no-mi-kage-no-mikoto 天御陰命 (SK). See also **Ame-ma-hitotsu**

Ame-no-o-habari (fierce manly sword) – sword used by Izanagi to kill the fire kami Kagu-tsu-chi
Ame-no-habari 天之尾羽張 (K1, Amë-nö-wo-pa-bari, Sweeping Blade of Heaven), Itsu-no-o-habari 伊都之尾羽張 (K1, Itu-nö-wo-pa-bari, Stern Sweeping Blade), Itsu-no-o-habari-no-kami 伊都之尾羽張神 (K1, Itu-nö-wo-pa-bari-nö-kamï, Stern Sweeping Blade), Ame-no-o-habari-no-kami 天尾羽張神 (K1, Amë-nö-wo-pa-bari-nö-kamï, Sweeping Blade of Heaven), Itsu-no-o-hashiri-no-kami (fierce manly quickness, perhaps) 稜威雄走神 (S9)

Ame-no-oshi-hi (heavenly push divine spirit) – a military kami sent to descend with Ninigi, progenitor of the Ōtomo linage group
天忍日命 (K1, Amë-nö-osi-pi-nö-mikötö, Grand Spirit of Heaven), Ama-no-oshi-hi-no-mikoto 天忍日命 (S9.4), Ame-no-oshi-hi-no-mikoto 天忍日命 (KGSI), Ame-no-oshi-hi-no-mikoto 天忍日命 (SK)

Ame-no-ta-jikara-o (heavenly hand power man) – kami who pulls Amaterasu out of the heavenly rock cave
Ame-no-ta-jikara-o 天手力男神 (K1, Amë-nö-ta-dikara-wo-nö-kamï, Strong-Armed Man of Heaven), Ta-jikara-o 手力男神 (K1), Ta-jikara-o 手力雄神 (S7), Ama-no-ta-jikara-o 天手力雄神 (S7.3), Ama-no-ta-jikara-o 天手力雄神 (KGSI)

Ame-no-toko-tachi (heaven always standing) – one of the first kami
Ame-no-toko-tachi 天之常立神 (K1, Amë-nö-tökö-tati-nö-kamï, Ever-Standing Heaven), Ama-no-toko-tachi-no-mikoto 天常立尊 (S1.6), Ama-no-toko-tachi-no-mikoto 天常立尊 (SK)

Ame-no-uzu-me (heavenly headdress woman) – a goddess associated with spirit possession and dance who lures Amaterasu out of the heavenly rock cave
天宇受売命 (K1, Amë-nö-uzume-nö-mikötö, Wreathed Woman of Heaven), Ame-no-uzu-me 天宇受売 (K1), Ame-no-uzu-me-no-kami 天宇受売神 (K1), Ama-no-uzu-me-no-mikoto 天鈿女命 (S7, S9.1), Ama-no-uzu-me 天鈿女 (S7.3, S9.1), Ama-no-uzu-me-no-mikoto 天鈿女命 (KGSI), Ama-no-uzu-me-no-mikoto 天鈿女命 (SK)

Ame-waka-hiko (heavenly young-lord) – son of Ama-tsu-kuni-tama, sent to pacify the central reed plain land, son-in-law of Ō-kuni-nushi, husband of Shita-teru-hime, killed by an arrow returned from heaven
天若日子 (K1, Amë-nö-waka-piko-nö-kamï, Young Lad of Heaven), Ame-waka-hiko 天稚彦 (S9, S9.1, S9.6)

Ame-yorozu-taku-hata-chi-hata-hime – See **Yorozu-hata-toyo-akitsu-hime**

Ana-no-watari (hole crossing) – evil kami of a water crossing, quelled by Yamato-take
    穴済の神 (Keikō 28.2), Anato-no-kami 穴戸神 (K2)
Ao-kashiko-ne – See **Aya-kashiko-ne**
Ashi-nazu-chi (leg rubbing spirit) – father-in-law of Susano-o, father of Kushi-ina-da-hime
    Ashi-nazu-chi 足名椎 (K1, Asi-na-duti, Foot-stroking Elder), Ashi-nazu-chi-no-kami 足名鈇神 (K1), Ina-da-no-miya-nushi-suga-no-ya-tsu-mimi-no-kami 稲田宮主須賀之八耳神 (K1, Inada-nö-miya-nushi-suga-nö-yatu-mimi-nö-kamï, Master of the Mighty Halls of Rice Paddies and Eightfold Majestic Might of Refreshed), Ashi-nazu-chi 脚摩乳 (S8, S8.3), Ina-da-no-miya-nushi-no-kami (rice ear paddy field shrine master) 稲田宮主神 (S8), Ina-da-no-miya-nushi-susa-no-ya-tsu-mimi 稲田宮主簀狭之八箇耳 (S8.1), Ashi-nazu-te-nazu 脚摩手摩 (S8.2), Ashi-nazu-chi 脚摩乳 (SK), Ina-da-no-miya-nushi-no-kami 稲田宮主神 (SK)
Ashi-nazu-te-nazu – See **Ashi-nazu-chi**
Aso-tsu-hiko (Aso lord) – god of the Aso area in Kyushu, husband of Aso-tsu-hime
    Aso-tsu-hiko 阿蘇都彦 (Keikō 18.6)
Aso-tsu-hime (Aso lady) – goddess of the Aso area in Kyushu, wife of Aso-tsu-hiko
    Aso-tsu-hime 阿蘇都媛 (Keikō 18.6)
Ata-tsu-hime – See **Kamu-ata-tsu-hime**
Awa-na-gi (foam man, perhaps) – father of Izanagi in a variant of the *Chronicles*, a river god in *Ancient Matters*
    Awa-na-gi-no-kami 沫那芸神 (K1, Awa-nagi-nö-kamï, Calm Foam Man), Awa-na-gi-no-mikoto 沫蕩尊 (S2.2), Awa-na-gi 沫蕩 (SK), Awa-na-gi-no-kami 沫那芸神 (SK)
Aya-kashiko-ne (beautiful, handsome or fear, apprehension, perhaps) – one of the first kami, wife of Omo-taru
    Aya-kashiko-ne-no-kami 阿夜訶志古泥神 (K1, Aya-kasiko-ne-nö-kamï, Awesome Indeed), Kashiko-ne-no-mikoto 惶根尊 (S2, S3.1), Aya-kashiko-ne-no-mikoto 吾屋惶根尊 (S2), Imu-kashiki-no-mikoto 忌樫城尊 (S2), Ao-kashiki-ne-no-mikoto 青樫城根尊 (S2, S2.1), Aya-kashiki-no-mikoto 吾屋樫城尊 (S2), Aya-kashiko-ne-no-mikoto 吾屋惶根尊 (SK), Kashiko-ne-no-mikoto 惶根尊 (SK), Kakari-hime-no-mikoto 蚊鴈姫尊 (SK)
Chi-gaeshi (road reversal) – the boulder used by Izanagi to block off the passage leading to Yomi
    Chi-gaeshi-no-ō-kami 道反之大神 (K1, Ti-gaeshi-nö-opo-kamï, Great Spirit Road Retreat), Sayari-masu-yomi-to-no-ō-kami 塞坐黄泉戸大神 (K1, Sayari-masu-yömi-do-nö-opo-kamï, Great Spirt Athwart the Underworld), Chi-gaeshi-no-ō-kami 道反大神 (S5.6), Yomi-to-ni-fusakari-masu-ō-kami (great kami blockage occupying the entry to Yomi) 泉門塞之大神 (S5.6), Chi-gaeshi-no-ō-kami 道反大神 (SK)

Chi-ji-hime – See **Yorozu-hata-toyo-aki-tsu-shi-hime**

Chi-shiki (road to catch up to) – a travel deity, created from Izanagi's shoes when he flees Yomi. In K1, an alternative name for Izanami.

Chi-shiki-no-ō-kami 道敷大神 (K1, Ti-siki-nö-opo-kamï, Great Spirit Path of Pursuit), Chi-shiki-no-kami 道敷神 (S5.6), Chi-shiki-no-ō-kami 道敷大神 (SK)

Fuki-aezu (thatching not connected) – son of Ho-ho-de-mi and Toyo-tama-hime, husband of Tama-yori-hime, father of Jinmu

Ama-tsu-hiko-hiko-nagisa-take-u-gaya-fuki-aezu-no-mikoto 天津日高日子波限建鵜葺草葺不合命 (K1, U-gaya-puki-aëzu-nö-mikötö, Seaside Brave Lad of Unfinished Comorant-Feather Thatching), Hiko-nagisa-take-u-kaya-fuki-aezu-no-mikoto (lord beach brave cormorant thatch roofing not connected) 彦波瀲武鸕鶿草葺不合尊 (S10, S10.1, S10.3, S11), Hiko-nagisa-no-mikoto 彦瀲尊 (KGSI), Hiko-nagisa-take-u-kaya-fuki-aezu-no-mikoto 彦波瀲武鸕鶿草葺不合尊 (SK)

Fu-na-to – See **Tsuki-tatsu-fu-na-to**

Fushi-ikazuchi (genuflect thunder) – A thunder god on Izanami's right foot in *Ancient Matters*

伏雷 (K1, Pusi-ikaduti, Bowing Thunder)

Futo-dama (great jewel, perhaps) – a god associated with ritual worship who helps lure Amaterasu out of the heavenly rock cave, progenitor of the Inbe lineage group

Futo-dama-no-mikoto 布刀玉命 (K1, Puto-tama-nö-mikötö, Solemn Soul), Futo-dama-no-mikoto 太玉命 (S7, S7.3, S9.1, S9.2), Imi-be-no-kami 忌部神 (S7.1), Futo-dama 太玉 (S7.2), Ama-no-futo-dama-no-kami 天太玉神 (SK), Ama-no-futo-dama-no-mikoto 天太玉命 (SK), Ama-no-futo-dama 天太玉 (SK), Futo-dama (SK), Futo-dama-no-mikoto (SK)

Futsu-nushi-no-kami (slicing master) – in the *Chronicles*, one of the kami who successfully pacifies the central reed plain land and secures the surrender of Ō-kuni-nushi

Futsu-nushi-no-kami 経津主神 (S5.6, S5.7, S9, S9.1, S9.2), Futsu-nushi-no-mikoto 布都怒志命 (IFD), Futsu-nushi-no-kami 経津主神 (SK)

Ha-akaru-tama (bright jewel) – a kami who gives Susano-o a curved jewel in a *Chronicles* variant

Ha-akaru-tama 羽明玉 (S5.2)

Ha-ko-kuni-no – See **Toyo-kumo-no**

Hani-yama-hime – See **Hani-yasu-bime**

Hani-yasu-bime (clay lady) – child of Izanagi and Izanami and kami of the earth in the *Chronicles*, child born from Izanami's feces in *Ancient Matters*

Hani-yasu-bime 波邇夜須毘売神 (K1, Pani-yasu-bime-nö-kamï, Lady Kneading Clay), Hani-yasu-no-kami 埴安神 (S5.6), Hani-yama-hime 埴山姫 (S5.2, S5.3), Hani-yama-hime 埴山媛 (S5.4), Hani-yasu-bime 埴安姫 (SK), Hani-yama-hime-no-kami 埴山姫神 (SK), Hani-yasu-bime-no-kami 埴安姫神 (SK)

Hara-yama-tsu-mi (field mountain divine spirit) – a mountain kami born from the left foot of the corpse of the fire kami in *Ancient Matters*
Hara-yama-tsu-mi-no-kami 原山津見神 (K1, Para-yama-tu-mi-nö-kamï, Mountain Field Majesty)

Haya-aki-tsu-hi – See **Haya-aki-tsu-hiko**

Haya-aki-tsu-hiko (fast mouth lord) – kami of the harbors in the *Chronicles* and of estuaries in *Ancient Matters*
Haya-aki-tsu-hiko-no-kami 速秋津比古神 (K1, Paya-aki-tu-piko-nö-kamï, Rushing River Mouth Lad), Haya-aki-tsu-hime-no-kami 速秋津比売神 (K1, Paya-aki-tu-pime-nö-kamï, Lady Rushing River Mouth), Minato-no-kami 水戸神 (K1), Haya-aki-tsu-hi-no-mikoto 速秋津日命 (S5.6)

Ha-yama-tsu-mi (extremity mountain divine spirit) – a mountain kami born from the right hand of the corpse of the fire kami in *Ancient Matters* and from the hands of the corpse in the *Chronicles*
Ha-yama-tsu-mi-no-kami 羽山津見神 (K1, Pa-yama-tu-mi-nö-kamï, Mountain Foot Majesty), Ha-yama-tsu-mi 麓山祇 (S5.7)

Haya-tama-no-o (honored spit man) – a god born from Izanagi's saliva when he seals his oath of divorce
Haya-tama-no-o 速玉男 (S5.10)

Hiko-ho-ho-de-mi (lord rice ear rice ear coming forth divine spirit) – Son of Ninigi and Kamu-ata-tsu-hime, husband of Toyo-tama-hime, son-in-law of the sea kami Wata-tsu-mi, father of Fuki-aezu, sometimes identified as Ho-no-ori See **Ho-no-ori.** Hiko-ho-ho-de-mi 彦火火出見尊 (9.5, distinct from Ho-no-ori, 9,7 distinct from Ho-no-yori, S9.8, S10, S10.1, S10.2, S10.3), 彦火火出見尊 (SK, distinct from Ho-no-ori)

Hiko-ho-no-ninigi – See **Ninigi**

Hiko-nagisa-take-u-kaya-fuki-aezu – See **Fukiaezu**

Hiko-sashiri (lord ??) – a kami associated with shield production
Hiko-sashiri 彦狭知神 (S9.2)

Hime-tatara-i-suke-yori-hime (lady panic aid possessed lady) – mother-in-law of Jinmu, wife of Ō-kuni-nushi, Ō-mono-nushi, or Koto-shiro-nushi depending on source
Hime-tatara-i-suke-yori-hime 比売多多良伊須気余理比売 (K1, Pime-tatara-isukë-yöri-pime, Lady Panicked Lady Summoned Sacred Ward), Hoto-tatara-i-susuki-hime 比売多多良伊須気余理比売 (K1, Potö-tatara-isusuki-pime-nö-mikötö, Lady Panicked Privates Poked), Hime-tatara-i-suzu-hime (lady standing many bells lady) 姫蹈鞴五十鈴姫 (S8.6)

Hi-no-haya-hi (fire swift spirit, perhaps) – a thunder kami created when Izanagi slays the fire kami, or, a son of Amaterasu and Susano-o and brother of Oshi-ho-mimi
Hi-no-haya-hi-no-kami 樋速日神 (K1, Pï-paya-pi-nö-kamï, Blazing Stormer), Hi-no-haya-hi-no-kami 熯速日神 (S5.6, S9), Hi-no-haya-hi-no-mikoto 熯速

APPENDIX 1   601

日命 (S5.6, S7.3), Hi-no-haya-hi-no-mikoto 熯之速日命 (S6.3), Hi-no-haya-hiko-no-mikoto 樋速日子命 (IFD), Hi-no-haya-hi-no-kami 熯速日神 (SK), Hi-no-haya-hi-no-mikoto 熯之速日命 (SK)

Hi-no-kami – See **Ama-terasu**

Hi-no-mae (before the sun) – a likeness of Amaterasu used to lure her out of the heavenly rock cave
Hi-no-mae-no-kami 日前神 (S7.1)

Hiru-ko (leech child) – the leech child, a crippled son of Izanagi and Izanami who is cast to the winds
Hiru-ko 水蛭子 (K1, Piru-go, Leech Child), Hiru-ko 蛭子 (K1), Hiru-ko 蛭児 (S4.1, S4.10, S5, S5.2), Hiru-ko 水蛭子 (SK), Hiru-ko 蛭児 (SK)

Hito-koto-nushi – See **Kazuraki-no-hito-koto-nushi**

Ho-deri (flame bright) – a son of Ninigi and Kamu-ata-tsu-hime
Ho-deri-no-mikoto 火照命 (K1, Po-deri-nö-mikötö, Bright Flame), Umi-sachi-biko 海佐知毘古 (K1, Umi-sati-biko, Lad Possessing the Fortune of the Seas). See also **Ho-no-suseri**

Ho-ho-de-mi – See **Ho-no-ori**

Ho-musuhi – See **Kagu-tsu-chi**

Ho-no-akari (flame redness) – a son of Ninigi and Kamu-ata-tsu-hime, associated with Nigi-haya-hi in later sources
Ho-no-akari 火明命 (S9, S9.2, S9.3, S9.5, S9.7), Ho-no-akari 火明命 (HFD), Ho-no-akari 火明命 (SK). See also **Nigi-haya-hi, Ame-no-ho-akari**

Ho-no-ikazuchi (flame thunder) – a thunder deity on Izanami's breast
Ho-no-ikazuchi 火雷 (K1, Po-nö-ikaduti, Blazing Thunder), Ho-no-ikazuchi 火雷 (S5.9)

Ho-no-ninigi – See **Ninigi**

Ho-no-ori (flame breaking) – a son of Ninigi and Kamu-ata-tsu-hime, husband of Toyo-tama-hime, son-in-law of the sea kami Wata-tsu-mi, father of Fuki-aezu, sometimes identified as Hiko-ho-ho-de-mi. See **Hiko-ho-ho-de-mi**
Ho-no-ori 火遠理命 (K1, Flickering Flame), Ama-tsu-hiko-hiko-ho-ho-de-mi-no-mikoto 天津日高日子穂穂手見命 (K1, Sprouting Rice Ears Mighty Lad of the Lofty Sun in Heaven), Yama-sachi-biko 佐知毘古 (K1, Yama-sati-biko, Lad Possessing the Fortune of the Mountains), Hiko-ho-ho-de-mi 彦火火出見尊 (S9, S9.6, S10.3), Ho-no-ori 火折尊 (S9.1, S9.5, S9.6, S10.1, S10.4), Ho-no-ori-hiko-ho-ho-de-mi-no-mikoto 火折彦火火出見尊 (S9.3), Ho-no-yo-ori 火夜織命 (S9.7), Yama-sachi-hiko (mountain fortune lord) 山幸彦 (S10.3), Ho-no-ori 火折尊 (SK)

Ho-no-ori-hiko-ho-ho-de-mi – See **Ho-no-ori**

Ho-no-suseri (flame raging) – son of Ninigi and Kamu-ata-tsu-hime
Ho-no-suseri 火須勢理命 (K1, Po-suseri-nö-mikötö, Bold Flame), Ho-no-susori 火闌降命 (S9, S10), Ho-no-suseri 火酢芹命 (S9.2, S9.3, S9.6, S9.8, S10.3, S10.4), Ho-no-susumi 火進命 (S9.3), Umi-sachi-hiko 海幸彦 (S10.3)

Ho-no-susori – See **Ho-no-suseri**

Ho-no-susumi (flame advancing) – a son of Ninigi and Kamu-ata-tsu-hime
Ho-no-susumi 火進命 (S9.3, S9.5). See also **Ho-no-suseri**, Ho-no-susumi 火進命 (SK)

Ho-no-to-hata-hime (rice ear flag lady) – daughter of Taka-mi-musuhi in a *Chronicles* variant
Ho-no-to-hata-hime 火之戸幡姫 (S9.6)

Ho-no-yo-ori – See **Ho-no-ori**

Hoshi-no-kami – See **Kagase-o**

Ichi-ki-shima-hime (market pestle island lady, perhaps) – daughter of Amaterasu and Susano-o
Ichi-ki-shima-hime 市寸島比売命 (K1, Ikiti-sima-pime-nö-mikötö, Lady Consecrated Isle), Sa-yori-bime-no-mikoto 狭依毘売命 (K1, Sa-yöri-bime-nö-mikötö, Lady Spirit Possessed), Ichi-ki-shima-hime 市杵島姫 (S6), Oki-tsu-shima-hime (open seas island woman) 瀛津島姫 (S6.1), Ichi-ki-shima-hime-no-mikoto 市杵島姫命 (S6.2, S6.3), Oki-tsu-shima-hime-no-mikoto 瀛津島姫命 (S6.1, S6.3), Ichi-ki-shima-hime-no-mikoto 市杵嶋姫命 (JH, CH), Sa-yori-hime-no-mikoto 佐依姫命 (SK)

I-hika (well shining) – earthly deity encountered by Jinmu; progenitor of the Obito of Yoshino
I-hika 井光 (Jinmu PA)

Ikazuchi-no-kami (thunder kami) – gods of thunder
雷神 (K1, Thunder Spirits) Ikazuchi-no-kami 雷神 (S5.7)

Iku-gui (lively peg) – one of the first kami
Iku-gui-no-kami 活杙神 (K1, Iku-gupi-nö-kamï, Thriving Tip), Iku-kui-no-mikoto 活樴尊 (S3.1), Iku-gui-ni-mikoto 活樴尊 (SK)

Iku-kui – See **Iku-gui**

Iku-tsu-hiko-ne (active lord) – son of Amaterasu and Susano-o and brother of Ninigi
Iku-tsu-hiko-ne-no-mikoto 活津日子根命 (K1, Iku-tu-pikone-nö-mikötö, Lively Little Lad), Iku-tsu-hiko-ne 活津彦根命 (S6, S6.1, S6.2, S6.3), Iku-metsu-hiko-ne 活目津彦根命 (S7.3), Iku-tsu-hiko-ne 活津彦根命 (SK)

Imi-be-no-kami – See **Futo-dama**

Ina-da-hime – See **Kushi-ina-da-hime**

Ina-da-no-miya-nushi – See **Ashi-nazu-chi**

Ina-da-no-miya-nushi-susa-no-yatsu-mimi – See **Ashi-nazu-chi, Te-nazu-chi**

Ina-se-hagi (No-yes-runner) – a messenger used by Take-mikazu-chi and Futsu-nushi when they pacify the central reed plain land
Ina-se-hagi 稲背脛命 (S9)

Isao-shi – See **I-takeru**

Ishi-kori-do-me (stone coagulate woman) – a kami of metalwork, including mirrors, who helps lure Amaterasu out of the heavenly rock cave
Ishi-kori-do-me-no-mikoto 伊斯許理度売命 (K1, Isi-köri-dome-nö-mikötö, Stone Mold Crone), Ishi-kori-do-me 石凝姥 (S7.1), Ishi-kori-tobe 石凝戸辺

(S7.3), Ishi-kori-do-me-no-mikoto 石凝姥命 (S9.1), Ishi-kori-do-me-no-kami 石凝姥神 (KGSI), Ishi-kori-do-me-no-mikoto 石凝姥命 (SK)

Ishi-kori-tobe – See **Ishi-kore-do-me-no-mikoto**

I-takeru (much bravery) – a son of Susano-o and kami of trees
I-takeru-no-kami 五十猛神 (S8.4), I-takeru-no-mikoto 五十猛命 (S8.4, S8.5), Isao-shi-no-kami 有高之神 (S8.4)

Itsu-no-o-hashiri – See **Ame-no-o-habari**

Iwai-no-ushi (human for ritual worship of divine auspicious signs) – a divination kami from a *Chronicles* variant who appears during the pacification of the central reed plain land
Iwai-no-ushi-no-kami 斎主神 (S9.2)

Iwa-naga-hime (rock long lady) – older sister of Kamu-ata-tsu-hime, rejected wife of Ninigi
Iwa-naga-hime 石長比売 (K1, Ipa-naga-pime, Lady Lasting Rock), Iwa-naga-hime 石長比売 (S9.2, S9.6), Iwa-naga-hime 石長比売 (SK)

Iwa-oshi-wake (rock superior lord) – father of a nameless kami encountered by Jinmu; the progenitor of the Kuisu people of Yoshino
Iwa-oshi-wake 磐排別 (Jinmu PA)

Iware-biko-ho-ho-de-mi – See **Jinmu**

Iwa-saku-ne-saku – See **Iwa-saku-no-kami**, **Ne-saku-no-kami**

Iwa-saku (rock splitter) – a sword god produced when Izanagi slays the fire kami Kagu-tsu-chi
Iwa-saku-no-kami 石析神 (K1, Ipa-saku-nö-kamï, Boulder Splitter), Iwa-saku-no-kami 磐裂神 (S5.6, S5.7), Iwa-saku-ne-saku-no-kami 磐裂根裂神 (S9), Iwa-saku-ne-saku-no-kami 磐裂根裂神 (SK)

Iwa-tsutsu-no-me (rock earth woman) – a sword goddess produced when Izanagi slays the fire kami Kagu-tsu-chi
Iwa-tsutsu-no-me-no-mikoto 磐筒女命 (S5.6, S5.9), Iwa-tsutsu-no-me-no-kami 磐筒女神 (S5.7)

Iwa-tsutsu-no-o (rock earth man) – a sword god produced when Izanagi slays the fire kami Kagu-tsu-chi
Iwa-tsutsu-no-o-no-kami 石筒之男神 (K1, Ipa-tutu-nö-wo-nö-kamï, Stone Mallet Man), Iwa-tsutsu-no-o-no-mikoto 磐筒男命 (S5.6), Iwa-tsutsu-no-o-no-kami 磐筒男神 (S5.7), Iwa-tsutsu-no-mikoto 磐土命 (S5.10), Iwa-tsutsu-no-o 磐筒男 (S9), Iwa-tsutsu-no-o 磐筒男 (SK)

Izanagi (he who invites) – creator god of the Japanese archipelago and its kami
Izana-gi-no-kami 伊耶那岐神 (K1, Izanagi-nö-kamï, He Who Beckoned), Izana-gi-no-mikoto 伊耶那伎命 (K1, Izanagi-nö-mikötö), Izana-gi-no-kami 伊耶那岐 (K1), Izana-gi-no-ōkami 伊耶那伎大神 (K1, Izanagi-nö-opo-kamï), Izana-gi-no-ōmikami 伊耶那岐大御神 (K1, Izanagi-nö-opo-mi-kamï), Izana-gi-no-mikoto 伊耶那岐命 (K1, Izanagi-nö-mikötö), Izana-gi-no-mikoto 伊弉諾尊 (S2, S2.2, S3, S3.1, S4, S4.1, S4.2, S5, S5.1, S5.6, S5.7, S5.8, S5.9, S5.10,

S5.11, S6, S7.3, S9.5, Jinmu 31), Izana-gi-no-kami 伊奘諾 (S4.3, S4.4, S5.2,), O-no-kami (male god) 陽神 (S4, S4.1, S4.5, S4.10), Izana-gi-no-kami 伊奘諾神 (Richū 5), Izana-gi-no-kami 伊弉奈枳 (IFD), Izana-gi-no-mikoto 伊差奈枳命 (IFD), Izana-gi-no-kami 伊奘諾 (KGSI), Izana-gi-no-mikoto 伊奘諾尊 (SK)

Izanami (she who invites) – creator goddess of the Japanese archipelago and its kami

Izana-mi-no-kami 伊耶那美 (K1, Izanami-nö-kamï, She Who Beckoned), Izana-mi-no-mikoto 伊耶那美命 Izanami-nö-mikötö (K1), Yomo-tsu-ō-kami 黄泉津大神 (K1, Great Spirit of the Underworld), Chi-shiki-no-ō-kami 道敷大神 (K1, Great Spirit Path of Pursuit), Izana-mi-no-mikoto 伊弉冉尊 (S2, S3, S3.1, S4, S4.1, S4.2, S5, S5.2, S5.3, S5.4, S5.5, S5.6, S5.9, S5.10), Izana-mi 伊奘冉 (S4.3, S4.4), Me-no-kami (female god) 陰神 (S4, S4.1, S4.5, S4.10), Izana-mi-no-mikoto 伊弉弥命 (IFD), Izana-mi 伊奘冉 (KGSI), Izana-mi-no-mikoto 伊奘冉尊 (SK)

Izasa-wake – See **Kehi-no-ō-kami**

Jinmu (divine warrior) – first emperor of the Japanese state, son of Fuki-aezu and Tama-yori-hime

Waka-mi-ke-nu-no-mikoto 若御毛沼命 (K1, Waka-mi-kë-nu-nö-mikötö, Young Master Mighty Offerings), Toyo-mi-ke-nu-no-mikoto 豊御毛沼命磐余彦帝 (K1, Töyö-mi-kë-nu-nö-mikötö, Master Plentiful Mighty Offerings), Kamu-yamato-iware-biko (K1, Kamu-yamatö-ipare-biko-nö-mikötö, Boulder Hamlet Lad of Sacred Yamato), Kamu-yamato-iware-hiko (S11, S11.1), Sano-no-mikoto 狭野尊 (S11.1), Iware-hiko 磐余彦 (S11.2), Kamu-yamato-iware-hiko-ho-ho-de-mi 神日本磐余彦火火出見尊 (S8.6, S11.2, S11.3), Iware-hiko-ho-ho-de-mi-no-mikoto 磐余彦火火出見尊 (11.4), Kamu-yamato-iware-hiko-no-sumera-mikoto (Jinmu), Ama-no-osu-kami 天圧神 (Jinmu PA)

Ka-ashi-tsu-hime – See **Kamu-ata-tsu-hime**

Kachi-haya-hi – See **Oshi-ho-mimi**

Kachi-haya-hi-ama-no-oshi-ho-mimi – See **Oshi-ho-mimi**

Kagase-o (shining man) – a star god killed by Take-mikazu-chi and Futsu-nushi

Kagase-o 香香背男 (S9), Hoshi-no-kami (star god) 星神 (S9), Ama-tsu-mika-hoshi (heavenly vigorous star) 天津甕星 (S9.2), Ama-no-kagase-o 天香香背男 (S9.2)

Kagu-tsu-chi (fire spirit) – the fire kami, kills Izanami while being born

Hi-no-kagu-tsu-chi-no-kami 火之迦具土神 (K1, Pï-nö-kagu-tuti-nö-kamï, Flickering Flame Elder), Kagu-tsu-chi-no-kami 迦具土神 (K1, Kagu-tuti-nö-kamï, Flickering Elder), Hi-no-yagi-haya-o-no-kami 火之夜芸速男神 (K1, Pï-nö-yagi-paya-wo-nö-kamï, Swift Burning Flame), Hi-no-kaga-hiko-no-kami 火之炫毘古神 (K1, Pï-nö-kaga-biko-nö-kamï, Blazing Flame Lad), Kagu-tsu-chi-no-kami 軻遇突智 (S5.2, S5.4, S5.6, S5.7), Ho-musuhi 火産霊 (S5.3), Ho-no-kami 火神 (S5.5), Kagu-tsu-chi-no-mikoto 軻遇突智命 (S5.8), Ho-no-musuhi-kagu-tsu-chi 火之産霊迦具突智 (SK), Ho-no-yaki-haya-o-no-kami

火焼速男命神 (SK), Ho-ho-yake-zumi-no-kami 火火焼炭神 (SK), Kagu-tsu-chi 軻遇突智 (SK), Katu-tsu-chi 迦具突智 (SK)

Kamu-ata-ka-ashi-tsu-hime – See **Kamu-ata-tsu-hime**

Kamu-ata-tsu-hime (divine lady of Ata) – husband of Ninigi, daughter of Ō-yama-tsu-mi, mother of Hiko-ho-ho-de-mi

Kamu-ata-tsu-hime 神阿多都比売 (K1, Kamu-ata-tu-pime, Lady Sacred of Net Hands), Ko-no-hana-no-saku-ya-bime 木花之佐久夜毘売 (K1, Kö-nö-pana-nö-sakuya-bime, Lady Blooming Tree Blossoms), Kamu-ata-tsu-hime 神吾田津姫 (S9), Kamu-ata-ka-ashi-tsu-hime (divine lady of Kashi) 神吾田鹿葦津姫 (S9, S9.2, S9.3), Ka-ashi-tsu-hime (lady of Kashi) 鹿葦津姫 (S9), Ko-no-hana-no-saku-ya-hime (lady of the blooming trees and flowers) 木花開耶姫 (S9, S9.2, S9.6, S9.8), Ata-ka-ashi-tsu-hime 吾田鹿葦津姫 (9.5), Toyo-ata-tsu-hime (rich lady of Ata) 豊吾田津姫 (S9.6), Ata-tsu-hime (lady of Ata) 吾田津姫 (S9.7), Ko-no-hana-saku-ya-bime 許乃波奈佐久夜比売命 (HFD)

Kamu-musuhi (divine generative force) – one of the first kami, father of Sukuna-bikona in the *Chronicles*, benefactor of Ō-kuni-nushi in *Ancient Matters*

Kamu-musuhi-no-kami 神産巣日神 (K1, Kamï-musubi-nö-kamï, Sacred Growth), Kamu-musuhi-no-mikoto 神産巣日之命 (K1), Kamu-musuhi-mi-oya-no-mikoto 神産巣日御祖命 (K1), Kamu-mi-musuhi-no-mikoto (divine august generative force) 神皇産霊尊 (S1.4, S9.7), Kamu-musuhi-no-kami 神産霊神 (KGSI), Kamu-musuhi 神産霊 (KGSI), Kamu-ru-mi-no-mikoto 神留弥命 (KGSI), Kamu-mi-musuhi-no-mikoto 神皇産霊尊 (SK), Kamu-mi-musuhi-no-mikoto 神魂尊 (SK), Kamu-mi-musuhi-mi-oya-no-mikoto 神皇産霊御祖尊 (SK), Kamu-mi-musuhi-no-kami 神皇産霊神 (SK), Kamu-mi-musuhi 神皇産霊 (SK), Kamu-mi-musuhi-no-mikoto 神魂命 (SK), Kamu-mi-musuhi-no-mikoto 神皇産霊命 (SK)

Kamu-nao-bi (divine fixing divine spirit) – a good kami produced during Izanagi's ablution after his escape from Yomi

Kamu-nao-bi-no-kami 神直毘神 (K1, Kamu-napobi-nö-kamï, Sacred Remedy), Kamu-nao-hi-no-kami 神直日神 (S5.6), Kamu-nao-hi-no-kami 神直日神 (SK)

Kamu-nao-hi – See **Kamu-nao-bi-no-kami**

Kana-yama-biko (metal mountain lord) – a kami of metal born from Izanami's vomit

Kana-yama-biko-no-kami 金山毘古神 (K1, Kana-yama-biko-nö-kamï, Metal Mountain Lad), Kana-yama-biko 金山彦 (S5.4), Kana-yama-biko-no-kami 金山彦神 (SK)

Kashiko-ne – See **Aya-kashiko-ne**

Kashiwa-no-watari-no-kami (kami of Kashiwa crossing) – an evil kami of water crossings, quelled by Yamato Take

Kashiwa-no-watari-no-kami 柏済の神 (Keikō 27.12)

Kaya-no-hime (grass field lady) – a goddess of grass, daughter of Izanagi and Izanami
Kaya-no-hime-no-kami 鹿屋野比売神 (K1, Kaya-nö-pime-nö-kamï, Lady Thatch), No-zu-chi-no-kami 野椎神 (K1, No-dzuti-nö-kamï, Moorland Elder), Kaya-no-hime 草野姫 (S5), No-zu-chi (spirit of the field) 野槌 (S5, S7.2), Kaya-hime-no-kami 鹿屋姫神 (SK)

Kazuraki-no-hito-koto-nushi (one word master of Kazuraki) – a kami that appears to Yūryaku while he is out on a hunt
Kazu-raki-no-hito-koto-nushi-no-ō-kami 葛城之一言主之大神 (K3, Pitö-kötö-nusi-nö-opo-kamï, Master One Word), Hito-koto-nushi-no-kami 一言主大神 (K3), Hito-koto-nushi-no-ō-kami 一言主之大神 (K3), Hito-koto-nushi-no-kami 一事主神 (Yūryaku 4.2), Kazuraki-no-hito-koto-nushi-no-kami 葛城之一言主之神 (SK)

Kehi-no-ō-kami (great kami of Kehi) – a kami from Tsuruga who switches names with Ōjin
Kehi-no-ō-kami 笥飯大神 (Jingū 13.2, Ōjin PA), Izasa-wake-no-kami 去来紗別神 (Ōjin PA)

Ko-goto-musuhi (generative force of words, perhaps) – parent of Ame-no-koyane
Ko-goto-musuhi 興台産霊 (S7.3)

Ko-no-hana-saku-ya-hime – See **Kamu-ata-tsu-hime**

Koto-katsu-kuni-katsu-naga-sa – (things super land super long narrow) an earthly kami encountered by Ninigi after he descends
Koto-katsu-kuni-katsu-naga-sa 事勝国勝長狭 (S9, S9.2, S9.4, S9.6), Shio-tsu-chi no oji 塩土老翁 (S9.4), Naga-sa 長狭 (S9.6). See also **Shio-tsu-chi-no-kami**

Koto-shiro-nushi (thing/word exchange master) – an oracle kami, son of Ō-kuni-nushi
Koto-shiro-nushi-no-kami 事代主神 (K1, Kötö-sirö-nushi-nö-kamï, Master Speaker for Others), Koto-shiro-nushi-no-kami 事代主神 (S.86, S9, S9.1, S9.2, Jinmu PA, Suizei PA, Annei PA, Itoku PA), Ame-ni-koto-shiro-sora-ni-koto-shiro-tama-kushi-iri-biko-itsu-no-koto-shiro-no-kami 天事代虚事代玉籤入彦厳之事代神 (Jingū PA), Koto-shiro-nushi-no-mikoto 事代主尊 (SK)

Ku-ku-no-chi (spirit of trees) – a kami of trees, child of Izanagi and Izanami
Ku-ku-no-chi-no-kami 久々能智神 (K1, Kuku-nö-ti-nö-kamï, Tree Trunk Elder), Ku-ku-no-chi 句句廼馳 (S5, S5.6), Ku-ku-no-chi 句々廼馳 (SK)

Kukuri-hime (unclear) – a goddess who appears when Izanagi flees Yomi
Kukuri-hime 菊理媛 (S5.10)

Kumano-kusu-hi (unclear) – son of Amaterasu and Susano-o, brother of Oshi-ho-mimi
Kumano-no-kusu-hi-no-mikoto 熊野久須毘命 (K1, Kumano-kusubi-nö-mikötö, Wonder Worker of Bear Moors), Kumano-kusu-hi-no-mikoto 熊野櫲樟日命 (S6, S6.2), Kumano-oshi-ho-mi-no-mikoto 熊野忍隅命 (S6.1, S6.3),

APPENDIX 1

Kumano-oshi-kuma 熊野忍隅命 (S6.3), Kumano-ō-sumi-no-mikoto 熊野大角命 (S7.3), Kumano-kusu-hi-no-mikoto 熊野櫲樟日命 (SK)

Kumano-no-ō-sumi – See **Kumano-kusu-hi**

Kumano-oshi-ho-mi – See **Kumano-kusu-hi**

Kumano-oshi-kuma – See **Kumano-kusu-hi**

Ku-na-to – See **Tsuki-tatsu-fu-na-to-no-kami**

Kuni-no-sa-tachi – See **Kuni-no-sa-tsuchi**

Kuni-no-sa-tsuchi (landed narrow earth, perhaps) – one of the first kami
Kuni-no-sa-tsuchi-no-mikoto 国狭槌尊 (S1, S1.1, S1.2, S1.4), Kuni-no-sa-tachi-no-mikoto 国狭立尊 (S1.1), Kuni-no-sa-tachi-no-mikoto 国狭立尊 (SK), Kuni-no-sa-tsuchi-no-mikoto 国狭槌尊 (SK)

Kuni-no-toko-tachi (land always standing) – one of the first kami
Kuni-no-toko-tachi-no-kami 国常立神 (K1, Kuni-nö-tökö-tati-nö-kamï, Ever-Standing Land), Kuni-no-toko-tachi-no-mikoto 国常立尊 (S1, S1.1., S1.2, S1.4, S1.5, S1.6, S2.2, S3), Kuni-no-soko-tachi-no-mikoto 国底立尊 (S1.1, S1.3), Kuni-no-toko-tachi-no-mikoto 国常立尊 (SK)

Kura-mitsu-ha (valley water ??) – a water kami born after the fire kami Kagu-tsu-chi is killed
Kura-mitsu-ha-no-kami 闇御津羽神 (K1, Kura-mitu-pa-nö-kamï, Ravine Water Gushing), Kura-mitsu-ha 闇罔象 (S5.6), Kura-mitsu-ha 闇罔象 (SK)

Kura-okami (valley ??) – a water kami born after the fire kami Kagu-tsu-chi is killed
闇淤加美神 (K1, Kura-okami-nö-kamï, Ravine Rain Serpent), Kura-okami 闇龗 (S5.6)

Kura-yama-tsu-mi (valley mountain spirit) – a mountain kami born after the fire kami Kagu-tsu-chi is killed; in *Ancient Matters*, born from the genitals of the corpse of the fire kami
Kura-yama-tsu-mi-no-kami 闇山津見神 (K1, Kura-yama-tu-mi-nö-kamï, Mountain Gorge Majesty), Kura-yama-tsu-mi 闇山祇 (S5.6), Kura-yama-tsu-mi-no-kami 闇山津見神 (SK), Kura-yama-tsu-mi 闇山祇

Kuro-ikazuchi (black thunder) – a thunder god on Izanami's stomach in *Ancient Matters* and on her bottom in the *Chronicles*
Kuro-ikazuchi 黒雷 (K1, Kuro-ikaduti, Darkening Thunder), Kuro-ikazuchi 黒雷 (S5.9)

Kushi-ina-da-hime (mystical rice ear paddy lady) – Daughter of Ashi-nazu-chi and Te-nazu-chi, wife of Susano-o
Kushi-na-da-hime 櫛名田比売 (K1, Kusi-nada-pime, Lady Wondrous Rice Paddies), Kushi-ina-da-hime 奇稲田姫 (S8), Ina-da-hime 稲田媛 (S8.1), Ma-kami-furu-kushi-ina-da-hime 真髪触奇稲田媛 (S8.2), Kushi-ina-da-hime 奇稲田媛 (8.3), Kushi-ina-da-mitoyo-manura-hime 久志伊奈太美等与麻奴良比売命 (IFD)

Kushi-tama-nigi-haya-hi – See **Nigi-haya-hi**

Masa-ka-a-katsu-kachi-haya-hi-ama-no-oshi-ho-mimi – See **Oshi-ho-mimi**

Masa-ka-a-katsu-kachi-haya-hi-ama-no-oshi-ho-ne – See **Oshi-ho-mimi**

Ma-saka-yama-tsu-mi (true edge mountain divine spirit) – a mountain kami born from the hip of the corpse of the fire kami in the *Chronicles* and from its head in *Ancient Matters*

Ma-saka-yama-tsu-mi-no-kami 正鹿山津見神 (Ma-saka-yama-tu-mi-nö-kamï, True Mountain Majesty), Ma-saka-yama-tsu-mi 正勝山祇 (S5.7)

Me-kami – See **Izanami**

Michi-no-naga-chi-ha (way long road boulder) – a kami created from Izanagi's belt when he flees Yomi

Michi-no-naga-chi-ha-no-kami 道之長乳歯神 (K1, Miti-nö-naga-ti-pa-nö-kamï, Long-winding Way Stones), Naga-chi-iwa-no-kami (long road boulder) 長道磐神 (S5.6), Naga-chi-iwa-no-kami 長道磐神 (SK), Michi-no-naga-chi-ha-no-kami 道長乳歯神 (SK)

Mi-ho-tsu-hime (august rice ear lady) – a daughter of Taka-mi-musuhi betrothed to Ō-mono-nushi in a *Chronicles* variant

Mi-ho-tsu-hime 三穂津姫 (S9.2)

Mika-no-haya-hi (vigorous swift spirit) – a thunder kami created when Izanagi slays the fire kami Kagu-tsu-chi

Mika-no-haya-hi-no-kami 甕速日神 (K1, Mika-paya-pi-nö-kamï, Stern Stormer), Mika-no-haya-hi-no-kami 甕速日神 (S5.6, S9), Mika-no-haya-hi-no-mikoto 甕速日命 (S5.6), Mika-no-haya-hi-no-kami 甕速日神 (SK), Mika-no-haya-hi-no-kami 甕速日神 (KGSI)

Mi-no – See **Toyo-kumo-no**

Mi-shima-no-mizo-kui-mimi (ditch opening ear kami of Mishima) – father of Tama-kushi-hime, grandfather of Hime-tatara-i-suzu-hime

Mi-shima-no-mizo-kui-mimi-no-kami 三島溝樴神 (Jinmu PA)

Mitsu-ha-no-me – See **Mizu-ha-no-me**

Mizo-kui-hime (ditch opening lady) – daughter of Mi-shima-no-mizo-kui-mimi, wife of Ō-mono-nushi / Ō-kuni-nushi / Koto-shiro-nushi, mother of Hime-tatara-i-suzu-hime

Mizo-kui-hime 溝樴姫 (S8.6), Tama-kushi-hime (jewel mysterious lady) 玉櫛姫 (S8.6)

Mizu-ha-no-me (water ?? woman) – a water kami born upon the death of Izanami after giving birth to the fire kami

Mizu-ha-no-me-no-kami 弥都波能売神 (K1, Mitu-pa-nö-me-nö-kamï, Water Gushing Woman), Mitsu-ha-no-me 罔象女 (S5.2, S5.3, S5.4), Mitsu-ha-no-me-no-kami 罔象女神 (SK)

Muka-hitsu-o-mo-o-so-ō-itsu-no-mitama-haya-sa-agari (unclear) – an unknown kami responsible for the death of Chūai

Muka-hitsu-o-mo-o-so-ō-itsu-no-mitama-haya-sa-agari 向匱男聞襲大歴五御魂速狭騰尊 (Jingū PA)

Naga-chi-iwa – See **Michi-no-naga-chi-ha-no-kami**

Naka-yama-tsu-mi (center mountain divine spirit) – a mountain kami born from the body of the corpse of the fire kami
Naka-yama-tsu-mi 中山祇 (S5.8)

Naka-tsu-tsu-no-o (middle harbor man) – produced by Izanagi during his ablution after his escape from Yomi, one of the three gods of the Sumiyoshi Grand Shrine
Naka-tsu-tsu-no-o-no-mikoto 中箇之男命 (K1, Naka-dutu-nö-wo-nö-mikötö, Middle Sail Man), Naka-tsu-tsu-no-o 中箇男 (K2), Naka-tsu-tsu-no-o-no-mikoto 中筒男命 (S5.6), Aka-tsu-tsu-no-mikoto 赤土命 (S5.10), Naka-tsu-tsu-no-o 中筒男 (Jingū PA, Jingū 1.2), Naka-tsu-tsu-no-o 中筒雄 (Jingū PA), Naka-tsu-tsu-no-o-no-mikoto 中筒男命 (SK), Aka-tsu-tsu-no-mikoto 赤土命 (SK)

Naka-tsu-wata-tsu-mi (middle sea divine spirit) – produced by Izanagi during his ablution after his escape from Yomi
Naka-tsu-wata-tsu-mi-no-kami 中津綿津見神 (K1, Naka-tu-wata-tu-mi-nö-kamï, Middle Ocean Majesty), Naka-tsu-wata-tsu-mi-no-mikoto 中津少童命 (S5.6), Naka-tsu-wata-tsu-mi-no-mikoto 中津少童命 (SK)

Naki-sawa-me (crying swamp woman) – produced from the tears of Izanagi after the death of Izanami
Naki-sawa-me-no-kami 泣沢女神 (K1, Naki-sapa-me-nö-kamï, Much Wailing Woman), Naki-sawa-me-no-mikoto 啼沢女命 (S5.6), Naki-sawa-me-no-kami 啼沢女神 (SK)

Nao-iri-no-mononobe (mononobe of Naoiri) – a kami venerated by Keikō during his conquest of Kyushu
Nao-iri-no-mononobe-no-kami 直入物部神 (Keikō 12.10)

Nao-iri-no-naka-omi (omi of inner Naoiri) – a kami venerated by Keikō during his conquest of Kyushu
Nao-iri-no-naka-omi-no-kami 直入中臣神 (Keikō 12.10)

Nari-ikazuchi (sounding thunder) – a thunder deity on Izanami's left foot in *Ancient Matters*
Naka-ikazuchi 鳴雷 (K1, Nari-ikaduti, Booming Thunder)

Ne-saku (root splitter) – a sword kami produced when Izanagi slays the fire kami Kagu-tsu-chi
Ne-saku-no-kami 根析神 (K1, Ne-saku-nö-kamï, Root Splitter), Ne-saku 根裂神 (S5.6, S5.7), Iwa-saku-ne-saku 磐裂根裂神 (S9), Iwa-saku-ne-saku 磐裂根裂神 (SK)

Nie-motsu (food presented to gods holder) – earthly deity encountered by Jinmu
Nie-motsu 苞苴擔 (Jinmu PA)

Nigi-haya-hi (flourishing swift divine spirit) – heavenly deity encountered by Jinmu, progenitor of the Mononobe, older brother of Ninigi in later sources
Nigi-haya-hi-no-mikoto 邇藝速日命 (K1, Nigi-paya-pi-nö-mikötö, Plentiful Rushing Sun), Nigi-haya-hi-no-mikoto 饒速日命 (Jinmu PA, Jinmu 31.4), Kushi-tama-nigi-haya-hi-no-mikoto 櫛玉饒速日命 (Jinmu PA), Ama-teru-kuni-teru-hiko-ama-no-ho-akari-kushi-tama-nigi-haya-hi-no-mikoto 天照国

照彦天火明櫛玉饒速日尊 (SK), Nigi-haya-hi-no-mikoto 饒速日尊 (SK). See also **Ho-no-Akari**

Ni-kutsu-hime (red footwear lady) – wife of Oshi-ho-mimi in a *Chronicles* variant
Ni-kutsu-hime 丹鳥姫 (S9.7)

Ninigi (flourish) – son of Oshi-ho-mimi, grandson of Taka-mi-musuhi and Amaterasu, father of Hiko-ho-ho-de-mi, husband of Kamu-ata-tsu-hime, often referred to as the "heavenly grandson" or the "heavenly descendant"
Ame-nigishi-kuni-nigishi-ama-tsu-hiko-hiko-ho-no-ninigi-no-mikoto 天邇岐志国邇岐志天津日高日子番能邇邇芸命 (K1, Ama-tu-piko-piko-po-nö-ninigi-nö-mikötö, Ripening Rice Ears Lad of Heaven), Hiko-ho-no-ninigi-no-mikoto 日子番能邇邇芸命 (K1), Ama-tsu-hiko-ho-no-ninigi-no-mikoto 天津日子番能邇邇芸命 (K1), Ama-tsu-hiko-hiko-ho-no-ninigi-no-mikoto (Heavenly lord rice ears red flourish) 天津彦彦火瓊瓊杵尊 (S9, S9.1), Ama-tsu-hiko-ho-no-ninigi-no-mikoto 天津彦彦火瓊瓊杵尊 (S9.2), Ho-no-ninigi-no-mikoto 火瓊瓊杵尊 (S9.6, S9.7, Jinmu PA), Ama-tsu-hiko-kuni-teru-hiko-ho-no-ninigi-no-mikoto 天津彦国光彦火瓊瓊杵尊 (S9.4), Ama-tsu-hikone-ho-no-ninigi-ne-no-mikoto 天津彦根火瓊瓊杵根尊 (S9.6), Ama-tsu-kuni-nigishi-hiko-ho-no-ninigi-no-mikoto 天国饒石彦火瓊瓊杵尊 (S9.6), Ama-no-gi-ho-ho-gise-no-mikoto 天之杵火火置瀬尊 (S9.7), Ama-no-ki-ho-ho-oki-se-no-mikoto 天之杵火火置瀬尊 (S9.7), Ama-no-kise-no-mikoto 天杵瀬命 (S9.7), Ama-no-nigi-shi-kuni-no-nigi-shi-ama-tsu-hiko-ho-no-ninigi-no-mikoto 天饒石国饒石天津彦火瓊瓊杵尊 (S9.8), Ama-tsu-hiko-no-mikoto 天津彦尊 (KGSI), Ama-tsu-hiko-ho-no-ninigi-no-mikoto 天津彦火瓊瓊杵尊 (SK)

No-no-ikazuchi (field thunder) – a thunder kami on Izanami's legs in the *Chronicles*
No-no-ikazuchi 野雷 (S5.9)

No-zu-chi – See **Kaya-no-hime-no-kami**

Ō-ana-muchi – See **Ō-kuni-nushi**

Ō-aya-tsu-hi (great ?? spirit) – kami produced during Izanagi's ablution after his escape from Yomi
Ō-aya-tsu-hi-no-mikoto 大綾津命 (S5.10)

Odo-yama-tsu-mi (?? mountain spirit) – a mountain kami born from the chest of the corpse of the fire kami
Odo-yama-tsu-mi-no-kami 淤藤山津見神 (K1, Odö-yama-tu-mi-nö-kamï, Younger Mountain Majesty)

Ō-getsu-hime (great food lady) – an agriculture goddess killed by Susano-o in *Ancient Matters* and, as Uke-mochi, by Tsuku-yomi in the *Chronicles*
大宜都比売 (K1, Opo-gë-tu-pime, Lady Great Sustenance), Ō-getsu-hime-no-kami 大気都比売神 (K1), Ō-getsu-hime 大気都比売 (K1), Ō-getsu-hime-no-kami 大宜津比売神 (K1), Uke-mochi-no-kami (food preserve) 保食神 (S5.11), Ō-getsu-hime 大宜都比売 (SK), Ō-getsu-hime-no-kami 大宜都比女神 (SK), Ō-mike-tsu-hime-no-kami 大御食都姫神 (SK), Ō-getsu-hime 大気都姫神 (SK)

Ō-hiru-me – See **Ama-terasu**
Ō-hiru-me-no-muchi – See **Ama-terasu**
O-kami – See **Izanagi**
Ō-ikazuchi (great thunder) – a thunder kami on Izanami's head in *Ancient Matters*
   Ō-ikazuchi 大雷 (K1, Opo-ikaduti, Grown Thunder), Ō-ikazuchi 大雷 (S5.9)
Oki-tsu-shima-hime – See **Ta-kiri-bime, Ichi-ki-shima-hime**
Ō-kuni-nushi (great land master) – descendant of Susano-o, completes creation of the land in *Ancient Matters* and a *Chronicles* variant, surrenders central reed plain land to the heavenly kami, worshipped at the Izumo Grand Shrine
   Ō-kuni-nushi-no-kami 大国主神 (KI, Opo-kuni-nusi-nö-kamï, Great Land Master), Ō-ana-muji-no-kami 大穴牟遅神 (K1, Opo-namudi-nö-kamï, Great Iron Mines Noble), Ashi-hara-no-shiko-o-no-kami 葦原色許男神 (K1, Asi-para-sikö-wo-nö-kamï, Grim Man of the Reed Plains), Ya-chi-hoko-no-kami 八千矛神 (K1, Ya-ti-pokö-nö-kamï, Eight Thousand Spears), Utsushi-kuni-tama-no-kami 宇都志国玉神 (K1, Utusi-kuni-tama-nö-kamï, Daylight Land Soul), Ō-ana-muchi-no-kami 大己貴神 (S8, S8.6, S9, S9.1, S9.2), Ō-kuni-nushi-no-kami 大国主神 (S8.1, S8.6), Ō-ana-muchi-no-mikoto (great ?? noble) 大己貴命 (S8.2, S8.6), Ō-ana-muchi-no-ō-kami 大己貴大神 (Jinmu 31.4), Ō-mono-nushi-no-kami (great object master) 大物主神 (S8.6, S9.2, Sujin 7.2, Sujin 8.12, Sujin 10.9), Kuni-tsukuri-no-ō-ana-muchi-no-mikoto 国作大己貴命 (S8.6), Ashi-hara-no-shiko-o (valiant reed plain man) 葦原醜男 (S8.6), Ya-chi-hoko-no-kami (many halberds) 八千矛神 (S8.6), Ō-kuni-tama-no-kami (great land soul) 大国玉神 (S8.6), Utsushi-kuni-tama-no-kami (visible land spirit) 顕国玉神 (S8.6), Utsushi-kuni-tama 顕国玉 (S9). See **Ō-mono-nushi-no-kami** (different kami in *Kojiki*, later name in *Nihon shoki*)
Oku-yama-tsu-mi (deep mountain spirit) – a mountain kami born from the stomach of the corpse of the fire kami
   Oku-yama-tsu-mi-no-kami 奥山津見神 (K1, Oku-yama-tu-mi-nö-kamï, Inner Mountain Majesty)
Ō-kuni-tama – See **Ō-kuni-nushi**
Okura-nushi (great storehouse master) – a kami encountered by Chūai
   Okura-nushi 大倉主 (Chūai 8.1)
Ō-magatsu-hi (great twisted spirit) – an evil kami produced during Izanagi's ablution after his escape from Yomi
   Ō-maga-tsu-hi-no-kami 大禍津日神 (K1, Opo-maga-tu-pi-nö-kamï, Great Mishap Bringer), Ō-aya-tsu-hi-no-kami (great ?? spirit) 大綾津日神 (S5.10), Ō-maga-tsu-hi-no-kami 大禍津日神 (SK)
Ō-miwa-no-kami – See **Ō-mono-nushi, Ō-kuni-nushi**
Omo-daru (face complete) – one of the first kami
   Omo-daru-no-kami 於母陀流神 (K1, Omö-daru-nö-kamï, Entirely Engorged), Omo-taru-no-mikoto 面足尊 (S2, S3.1), Omo-taru-no-mikoto 面足尊 (SK)

Omoi-kane (thoughts many) – son of Taka-mi-musuhi who formulates plans for luring Amaterasu out of the heavenly rock cave and for pacifying the central reed plain land

Omoi-kane-no-kami 思金神 (K1, Omöpi-kane-nö-kamï, Thought Over), Tokoyo-no-omoi-kane-no-kami 常世思金神 (K1, Tökö-yö-nö-omöpi-kane-nö-kamï, Evermore Thought Over), Omoi-kane-no-kami 思兼神 (S7, S7.1, S9.1), Omoi-kane-no-kami 思兼神 (KGSI), Omoi-kane-no-kami 思兼神 (JH, TH), Yagokoro-omoi-kane-no-kami 八意思兼神 (SK), Omoi-kane-no-kami 思金神 (SK), Tokoyo-no-omoi-kane-no-kami 常世思金神 (SK), Yagokoro-omoi-kane-no-mikoto 八意思金命 (SK)

Ō-mono-nushi (great object master) – earthly kami associated with Ō-kuni-nushi in the *Chronicles,* worshipped at the Miwa shrine, causes a plague in the reign of Sujin

Ō-mono-nushi-no-kami 大物主神 (K2, Opo-mönö-nusi-nö-kamï, Master Great One), Ō-mono-nushi-no-ō-kami 大物主大神 (K2, Opo-mönö-nusi-nö-opo-kamï, Mighty Spirit Master Great One), Ō-mono-nushi-no-kami 大物主神 (S8.6, S9.2, Sujin 7.2, Sujin 8.12, Sujin 10.9), Ō-mono-nushi-no-ō-kami 大物主大神 (Sujin 7.8, Sujin 8.12), Ō-miwa-no-kami 大三輪の神 (S8.6)

Omo-taru – See **Omo-daru-no-kami**

Ō-nao-bi (great fixing divine spirit) – an good kami produced during Izanagi's ablution after his escape from Yomi

Ō-nao-bi-no-kami 大直毘神 (K1, Opo-naobi-nö-kamï, Great Remedy), Ō-nao-hi 大直日 (S5.6, S5.10), Ō-nao-hi-no-kami 大直日神 (SK), Ō-nao-hi-no-mikoto 大直日命 (SK)

Ō-nao-hi – See **Ō-nao-bi-no-kami**

Ōsaka-no-kami (kami of Osaka) – a kami who comes to Sujin in a dream

Ōsaka-no-kami 大坂神 (Sujin 9.3)

Ō-se-ii-no-mi-kuma-no-ushi (unclear) – son of Ame-no-ho-hi

Ō-se-ii-no-mi-kuma-no-ushi 大背飯三熊大人 (S9), Take-mi-kuma-no-oshi 武三熊之大人 (S9)

Oshi-ho-mimi (powerful superior mysterious power) – son of Amaterasu and Susano-o, father of Ninigi

Masa-katsu-a-katsu-kachi-haya-hi-ame-no-oshi-ho-mimi-no-mikoto 正勝吾勝々速日天之忍穂耳命 (K1, Masa-katu-a-katu-kati-paya-po-amë-nö-osi-po-mimi-nö-mikötö, Truly Winning Have I Won with Rushing Might Ruling Grand Rice Ears of Heaven), Masa-katsu-a-katsu-kachi-haya-hi-ame-no-oshi-ho-mimi-no-mikoto 正勝吾勝々速日天忍穂耳命 (K1), Masa-ka-a-katsu-kachi-haya-hi-ama-no-oshi-ho-mimi-no-mikoto (truly I win swift divine spirit heavenly powerful superior mysterious power) 正哉吾勝勝速日天忍穂耳尊 (S6, S9, S9.1, S9.8), Masa-ka-a-katsu-kachi-haya-hi-ama-no-oshi-hone-no-mikoto 正哉吾勝勝速日天忍骨尊 (S6.1, S6.2), Kachi-haya-hi-ama-no-oshi-ho-mimi-no-mikoto 勝速日天忍穂耳尊 (S6.3, S9.1),

Masa-ka-a-katsu-kachi-haya-hi-ama-no-oshi-hone-no-mikoto 正哉吾勝勝速日天忍穂根尊 (S7.3), Ama-no-oshi-ho-mimi-no-mikoto 天忍穂耳尊 (S9.2), Ama-no-oshi-ho-ne-no-mikoto 天忍穂根尊 (S9.6), Ama-no-oshi-hone-no-mikoto 天忍骨命 (S9.7), Kachi-haya-hi-no-mikoto 勝速日命 (S9.7), Ama-no-ō-mimi-no-mikoto 天大耳尊 (S9.7), A-katsu-no-mikoto 吾勝尊 (KGSI), Masa-ka-a-katsu-kachi-haya-hi-ama-no-oshi-ho-mimi-no-mikoto 正哉吾勝々速日天押穂耳尊 (TH, TKH), Ama-no-oshi-ho-mimi-no-mikoto 天忍穂耳尊 (SK)

Ō-toma-be – See **Ō-to-no-be**

Ō-tomi-be – See **Ō-to-no-be**

Ō-tomi-ji – See **Ō-to-no-ji**

Ō-to-no-be (great door woman) – one of the first kami
Ō-to-no-be-no-kami 大斗乃弁神 (K1, Opo-to-nö-be-nö-kamï, Great Entry Mistress), Ō-toma-be-no-mikoto (great woven mat woman) 大苫辺尊 (S2), Ō-toma-hime-no-mikoto 大戸摩姫尊 (S2), Ō-tomi-be-no-mikoto 大富辺尊 (S2), Ō-toma-be-no-mikoto 大苫辺尊 (SK), Ō-to-no-be 大戸之辺 (SK), Ō-tomi-be 大富辺 (SK), Ō-toma-hime 大戸摩姫 (SK)

Ō-to-no-ji (great door path man) – one of the first kami
Ō-to-no-ji-no-kami 意富斗能地神 (K1, Opo-to-nö-di-nö-kamï, Great Entry Elder), Ō-to-no-ji-no-mikoto 大戸之道尊 (S2), Ō-to-no-be 大戸之辺 (S2), Ō-toma-hiko-no-mikoto 大戸摩彦尊 (S2), Ō-tomi-ji-no-mikoto 大富道尊 (S2), Ō-toma-hiko-no-mikoto 大苫彦尊 (SK), Ō-to-no-ji 大戸之道 (SK), Ō-tomi-ji 大富道 (SK), Ō-toma-hiko 大戸摩彦 (SK)

Ō-yama-tsu-mi (great mountain spirit) – a mountain kami, born from the head of the corpse of the fire kami in the *Chronicles*, parent of Kamu-atsu-tsu-hime Ō-yama-tsu-mi-no-kami 大山津見神 (K1, Opo-yama-tu-mi-nö-kamï, Great Mountain Majesty), Yama-tsu-mi 山祇 (S5.6), Ō-yama-tsu-mi-no-kami 大山祇神 (S5.7, S9, S9.2, S9.5, S9.6, S9.8), Ō-yama-tsu-mi 大山祇 (S5.8), Yamazu-chi 山雷 (S7.2)

Ō-ya-tsu-hime (great house lady) – daughter of Susano-o, sister of I-takeru Ō-ya-tsu-hime-no-mikoto 大屋津姫命 (S8.5)

Sai-mochi (sword holder) – kami created from the sword of Ina-hi, brother of Jinmu Sai-mochi-no-kami 鋤持神 (Jinmu PA)

Saku-ikazuchi (splitting thunder) – thunder kami on Izanami's genitals 裂雷 (K1, Saku-ikaduti, Splitting Thunder), Saku-ikazuchi 裂雷 (S5.9)

Saru-ta-biko (monkey rice paddy lord, perhaps) – earthly kami who comes to the crossroads of heaven to greet Ninigi, associated with Ise, later drowns in *Ancient Matters*
Saru-ta-biko-no-kami 猿田毘古神 (K1, Saruta-biko-nö-kamï, Monkey Guard Lad), Saru-ta-biko-no-ō-kami 猿田毘古大神 (K1, Saruta-biko-nö-opo-kamï, Great Spirit Monkey Guard Lad), Saru-ta-biko-no-o-kami 猿田毘古之男神 (K1, Male Spirit Monkey Guard Lad), Soko-do-ku-mi-tama 底度久御魂 (K1,

Sökö-doku-mi-tama, Bottom Sinking Mighty Soul), Tsubu-ta-tsu-mi-tama 都夫多都御魂 (K1, Tubu-tatu-mi-tama, Bubbling Up Mighty Soul), Awa-sa-ku-mi-tama 阿和佐久御魂 (K1, Awa-saku-mi-tama, Bursting Foam Mighty Soul), Saru-ta-hiko-no-ō-kami 猨田彦大神 (S9.1), Saru-ta-hiko-no-kami 猨田彦神 (S9.1), Saru-ta-hiko-no-ō-kami 猨田彦大神 (KGSI), Saru-ta-hiko-no-ō-kami 猨田彦大神 (SK), Saru-ta-hiko-no-kami 猨田彦神 (SK)

Saru-ta-hiko – See **Saru-ta-biko**

Shiga (unclear) – a kami venerated by Keikō during his conquest of Kyushu
Shiga-no-kami 志我神 (Keikō 12.10)

Shigi-yama-tsu-mi (undergrowth mountain divine spirit, perhaps) – a mountain kami born from the left hand of the corpse of the fire deity in *Ancient Matters* and the feet of the corpse in the *Chronicles*
Shigi-yama-tsu-mi-no-kami 志芸山津見神 (K1, Sigi-yama-tu-mi-nö-kamï, Mountain Forest Majesty), Shigi-yama-tsu-mi 鵄山祇 (S5.7)

Shihi-no-netsu-hiko – See **Uzu-hiko**

Shi-naga-to-ma – See **Shi-natsu-hiko**

Shi-naga-tsu-hiko – See **Shi-natsu-hiko**

Shi-na-tsu-hiko – a wind kami produced by Izanagi's breath
Shi-na-tsu-hiko-no-kami 志那都比古神 (K1, Sina-tu-piko-nö-kamï, Long Blowing Lad), Shi-naga-to-ma-no-mikoto (long wind place) 級長戸辺命 (S5.6), Shi-naga-tsu-hiko-no-mikoto (long wind lord) 級長津彦命 (S5.6), Shi-naga-tsu-hiko-no-mikoto 級長津彦命 (SK), Shi-naga-to-be-no-kami 級長戸辺神 (SK)

Shio-tsu-chi (sea current spirit) – a kami of the ocean currents, helps Hiko-ho-ho-de-mi reach the palace of the sea kami, helps Ninigi and Jinmu in the *Chronicles*
Shio-tsu-chi-no-kami 塩椎神 (K1, Sipo-tuti-nö-kamï, Current Elder), Shio-tsu-chi-no-oji 塩土老翁 (S9.4, S10, S10.1, S10.3, Jinmu PA), Shio-tsu-tsu-no-oji 塩筒老翁 (S10.4). See also **Koto-katsu-kuni-katsu-naga-sa**

Shio-tsu-tsu – See **Shio-tsu-chi**

Shita-teru-hime (red shining lady) – daughter of Ō-kuni-nushi, wife of Ame-waka-hiko
Shita-teru-hime-no-mikoto 下光比売命 (K1, Sita-teru-pime-nö-mikötö, Lady Downward Shining), Shita-teru-hime 下照比売 (K1, Sita-teru-pime, Lady Downward Shining), Taka-hime-no-mikoto 高比売命 (K1, Taka-pime-nö-mikötö, Lady Lofty), Shita-teru-hime 下照姫 (S9), Taka-hime 高姫 (S9), Waka-kuni-dama 稚国玉 (S9), Shita-teru-hime 下照媛 (S9.1), Shita-teru-hime 下照姫 (SK), Shita-teru-hime-no-mikoto 下照姫命 (SK)

Soko-tsu-tsu-no-o (deep harbor man) – produced by Izanagi during his ablution after his escape from Yomi; one of the three gods of the Sumiyoshi Grand Shrine
Soko-tsu-tsu-no-o-no-mikoto 底筒之男命 (K1, Sökö-dutu-nö-wo-nö-mikötö, Bottom Sail Man), Soko-tsu-tsu-no-o 底筒男 (K2), Soko-tsu-tsu-no-o-no-mikoto 底筒男命 (S5.6), Soko-tsu-tsu-no-mikoto 底土命 (S5.10), Soko-tsu-tsu-no-o 底

APPENDIX 1

筒男 (Jingū PA, Jingū 1.2), Soko-tsu-tsu-no-o 底筒雄 (Jingū PA), Soko-tsu-tsu-no-o-no-mikoto 底筒男命 (SK), Soko-tsu-tsu-no-mikoto 底土命 (SK)

Soko-tsu-wata-tsu-mi (deep sea divine spirit) – produced by Izanagi during his ablution after his escape from Yomi

Soko-tsu-wata-tsu-mi-no-kami 底津綿津見神 (K1, Sökö-tu-wata-tu-mi-nö-kamï, Bottom Ocean Majesty), Soko-tsu-wata-tsu-mi-no-mikoto 底津少童命 (S5.6), Soko-tsu-wata-tsu-mi-no-mikoto 底津少童命 (SK)

Suga-no-yu-yama-nushi-mi-na-saro-hiko-ya-shima-shino (unclear) – a son of Susano-o and Kushi-ina-da-hime, ancestor of Ō-kuni-nushi

Suga-no-yu-yama-nushi-mi-na-saro-hiko-ya-shima-shino 清之湯山主三名狹漏彦八島篠 (S8.1), Suga-no-kake-na-saka-karu-hiko-ya-shima-de-no-mikoto 清之繋名阪輕彦八島手命 (S8.1), Suga-no-yu-yama-nushi-mi-na-saro-hiko-ya-shima-no 清之湯山主三名狹漏彦八島野 (S8.1)

Su-hichi-ni (sandy earth) – one of the first kami

Su-hichi-ni-no-kami 須比智邇神 (K1, Su-pidi-ni-nö-kamï, Little Silted Mud), Su-hiji-ni-no-mikoto 沙土煮尊 (S2, S3.1), Su-hiji-ne-no-mikoto 沙土根尊 (S2), Su-hiji-ni-no-mikoto 沙土煮尊 (SK), Su-hiji-ne-no-mikoto 沙土根尊 (SK)

Su-hiji-ni – See **Su-hichi-ni**

Sukuna-biko-na-no-kami (small lord) – son of Taka-mi-musuhi in the *Chronicles* and Kamu-musuhi in *Ancient Matters*; aids Ō-kuni-nushi to complete creation of the land

Sukuna-biko-na-no-kami 少名毘古那神 (K1, Sukuna-biko-na-nö-kamï, Little Lad), Sukuna-biko-na 少名毘古那 (K1), Sukuna-mi-kami 須久那美迦微 (K2), Sukuna-biko-na-no-mikoto 少彦名命 (S8.6), Sukuna-mi-kami 周玖那弥伽未 (Jingū 13.2), Ō-na-suku-hiko-ne-no-mikoto 大汝少日子根命 (HFD), Sukuna-biko-no-mikoto 須久奈比古命 (IFD), Sukuna-biko-na-no-kami 少彦名神 (KGSI)

Sukuna-mi-kami – See **Sukuna-biko-na**

Susa-no-o (man of Susa; raging man) – son of Izanagi and Izanami, brother of Amaterasu, ancestor of Ō-kuni-nushi

Take-haya-susa-no-o-no-mikoto 建速須佐之男命 (K1, Take-paya-susa-nö-o-nö-mikötö, Reckless Rushing Raging Man), Susa-no-o-no-mikoto 須佐之男命 (K1, Susa-nö-o-nö-mikötö, Raging Man), Susa-no-o-no-mikoto 須佐能男命 (K1, Susa-nö-o-nö-mikötö, Raging Man), Haya-susa-no-o-no-mikoto 速須佐之男命 (K1, Paya-susa-nö-o-nö-mikötö, Rushing Raging Man), Susa-no-o-no-mikoto 素戔嗚尊 (S5, S5.1, S5.2, S5.6, S5.11, S6, S6.1, S6.2, S6.3, S7, S7.1, S7.2, S7.3, S8, S8.1, S8.2, S8.3, S8.4, S8.5), Kamu-susa-no-o-no-mikoto 神素戔嗚尊 (S5), Haya-susa-no-o-no-mikoto 速素戔嗚尊 (S5), Kamu-susa-no-o-no-mikoto 神須佐乃袁命 (IFD), Kamu-susa-no-o-no-mikoto 神須佐能袁命 (IFD), Kamu-susa-no-o-no-mikoto 神須佐乃乎命 (IFD), Susa-no-o-no-mikoto 須佐乎命 (IFD), Susa-no-o-no-mikoto 須佐能袁命 (IFD), Susa-no-o-no-mikoto 須佐袁命 (IFD), Susa-no-o-no-mikoto 須作能乎命

(IFD), Susa-no-o-no-mikoto 須佐能乎命 (IFD), Susa-no-o-no-kami 素戔嗚神 (KGSI), Susa-no-o-no-mikoto 素戔烏尊 (SK), Take-haya-susa-no-o-no-mikoto 建速素戔烏尊 (SK), Haya-susa-no-o-no-mikoto 速素戔烏命 (SK), Kamu-susa-no-o-no-mikoto 神素戔烏尊 (SK), Take-susa-no-o-no-mikoto 建素戔烏尊 (SK), Haya-take-susa-no-o-no-mikoto 速建素戔烏尊 (SK), Haya-susa-no-o-no-mikoto 速素戔烏尊 (SK)

Ta-jikara-o – See **Ame-no-ta-jikara-o**

Tagitsu-hime – See **Ta-kitsu-hime**

Taka-hime – See **Shita-teru-hime**

Taka-mi-musuhi (high august generative force) – one of the first kami, grandfather of Ninigi; called the "imperial ancestor" in the *Chronicles*

Taka-mi-musuhi-no-kami 高御産巣日神 (K1, Taka-mi-musubi-nö-kamï, Lofty Growth), Taka-gi-no-kami 高木神 (K1, Taka-kï-nö-kamï, Lofty Tree), Taka-mi-musuhi-no-mikoto 高皇産霊 (S1.4, S8.6, S9, S9.2, S9.4, S9.6, S9.7, S9.8, Jinmu PA, Kenzō 3.2, Kenzō 3.4), Taka-mi-musuhi 高皇産霊 (S7.1, Sujin 3.4), Taka-mi-musuhi-no-kami 高皇産霊神 (KGSI), Taka-mi-musuhi-no-mikoto 高皇産霊尊 (KGSI), Taka-mi-musuhi 高皇産霊 (KGSI), Kamu-ru-ki 神留伎命 (KGSI), Taka-mi-musuhi-no-mikoto 高皇産霊尊 (JK, JH, TH, CH), Taka-mi-musuhi-no-mikoto 高魂尊 (TH, KK, KZH), Taka-gi-no-mikoto 高木命 (SK), Taka-mi-musuhi 高皇産霊 (SK)

Taka-okami (high ??) – a kami produced from the corpse of the fire deity in a *Chronicles* variant

Taka-okami 高龗 (S5.7)

Take-ha-zu-chi (brave blade spirit) – a weaver kami who forces the surrender of the star kami

Take-ha-zu-chi-no-mikoto 建葉槌命 (S9)

Take-mikazu-chi-no-o (brave vigorous spirit man; brave august lightning man) – a thunder kami born when Izanagi slays the fire deity Kagu-tsu-chi; pacifies the central reed plain land so that Ninigi can descend

Take-mikazu-chi-no-o-no-kami 建御雷之男神 (K1, Take-mika-duti-nö-wo-nö-kamï, Brave Mighty Thunderbolt Man), Take-mikazu-chi-no-kami 建御雷神 (K1, Take-mika-duti-nö-kamï, Brave Mighty Thunderbolt Man), Take-futsu-no-kami 建布都神 (K1, Take-putu-nö-kamï, Brave Slasher), Toyo-futsu-no-kami 豊布都神 (K1, Töyö-putu-nö-kamï, Plentiful Slasher), Take-mikazu-chi-no-mikoto 武甕槌命 (K2, Take-mika-duti-nö-mikötö, Brave Flagon Elder), Take-mikazu-chi-no-kami 武甕槌神 (S5.6, S9, S9.1, S9.2), Take-mikazu-chi-no-kami 武甕雷神 (Jinmu PA), Take-mikazu-chi-no-kami 武甕槌神 (KGSI), Take-mikazu-chi-no-o-no-kami 建甕槌之男神 (SK), Take-futsu-no-kami 建布都神 (SK), Toyo-futsu-no-kami 豊布都神 (SK), Take-mikazu-chi-no-o-no-kami 武甕雷男神 (SK), Take-mikazu-chi-no-kami 武甕槌神 (SK), Take-mikazu-chi 武甕槌 (SK), Take-mikazu-chi-no-kami 武甕雷神 (SK)

APPENDIX 1

Take-mi-kuma-no-ushi – See **Ō-se-ii-no-mi-kuma-no-ushi**

Ta-kiri-bime (many mist lady) – daughter of Susano-o and Amaterasu
Ta-kiri-bime-no-mikoto 多紀理毘売命 (K1, Takïri-bime-nö-mikötö, Lady Mist), Oki-tsu-shima-hime-no-mikoto 奥津島比売命 (K1, Oki-tu-sima-pime-nö-mikötö, Lady Offshore Isle), Ta-kori-hime 田心姫 (S6, S6.1), Ta-kori-hime-no-mikoto 田心姫命 (S6.2), Ta-kiri-hime-no-mikoto 田霧姫命 (S6.3), Oki-tsu-shima-hime 瀛津嶋姫命 (SK), Ta-kori-hime 田心姫 (SK), Ta-kiri-hime 田霧姫 (SK), Ta-kori-hime-no-mikoto 田心姫命 (SK), Oki-tsu-shima-hime-no-mikoto 奥津嶋姫命 (SK)

Ta-kiri-hime – See **Ta-kiri-bime**

Ta-kitsu-hime (rushing water lady) – daughter of Susano-o and Amaterasu
Ta-kitsu-hime-no-mikoto 多岐都比売命 (K1, Takitu-pime-nö-mikötö, Lady Seething Torrent), Ta-kitsu-hime-no-mikoto 田寸津比売命 (K1), Tagitsu-hime 湍津姫 (S6, S6.1), Tagitsu-hime-no-mikoto 湍津姫命 (S6.2, S6.3), Tsushima-hime-no-mikoto 津嶋姫命 (JH, CH), Tagitsu-hime-no-mikoto 湍津姫命 (SK), Takitsu-hime-no-mikoto 多岐都姫命 (SK), He-tsu-shima-hime-no-mikoto 辺津嶋姫命 (SK)

Ta-kori-hime – See **Ta-kiri-bime**

Taku-hata-chi-ji-hime – See **Yorozu-hata-toyo-akitsu-shi-hime**

Tama-no-oya (jewel ancestor) – kami associated with jewel-making, ancestor of the jeweler hereditary guild
Tama-no-oya-no-mikoto 玉祖命 (K1, Tama-no-ya-nö-mikötö, Jewel Ancestor), Toyo-tama (rich jewel) 豊玉 (S7.2), Ama-no-akaru-tama 天明玉 (S7.3), Tama-no-ya 玉屋命 (S9.1), Kushi-akaru-tama-no-kami 櫛明玉神 (S9.2), Kushi-akaru-tama-no-mikoto 櫛明玉命 (KGSI), Kushi-akaru-tama-no-kami 櫛明玉神 (KGSI)

Tama-yori-bime (jewel drawing lady) – daughter of the sea kami, sister of Toyo-tama-hime, wife of Fuki-aezu
Tama-yori-bime 玉依毘売 (K1, Tama-yöri-bime, Lady Summoned Soul), Tama-yori-hime 玉依姫 (S10, S10.1, S10.3, S10.4, S11, Jinmu PA)

Tama-yori-hime (spirit drawing lady) – granddaughter of Taka-mi-musuhi and wife of Oshi-ho-mimi in a *Chronicles* variant
Tama-yori-hime 玉依姫命 (S9.7) See **Tama-yori-bime**

Ta-oki-ho-oi (hand place ??) – kami associated with the production of hats
Ta-oki-ho-oi-no-kami 手置帆負神 (S9.2)

Te-nazu-chi (hand rub spirit) – mother of Kushi-ina-da-hime, mother-in-law of Susano-o
Te-nazu-chi 手名椎神 (K1, Te-na-duti, Hand-stroking Elder), Te-nazu-chi-no-kami 手名椎神 (K1), Te-nazu-chi 手摩乳 (S8, S8.3), Ina-da-miya-nushi-no-kami 稲田宮主神 (S8), Ina-da-no-miya-nushi-susa-no-ya-tsu-mimi 稲田宮主簀狭之八箇耳 (S8.2), Te-nazu-chi 手摩乳 (SK), Ina-da-miya-nushi-no-kami 稲田宮主神 (SK)

To-yama-tsu-mi (door mountain spirit) – mountain kami born from the right foot of the corpse of the fire deity in *Ancient Matters*
 To-yama-tsu-mi-no-kami 戸山津見神 (K1, To-yama-tu-mi-nö-kamï, Outer Mountain Majesty)

Toyo-kabu-shino – See **Toyo-kumo-no**

Toyo-kuhi-no – See **Toyo-kumo-no**

Toyo-kumi-no – See **Toyo-kumo-no**

Toyo-kumo-no (richly clouded swamp) – one of the first kami
 Toyo-kumo-no-no-kami 豊雲野神 (K1, Töyö-kumo-no-nö-kamï, Abundant Clouds Moor), Toyo-kumu-nu-no-mikoto (richly watered swamp) 豊斟渟尊 (S1), Toyo-kuni-nushi-no-mikoto (rich land master) 豊国主尊 (S1.1), Toyo-kumi-no-no-mikoto 豊組野尊 (S1.1), Toyo-kabu-shino-no-mikoto 豊香節野尊 (S1.1), Uki-funo-no-toyo-kai-no-mikoto 浮経野豊買尊 (S1.1), Toyo-kuni-no-no-mikoto (rich land fields) 豊国野尊 (S1.1), Toyo-kuhi-no-no-mikoto 豊齧野尊 (S1.1), Hako-kuni-no-no-mikoto 葉木国野尊 (S1.1), Mi-no-no-mikoto 見野尊 (S1.1), Toyo-kuni-nushi-no-mikoto 豊国主尊 (SK), Toyo-kumu-no-no-mikoto 豊斟渟尊 (SK), Toyo-ka-bushi-no-toyo-no-mikoto 豊香節野豊尊 (SK), Uki-funo-no-toyo-kai-no-mikoto 浮經野豊買尊 (SK), Toyo-ha-no-mikoto 豊歯尊 (SK)

Toyo-kumu-no – See **Toyo-kumo-no**

Toyo-kumu-nu – See **Toyo-kumo-no**

Toyo-kuni-no – See **Toyo-kumo-no**

Toyo-kuni-nushi – See **Toyo-kumo-no**

Toyo-tama – See **Tama-no-oya**

Toyo-tama-bime (rich jewel lady) – daughter of the sea kami, wife of Hiko-ho-ho-de-mi, mother of Fuki-aezu
 Toyo-tama-bime 豊玉毘売 (K1, Töyö-tama-bime, Lady Bountiful Soul), Toyo-tama-hime-no-mikoto 豊玉毘売命 (K1), Toyo-tama-hime 豊玉姫 (S10, S10.1, S10.2, S10.3, S10.4)

Toyo-tama-hiko – See **Wata-tsu-mi**

Tsubura-hime (unclear) – kami encounter by Chūai
 Tsubura-hime 菟夫羅媛 (Chūai 8.1)

Tsuchi-ikazuchi (earth thunder) – thunder kami on the right hand of Izanami in *Ancient Matters* and on her stomach in the *Chronicles*
 Tsuchi-ikazuchi 土雷 (K1, Tuti-ikaduti, Earthen Thunder), Tsuchi-ikazuchi 土雷 (S5.9)

Tsuki-no-kami – See **Tsuku-yomi**

Tsuki-tatsu-fu-na-to (post stand road fork) – crossroads kami created by Izanagi's belt when he flees Yomi; made to guide the heavenly kami during their pacification of the central reed plain land in the *Chronicles*
 Tsuki-ta-tsu-fu-na-to-no-kami 衝立船戸神 (K1, Tuki-tatu-pina-to-nö-kamï, Post at the Road Bend), Fu-na-to-no-kami, Ku-na-to-no-kami (road fork; passage prohibition) 岐神 (S5.6, S5.9, S9.2), Ku-na-to-no-sae 来名戸之祖神

APPENDIX 1

(S5.9), Fu-na-to-no-kami 岐神 (SK), Ku-na-to-no-sae 来名戸神 (SK), Tsuki-ta-tsu-fu-na-to-no-kami 衝立船戸神 (SK)

Tsuku-yomi (moon counting) – moon kami, brother of Amaterasu and Susano-o
Tsuku-yomi-no-mikoto 月読命 (K1, Tuku-yömi-nö-mikötö, Moon Counting), Tsuki-no-kami (moon kami) 月神 (S5, Kenzō 3.2), Tsuku-yumi-no-mikoto (moon bow) 月弓尊 (S5, S5.1), Tsuku-yomi-no-mikoto 月夜見尊 (S5, S5.11), Tsuku-yomi-no-mikoto 月読尊 (S5, S5.6), Tsuki-no-kami 月神 (KGSI), Tsuku-yomi-no-mikoto 月読尊 (OH, JH), Tsuku-yomi 月夜見 (SK), Tsuku-yumi 月弓 (SK), Tsuku-yomi-no-mikoto 月読命 (SK), Tsuku-yummy-no-mikoto 月弓尊 (OH, JH), Tsuku-yomi-no-mikoto 月夜見尊 (SK)

Tsuku-yumi – See **Tsuku-yomi**

Tsuma-tsu-hime (squared lumber lady, perhaps) – daughter of Susano-no and sister of I-takeru and Ō-ya-tsu-hime
Tsuma-tsu-hime-no-mikoto 柧津姫命 (S8.5)

Tsuno-gui-no-kami (horn peg) – one of the first kami
角杙神 (K1, Tuno-gupi-nö-kamï, Swelling Tip), Tsuno-kui 角橸尊 (S3.1), Tsuno-kui 角橸尊 (SK), Tsuno-ta-tsu-tama 角龍魂尊 (SK)

Tsuno-kui – See **Tsuno-gui**

Tsunuga – See **Kehi-no-ō-kami**

Uhi-ji-ne – See **Uji-hi-ni**

U-hiji-ni (muddy earth) – one of the first kami
U-hiji-ni-no-kami 宇比地邇神 (K1, U-pidi-ni-nö-kamï, Little Floating Mud), U-hiji-ni-no-mikoto 埿土煮尊 (S2, S3.1), U-hiji-ne-no-mikoto 埿土根尊 (S2), U-hiji-ni-no-mikoto 埿土煮尊 (SK), U-hiji-ne-no-mikoto 埿土根尊 (SK)

Uka-no-mi-tama (soul of rice storage) – a rice kami created by Izanagi
Uka-no-mi-tama-no-kami 宇迦之御魂神 (K1, Uka-nö-mi-tama-nö-kamï, Mighty Soul of Sustenance), Uka-no-mi-tama 倉稲魂 (S5.6), Ina-kura-tama-no-mikoto 稲倉魂命 (SK), Ina-kura-tama-no-kami 稲倉魂神 (SK), Uka-no-mi-tama-no-kami 宇迦能御玉神 (SK)

Uke-mochi – See **Ō-getsu-hime**

Uki-funo-no-toyo-kai – See **Toyo-kumo-no**

Umashi-ashikabi-hikoji (good reed man) – one of the first kami
Umashi-ashikabi-hikoji-no-kami 宇摩志阿斯訶備比古遅神 (K1, Umasi-asi-kabï-piko-di-nö-kamï, Fine Budding Reed Lad), Umashi-ashikabi-hikoji-no-mikoto 可美葦芽彦舅尊 (S1.2, S1.3, S1.6), Umashi-ashikabi-hikoji-no-mikoto 可美葦牙彦舅尊 (SK)

Umi-sachi-hiko – See **Ho-deri**, **Ho-no-suseri**

Utsushi-kuni-tama – See **Ō-kuni-nushi**

Uwa-tsu-tsu-no-o (surface harbor man) – produced by Izanagi during his ablution after his escape from Yomi; one of the three gods of the Sumiyoshi Grand Shrine
Uwa-tsu-tsu-no-o-no-mikoto 上筒之男命 (K1, Upa-dutu-nö-wo-nö-mikötö, Surface Sail Man), Uwa-tsu-tsu-no-o 上筒男 (K2), Uwa-tsu-tsu-no-o-no-mikoto

表筒男命 (S5.6), Iwa-tsutsu-no-mikoto 磐土命 (S5.10), Uwaa-tsu-tsu-no-o 表筒男 (Jingū PA, Jingū 1.2), Uwa-tsu-tsu-no-o 表筒雄 (Jingū PA), Uwa-tsu-tsu-no-o-no-mikoto 表筒男命 (SK), Iwa-tsutsu-no-mikoto 磐土命 (SK)

Uwa-tsu-wata-tsu-mi (surface sea divine spirit) – produced by Izanagi during his ablution after his escape from Yomi
Uwa-tsu-wata-tsu-mi-no-kami 上津綿津見神 (K1, Upa-tu-wata-tu-mi-nö-kamï, Surface Ocean Majesty), Uwa-tsu-wata-tsu-mi-no-mikoto 表津少童命 (S5.6), Uwa-tsu-wata-tsu-mi-no-mikoto 表津少童命 (SK)

Uzu-hiko (extraordinary lord; whirlpool lord, perhaps) – a kami encountered by Jinmu; guides Jinmu's boat out of Kyushu
珍彦 (Jinmu PA), Sao-ne-tsu-hiko 槁根津日子 (K2, Sawo-ne-tu-piko, Little Pole Lad), Shihi-no-ne-tsu-hiko 椎根津彦 (Jinmu PA)

Waka-hiru-me – See **Ame-no-hata-ori-me**

Waka-ikazuchi (young thunder) – a thunder kami on Izanami's left hand in *Ancient Matters* and on her back in the *Chronicles*
Waka-ikazuchi 若雷 (K1, Waka-ikaduti, Young Thunder), Waka-ikazuchi 稚雷 (S5.9)

Waka-kuni-tama – See **Shita-teru-hime**

Waka-musuhi (young generative force) – agriculture kami, child of Kagu-tsu-chi and Hani-yama-hime
Waka-musuhi-no-kami 和久産巣日神 (K1, Waku-musubi-nö-kamï, Fresh Growth), Waka-musuhi 稚産霊 (S5.2), Waka-musuhi-no-kami 稚皇産霊神 (SK)

Wata-tsu-mi (divine spirit of the sea) – kami of the sea, child of Izanagi and Izanami, father of Toyo-tama-hime and Tama-yori-hime, father-in-law of Hiko-ho-ho-de-mi
Wata-tsu-mi-no-kami 綿津見神 (K1, Wata-tu-mi-nö-kamï, Ocean Majesty), Ō-wata-tsu-mi-no-kami 大綿津見神 (K1, po-wata-tu-mi-nö-kamï, Great Ocean Majesty), Wata-tsu-mi 綿津見 (K1, Wata-tu-mi, Ocean Majesty), Wata-tsu-mi-no-ō-kami 綿津見大神 (K1, Wata-tu-mi-no-opo-kamï, great spirit Ocean Majesty), Umi-no-kami 海神 (K1), Wata-tsu-mi-no-mikoto 少童命 (S5.6), Umi-no-kami/Wata-tsu-mi 海神 (S10, S10.1, S10.2, S10.3, S10.4, Jinmu PA, Keikō 40), Toyo-tama-hiko 豊玉彦 (S10.1), Wata-tsu-mi 海童 (Jinmu PA), Wata-tsu-mi 海若 (IFD), Tsukushi-no-shika-no-kami 筑紫斯香神 (SK), Wata-tsu-mi 海童 (KH, TNH)

Wazurai-no-kami – See **Wazurai-no-ushi**

Wazurai-no-ushi (illness) – an evil kami born during Izanagi's ablution after his escape from Yomi
Wazurai-no-ushi-no-kami 和豆良比能宇斯能神 (K1, Wadurapi-nö-usi-nö-kamï, Master Miasma), Wazurai-no-kami 煩神 (S5.6), Wazurai-no-kami 煩神 (SK), Wazurai-no-ushi-no-kami 和豆良比能宇斯能神 (SK), Wazurai-no-ushi-no-kami 和爪良比能守斯能神 (SK)

APPENDIX 1

Yama-no-ikazuchi (mountain thunder) – a thunder kami on Izanami's hands in the *Chronicles*
Yama-no-ikazuchi 山雷 (S5.9)

Yama-sachi-hiko – See **Ho-no-ori**

Yamata-no-orochi (eight fork serpent) – eight-headed snake killed by Susano-o
Yamata-no-orochi 八俣遠呂智 (K1, Ya-mata-nö-woröti, Eight-headed Dragon), Koshi-no-yamata-no-orochi 高志之八俣遠呂智 (K1), Yamata-no-orochi 八岐大蛇 (S8, S8.2), Orochi 大蛇 (S8, S8.2, S8.3, S8.4), Orochi 蛇 (S8, S8.2, S8.3, S8.4), Yamata-no-orochi 八岐大蛇 (KGSI), Orochi 大蛇 (KGSI), Yamata-no-orochi 八岐大蛇 (SK), Orochi 大蛇 (SK)

Yamato-ō-kuni-tama (great land spirit of Yamato) – kami venerated by Suinin; enshrined on Cape Nagaoka
Yamatao-ō-kuni-tama-no-kami 倭大国魂神 (Suinin 6, Suinin 7.8, Suinin 7.11), Yamato-no-ō-kuni-tama 日本大国魂神 (Suinin 6), Yamato-no-ō-kami 倭大神 (Suinin 25.3)

Yama-tsu-mi – See **Ō-yama-tsu-mi**

Yama-zu-chi – See **Ō-yama-tsu-mi**

Yame-tsu-hime (lady of Yame) – a kami encountered by Keikō during the latter's conquest of Kyushu
Yame-tsu-hime 八女津媛 (Keikō 18.7)

Yaso-magatsu-hi (many disasters divine spirit) – an evil kami produced during Izanagi's ablution after his escape from Yomi
Yaso-maga-tsu-hi-no-kami 八十禍津日神 (K1, Yaso-maga-du-pi-nö-kamï, Many Mishaps Bringer), Yaso-maga-tsu-hi-no-kami 八十枉津日神 (S5.6), Yaso-maga-tsu-hi-no-kami 八十禍津日神 (SK)

Ya-ta-garasu (eight shaftment crow) – a crow sent by Amaterasu to guide Jinmu into the Nara Basin
Ya-ta-garasu 八咫烏 (K2, Raven of Many Feet), Ya-ta-garasu 頭八咫烏 (Jinmu PA)

Yomi-to-ni-sa-yarimasu – See **Chi-gaeshi**

Yomo-tsu-koto-saka-no-o (Yomi words separation man) – kami created during the divorce of Izanagi and Izanami
Yomo-tsu-koto-saka-no-o 泉津事解之男 (S5.10)

Yorozu-hata-toyo-aki-tsu-shi-hime (myriad flags rich autumn lady; myriad flags dragonfly lady) – daughter of Taka-mi-musuhi, wife of Oshi-ho-mimi, mother of Fuki-aezu
Yorozu-hata-toyo-aki-tsu-shi-hime-no-mikoto 万幡豊秋津師比売命 (K1, Yörödu-pata-töyö-aki-tsu-si-pime-nö-mikötö, Lady Blowing Banners of Bountiful Autumn), Taku-hata-chi-ji-hime (paper mulberry flags thousand thousand lady) 栲幡千千姫 (S9), Yorozu-hata-toyo-aki-tsu-hime-no-mikoto 万幡豊秋津媛命 (S9.1), Yorozu-hata-hime 万幡姫 (S9.2, S9.7), Taku-hata-chi-ji-hime-yorozu-hime-no-mikoto 栲幡千千姫万幡姫命 (S9.6),

Chi-ji-hime-no-mikoto 千千姫命 (S9.6), Ama-yorozu-taku-hata-chi-hata-hime 天万栲幡千幡姫 (S9.7, S9.8), Taku-hata-chi-hata-hime 栲幡千幡姫 (S9.7), Taku-hata-chi-ji-hime-no-mikoto 栲幡千千姫命 (KGSI), Taku-hata-chi-ji-hime-yorozu-hata-hime-no-mikoto 栲幡千千姫万幡姫命 (SK), Yorozu-hata-toyo-aki-tsu-shi-hime-no-mikoto 万幡豊秋津師姫命 (SK), Taku-hata-chi-ji-hime-no-mikoto 栲幡千千姫命 (SK)

Appendix 2
Songs in the *Chronicles*

POEM NUMBER	FIRST LINE	LOCATION
1	Eightfold clouds rise†	S8
2	Like beads strung together	S9.1
3	At the shallows crossed	S9.1
4	Though seaweed from the depths	S9.6
5	On the island†	S10.3
6	Though people say	S10.3
7	At the high hunting ground in Uda	Jinmu PA
8	Like snails	Jinmu PA
9	In the great hall	Jinmu PA
10	Just now	Jinmu PA
11	Though people say	Jinmu PA
12	Line up the shields	Jinmu PA
13	Fiercely, fiercely	Jinmu PA
14	Fiercely, fiercely	Jinmu PA
15	This sacred wine	Sujin 8.12
16	Sweet wine†	Sujin 8.12
17	Sweet wine†	Sujin 8.12
18	Alas, Mi-maki-iri-biko	Sujin 10.9
19	Perhaps because they are passed from hand to hand	Sujin 10
20	The scabbard of the sword worn	Sujin 60.7
21	From the direction	Keikō 17.3
22	Yamato is	Keikō 17.3
23	Those of you	Keikō 17.3
24	Swiftly vanishing morning frost†	Keikō 18.7
25	Since passing Tsukuba	Keikō 40.10
26	Counting them up	Keikō 40.10
27	O solitary pine	Keikō 40.10
28	To the pine grove	Jingū PA

(continued)

POEM NUMBER	FIRST LINE	LOCATION
29	Well, my lord	Jingū PA
30	I am irritated	Jingū PA
31	At the crossing at Seta	Jingū PA
32	This august wine	Jingū 13.2
33	The people who made	Jingū 13.2
34	When I survey	Ōjin 6.2
35	Come, my lord	Ōjin 13.9
36	I knew not the length	Ōjin 13.9
37	Though I had heard	Ōjin 13.9
38	The maiden	Ōjin 13.9
39	Where the live oaks grow	Ōjin 19.10
40	The island of Awaji	Ōjin 22.4
41	Karano	Ōjin 31.8
42	Dear people	Nintoku PA
43	Dear spindle tree	Nintoku PA
44	This maiden, my vassal	Nintoku 16.7
45	Hayamachi of Harima	Nintoku 16.7
46	Those of good breeding	Nintoku 22.1
47	It is well enough to double	Nintoku 22.1
48	Like adjacent beaches	Nintoku 22.1
49	It is not good	Nintoku 22.1
50	It would be better to accompany	Nintoku 22.1
51	Boat people of Naniwa	Nintoku 30.9
52	To Yamashiro	Nintoku 30.9
53	I travel up	Nintoku 30.9
54	Traveling up past the palace	Nintoku 30.9
55	When I see my older brother	Nintoku 30.10
56	Iwa-no-hime	Nintoku 30.10
57	Like the rustling	Nintoku 30.10
58	Like the pure white	Nintoku 30.10
59	The heavenly metal loom	Nintoku 40.2
60	The falcon	Nintoku 40.2
61	They're like climbing a ladder	Nintoku 40.2
62	Uchi no Ason	Nintoku 50.3
63	My great king	Nintoku 50.3
64	When I asked the way	Richū PA

APPENDIX 2

POEM NUMBER	FIRST LINE	LOCATION
65	'Tis twilight, when my beloved	Ingyō 8.2
66	Untie	Ingyō 8.2
67	Beautiful as a flower†	Ingyō 8.2
68	Continually	Ingyō 11.3
69	I build a rice paddy in the mountains	Ingyō 23.3
70	Even were my great lord	Ingyō 24.6
71	Maiden of Karu	Ingyō 24.6
72	In the shade of the gate	Ankō PA
73	A bell tied to the garter	Ankō PA
74	The minister, my husband	Yūryaku PA
75	On Mt. Omura	Yūryaku 4.2
76	Afraid of the growl of the wild boar	Yūryaku 5.2
77	The mountains of Hatsuse	Yūryaku 6.2
78	Until the five hundred dangling	Yūryaku 12.4
79	For Koshima-ko	Yūryaku 13.3
80	How grievous	Yūryaku 13.3
81	Black horse of Kai	Yūryaku 13.3
82	Oshiro	Yūryaku 23.8
83a	May the creeping vines	Kenzō PA
83	Though the willow on the riverbank	Kenzō PA
83b	Yamato is	Kenzō PA
83c	The divine cedar at Furu	Kenzō PA
84	What I wish to see	Kenzō PA
85	Across the barren land	Kenzō 1.2
86	Okime	Kenzō 2.9
87	Looking upon the waves breaking	Buretsu PA
88	Say you, Prince, to loosen her	Buretsu PA
89	I stand wearing	Buretsu PA
90	Though you mean to build	Buretsu PA
91	Many-sided is the brushwood hedge	Buretsu PA
92	Kami, to the strummed zither	Buretsu PA
93	Though the august paper mulberry sash	Buretsu PA
94	From Isonokami	Buretsu PA
95	In the valley of Mt. Nara	Buretsu PA

Note: See the list of abbreviations in Appendix 1.

Text-Critical Endnotes

Endnotes to Book 1

i The first paragraph of the Main Version derives from the Chinese texts *Writings of the Huainan Masters* (*Huainanzi* 淮南子) and *Record of Threes and Fives* (*Sanwu liji* 三五歷紀). The latter text is cited on the basis of quotations of it in *Classified Extracts from Literature* (*Yiwen leiju* 藝文類聚).

ii The simile of floating oil also appears in the *Ancient Matters* narrative of creation.

iii The concept of "generative force" (*musuhi/musubi*) suggests the spontaneous appearance of organic material like moss or mold and is a central force in *Ancient Matters*, as are these three kami. In the *Chronicles*, they are relegated to Variant 4, though Taka-mi-musuhi will later appear in the main narrative. Similarly, the High Heavenly Plain appears frequently in the *Ancient Matters* creation narrative, but not in the main version of the *Chronicles*.

iv The Kanbun 9 edition of the *Chronicles* has "snow floating on the sea," but this is usually taken to be a mistake for the similar character for "cloud."

v *Ancient Matters* also identifies seven generations of kami, but counts them differently.

vi Awaji is a large island in the inland sea. The name may be derived from *ahaji*, "ashamed of oneself," or from *ahamu*, "to regard lightly."

vii Great Yamato of Rich Autumns refers to the island of Honshu; autumn recalls the harvest season. An original note adds that all appearances of the characters "Origin of the Sun," meaning "Japan," should be read "Yamato." Iyo-no-futana is the island of Shikoku. Tsukushi is the island of Kyushu. Oki and Sado are two large islands in the Sea of Japan. Ō Island is unclear; there are numerous islands with this name in the archipelago. Koshi refers to Northern Japan, around present-day Niigata Prefecture. Kibiko Island is the Kojima Peninsula in Okayama Prefecture; it was an island in the ancient period.

viii It is not clear where Ko Island (small island) refers to; it forms a pair with Ō Island (big island).

ix The Hananoiwa Shrine in present-day Arima District, Kumano City, Mie Prefecture, claims to mark Izanami's grave.

x Grammatically speaking, the unstated subject of "weakened from hunger" is Izanagi, since he is the subject of the previous sentence, but commentators have suggested it should be "the people of the world," whose hunger leads to a rice kami being born.

xi Yomi is the Japanese underworld. In popular lore, it is the final destination for souls on earth, but in the ancient mythological sources, Izanami is the only one to go there upon death, and Izanagi then closes off the way. Izanagi's visit resembles the narrative in *Ancient Matters*. Here, however, the interaction between Izanagi and Izanami is much shorter.

xii Why Izanami says "Yet" 雖然 before she retires is unclear.

xiii In *Ancient Matters*, the crossroads deity Chi-mata appears when Izanagi throws down his shoes, and Chi-shiki is an alternative name for Izanami.

xiv A version of the narrative similar to this variant appears in *Ancient Matters*, but with Amaterasu asking Susano-o instead of Tsuku-yomi, and with the agriculture kami named Ō-getsu-hime instead of Uke-mochi. The version of the myth here explains the estrangement between the sun and the moon.

xv Linguists have suggested a link between the body parts and the resultant products based on Korean.

xvi Susano-o's statement in Section Six is the only mention of the High Heavenly Plain in the Main Version, but variation among manuscripts suggests that this was originally "high heaven" and that "plain" was added by a later copyist.

xvii This paragraph seems out of place and may have been intended as a note. Commentators have speculated that it might belong in Section 5, or that it might have been meant as a note to Section 6. Notably, Izanami, who did not die in the Main Version of Section 5, has vanished, and the heavenly kami to whom Izanagi reports are also not part of the Main Version. The Lesser Palace of the Sun is unclear.

xviii Amaterasu refers to the charges pronounced by Izanagi and Izanami in the Main Version of Section 5.

xix The string of beads has a special name, "Yasaka-ni no iho-tsu-misumaru," but the precise meaning is unclear. Yasaka-ni means "eight-span-jewel," but this is too large for a bead. Perhaps it refers to the length of the string connecting the beads. I-ho-tsu means "five-hundred-unit," or simply "many." Misu-maru means "august-long thread," referring to the connecting string.

xx Some commentators have proposed that the name Ichi-ki-shima-hime equates with "itsuki" for "ablution." Variant 3 suggests that this kami is the same as Oki-tsu-shima-hime, "deep sea island lady," but *Ancient Matters* identifies Oku-tsu-shima-hime as Ta-kiri-bime, given here as Ta-kori-hime.

xxi Usa is in modern-day Oita Prefecture, on the southern island of Kyushu.

xxii The vernacular reading is shared by both appearances of "likeness," but only the former makes this meaning explicit in the characters. The latter occurrence literally reads "She made a kami." The Hinokuma (Hinomae) and Kunikakasu Shrines in Wakayama Prefecture ostensibly house a likeness xxiii Variant 3 proposes an alternate chronology for Sections 6 and 7 in which the oath between Amaterasu and Susano-o happens after Susano-o is banished and returns to see her. This is plausible since Susasno-o's destruction of Amaterasu's rice fields is not caused by his victory in their oath in the Main Version of the *Chronicles*, but *Ancient Matters* makes this causation explicit.

mirror and a halberd mirror made by Ishi-kori-do-me, though in Variant 2, the mirror is located in Ise Province.

xxiv The Hi River is the present-day Hii River that flows through western Shimane Prefecture. The river, prone to flooding, now empties into Lake Shinji, but in the ancient period, it flowed west across Shimane Prefecture into the Sea of Japan.

xxv The river to which this passage refers is unclear.

xxvi The Atsuta Shrine in Nagoya still venerates this sword.

xxvii The Isonokami Shrine is perhaps the Isonokami Futsumitama Shrine in present-day Akaiwashi City, Okayama Prefecture.

xxviii Kibi is a region of Japan along the inland sea; it includes Akaiwashi City and may connect this passage to the Isonokami Shrine in Variant 2, though the name of the sword is different.

xxix Soshimori is a place-name on the Korean peninsula. No definitive identification with any existing location has been established, though this passage was often used in the early twentieth century to justify Japanese colonization of the Korean peninsula.

xxx Torikami is Mt. Sentsū on the border of present-day Shimane and Tottori Prefectures; sentsū means "boat passage."

xxxi Variant 6 is linked to Variant 1 through the use of the name Ō-kuni-nushi; these are the only two times this name is used in the *Chronicles*. Yoshida commentators have suggested that this portion should be its own section rather than being a variant of Section 8. The content had important doctrinal implications for the Yoshida and Suika sects of Shinto.

xxxii Kumano is a place-name in present-day Matsue City, Shimane Prefecture. The Land of Tokoyo is across the sea. Awa Island may be so named because awa means "millet"; a location by this name exists in Yonago City, Tottori Prefecture.

xxxiii Mt. Mimoro, also known as Mt. Miwa, is in present-day Sakurai City, Nara Prefecture. Ōmiwa ("great miwa") derives its name from this mountain. The Kamo were a lineage group from the southwestern Nara Basin, and the Ōmiwa, from the southeastern Nara Basin.

xxxiv In *Ancient Matters*, Jinmu's empress has the alternative name Hime-tatara-isuzu-hime, which is used in Variant 6 of the Jinmu book and in the Suizei book of the *Chronicles*, but her original name in *Ancient Matters* is Hoto-tatara-isusugi-hime "vagina standing surprise running lady." This is because her father, Koto-shiro-nushi, changed himself into an arrow, swam up the sewer, and impregnated her mother while she was using the toilet. The episode explains the mother's names Mizo-kui-hime "ditch peg lady" and Tama-kushi-hime "jeweled stake lady."

xxxv The location of this beach is unknown. In Section 9, heavenly kami descend to Itasa beach. In *Ancient Matters*, they descend to Isasa beach.

Endnotes to Book 2

i The Ayumi River is the present-day Ai River in Fuwa District, Gifu Prefecture. Mt. Moyama is perhaps Mt. Sōzo in Tarui Town, Fuwa District, Gifu Prefecture.

ii Koto-shiro-nushi appears in Section 8.6 of the "Age of the Gods." Cape Miho is at the eastern tip of the Shimane Peninsula in present-day Matsue City, Shimane Prefecture.

iii So is present-day Soo City, Kagoshima Prefecture, and Miyakonojō City, Miyazaki Prefecture. Taka-chi-ho means "high thousand rice ears." There are two peaks claiming to be Takachiho, one in Takachiho Town, Miyazaki Prefecture, and one near Mt. Kirishima on the border of Kagoshima and Miyazaki prefectures.

iv Cape Kasasa is perhaps Cape Noma in present-day Minami Satsuma City, Kagoshima Prefecture.

v The characters for the kami Ho-no-susori here differ from those in Variants 2, 3, 6, and 8, and in *Ancient Matters*, where he is called Ho-no-suseri. The Kanbun 9 edition mistakes the vernacular reading in these instances. The kami appears when the fire first burned or reached its peak, suggesting that "suseri" derives from "raging." However, the birth circumstances and name in the Main Version differ, rendering the meaning unclear.

vi "Hiko-ho-ho-de-mi," the name of Jinmu's grandfather and Jinmu, means "lord rice ear rice ear coming forth divine spirit." "Ho" is a pun on "fire," the grandfather having been born during a conflagration.

vii Ninigi's tomb is traditionally held to be the Nitta Shrine in the Miyauchi area of Satsumasendai City, Kagoshima Prefecture.

viii Sanagata is unclear, but the Isuzu River flows through the Ise Grand Shrine in present-day Mie Prefecture.

ix Azuma is Eastern Japan. The Katori Shrine in Katori City, Chiba Prefecture, is devoted to the worship of Futsu-nushi.

x Ama-no-hi-sumi is perhaps "heavenly-sun-set" or "heavenly-sun-dwell," perhaps referring to Izumo's geographical location to the west of the Yamato basin.

xi Perhaps this place is the Takaya Shrine in present-day Kagoshima Prefecture.

xii Hiko-ho-ho-de-mi's tomb is traditionally held to be a round tumulus at Suganokuchi in the Mizobechō-fumoto area of Kirishima City, Kagoshima Prefecture.

xiii "Kamu-yamato-iware-hiko" means "Divine Lord of Yamato and Iware." Yamato refers to the Japanese realm and to Yamato Province; Iware is a place-name in Yamato that appears during Jinmu's conquest narrative.

xiv Mt. Ahira is in present-day Kanoya City, Kagoshima Prefecture. Fuki-aezu's tomb is traditionally held to be in the Aira area of Kanoya City.

xv The meaning of "Sa-no" is unclear. "Quickly ripening rice" and "Divine rice ears" have been proposed, along with the literal "Narrow field," suggesting that Jinmu's yield is presently small but will grow to include the whole realm when he assumes his full title as lord of Yamato.

Endnotes to Book 3

i The title of "emperor" and, later, "empress," are both anachronisms. Originally, use of "emperor" was thought to have begun during the reign of Emperor Suiko 推古天皇 (554–628, r. 593–628), based on its usage in diplomatic contact with the Sui Dynasty and the inscription on the Tenjukoku Embroidery (*Tenjukoku Mandala Shūchō* 天寿国曼荼羅繡帳, 7th cen., Nara National Museum), but more recent research has convincingly challenged this hypothesis. Wooden strips using this word have been excavated from the late seventh century, and the title was likely applied first to Emperor Tenmu 天武天皇 (d. 686, r. 673–686) and then systematized for other sovereigns by the series of legal codes produced during the late seventh and early eighth century. That systemization was then applied retroactively in the *Chronicles* of 720. Traditionally, it is believed that the Chinese-style names for each sovereign were created by Ōmi no Mifune 淡海三船 (722–785), based on references to the Chinese canon. Jinmu means "divine warrior" and derives from the first of the "Appended Words" (*Xici zhuan* 繫辭傳) wing of the *Classic of Changes* (*Yijing* 易經), where it describes a sage of perspicacious knowledge and divine martial skill, but who did not kill others. In Japanese naming practice, an individual might have both a "real" name and a posthumous name; in this case, Hiko-ho-ho-de-mi is the name that Jinmu was called during his life. Kamu-yamato-iware-hiko was his posthumous name, and Jinmu was the Chinese-style name given to him in the eighth century. "Hiko-ho-ho-de-mi," also the name of Jinmu's grandfather, means "lord rice ear rice ear coming forth divine spirit." "Ho" is a pun on "fire," the grandfather having been born during a conflagration.

ii This sentence derives from the description of King Wen of Zhou 周文王 (d. 1050 BCE) in the *History of the Former Han* (*Hanshu* 漢書), thus linking the posthumously honored founder of the Zhou Dynasty with the legendary founder of the Yamato Dynasty in Japan. This assessment also explains why Jinmu was named crown prince despite having three older brothers. In this keeping with his role of dynastic founder in the Chinese sense, Jinmu builds a palace to serve as capital, accedes to the throne, gives his wife and heir official status, provides faithful servants with land and titles, and creates altars outside of the capital for the worship of his imperial ancestors.

iii The Atai of Yamato were the Provincial Miyatsuko of Yamato.

iv Oka is at the mouth of the Onga River in Fukuoka City, Fukuoka Prefecture.

v E Palace is unknown. The same E River appears in Section 8.2 of the "Age of the Gods."

vi Kibi is present-day Okayama Prefecture. The Takashima Shrine on Takashima Island in Okayama City claims to be this legendary location.

vii Naniwa is an area in present-day Osaka where the Yodo River meets Osaka Bay.

viii Kusaka Village and the harbor at Shirakata are in present-day Higashi Ōsaka City. This area is now inland, but in antiquity Osaka Bay extended further to the east.

ix Tatsuta is present-day Ikaruga Town in Nara Prefecture. Blocked by the Ikoma mountain range to the east, Jinmu meant to lead his troops south around the mountains, but then turned back and instead traversed the range.

x The location of Kusae Hill, while uncertain, is presumably on the western side of Mt. Ikoma in Kōchi.

xi Yamaki Port is in the present-day Sennan District of Osaka Prefecture.

xii The Kamayama shrine is in Wakayama City.

xiii Nakusa is in the present-day Kaisō district of Wakayama Prefecture.

xiv Sano is in Shingū City, Wakayama Prefecture. Kumano is present-day eastern Wakayama Prefecture and Southern Mie Prefecture. Miwa perhaps refers to the Kamikura Shrine in Shingū City, Wakayama Prefecture, which features a large, shield-like boulder.

xv There are multiple possible locations for Arasaka, but it is in the southern part of present-day Mie Prefecture along the Pacific Ocean.

xvi In the *Chronicles*, an unread character meaning "head" has been added to the beginning of the name, suggesting that the crow's head alone was eight shaftments long, though in *Ancient Matters* it is the length of the entire crow. Eight shaftments is about 1.3 meters.

xvii Uda is present-day Uda City, Nara Prefecture. The character used for "ukachi" refers to threading something through a hole, perhaps referring to how the army weaved through the mountains.

xviii The place-name Kunisu exists in Yoshino Town, Nara Prefecture.

xix Ada is a place-name in Nara Prefecture. U-kai means "cormorant-raise," suggesting the use of these birds for fishing, though here the person is using a weir.

xx Iware Village is in present-day western Sakurai City and eastern Kashihara City.

xxi Heavenly Mt. Kagu is in present-day Kashihara City, Nara Prefecture.

xxii Shiki Village is on the western foothills of Mt. Miwa, present-day Sakurai City, Nara Prefecture. The name of Takaohari was later changed to Kazuraki ("Climbing vines fort") based on the arrowroot nets used to subdue the rebels there. Kazuraki is present-day Katsuragi City on the western edge of the Nara Basin.

xxiii The Niu River is unclear, but perhaps refers to the area near the Niukawakami Shrine in present-day Yoshino City, Nara Prefecture. Asabara refers to the area near Haibara along the Uda River in Uda City.

xxiv The final lines of this poem are repeated in poems 9, 13, and 14, and were used as a refrain by Japanese forces in World War II.

xxv Osaka Village is the present-day Otsusaka area in Sakurai City, Nara Prefecture.

xxvi Tobi Village is the present-day Tomio area of Nara City.

xxvii The location of Hata is uncertain, but the district of Soho is in northern Nara Prefecture. Nii-ki-tobe is derived from the place-name Nii-ki, present-day Yamatokōriyama City.

xxviii Wani Hill is in present-day Tenri City. Kose-hafuri suggests a head priest in the place Kose, perhaps responsible for worshipping a local kami, but a Kose that corresponds with Wani Hill is unknown.

xxix Hosomi-no-nagara is unknown, as is Ino-hafuri, "head priest of Ino."

xxx Mt. Kazuraki stands in present-day Gose City, Nara Prefecture, and the Kazuraki (Katsuragi) area comprises the western part of the Nara Basin.

xxxi Iwamu might mean "to encamp," but it is unusual for "mu" to be replaced with "re" to form Iware. The compiler found it important to ground the "Iware" in Jinmu's name in an event from his campaign.

xxxii Mt. Unebi stands in present-day Kashihara City, Nara Prefecture.

xxxiii The year 660 BCE was used as Year 1 for the Japanese calendar during the modern imperial era, resulting in massive celebrations of the 2600th anniversary of the state in 1940. The conversion of the date to the Gregorian Calendar gives February 11, which is still celebrated in Japan as National Foundation Day. Courtier Miyoshi no Kiyoyuki 三善清行 (847–919) suggested in a 901 writing that the year Metal Rooster was of particular significance for the founding of a state, based on his studies of the *Classic of Changes*. Kiyoyuki further suggested that the Metal Rooster occurring after 22 cycles of the 60-year sexagenary cycle would be especially important; this would mean that 661 CE was also a revolutionary year. According to the *Chronicles*, Emperor Tenji 天智天皇 (626–672, r. 668–672) took power in this year, though he did not formally take the throne until 668. In 901, when Kiyoyuki wrote, the court traced its lineage to Tenji. The *Classic of Changes* itself, however, suggests that 21 cycles of 60 years, not 22, which would be 601 CE, is especially important. This would be the ninth year of Emperor

Suiko's reign, and according to the *Chronicles*, in this year, her nephew and regent Prince Shōtoku 聖徳太子 (574–622) completed his palace in Ikaruga. Shōtoku was considered a sage during the eighth century, and the compilers of the *Chronicles* likely used calendrical manipulation to make both Jinmu and Shōtoku into revolutionary figures.

xxxiv Kamu-ya-i is called Kamu-ya-i-mimi in the Suizei book and in *Ancient Matters*. In *Ancient Matters*, there is another son, Hiko-ya-i, born before Kamu-ya-i-mimi. *New Selected Record* suggests that Hiko-ya-i is, rather, the son of Kamu-ya-i-mimi. Kamu-nu-na-kawa-mimi means "divine lagoon river" and could refer to a place-name.

xxxv "Kamu-yamato-iware-hiko-ho-ho-de-mi" combines two other names given to Jinmu, rendered "Divine lord of Yamato and Iware" and "rice ear, rice ear coming forth divine spirit."

xxxvi Tsukisaka Village is the Toriya area in present-day Kashihara City, Nara Prefecture.

xxxvii Kume Village is in the Kume area of Kashihara City along the Kume River.

xxxviii Takeda Village is the Higashi Takeda area in Kashihara City. Based on *Ancient Matters*, the Moitori are perhaps the Mizu-tori, "water bearers," of Uda, the site of a major river.

xxxix The name Kuro-haya does not appear elsewhere, and its meaning is unclear.

xl Tsurugi-ne is "sword root." While this figure is not named before this, he perhaps played a leading role at the battle of Takaohari, the area later renamed Kazuraki.

xli Kazuno is perhaps the Kado district, now part of the Kamigyō Ward of Kyoto City, Kyoto Prefecture.

xlii Perhaps Mt. Torimi in Sakurai City or the Torimi area in Nara City. The two shrine locations are unclear.

xliii Hohoma Hill in Wakigami is in northeastern Gose City, Nara Prefecture.

xliv Jinmu's tomb appears in Tenmu 1. The legendary location was later lost, but the Tokugawa Shogunate established a site in 1863 in present-day Kashihara City. On April 3, the Gregorian Calendar equivalent date of Jinmu's passing, a festival takes place on the site to commemorate Jinmu and the imperial line.

Endnotes to Book 4

i Book 4 of the *Chronicles* is sometimes called the "Eight Generations of Empty History" owing to the paucity of each entry. However, the book serves several important functions. These eight emperors and their extended reigns and lifespans serve to push the founding of the reign back to the auspicious year 660 BCE. The history of these reigns follows a loose pattern. First, a pre-accession record includes each emperor's lineage, children, mother's lineage, character traits, crown prince, and year the previous emperor died. Then each reign includes an accession, promotion of the old empress to empress dowager, and year given in the sexagenary cycle, followed by the establishment of the capital, interment of the previous emperor, establishment of the empress and crown prince, death, and burial site. The eight reigns also suggest the minimum features that the compilers of the *Chronicles* considered indispensable to and constitutive of a historical reign. The geographical locations of the empresses, consorts, and ancestral figures suggest the consolidation of the Yamato state in and around the Nara Basin and of its relations with the neighboring states of Kibi and Koshi.

ii Suizei means "soothing stability" and derives from part 1 of the "Biography of Wang Mang" 王莽傳 in the *History of the Former Han*, perhaps in reference to the completion of rituals associated with the effective functioning of the state.

iii The same phrase, "refined in his appearance," is later used in the Nintoku and Tenmu books. It derives from the "Annals of Emperor Ming" 明帝紀 in the *History of Wei* in the *History of the Three Kingdoms*.

iv Ama-tsu-ma-ura means "heavenly-eyed-diviner." It is an unusual name for an individual and suggests a kami. Commentaries suggest that this name may refer to the descendants of Ama-tsu-ma-ura. A similarly named kami Ama-tsu-ma-ra is the ancestor of the smithing hereditary guild in *Ancient Matters*.

v Kataoka is present-day Ōji Town, Nara Prefecture.

vi Takaoka Palace is traditionally claimed to be in the present-day Moriwaki area of Gose City, Nara Prefecture.

vii The phrases "the crown prince acceded to the imperial throne" and "the empress was honored with the title of empress dowager," which occur often in the early years of reigns in the *Chronicles*, recall the opening lines of the "Annals of Emperor Hui" 惠帝紀 in the *History of the Former Han*. Both Suizei and Hui were second emperors. The *Chronicles* thus presents the Yamato Dynasty as akin to the Han.

viii Shiki-tsu-hiko is "Lord of Shiki," referring perhaps to his mother's lineage. Tamate is perhaps the Tamate area in present-day Gose City, Nara Prefecture.

ix Annei means "tranquil and peaceful" and is used to describe the peaceful reigns of Kings Cheng and Kang of Zhou in the "Annals of Zhou" 周本紀 in the *Records of the Historian* (*Shiji* 史記). The word used here and elsewhere to describe him as the oldest son more specifically means the oldest son borne by the empress and excludes children of consorts. Occasionally, the word is also used as a substitute for "crown prince" in entries describing accession (Annei, Kōrei, Kaika).

x Suizei's burial location, Tsukita-no-oka-no-ue Tomb, while disputed in the commentaries, is traditionally held to be in the Shijō area of Kashihara City in Nara Prefecture.

xi Katashio is the Mikurado area in present-day Yamatotakada City, Nara Prefecture.

xii The first half of "Ō-yamato-hiko-suki-tomo" means "Great Yamato Lord." "Suki" means "spade," and the meaning of "tomo" is unclear.

xiii Itoku means "esteemed virtue" and appears in Zheng Min 烝民, "Decade of Dang" (Dang zhi shen 蕩之什) section of the "Major Court Hymns" (Da ya 大雅) in the *Classic of Poetry* (*Shijing* 詩經).

xiv Karu is the present-day Ōgaru area in Kashihara City, Nara Prefecture.

xv The first half of "Mima-tsu-hiko-kaeshi-ne" means "Lord of Mima." The meaning of "kaeshi-ne" is unclear.

xvi Kōshō means "filial illumination" and begins a series of four sovereigns with "filial" in their names. The *Collected Commentary on the Chronicles* (*Shoki shikkai* 書紀集解) suggests that this is modeled on Emperor Hui of Han 漢惠帝 (210–188 BCE, r. 195–188 BCE), after whom all Han emperors have the word "filial" in their courtesy names. Kōshō's name is thus parallel to that of Emperor Zhao of Han 漢昭帝 (94–74 BCE, r. 87–74 BCE).

xvii Itoku's burial location is traditionally held to be in the Ikejiri area of Kashihara City, Nara Prefecture.

xviii Yamato-tarashi-hiko-kuni-oshi-hito is "Yamato replete lord and majestic human of the land." Ama-tarashi-hiko-kuni-oshi-hito is "heavenly replete lord and majestic human of the land." The Wani lineage group boasted of numerous empresses and consorts in later eras—a fact suggesting major political influence. The Wani were concentrated in what is now the Wani area of Tenri City, Nara Prefecture. Like the Ō lineage group, the Wani lineage is provided in *Ancient Matters*, but not in the *Chronicles*, indicating a major difference in the objectives of the two works.

xix Kōan means "filial tranquil" and was the courtesy name of Emperor An of Han 漢安帝 (94 –125, r. 106 –125).

xx Kōshō's burial location is traditionally held to be in the Mimuro area of Gose City, Nara Prefecture. That he was not buried until thirty-eight years after his death is widely speculated about in commentaries.

xxi Ō-yamato-neko-hiko-futo-ni means "Grand Yamato *neko* lord magnificent jewel," where *neko* is an honorific title.

xxii Kōrei means "filial soul" and was the courtesy name of Emperor Ling of Han 漢靈帝 (156–189, r. 168–189).

xxiii Kōan's burial location is traditionally held to be in the Muro area of Gose City, Nara Prefecture.

xxiv Kuroda is the Kuroda area in present-day Tawaramoto Town, Shiki District, Nara Prefecture.

xxv The first half of "Ō-yamato-neko-hiko-kuni-kuru" is the same name as the previous emperor: Grand Yamato *neko* lord, where *neko* is an honorific title. "Kuni-kuru" means "Drawing the land near."

TEXT-CRITICAL ENDNOTES 637

xxvi Kōgen means "the origin of filiality" and was the courtesy name of Emperor Yuan of Han 漢元帝 (75–33 BCE, r. 48–33 BCE).

xxvii Kōrei's burial location is traditionally held to be in the Honmachi area of Ōji Town, Kita Katsuragi District, Nara Prefecture.

xxviii "Yamato-neko-hiko" also appears in the names of Kōrei and Kōgen. "Waka" means "young" and perhaps is intended to contrast Kaika with these two forebears. "Ō" means "great"; the Kanbun 9 version glosses the character as "futo," but based on *Ancient Matters*, it should be "ō." "Bibi" is the same as "mimi," which appears in many names and could mean "mysterious power" or "rice ears."

xxix The lineages started by Ō-hiko were scattered across Japan. The Omi of Ahe were a powerful ancient lineage group. The Omi of the Kashiwade were an allied miyatsuko group responsible for providing and preparing court meals. The Omi of Ahe in Iga, differentiated in the original from the first lineage noted by the characters used for "Ahe," were concentrated in present-day Iga City, Mie Prefecture. The Yama-no-kimi of Sasaki were concentrated in the present-day Azuchi area of Ōmihachiman City, Shiga Prefecture. The Omi of Iga were concentrated in present-day Iga City, Mie Prefecture.

xxx Kaika means "commence civilization" and appears in the "Biography of Gu Jizhi" 顧覬之傳 in the *History of the Liu Song* (*Song shu* 宋書).

xxxi Kasuga is in present-day Nara City, Nara Prefecture.

xxxii Kōgen's burial location is traditionally held to be in the Ishikawa area of Kashihara City, Nara Prefecture.

xxxiii Kaika's burial location, Izakawa-no-sakamoto Tomb, is traditionally held to be in the Aburasaka area of Nara City, Nara Prefecture.

Endnotes to Book 5

i "Mi-maki" "i-nie," and "iri" are unclear; "iri" might be a title of affection. "Biko" means "lord."

ii Sujin means "revere divinity" and is perhaps taken from a speech in the first book of the "Discourses of Zhou" ("Zhou yu" 周語) in *Discourses of the States* (*Guoyu* 國語).

iii Ō-heso-ki appears in *Original Records* as a descendant of Nigi-haya-hi, the patron kami of the Mononobe.

iv This sentence is derived from the description of Emperor Cheng of Han 漢成帝 (51–7 BCE, r. 33–7 BCE) in the *History of the Former Han*.

v In the pre-accession record of Suinin, Mi-maki-hime is given as the daughter of Ō-hiko. She is given as Mi-ma-tsu-hime in *Ancient Matters*.

vi "Ikume" is unclear." "Iri" might be a title of affection. "Biko" means "lord." "Isa-chi" might derive from "isamashi," meaning "brave, valiant," and "chi" means "divine spirit."

vii Ikume-iri-biko-isa-chi is perhaps "place-name *term of affection* lord valiant spirit." In *Ancient Matters*, the children after Suinin are given as Iza-no-ma-waka, Kuni-kata-hime, Chiji-tsuku-yamato-hime, Iga-hime, and Yamato-hiko. Iga-hime perhaps equates with Iga-tsuru-hiko, though birth order and sex differ.

viii In *Ancient Matters*, Ara-kawa-tobe is given as the Provincial Miyatsuko of Ki. *Original Records* gives Ō-ni-i-kawa as the husband of the daughter of Ara-kawa-tobe of Ki, Naka-tsu-hime. Arakawa is the present-day Momoyama area of Kinokawa City, Wakayama Prefecture. *Ancient Matters* gives Toyo-ki-iri-biko as the ancestor of the Kimi of Kamitsukeno and Shimotsukeno, present-day Gunma and Tochigi Prefectures, and Toyo-suki-iri-bime as the priestess of the Ise Grand Shrine. On the latter, see Sujin 6.

ix Going by his name, the Sukune of Ōama might well refer to the next consort, Ō-ama-hime of Owari. This would make him the leader of the fisher hereditary guild from Owari Prefecture.

x *Ancient Matters* gives Ō-ama-hime as ancestor of the Muraji of Owari. *Original Records* gives Take-unahi, a descendant of Nigi-haya-hi, as father of Ō-ama-hime of Owari, and gives her the alternative name Takana-hime of Kazuraki. Yasaka-iri-biko is the father of Yasaka-iri-bime and Oto-hime, who appear in Keikō 4.2. *Ancient Matters* gives a son, Ō-iri-ki, before Yasaka-iri-biko. Nunaki-iri-bime is given as Nunaki-no-iri-bime in *Ancient Matters* and as Nunaki-waka-hime in the note to Suinin 25.3. Tōchi-ni-iri-bime is given in *Ancient Matters* as Tōchi-no-iri-bime; Tōchi perhaps refers to the former Tōichi District of Yamato Province, present-day Shiki District.

xi Yamato-ō-kuni-tama is "Yamato great land soul." The "Yamato" in Yamato-ō-kuni-tama is written with both the character 和 and the characters 日本, though they are glossed the same in Japanese. Worship of this kami is related to governance of the state as a whole. A continued entry related to worship of Amaterasu and Yamato-ō-kami appears in the note to Suinin 25, but it also introduces discrepancies about when worship of these kami actually began and between the similarly named Nunaki-iri-bime and Nunaki-waka-hime.

xii Asajihara is the Kasa area in Sakurai City, Nara Prefecture.

xiii Ō-mono-nushi appears in S9.2, when Ama-no-koyane and Futo-dama are instructed to worship him. In the same variant, Ō-mono-nushi goes to heaven with Koto-shiro-nushi after Ō-ana-muchi (Ō-kuni-nushi) has surrendered. Conversely, in S8.6, Ō-mono-nushi is stated to be a variant name of Ō-ana-muchi, and in this variant, Ō-ana-muchi's spirit of fortune and spirit of discernment wish to dwell on Mt. Miwa, where Ō-mono-nushi is worshipped.

xiv Sue is present-day Mt. Tōki in Sakai City, Ōsaka Prefecture. The name suggests that the area was associated with ceramics, as does that of

Sue-tsu-mimi, "ceramics' mysterious power." The additional account is unusual in this case, as it is written in full-size characters.

xv The day given is inconsistent across manuscripts.

xvi Sumisaka is in present-day Uda City, Nara Prefecture. Ōsaka is perhaps the Ōsaka-Yamaguchi Shrine in Kashiba City, Nara Prefecture.

xvii Wani is the Wani area in present-day Tenri City, Nara Prefecture.

xviii The Miwa kami, Ō-mono-nushi, appeared as a snake also in Yūryaku 7.7.

xix A similar episode appears in *Ancient Matters* when Susano-o scares a weaver kami and she accidentally stabs herself in the vagina with the shuttle and dies. However, while a weaver holding a shuttle is plausible, it is unusual that Yamato-to-to-hi-momo-so-bime has chopsticks in her dressing room. The story was likely created based on the name of the tomb, Hashihaka, "chopsticks tomb." The tomb itself, in Sakurai City, Nara Prefecture, is one of the oldest large-scale mound tumuli in Japan, dating from the third century CE. Researchers have posited that the tomb might belong to Pimiko, a legendary queen of Yamatai recorded in the *History of the Three Kingdoms*.

xx Much of this edict derives from the "Annals of Emperor Cheng of Han" in the *History of the Former Han*. Emperor Cheng's repeated worship of the gods and his movement of their shrines parallels the events in this book.

xxi Sujin's title of "first emperor to rule the state" resembles that of Jinmu, who "ruled all under heaven as the first emperor." The Japanese gloss for the respective characters used for "first" is the same. However, Jinmu's title uses 始 and Sujin's uses 肇, here akin to "established" or "formalized," a reference to Sujin's creation of the census and taxation systems.

xxii Kamitsuke and Shimotsuke are present-day Gunma and Tochigi Prefectures in eastern Japan.

xxiii Take-hina-teru does not appear in the "Age of the Gods" in the *Chronicles*, but *Ancient Matters* gives Take-hira-tori as the son of Ama-no-ho-hi and the ancestor of the Provincial Miyatsuko of Izumo. The *Shinto Prayer of the Provincial Miyatsuko of Izumo* (*Izumo no kuni no miyatsuko no kanyo goto* 出雲国造神賀詞) identifies Ame-no-take-hina-tori, son of Ama-no-ho-hi, as the distant ancestor of the Provincial Miyatsuko of Izumo. In the *Chronicles*, Ama-no-ho-hi is the ancestor of the Omi of Izumo.

xxiv *Original Records* identifies Take-moro-sumi as a descendant of Nigi-haya-hi, and an Ō-mo-sumi as his younger brother.

xxv Future lineages for Ii-iri-ne, Umashi-kara-hisa, and U-kazu-kune are given in *New Selected Records*.

xxvi The episode with the wooden sword recalls the defeat of the Izumo champion by Yamato Take in *Ancient Matters*. The poem appears in that context in *Ancient Matters*.

xxvii Hikami is the present-day Hikami area of Tanba City, Hyōgo Prefecture.

xxviii This passage derives from the "Annals of Emperor Wen of Han" 漢文帝 (d. 157 BCE, r. 180–157 BCE) in the *History of the Former Han*.

xxix Sayama is present-day Ōsakasayama City, Osaka Prefecture. Hanita is perhaps the Handa area. In the Suinin book of *Ancient Matters*, a Sayama Reservoir is built.

xxx Sujin's burial place is traditionally held to be at the Andon'yama Tumulus in the Yanagimoto area of Tenri City, Nara Prefecture.

Endnotes to Book 6

i Suinin means "dangling benevolence" and derives from the "Shanmou" 善謀 section of *Matters Newly Arranged* (*Xinxu* 新序), by Liu Xiang 劉向 (79–8 BCE). Suinin's benevolence is epitomized by his outlawing the practice of following one's lord in death near the end of this book. He is described as the third son of Sujin on account of his two half-brothers. Ō-hiko was a son of Emperor Kōgen.

ii Descriptions of Suinin's character derive from notes for Emperor Ming of Wei 魏明帝 (d. 239, r. 226–239) in *Commentary on the History of the Three Kingdoms* (*Sanguo zhi zhu* 三國志注), by Pei Songzhi 裴松之 (372–451); Book 41 of *Selections of Refined Literature* (*Wen xuan* 文選); the "Annals of Gaozu" 高祖本紀 in the *Records of the Historian*; the *Doctrine of the Mean* (*Zhongyong* 中庸) in the *Records of Rituals* (*Liji* 禮記); the biography of Zheng Chong 鄭沖 in the *History of the Jin Dynasty* (*Jinshu* 晉書); and the biography of the four princes of Wen 文四子 in the *History of the Sui Dynasty* (*Sui shu* 隋書).

iii The name "Saho-hime" derives from the area around the Saho River in present-day Nara City. "Hime" is reserved for women of imperial stock prior to the Keikō book, but it is not clear here which emperor was her father. In *Ancient Matters*, she was the daughter of Kaika.

iv Makimuku is in present-day northern Sakurai City, Nara Prefecture.

v The title Kokishi, glossed on the character for king, appears as "Konikishi" in the Jingū and other books of the *Chronicles*. Book 49 of the *History of the Zhou Dynasty* (*Zhou shu* 周書) uses a similar word as the title for a king of Paekche.

vi The enmity between Silla and Kaya is followed up on in Keitai 23.3.

vii The first note on Sonakashichi suggests that he was from Ōkara (Kŭmgwan Kaya) and intended to naturalize rather than present tribute. Kei Beach is present-day Tsuruga City, Fukui Prefecture.

viii Tsunuga is present-day Tsuruga City.

ix Ōkara is another name for the Korean kingdom Kŭmgwan Kaya. The story later explains why Ōkara would be called Mimana. Tsunuga is perhaps a combination of the place-name given in the story and the *kakkan* rank of Silla and other Korean aristocracies, which could be written using the character for "horn." Arashito is perhaps related to Arishito, who appears in Keitai 23.3, and here perhaps reflects a confusion or confluence of a Korean name and a Korean rank. Ushiki is unclear. Arishichi likely refers to Arashito or Arishito. Kanki frequently appears as a moniker for Kaya kings in the *Chronicles*.

x Anato is the strait between Honshu and Kyushu, off present-day Yamaguchi Prefecture.

xi The name Mimana resembles that of Emperor Mi-maki, but in fact the name likely derives from Korean *nimnae*. An account of Ame-no-hi-hoko that blends some elements from the note on Sonakashichi given here appears in the Ōjin book of *Ancient Matters*.

xii Kunisaki is present-day Kunisaki City, Oita Prefecture.

xiii Tajima is across the Sea of Japan from the eastern coast of the Korean Peninsula and Silla.

xiv Ō-tomo-nushi is given in *Original Records* as a descendant of Susano-o and is named Kimi of Ōmiwa during the reign of Sujin.

xv The emperor's older brother, Toyo-ki-iri-biko, was given as the first ancestor of the Kimi of Kamitsuke in Sujin 48.4. *New Selected Record* gives Ya-tsuna-da as the son of Toyo-ki-iri-biko.

xvi Tagima is the present-day Tagima area of Katsuragi City, Nara Prefecture.

xvii Kazuno, later called Kadono, is in the present-day Sakyō Ward of Kyoto City. Otokuni also appears in Keitai 12.3.

xviii Ō-tarashi-hiko-oshiro-wake means "great bountiful, powerful ruler *affectionate term for young man*."

xix There was no day of the Wood Rat this month; perhaps this is an error for the Wood Rat day corresponding with Ninth Month, seventeenth day, or perhaps for Wood Horse day, which would be Tenth Month, eighteenth day.

xx Kuka-nushi is perhaps related to Kuka-tachi, a divination performed using hot water, as seen in Ingyō 4.9. Anashi Village is the present-day Anashi area in Sakurai City, Nara Prefecture.

xxi Sugawara-no-Fushimi Tomb is traditionally held to be in the Amagatsuji-nishi area of Nara City, Nara Prefecture. A small island in the moat surrounding the tomb is held to be the resting place of Tajima-mori.

Endnotes to Book 7

i Keikō means "luminous goings." The term appears in poem 218 of the *Classic of Poetry*, in the Decade of Sang Hu 桑扈之什. It perhaps refers to Emperor Keikō's seven-year-long tour of Tsukushi, which occupies much of the book.

ii In *Ancient Matters*, the empress's lineage is given as daughter of Wakatake, Lord of Kibi (Kibi-tsu-biko), with Waka-iratsume given as her younger sister. Inabi is the former Inami District of Hyōgo Prefecture. Iratsume is an honorary title for women.

iii Beginning with the Keikō book, the children of emperors begin to be called "Imperial Prince" and "Imperial Princess." In *Ancient Matters*, the younger brother kills the older one, but that narrative is absent in the *Chronicles*. Ō-usu will later be enfeoffed in Mino, and O-usu will die in service to the empire.
iv Lifting a three-legged cauldron to demonstrate strength appears in the Annals of Xiang Yu 項羽本紀 in the *Records of the Historian*.
v Present-day southern part of Wakayama City, Wakayama Prefecture.
vi Kukuri Palace is present-day Kani City, Gifu Prefecture. Kukuri Palace appears in *Myriad Poems* XIII:3242.
vii *Ancient Matters* provides a slightly different genealogy for Keikō's consorts and offspring. Ōjin's three consorts are daughters of Homuda-no-ma-waka, son of Ioki-no-iri-biko. Ioki-no-iri-biko married the daughter of the ancestor of the Muraji of Owari. Waka-yamato-neko is given in *Ancient Matters* as Yamato-neko. As in the note for Keikō 2.3, his mother is Inabi-no-iratsume of Harima. Ō-su-wake is not seen. Motoori Norinaga 本居宣長 (1730–1801) notes that the name of Emperor Ninken is given as Ō-shi or Ō-su. Thereby, Ō-su-wake could be the same child as Oshi-wake. Nu-no-shi-no-iratsume is given as the child of another consort, the same mother as Toyo-to-wake. Nunaki-no-iratsume is given as the child of another consort, the same mother as that of Kago-yori-hime, Waka-ki-no-iri-biko, Kibi-no-ye-hike, Takaki-hime, and Oto-hime. I-saki-no-iri-biko is perhaps the Waka-ki-no-iri-biko given in *Ancient Matters*. In *Original Records*, he is the ancestor of the Atai of the Hase hereditary guild of Mikawa. Norinaga suggests that perhaps Taka-ki-no-iri-bime has been confused with the consort of Ōjin, who bears the same name. Iono is not seen in *Ancient Matters*. She is sent to worship Amaterasu in Keikō 20.2. Norinaga gives the mother of Kamu-kushi as Inabi-no-iratsume of Harima. *New Selected Records* gives Kamu-kushi-wake as an alternative name for the ancestor of the Kimi of Sanuki. The entry for Jōwa 3.3 (836 CE) in *Continued Chronicle of Later Japan* (*Shoku Nihon kōki* 続日本後紀) gives the Kimi of Sanki as descendants of Kamu-kushi. *Ancient Matters* also gives Kamu-kushi as the ancestor of the Saka hereditary guilds (Sakabe) of Ki and Uda. *New Selected Records* gives Kamu-kushi-wake as ancestor of the Kimi of the Saka hereditary guild of Izumi, while Inase-no-iri-biko is not, though the Suinin book of *Ancient Matters* notes that Suinin's daughter Azami-tsu-hime married one Inase-biko. *New Selected Records* gives him as the ancestor of the Atai of the Saeki. Take-kuni-kori-wake, Himuka-no-so-tsu-biko, Kuni-chi-wake, and Kuni-so-wake are not seen in *Ancient Matters*. Toyo-to-wake is given as the son of another consort. *Original Records* gives Toyo-to-wake as the ancestor of the Kimi of the Mizuma of Mishima; the Obito of Anchi, Wakugo, and Awa; and the Kimi of Hinowake in Tsukushi.
viii Waka-tarashi-hiko means "young bountiful lord."

ix Yamato Take, Waka-tarashi-hiko, and Ioki-no-iri-biko are all directly connected the imperial line: Yamato Take as the father of Chūai, Waka-tarashi-hiko as Seimu, and Ioki-no-iri-biko as the grandfather of Naka-tsu-hime, empress to Ōjin and mother of Nintoku. *Ancient Matters* says instead that these three all bore the title of crown prince. *Ancient Matters* tends toward presenting the imperial succession as being determined by the course of events, while the legitimate successor is overdetermined in the *Chronicles*, where eventual sovereigns use a different character for their title of "mikoto" than other imperial family members. However, even the *Chronicles* details dreams, portents, and other events that ultimately make clear which child should inherit the throne. *Ancient Matters* commentator Motoori Norinaga argues that this reveals a difference between the Chinese model of succession (in which a crown prince was named, and which was adopted by the *Chronicles* due to its reliance on Chinese historiographical norms) and succession in ancient Japan (which might go to any child depending on their individual qualities and the circumstances).

x The Kumaso dwelt in southern Kyushu. The name might derive from the Kuma District of Higo, present-day Hitoyoshi City, and the So District of Ōsumi, present-day Kirishima City. However, in the *Chronicles*, the conquest of the Kuma District occurs later, in Keikō 18, and the Kumaso are associated only with the So District, in Keikō 12.12. They are often theorized as being of a South Seas origin and related to the Hayato, who served the eighth-century court and are referred to in S10 of the "Age of the Gods." No mention of previous tribute from the Kumaso is provided, but this may refer to the entries in Sujin 11 and 12, when various foreigners pledged their allegiance. In the *Chronicles*, tribute was largely imagined to come from foreign states: Mimana, Silla, Paekche, and Goguryŏ on the Korean peninsula and Wu in China. The inclusion of the Kumaso and the Emishi as tributaries suggests that the compilers viewed them as foreign states.

xi There is an unusually high amount of correspondence between the information about Kyushu presented in the *Chronicles* in Keikō 11 and the *fudoki* gazetteers, which suggests that one text was used in the compilation of the other. As the texts were written around the same time, it is not certain which was the original.

xii Saba is the present-day Saba area of Hōfu City, Yamaguchi Prefecture.

xiii The Omi of Ō appear in the Suizei book, but there, in *Ancient Matters*, and in *New Selected Records*, they are descended from Kamu-ya-i-mimi. The Omi of Kunisaki were concentrated in the Kunisaki District of Higo, the present-day Kunisaki Peninsula in Oita Prefecture. Their ancestor is given in *Ancient Matters* as Hiko-sashi-kata-wake, a son of Kōrei. The Kimi of Mononobe perhaps refers to the Mononobe of northern Kyushu.

xiv The Usa River perhaps refers to the Yakkan River in present-day Usa City, Oita Prefecture.

xv The Mike River is the Yamakuni River between present-day Oita Prefecture and Fukuoka Prefecture.
xvi The Takaha River perhaps refers to the Tagawa District in present-day Fukuoka Prefecture, which the Hikosan River flows through.
xvii Nagao is an area in Yukuhashi City, Fukuoka Prefecture. Miyako is a district in Fukuoka Prefecture adjacent to Yukuhashi City.
xviii Ōkita is present day Ōita City, Ōita Prefecture.
xix Hayami Village is the present-day Hayami District, Ōita Prefecture.
xx Present-day Taketa City, Ōita Prefecture.
xxi This location is marked by Miyakono Shrine in present-day Taketa City, Ōita Prefecture.
xxii The Inaba River flows through present-day Taketa City, Ōita Prefecture.
xxiii Kihara is the Kibaru area is in present-day Taketa City, Ōita Prefecture.
xxiv The Takaya Shrine in present-day Miyazaki City, Miyazaki Prefecture, claims to mark the spot of Keikō's palace.
xxv So is in present-day Kirishima City, Kagoshima Prefecture. Atsu-kaya and Sa-kaya literally mean "thick kaya" and "thin kaya," which suggests that the two are siblings. "Kaya" is perhaps a place-name. "Kaya" appears earlier in the names of the two Kumaso women.
xxvi Koyu is the present-day Koyu District of Miyazaki Prefecture.
xxvii The Heguri mountains refers to the hills in Heguri Town, Ikegoma District, Nara Prefecture.
xxviii In *Ancient Matters*, this song is composed by Keikō's son Yamato Take before he dies. In that text, it is broken into three separate poems. These poems are conventionally numbered in the *Chronicles* based on their format in *Ancient Matters*.
xxix Perhaps present-day Hosono-Hinamori in Kobayashi City, Miyazaki Prefecture. Hina-mori means "rustic guardian" and appears as a place-name in other places of strategic importance, which suggests that it originally referred to a location where border guards were stationed.
xxx The Iwase River flows through Kobayashi City, Miyazaki Prefecture.
xxxi Kuma District is present-day Kuma District and Hitoyoshi City, Kumamoto Province.
xxxii Ashikita is present-day Ashikita District and Minamata City, Kumamoto Prefecture.
xxxiii Ashikita and Mizushima appear in *Myriad Poems* III:246.
xxxiv Yatsushiro District is present-day Yatsushiro District and Yatsushiro City, Kumamoto Prefecture.
xxxv In the *Gazetteer of Higo Province* (*Higo no kuni fudoki* 肥後国風土記) and *Gazetteer of Hizen Province* (*Hizen no kuni fudoki* 肥前国風土記), the rationale for naming the region the "land of fire" appears in the reign of Sujin and is then later confirmed by Keikō in a very similar episode. The

similarities suggest that the texts, which were compiled around the same time, influenced each other.

xxxvi Aso is present-day Aso District and Aso City, Kumamoto Prefecture.

xxxvii Michinoshiri in Tsukushi is Chikugo Province. Mike is present-day Omuta City and Miyama City.

xxxviii Mt. Kishima is in present-day Takeo City, Saga prefecture. Mt. Aso is in present-day Aso City, Kumamoto Prefecture.

xxxix Yame District is present-day Yame District and Yame City, Fukuoka Prefecture. Mt. Fuji is perhaps in the Fujiyama area of Kurume City, Fukuoka Prefecture.

xl Minuma is present-day Mizuma District and part of Kurume City, Fukuoka Prefecture.

xli Ukiha is present-day Ukiha City, Fukuoka Prefecture.

xlii The Hokuriku region comprises northwestern Honshu along the Sea of Japan. Azuma refers to the Kantō and Tōhoku regions of eastern and northeastern Honshu. These regions were added to the Yamato empire in Sujin 10.

xliii Ishiura is present-day Kuwana City, Mie Prefecture. Inaki appears in Seimu 5 and Taika 1 of Kōtoku's reign. The *History of the Sui Dynasty*, Book 81 "Eastern Barbarians," notes that the people of Wa had "Inagi" who functioned as village chiefs, which would make the Inaki administrators of an area smaller than a provincial miyatsuko. Tago is perhaps the present-day Takō area of Mizuho Ward, Nagoya City, Aichi Prefecture. Chichika is unclear.

xliv Takeru means "ferocious, violent" and is used to describe enemy leaders. Torishi may be read "Toroshi." Kaya is perhaps a place-name; it appears in the names of the Kumaso women in Keikō 12. In *Ancient Matters*, Torishikaya includes both an older and younger brother. Kawakami is perhaps a place-name.

xlv Kibi is present-day Okayama Prefecture and eastern Hiroshima Prefecture. The Ana Sea is perhaps in Fukuyama City, Hiroshima Prefecture.

xlvi The Kashiwa Crossing is the Nozato and Kashiwazato areas in Nishiyodogawa Ward, Osaka City, Osaka Prefecture.

xlvii The standard appellation of "mikoto" is missing from Yamato Take's name in this instance.

xlviii Keikō's edict is a pastiche of descriptions of barbarians taken from texts in the Classical Chinese canon.

xlix A three-span sword is used by Emperor Gaozu of Han in the *History of the Former Han* and in the *Records of the Historian* biography of Han Changru 韓長孺 to signify conquering the realm.

l Yakitsu is present-day Yaizu City, Shizuoka Province.

li Kamitsufusa is Kazusa Province. Yamato Take crosses the Uraga Channel between the Miura and Bōsō peninsulas.

lii In *Ancient Matters*, Oto-tachibana-hime is called an empress. The Hozumi appear in the Kaika book.
liii Hashiru-mizu is present-day Yoksuka City, Kanagawa Prefecture.
liv Michinoku is Mutsu Province.
lv Ashiura is unclear. Tamanoura is perhaps present-day Kujūkuri Beach in Sōsa City, Chiba Prefecture.
lvi Taka is perhaps the Taga Shrine in the Taihaku Ward of Sendai City, Miyagi Prefecture, or Takayanagi in Natori City, Miyagi Prefecture, or the Taka Shrine in Minami Sōma City, Fukushima Prefecture.
lvii Sakaori is an area in present-day Kōfu City, Yamanashi Prefecture. A shrine there claims to mark this location.
lviii Tsukuba is present-day Tsukuba City, Ibaraki Prefecture. Niibari is in the eastern area of present-day Chikusei City, Ibaraki Prefecture.
lix Koshi is present-day Fukui, Toyama, and Niigata Prefectures.
lx Kamitsukeno is present-day Gunma Prefecture. Usui Hill / Mt. Usui is on the border between present-day Annaka City, Gunma Prefecture, and Karuizawa Town, Nagano Prefecture. It appears in *Myriad Poems* XIV:3402 and XX:4407.
lxi Shinano Pass is the present-day Misaka Pass connecting Nakatsugawa City, Gifu Prefecture, with Achi Village, Nagano Prefecture. The steepness of the pass led to a detour being created in 713 CE.
lxii In *Ancient Matters*, Yamato Take meets Miyazu-hime on the way to the east and promises to return. In the *Chronicles*, this episode is omitted, but the text still sees him "return again" to Owari.
lxiii Mt. Ibuki is in present-day Maibara City, Shiga Prefecture. The sword is Kusa-nagi. This episode explains why the sword ended up at the Atsuta Shrine in Owari Province, present-day Nagoya City.
lxiv Isame is the present-day Samegai ("sobering well") area in Maibara City, Shiga Prefecture.
lxv Otsu is the present-day Tado area in Kuwana City, Mie Prefecture.
lxvi Nobono is perhaps the fields stretching from present-day northern Suzuka City to eastern Kameyama City, Mie Prefecture.
lxvii Kotohiki is the present-day Toyoda area of Gose City, Nara Prefecture.
lxviii Furuichi Village is the present-day Furuichi area of Habikino City, Osaka Prefecture.
lxix The Atsuta Shrine is in present-day Nagoya City, Aichi Prefecture.
lxx Some editions amend Ise to Iyo, based on *New Selected Records* and Iyo's geographical proximity to the other provinces named, which are all near the Seto Inland Sea.
lxxi "Tarashi" means "replete" and derives from the names of Chūai's forebears. "Naka-tsu-hiko" means "middle lord" and perhaps refers to Chūai's being the second son of Yamato Take, after his older brother Ina-yori-wake.

lxxii In *Ancient Matters*, Ina-yori-wake is the son of a different woman similarly named Futaji-hime, daughter of the ancestor of the Provincial Miyatsuko of Yasu in Ōmi. Inukami is a place-name in Ōmi, present-day Inukami District, Shiga Prefecture.

lxxiii Awa is the southern portion of the Bōsō Peninsula (Chiba), not to be confused with Awa (Tokushima).

lxxiv Kanihata Palace is held to be in the Kasado area of Suzuka City, Mie Prefecture.

lxxv Anakui Village is perhaps near the Anaguri Shrine, present-day Nara City, Nara Prefecture.

lxxvi The Sakate Reservoir is in present-day Sakate, Tawaramoto Town, Shiki District, Nara Prefecture.

lxxvii The corresponding entry in *Ancient Matters* has "During this imperial reign, the Ta lineage group was established for Yamato imperial fiefs." This more likely entry suggests that what was established was a Ta (paddy rice field) lineage group charged with producing rice from imperial fiefs, not an imperial fief named Tabe.

lxxviii Taka-anaho is the present-day Anō area of Ōtsu City, Shiga Prefecture.

lxxix Seimu means "accomplishing undertakings" and appears in the "Appended Words" wing of the *Classic of Changes*.

lxxx The Yama-no-be-no-michi-no-e Tomb is traditionally held to be the Shibutani-mukaiyama Tumulus in the present-day Shibutani area of Tenri City, Nara Prefecture.

lxxxi A record of provincial miyatsuko is also given in the *Original Records*. Noteworthy is that in the *Original Records* version of events, the province system is set up by Jinmu, who rewarded accomplishments with positions of provincial miyatsuko and, over those who rebelled against him, established agatanushis. Of the 74 references to provincial miyatsuko in the *Chronicles* that specify the name of a province, all but one are included in the *Original Records*, and while the establishment of provincial miyatsuko in the *Original Records* spans multiple reigns, nearly half occur in Seimu's reign, which suggests that that text was conscious of the *Chronicles* entry for Seimu 5.

lxxxii Much of Seimu's edict is taken from Chinese texts, especially the *Selections of Refined Literature*.

Endnotes to Book 8

i Chūai is perhaps "younger brother short lived," taking the first character from Chūai's vernacular Japanese name and the last character to mean "short lived" based on the *Shi fa jie* 諡法解 in the *Leftover Books of Zhou* (*Yi Zhou shu* 逸周書). This combination recalls the prediction that Chūai would die young for defying the will of the kami.

ii In *Ancient Matters*, Seimu has one son, and the names of Seimu's wife and son closely resemble those of Yamato Take in the *Chronicles*.
iii Seimu's tomb is traditionally held to be the Sakiishizukayama Tumulus in present-day Nara City, Nara Prefecture.
iv Koshi Province is present-day Niigata, Toyama, Ishikawa, and Fukui prefectures.
v Okinaga-tarashi-hime combines the "tarashi" (bountiful) that appears in the names of Keikō, Seimu, and Chūai, with "Okinaga," which is derived from her father's name, Okinaga no Sukune. Okinaga is a place-name in Sakata, Ōmi Province, present-day Sakata District, and appears in the first Tenmu book as the site of the Yokogawa River and as the setting for *Myriad Poems* XIII:3323. In the Bidatsu book, the empress of Bidatsu, Hiro-hime, is the daughter of Okinaga-no-mate no Kimi and Bidatsu, and Hiro-hime's grandson, Jomei, was named Okinaga-tarashi-hi-hiro-nuka, and his empress, later ruling as Emperor Kōgyoku, was named Ame-toyotakara-ikashi-hi-tarashi-hime. Hence, the title "tarashi" is concentrated around two sets of rulers: Keikō, Seimu, Chūai, and Jingū, and around Jomei and Kōgyoku. The Ōjin book of *Ancient Matters* notes that Takanuka-hime of Kazuraki was the fifth-generation descendant of Ame-no-hihoko, thus linking Jingū's lineage with the Korean peninsula. The *Chronicles* notes in Jingū 69 that the name Okinaga-tarashi-hime was given posthumously.
vi Tsunuga is present-day Tsuruga City, Fukui Prefecture, where Chūai is enshrined at the Kehi Shrine.
vii Tokorotsu is perhaps the Shinzaike area of present-day Wakayama City, Wakayama Prefecture.
viii Anato is present-day Shimonoseki City, Yamaguchi Prefecture.
ix Toyura Harbor is in present-day Shimonoseki City, Yamaguchi Prefecture.
x Nuta is perhaps the Tsunegami Peninsula in Tsuruga City, Fukui Prefecture.
xi The Iminomiya Shrine in Shimonoseki City, Yamaguchi Prefecture, claims to be the site of this palace.
xii Oka is present-day Onga District, Fukuoka Prefecture.
xiii Saba Harbor in Suwa is the present-day Saba area in Hofu City, Yamaguchi Prefecture.
xiv Mukatsuno is the port in present-day Yamaga Town, Hayami District, Ōita Prefecture. Nagoya is perhaps the Tobata Ward of Kitakyūshū City, Fukuoka Prefecture.
xv Motori and Ahe are perhaps Mutsure and Ai islands, Fukuoka Prefecture. Shiba is perhaps an island in the Dōkai Bay. The Sakami Sea is perhaps Sakami in the Wakamatsu Ward of Kitakyūshū City, Fukuoka Prefecture.
xvi Cape Yamaka is perhaps Cape Tōmigahana, Kitakyūshū City, Fukuoka Prefecture.
xvii The Kuki Sea is the Dōkai Bay, Kitakyūshū City, Fukuoka Prefecture.

xviii Ito is present-day Ito City, Fukuoka Prefecture.
xix There is a Hiko Island in present-day Shimonoseki City, Yamaguchi Prefecture, but Chūai has already gone past this location, and it geographically overlaps with the land given as tribute to Chūai by Wani earlier in the episode. Iote's home territory is farther west.
xx Naga is perhaps na-ga-agata, "district of Na." The Na River appears in the Jingū book, and the Na Harbor in the Senka book. Na also appears on the gold seal excavated in Shikinoshima, claimed to be a gift from the Chinese emperor and appearing in Chinese historical records. It is the present-day Hakata area of Fukuoka City. Kashihi Palace is marked by the Kashii Shrine in the Kashii area of present-day Fukuoka City, Fukuoka Prefecture.
xxi Ikatsu, Omi of the Nakatomi, appears in the pre-accession record of Jingū and may be the same person as Ikatsu, Muraji of the Nakatomi. Ikatsu, Omi of the Nakatomi, also appears in Ingyō 7, but this is 219 years later. Ōtomonushi, Kimi of Ōmiwa, appears in Suinin 3, 227 years earlier. Ikui, Muraji of the Mononobe, is given in *Original Records* as the son of Mononobe no Tōchine, seen in Suinin 25. Takemotsu, Muraji of the Ōtomo, is given in the Jōgan 3.11 entry of *True History of Three Reigns of Japan* (*Nihon sandai jitsuroku* 日本三代実録, 901) as the son of Takehi, Muraji of the Ōtomo, who was dispatched eastward with Yamato Take in Keikō 40.

Endnotes to Book 9

i "Jingū" means "divine accomplishment" and appears in Book 40 of *Selections of Refined Literature*. It refers to Jingū's especially close connection to the kami and her mythical conquest of the Korean peninsula. Jingū is the only empress to whom a book of the *Chronicles* is dedicated, and is perhaps based on the "Annals of Lü Zhi" 高后紀 in the *History of the Former Han* or the "Annals of Empresses" 皇后紀 books in the *History of the Later Han* (*Hou han shu* 後漢書). However, Jingū also has a founding year and is described in the *Gazetteer of Hitachi Province* (*Hitachi no kuni fudoki* 常陸国風土記) as an ruling emperor. She is counted as a ruling emperor in sources through the early modern period, such as *Table of the Rulers of Japan* (*Nihon ōdai ichiran* 日本王代一覧, 17th cent.), but was not included in the count of Japanese emperors decided by the modern Japanese nation-state in the late nineteenth century.

ii The phrase "From a young age, she was astute and intelligent" appears in the *Han Records of the Eastern Lodge* (*Dongguan Han ji* 東觀漢記) and the *Classified Extracts from Literature* to describe Emperor Ming of Han 漢明帝 (28–75, r. 57–75).

iii The details of Jingū's quest to "purge evils" are given in detail in the Chūai book of *Ancient Matters*. A palace for ritual worship appears in the Suinin book of the *Chronicles*, where one is built for Amaterasu in Ise. Commentators diverge on whether the character of this palace, which seems intended specifically for receiving oracles, differs from those used for general ritual worship. Oyamada is perhaps the Yamada area of present-day Munakata City, Fukuoka Prefecture.

iv In the Chūai book of *Ancient Matters*, Chūai himself plays the zither at an oracle possession of Jingū. The zither features more prominently in the alternative account given below. An "interpreter" also appears in *Ancient Matters*, where it appears to refer to a person charged with explaining the oracle.

v This kami is presumably Amaterasu, whom Jingū worships after conquering Silla, and whose main shrine is in Watarai.

vi In the original, Isuzu, Watarai, and Ise are all prefaced by pillow words.

vii Tsuki-sakaki-itsu-no-mitama-ama-sakaru-muka-tsu-hime is "standing-sakaki-tree-fierce-divine-spirit-heaven-distancing-far-off-lady." "Distancing far off" refers to Amaterasu's command later in the book that "my spirit of violence should not draw near to the empress."

viii A pillow-word emphasizes the swaying of the rice ears in the original. Later, Jingū worships Waka-hiru-me, presumably the same as this kami. The name suggests a daughter or younger sister of Ō-hiru-me (Amaterasu). Waka-hiru-me appears in S 7.1 of the "Age of the Gods." Agatafushi in Oda perhaps refers to the Izawa Shrine in the Arashima District of present-day Toba City, Mie Prefecture.

ix Ame-ni-koto-shiro-sora-ni-koto-shiro-tama-kushi-iri-biko-itsu-no-koto-shiro means "in heaven thing/word-exchange in the sky thing/word exchange spirit mysterious power *affectionate term for young man* fierce thing/word exchange." Usually known as Koto-shiro-nushi, this kami appears in S8.6 of the "Age of the Gods." Tama-kushi perhaps refers to Tama-kushi-hime, with whom Koto-shiro-nushi had intercourse. Jingū worships Koto-shiro-nushi after conquering Silla.

x These are the three kami of the Sumiyoshi Grand Shrine; they were created at Tachibana in Odo when Izanagi cleansed himself upon his return from Yomi in S7.6 of the "Age of the Gods." The kami of Sumiyoshi were associated with the ocean and seafaring. Jingū worships them after conquering Silla.

xi Notorita is perhaps present-day Shimabara City, Nagasaki Prefecture, or the Akizuki area of Asakura City, Fukuoka Prefecture.

xii Matsuo Palace is perhaps in the present-day Kurida area of Chikuzen Town, Asakura District, Fukuoka Prefecture.

xiii *New Selected Records* gives this episode as happening in the reign of Emperor Ōjin, occurring in Kibi, and associated with Kamo-no-wake, who was sent to attack the Kumaso in an earlier entry of the *Chronicles*. Mikasa is the former Mikasa District, now split between Chikushino, Ōnojō, and Dazaifu Cities.

xiv Sosokino is perhaps in the present-day Yanotake area of Asakura City, Fukuoka Prefecture. A marker there commemorates Jingū's defeat of Kumawashi.

xv The former Yasu Town is now part of Chikuzen Town, Asakura District, Fukuoka Prefecture.

xvi Yamato District comprises part of present-day Miyama City, Fukuoka Prefecture. The hypothesis that this place-name might refer to the Yamatai in Chinese historical writing about the Japanese archipelago is now rejected, based on linguistic evidence. Tabura-tsu-hime means "swindling lady."

xvii Tamashima Village is the former Hamatama Town, Higashi Matsuura District, now Karatsu City, Saga Prefecture. The Ogawa River is the Tamashima River. A number of poems in *Myriad Poems* V associate this location with women catching sweetfish.

xviii The Na River is the Nakagawa River, which flows through Fukuoka Prefecture and empties into Hakata Bay.

xix Todoroki Hill is perhaps Antoku in present-day Nakagawa City, Fukuoka Prefecture.

xx This speech consists of quotations from the *Art of War* (*Sun zi bing fa* 孫子兵法), *Records of the Historian*, *History of the Former Han*, *History of the Later Han*, *Master Wu* (*Wuzi* 吳子), and *Zuo Tradition* (*Zuozhuan* 左傳).

xxi This response derives from that given by government officials to Empress Lü in the *History of the Former Han*. Lü Zhi 呂雉 (241–180 BCE) served as regent of the Han Dynasty from 195 to 180 BCE and is an obvious parallel to Jingū, who would later rule as regent herself.

xxii Miwa Town is present-day Chikuzen Town, Fukuoka Prefecture. The Ōnamuchi Shrine there claims to mark this location.

xxiii Perhaps Ai Island off the north coast of Fukuoka Prefecture; it appears in the Chūai book written with different characters. A "messenger from the western sea route" appears in the Kōtoku and Saimei books; the phrase refers to the route to the Korean peninsula.

xxiv Shika Island. The island is well-known as the location where a gold seal of Chinese origin was excavated, and its fisherman famously feature in *Myriad Poems* XVI:3860–3869.

xxv This speech consists of quotations from the *History of the Former Han* and *Master Wu*.

xxvi Yosami is a place-name that appears in the Sujin book. Abiko is a title of nobility for an allied miyatsuko. The ancestor of the Abiko of Yosami is given in the Kaika book of *Ancient Matters* as Kaika's son Take-toyo-hazura-wake. Yosami appears in *New Selected Records* and *Continued Chronicles of Japan* (*Zoku Nihon ki* 続日本紀, 797) in connection with Sumiyoshi. The *Sumiyoshi Record of the Age of the Gods* (*Sumiyoshi taisha jindai ki* 住吉大

社神代記) records an Ōtarumi and an Otarumi charged with worship upon Jingū's return from Korea.

xxvii Ito District appears in the Chūai book. The legend surrounding Jingū's use of a rock to prevent childbirth also appears in *Ancient Matters*, the *Gazetteer of Chikuzen Province* (*Chikuzen no kuni fudoki* 筑前国風土記), and *Myriad Poems* V:813–814.

xxviii Wani is present-day Wani Beach in the Kamitsushima area of Tsushima City, Nagasaki Prefecture.

xxix The white plait and the collection of registers recalls the surrender of the children and consorts of the Qin King in the Annals of Emperor Gaozu in the *History of the Former Han*. The sealing of the registers signified that they would not be used; i.e., that the right of governance has been completely surrendered to Jingū.

xxx The Arinare River could be the Yalu, but more likely is the Alchŏn (Pukchŏn) flowing through northern Kyŏngju City, South Korea.

xxxi Calls for the putting the king to death and a rejection due to it being inauspicious appear after the surrender of the Qin King in the Annals of Emperor Gaozu in the *History of the Former Han*.

xxxii The *Samguk sagi* 三國史記 records Misahŭn going to Wa (Japan) in 402 CE, the year of Naemul's death, after Naemul was succeeded by King Silsŏng (r. 402–417 CE), who may have been trying to distance Naemul's sons from Silla. *Samguk yusa* 三國遺事 gives 390 CE as the year of Misahŭn's departure. "Hatori" is perhaps meant for the fourth rank of the Silla Bone Rank system p'ajin-ch'ŏn; it later appears written as "hotsukan." Kanki is used to designate kings from the states of the Kaya Confederacy.

xxxiii Koguryŏ is given as "Koma," and Paekche as "Kudara." Both are perhaps taken from place-names expanded to refer to the state as a whole. Ku-tara could be "big settlement."

xxxiv Umi is present-day Umi Town, Kasuya District, Fukuoka Prefecture.

xxxv This alternative account begins with the events given in the ninth month of Chūai 8 in the Chūai book.

xxxvi Saba also appears in Keikō 12 and Chūai 8. Utsu-hiko means "reality lord"; kuni-hiko is "land lord." The two may identify lineages. Matsuya may be a place-name, and matsuya-tane a corruption of matsuya-tsu-ane, "older sister of Matsuya." Or, Matsuyatane may be one place-name.

xxxvii This episode has a passing similarity to the biography of Sŏk Uro in Book 45 of the *Samguk sagi*, in which a Silla wife gets revenge on a Wa (Japan) emissary for Wa's killing her husband when the Wa King was angered by Silla. However, in that version of the story, the Wa army that invades in response to the wife's revenge is defeated.

xxxviii Anato appears in the Chūai book.

xxxix Homutachi is the Agatanushi of Anato in the Chūai book. The *Sumiyoshi Record of the Age of the Gods* notes that Ta-momi (hand rubber) rubbed Jingū's skirt and was renamed accordingly and named the principal of the Sumiyoshi Shrine. Tsu-mori (port guardian) suggests the role of this position; a figure with the same office appears in the Kinmei book in connection with foreign relations.

xl Kagosaka and Oshikuma's rebellion also appears in *Ancient Matters*, but there, Jingū is concerned about the disposition of the people upon her return to Japan and pretends that her child has died to test the waters, upon which Kagosaka and Oshikuma try to seize the throne.

xli Togano could be the Togano area in Kita Ward, Osaka City, a field near the Toga River in Nada Ward, Kobe City, or the Yumeno area in Hyōgo Ward, Kobe City. Deer from Togano appear in Nintoku 38.

xlii Suminoe is present-day Sumiyoshi Ward, Osaka City. It is also the location of Sumiyoshi Grand Shrine.

xliii The Muko River in Hyōgo Prefecture flows into Osaka Bay; the port was probably at the river mouth. Jingū's divination resulted in instructions for four places of worship, one each for Amaterasu, Waka-hiru-me, Koto-shiro-nushi, and the three Sumiyoshi kami. These are the same four kami who revealed themselves to Jingū before the conquest of Silla. The locations that they identify suggest the Hirota Shrine in Nishinomiya City, the Ikuta Shrine in Chūō Ward, Kobe City, the Nagata Shrine in Nagata Ward, Kobe City, and the Sumiyoshi Grand Shrine in Sumiyoshi Ward, Osaka City. All four shrines are in the former Setsu Province and are close to each other.

xliv Neko of Yamashiro appears in *New Selected Records* as the Atai of Yamashiro, but Hayama-hime and her younger sister Naga-hime do not appear anywhere else.

xlv There are two competing explanations for the location specified by the Sumiyoshi kami. One is the Sumiyoshi-honmachi area of Higashi Nada Ward, Kobe City, and the other is the current Sumiyoshi Grand Shrine in Sumiyoshi Ward, Osaka City. Norinaga argues for the former, noting that there is a Sumiyoshi shrine, that the geography resembles a long cape or tail (Naga-o), and that this site is close to Muko, where Jingū performed divination. In this explanation, the Sumiyoshi kami were moved to the current Sumiyoshi Grand Shrine according to a record in the Nintoku book of *Ancient Matters*. However, Oshikuma also camps at Sumiyoshi (Suminoe), and since the Sumiyoshi in Kobe is west of the Muko River, if that were where Oshikuma had camped, then Jingū would have had to bypass the enemy army in order to arrive at Muko and perform divination. Furthermore, the entry in the Nintoku book of *Ancient Matters* refers to the establishment of the port at Sumiyoshi, not the shrine. In the eighth century, when the *Chronicles* was compiled, the Sumiyoshi Grand Shrine was closer to the ocean, but Osaka Bay has since been filled in.

xlvi Uji is present-day Uji City, Kyoto Prefecture.

xlvii Hidaka is present-day Hidaka District, Wakayama City.

xlviii The Shino Hachiman Shrine in Gobō City, Wakayama Prefecture, claims to mark the location of Shino Palace.

xlix Shino Shrine is unclear, but Jingū and Ōjin were staying at Shino Palace. Amano is in Katusragi Town, Ito District, Wakayama Prefecture. The Niutsuhime Shrine in this location, and the *Gazetteer of Harima Province* (*Harima no kuni fudoki* 播磨国風土記) attributes the founding of this shrine to Jingū's conquest of Silla.

l The ancestor of the Omi of Wani, Neko of Naniwa Takefurukuma, appears in Nintoku 65 and in the Chūai book of *Ancient Matters*. The distant ancestor of the Omi of Wani, Hiko-kuni-buku, appears in Sujin 9, and the first ancestor of the Omi of Wani, Ama-tarashi-hiko-kuni-oshi-hito, appears in Kōshō 68. A more detailed lineage is given in *New Selected Records*, assuming that the Takefurukuma here is the same as the Naniwa no Sukune in that text.

li Kazuno is the present-day Kazuno area of Kyoto City, Kyoto Prefecture. Ki is the lineage group name. This lineage group does not appear elsewhere. Tago is a family name.

lii Ōsaka is in present-day Ōtsu City, Shiga Prefecture.

liii Kurusu is in the present-day Zeze area of Ōtsu City, Shiga Prefecture. Sasanami is a name for Shiga.

liv This song appears, with some variation, in the Chūai book of *Ancient Matters*.

lv The Seta River (Uji River, Yodo River) begins at Lake Biwa, here called the Ōmi Sea.

lvi Tanakami is the present-day Tanakami-Sekinotsu area of Ōtsu City, Shiga Prefecture.

lvii Chūai is traditionally held to be interred in the Okamisanzai Tumulus in present-day Fujiidera City, Osaka Prefecture.

lviii The king is not named, but an episode in which King Nulchi of Silla (r. 417–458 CE) sends a retainer, Pak Che-sang, to Wa to retrieve his younger brother Misahŭn (Mishikochi-hatori/Mishikochi-hotsukan in the *Chronicles*), who had been exiled to Wa by his uncle, the former king, appears in the *Samguk sagi* text for 418 CE. Ureshihotsu is perhaps a variant of Uru-sohorichika, who is named as the King of Silla in one of the alternative accounts of Jingū's conquest above. Momarishichi is perhaps Che-sang. Horamochi is unclear.

lix Kazuraki is both a family name and a place-name in Yamato, present-day Nara Prefecture. In Jingū 62, Sotsuhiko is sent to attack Silla; the *Record of Paekche* cited in the *Chronicles* gives his name as Sachihiko and a date of 382 CE. Sotsuhiko's daughter Iwa-hime becomes empress to Nintoku and the mother of Richū, Hanzei, and Ingyō. Richū's consort Kuro-hime, the daughter of Ashita no Sukune, was mother of Imperial Prince Ichi-no-he-no-oshiha, the father of Kenzō and Ninken, and according to *Ancient Matters*, Ashita no Sukune was the son of Sotsuhiko. All together, this suggests a tight connection between the Kazuraki lineage group and this series of legendary sovereigns. Sotsuhiko also appears in Ōjin 14 and 16, Nintoku 41, and also in connection with the states of the Korean peninsula.

lx Perhaps Sahi refers to Wani, the Tsushima port town that Jingū stops at on the way to Korea. Alternatively, in Jingū 47, "Sahi" is used as a general moniker for Silla.

lxi Tatara is Tataep'o, a beach in the Saha District of Pusan City, South Korea. The characters used here mean "foot bellows," perhaps recalling iron production on the Korean peninsula. The same location is spelled phonetically in Keitai 23. Sawara Fortress is Sapryang, present-day Yangsan City, South Kyŏngsang Province.

lxii Kuwahara, Sabi (perhaps Sami), Takamiya, and Oshinumi are west of Mt. Kazuraki in present-day Gose City, Nara Prefecture. Ayahito refers to immigrant lineages. The characters suggest from China, but the moniker was used to include peoples from the Korean peninsula as well. These immigrant lineage groups were often associated with advanced technology and the production of goods.

lxiii The Kehi Shrine stands in Tsuruga City, Fukui Prefecture. An episode in which this kami is named by switching names with the crown prince, Ōjin, appears in the Ōjin pre-accession record and in more detail in the Chūai book of *Ancient Matters*. Kehi means "Food-divine spirit."

lxiv Note the similarity to poem 15. The words "august wine" in poem 15 and "sacred wine" here are homophones, but use different characters.

lxv Ming of Wei (Cao Rui 曹叡) was emperor of the state of Cao Wei 曹魏. Since he died in the first month of 239 CE, the ruler should be Cao Fang 曹芳 (r. 239–254 CE). The characters for "Emperor Ming" and source of this error do not appear in the actual *History of Wei* in the *History of the Three Kingdoms*. The Jingchu 景初 era lasted from 237 to 239 CE. The *History of Wei* says "second year"; the *History of Liang* (*Liang shu* 梁書) gives "third year" for this entry, which is the correct date. The Queen of Wa was Pimiko 卑弥呼. Nan Doumi 男斗米 appears multiple times in the *History of Wei* with the name Nan Shengmi 難升米; presumably the latter spelling is correct. The Daifang Commandery was built by the Han Dynasty on the Korean peninsula in what is present-day Hwanghae Province, disputed between North and South Korea, but controlled by the North.

lxvi The *History of Wei* in the *History of the Three Kingdoms* adds a subject to this sentence, "Commander Gong Zun," 太守弓遵, who was acting on imperial orders. Ti Xi 梯㒞 is given there as Ti Jun 梯俊.

lxvii The *History of Wei* in the *History of the Three Kingdoms* gives Iseiki 伊聲者 for Iseisha 伊聲者, Yayayaku 掖邪狗 for Yayayaku 掖耶約, and itemizes the tribute.

lxviii The *Chronicles* cites the *Record of Paekche*, *New Selections of Paekche*, and *Annals of Paekche* at various points, eighteen places in total, but these texts to do not survive. The events and people related to the Korean states described in the latter part of this book would normally be dated to the late fourth century according to the Korean sources *Samguk sagi* and *Samguk yusa*, but the compilers of the *Chronicles* have moved them back 120 years. However, because the Chinese sexagenary calendar cycle repeats after sixty years, this discrepancy appears only when the years are converted to a calendar that numbers the years sequentially and would not have been immediately apparent in the original.

lxix Hishiho is Pihwa Kaya, present-day Ch'angnyeong County, South Kyŏngsang Province. Arihishino-kara is Kŭmgwan Kaya, present-day Kimhae City, South Kyŏngsang Province. Tokuno-kuni is present-day Kyŏngsan City, North Kyŏngsang Province. Ara is Ara Kaya (Ana Kaya), present-day Haman County, South Kyŏngsang Province. Tara is present-day Hapch'ŏn County, South Kyŏngsang Province. Tokujun is present-day Daegu City. Kara is Koryŏng Kaya, better known as Taegaya, in present-day Koryŏng County, North Kyŏngsang Province.

lxx Kokei is present-day Kangjin County in South Chŏlla Province, South Korea. Tomutare is present-day Cheju Island; it appears again in Ōjin 8, then in the Keitai book under the name Tanma in Keitai 2.

lxxi Hiri is perhaps present-day Chŏnju City, North Chŏlla Province, or Naju City, South Chŏlla Province. Hechu is present-day Kimje City, North Chŏlla Province. Homuki is Kongju City, South Ch'ungch'ŏng Province. Hanko is Naju City, South Chŏlla Province. A similar entry with four place-names near these appears in Keitai 6.

lxxii Orusuki is present-day Kongju City, Kyŏnggi Province. It appears as Wirye in the *Samguk sagi* and Yūryaku 20, and was the capital of Paekche until 475, when it fell to Koguryŏ.

lxxiii Mt. Kosa is the present-day Kobu area of Chŏngŭp City, North Chŏlla Province.

lxxiv Tasa Fortress was near the mouth of the Sŏmjin River, which forms the division between present-day South Chŏlla Province and South Kyŏngsang Province.

lxxv Kokuna is perhaps present-day Koksan County in North Hwanghae Province, North Korea. In 371 CE, King Kŭnch'ogo and his son Kŭn'gusu attacked the state of Koguryŏ and captured P'yŏngyang, expanding Paekche's territory northward.

lxxvi The Gosashi Tumulus in Nara City is presently held to be Sakino-tatanami Tomb, but owing to confusion with the tomb of Seimu, Jingū's assigned resting place has varied over the centuries.

Endnotes to Book 10

i Homuta is given in Jingū 3 as Homuta-wake. "Wake" was a term of endearment used for men and later used as a title of nobility granted to regional powerful lineage groups by the central governing authority. In the Chūai book of *Ancient Matters*, Homuta is given as "Ōtomo-wake, also known as Homuda-wake," and in the *Gazetteer of Harima Province*, as "Emperor Homuta." The characters here are phonetic, but those meaning "in the womb," glossed "Homuta," appear in Keitai 6. In *Ancient Matters*, the father of Ōjin's empress Naka-tsu-hime is given as Homuda-no-mawaka-no-hiko, which suggests that "Homuta" derives from a place-name. In Yūryaku 9, there is a Homuta Tomb. The Homuta area is in present-day Habikino City, Osaka Prefecture. The simple quality of Homuta's name, compared to the comparatively adorned names of previous emperors, suggests a change in the ruling dynasty. Ōjin means "responding to the divine" and refers to the oracle that prophesied his birth.

ii In the Jingū book, this place is given as Umi, present-day Umi Town, Kasuya District, Fukuoka Prefecture. Kada is unclear, but is perhaps the Hirakata area of Ogōri City or the Maebara area of Itoshima City, Fukuoka Prefecture.

iii "Intelligent from a young age" and "In his manner and bearing, he had the miraculous appearance of a sage" appear in the biography of Emperor Zhang of Han 漢章帝 (56–88 CE, r. 75–88), in the *Han Records of the Eastern Lodge*.

iv There is no attested source from the Nara period referring to elbow-pads as "homuta." This was perhaps an archaic usage at that time. Alexander Vovin suggests a Korean etymology meaning "arm cover," in keeping with a larger theory of dynastic change beginning with Ōjin and linked to migrants from the Korean peninsula.

v There is an error in the entry indicating the sexagenary cycle for the first day of the month.

vi In *Ancient Matters*, Naka-tsu-hime's father is given as Homudano-mawakano-hiko and her grandfather as Ihokino-iribiko. Ihokino-iribiko is also given as her grandfather in the pre-accession record of Nintoku. Ihokino-iribiko was a son of Emperor Keikō and Consort Yasaka-iri-bime, and the younger brother of Emperor Seimu.

vii *Ancient Matters* gives Arata-no-iratsume of Ki. Ōsazaki is taken from the name of a bird, the Eurasian wren, according to the explanation given in Nintoku 1.

viii *Ancient Matters* gives one more daughter, Mi-no-iratsume. Her omission here may be why the later entry counts twenty children but only nineteen are listed.

ix In *Ancient Matters*, Ōjin marries Miya-nushi-yakahae when he meets her during a tour of Ōmi. The characters used for "omi" in Hifure-no-omi's name may be taken from a Korean title often used in the *Nihon shoki* as a hereditary title for lineage groups with Korean origins.

x "Kawa-mata-naka-tsu-hiko" is "Kuhi-mata-naga-hiko" in *Ancient Matters*. In the Keikō book of *Ancient Matters*, Kuhi-mata-naga-hiko is the son of Oki-nagata-wake, son of Yamato Take. Oto-hime is given in *Ancient Matters* as Okinaga-ma-waka-naka-tsu-hime.

xi The Muraji of Sakurai-tabe oversaw the hereditary guild for rice production (tabe) of Sakurai. They are promoted to Sukune in Tenmu 13. *Ancient Matters* gives the lineage "Itoi-hime, daughter of Shimatarine, ancestor of the Muraji of Sakurai-tabe."

xii Izumi is present-day Akune and Izumi Cities, Kagoshima Prefecture.

xiii The Keikō book of *Ancient Matters* gives Ōusu as the ancestor of the Kimi of Ōta.

xiv *Ancient Matters* gives Ō-yama-mori as ancestor of the Kimi of Hijikata, Heki, and Harihara.

xv The Wake of Fukakawa are not seen elsewhere. Fukakawa is perhaps the Furukawa area in Hida City, Gifu Prefecture.

xvi This road is not known. Ōjin 15 gives a place-name Umayasaka at Karu Hill. Ōjin 11 gives Umayasaki Reservoir. And Jomei 12 gives Umayasaka Palace.

xvii These men are sons of Takeuchi no Sukune in the Kōgen book of *Ancient Matters*, which also lists their descendants. Tsuno no Sukune of Ki is the ancestor of the Omi of Ki, Tsunu, and Sakamoto. He too is dispatched to Paekche under similar circumstances in Nintoku 41. The Omi of Ki were promoted to ason in Tenmu 13. Hata no Yashiro no Sukune is ancestor of the Omi of Hata, Hayashi, Hami, Hoshikawa, Ōmi, and Hatsusebe. The Omi of Hata were promoted to ason in Tenmu 13. Ishikawa no Sukune is named Soga no Ishikawa no Sukune and ancestor of the Omi of Soga, Kawabe, Tanaka, Takamuka, Owarida, Sakurai, and Kishida. Tsuku no Sukune is named Tsuku no Sukune of Heguri and ancestor of the Omi of Heguri and Sawara and the Muraji of Umakui. Nintoku 1 also gives Tsuku no Sukune as the first ancestor of the Omi of Heguri and notes that he was born on the same day as Emperor Nintoku, with whom he exchanged names.

xviii Uji Field presumably is a field in present-day Uji City, Kyoto Prefecture. The region of Kuzuno lies in the present-day Ukyō Ward of Kyoto City, which means that Ōjin is looking northwest from his viewpoint in Uji.

xix A similar entry in *Ancient Matters* claims that it was people from Silla who built the reservoir and that it was named Kudara no ike, "Paekche Reservoir."

This is the first of numerous entries detailing public works projects, which are concentrated in the Ōjin and Nintoku books.

xx "Kennamu" and "Tōkan" are unclear. Shishimu corresponds with the Zhiqin state of the "Biographies of the Wuhuan, Xianbei, and Dongyi" book of the *History of Wei* in the *History of the Three Kingdoms*, which uses the same characters as "Shishimu" and is perhaps the Chisim area in the *Samguk sagi*, present-day Hongsŏng County, South Ch'ungch'ŏng Province, South Korea. Kokuna is Koksŏng County, South Chŏlla Province. Another possible interpretation takes "Tōkan" (lit. "East Korea") as the combination of the three locations preceding it, not as a separate land. The entry for Ōjin 16 gives Kamura, Kōnan, and Nirimu Fortresses as the three lands of Tōkan, and this explanation identifies Kennamu as Kamura, Shishimu as Nirimu, and Kokuna as Kōnan. One interpretation of the "lack of propriety" shown by Paekche is that it is a codeword for the Paekche's surrender to Koguryŏ during the corresponding time period.

xxi Umashiuchi no Sukune is given in the Kōgen book of *Ancient Matters* as the son of Kōgen's own son Hiko-futsu-oshino-makoto and China-bime of Kazuraki, the daughter of Ōnabi, ancestor of the Muraji of Owari.

xxii Iki Island lies in the Korea Strait between Kyushu and Tsushima. *New Selected Records* gives Ama-no-koyane as the ancestor of the Atai of Iki.

xxiii Tsurugi Reservoir also appears in the Ōjin book of *Ancient Matters*. It is in the present-day Ishikawa area of Kashihara City, Nara Prefecture. Karu Reservoir is unclear; Yamato no Karu Reservoir and Karu no Sakaori Reservoir appear in the Suinin and Sujin books of *Ancient Matters*. Kanokaki and Umayasaka are unclear; the latter may refer to the roadway built in Ōjin 3.

xxiv Kuhatsu Village is the present-day Kuhatsu area in Higashi Sumiyoshi Ward, Osaka City.

xxv Kako Harbor is at the mouth of the Kako River in Kakogawa and Takasago Cities, Hyogo Prefecture.

xxvi The *Gazetteer of Harima Province* suggests that the name "Fawn Harbor" was derived from the emperor's assertion that a hill he saw looked like a fawn.

xxvii Along with the entry in Ōjin 16, this entry gives the origins of the powerful Hata allied lineage group. *New Selected Records* gives Yutsuki as a descendant of Qin Shi Huang 始皇帝 (259–210 BCE, r. 221–210 BCE). The same character is used for "Hata" and "Qin."

xxviii This episode corresponds with that in *Ancient Matters*, which further notes that Wani brought *The One Thousand Character Text* (*Qianzi wen* 千字文) and the *Analects* (*Lunyu* 論語) with him. In the *Chronicles*, a formal transmission of the Confucian Classics to Japan occurs later, in Keitai 7. In *Ancient Matters*, Achiki is given as Achikishi, with "kishi" referring to the fourteenth *kilsa* rank of the Silla Bone Rank system.

xxix Wani is given as "Wani-kishi" in *Ancient Matters*, based on the Silla Bone Rank system. The *Continued Chronicles of Japan* entry for 791.4.8 records a lineage group claiming descent from Wani.
xxx "Arata-wake, ancestor of the Kimi of Kamitsukeno" appears in Enryaku 9.7.17 [790 CE] of the *Continued Chronicles of Japan*. That entry was likely based on this one. Achiki is given as Achi in *Ancient Matters*. In Tenmu 12, the group was given the hereditary title of nobility muraji.
xxxi *Ancient Matters* gives a more detailed entry claiming that Wani brought with him *Analects* in ten books and *The One Thousand Character Text*. The latter text was not compiled until the sixth century. The Obito of Fumi, also called the Fumi lineage group of Kōchi, were an immigrant lineage group specializing in reading and writing and were concentrated in the Furuichi District of Kōchi Province (Osaka), present-day Habikino City. The group was given the hereditary title of nobility muraji in Tenmu 12 and that of imiki in Tenmu 14.
xxxii *Samguk sagi* gives King Asin's death as 405 CE, two sexagenary cycles after the date given here.
xxxiii *Samguk sagi* provides a longer narrative in which the younger brother of King Chŏnji took the throne to wait for Chŏnji's return from Wa, but was killed by their uncle. The uncle was later killed, and Chŏnji was made king. Kamura is perhaps Hamyŏl, North Chŏlla Province. Nirimu is perhaps in Kimje City, North Chŏlla Province, or somewhere in South Ch'ungch'ŏng Province.
xxxiv An Omi of Ikuha appears in Nintoku 12. The Kōgen book of *Ancient Matters* gives Nagaeno-sotsuhiko of Kazuraki as the ancestor of the Omi of Ikuha; *New Selected Records* gives Sotsuhiko of Kazuraki. Sotsuhiko here is the Sotsuhiko of Kazuraki referred to in Ōjin 14. Note the similar anecdote recorded in Jingū 62.
xxxv A similar episode is recorded in *Ancient Matters*, but without the entry on Yoshino Palace. This palace was frequently used as a royal getaway from the seventh century. Ruins from the seventh century, but not earlier, have been excavated at Miyataki in Yoshino Town, Nara Prefecture.
xxxvi Naniwa is present-day Osaka City. Ōsumi is perhaps present-day Higashi Yodogawa Ward. An Ōsumi Island appears in Ankan 2 and may be the same place.
xxxvii Mitomo-wake appears in *New Selected Records* and the *True History of Three Reigns of Japan* in connection with Kibi.
xxxviii Perhaps Ōtsu ("great port") refers to Naniwa Harbor. In Jingū 1, the kami of Sumiyoshi request that they be enshrined "in Nagao in Nunakura in Ōtsu."
xxxix Hada is perhaps the eastern part of present-day Sōja City, Okayama Prefecture. Ashimori is perhaps the Ashimori area of Okayama City, Okayama Prefecture.

xl An alternative genealogical record of the rulers of Kibi is given in the Kōrei book of *Ancient Matters*.

xli Shimotsumichi is the present-day western side of Sōja City and the Makibi area of Kurashiki City, Okayama Prefecture. The Omi of Shimotsumichi were promoted to ason in Tenmu 13; those from Makibi were promoted to Ason of Kibi in Tenpyō 18 [746 CE].

xlii Kamitsumichi is present-day eastern Okayama City. The Omi of Kamitsumichi appear in Yūryaku 7 and the pre-accession record of Seinei. They were promoted to ason and named Provincial Miyatsuko of Kibi in Tenpyō-hōji 1 [757 CE]. The Omi of Kaya administered the Takamatsu and Ashimori areas of Okayama City and eastern Sōja City.

xliii Mino District is present-day northern Okayama City, west of the Asahi River.

xliv This place-name is unclear. The Omi of Kasa appear in Nintoku 67 and Taika 1 [645]; they were promoted to ason in Tenmu 13.

xlv Sono District is the present-day northern Makibi area of Kurashiki City, Okayama Prefecture.

xlvi Toki appears later in Ōjin 39. Presumably, there is a mistake. King Chŏnji (Toki) died in 420, according to the *Samguk sagi*, leaving a six-year difference even with the standard two sexagenary cycles inserted. The *Chronicles* and *Samguk sagi* continue to be out-of-sync from this point until the death of King Kaero in 475 CE, perhaps due to different source materials.

xlvii Moku Manchi is perhaps Mokhyŏpmanch'i in the Kaero book of the *Samguk sagi*; Mokhyŏpmanch'i may be a scribal error for the similar Mokryŏmanch'i. In the citation that follows, he appears as Mokura Konshi. Manuscripts of the *Chronicles* other than the Tanaka version have "Mokumanchi of Yamato," which suggests Japanese origins, but the Tanaka version is considered to be older and more authentic on this point, and thus makes peninsular origins a strong possibility. Note the corresponding entry for Mokura Konshi in Jingū 49.

xlviii There is no entry noting when the emperor arrived at this palace. The opening of the Ōjin book of *Ancient Matters* seats Ōjin's rule at "Akira Palace in Karu Island." The *Continued Chronicles of Japan* records a "Toyoakira Palace on Karu Island." Norinaga notes that "Island" need not refer to a land surrounded by sea in the original, but may simply be a demarcated area.

Endnotes to Book 11

i The similarity of Saza in "Ōsazaki" to "San," one of the Five Kings of Wa, suggests equivalence, though San is succeeded by his younger brother Chin and Nintoku by his son, Hanzei. Nintoku means "Benevolent Virtue" and refers to the nature of Nintoku's reign, touted as a model of benevolent kingship.

ii The phrase "From a young age, he was astute and intelligent" appears in the *Han Records of the Eastern Lodge* and the *Classified Extracts from Literature* to describe Emperor Ming of Han; the full sentence appears verbatim to describe Empress Jingū.

iii A similar phrase appears in the chapter "Four Barbarian Tribes" 四夷 in Book 97 of the *History of the Jin* (*Jin shu* 晉書).

iv This description of kingship is taken from the "Annals of Empress Lü Zhi" in the *History of the Former Han*.

v Uji-no-waki-iratsuko alludes to the description of a kingdom lacking wise men in the "Ba Yi" 八佾 chapter of *Analects*.

vi Use of "Indeed" (Jp. *Sore*) for emphasis is especially pronounced in Books 11–13.

vii This sentence derives from the "Annals of Emperor Wen" in the *History of the Former Han*.

viii Similar phrases appear in Pei Songzhi's *Commentary on the History of the Three Kingdoms* on the "Annals of Emperor Wen" (Cao Pi) in the *History of Wei*, and later, in the pre-accession record of Emperor Ingyō.

ix This phrase is based on the *Selections of Refined Literature*. The Sinitic text gives "state," but the vernacular gloss "realm."

x The poem in *Ancient Matters* begins with "Chihayaburu," a pillow word for Uji, but in the *Chronicles* this has been changed to "Chihaya-hito," the meaning of which is unclear.

xi Kawara is present-day Kawara in the Tanabe area of Kyōtanabe City, Kyoto Prefecture. An explanation for this place-name is given in Sujin 10. In the Ōjin book of *Ancient Matters*, this place is called "Kawara" because of the sound made by the hooks used to drag in Ō-yama-mori's corpse when they struck his armor.

xii The *Ancient Matters* version of this song has "at the rapids of the crossing" instead of "at the crossing place." "My lord" might be understood as the address used by a wife to a husband. The "beloved" is perhaps Ō-yama-mori's wife. In the original, the word "Azusa-yumi" (Catalpa bow) precedes "spindle tree" to provide rhythm.

xiii Mt. Nara is in the north of present-day Nara City.

xiv In *Ancient Matters*, Uji-no-waki-iratsuko simply expires, and there is no resurrection. Tsuda Sōkichi has suggested that the version in the *Chronicles* is meant to emulate suicides in Chinese historical tales. The use of "expire" in *Ancient Matters* puts Uji-no-waki-iratsuko on the level of an emperor, versus "perish" used here.

xv Uji-no-waki-iratsuko's death is commemorated in *Myriad Poems* IX:1795 and by Fujiwara Yoshino (786-846) in an 840.5.6 address recorded in the *Continued Chronicle of Later Japan*. Mt. Uji is perhaps Mt. Todōmaru in Uji City.

xvi A memorial marking the location of Takatsu Palace can be found on the campus of Osaka Prefectural Kōzu High School, but there is no evidence that this location was in fact Nintoku's palace.

xvii This sentence is taken from *Six Secret Teachings* (*Liu Tao* 六韜).

xviii *Ancient Matters* and the Tenpyō 1 (729.8.24) pronouncement naming Kōmei as empress in the *Continued Chronicles of Japan* both have "Iwa-no-hime, daughter of Sotsuhiko of Kazuraki." In the latter work, this event is being used a precedent for naming the daughter of a vassal as empress. Poems II:85–90 in the *Myriad Poems* are attributed to Iwa-no-hime.

xix "Mitsu-ha" means "beautiful teeth," and "wake" is a term of endearment added to the ends of names.

xx Ōe-no-izaho-wake [Richū] is given in the Nintoku book of both the *Chronicles* and *Ancient Matters* as Ōe-no-izaho-wake, but with different characters for "Ōe." One possible meaning is "older brother Izaho"; another is "Izaho of Ōe," referring to a place-name in Naniwa. Sumi-no-e-no-naka is killed in the pre-accession record of Richū. *Ancient Matters* gives Mitsu-ha-wake as Tajiji-no-mizuha-wake; he is considered to be Chin in the Five Kings of Wa. A sword excavated from the Etafunayama Tumulus in Kumamoto Prefecture is inscribed with characters closely resembling "Tajihi" and "ha" in "Tajiji-no-mizuha-wake," but later excavation of a sword with a more legible inscription from the Inariyama Tumulus in Saitama Prefecture suggests that the Etafunayama sword has the same inscription of "Waka-takeru" and refers to Emperor Yūryaku. "O" in O-asazuma-wakugo-no-sukune could mean brave, valiant, or small, and could be shared with the "O" at the beginning of Yūryaku's name. Asazuma is a place-name in the Katsujō District of Yamato, part of present-day Gose City, and is the birthplace of Ingyō's mother. "Wakugo" appears in the names of Kenzō and Ninken and means "young child." The term is commonly attached to place-names to create a personal name. "Sukune" is a term of affection indicating "smaller" or "younger." King Sai or Sei of the Five Kings of Wa could be from the Asa or the zu of Ingyō's name.

xxi Nintoku's relationship with Kami-naga-hime is given in Ōjin 11 and 13. In *Ancient Matters*, Ō-kusaka is given as Hatabino-ō-iratsuko, with the alternative name Ō-kusaka. Kusaka is a place-name in present-day Ōsaka Prefecture. In Yūryaku 1.3, she is given as Hatabi of Kusaka, with the alternative name Tachibana-no-hime. In Ankō 1.2 and the Ankō book of *Ancient Matters*, Ankō attempts to make Hatabi the consort for his younger brother, who would later become Emperor Yūryaku, and she becomes his empress in Yūryaku 1.3. In Richū 1.9, she is Richū's consort, and in Richū 6, she is named empress. The latter marriage is not in *Ancient Matters* and is much later in time in the *Chronicles*, which suggests either another person with the same name or some issue with the source material.

xxii This episode, also appearing in *Ancient Matters*, establishes Nintoku as a ideal Confucian sage-king. The *New Collection of Poems Old and New* (*Shinkokin wakashū* 新古今和歌集, 1205) and the *Collection of Japanese and Chinese Poems for Singing* (*Wakan rōeishū* 和漢朗詠集) include a poem about this episode attributed to Nintoku, though it is more likely a revision of the 906 *Nihongi* banquet poem by Fujiwara no Tokihira 藤原時平 (871–909), which is also about Nintoku.

xxiii This phrase is taken from *Sizi jiangde lun* 四子講德論, by Wang Bao 王褒, in the *Selections of Refined Literature*.

xxiv This sentence and the one preceding it are likely taken from *Six Secret Teachings*.

xxv This sentence is perhaps taken from *Xunzi* 荀子 (ca. 280s–230s BCE).

xxvi The full version of this phrase, "to not even collect objects dropped on the road," appears in Kōgyoku 1 and elsewhere in the Chinese canon.

xxvii Because the river course has changed over time, the precise location of this public works project is unknown, but the river ultimately emptied into present-day Osaka Bay. The Ōkawa, or upper section of the Kyū-Yodo River, is the most likely candidate.

xxviii Repair and maintenance of this dyke appears in the Tenpyō-shōhō 2 [750 CE], Hōki 1 [770 CE], and Hōki 3 [772] entries of the *Continued Chronicles of Japan*. The two Tsutsumine Shrines in Kadoma City, Osaka Prefecture, claim to be built in order to honor the kami of Mamuta Dyke.

xxix Musashi Province is present-day Tokyo Prefecture, most of Saitama Prefecture, and part of Kanagawa Prefecture. Kowakubi is not seen elsewhere. Kōchi is present-day Osaka Prefecture. The Muraji of Murata are given in *New Selected Records* as descendants of Hiko-yai-mimi, who is not seen in the *Chronicles*, but is perhaps related to a son of Jinmu named Hiko-yai in *Ancient Matters*. The Muraji of Murata are promoted to sukune in Tenmu 13.

xxx A Chinese compound referring to the god of the Yellow River is used, but the gloss renders this as kami. "Veneration" in this case meant human sacrifice.

xxxi The gloss for "oath" refers to the same kind of oath used to determine truth as seen elsewhere in the *Chronicles*, but the Chinese character refers to a request or prayer.

xxxii Kowakunibi Gap is perhaps in the Senbayashi area of Asahi Ward, Osaka City. Koromonoko Gap is in the Taima area of Neyagawa City. The two locations are about eight kilometers apart.

xxxiii *New Selected Records* gives the Omi of Ikuha as the descendants of Sotsuhiko of Kazuraki.

xxxiv The great ditch might go north from the Kizu River or refer to the Naga Reservoir, both in the Ebisumae area of Tono in Jōyō City, Kyoto Prefecture. Kurukuma is northwest Jōyō City and southern Kumiyama Town, Kuse

TEXT-CRITICAL ENDNOTES

District, Kyoto Prefecture. Another flood control project in Kurukuma is given in Suiko 15.

xxxv The Yokono Dyke was in the present-day Tatsumiminami area of Ikuno Ward, Osaka City, perhaps on the Hirakawa River.

xxxvi Ikai Harbor is the present-day Ikaino area of Ikuno Ward, Osaka City, which used to be on the east bank of the Hirakawa River.

xxxvii Obashi is the present-day Obase area of Tennōji Ward, Osaka City.

xxxviii Archaeological excavation has revealed that such a route ran from the remains of a palace discovered in Osaka, probably Naniwa Nagaratoyosaki Palace of Emperor Kōtoku, to the south. The compiler of the *Chronicles* has backdated its creation to Nintoku.

xxxix Tajihi Village is present-day Tanpi area of Habikino City, Osaka Prefecture.

xl Komuku is present-day Kanan Town, Minami Kawachi District, Osaka Prefecture.

xli The Ishi River flows northward through southeast Osaka Prefecture from Kawachinagano City before emptying into the Yamato River. The four locations here are unclear.

xlii Kuwata is present-day Kameoka City, Kyoto Prefecture.

xliii "Deep among the waters" may be a pillow word. It resembles a similar pillow word used in a poem in Keitai 7 applied to "uo" (fish), which is similar in initial sound to "omi" (vassal). The syllabic meter of the poem, 5-7-7, suggests a short poem meant to be replied to.

xliv Inase-iri-biko is given as the first ancestor of the Wake of Harima in Keikō 4. *Original Records* gives the establishment of the Provincial Miyatsuko of Harima to the reign of Keikō's successor, Seimu. Hayamachi is not seen elsewhere.

xlv Asazuma is the present-day Asazuma area of Gose City, Nara Prefecture, but Hika is unclear. Asazuma is in Kazuraki, the home of the empress.

xlvi Cape Kumano is in present-day Shingū City, Wakayama Prefecture.

xlvii In *Ancient Matters*, the empress hears the news from an official passing through Naniwa to Kibi.

xlviii The "tori" of Toriyama ("Bird Mountain") evokes images of a messenger.

xlix The Yamashiro River is the Kizu River. The empress has gone up the Yodo River and turned into the Kizu.

l Tsutsuki Hill is near present-day Kannon Temple in Kyōtanabe City, Kyoto Prefecture. In *Ancient Matters*, the empress stays in Tsutsuki at the home of a Korean named Nurinomi.

li Kuchimochi is not seen elsewhere. Kuchi means "mouth" and suggests delivering an oral message. In *Ancient Matters* he is given as Kuchiko.

lii Kuniyori-hime is given in *Ancient Matters* as Kuchi-hime.

liii *Ancient Matters* does not describe the death of Iwa-no-hime or the later naming of Yata as empress. However, it does note the creation of the Yata hereditary guild. Iwa-no-hime's burial site is traditionally reckoned to be the Hishiage Tumulus, a keyhole-shaped burial mound in Nara City, Nara Prefecture.

liv Togano appears in Jingū 1, but this place is perhaps different. *Commentary on the Nihongi* (*Shaku Nihongi*, 釈日本紀) suggests a location corresponding with the present-day Yumeno area of Hyōgo Ward, Kobe City, but from this place, deer would not be audible in Naniwa (Osaka), where the emperor and empress were in the palace. Another Togano nearer to Naniwa is in present-day Kita Ward of Osaka City.

lv Ina Disctrict is perhaps the area on the Ina River that originates in present-day Inagawa Town, Kawabe Disctrict, Hyōgo Prefecture, and flows south to Osaka Bay.

lvi Nuta is perhaps present-day Takehara City, Hiroshima Prefecture. The Saekibe of Aki appear in Keikō 51. The Sinographs used for "relocate" are used in the Civil and Penal Codes for moving a pardoned criminal to a new area to avoid retaliation by the victim's family, though the vernacular gloss simply gives "send, dispatch."

lvii A similar story appears in the *Gazetteer of Settsu Province* (*Settsu no kuni fudoki* 摂津国風土記), quoted in the *Commentary on the Nihongi*.

lviii In *Ancient Matters*, the couple flee to Mt. Kurahashi in Yamato.

lix Soni is present-day Soni Valley east of the Murō area in Uda City, Nara Prefecture. In *Ancient Matters* the couple are killed at Soni.

lx Komoshiro in Ise is unclear.

lxi Perhaps the Ioki River refers to the Kumozu River, which flows through the present-day Ieki area of Tsu City, Mie Prefecture.

lxii The Kimi of Ōmi no Yama is unclear; it may refer to the administrator of the Yama hereditary guild of Ōmi Province. In *Ancient Matters*, it is the wife of Ōtate, Muraji of the Yama hereditary guild, who has these jewels. The Kimi of Sasaki no Yama in Ōmi appears in the pre-accession record of Yūryaku. Iwasaka-hime may be taken from the place-name Iwasaka in Sakurai City, Nara Prefecture. Inner palace ladies were often provided to the imperial clan by powerful lineage groups.

lxiii Ishikawa is in present-day Habikino City, Osaka Prefecture.

lxiv Yosami Reservoir appears in Sujin 62. It is perhaps the present-day Abiko and Niwai areas of Higashi Sumiyoshi Ward, Osaka City. Abiko was a title of nobility and appears as a place-name throughout Japan.

lxv The Mozu area spans from the present-day Nakamozu area, Kita Ward, to the Hamadera-ishizu area, Nishi Ward, of Sakai City. Ishizuhara appears in Nintoku 67.

lxvi According to *Commentary on the Civil Codes* (*Ryō no gige* 令義解), there were seventeen households of this group in Yamato, Kōchi, and Setsu Provinces.

lxvii Mamuta Dyke appears in Nintoku 11. In *Ancient Matters*, this story is set in Himeshima, perhaps the present-day Himeshima area of Nishi-yodogawa Ward, Osaka City.

lxviii Ishi Port is perhaps present-day Katsuura City and Isumi District, Chiba Prefecture, or Ishinomaki City and Oshika District, Miyagi Prefecture.

lxix In Suiko 1, the Shitennō Temple is built in Arahaka of Naniwa, present-day Tennōji Ward of Osaka City. Arahaka means "abandoned tomb," and the Chausuyama Tumulus is nearby.

lxx Meki is not seen elsewhere.

lxxi Tsuke is the present-day Tsuge-mura area of Nara City, Nara Prefecture.

lxxii The Himoro (ice room) Shrine in the Fukusumi area of Tenri City, Nara Prefecture, claims to mark this location.

lxxiii Ishitsuhara is the present-day Hamadera-ishizu area in Nishi Ward, Sakai City.

lxxiv The division of Kibi into Upper, Central, and Lower did not happen until the seventh century. A Kawashima District appears in Ōjin 22.9. The river is perhaps the Takahashi River in Okayama Prefecture. The sinographs give only "great snake," but the vernacular specifies the element of water, as opposed to other giant snakes in the *Chronicles*.

lxxv The passage from "woke up early" to "flowed outward" is taken from the *Writings of the Huainan Masters*.

lxxvi *Ancient Matters* gives his age at death as eighty-three in 427 CE. Of the Five Kings of Wa, San in the *History of Liang* dies in 425 CE and is traditionally thought to be Nintoku, based on his Japanese name "Ōsasaki," though a competing explanation identifies Nintoku's successor, Richū, as San.

lxxvii Nintoku's tomb is traditionally considered to be the Daisenryō Tomb, the largest tomb in Japan and part of a large cluster of tombs in Sakai City, Osaka Prefecture.

Endnotes to Book 12

i "Izaho-wake" is an abbreviated name for Ōe-no-izaho-wake. "Izaho" is unclear. "Wake" is a term of endearment often added to the ends of names. "Richū" means "tread center" and is probably taken from the tenth hexagram, in the King Wen sequence, of the *Book of Changes*. "Tread" refers to treading on the tail of a tiger without being bitten, that is, to the weak stepping on the strong and still making progress. The fifth line of the trigram is "strong and in the center, and even while treading on [assuming] one's divinely assigned position [imperial rank], does not fail."

ii One theory equates Richū with San of the Five Kings of Wa because there is a "za" in his name, the next King of Wa, Chin, was his younger brother, and Richū was followed by his younger brother Hanzei.

iii Sumie-no-nakatsu also rebels in *Ancient Matters*, but there is no mention of rape. Perhaps the *Chronicles* is attempting to provide a rationale for the rebellion, or *Ancient Matters* to elide over the matter.

iv In *Ancient Matters*, the Atai of Aya, Achi no Omi, saves the young sovereign, but the other two men, Tsuku no Sukune and Ōmae no Sukune, are not mentioned. Tsuku no Sukune, who appears in the pre-accession record of Nintoku, is the son of Takeuchi no Sukune. Mononobe no Ōmae no Sukune is given in the *Original Records* as the descendant of the heavenly kami Nigi-haya-hi, and he becomes Ō-muraji in the reign of Emperor Ankō.

v In *Ancient Matters*, Sumie-no-nakatsu opportunistically sets fire to the palace when Richū is passed out drunk. That text specifies that it was Naniwa Palace that burned.

vi Haniu Hill is the present-day Nonoue area of Habikino City, Osaka Prefecture.

vii Ōsaka is the present-day Ōsaka area in Kashiba City, Nara Prefecture. Richū is escaping Kōchi to Yamato via the Anamushi Pass.

viii Mt. Asuka is in the mountains of the present-day Komagatani area of Habikino City, Osaka Prefecture. It should be distinguished from the Mt. Asuka in Nara Prefecture.

ix Tagima is the present-day Taima area in Katsuragi City, Nara Prefecture. The maiden is advising him to use the Takenouchi Pass.

x Mt. Tatsuta is in the mountains west of present-day Sangō Town, Ikoma District, Nara Prefecture. Richū's ultimate destination is the Isonokami Shrine, east of Mt. Tatsuta.

xi Noshima is the present-day Noshima area of northwest Awaji City, Hyōgo Prefecture. Its fishermen appear in *Myriad Poems* VI 933–934, and those of Awaji in Ōjin 22.3 and the Nintoku pre-accession record.

xii Agoko appears in the pre-accession record of Nintoku, where he is dispatched to Korea. He is recalled by his older brother, who drafts eighty fishermen from Awaji into service.

xiii Kakihami is unknown. Kurusu is perhaps in the northern part of present-day Gose City, Nara Prefecture.

xiv In *Ancient Matters*, Tsuku no Sukune is not sent with him.

xv The question derives from a passage in the "Yan Yuan" 顏淵 chapter of the *Analects*: "How would it be to kill the unprincipled on behalf of the principled?"

xvi In *Ancient Matters*, Mitsu-ha-wake rewards the man, then kills him.

xvii In *Ancient Matters*, Mitsu-ha-wake stays at Isonokami to worship the kami there, but in the *Chronicles* he rushes back to Yamato.

xviii The location of Murahase is unclear.

xix The capital was built in Iware in Richū 2, and the origins of the name of the palace there are given in Richū 3. Jingū 3.1 identifies her palace also as Wakasakura in Iware. *Gleanings from Ancient Tidings* (*Kogo shūi* 古語拾遺, 807) suggests that Jingū's palace was Wakasakura, and that Richū's was the Later Wakasakura. The location is perhaps the Ike-no-uchi area of Sakurai City, Nara Prefecture.

xx The Heguri, Soga, and Mononobe lineage groups would all end up serving at the highest levels of state administration as Ō-omi or Ō-muraji. This entry serves to backdate their meritorious service. Machi no Sukune of Soga is perhaps the father of Soga no Karako, who appears in Yūryaku 9.3. In *Gleanings from Ancient Tidings*, he is appointed chief officer of the three treasuries (sacred, imperial, and state). Mononobe no Ikofu is the tenth-generation descendant of the kami Nigi-haya-hi according to the *Original Records*. Tsubura no Ōmi is given as Tsubura no Ō-omi of Kazuraki in Yūryaku 1.3 His daughter Kara-hime would become consort to Yūryaku.

xxi Perhaps the same as the Ichishi Reservoir of Iware in Richū 3.11. A reservoir with the same name appears in a poem in Keitai 7.9 and *Myriad Poems* III:416. It was perhaps located in the Ike-no-uchi area of Sakurai City, Nara Prefecture.

xxii Areshi is perhaps referred to in the *Original Records* in reference to the establishment of the Allied Miyatsuko of Kashiwade, but the reference is inconclusive.

xxiii Nagamai, Muraji of the Mononobe, appears in *New Selected Records* as the fourth-generation descendant of Nigi-haya-hi.

xxiv Mt. Wakinokami-no-muro is perhaps a mountain in the present-day Muro area of Gose City, Nara Prefecture.

xxv *New Selected Records* traces two Miyatsuko of the Wakasakurabe lineage groups to Nigi-haya-hi, patron kami of the Mononobe. The Omi of Wakasakurabe are promoted to ason in Tenmu 13.11.

xxvi Similar passages appear in the Du Yu 杜預 commentary to the *Zuo Tradition*, the *Records of the Historian*, and the *History of the Former Han*.

xxvii The Isonokami Canal was built in the present-day Furu area of Tenri City, Nara Prefecture. A canal to Isonokami Canal was built in Saimei 2.

xxviii "From whence the birds come and go" is a pillow word for "ha" (feather), usually used in verse. A Mt. Hasa appears in a poem in Ingyō 24.6. It is perhaps in the present day Ōgaru area of Kashihara City, Nara Prefecture.

xxix The Civil and Penal Codes provide for sixty people in a hereditary guild serving the Office of the Treasury and forty people in a hereditary guild for the smaller Office of the Exchequer. The language here could apply to either, but as the former was established by Yūryaku, the assumption here is that the latter is referred to here. This accords with the account of two treasuries in the *Gleanings from Ancient Tidings*. Along with *Ancient Matters*, that text also associates these offices with immigrants from the Korean peninsula.

xxx Funashi-wake, Futo-hime-no-iratsume, and Taka-tsuru-no-iratsume are not seen elsewhere.

xxxi Washi-sumi is not seen elsewhere.

xxxii The ancestor of the Provincial Miyatsuko of Sanuki is given as Imperial Prince Kamikushi in Keikō 4.2. Ashikui-wake of Awa Province are not seen elsewhere. Perhaps they resided in the present-day Shishikui area of Kaiyō Town, Kaifu District.

xxxiii *Ancient Matters* gives his age at death as sixty-four.

xxxiv Richū's tomb is traditionally held to be the southern Mozu-no-mimi-hara tomb or Kami-ishi-zu-misanzai Tumulus in present-day Sakai City, Osaka Prefecture.

xxxv Hanzei means "return to propriety" and is perhaps taken from the *Gongyang Commentary on the Spring and Autumn Annals* (*Gongyang zhuan* 公羊传).

xxxvi The location of this palace is unknown.

xxxvii *Ancient Matters* likens his teeth to a string of jewels.

xxxviii The Annei book of *Ancient Matters* notes a Mi-i (august well) Palace in Awaji, and the Nintoku book of *Ancient Matters*, the presentation of water from a spring in Awaji. These two mentions may correspond to a single location.

xxxix Tajihi as used in the emperor's name may refer in fact to the Tajihi area of Kōchi, now part of Sakai, Ōsakasayama, and Matsubara Cities, Osaka Prefecture. A similar legend appears in more detail in *New Selected Records* for the lineage of Tajihi no Sukune.

xl Kogoto, ancestor of the Omi of the Ōyake, is given in *Ancient Matters* as Kogoto no Omi of Wani. The Ōyake were a powerful lineage group from the northeast Nara Basin and were related to the Wani, who occupied the same area. The Kōshō book of *Ancient Matters* gives their origin as Ame-oshi-tarashi-hiko, son of Kōshō. They are promoted to ason in Tenmu 13.11. This is the only use of "empress-consort, second degree" in the *Chronicles*, akin to the singular use of "empress-consort" in the Richū book above.

xli Imperial Princess Takara is male in *Ancient Matters*, Takara no Miko. In the same work, Imperial Prince Takabe is female, Takabe-no- iratsume.

xlii The location of this palace is unknown. Tajihi District in Kōchi Province, the present-day Ueda area of Matsubara City has been suggested.

xliii This phrase is taken from the Annals of Emperor Cheng in the *History of the Former Han*. A similar phrase appears in Sujin 12.9.

xliv A number of manuscripts give "sixth year" instead of "fifth year," perhaps because this resolves an open year between Hanzei and Ingyō. However, the calendar date given accords only with the fifth year. *Ancient Matters* gives his age at death as sixty and his place of burial as Mozuno.

Endnotes to Book 13

i "Ingyō" is taken from the "Yao dian" 堯典 book of the *Classic of Documents* (*Shangshu* 尚書) and means "genuinely respectful."

ii "Gracious and unassuming" was a phrase normally paired with "appearance" and translated as "refinement" that was used for Emperors Suizei and Nintoku. It appears here as only "from refinement." Based on the appearance of this phrase in the "Annals of Emperor He of Han," in *Han Records of the Eastern Lodge*, and the *Classified Extracts from Literature* citations of the *Han Records of the Eastern Lodge*, here the meaning is "from a young age, he was clever." A boy would usually tie up his hair around age seventeen or eighteen.

iii This sentence and the one preceding it are derived from the "Annals of Emperor Wen of Han" in the *History of the Former Han*.

iv The last half of this sentence is derived from the "Annals of Emperor Wen" in the *History of the Former Han*.

v The two clauses of this sentence are both taken from the *Selections of Refined Literature*.

vi This passage derives from the "Annals of Emperor Guangwu" 光武帝紀 in the *History of the Later Han*.

vii This passage and the one preceding it derive from the "Annals of Emperor Wen" in the *History of the Former Han*.

viii Oshi-saka-no-ō-naka-tsu-hime is given in the pre-accession record of Ankō as the daughter of Imperial Prince Waka-nuke-futa-mata, a son of Emperor Ōjin. The Ōjin book of *Ancient Matters* gives her mother as Waka-nuke-futa-mata's aunt, named Momo-shiki-iro-be, with the alternative name Oto-hime-ma-wake-hime. Oshi-saka is in the Shikijō District of Yamato, now part of Sakurai City, Nara Prefecture.

ix This passage derives from the Annals of Emperor Wen in the *History of the Former Han*.

x "Anaho" is a place-name in Nara Prefecture, in the present-day Isonokami area of Tenri City. Ankō's palace was called "Anaho Palace of Isonokami."

xi "Ō-hatsuse-no-waka-take" means "Great young brave of Hatsuse." Hatsuse is in present-day Nara Prefecture and refers to the area along the Hasegawa River. Yūryaku built his palace in Asakura, in Hatsuse.

xii Kinashi is perhaps a place-name; Karu is a place-name in Yamato Province. Kinashi-no-karu would later be named crown prince, but would not accede to the throne. Nagata-no-ō-iratsume is given as an alternative name for a daughter of Richū, Imperial Princess Nakashi, in the pre-accession record of Yūryaku. Commentators are divided on whether there is an error here or there. Sakai is probably a place-name. Or, when Sakai-no-kuro-hiko is killed in the Yūryaku book, the Muraji of the Sakai hereditary guild, Nie no Sukune, holds Sakai-no-kuro-hiko's corpse in his arms, which leads to the suggestion that Sakai-no-kuro-hiko's nurse was from the Sakai lineage group. Imperial Princess Karu-no-ō-iratsume has the alternative name So-tōri-no-iratsume in *Ancient Matters*, but in the *Chronicles*, So-tōri-no-iratsume is the younger sister of the empress. Yatsuri and Tachibana are both place-names in present-day Takaichi District, Nara Prefecture. Sakami is a place-name in present-day Honkanbe in the Imaise area of Ichinomiya City, Aichi Prefecture. Ō means "grand." Hatsuse is a place-name in the present-day Hase and Kurozaki areas of Sakurai City, Nara Prefecture. Yūryaku builds his palace in Asakura, Hatsuse.

xiii Ingyō's attempt to right the confusion associated with lineage groups and their titles is frequently praised as a signature achievement, for example, in *Ancient Matters* and the *New Selected Records*. Such trials as that by boiling water also appear in Ōjin 9.4 and Keitai 24.9, and in the "Dongyi" 東夷 book of the *History of the Sui Dynasty*.

xiv Umakashi Hill is in present-day Asuka Village, Takaichi District, Nara Prefecture.

xv Legend holds that the Muromiyayama Tumulus is the tomb of Takeuchi no Sukune, though the tomb of Sotsuhiko of Kazuraki has also been suggested. The tumulus is in present-day Gose City, Nara Prefecture.

xvi Oharida is in present-day Asuka Village, Takaichi District, Nara Prefecture, and was the location of Suiko's palace.

xvii Hanzei is traditionally held to be buried in the Tadeiyama Tumulus, present-day Sakai City, Osaka Prefecture.

xviii In the *Chronicles*, So-tōri-no-iratsume is the alternative name of Oto-hime, younger sister of Oshi-saka-no-ō-naka-tsu-hime, but in *Ancient Matters*, it is another name for Imperial Princess Karu-no-ō-iratsume, daughter of Ingyō and Oshi-saka-no-ō-naka-tsu-hime. As Karu-no-ō-iratsume features prominently in the events of Ingyō 23 two decades later, it seems unlikely that this is a single individual. Norinaga suggests that since the Fujiwara hereditary guild would later be created for So-tōri-no-iratsume, she was actually Fujiwara no Kotofushi, and that So-tōri should be read Soto-fushi. Fujiwara no Kotofushi was a daughter of Ōjin in *Ancient Matters*. Conversely, the lineage group could be named after her palace, Fujiwara Palace, a pattern seen in the Senka book of the *Chronicles*.

xix Sakata is the Sakata District of Shiga Prefecture, now part of Maibara City.

xx Ichii is the present-day Ichi area of Tenri City, Nara Prefecture. A poem in the Ōjin book of *Ancient Matters* links the Ichii lineage group with the Wani, which occupied the same area. The Ichii were promoted to ason in Tenmu 13.11.

xxi The *House Record of the Fujiwara* (*Tōshi kaden* 藤氏家傳, 760) claims that its paragon Fujiwara no Kamatari was born at the Fujiwara estate in the Takaichi Distrcit of Yamato Province. *Myriad Poems* II:103, presented by Tenmu to Kamatari's daughter, locates the estate at Ōhara, the present-day Ohara area of Asuka Village, Takaichi District, Nara Prefecture. Alternatively, he might have been born in Fujiwara Palace, since Jitō ruled from there. Fujiwara Palace is in the present-day Takadono area of Kashihara City, Nara Prefecture.

xxii Chinu refers to Izumi Province, the southern part of present-day Osaka Prefecture. Chinu is given here as being in neighboring Kōchi, but Chinu did not divide from Izumi until 716 CE.

xxiii Hineno also appears in Yūryaku 14.4. It is perhaps the present-day Hineno area in Izumisano City, Osaka Prefecture.

xxiv Ōtomo no Muroya is promoted to Ō-Muraji in the pre-accession record of Yūryaku. An entry for Jōgan 3.11 (860 CE) in the *True History of Three Reigns of Japan* also refers to Ō-Muraji Muroya in the time of Ingyō.

xxv Akashi is present-day Akashi City, Hyōgo Prefecture.

xxvi Naga Village is perhaps the Nakagawa area in present-day Anan City, Tokushima Prefecture.

xxvii In *Ancient Matters*, it is Ki-nashi-no-karu who is banished to Iyo on the island of Shikoku, an event referred to in the subsequent poem.

xxviii Along with Mt. Amanokaguyama, Mt. Miminashi and Mt. Unebi formed a set of three mountains of topographical significance in the southern Nara Basin.

xxix Kotohiki Slope is perhaps the same as Kotohiki Field, which appears in Keikō 40, where it too is along the path from Nara to Osaka.

xxx *Ancient Matters* gives his tomb as Ega-no-nagae in Kōchi. Traditionally, Ingyō's resting place is taken to be the Ichinoyama Tumulus in Fujidera City, Osaka Prefecture.

xxxi As both the *Chronicles* and *Ancient Matters* give Sakai-no-kuro-hiko as Ingyō's second son, the account in the note appears to be the correct one. Anaho is a place-name in the present-day Isonokami area of Tenri City, Nara Prefecture. Ankō appears in the biography of Sun Chen 孫綝 (232–259) in the *History of Wu* (*Wu shu* 吳書) in the *History of the Three Kingdoms* and means "peaceful tranquility." Kō of the Five Kings of Wa is derived from the "ho" of Anaho, Ankō's name.

xxxii In *Ancient Matters*, Ōmae no Sukune captures the prince and surrenders him to the court, upon which he is banished to Iyo.

xxxiii The Anaho Shrine in the present-day Ta area of Tenri City, Nara Prefecture, claims to mark the location of this palace.

xxxiv According to Hanzei 1.8, his daughters were Imperial Princess Kahi, Imperial Princess Tsubura, and Imperial Princess Takara. According to the Hanzei book of *Ancient Matters*, also Takabe-no-iratsume. Given that over forty years had passed since Hanzei had first taken the throne, his daughters themselves would likely be in their forties by this point. Perhaps the chronology of the *Chronicles* has been stretched on this point, or perhaps it is meant to refer to Hanzei's granddaughters. If the latter case, then the note that their names are not recorded would make sense.

xxxv A gilt bronze crown resembling a standing tree was excavated from the Fujinoki Tumulus in Nara Prefecture. A number of crowns in this style have been excavated on the Korean peninsula.

xxxvi Hatabi and Ō-hatsu-se are aunt and nephew, and both had an emperor for a father. *Ancient Matters* gives Ō-kusaka's line as, "How could my younger sister be the sleeping mat for someone of the same class of lineage group?"

xxxvii Ankō's tomb is traditionally held to be at the ruins of Hōrai Fortress in the Hōrai area of Nara City, Nara Prefecture. *Ancient Matters* gives Ankō's age at death as fifty-six.

Endnotes to Book 14

i Yūryaku is named Ō-hatsuse in Ingyō 41.12 and the Ingyō book of *Ancient Matters* and Ō-hatsuse-no-waka-take in the Yūryaku book of *Ancient Matters*. In Yūryaku 4.2 he gives his own name as Waka-take. Bu of the Five Kings of Wa and the King Wakatakiru on the swords excavated from the Inariyama and Eta Funayama Tumuli are assumed to refer to Yūryaku. The name Yūryaku means "masculine planning" and is taken from the *Rhapsody on the Western War* (*Xi zheng fu* 西征賦) in the *Selections of Refined Literature*.

ii This phrase is taken from the "Annals of Emperor An" 孝安帝紀 in the *History of the Later Han*.

iii *Ancient Matters* gives his age at this time as seven.

iv In the *Ancient Matters* version of the episode, Mayowa beheads Ankō using the sword lying at the emperor's side.

v In *Ancient Matters*, Yūryaku does not suspect his brothers, but is angered rather by their nonchalance at the emperor's death, and kills them.

vi In the *Chronicles*, he flees to the house of Tsubura, but in *Ancient Matters*, Yūryaku buries him alive.

vii There is no direct connection between Mayowa and Tsubura, but Tsubura was of the Kazuraki lineage group, as was Imperial Prince Ichi-no-he-no-oshiwa, Yūryaku's rival for the throne. Either Mayowa could be putting trust in Ichi-no-he-no-oshiwa, or Yūryaku could be using this opportunity to destroy the Kazuraki.

viii This saying is taken from the "Zi Han" 子罕 chapter of the *Analects*: "The commander of an army can be captured, but the will of even a common man cannot be taken from him."

ix *Ancient Matters* gives "five imperial fiefs in Kazuraki." In Suiko 32.10, Soga no Umako asks the emperor to return the fief to his lineage group, but she denies him. In *Ancient Matters*, Tsubura simply renders these properties and Kara-hime to Yūryaku, then returns to his house to fight to the death.

x Imaki also appears in Taika (Kōtoku) 5.3. It is thought to span present-day Gose and Gojō Cities, Takaichi District, and the Ōyodo area of Yoshino District.

xi Kayano is the present-day Kamigano and Kano areas of Aishō Town, Echi Distict, Shiga Prefecture. Karafukuro appears in Kenzō 1.5.

xii The location of this well is unclear, but presumably it is near Mt. Miwa in Nara Prefecture.

xiii Hatsuse is a place-name in the present-day Hase and Kurozaki areas of Sakurai City, Nara, but the location of Asakura is unknown. Tradition held the palace to be in the Kurosaki or Iwasaka area of Sakurai City, though there are several theorized locations. The Hakusan Shrine in Kurosaki claims to mark the location of the palace. Archeological excavation suggests the Wakimoto Ruins in Wakimoto, Sakurai City. *New Selected Records* provides an episode linking the Asakura Palace to another palace built in Yūryaku 12.4 and to the courtier Sake no Kimi of the Hada, but in the *Chronicles*, these are separate locations.

xiv The word used for the Ise Shrine (*yashiro*) here, in Keitai 1.3, and in Bidatsu 7.3, is unusual. Usually this shrine is called a "miya."

xv Fukame is not seen elsewhere.

xvi The glosses in the original note for "lady" and "madam" are unclear, but are perhaps given in the Paekche language. Ishikawa no Tate is unclear, but might refer to a place-name in Kōchi (Osaka). Another Ishikawa-based lineage group, appearing in Nintoku 41, is similarly connected to immigrants from Paekche. The *New Compiled Records of Paekche* is cited here, in Yūryaku 5.7, and in Buretsu 4. The year Yūryaku 2 is Earth Dog [458 CE]. However, this year is too early to accord with King Bu of the Five Kings of Wa, who is usually associated with Yūryaku. Conversely, moving the sexagenary cycle forward sixty years to Earth Snake of 489 CE significantly postdates the reign of 455–475 usually assigned to Kaero, which is based on the *Samguk sagi*. One theory suggests that the *Chronicles* has mistaken Kaero for his father King Piyu (427–455). In Ōjin 39 [308 CE], the King of Paekche sends seven women to Yamato, led by Shisetsu-hime. This year is 119 years before 429 CE, almost exactly two sexagenary cycles, and the "Annals of Paekche," *Samguk sagi*, records messengers coming from Wa in 428 CE, which suggests that the entry here and in Ōjin are variants of the same episode.

xvii This line and the following four sentences are taken from the *Western Metropolis Rhapsody* (*Xi jing fu* 西京賦) in the *Selections of Refined Literature*.

xviii It is not clear if Ōtsu refers to Ōtsu in Izumi, present-day Izumiōtsu City, or Ōtsu in Naniwa, present-day Osaka City.

xix Nagano, Omi of Kashiwade is not seen elsewhere. The Omi of Kashiwade appear in Kōgen 7 as descendants of Ō-biko, son of Kōgen.

xx Uda is a place-name, present-day Uda City, Nara Prefecture. A Mitobe lineage group descended from Ho-akari appears in *New Selected Records*, but written with different characters. Masakita Takame is unclear and might be parsed differently.

xxi Saho is a place-name. The Saho River runs through present-day Nara City.

xxii The character used for "hereditary guilds" for scribes differs from that used elsewhere, though the vernacular reading is the same. The place-name Kawakami occurs in several places in the archipelago; here it is not clear which place is meant.

xxiii Ao and Hakatoko will be dispatched to Wu in Yūryaku 8 and 12 and will return in Yūryaku 10 and 14, respectively. Both men are presumably of Korean origins. Musa is perhaps taken from a place-name; the Musa Shrine stands in the Mise area of Kashihara City, Nara Prefecture. *New Selected Records* identifies Musa as being descended from immigrants from Wu. The title of nobility Suguri is perhaps taken from Korean; the sinographs give its meaning as "village master." Hinokuma is the present-day Hinokuma area of Asuka Town, Takaichi District, Nara Prefecture. Both locations fall within the area dominated by the Aya lineage group. Tami no Tsukai could be an abbreviation for the title of nobility "Obito of the Tami no tsukai" or "Obito of the messenger for the people," which appears elsewhere, or Hakatoko could work as a messenger and not have a title himself.

xxiv Ioki is the old name for the Kumozu River, which flows through present-day Ieki in the Hakusan area of Tsu City, Mie Prefecture.

xxv In the *Ancient Matters* version of this episode, the kami has identical clothing and an identical retinue to those of Yūryaku.

xxvi In the *Ancient Matters* version of this episode, the kami explains that he can bring about good or ill with a single word. Several shrines venerate this kami, the principle one being the Kazuraki Hitokotonushi Shrine in Gose City, Nara Prefecture. The same shrine also venerates Yūryaku. The pronouns used by Yūryaku and Hito-koto-nushi in the *Chronicles* place Yūryaku in a higher status, but in *Ancient Matters*, the two are social equals.

xxvii This sentence and the one preceding it derive from the *Western Metropolis Rhapsody* in the *Selections of Refined Literature*.

xxviii The Kume River is the Taketori River, which merges with the Soga River west of Mt. Unebi. In *Ancient Matters*, the kami escorts Yūryaku farther, to Hatsuse near Yūryaku's palace.

xxix "Kawakami" could refer to the Nishikawa area in Kawakami Village, Yoshino District, but as it also appears to be close to Yoshino Palace, it could refer to the Miyataki area of Yoshino Town, Yoshino District, Nara Prefecture.

xxx Because this poem switches from third to first person and appears to have several roles, commentators have suggested that it was meant as a performance explaining the origin of the moniker "Akizu-shima" or "dragonfly island." Another origin story for this name is given in Jinmu 31.4. Omura perhaps refers to a peak in the present-day Omura area of Higashi Yoshino Village, Yoshino District, Nara Prefecture. An "omure" and "omuro" appear in poems in the Saimei book of the *Chronicles* and the Yūryaku book of *Ancient Matters* and may refer to the same location. O-mure could mean peak-multitude (*wo-mure*).

xxxi The field of the dragonfly is the meaning according to the characters, but also possible is "bright field," which suggests a field that suddenly brightens when the sun crests the mountains shading it.

xxxii The following episode, for which Yūryaku is famous, appears in shortened version in *Ancient Matters*.

xxxiii This line and the rest of the episode are derived from the *Classified Extracts from Literature* citations of *Zhuang zi*, chapter 66 on hunting.

xxxiv Kakara Island is identified with a Nirimu Island cited in a Paekche record in Buretsu 4. There, Nirimu Island is located in the Kakara Sea. *Nirimu* is a Paekche word meaning "sovereign." The island is perhaps Kakara Island in present-day Karatsu City, Saga Prefecture.

xxxv According to the *Samguk sagi*, Muryŏng is rather identified as the second son of King Tongsŏng and father of King Sŏngmyŏng.

xxxvi The Metal Ox referred to in the note occurred during Kaero's reign, in 461 CE. However, in 462 Kō of the Five Kings of Wa sent a mission to the Liu Song. This is prior to Yūryaku (Bu) acceding to the throne, and so commentators suggest it might have occurred during Ankō's reign.

xxxvii The precise meanings of "standing straight" and "running along" are unclear, but from context, they clearly refer to the physical characteristics of the mountains. *Myriad Poems* XIII:3331 is quite similar.

xxxviii A "Hatsuse Way" appears in *Myriad Poems* XI:2511.

xxxix *Myriad Poems* IX:1738 uses Sugaru to designate the thin midsection of a thread-waisted wasp.

xl In *Ancient Matters*, Jinmu's son Kamu-yai-mimi is given as the ancestor of the Muraji of the Chihisako-be, or small children hereditary guild. In Tenmu 13.12, this muraji is promoted to sukune.

xli A similar episode is given in *Record of Miraculous Events in Japan* (*Nihon ryōi ki* 日本霊異記). Mimoro Hill refers to Mt. Miwa. The Ōmiwa Shrine has a torii gate and a hall for worship, but unlike some other shrines, there is no particular object that represents the kami. Rather, the kami is the

xlii mountain itself. For this reason, it would be impossible to catch the kami, as Yūryaku suggests.
xlii Ōzora is not seen elsewhere. By the name, the Yuge hereditary guild of Kibi was probably involved in the production of bows. Sakitsuya is not seen elsewhere. The Omi of Shimotsumichi of Kibi appear in Ōjin 22.9.
xliii *Original Records* identifies Tasa as a child of Naka-hiko who was enfeoffed as Provincial Governor of Kamitsumichi during the reign of Ōjin.
xliv These sentences of praise are taken from various sections of the *Selections of Refined Literature*.
xlv This latter sentence may derive from the *Selections of Refined Literature*.
xlvi Here the characters "central state" are glossed "mikado" for "emperor." The reference is to Yamato. The use of this term with regard to Silla posits Yamato as the center and Silla as the periphery.
xlvii Ōshima also appears in Keitai 23.3. Its location is unknown, but perhaps it is Namhae Island in South Kyŏngsang Province, South Korea.
xlviii Kusu-hime is not seen elsewhere.
xlix Ato is perhaps the Atobe area in the present-day Kameichō area of Yao City, Osaka Prefecture. For this reason, commentators have read this line as "the land of Yamato," and not "Yamato Province." However, it could instead refer to the former Ato Village in Shikige District, Yamato Province. This perhaps corresponds with the Ato seen in Suiko 18.10, which is near Suiko's palace of Oharida, likely in present-day Asuka Village, Nara Prefecture. A Kimi of Hirokitsu appears in *New Selected Records* in both Yamato and Kōchi Provinces.
l Tsuka arrives from abroad with his father Achi in Ōjin 20.9. The Sue-style ceramics hereditary guild (sue-tsukuri), from the southern Korean peninsula, produced the Sue style of pottery, but because early legal records do not incorporate them into the oversight mechanisms of the Civil and Penal Codes, it is presumed that they were dissolved or disbanded. The saddle-makers hereditary guild (kura-tsukuri) would be incorporated into the Ministry of the Treasury under the Civil and Penal Codes. There is a Kamikuratsukuri area in present-day Osaka City. The painters hereditary guild (e-kaki) would be incorporated into the Ministry of Central Affairs under the Civil and Penal Codes. Group members appear to be settled in multiple locations: Yamato in Tenmu 6.5 and in the *Continued Chronicles of Japan* in Tenpei 17.4 [745 CE], Kōchi in *New Selected Records*, and other places in Shōsōin documents. The brocade weaving hereditary guild (nishikori, from brocade *nishiki* + weaving *ori*) would be incorporated into the Ministry of the Treasury under the Civil and Penal Codes. Their administrator, the Miyatsuko of the Nishikori, appears in Tenmu 10.4. Nishigori was a district in Kōchi Province, and Nishikori Village is now part of Tondabayashi City,

Osaka Prefecture. The interpreters (osa) also appear in Suiko 15.7 and 16.9. "Osa" is perhaps derived from Korean; this would later become the name of a lineage group. *New Selected Records* identifies them as the descendants of Takeuchi no Sukune and of the same lineage as the Ki lineage group, and claims that they pledged allegiance to Japan (naturalized) in the Kinmei era. Momohara is unclear but may refer to the present-day Asuka Village area of Nara Prefecture. The Momohara Tomb that appears in Suiko 34.5 is thought to be the Ishibutai Tumulus in Asuka Village. In Sushun 1, Makami-no-hara is the site of the Hōkō Temple, present-day Asuka Temple in Asuka Village.

li In the manifest presented by King Bu of Wa in 478, recorded in the *History of the Liu Song*, vol. 97, "Yi Man" 夷蠻, there is a complaint that Koguryŏ was behaving inappropriately.

lii Perhaps the Silla word for chicken "tark" resembled the Koguryŏ word for soldier, "tar" or "tak."

liii This sentence is taken from the "Annals of Gaozu" in the *History of the Former Han*.

liv The phrase "hung up like a pennant" appears in the *Selections of Refined Literature* and the *History of Wei* in the *History of the Three Kingdoms*. The latter is also quoted in Yūryaku 9.5 and so was likely the source here as well. It means to be completely at the will of someone else, the person who can wave the pennant about.

lv These figures are not seen elsewhere.

lvi From this sentence until "leading to a great defeat" derives from the "Annals of Emperor Wu" in the *History of Wei* in the *History of the Three Kingdoms*.

lvii Katabu is not seen elsewhere.

lviii Toyoho is not seen elsewhere. Ainohara also appears in Keitai 25.12. It is the present-day Ōda area of Ibaraki City, Osaka Prefecture.

lix Perhaps the Munakata kami from the previous entry. The "Annals of Silla" in the *Samguk sagi* note a failed invasion from Wa early in the fifth and sixth years of the reign of King Chabi (r. 458–479).

lx The metaphor of the wolf cub is taken from the "Biography of Lü Bu" 呂布 (d. 199) in the *History of Wei* in the *History of the Three Kingdoms*.

lxi This final sentence is stitched together from quotations in the *Selections of Refined Literature*.

lxii Ōshiama is not seen elsewhere.

lxiii This sentence and the passage that follows derive from the "Annals of Emperor Gaozi" in the *History of the Former Han*. This intertextual reference to a successful campaign masks the defeat of the Yamato army by Silla.

lxiv The name of the Muraji of the Kume of Okazaki in Ki is not given.

lxv Tsumaro is not seen elsewhere.

lxvi This sentence and the one following it are derived from the "Annals of Emperor Wu" in the *History of Wei* in the *History of the Three Kingdoms*.
lxvii The basis for this statement is unclear. The Ōtomo base of power was the southeast part of the Nara Basin and the Ki in the Heguri area on the western edge of the basin. However, both lineage groups expanded in the Osaka Bay area: the Ōtomo in Settsu and Izumi Provinces and the Ki in neighboring Kii Province. Oyumi's tomb is near the border between Izumi and Kii.
lxviii Otori is not seen elsewhere. Tamuwa Village is the present-day Tannowa area of Misaki Town, Nansen District, Osaka Prefecture. There are several large tumuli in this area, including the Sairyō and Nishi Koyama Tumuli. Excavation of the latter has yielded metal products of peninsular origin.
lxix The land of Tsu is in present-day Yamaguchi Prefecture, and included the former Tsuno District, present-day Kudamatsu and Shūnan cities, and at least two other neighboring districts, though its precise composition is unclear.
lxx Asukabe is the present-day Asuka area of Habikino City, Osaka Prefecture. The Fubito of Tanabe were an immigrant lineage begun by Hakuson. There is a corresponding entry in *New Selected Records*. Tanabe is perhaps the present-day Tanabe area in Kashiwara City, Osaka Prefecture. Furuichi is the present-day Furuichi area of Habikino City. Karyō is not seen elsewhere.
lxxi Homuta Tomb perhaps refers to the tomb of Ōjin. Unusually, this tomb is not mentioned in the entries on Ōjin's death or the immediately following accession of his successor. The tomb is traditionally held to be the Kondogobyōyama Tomb in the present-day Homuta area of Habikino City, Osaka Prefecture. Ichibiko is the old word for strawberry, but the location of Ichibiko Hill is unclear.
lxxii This sentence and the one beginning "The sorrel took off" below are derived from the *Rhapsody on Sorrel and Dapple Grey Horses* (*Zhe bai ma fu* 赭白馬賦) in the *Selections of Refined Literature*.
lxxiii Nemaro is not seen elsewhere. Mine District is perhaps the former Mine Town, present-day Miyaki Town, Saga Prefecture.
lxxiv Kurumoto District is present-day Rittō and Kusatsu cities, Shiga Prefecture; the area was formerly called Kurita District. Tanakami Beach refers to the place where the Tagami River, now called the Daido River, merges with the Seta River south of Lake Biwa in Shiga Prefecture.
lxxv The servants of Kawase would be managed by the Miyatsuko of the Kawase servants (Kawase no toneri no miyatsuko). This lineage group was promoted to muraji in Tenmu 12.9. Kawase is an area in Hikone City, Shiga Prefecture. Kawase is some distance from Kurumoto, and the connection between these locations is unclear.
lxxvi Kuishin is not seen elsewhere.

lxxvii Yakatamaro is not seen elsewhere. Sakate is an area in present-day Tawaramoto Town, Shiki District, which abuts Iware. A Sakate Reservoir appears in Keikō 57.9. Wu style music in the traditional Japanese court appears not to have used a zither. A six-string zither from Koguryŏ and a twelve-string zither from Silla were both developed. Which zither this entry refers to is not clear.

lxxviii Yohoro were people conscripted for public service; the conscripted watchmen (*tsukae no yohoro*) performed surveillance and guard duties. Shinano and Musashi provinces were on the frontier in Eastern Japan. Both provinces appear to have been incorporated into the Yamato state around the fifth century CE.

lxxix Mita is not seen elsewhere. Tsuke is the present-day Tsuge area of Nara City, formerly Tsuge Village, Yamabe District, Nara Prefecture. The insertion of editorial judgment in the original note has led some commentators to suggest that the note was added later, though such judgment is a general feature of the Yūryaku book and can be attributed to its editor/compiler.

lxxx Yamabe is a place-name in both the Nara Basin and Ise, among other places.

lxxxi Eka Market is the present-day Kō area of Fujiidera City, Osaka Prefecture, near the confluence of the Yamato and Ishi rivers.

lxxxii Nagano Village is the present-day Oka area in Fujiidera City, Osaka Prefecture. The Karakuni Shrine in Fujiidera incorporated what was formerly called Nagano Shrine.

lxxxiii The location of Miikuma is unclear, though it was presumably along the coast on account of the plundering of merchant vessels.

lxxxiv The absence of honorific speech in the vernacular, despite the grammatical subject being the emperor, reflects a Heian-period usage paradigm in which improper actions would not use the honorific register.

lxxxv Kai was famous for its horses, though that distinction arose later in history than this legendary episode would suggest, probably in the seventh century.

lxxxvi This episode is very similar to the entries given in Ōjin 37.2 and 41.2. The fishing people of Shihatsu appear in *Myriad Poems* VI:999 in relation to Sumiyoshi in Osaka.

lxxxvii Hinokuma is the present-day Hinokuma area of Asuka Town, Takaichi District, Nara Prefecture. Kurehara is another name for Kurihara, also in Asuka Town.

lxxxviii The house of the ancestor of the miyatsuko of the tailor hereditary guild (*kinu-nui-be*) of Asuka, called Konoha, is destroyed in Sushin 1.3 in order to build Hōkō Temple, present-day Asuka Temple in Asuka Village. The tailor hereditary guild of Ise was perhaps located Kurebe Village, in Ichishi District of Ise Province, presently split between Tsu and Matsubara cities, Mie Prefecture.

lxxxix Isonokami is the present-day Isonokami area of Tenri City, Nara Prefecture, but Takanuki Field is unknown.

xc Hine was a district in Izumi Province; it is present-day Sennan District. The Agatanushi of Chinu, hereditary guild of Kusaka, and Omi of Sakamoto, who appear later in the episode, were all from Hine. The name Ne no Omi (Omi of Ne) may be derived from this place-name as well.

xci Perhaps the hereditary guild of Kusaka (Kusaka-be). Kusaka is a place-name in present-day Higashi Osaka City.

xcii Another individual named One, Agatanushi of Mino in Kōchi Province, joins a revolt in the pre-accession record of Seinei, which has led to speculation that they are the same individual. However, their respective geographical strongholds are quite distant from each other.

xciii This accords with the account given in Ankō 1.2. The same phrase "began from this time" is used in Yūryaku 9.5 for the Omi of Tsu. *Ancient Matters* and *New Selected Records* identify both lineages as originating from the son of Takeuchi no Sukune, Tsu no Sukune of Ki.

xciv Called the Yutsuki in Ōjin 14 but using the same character as Hada, the people of this group came from 120 districts. Commentators suggest that that entry, this one, and the following dispersal of the Hada in Yūryaku 16.7 provide an origin story for the wide dispersal of textile workers from the continent that later settled in the archipelago. The origin story in *New Selected Records* sets the dispersal in the Nintoku era. The Miyatsuko of Hada was an allied miyatsuko charged with managing the Hada people. That lineage group was given the title muraji in Tenmu 12.9 and imiki in Tenmu 14.6.

xcv Nie-no-haji-be. There is doubt about whether the Haji were as widespread as this episode claims. The Haji were associated with ceramics for ritual worship. Perhaps the episode was created by later members of the Haji, to whom control of the imperially created Nie-no-haji-be had been entrusted, to explain the relationship between the groups. Ake is not seen elsewhere. Kusasa is present-day Nose Town, Toyono District, Osaka Prefecture, where the Kusasa Shrine is located. Uchi is present-day Uchizatouchi area in Yawata City, Kyoto Prefecture, where the Uchi Shine is located. Fushimi is present-day Fushimi Ward, Kyoto City. Fujikata is perhaps the present-day Fujikata area in Tsu City, Mie Prefecture.

xcvi Ushiro and Asake no Iratsuko are not seen elsewhere.

xcvii Aohaka perhaps refers to the Mihakayama Tumulus in the present-day Sanagu area of Iga City, Mie Prefecture.

xcviii Ō-onote is not seen elsewhere. Kiku was formerly Kiku District, Fukuoka Prefecture, and included parts of presented-day Kita Kyushu City, Yahatahigashi District, and Yukuhashi City.

xcix Hesuoto perhaps derives from the Paekche language.

c This speech derives from the "Annals of Emperor Gaozu" in the *History of the Sui Dynasty*.

ci The word used for Koguryŏ in the note is pejorative, imposing a Paekche viewpoint on the text. The great stronghold and capital of Paekche was in the Han River Valley, present-day Seoul, South Korea. Ire refers to the first capital of Paekche, Wiryesŏng.

cii Kumunari is present-day Kongju City, and as Ungjin, was the capital of Paekche from 475 to 518 CE. King Munju is traditionally counted as the son of Kaero, based on the *Samguk sagi*, but the late note gives an alternative explanation.

ciii Neither interpretation of Munju's lineage in the note accords with the *Samguk sagi*. Another version of the miraculous rescue of Paekche in which Yūryaku confers with an oracle is given in Kinmei 16.2. The *Nihon kuki* is not seen elsewhere. Aroshitakori is perhaps an error for Aroshi-tari-kori (Lower Tari District). Upper and Lower Tari appear in Keitai 6.12. There are two theories for the location of Tari: the area from northeastern North Chŏlla Province to southeastern South Ch'ungch'ŏng Province, and the southwestern area of South Chŏlla Province. The passage here must refer to the former, given the location of the new Paekche capital at Ungjin in South Ch'ungch'ŏng Province.

civ The well-known folktale of Urashima Tarō appears in several early sources. The version in *Myriad Poems* IX:1740 and the citations of the "Gazetteer of Tango Province" (*Tango no kuni fudoki* 丹後国風土記) in the *Commentary on the Nihongi* are presumed to be older than the account here. There are several changes in the details between versions. The rationale for its inclusion at this historical moment in the *Chronicles* is unclear. Perhaps the compilers of the *Chronicles* placed the story in the Yūryaku book because the "Tango Gazetteer" does so as well, suggesting a common source material. Or perhaps because in the "Tango Gazetteer," Urashima is given as the ancestor of the Obito of the Kusaka hereditary guild, the compilers wished to stress the connection with this group, which was established in Yūryaku 14.4. Finally, like the encounter with the kami Hito-koto-nushi, the incorporation of supernatural events associated with sages emphasizes the sitting ruler's virtue.

cv These two figures are not seen elsewhere, and a place-name for Achi in Kyushu is not clear.

cvi This sentence and much of the edict that follows in month eight are heavily derived from the "Annals of Emperor Gaozu" in the *History of the Sui Dynasty*.

cvii The statement on caps and clothing is taken from an edict in the "Annals of Emperor Gaozu" in the *History of the Sui Dynasty*, but it has been amended to accord with a phrase appearing later in that same book.

cviii This proverb appears throughout the Classical Chinese corpus. Given the surrounding material here, it is likely taken from the *History of the Sui Dynasty*.
cix Oshiro is not seen elsewhere.
cx Saba Port is perhaps the present-day Saba area in Fukuyama City, Hiroshima Prefecture. Another place named Saba is seen in Keikō 12.9 and Suiko 11.2, but it is too far from Kibi.

Endnotes to Book 15

i "Shiraka" means "white hair." The other elements of Seinei's name appear in other emperors' names and mean "Brave, young, and forceful ruler of the wide land of Yamato."
ii Seinei is alternatively named Shiraka-no-ō-yamato-neko in the Seinei book of *Ancient Matters* and Shiraka in the Yūryaku book of *Ancient Matters*. Shira means "white" and ka means "hair," presumably referring to his being born with white hair, as noted in the following passage. Take-hiro-oshi-kuni is an appellation of praise closely resembling those given to Ankan and Senka. Relative birth order between wives is not given in the Yūryaku book, but here Yūryaku's two sons—Iwaki and Hoshikawa—by his consort Waka-hime, are older than Seinei, his son by Kara-hime. Seinei means "pure tranquility" and appears in the second book of "Annals of Emperor Guangwu" in the *History of the Later Han* as a description for the realm being at peace.
iii "The younger" refers to Hoshikawa's being the second son of Waka-hime. *Gleanings from Ancient Tidings* and *New Selected Records* claim that it was during Yūryaku's reign that a national treasury, as opposed to the imperial exchequer, was established. See Book 12, endnote xxix.
iv The phrase "his mother the consort" identifies Kara-hime as a consort of rank three or above, though this rating system did not exist until the later implementation of the Civil and Penal Codes.
v The phrasing used for "thereby" is particular to the Seinei, Keitai, Ankan, and Kinmei books.
vi The Agatanushi of Mino in Kōchi are promoted to muraji in Tenmu 13.1. They were perhaps based near the present-day Mino-no-Agatanushi Shrine in Yao City, Osaka Prefecture.
vii Ayahiko is not seen elsewhere. Ōkata, Kishi of Kusakabe, is named Muraji of Naniwa in Tenmu 12.1, and the Kishi of Kusakabe are promoted to muraji in Tenmu 12.10. *New Selected Records* suggests that the Muraji of Naniwa were of peninsula origin.
viii The phrase "my shortened lifespan" comes from the *Golden Light Sutra* 金光明経. Phrases from this sutra are frequent in the Seinei, Kenzō, Ninken, Buretsu, Keitai, and Kinmei books.

ix Ōie is not seen elsewhere. The use of hectares (*chō*) is anachronistic, as the measure was implemented with the Civil and Penal Codes. The earlier system used the *shiro*.

x This phrase is derived from the "Annals of Emperor Guangwu" in the *History of the Later Han*. Mikakuri is unclear.

xi Yūryaku is traditionally held to be buried in the Shimamaruyama Tumulus, also called the Takawashi-maruyama Tumulus, in present-day Habikino City, Osaka Prefecture.

xii The creation of the Shiraka-be is recounted again in Keitai 1.2 and given in the Seinei book of *Ancient Matters*. Above and in these two instances, Seinei created the group because he had no children. Conversely, in the Yūryaku book of *Ancient Matters*, Yūryaku creates the group on behalf of his son Seinei. The Shiraka-be appears in various provinces throughout the archipelago.

xiii In *Ancient Matters*, Shijimi is the personal name of a Harima local. It likely refers to the Shijimi area of present-day Miki City, Hyōgo Prefecture. The Miyatsuko of the Oshinumi hereditary guild are given in *Ancient Matters* as the descendants of Take-toyo-hazura-wake, a son of Emperor Kaika.

xiv This phrase derives from the "Annals of Emperor Xuan" 宣帝紀 in the *History of the Former Han*.

xv In *Ancient Matters*, Seinei is already dead, and so the report is given to Princess Iidoyo.

xvi This phrase derives from the "Annals of Emperor Guangwu" in the *History of the Later Han*.

xvii Tsu follows the vernacular. The sinographs give Settsu Province, which was a later reference.

xviii This phrase derives from the "Annals of Emperor Ling" 孝靈帝紀 in the *History of the Later Han*. Blue palanquins were used by imperial princes.

xix The pre-accession record of Kenzō notes that Iidoyo ruled from Oshinumi-no-tsu-no-sashi Palace. Oshinumi is in the present-day Shinjō area of Katsuragi City, Nara Prefecture.

xx This phrase derives from the "Annals of Emperor Gaozu" in the *History of the Sui Dynasty*. Several other references to this record of annals and the paucity of information on Seinei's reign in *Ancient Matters* suggest that this Chinese work was the primary source for constructing Seinei's annals in the *Chronicles*.

xxi This phrase derives from the "Annals of Emperor Gaozu" in the *History of the Sui Dynasty*.

xxii These phrases derive from the "Annals of Emperor Gaozu" in the *History of the Sui Dynasty*.

xxiii This phrase derives from the "Annals of Emperor Gaozu" in the *History of the Sui Dynasty*.
xxiv This phrase derives from the "Annals of Emperor Ming" in the *History of the Later Han*.
xxv This phrase derives from the "Annals of Emperor Gaozu" in the *History of the Sui Dynasty*.
xxvi These phrases derive from the "Annals of Emperor Gaozu" in the *History of the Sui Dynasty*.
xxvii Seinei is traditionally held to be buried in the Shiragayama Tumulus, present-day Habikino City, Osaka Prefecture.
xxviii In *Ancient Matters*, Kenzō is named Oke-no-iwasu-wake. O, or wo, means "small," referring to his status as the younger brother. Ke is unclear. Kume-no-wakugo means "young son of the Kume" and may refer to being discovered by Odate, who was of the Kume hereditary guild. Kenzō means "revealed ancestor" and perhaps refers to his making his imperial heritage publicly known. It derives from an appellation given to Emperor Ming of Han in the *History of the Later Han*, where he is called Emperor Xianzong (Jp. Kenzō) Xiaoming.
xxix I-natsu-hime is not seen elsewhere.
xxx Shima-no-wakugo means "young one of Shima."
xxxi The pre-accession record of Ninken gives his courtesy name as Shima-no-iratsuko and his real name as Ōshi. The rationale for these names is unclear.
xxxii Later, Princess Iidoyo rules from Oshi-numibe-no-tsu-no-sashi Palace. The gloss styles Iidoyo as "Imperial Princess," but the sinographs only as "Princess."
xxxiii Prince Tachibana is not seen elsewhere. Ninken has a daughter, Imperial Princess Tachibana, and the Senka book of *Ancient Matters* gives a Tachibana-no-naka-tsu-hime as a daughter of Kenzō.
xxxiv The second clause of this expression derives from the *Writings of the Huainan Masters*.
xxxv The latter half of this sentence is derived from the "Annals of Emperor Guangwu" in the *History of the Later Han*.
xxxvi Iwaya is in the present-day Shimiji area of Miki City, Hyōgo Prefecture.
xxxvii The quotation is derived from book 21 of the *Classified Extracts from Literature*.
xxxviii Iidoyo's tomb is traditionally held to be the Kita-hana-uchi-ō-tsuka Tumulus in present-day Katsuragi City, Nara Prefecture.
xxxix This speech is derived from book 21 of the *Classified Extracts from Literature*.
xl These phrases are derived from the "Annals of Emperor Wu" in the *History of Liang*.

xli These phrases are derived from the *Classified Extracts from Literature* and the "Annals of Emperor Guangwu" in the *History of the Later Han*.
xlii This speech is derived from the "Annals of Emperors An and Shun of Han" in the *History of the Later Han*.
xliii Commentators are divided on whether this palace was in the Asuka of Yamato Province or the Asuka of Kōchi Province (Osaka).
xliv These lines derive from book 52 of the *Classified Extracts from Literature*.
xlv This quotation derives from the *Classified Extracts from Literature* citation of the *Classic of Rites*.
xlvi This quotation derives from the *Classified Extracts from Literature* citation of the *Classic of Songs*.
xlvii This quotation derives from the *Classified Extracts from Literature*.
xlviii These lines derive from the *Golden Light Sutra*.
xlix These lines are taken from the "Annals of Emperor Ming" in the *History of the Later Han*. The use of coin is an anachronism.
l The Takamioya Shrine in present-day Iki City, Nagasaki Prefecture is dedicated to Taka-mi-musuhi. *Original Records* names the moon kami as the ancestor of the Agatanushi of Iki.
li The Amateru Shrine in present-day Tsushima City, Nagasaki Prefecture, is dedicated to Ame-no-hi-no-mitama, a sun kami distinct from Amaterasu. *Original Records* names Ame-no-hi-no-mitama as the ancestor of the Agatanushi of Tsushima.
lii The wording "palace administration" is likely taken from the "Annals of Emperor Guangwu" in the *History of the Later Han*.
liii Chwaro is unclear; a Saro-matsu appears in the *Chronicles* citation of the *Annals of Paekche* in Kinmei 2.7. Nagit'a-gappae is unclear; a Nakanda-kōhai appears in the *Chronicles* citation of the *Annals of Paekche* in Kinmei 5.2. Chŏng-mag-ihae is not seen elsewhere. Nirimu appears in an original note to Ōjin 16 as Nirimu Fortress, but this makes the original note unclear. Perhaps the "Koma" (Koguryŏ) in the note is meant to be "kom" (bear) in reference to Komanaru (mod. Kr. Ungchin) in Paekche.
liv Shitoro-moro is in the present-day Taein area of Chŏngŭp City, North Chŏlla Province.
lv This sentence and the one preceding it derive from the "Annals of Emperor Guangwu" in the *History of the Later Han*.
lvi O in Oke's name means "large," in contrast to his younger brother O-ke (Wo-ke; Kenzō), who is "small." The meaning of ke is unknown. Ōshi resembles the name of Ninken's father Oshiwa. Shima-no-iratsuko resembles the name Shima-no-wakugo given in the pre-accession record of Kenzō's citation of *Record of Successions to Titles of Nobility*. Ninken means benevolent intelligence and appears in the genealogy of the House of Song Wei Zi 宋微子世家 in *Records of the Historian*.

lvii The meaning of "Ōsu" is unclear, but it seems related to Ninken's other name "Ōshi."
lviii This sentence perhaps derives from the "Annals of Emperor Zhang" in the *Han Records of the Eastern Lodge*.
lix The Ninken book of *Ancient Matters* gives Takaki-no-iratsume. Takahashi is a place-name in the Yajō area of Nara City, Nara Prefecture.
lx Asazuma does not appear in *Ancient Matters*. Perhaps she is the same as the Takara-no-iratsume who appears there. Asazuma is a place-name in present-day Gose City, Nara Prefecture.
lxi Given as Tashiraka-no-iratsume in *Ancient Matters*. Empress to Keitai.
lxii Given as Kusubi-no-iratsume in *Ancient Matters*, where her birth order is switched with Tashiraka.
lxiii She appears as Imperial Princess Tachibana-no-nakatsu in Senka 1.3, when she was named empress. She does not appear in the Ninken book of *Ancient Matters*, but does appear in the Senka book of *Ancient Matters* as Tachibana-no-naka-tsu-hime.
lxiv Imperial Princess Mawaka is given in *Ancient Matters* as a boy, Prince Mawaka. Mawaka could be a name for either sex.
lxv Kenzō is traditionally held to be buried in the Tsukiyama Tumulus in present-day Yamatotakada City, Nara Prefecture.
lxvi Both Kashima and Hohe no Kimi are not seen elsewhere.
lxvii Hishiki Village is perhaps the Hishiki area in present-day Nishi Ward, Sakai City, Osaka Prefecture.
lxviii Tamatsukuri perhaps refers to the Tamatsukuri area of present-day Chūō and Tennōji Wards of Osaka City. Karama appears in *New Selected Records* as a descendant of Takeuchi no Sukune.
lxix Sumuchi is the present-day Sumi-no-dō area of Daidō City, Osaka Prefecture.
lxx Suruki and Nuruki are not seen elsewhere.
lxxi Nukata Village is perhaps the present-day areas of Nukatabe-kitamachi, Nukatabe-teramachi, and Nukatabe-minamimachi, in Yamatokōriyama City, Nara Prefecture.
lxxii This passage and the quotation preceding it derive from the "Annals of Emperor Ming" in the *History of the Later Han*.
lxxiii The Bokeyama Tumulus in Fujiidera City, Osaka Prefecture, is traditionally taken to be Ninken's burial site.

Endnotes to Book 16

i O-hatsue (small Hatsuse, Buretsu) forms a natural pair with Ō-hatsue (large Hatsuse, Yūryaku). Hatsuse is a place-name, the present-day Hase area of Sakurai City, Nara Prefecture. Yūryaku's capital was Hatsuse-no-asakura Palace; Buretsu's was Hatsuse-no-namiki Palace. Waka-sazaki (young wren, Buretsu) also forms a natural pair with Ō-sazaki (great wren, Nintoku).

The cultured reign of Nintoku and the martial reign of Yūryaku are thus combined in a single figure. Buretsu means "martial order" and is taken from the "Discourses on Zhou" in the *Discourses of the States*. The name Buretsu emphasizes Buretsu's martial qualities and is apt in describing a sovereign whose actions were despotic and cruel. As the final ruler in the lineage established by Nintoku, Buretsu is also associated with dynastic failure. Buretsu thus illustrates the Chinese ideology that associates evil rulers with dynastic failure.

ii This sentence and the two that precede it derive from the description of Ming of Han in the "Emperors and Kings" book of the *Classified Extracts from Literature*. The same phrases appear in the "Annals of Emperor Ming" in the *History of the Later Han*, but the similarity of the first three sentences of the Buretsu book to the description of Ming of Han suggests the former text was used.

iii In *Ancient Matters*, Shibi is the ancestor of the Omi of Heguri, and the battle of songs is with Seinei, not Buretsu, over a woman named Ofuo, the daughter of the Obito of Uda.

iv The Tsubaki Market is Tsubaichi in the present-day Kanaya area of Sakurai City, Nara Prefecture.

v This sentence and the one following it are adapted from the "Annals of Emperor Guangwu" in the *History of the Later Han*.

vi This quotation derives from the *Golden Light Sutra*.

vii This quotation derives from the "Annals of Emperor Wu" in the *History of Wei* in the *History of the Three Kingdoms*.

viii The expression "what he desired would not come to pass" refers to the content of the pre-accession record of Buretsu, where Matori desires to become King of Yamato.

ix This sentence derives from the "Annals of Emperor Guangwu" in the *History of the Later Han*.

x Much of this passage derives from the "Diwang" 帝王 section of the *Classified Extracts from Literature*. The "great lands of treasure" perhaps refers to the Korean peninsula in light of the phrasing used in the Chūai book.

xi This sentence derives from the "Annals of Emperor Guangwu" in the *History of the Later Han*.

xii This sentence derives from *Mr. Lü's Spring and Autumn Annals* (*Lüshi chunqiu* 呂氏春秋).

xiii Kinoe is perhaps in present-day Kōryō Town, Kita Katsuragi District, Nara Prefecture.

xiv Otara is not seen elsewhere.

xv In the *Samguk sagi*, Shima (Munyŏng) is the second son of King Matsuta (Mata, Malda, Dongmyŏng).

xvi Saa is not seen elsewhere.

xvii The Kimi of Yamato is not seen elsewhere, though an Omi of Yamato with ties to the Paekche royal house is given in *New Selected Records*.

xviii Part of this sentence and much of the rest of the entries for this month are derived from passages in *Biographies of Notable Women* (*Lienü zhuan* 列女傳, first century BCE).

Index of Key Names and Places

For kami, see Appendix 1: Glossary of Kami in the *Chronicles*.

Achi no Omi, 363, 371, 373, 427, 668
Achiki, Fubito of, 361, 659
Ada, Ukai of, 145
Ahira-tsu-hime, 127
Ahe, Omi of, 182, 183, 489, 569, 637
Ahe in Iga, Omi of 182, 637
Ajikki (Achiki), 361
Aki, 27, 59, 129, 285, 666
Ama-tarashi-hiko-kuni-oshi-hito, 177, 179, 636, 654
Ame-no-hi-hoko, 221, 223, 241, 641
Amu, Kimi of, 249
Analects, 659, 660, 662, 668, 674
Anaho, Miyatsuko of, 530
Anato, 219, 285, 295, 297, 301, 303, 317, 319, 641, 648, 652, 653
　Agatanushi of, 301
Annals of Paekche, 569, 656, 675, 687
Ara (Kaya), 339, 656
Arihishino-kara (Kaya), 339, 656
Arinare River, 313, 652
Aso (person), 455
Aso (place), 259, 261
Ata, Kimi Ohashi of, 105
Ata-hime, 199, 201
Atsuta, 63, 283, 629, 646
Awa, 15, 17, 19, 67, 285, 629, 642, 647
　Ashikui-wake of 443, 670
　Province, 53, 443, 465, 670
Awaji, 11, 15, 17, 19, 35, 221, 241, 295, 319, 359, 365, 367, 379, 429, 439, 463, 627, 668, 670

Aya
　Atai of, 363, 427, 668
　of Yamato, 505, 533, 539
Ayuki, 241
Azuma, 89, 265, 277, 351, 630, 645
Azumi, Muraji of, 29, 351, 429, 435, 437

Biographies of Notable Women, 690
Biwa (lake), 135, 654, 680

Cape Kasasa, 79, 95, 99, 630
Central Reed Plain Land, 33, 45, 49, 53, 55, 67, 71, 75, 83, 85, 87, 89, 91, 99, 233
Chihisako-be, Muraji of, 499, 677
Chinu, 133, 191, 237, 239, 461, 463, 525, 673, 682
　Agatanushi of, 525, 682
Civil and Penal Codes, 387, 441, 476, 505, 513, 521, 565, 666, 669, 678, 684, 685
Classic of Changes, 631, 633, 647
Classic of Documents, 671
Classic of Poetry, 636, 641
Classified Extracts from Literature, 627, 649, 662, 671, 677, 687, 689
Collected Commentary on the Chronicles, 636
Commentary on the Civil Codes, 417, 667
Commentary on the History of the Three Kingdoms, 640, 662
Commentary on the Nihongi, 666, 683

Commentary on the Spring and Autumn Annals, 670
Continued Chronicle of Later Japan, 642, 662
Continued Chronicles of Japan, 563, 651, 660, 661, 663

Daifang Commandery, 333, 655
Discourses of the States, 637, 689

Eight Great Islands, 9, 11, 15, 19, 25, 65
Emishi, 151, 153, 265, 269, 275, 277, 279, 283, 287, 351, 409, 419, 421, 537, 545, 643

Feast of First Rice, 46, 47, 51, 73, 95, 413, 542, 543, 549
Floating Bridge of Heaven, 9, 13, 79, 85, 95
Fujiwara no Kamatari, 673
Fukakawa, Wake of, 351, 658
Fukuoka, 29, 37, 632, 644, 645, 648–52, 657, 682
Fumi, Obito of the, 361, 515, 660

Gazetteer of Higo Province, 644
Gazetteer of Hitachi Province, 649
Gazetteer of Hizen Province, 644
Gazetteer of Settsu Province, 666
Gleanings from Ancient Tidings, 669, 670, 684
Golden Light Sutra, 684, 687, 689
Great Yamato of Rich Autumns, 11, 15, 17, 19, 627

Hada (lineage grouo), 519, 527, 682
    Kimi of, 519, 675
    Miyatsuko of, 519, 527, 682
Haji (lineage group), 237, 682
    Muraji of the, 37, 55, 237, 421, 513, 529
    Omi of, 237

Hakuson, 515, 680
Hani-yasu-biko, 195, 201, 203, 231
Harihara, Kimi of, 351
Harima, 221, 245, 285, 319, 359, 521, 543, 642, 685
    Governor of, 549, 555, 563, 571
    Provincial Miyatsuko of, 395, 665
    Wake of, 249, 665
Hashihaka, 197, 205, 207, 639
Hayabusa-wake, 351, 409, 411
Hayato, 79, 105, 113, 435, 541, 545, 643
Heavenly Mt. Kagu, 47, 49, 53, 145, 147, 161, 201, 632
Heguri, 257, 289, 361, 427, 437, 482, 541, 644, 658, 669, 680
    Omi of, 385, 483, 579, 658, 689
    Matori, 483, 541, 579, 585, 587, 689
    Shibi, 579, 581, 583, 585, 689
Hi (land), 259
    Provincial Miyatsuko of, 255,
    Wake of, 249
High Heavenly Market, 49, 91
High Heavenly Plain, 5, 17, 29, 33, 91, 165, 627
Hijikata, Kimi of, 351, 658
Hime-tatara-i-suzu-hime, 67, 165, 169, 608
Himuka, 27, 79, 89, 93, 95, 99, 107, 123, 127, 131, 249, 255, 257, 261, 307, 351, 357, 359, 385
    Provincial Miyatsuko of, 255
Hinokuma, Tami no Tsukai of, 489, 505, 517, 519, 676
Hishiho (Pihwa Kaya), 339, 656
History of Liang, 655, 667
History of the Former Han, 631, 635, 637, 639, 640, 645, 649, 651, 652, 662, 669, 671, 679, 685
History of the Jin Dynasty, 640
History of the Later Han, 649, 651, 671, 674, 684–89
History of the Liu Song, 371, 637, 679

History of the Sui Dynasty, 339, 640, 645, 672, 683, 685
History of Wei, 333, 335, 635, 655, 656, 659, 679, 680, 689
History of Wu, 673
Homutsu-wake, 217, 225, 227, 229, 231
Hoshikawa, 535, 537, 539, 541, 658, 684
House Record of the Fujiwara, 673
Hozumi,
    Omi of, 183, 191, 233
    Sukune of the, 273, 285

Ichi-no-he-no-oshiwa, 481, 543, 545, 547, 561, 674
Iga, Omi of, 182, 183, 637
Ii-iri-ne, 211, 213, 639
Iidoyo, 543, 545, 547, 555, 557, 685, 686
Iki, 11, 17, 355, 569, 659, 687
Ikuha, Omi of, 393, 397, 405, 575, 660, 664
Ikuha-no-toda no Sukune, see Toda-no-Sukune
Iku-me, 209, 211, 213, 219
Ikume-iri-biko-isa-chi, 187, 217, 245, 293, 638
Ina-hi, 123, 125, 137
Ina-yori-wake, 285, 646, 647
Inbe, 47, 49, 51, 53, 87, 91
I-ni-shiki-iri-biko, 229, 235, 237, 239
Inukami, Kimi of, 285, 321
Ioki-no-iri-biko, 247, 249, 642, 643
Ise, 51, 89, 149, 231, 233, 273, 279, 281, 285, 287, 413, 519, 523, 529, 646, 649, 650, 666, 681
    Kimi of, 191
    Province of, 305, 529, 529, 629, 681
Ise Grand Shrine, 191, 233 (Watarai Shrine), 271, 273, 279, 283, 411, 483, 489, 490, 630, 638, 675

Isonokami, 239, 433, 435, 439, 473, 525, 529, 553, 573, 575, 585, 629, 668, 669, 671, 673, 682
Isonokami Shrine (Nara), 239, 241, 343, 433, 491, 629
Isonokami Shrine (Okayama), 63, 629
I-suzu-yori-hime, 171, 173
Ito, Agatanushi of, 297
Itsukai, Muraji of the, 173
Itsu-se, 125, 133, 137, 157
Iwa-no-hime, 385, 399, 403, 405, 407, 427, 663, 666
Iware, 145, 161, 331, 435, 437, 517, 541, 569, 631, 632–34, 669, 681
Iyo, 11, 15, 17, 19, 285, 467, 543, 549, 627, 646, 673
    Province of, 249, 285, 471
    Wake of, 249
Izumo, 37, 55, 57, 59, 61, 63, 65, 67, 69, 75, 85, 89, 207, 213, 219, 227, 231, 233, 237, 377, 551, 630, 639
    Omi of, 37, 55, 89, 211, 213, 377, 639
    Province of, 37
    Provincial Miyatsuko of, 37, 377, 639
Izumo Grand Shrine, 211
Izumo-furu-ne, 211, 213

Jeweled Spear of Heaven, 9, 13, 15, 17, 19

Kagosaka, 295, 319, 321, 329, 653
Kai, 265, 275, 277, 523, 681
Kamitsufusa (Kazusa), 273, 285, 645
Kamitsukeno, 277, 287, 646
    Kimi of, 211, 225, 286, 361, 419, 638, 641, 660
Kamitsumichi, Omi of, 369, 485, 501, 539, 541, 661
Kamo, Kimi of, 67, 175
Kamu-nu-na-kawa-mimi, 165, 167, 169, 171, 173, 634

Kamu-ya-i, 165, 169, 171, 634, 643
Kara (Korea), 65, 339, 341, 343, 345, 361, 503, 656
Kasa, Omi of, 307, 369, 423, 661
Kashihara, 163, 165, 167, 175, 179, 632, 633–37, 659, 669, 673, 676
Kashiwade, 489
   Allied Miyatsuko of, 669
   Omi of, 182, 183, 285, 437, 439, 507, 509, 637, 676
   Ōtomo Lineage, 285
Kasuga, 181, 183, 185, 287, 459, 485, 521, 585, 637
   Agatanushi of, 171
   Omi of, 239, 573
   Omi of Kasuga-no-ono, 521
Kawakami Takeru, 265, 267
Kawase, Miyatsuko of, 680
Kaya Confederacy, 215, 315, 335, 361, 373, 503, 507, 640, 641, 652, 656
Kaya (Okayama), Omi of, 369, 661
Kazuno, 229, 634, 641, 654
   Agatanushi of, 167
   Obito of, 323
Kazuraki, 145, 159, 171, 265, 305, 331, 361, 389, 401, 427, 437, 455, 479, 482, 483, 487, 491, 495, 501, 539, 541, 545, 557, 633, 634, 638, 648, 654, 655, 659, 660, 663–65, 669, 672, 674–76
   Provincial Miyatsuko of, 167
Kennamu, 353, 659
Ki, Kii, 129, 187, 245
   Atai of, 247, 323, 355
   Omi of, 658
   Province, 25, 51, 65, 91, 295, 321, 323, 399, 680
   Provincial Miyatsuko of, 247, 638
Kibi, 63, 129, 181, 267, 271, 277, 279, 285, 365, 369, 411, 501, 503, 511, 513, 535, 539, 561, 629, 632, 635, 641, 642, 650, 660, 661, 665, 667, 678, 684
   Ason of, 661
   Omi of, 181, 307, 365, 423, 501, 507, 537, 541, 563
   Omi of Kuboya of, 485
   Province, 423, 537
   Provincial Miyatsuko of, 661
Kibiko Island, 11, 15, 17, 19, 627
Kibi-tsu-hiko, 181, 195, 213
Kinashi-no-karu, 451, 465, 467, 671
Kinu-nui-be, Miyatsuko of the, 681
Kōchi, 133, 183, 215, 237, 283, 391, 423, 439, 443, 461, 469, 539, 545, 632, 660, 664, 668, 670, 673, 675, 678, 682, 684, 687
   Agatanushi of Mino in, 684
   Aya of, 503
   Fumi of, 660
   Province of, 207, 331, 417, 429, 449, 515, 660, 667
   Provincial Miyatsuko of, 37
Koguryŏ, 315, 349, 353, 369, 371, 393, 421, 505, 507, 509, 530, 531, 533, 569, 575, 577, 652, 656, 659, 679, 681, 683, 687
   King of, 369, 371, 505, 507
Kokuna, 343, 353, 656, 659
Kose, 159, 289, 482, 633
Koshi, 11, 15, 17, 183, 219, 277, 293, 295, 349, 627, 635, 646, 648
Kukumata, Miyatsuko of, 295
Kumano, 25, 37, 39, 43, 45, 55, 65, 67, 77, 137, 377, 399, 606, 607, 627, 629, 632, 665
Kumaso, 251, 255, 265, 267, 269, 271, 281, 295, 301, 303, 307, 643, 644, 645, 650
Kume (lineage group), 95, 139, 143, 149, 151, 157, 165, 487, 511, 539, 543, 549, 555, 563, 583, 679, 686
   Muraji of, 511, 539, 679

Kume (place), 165, 225, 235, 361, 493, 541, 634, 676
Kunimi Hill, 145, 149
Kunisaki, Omi of, 251, 643
Kunisu, 144, 145, 363, 632
Kusa-nagi, 57, 63, 65, 87, 273, 283, 646

Makimuku, 217, 243, 251, 287, 379, 640
Mayowa, 475, 477, 479
Metori, 351, 409, 411, 413, 415
Mibu hereditary guild, 389, 427
Michi-no-omi, 89, 139, 143, 149, 151, 153, 165
Michinushi of Tanba, 199, 227, 245
Mike-iri-no, 125, 137
Mimana, 191, 215, 217, 219, 353, 361, 369, 415, 501, 503, 507, 531, 569, 571, 640, 641, 643
Mine, Agatanushi of, 517
Mino, 75, 83, 247, 249, 251, 265, 269, 277, 369, 539, 642, 661, 682, 684
    Agatanushi of, 682
    Province of, 75, 83, 269
    Omi of, 369
Minuma
    Agatanushi of, 261
    Kimi of, 45, 517
Mio, Kimi of, 237
Mishima, 67, 509, 608, 642
Miwa, 137, 187, 193, 195, 197, 205, 209, 211, 221, 311, 481, 629, 632, 633, 638, 639, 651, 675, 677
    Kimi of, 221, 481
    Kimi of Ōmiwa, 67, 303, 523, 629, 641, 649, 677
Miyatsuko of Totori, 231
Miyazu-hime, 277, 279, 646
Miyoshi no Kiyoyuki, 633
Moitori of Uda, 167
Mononobe, 128, 159, 187, 193, 231, 233, 239, 251, 303, 427, 437, 471, 483, 485, 501, 519, 521, 529, 579, 609, 637, 643, 649, 668, 669
    Muraji of the, 239, 303, 483
    no Ikofu, 437, 669
    no Me, 485, 519, 521, 529
    no Nagamai, 437, 669
    no Ōmae, 427, 429, 471, 668, 673
    no Tōchine, 233, 649
    no Ushiro, 529, 682
    Obito of the, 239
Mori, Kimi of, 269
Moroagata, Moroagata, Kimi of, 257, 357, 359
Motoori Norinaga, 392, 471, 642, 643, 653, 661, 672
Mt. Ikoma, 133, 135, 632
Mt. Mimoro, 67, 283, 629
Mt. Moyama, 75, 83, 630
Mugetsu, Kimi of, 269
Munakata, 37, 41, 373, 439, 509, 650, 679
    Munakata District, 37
    Kimi of, 37
Murata, Muraji of, 664
Musa, Suguri of, 489, 505, 517, 519, 523
Musashi, 277, 391
    Province, 339, 517, 664, 681
    Provincial Miyatsuko of, 55

Naga-sune-hiko, 133, 155, 157, 159
Nakatomi, 49, 51, 87, 129
    Muraji of the, 47, 53, 231, 233, 303, 649
    Omi of the, 305, 457, 649
Nakatsu, 385, 427, 429, 433, 435
Naka-tsu-hime, 349, 375, 385, 638, 643, 657
Naniwa, 131, 133, 221, 267, 321, 365, 373, 383, 385, 397, 399, 421, 423, 429, 433, 435, 467, 469, 509, 525, 541, 561, 573, 575, 632, 654, 660, 663, 665–68, 676, 684
    Imiki of, 475

Naniwa (*continue*)
    Kishi of, 475, 507
    Muraji of, 475, 684
    Neko of, 423, 654
Ne (land), 21, 29, 33, 35, 53, 55, 59, 65
Ne no Omi, 473, 475, 477, 525, 527, 682
New Selected Records, 363, 415, 419,
    440, 480, 501, 519, 529, 639, 642,
    643, 646, 650, 651, 653, 654, 659,
    660, 664, 669, 670, 672, 675,
    676, 678–80, 682, 684, 688, 690
New Selections of Paekche, 656
Newly Compiled Record of Paekche,
    589
Nishikori, Miyatsuko of the, 678
Niu River, 147, 149, 633
Nomi no Sukune, 227, 229, 237
Nukatabe, 55, 339
    Muraji of the, 55
    Obito of Tsukimoto, 339
Nukata-no-ō-naka-tsu-hiko, 351, 376,
    377, 379, 421
Nunaki-iri-bime, 187, 189, 638
Nunaki-waka-hime, 233, 638

Ō (lineage group), 171, 636
    no Yasumaro, 171
Ōama, Sukune of, 187, 638
Odo, 27, 33, 119, 307, 650
Ōeno-izaho-wake, 389, 407
Ohatsuse, Miyatsuko of, 397
Ō-hiko, 182, 183, 195, 199, 201, 217, 285,
    569, 637, 640
Oka, 129, 297, 632, 648, 681
    Agatanushi of, 297
Oki, 11, 15, 17, 19, 39
Ō-kusaka, 385, 447, 473, 475, 477, 483,
    525, 527, 663, 674
Old Man Shio-tsu-chi, 97, 103, 107,
    115, 127
Ōmi (person), 191

Ōmi, (place), 221, 231, 277, 287, 327,
    457, 481, 561, 567, 647, 654, 658,
    666, 669
    Kimi of, Kimi of Ōmi no Yama, 413,
    666
    Province, 353, 517, 561, 648, 666
Ōmi no Mifune, 631
Ō-muraji, 233, 239, 437, 482, 483, 485,
    487, 505, 509, 511, 513, 515, 519,
    521, 533, 535, 539, 541, 543, 555,
    559, 579, 583, 587, 589, 668, 669
The One Thousand Character Text, 659,
    660
Onogoroshima, 9, 13, 15, 17
Ō-omi, 233, 289, 479, 482, 483, 485,
    539, 541, 555, 559, 579, 587, 669
Original Records, 128, 183, 637, 638,
    639, 641, 642, 647, 649, 665, 668,
    669, 678, 687
Osaka, 29, 37, 135, 207, 445, 449, 473,
    632, 640, 645, 646, 653, 654, 657,
    659, 660, 663–68, 670, 672, 673,
    675, 676, 678–82, 684–88
Osaka (Nara), 145, 149, 151, 155, 197,
    633
Ōsaka, 195, 201, 205, 327, 429, 632,
    638, 639, 654, 663, 668
Ōshikōchi, Atai of, 37, 509
Oshikuma, 295, 319, 321, 323, 325, 327,
    329, 653
Oshinumi, Miyatsuko of the, 543, 685
Oshisaka (clan), 239, 451
Oshi-saka-no-ō-naka-tsu-hime, 449,
    451, 469, 487, 658, 671, 672, 686,
    688
Ō-tata-neko, 191, 193, 195
Otohiko no Kimi, 265, 267
Oto-kimi, 501, 503, 505
Ōtomo, 95, 139, 165, 233, 275, 509, 513,
    583, 673, 680
    Kashiwade of, 285

INDEX OF KEY NAMES AND PLACES

no Kanamura, 509, 583, 585. 587
no Katari, 205, 511
Muraji of the, 95, 231, 271, 275, 285, 303, 483, 509, 511, 649
no Muroya, 463, 483, 505, 509, 511, 513, 515, 533, 539, 541, 543, 589, 673
no Takehi,
Oto-tachibana-hime, 273, 277, 285, 646
O-usu, see Yamato Take
Ō-usu, 245, 249, 269, 642
Owari, 187, 265, 277, 279, 283, 638, 646
  Province, 63, 646
  Muraji of, 79, 99, 101, 177, 455, 638, 642, 659
Ōyake, Omi of, 670
Ō-yama-mori, 351, 373, 376, 377, 379, 381, 658, 662

Paekche, 315, 331, 335, 339, 341, 343, 345, 349, 351, 353, 361, 369, 371, 415, 417, 487, 497, 503, 505, 509, 513, 517, 530, 531, 533, 569, 571, 587, 589, 591, 640, 643, 652, 654, 656, 658, 659, 675, 677, 682, 683, 687, 690

Record of Paekche, 339, 656
Record of Threes and Fives, 627
Records of Rituals, 640
Records of the Eastern Lodge, 649, 657, 662, 671, 688
Records of the Historian, 635, 640, 642, 645, 651, 669, 687

Saba, Agatanushi of, 315
Sado, 11, 15, 17, 19, 627
Saeki (clan), 285, 409, 481, 537, 547, 575, 666
  Atai of, 415, 642

of Harima, 411
  Miyatsuko of, 575
  Muraji of, 583
Saho-biko, 223, 225, 227, 229, 519
Saho-hime, 217, 519, 640
Sakai (clan), 480, 481, 672
  Muraji of the, 479, 480, 671
Sakamoto, Omi of, 473, 515, 527, 682
Sakanokori, Omi of, 393
Sake no Kimi, 415, 417, 519, 675
Samguk sagi, 345, 353, 530, 571, 652, 656, 659–61, 675, 677, 679, 683, 689
Samguk yusa, 652, 656
Sanuki, 529, 642, 670
  Kimi of Aya in, 285
  Kimi of, Sanuki, 642
  Province of, 249, 284, 285,
  Provincial Miyatsuko of, 443, 670
Sarume, Kimi of, 49, 89
Selections of Refined Literature, 640, 647, 649, 662, 664, 671, 675, 676, 678, 679, 680
Shihi-no-ne-tsu-hiko, 129, 147, 149, 155
Shiki, 145, 153, 161, 187, 197, 233, 355, 633, 635, 636
  Agatanushi of, 167, 171, 173, 175, 177, 179, 181
  District, 51, 638, 647, 681
Shima no Sukune, 335, 337
Shimotsuke, Kimi of, 211, 286, 638, 639,
Shimotsumichi, 661, 678
  Omi of, 365, 501
Shinano, 277, 517, 589, 646, 681
Shishimu, 353, 659
Shōtoku (Prince), 634
Silla, 63, 215, 219, 221, 241, 303, 305, 307, 313–15, 317, 319, 321, 331, 337, 339, 343, 345, 349, 353, 361, 363, 369, 371, 393, 397, 419, 451, 467,

Silla (*continue*)
    469, 503, 505, 507, 509, 511, 521, 537, 640, 641, 643, 650, 652–55, 658–60, 678, 679, 681
Six Secret Teachings, 663, 664
Soga (clan), 289, 437, 482, 509, 658, 669, 675
    Machi no Sukune, 437, 669
    Karako, 509, 669
    no Ishikawa, 658
    Omi of, 658
    River, 676
Sono, Omi of, 369
So-tōshi-no-iratsume, 457, 459, 461, 463
Sotsuhiko, 331, 343, 361, 363, 389, 415, 427, 437, 455, 501, 545, 654, 655, 660, 663, 664, 672
Spring and Autumn Annals, 670, 689
Sue (place), 191, 638
    Ceramics, 505, 678
Sue-tsu-mimi, 191, 639
Suga, 57, 59
Sugaru, 499, 501, 677
Suguri (title), 527, 676
Sumisaka, 144, 145, 155, 161, 195, 197, 499, 639
Sumiyoshi Grand Shrine, 29, 609, 619, 650, 653, 654

The Sumiyoshi Record of the Age of the Gods, 651, 653
Table of the Rulers of Japan, 649
Tachibana, 27, 33, 119, 307, 483, 521, 545, 573, 650, 663, 672, 686, 688
Tagima no Ke-haya, 227, 229
Ta-gishi-mimi, 127, 137, 169, 171
Tago, Kishi of, 323
Tajima-mori, 221, 223, 243, 641
Takachiho, 79, 89, 93, 95, 99, 630
Takebe, Kimi of, 284, 285

Takeda, Agatanushi of, 167
Take-hani-yasu-biko, 183, 199, 201
Take-nu-na-kawa-wake, 195, 213
Takeuchi no Sukune, 183, 246, 247, 261, 265, 283, 289, 303, 305, 309, 321, 323, 325, 327, 331, 333, 337, 341, 353, 355, 385, 415, 417, 455, 482, 483, 658, 668, 679, 682, 688
Tanabe, Fubito of, 515, 680
Tanba, 185, 199, 213, 227, 229, 241, 245, 529, 533, 537, 639
Tara, 339, 656
Tasa Fortress, 341, 656
Tatsuta, 133, 135, 429, 632, 668
Tenjukoku Embroidery, 631
Toda no Sukune, 361, 392, 393, 397
Tōkan, 353, 361, 659
Tokoyo (land), 47, 67, 137, 231, 243, 333, 533, 629
Tokujun, 335, 337, 339, 656
Tokuno-kuni, 339, 656
Tomutare, 339, 353, 656
Tōshi, Agatanushi of, 181
Totori, Allied Miyatsuko of, 229, 231
Toyura, 295, 297
    Palace, 297, 303, 319, 648
Tranquil River of Heaven, 45, 47, 89
True History of Three Reigns of Japan, 649, 660, 673
Tsu Province, 373, 529, 543, 555
Tsubura no Ōmi, 437, 479, 483, 539, 669
Tsuke, Inaki of, 421, 451
Tsuku no Sukune, 353, 361, 385, 427, 435, 437, 482, 658, 668
Tsukushi, 11, 15, 17, 19, 27, 37, 43, 45, 65, 79, 89, 129, 211, 215, 251, 257, 259, 261, 263, 297, 305, 315, 349, 355, 373, 439, 441, 467, 497, 517, 529, 533, 589, 627, 641, 642, 645
    Provincial Miyatsuko of, 129, 183
Tsuno no Sukune, 353, 415, 658

Tsunuga, 219, 295, 333, 349, 587, 619, 640, 648
Tsushima, 11, 17, 331, 467, 509, 569, 617, 652, 655, 659, 687

Uda, 139, 143, 144, 145, 147, 155, 163, 167, 231, 297, 413, 489, 499, 517, 632–34, 639, 642, 666, 676, 689
Uji River, 221, 293, 327, 654
Uji-no-waki-iratsuko, 351, 361, 369, 373, 375, 383, 385, 662
Umakai (clan), 439, 469
   Muraji of the, 533
Unebi, 165, 167, 171, 175, 177, 469, 633, 673, 676
Urashima Taro, 531, 533

Wa, 335, 353, 499, 645, 652, 654, 660, 679
   Five Kings of Wa, 371, 661, 663, 667, 668, 673–75, 677
   King of, 335, 343, 679
   Queen of, 333, 347, 655
Wakasakurabe,
   Miyatsuko of the, 669
   Omi of the, 439, 669
Wangin (Wani), 361
Wani, Omi of, 177, 185, 201, 231, 323, 351, 405, 423, 573, 579, 654, 670
Wani Hill, 159, 199, 633
Watarai Shrine, 233
Writings of the Huainan Masters, 627, 667
Wu, 347, 371, 373, 421, 499, 505, 517, 519, 523, 525, 643, 651, 673, 676, 679, 680, 681, 686, 689

Xunzi, 664

Yama-no-kimi, 182, 183, 637

Yamashiro, Atai of, 37, 199, 201, 207, 237, 321, 323, 393, 401, 405, 407, 529, 569, 653, 665
Yamato District (Fukuoka), 307, 651
Yamato (Japan), 19, 65, 67, 145, 161, 193, 195, 201, 219, 221, 245, 257, 265, 267, 291, 313, 315, 317, 335, 345, 369, 417, 419, 482, 483, 489, 493, 497, 503, 507, 513, 527, 530, 531, 533, 553, 571, 579, 587, 589, 627, 631, 634–36, 645, 661, 663, 675, 678, 679, 681, 684, 689
Yamato (Nara), 145, 167, 173, 177, 189, 191, 199, 233, 237, 257, 267, 281, 283, 287, 297, 377, 379, 401, 429, 433, 435, 437, 459, 485, 487, 493, 505, 555, 630, 631, 647, 654, 659, 666, 668, 671, 678,
   Agatanushi of, 459
   Atai of, 129, 221, 227, 233, 378, 379, 421, 433, 632
   Atai of Aya in, 363, 505, 533, 539
   Kimi of, 591, 690
   Muraji of, 515
   Omi of, 690
   Province, 51, 207, 293, 393, 417, 449, 577, 631, 638, 667, 671, 673, 678, 687
   Provincial Chieftain of, 165, 489
   Provincial Miyatsuko of, 165, 433, 487, 632
   River, 135, 665, 681
   Umakai-be of, 469
Yamato Take, 57, 231, 245, 249, 261, 265, 267, 269, 271, 273, 275, 277, 279, 281, 283, 285, 291, 293, 421, 491, 555, 639, 643, 644, 645, 646, 648, 649, 658
   O-usu, 245, 281, 285, 642
Yamato-hiko, 187, 235
Yamato-hime, 229, 231, 233, 273, 283

Yamato-to-to-hi-momo-so-bime, 181, 183, 191, 199, 205, 639
Yasaka-iri-bime, 247, 285, 289, 638, 657
Yata, 351, 385, 397, 399, 407
Ya-ta-garasu, 139, 153, 167
Ya-tsuna-da, 225, 227, 286, 287, 641
Yodo River, 135, 632, 654, 665
Yomi, 21, 27, 31, 628, 650
Yosami, Abiko of, 259, 311, 415, 651, 666
Yoshino, 144, 145, 363, 487, 493, 632, 633, 660, 662, 675, 677
  Obito of, 145
Yuge, Muraji of the, 509

Zuo Tradition, 651, 669